Lecture Notes in Computer Science 8523

Commenced Publication in 1973
Founding and Former Series Editors:
Gerhard Goos, Juris Hartmanis, and Jan van Leeuwen

T0212815

Panayiotis Zaphiris   Andri Ioannou (Eds.)

Learning and Collaboration Technologies

Designing and Developing Novel Learning Experiences

First International Conference, LCT 2014
Held as Part of HCI International 2014
Heraklion, Crete, Greece, June 22-27, 2014
Proceedings, Part I

 Springer

Volume Editors

Panayiotis Zaphiris
Andri Ioannou
Cyprus University of Technology
Department of Multimedia and Graphic Arts
Lemesos, Cyprus
E-mail: {panayiotis.zaphiris; andri.i.ioannou}@cut.ac.cy

ISSN 0302-9743   e-ISSN 1611-3349
ISBN 978-3-319-07481-8   e-ISBN 978-3-319-07482-5
DOI 10.1007/978-3-319-07482-5
Springer Cham Heidelberg New York Dordrecht London

Library of Congress Control Number: 2014939302

LNCS Sublibrary: SL 3 – Information Systems and Application,
incl. Internet/Web and HCI

Typesetting: Camera-ready by author, data conversion by Scientific Publishing Services, Chennai, India

Printed on acid-free paper

Springer is part of Springer Science+Business Media (www.springer.com)

Foreword

The 16th International Conference on Human–Computer Interaction, HCI International 2014, was held in Heraklion, Crete, Greece, during June 22–27, 2014, incorporating 14 conferences/thematic areas:

Thematic areas:

- Human–Computer Interaction
- Human Interface and the Management of Information

Affiliated conferences:

- 11th International Conference on Engineering Psychology and Cognitive Ergonomics
- 8th International Conference on Universal Access in Human–Computer Interaction
- 6th International Conference on Virtual, Augmented and Mixed Reality
- 6th International Conference on Cross-Cultural Design
- 6th International Conference on Social Computing and Social Media
- 8th International Conference on Augmented Cognition
- 5th International Conference on Digital Human Modeling and Applications in Health, Safety, Ergonomics and Risk Management
- Third International Conference on Design, User Experience and Usability
- Second International Conference on Distributed, Ambient and Pervasive Interactions
- Second International Conference on Human Aspects of Information Security, Privacy and Trust
- First International Conference on HCI in Business
- First International Conference on Learning and Collaboration Technologies

A total of 4,766 individuals from academia, research institutes, industry, and governmental agencies from 78 countries submitted contributions, and 1,476 papers and 225 posters were included in the proceedings. These papers address the latest research and development efforts and highlight the human aspects of design and use of computing systems. The papers thoroughly cover the entire field of human–computer interaction, addressing major advances in knowledge and effective use of computers in a variety of application areas.

This volume, edited by Panayiotis Zaphiris and Andri Ioannou, contains papers focusing on the thematic area of learning and collaboration technologies, addressing the following major topics:

- Design of learning technologies
- Novel approaches in eLearning

- Student modeling and learning behavior
- Supporting   problem-based,   inquiry-based,   project-based and blended learning

The remaining volumes of the HCI International 2014 proceedings are:

- Volume 1, LNCS 8510, Human–Computer Interaction: HCI Theories, Methods and Tools (Part I), edited by Masaaki Kurosu
- Volume 2, LNCS 8511, Human–Computer Interaction: Advanced Interaction Modalities and Techniques (Part II), edited by Masaaki Kurosu
- Volume 3, LNCS 8512, Human–Computer Interaction: Applications and Services (Part III), edited by Masaaki Kurosu
- Volume 4, LNCS 8513, Universal Access in Human-Computer Interaction: Design and Development Methods for Universal Access (Part I), edited by Constantine Stephanidis and Margherita Antona
- Volume 5, LNCS 8514, Universal Access in Human–Computer Interaction: Universal Access to Information and Knowledge (Part II), edited by Constantine Stephanidis and Margherita Antona
- Volume 6, LNCS 8515, Universal Access in Human–Computer Interaction: Aging and Assistive Environments (Part III), edited by Constantine Stephanidis and Margherita Antona
- Volume 7, LNCS 8516, Universal Access in Human–Computer Interaction: Design for All and Accessibility Practice (Part IV), edited by Constantine Stephanidis and Margherita Antona
- Volume 8, LNCS 8517, Design, User Experience, and Usability: Theories, Methods and Tools for Designing the User Experience (Part I), edited by Aaron Marcus
- Volume 9, LNCS 8518, Design, User Experience, and Usability: User Experience Design for Diverse Interaction Platforms and Environments (Part II), edited by Aaron Marcus
- Volume 10, LNCS 8519, Design, User Experience, and Usability: User Experience Design for Everyday Life Applications and Services (Part III), edited by Aaron Marcus
- Volume 11, LNCS 8520, Design, User Experience, and Usability: User Experience Design Practice (Part IV), edited by Aaron Marcus
- Volume 12, LNCS 8521, Human Interface and the Management of Information: Information and Knowledge Design and Evaluation (Part I), edited by Sakae Yamamoto
- Volume 13, LNCS 8522, Human Interface and the Management of Information: Information and Knowledge in Applications and Services (Part II), edited by Sakae Yamamoto
- Volume 15, LNCS 8524, Learning and Collaboration Technologies: Technology-rich Environments for Learning and Collaboration (Part II), edited by Panayiotis Zaphiris and Andri Ioannou
- Volume 16, LNCS 8525, Virtual, Augmented and Mixed Reality: Designing and Developing Virtual and Augmented Environments (Part I), edited by Randall Shumaker and Stephanie Lackey

- Volume 17, LNCS 8526, Virtual, Augmented and Mixed Reality: Applications of Virtual and Augmented Reality (Part II), edited by Randall Shumaker and Stephanie Lackey
- Volume 18, LNCS 8527, HCI in Business, edited by Fiona Fui-Hoon Nah
- Volume 19, LNCS 8528, Cross-Cultural Design, edited by P.L. Patrick Rau
- Volume 20, LNCS 8529, Digital Human Modeling and Applications in Health, Safety, Ergonomics and Risk Management, edited by Vincent G. Duffy
- Volume 21, LNCS 8530, Distributed, Ambient, and Pervasive Interactions, edited by Norbert Streitz and Panos Markopoulos
- Volume 22, LNCS 8531, Social Computing and Social Media, edited by Gabriele Meiselwitz
- Volume 23, LNAI 8532, Engineering Psychology and Cognitive Ergonomics, edited by Don Harris
- Volume 24, LNCS 8533, Human Aspects of Information Security, Privacy and Trust, edited by Theo Tryfonas and Ioannis Askoxylakis
- Volume 25, LNAI 8534, Foundations of Augmented Cognition, edited by Dylan D. Schmorrow and Cali M. Fidopiastis
- Volume 26, CCIS 434, HCI International 2014 Posters Proceedings (Part I), edited by Constantine Stephanidis
- Volume 27, CCIS 435, HCI International 2014 Posters Proceedings (Part II), edited by Constantine Stephanidis

I would like to thank the Program Chairs and the members of the Program Boards of all affiliated conferences and thematic areas, listed below, for their contribution to the highest scientific quality and the overall success of the HCI International 2014 Conference.

This conference could not have been possible without the continuous support and advice of the founding chair and conference scientific advisor, Prof. Gavriel Salvendy, as well as the dedicated work and outstanding efforts of the communications chair and editor of *HCI International News*, Dr. Abbas Moallem.

I would also like to thank for their contribution towards the smooth organization of the HCI International 2014 Conference the members of the Human–Computer Interaction Laboratory of ICS-FORTH, and in particular George Paparoulis, Maria Pitsoulaki, Maria Bouhli, and George Kapnas.

April 2014   Constantine Stephanidis
                                         General Chair, HCI International 2014

Organization

Human–Computer Interaction

Program Chair: Masaaki Kurosu, Japan

Jose Abdelnour-Nocera, UK
Sebastiano Bagnara, Italy
Simone Barbosa, Brazil
Adriana Betiol, Brazil
Simone Borsci, UK
Henry Duh, Australia
Xiaowen Fang, USA
Vicki Hanson, UK
Wonil Hwang, Korea
Minna Isomursu, Finland
Yong Gu Ji, Korea
Anirudha Joshi, India
Esther Jun, USA
Kyungdoh Kim, Korea

Heidi Krömker, Germany
Chen Ling, USA
Chang S. Nam, USA
Naoko Okuizumi, Japan
Philippe Palanque, France
Ling Rothrock, USA
Naoki Sakakibara, Japan
Dominique Scapin, France
Guangfeng Song, USA
Sanjay Tripathi, India
Chui Yin Wong, Malaysia
Toshiki Yamaoka, Japan
Kazuhiko Yamazaki, Japan
Ryoji Yoshitake, Japan

Human Interface and the Management of Information

Program Chair: Sakae Yamamoto, Japan

Alan Chan, Hong Kong
Denis A. Coelho, Portugal
Linda Elliott, USA
Shin'ichi Fukuzumi, Japan
Michitaka Hirose, Japan
Makoto Itoh, Japan
Yen-Yu Kang, Taiwan
Koji Kimita, Japan
Daiji Kobayashi, Japan

Hiroyuki Miki, Japan
Hirohiko Mori, Japan
Shogo Nishida, Japan
Robert Proctor, USA
Youngho Rhee, Korea
Ryosuke Saga, Japan
Katsunori Shimohara, Japan
Kim-Phuong Vu, USA
Tomio Watanabe, Japan

Engineering Psychology and Cognitive Ergonomics

Program Chair: Don Harris, UK

Guy Andre Boy, USA
Shan Fu, P.R. China
Hung-Sying Jing, Taiwan
Wen-Chin Li, Taiwan
Mark Neerincx, The Netherlands
Jan Noyes, UK
Paul Salmon, Australia

Axel Schulte, Germany
Siraj Shaikh, UK
Sarah Sharples, UK
Anthony Smoker, UK
Neville Stanton, UK
Alex Stedmon, UK
Andrew Thatcher, South Africa

Universal Access in Human–Computer Interaction

**Program Chairs: Constantine Stephanidis, Greece,
and Margherita Antona, Greece**

Julio Abascal, Spain
Gisela Susanne Bahr, USA
João Barroso, Portugal
Margrit Betke, USA
Anthony Brooks, Denmark
Christian Bühler, Germany
Stefan Carmien, Spain
Hua Dong, P.R. China
Carlos Duarte, Portugal
Pier Luigi Emiliani, Italy
Qin Gao, P.R. China
Andrina Granić, Croatia
Andreas Holzinger, Austria
Josette Jones, USA
Simeon Keates, UK

Georgios Kouroupetroglou, Greece
Patrick Langdon, UK
Barbara Leporini, Italy
Eugene Loos, The Netherlands
Ana Isabel Paraguay, Brazil
Helen Petrie, UK
Michael Pieper, Germany
Enrico Pontelli, USA
Jaime Sanchez, Chile
Alberto Sanna, Italy
Anthony Savidis, Greece
Christian Stary, Austria
Hirotada Ueda, Japan
Gerhard Weber, Germany
Harald Weber, Germany

Virtual, Augmented and Mixed Reality

**Program Chairs: Randall Shumaker, USA,
and Stephanie Lackey, USA**

Roland Blach, Germany
Sheryl Brahnam, USA
Juan Cendan, USA
Jessie Chen, USA
Panagiotis D. Kaklis, UK

Hirokazu Kato, Japan
Denis Laurendeau, Canada
Fotis Liarokapis, UK
Michael Macedonia, USA
Gordon Mair, UK

Jose San Martin, Spain
Tabitha Peck, USA
Christian Sandor, Australia

Christopher Stapleton, USA
Gregory Welch, USA

Cross-Cultural Design

Program Chair: P.L. Patrick Rau, P.R. China

Yee-Yin Choong, USA
Paul Fu, USA
Zhiyong Fu, P.R. China
Pin-Chao Liao, P.R. China
Dyi-Yih Michael Lin, Taiwan
Rungtai Lin, Taiwan
Ta-Ping (Robert) Lu, Taiwan
Liang Ma, P.R. China
Alexander Mädche, Germany

Sheau-Farn Max Liang, Taiwan
Katsuhiko Ogawa, Japan
Tom Plocher, USA
Huatong Sun, USA
Emil Tso, P.R. China
Hsiu-Ping Yueh, Taiwan
Liang (Leon) Zeng, USA
Jia Zhou, P.R. China

Online Communities and Social Media

Program Chair: Gabriele Meiselwitz, USA

Leonelo Almeida, Brazil
Chee Siang Ang, UK
Aneesha Bakharia, Australia
Ania Bobrowicz, UK
James Braman, USA
Farzin Deravi, UK
Carsten Kleiner, Germany
Niki Lambropoulos, Greece
Soo Ling Lim, UK

Anthony Norcio, USA
Portia Pusey, USA
Panote Siriaraya, UK
Stefan Stieglitz, Germany
Giovanni Vincenti, USA
Yuanqiong (Kathy) Wang, USA
June Wei, USA
Brian Wentz, USA

Augmented Cognition

**Program Chairs: Dylan D. Schmorrow, USA,
and Cali M. Fidopiastis, USA**

Ahmed Abdelkhalek, USA
Robert Atkinson, USA
Monique Beaudoin, USA
John Blitch, USA
Alenka Brown, USA

Rosario Cannavò, Italy
Joseph Cohn, USA
Andrew J. Cowell, USA
Martha Crosby, USA
Wai-Tat Fu, USA

Rodolphe Gentili, USA
Frederick Gregory, USA
Michael W. Hail, USA
Monte Hancock, USA
Fei Hu, USA
Ion Juvina, USA
Joe Keebler, USA
Philip Mangos, USA
Rao Mannepalli, USA
David Martinez, USA
Yvonne R. Masakowski, USA
Santosh Mathan, USA
Ranjeev Mittu, USA

Keith Niall, USA
Tatana Olson, USA
Debra Patton, USA
June Pilcher, USA
Robinson Pino, USA
Tiffany Poeppelman, USA
Victoria Romero, USA
Amela Sadagic, USA
Anna Skinner, USA
Ann Speed, USA
Robert Sottilare, USA
Peter Walker, USA

Digital Human Modeling and Applications in Health, Safety, Ergonomics and Risk Management

Program Chair: Vincent G. Duffy, USA

Giuseppe Andreoni, Italy
Daniel Carruth, USA
Elsbeth De Korte, The Netherlands
Afzal A. Godil, USA
Ravindra Goonetilleke, Hong Kong
Noriaki Kuwahara, Japan
Kang Li, USA
Zhizhong Li, P.R. China

Tim Marler, USA
Jianwei Niu, P.R. China
Michelle Robertson, USA
Matthias Rötting, Germany
Mao-Jiun Wang, Taiwan
Xuguang Wang, France
James Yang, USA

Design, User Experience, and Usability

Program Chair: Aaron Marcus, USA

Sisira Adikari, Australia
Claire Ancient, USA
Arne Berger, Germany
Jamie Blustein, Canada
Ana Boa-Ventura, USA
Jan Brejcha, Czech Republic
Lorenzo Cantoni, Switzerland
Marc Fabri, UK
Luciane Maria Fadel, Brazil
Tricia Flanagan, Hong Kong
Jorge Frascara, Mexico

Federico Gobbo, Italy
Emilie Gould, USA
Rüdiger Heimgärtner, Germany
Brigitte Herrmann, Germany
Steffen Hess, Germany
Nouf Khashman, Canada
Fabiola Guillermina Noël, Mexico
Francisco Rebelo, Portugal
Kerem Rızvanoğlu, Turkey
Marcelo Soares, Brazil
Carla Spinillo, Brazil

Distributed, Ambient and Pervasive Interactions

Program Chairs: Norbert Streitz, Germany,
and Panos Markopoulos, The Netherlands

Juan Carlos Augusto, UK
Jose Bravo, Spain
Adrian Cheok, UK
Boris de Ruyter, The Netherlands
Anind Dey, USA
Dimitris Grammenos, Greece
Nuno Guimaraes, Portugal
Achilles Kameas, Greece
Javed Vassilis Khan, The Netherlands
Shin'ichi Konomi, Japan
Carsten Magerkurth, Switzerland

Ingrid Mulder, The Netherlands
Anton Nijholt, The Netherlands
Fabio Paternó, Italy
Carsten Röcker, Germany
Teresa Romao, Portugal
Albert Ali Salah, Turkey
Manfred Tscheligi, Austria
Reiner Wichert, Germany
Woontack Woo, Korea
Xenophon Zabulis, Greece

Human Aspects of Information Security, Privacy and Trust

Program Chairs: Theo Tryfonas, UK,
and Ioannis Askoxylakis, Greece

Claudio Agostino Ardagna, Italy
Zinaida Benenson, Germany
Daniele Catteddu, Italy
Raoul Chiesa, Italy
Bryan Cline, USA
Sadie Creese, UK
Jorge Cuellar, Germany
Marc Dacier, USA
Dieter Gollmann, Germany
Kirstie Hawkey, Canada
Jaap-Henk Hoepman, The Netherlands
Cagatay Karabat, Turkey
Angelos Keromytis, USA
Ayako Komatsu, Japan
Ronald Leenes, The Netherlands
Javier Lopez, Spain
Steve Marsh, Canada

Gregorio Martinez, Spain
Emilio Mordini, Italy
Yuko Murayama, Japan
Masakatsu Nishigaki, Japan
Aljosa Pasic, Spain
Milan Petković, The Netherlands
Joachim Posegga, Germany
Jean-Jacques Quisquater, Belgium
Damien Sauveron, France
George Spanoudakis, UK
Kerry-Lynn Thomson, South Africa
Julien Touzeau, France
Theo Tryfonas, UK
João Vilela, Portugal
Claire Vishik, UK
Melanie Volkamer, Germany

HCI in Business

Program Chair: Fiona Fui-Hoon Nah, USA

Andreas Auinger, Austria
Michel Avital, Denmark
Traci Carte, USA
Hock Chuan Chan, Singapore
Constantinos Coursaris, USA
Soussan Djamasbi, USA
Brenda Eschenbrenner, USA
Nobuyuki Fukawa, USA
Khaled Hassanein, Canada
Milena Head, Canada
Susanna (Shuk Ying) Ho, Australia
Jack Zhenhui Jiang, Singapore
Jinwoo Kim, Korea
Zoonky Lee, Korea
Honglei Li, UK
Nicholas Lockwood, USA
Eleanor T. Loiacono, USA
Mei Lu, USA

Scott McCoy, USA
Brian Mennecke, USA
Robin Poston, USA
Lingyun Qiu, P.R. China
Rene Riedl, Austria
Matti Rossi, Finland
April Savoy, USA
Shu Schiller, USA
Hong Sheng, USA
Choon Ling Sia, Hong Kong
Chee-Wee Tan, Denmark
Chuan Hoo Tan, Hong Kong
Noam Tractinsky, Israel
Horst Treiblmaier, Austria
Virpi Tuunainen, Finland
Dezhi Wu, USA
I-Chin Wu, Taiwan

Learning and Collaboration Technologies

**Program Chairs: Panayiotis Zaphiris, Cyprus,
and Andri Ioannou, Cyprus**

Ruthi Aladjem, Israel
Abdulaziz Aldaej, UK
John M. Carroll, USA
Maka Eradze, Estonia
Mikhail Fominykh, Norway
Denis Gillet, Switzerland
Mustafa Murat Inceoglu, Turkey
Pernilla Josefsson, Sweden
Marie Joubert, UK
Sauli Kiviranta, Finland
Tomaž Klobučar, Slovenia
Elena Kyza, Cyprus
Maarten de Laat, The Netherlands
David Lamas, Estonia

Edmund Laugasson, Estonia
Ana Loureiro, Portugal
Katherine Maillet, France
Nadia Pantidi, UK
Antigoni Parmaxi, Cyprus
Borzoo Pourabdollahian, Italy
Janet C. Read, UK
Christophe Reffay, France
Nicos Souleles, Cyprus
Ana Luísa Torres, Portugal
Stefan Trausan-Matu, Romania
Aimilia Tzanavari, Cyprus
Johnny Yuen, Hong Kong
Carmen Zahn, Switzerland

External Reviewers

Ilia Adami, Greece
Iosif Klironomos, Greece
Maria Korozi, Greece
Vassilis Kouroumalis, Greece

Asterios Leonidis, Greece
George Margetis, Greece
Stavroula Ntoa, Greece
Nikolaos Partarakis, Greece

HCI International 2015

The 15th International Conference on Human–Computer Interaction, HCI International 2015, will be held jointly with the affiliated conferences in Los Angeles, CA, USA, in the Westin Bonaventure Hotel, August 2–7, 2015. It will cover a broad spectrum of themes related to HCI, including theoretical issues, methods, tools, processes, and case studies in HCI design, as well as novel interaction techniques, interfaces, and applications. The proceedings will be published by Springer. More information will be available on the conference website: http://www.hcii2015.org/

General Chair
Professor Constantine Stephanidis
University of Crete and ICS-FORTH
Heraklion, Crete, Greece
E-mail: cs@ics.forth.gr

Table of Contents – Part I

Design of Learning Technologies

Novel Approaches in eLearning

Student Modeling and Learning Behaviour

Supporting Problem-Based, Inquiry-Based, Project Based and Blended Learning

Table of Contents – Part II

Virtual and Augmented Learning Environments

Mobile and Ubiquitous Learning

Technology@School

Collaboration, Learning and Training

Design of Learning Technologies

Course Sprints: Combining Teacher Training, Design Thinking and Hackathons

Gemma Aguado, Carles Fernández, Muriel Garreta-Domingo,
Roger Griset, and Alícia Valls

Learning Services, Universitat Oberta de Catalunya, Barcelona, Spain
{gaguado,cfernandezba,murielgd,rgriset,avallssa}@uoc.edu

Abstract. In this work we present a teaching support action – Course Sprint - for the design and implementation of a course in a new virtual classroom. A Course Sprint is an intense and collaborative activity that brings together educators and instructional designers experts in teaching and learning technologies. The main objective is to create or redesign a set of learning activities considering the defined learning objectives and competences in the teaching program using creative thinking. The need of such an activity originated with the deployment of a new learning environment: how to get teachers to adopt this updated virtual environment for teaching and learning? The new classroom is activity-centered as opposed to calendar-centered and, therefore, requires teachers to change the design of the course and the learning activities.

Keywords: collaborative learning, informal learning, online learning, instructional design, higher education, teacher trainning, coaching, continuous professional development.

1   Introduction

In order to adapt the instructional design to the constant changes of learners, the context, and the learning resources available teachers should review and redesign courses and activities constantly. Nevertheless, often the lack of time and support to undertake this redesign process pushes educators to repeat year after year the same learning process, using the same activities, content and strategies for teaching and learning.

Technology for teaching and learning is another element that is directly affecting the education sector and showing the importance of review teaching plans. As a result, in online learning, which is the case of our University, it is even more important to provide teachers with adequate support for redesign their courses efficiently.

Much of the design methodologies currently available are very time consuming and do not specifically take into account the teaching goals and competence level neither consider the most common possibility of having an existing learning design that needs to be redesigned.

P. Zaphiris and A. Ioannou (Eds.): LCT 2014, Part I, LNCS 8523, pp. 3–12, 2014.

In this work we present a teaching support action for the implementation of a subject in a new virtual classroom. Here the design of new virtual classroom works as a perfect excuse for teachers to review their instructional designs. We call this action "Course Sprint" (CS). A CS is a collaborative and intense activity with faculty members, tutors and instructional designers to (re) design the learning activities of a course in 4 hours taking into account the learning objectives of the course and the available technology for teaching and learning.

2   Background

For the ideation of the CS we considered the main characteristics of our context, our teacher's needs and we analyzed current trends in support actions for instructional designers and continuous professional development for teachers.

2.1   Context

The Open University of Catalonia (http://www.uoc.edu) is a fully online university that develops all teaching and learning activities through a virtual campus. There are 256 faculty members from different departments responsible for the design, implementation and monitoring of the courses developed in the virtual classroom. Tutors are responsible for the class activity, the follow-up of the students' learning process and the evaluation of continuous assessment exercises and final exams. Currently, we have 3.406 tutors for the 2.562 courses being offered.

The definition and design of the learning activities is often done collaboratively among faculty members and tutors as both are implied in the teaching process. Both teachers and tutors have a tight agenda, having little time for participating in long processes of instructional design. Also, the fact that tutors work totally online and have a full-time job – besides collaborating at the UOC - makes it difficult to find time for face to face meetings.

The rapid changes in technology and in online learning as well as the requirements brought by the European Higher Education Area (EHEA) [5] pushes for the constant evolution of the learning management system. As part of this evolution, a new classroom environment has been designed and iteratively improved during two academic years. For the current year, the goal was to have a more massive pilot of this new classroom. As a result, we designed several accompaniment actions to promote the change to this new classroom: from the more traditional and formal training sessions to Course Sprints. As a result, this new classroom is currently available in 333 subjects (13%), affecting 113 faculty members, 430 tutors and 14.510 students.

The new classroom is activity-centered as opposed to calendar-centered and, therefore, requires teachers to change their mindset and the design of the course. In consequence, the adoption of this new environment implies for educators to both learn a new web application and the (re)design the learning activities. Our goal was to design and implement the right accompaniment actions to help teachers in this process.

2.2   Instructional Design Theories and Models

Instructional design is a discipline aimed at the development of learning experiences and environments which promote the acquisition of specific knowledge and skill by students [10]. There are different design models that offer support and guidance for the creation of learning experiences. There are also other models of design not related directly with education that offers us good input: such as design thinking or lean entrepreneurship.

Many of the models are quite similar in that they essentially mostly address the same four components in some form or another: 1) the learners; 2) the learning objectives; 3) the method of instruction; and 4) some form of assessment or evaluation. Some of them such as ADDIE [6] are more focused on the process and others are more centered on working on the different components that compose the instruction like Dick and Carey Model [4]. Being these models very time consuming and very rigid in their implementation, some other models were proposed based on flexibility and iterative processes like Kemp's Model [12] or Rapid Prototyping Model [11].

The IMS Learning Design specification [8] was also taken into account. This specification is able to use any pedagogical model to get units of learning run-able and editable in an interoperable way. IMS-LD augments other well-known e-learning specifications aforementioned, like SCORM, IMS Content Packaging, IMS Question and Test Interoperability or IMS Simple Sequencing. Furthermore, IMS-LD describes among other things the roles, the activities, the basic information structure, the communication among different roles and users; and all these under the pedagogical approach decided by the teacher and-or the e learning designer. Although it seems like a good approach to consider in our online learning environment, the IMS-LD is too complex and theoretical and the software available to help create learning objects is not mature enough.

These models as such were discarded as an option to promote the adoption of the new virtual environment. Teachers would not take the time to go through the documentation and the training was too theoretical and far from the real implementation problems. However, we did get inputs and insights to help us shape the support action we were aiming for.

Other less education related approaches like Design Thinking [3] also provide an adequate framework. However, again, the process spreads over time and, as a result, requires too much involvement for teachers. Our goal was to design a solution that would provide a one-time and not too long involvement; instead of day-long or sessions spread during different days. Design thinking promotes the combination of empathy for the context of a problem, creativity in the generation of insights and solutions, and rationality to analyze and fit solutions to the context. All these elements as well as the creativity aspect are important for the design of the learning activities support.

Lean Entrepreneurship and its uses in education were analyzed as well as the T-PACK methodology and the ISTE coaching proposal. The Lean Startup [9] provides a scientific approach to creating and managing startups with the goal of offering a desired product to customers' hands faster. The Lean Startup (LS) method is about how to drive a startup-how to steer, when to turn, and when to persevere-and grow a business with maximum acceleration. It is a principled approach to new product development. A core component of Lean Startup methodology is the build-measure-learn feedback loop. This makes the LS very interesting in education as a perfect way of constantly evaluating the learning experiences adapting it to learners and context. In this sense, it is similar to the iterative nature of design thinking and more generally of user-centered design approaches.

The Technological Pedagogical Content Knowledge (TPACK) model [14] attempts to identify the nature of knowledge required by teachers for technology integration in their teaching, while addressing the complex, multifaceted and situated nature of teacher knowledge. An possible solution for the implementation of a TPACK model are the technology coaches defined by ISTE [13]; who assist teachers in using technology effectively for assessing student learning, differentiating instruction, and providing rigorous, relevant, and engaging learning experiences for all students.

All these different models, theories and approaches to instructional design helped us better design the accompaniment action and take the aspects and ideas that best fit our context and the needs and characteristics of faculty members and tutors.

Being a multidisciplinary department with many of its members software developers, we also looked at agile methodologies and especially at hackathons [7] which are collaborative and intense activities. During these events, computer programmers and other profiles involved in software development, including graphic designers, interface designers and project managers, collaborate intensively on software projects. The focus is on producing an end-product by the end of the event. This specific characteristic was key in the type of action we were looking for.

Booksprints [1] are similar to hackathons, they bring together a group to produce a book in 3-5 days. There are five main parts of a Book Sprint:

1. Concept Mapping: development of themes, concepts, ideas, developing ownership, etc.
2. Structuring: creating chapter headings, dividing the work, scoping the book (in Booktype, for example).
3. Writing: distributing sections/chapters, writing and discussion, but mostly writing.
4. Composition: iterative process of re-structure, checking, discussing, copy editing, and proofing.
5. Publication

This structure was also very useful and adequate to the (re)design of learning activities and can be mapped to the process of creating these activities and then implementing them into the new classroom.

3   Characteristics of the New Support Action

Learning from the several aspects we gathered from current instructional design models as well as software and design development processes together with our specific context and end-users, the new support action for faculty members and tutors had to cover the following characteristics and aspects:

- Promote adoption of the new virtual classroom environment. Now is activity-centered as opposed to calendar-centered and, therefore, requires teachers to change their mindset and the design of the course.
- Train faculty members and tutors about this new classroom and its characteristics.
- Short and self-contained. The lack of time of our target users and the fact that they are spread in different locations are a big constraint.
- Different agents implied in the design of each course/subject. In our university there are two different agents responsible of designing and teaching in each subject: The teacher and the tutor. Both teachers and tutors assist to the Course Sprint.
- Awareness of the students' needs as well as the differences between teachers of different departments and with a diverse interest in learning technology. Teachers need different types of support depending on the characteristics of the subjects they teach and also the students' needs. There are subjects that are completely new, others that are already designed but need some revision. There are some subjects with big number of desertion, others that are well considered but have not been revised for a long period of time, for instance.

4   The Course Sprint Structure

During Course Sprints [2] faculty members and tutors design the learning activities taking into account the learning objectives of the course and also the competences students have to acquire during the semester. Contents are considered as resources for students to solve the activities and not as the main tool of the learning process. We also offer teachers the possibility of including Open Educational Resources as reliable material that can be included to help students to work the activities of the minor.

The 4-hours session is structured in the following phases:

1. Introduction of the new virtual classroom and the teaching and learning tools available in the virtual classroom (wikis, blogs, microblogs, etc.). During 30 minutes we make an introduction to the new classroom for teachers to familiarize with the new classroom design.
2. Analysis of the virtual mind map created with the goals and competences that the course needs to cover. Before the brainstorming activity, we introduce the mind map we have created for the session. The main map is based on goals and skills that the course/subject needs to cover and want to help teachers to think about possible learning activities.
3. Brainstorming of learning activities based on the mind map. Using the virtual mind mapping tool, teachers include, first, individually, afterwards as a group and during

30 minutes, all the activities they think are adequate for students to achieve the goals and skills established. This stage of the session is very important as usually teachers establish the activities based on content and not on goals and skills. It requires them to define activities from a new point of view.

4. Introduction to Open Educational Resources (OER) research techniques. Library staff explain basic research techniques for teachers to be autonomous to find and include OER in their learning activities.

5. Selection of the learning activities to design. Using the virtual mind map, faculty members and tutors explain the activities he/she have added to the map trying to find similar ones proposed by others and trying also to estimate the time required to the student and its place in the course planning. We define a group of parameters for each activity: public/private, product (final result of the activity), individual/group.

6. Design of activities. From the selection made in step 5, we organize teachers in groups for developing the activities using the templates previously prepared. In this template we propose a flexible organization for the description of each activity.

7. Search for online resources to complement the activities. A specialist in documentation and OER research is present during the session helping teachers find new resources associate to the activities they propose. These resources are a complement to the mandatory material associated to the course or subject. It is also a good moment for teachers to ask doubts about research techniques to the specialist.

8. Publish the activities in the new virtual classroom. Once the activities are developed, teacher access to the new classroom and published it. Teacher learns with this practical exercise how the new classroom works acquiring the basic knowledge for being autonomous in the management of their virtual classrooms.

In order to prepare each session and adapt the structure to the specific needs and characteristics of the teachers and the course, previous to running a Course Sprint, it is very important to meet faculty members to know their concrete needs for adapting the sessions. Depending on that some of the phases of the CS were longer, shorter or eliminated.

As mentioned for step 2, also previous to the Course Sprint, we create some documentation that was used for the dynamic of the sessions. First of all, we create an online collaborative space for the brainstorming phase. This space is configured specially for each course we are going to work. Here, we include objectives (blue in the figure) and skills (black in the figure) that had to be worked in the concrete subject. All this information is taken from the syllabus that faculty members previously facilitate us.

During the session – stage 3 - teachers create the possible activities (pink in the figure) they are going to work with students taking into account the desired learning goals and competences. This online system offers us the possibility of working first in an individual way and collaboratively afterwards.

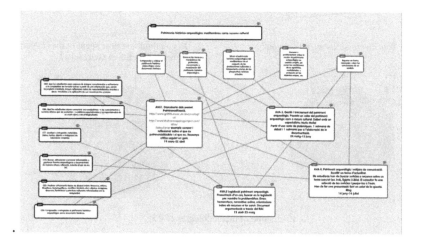

Fig. 1.

We have also created templates for the design of the activities phase. In this phase, teachers, based on the brainstorming phase, select and develop the activities that are going to be part of their course. Here we work the concrete definition of each activity using the template as a way of helping teachers to refine each activity description. Some sections are suggested in the templates for the definition of each activity: Description and instructions; Objectives; Skills; Contents; Materials and resources; Teaching and learning tools; Important dates; Dedication and pending issues. These sections are just a starting point, teachers can change them if needed.

All this material stays available for teachers to be used after the CS session.

5   Evaluation and Results

We have run 21 Course Sprints with 71 teachers from different specialties during the 4 months previous to the start of the semester; which is when teachers revise the syllabus and learning activities of their courses. Most of the sessions were face to face. However, when there were tutors that could not assist, we offered them to participate via a videoconferencing tool.

The evaluation of the CS experience has been made using qualitative, informal and quantitative methods collecting data with different instruments.

We created a questionnaire in which we asked about different aspects of the CS: utility of the CS, relation between time spent and benefits, methodology valuation, resources evaluation, utility of the products of the session and an open-ended question about possible improvements of the CS. The figures below show the responses of 16 of the participants.

1. Was this sessions useful for you?

2. Do you think the time spent in the session relates to benefits in the results?

3. Evaluation of methodologies of CS

Brainstorming

Activity development

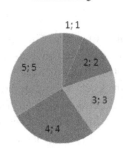

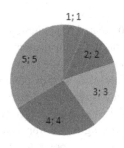

Fig. 2.

At the open-ended question about possible improvements of the CS, teachers gave us positive feedback about the adequacy of the session to the established goals. Also gave us some ideas for the improvement of the session related especially with the length, proposing doing the CS in 2 sessions for example or working part of the session online before the face to face meeting. On the other hand they valued punctuality and organization the most.

From the feedback on the sessions, we gather that the experience has been very positive. In a short period of time, teachers get to know the new environment, (re)design the learning activities and have the virtual classroom ready to start the semester. We have also seen that teachers that do not go through this course have a hard time when they switch to the new classroom. When they go through the Course Sprint previously, they already know the new system and it was much easier to adapt and guide their students though the new interface and their functionalities.

Also, the more Course Sprints we made the more we learn about teachers and their needs. That offers us the possibility get data to keep working on the enhancement of both the virtual learning environment and tools and the accompaniment actions we offer.

6   Conclusions

Technology by itself does not change the teaching methodology and practice. In this paper we have presented how we have created a support action to use the changes made in our learning environment as a perfect reason to motivate teachers to rethink their teaching tools and methodologies. Our goal was to support teachers in the design of the courses and learning activities. We do not expect them to learn first about instructional design or the available teaching and learning technologies.

The method itself very flexible, and has allowed us to place the focus on specific aspects depending on the needs of the participants by adding or removing time from others. The situation of the programs, subjects or teachers may be very different from one another, and in this sense the CS has demonstrated to easily meet the needs of each session. For example, some teachers may require support in the definition of learning objectives, while others may only be interested to focus in the design of innovative learning activities. Other teachers come with a clear idea on what they want to do, but they need to know which ICT tools can be used for their ideas.

A really interesting collateral effect of this collaborative activity with the educators and instructional designers is that they are obliged to deal together with most of the issues of that course, and this is a way to make communication flow and share important aspects of that course. Making decisions in a group is also a way to make teachers more comfortable with their tasks and make sure all the participants in the course design share a particular view.

Another parallel effect is that, by supporting a teacher on the course design of a specific subject, probably we will be indirectly improving other subjects he or she is teaching. Based on our experiences, the sessions with teachers made new ideas emerge in our teachers' minds, and many of them may take advantage of these ideas to introduce changes in other subjects. Besides, at the end, the best impact is done on the students, who will enjoy of a better learning experience.

Course Sprint sessions are teacher training sessions. In this sense, CS is a powerful contribution to the teacher training programme in a particular institution, with the added value that as you train a teacher, you are also getting a subject designed. This is an essential factor to consider: teachers will be more engaged and open to teacher training actions if they can see that the training provides a useful product for them.

The role of the facilitator, coach or expert in educational sciences and ICT is the most appropriate to support teachers in CS sessions. These facilitators need to learn about the course to be (re)designed, have a clear idea of the competences and objectives related to it, and think of a methodology or potential activities to reach the learning objectives. The knowledge about a considerable range of ICT tools is necessary as well as the most important pedagogical strategies. Creativity, spontaneity, real listening skills and flexibility are some of the essential abilities that this facilitator should bring to the process.

These conclusions will be widen once the courses that were designed through CS are finished. By that time, we will be able to collect data about the evaluation of such courses and then we will compare it with the same course designed without the CS session. For now, we know that the experience is positive for educators and helps accomplish our main goal: to facilitate the adoption of the new classroom through a short and handson activity so educators would both get to know the environment and (re)design the learning activities.

References

1. Booksprint, http://www.booksprints.net/about/
2. Course Sprint Video, http://goo.gl/1hNHRiXX
3. Design Thinking, http://designthinkingforeducators.com
4. Dick, W., Carey, L.: The Systematic Design of Instruction, 4th edn. Harper Collins Publishing, New York (1996)
5. European High Education Area, http://www.ehea.info/
6. Siemens, G.: Instructional Design in Elearning (2002),
   http://www.elearnspace.org/Articles/InstructionalDesign.htm
7. Hackathon, http://en.wikipedia.org/wiki/Hackathon
8. IMS Global Learning Consortium,
   http://www.imsglobal.org/learningdesign/
9. Lean Startup, http://theleanstartup.com/
10. Merrill, M.D., Drake, L., Lacy, M.J., Pratt, J.: Reclaiming instructional design. Educational Technology 36(5), 5–7 (1996),
    http://mdavidmerrill.com/Papers/Reclaiming.PDF
11. Wang, M., Brown, F., Jason, W.P.: Current Instructional Design Models and Principles for Effective E-and Mobile Learning. San Diego University (2012),
    http://edweb.sdsu.edu/courses/edtec596/ml/Slides/week9/
    DesignPrinciples_BrownWang.pdf
12. Morrison, G.R., Ross, S.M., Kemp, J.E.: Designing effective instruction, 4th edn. John Wiley & Sons, New York (2004)
13. Standards for coaches,
    http://www.iste.org/standards/standards-for-coaches
14. TPACK, http://www.tpack.org/

Canvas to Improve the Design Process
of Educational Animation

André L. Battaiola, Márcia Maria Alves, and Rafael Eduardo Paulin

Paraná Federal University – PPGDesign, Design Department – General Carneiro, 460,
80060-150 - Curitiba, Paraná, Brazil
{ufpr.design.profe.albattaiola,alvesmarcia,
rafapaulin}@gmail.com

Abstract. Educational animation as a resource for learning has proliferated due to the inclusion of technology in schools and the possibilities brought by new media and graphic design software. By using animation for learning this feature gains more stakeholders with different goals (learning and teaching) and becomes a complex product. Aiming this, it is necessary to use auxiliary tools to cover all the functions of the project. The Business Model Generation (BMG) is a tool that displays all stakeholders of a business and their relationships. This article tries to apply the idea of this tool as an auxiliary canvas for creating requirements for animation. For those presents the BMG canvas and proposes a canvas for design educational animations. Finally, to show its uses two animation samples were evaluated by the model built, to demonstrate the ability of the canvas to be used as a tool for collaborative requirements elicitation.

Keywords: animation, design, educational animation, and canvas.

1   Introduction

Nowadays, the use of animations as learning objects has been expanded [1]. The entertainment characteristic of animation helps to improve motivation in the teaching / learning process. On the other hand, the educational animation design becomes more complex, considering that more elements and stakeholders must be taken into account to produce an efficient educational animation.

The stakeholders group includes, basically, four types: content creators (educators in general), designers (animation conception and production), teachers as users (indirect users) and apprentices (direct users).

The design process must consider all requirements of this group, thus this process needs a tool that helps to manage and conciliate decisions in a collaborative way. To solve this problem, this paper proposes the use of a canvas based on the model presented in "Business Model Generation Canvas" [25, 26]. The proposed canvas allows both a modular and a holistic view of all design process. Besides, it allows collaborative design.

In the area of education, the use of Canvas Business Model Generation is also justified because in addition to facilitating the design of materials, it can aid in the analy-

P. Zaphiris and A. Ioannou (Eds.): LCT 2014, Part I, LNCS 8523, pp. 13–24, 2014.
© Springer International Publishing Switzerland 2014

sis of the context of learners and provide them a better fit of the proposed tasks. The analysis cultural, social and cognitive of users can help the design team elaborate the requirements of the project and put into practice the concepts of learning that focuses on apprentice learner theory (constructivism, constructionism, meaningful learning, situated learning, tangential). Having clearer understanding of the target audience could generate more motivating and engaging materials for learners.

This article examines the production of educational animations, a tool for business model proposal, and presents examples of the use of the model as a form of assessment that may evidence the actions that have been and could be taken, if the model is used at the conception phase of a given animation. The examples show some uses of the canvas.

2   Animation Educational and Participative Design

The first step to develop the canvas was modules of definition and specification. This goal required a literature review.

There are different settings for the animation definition. Lowe and Schnotz [15] define it as pictorial representation that varies over time, a form of representation and information transmission. Thomaz and Johnston [30] emphasize the animation as a media to motivate and transmit emotions. Since the study was focused on educational animation, it is expected that both visions appear balanced in design process.

This process is often guided through steps, and the entertainment industry established some animation design models [3, 11, 12, 20, 27, 29, 30, 32]. Basically, the models present four phases: conception, pre-production, production and post-production.

The conceptual phase reaches the end with the Animatic production. The Animatic is a preview of the animation, a kind of animated storyboard with times, sounds and movements planned [11]. The other phases are responsible to complete the production accordingly to the animatic.

The presented models are appropriate to develop animations focused in entertainment but they do not address educational issues, even in the conceptual phase. In addition, the lack of a process to develop educational animations usually transfers the animation concept phase to designers or to the teachers. The conception is based on designers/teachers experience and feelings, it depends of each particular designer or designer team allocated to develop the animation, thus the conception phase does not consider or consider partially the real needs of the stakeholders and the project objectives.

As already mentioned before, it is considered in this paper as stakeholders of educational animations: content creators (educators in general), designers (animation conception and production), the teachers' users (indirect users) and apprentices (direct users). To serve them, the adoption of design practices that enable collaboration and effective participation of stakeholders in the process of generating these animations is needed. This article refers to the processes of user-centered design, and more specifi-cally the participatory design. There are several definitions for participatory design, to Muller, and Haslwanter Daytorn [24] this term arising from studies of HCI can be defined as "is that the ultimate users of the software make effective contributions that reflect their own perspectives and needs, somewhere in the design and development lifecycle of the software".

However, this research adopts what Baranaukas, Martins and Valente [5] call co-design, a form of design that has bases in participatory design, but it gathers people who do not share the same work context (teachers, students and developers), and who will benefit from the product's results, view that has been an emphasis on human mediation for making animation. Co-design is understood "*as the action to work to-gether with people through various artifacts (including pencils and paper prototype systems, narratives, ethnographic research, etc.) to clarify the meanings they con-struct* " this option is necessary if one wants to narrow the gap between the results or the product of the expectations of the people most impacted by the projected solution.

Thinking of these perspectives many tools were surveyed. In HCI there are many tools and techniques for software design. Muller, Haslwanter and Daytorn offer 61 ways to work with participatory design, with the main advantages for its use in projects being the possibility of democratic and social participation of different professionals, efficiency and effectiveness and provided a greater acceptance by users [24].

By presenting these advantages, it was adopted the use of participatory and user-centered design tools as a basis for the design of educational animations.

Of course there are big productions made by film studios that have a comprehen-sive roadmap and can certainly balance these items. However designers, professionals and teachers who do not hold this training or resources make a large part of the learn-ing materials, mainly for public schools. Therefore, to assist these developers sug-gested the Business Model Generation. It is a tool for business planning, but it can assist in the development of materials for education.

This Canvas has some features that can help developers and teachers, therefore, treat the course material as a product and direct it to the students is a proposal that meets all the new trends of the interacting education.

3   Business Model Generations

According to Osterwalder, A. & Pigneur, Y., the Business Model Generation Canvas is structured to describe, analyze and design business models. The union of business techniques, strategies and concepts, forms this tool.

Figure 2 shows nine categories defined by the model; they address specific issues to plan a business. Modules show the task segmentation and prioritization (inputs and outputs) and that they can be completed collaboratively (with stickers), what differen-tiates the canvas of a conceptual map [9, 25, 26].

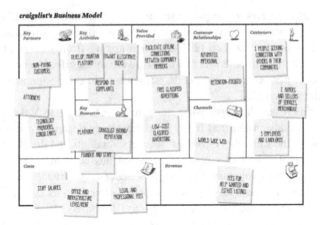

Fig. 1. Business Model Canvas [25]

The business model was adopted because the animation is treated as a product that needs to pass through processes and need to understand and work with different areas of expertise. Such processes depend on settings and complex concepts in education, technology and design, different fields that do not always share their concepts.

Educational animation can be considered products that need to be designed to provide situations and teach, which does not necessarily only depend on technical factors. The playful, motivation and entertainment can assist in this process.

In the book Business Model Generation has numerous motives and uses that canvas has acquired in worldwide. Among the main reasons for its adoption by entrepreneurs the BMG authors mention these: the canvas allows the visualization of links between parts of a process, addresses the problem (the business) holistically, presenting and exhibiting the most varied details; unifies different language experts which helps to clarify the perception of process and product; confronts actions with prospects of success and shows the entire staff implications, actions and prospects of the business.

All these vantages can be used for designing animations: best view, the holistic view, the exposure of details, the unification of process' terms can assist in the production of animation. The use of this tool can professionalize the production of educational animation and consequently improve education itself by offering an alternative to this medium be used efficiently not only just for entertainment, but also for learning.

4   Structuring the Model

The BMG canvas was the inspiration to define a canvas that helps the development of the conceptual phase of an educational animation. The proposed canvas, as a modular and collaborative tool, can help to solve or minimize this problem. Note that the current canvas is restricted to the conceptual phase, a crucial part of the educational animation design.

Figure 2 shows the initial proposal of a canvas-based business model. The model uses four modules and an integration scheme. These modules were designed to meet the 4 stakeholders and list the necessary elements to suit each group and the resources that need to be defined for each animation. The elements of each module were defined based on a bibliographic research and each module treats a specific part of the design process:

1. Content - what teach? - Type, subject, age, pedagogical line [1, 2, 7, 10, 21, 23, 33];
2. Objectives - why teach? - Motivate, illustrate, involve, visualize, thrill [1, 2, 7, 31, 33];
3. Resources - how teach? - Physical support, required resources and presentation types [1, 2, 3, 4, 6, 7, 8, 13, 14, 15, 16, 17, 18, 19, 21, 22, 28, 31];
4. Target-public – for whom? Indirect and direct users [2].

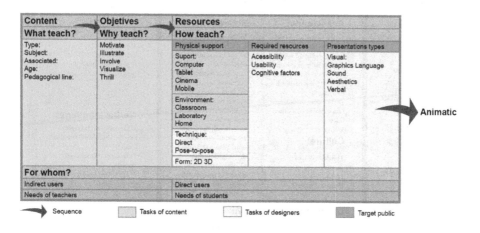

Fig. 2. First Canvas for design of educational animations

However, this initial model does not hierarchizes input or output for the shares and no inserts modules and possible elements that could go into each phase, so he was re-structured as shown in figure 3, where it has an order which lists objectives, content and resources. These modules are based on the key decisions to be made in the conceptual phase.

The modules created are only for illustration and may be added others according to the needs of the project. With this we can generate relationships, justify actions and allow the participation of other experts and other areas that may generate demands for the animation.

Fig. 3. Ultimate canvas for the Design of educacional animations

How the interests of stakeholders are different, with the generation of this canvas leave clearer decisions and requirements of the project for all involved. These modules are the result of recommendations from the dissertation of Alves [2]. Therefore, for each module have a set of questions that can be answered to establish the requisites (Table 1).

This representation shows a wider view of the animation providing an overview of the project requirements and of the stakeholders (teachers and designers), demonstrating how each action was taken and justifying each step of production.

The modules are interconnected and each choice provides a new perspective for the construction or the possibility of inclusion of other elements.

Table 1. Questions to fill the canvas

Evaluation of educational animation	
Objectives - Why?	
1) Principal goal: Why animate content?	
2) Secondary goal: There is some content associated with?	
Functions - Stakeholders	
For students:	For teachers:
Motivate? / Explain content? / Show the contents? / Entertain the student? / Illustrate content? / Display the contents? / Generate interaction? / Other	Motivate the students? / Explain content? / Show the contents? / Entertain the students? / Facilitate learning? / Display the contents? / Illustrate content? / Contextualizing? / Generate interaction? / Other
Content - What?	
Theme:	What is the theme of the animation?
Age:	What is the age group for the Project?
Type:	Fact / Procedure / Concepts / Principles / Attitudes / Values
Media:	TV / Computer / Tablet / Mobile / Cinema
Technics:	Direct / Pose to pose
Rules for content:	What is the government legislation? Standards?
Associated with:	What is discipline?
Environment:	Classroom / Laboratory / Home / Auditorium
Accessibility:	1) What is the target? 2) The animation has alternative texts or images? 3) You will be allowed to migrate from one media to another? What? 4) What file format will be available? 5) How does the interaction in the case of disabilities?
Usability	Usability principles.
Culture:	1) Adaptation of language, elements? / Others
Motivation:	1) The animation will be based on a narrative? 2) The animation has characters? 3) What is the content? Technical, serious, playful, humorous? 4) Will be used Language features? Metaphors, analogies? 5) How wills the aesthetic of animation? Which style, dash, drawing animation? 6) What is the degree of fidelity of representation towards the real object? 7) What degree of control and user interaction on the animation?
Resources - How?	
Visual language:	Syntactic composition: 1) Analyzes the Position: position of the frames (physical position or sequence of animation that can be analyzed through the structuring of keyframes). 2) Analyzes the size: the size and scale of the elements within the frame of the animation. In the case of events the issue of macro and micro situations that make up the information. 3) Analyzes the value: texture, volume and colors; use of dimensions (2D, 3D). 4) Analyzes the framing shots. 5) Drive a study of the orientation of the material: the gaze direction by direction indicators (arrows, textual, narration or sound) or motion. 6) Conducts studies of color: hue and saturation, textures, real and artificial, static color patterns and color patterns of events and dramatic situations.

Table 1. (*continued*)

	7) Evaluates the emphatic contents.
	8) Considers information as cause and effect.
	9) Groupings: connector elements, composers of the forms.
	10) Disposition of information: a way to organize the graphical representation.
	11) Analysis of movement: explicit and near real movement or unreal movement, but representative.
	12) Analysis of time: timing, acceleration and deceleration.
	13) Setting events: continuity, overlapping action, secondary action, transformation of information into narrative, scenes, sequences, plans and frameworks, use of exaggeration, anticipation, stretch and shrink.
Verbal language:	1) How the text is inserted into the animation? Subtitles? Sound?
	2) How the text relates to visual?
	3) There are visual texts?
Sounds:	1) How is the sound?
	2) True to the object represented?
	3) Playful? Illustrative? Narrative audio?

This model is still being tested but, to justify the choice of the Business Model Generation, an initial test with existing animations has been made. This strategy was adopted to justify the use of BMG and show the effects could provide a canvas in the design of educational animations process.

For this, 2 animations were selected in an intentional non-probabilistic sample to demonstrate how the canvas would work before applying it in a real design process. The selected animations are freely available on *Youtube®*. The two animations were selected because they have similar contents but different goals. The first is a playful and informative while, the other presents technical and informative content. The authors performed the assessment presented; therefore, the participation of experts and training of the variables that could be done by more people (which will be done in the future) would be necessary. The next section shows the results of these analyses.

The animations were chosen due to submit the same theme (greenhouse) but with different structures and different ways of presenting information. To demonstrate these differences form the canvas following built based on the proposed model.

The first animation (Figure 4) analyzed belongs to a series of Brazil animations called Collective conscious, created for *Canal Futura®*, a TV channel linked to education. The animation was created by *Akatu®*, which values the conscious consumption, HP and *Canal Futura®* company.

The analysis revealed some characteristics displayed by animation that may have been thought of in his briefing. The fun aspect, intended to teach values and concepts and generate reflection, it is reflected in the attitudes of the characters and the metaphors used. The use of colors, emotional, and moral appeals give an aspect of humor and attract learners' attention. The canvas can explicit the elements that have been used in the presentation, which provides the possibility of generating an assessment document that can be used as requirements document for the creation.

The second animation evaluated (Figure 5) also addresses the greenhouse and it was designed by *Mamute Midia®* for the INPE (Portuguese for Brazilian National Space Research Institute). Its analysis shows similar information when compared to the first animation, but with a different design. The animation turned into an animated infographic in 3D, with visual text (written) and spoken data. This animation uses analogies and even accessibility options (texts spoken and written). It aims to transmit technical information and to offer points of interaction with the content for the students.

The two canvas built showed different actions taken for each animation to try to achieve the needs of each one.

The canvas can also show that each requirement can require some different elements. For example, the first issue presented need the motivational factors that allowed the adoption of animated characters that was not used in the second animation that valued the real information and the teaching content.

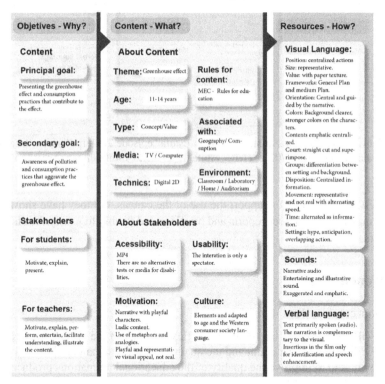

Fig. 4. Canvas of evaluation: Animation "Consciente Coletivo" episode 2. <http://www.youtube.com/watch?v=EEWturRPRuI&feature=c4-overview-vl&list=PL0799B2AEDB98CC4D> Access in Feb 01. 2014.

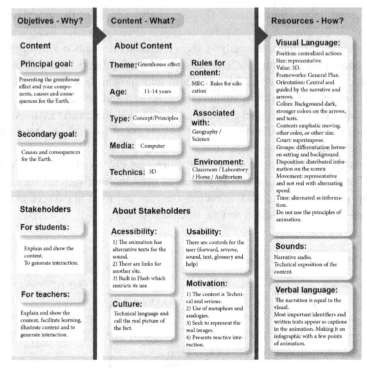

Fig. 5. Canvas of evaluation: Animation "Efeito Estufa" episode 2. <http://videoseducacionais.cptec.inpe.br/swf/mud_clima/02_o_efeito_estufa/02_o_efeito_estufa.shtml> Access in Feb 01. 2014.

This test is insufficient to support the use of the canvas, but they have showed that their use may become clearer reports and briefings and visibly to justify the choices of developers.

5   Conclusion

The authors consider that this model:

a) will allow an holistic, modular and flexible view of the design process,
b) will increase the amount and the quality of the participatory decisions and
c) will help to improve the quality of the educational animations produced.

The idea of Business Canvas can help the designers to work in an interdisciplinary and collaborative perspective, can reduce design errors and approximate the perspective of materials for teachers and students by providing best learning experience.

As future work, more tests on actual production situations animations are needed to evaluate the use of canvas as a form of animation design. The next step will consist of a consultation with experts and a case study on the use of the tool in a given period of time in a company's actual educational animation.

Acknowledgments. The financing of CAPES.

References

1. Ainsworth, S.: How do animations influence learning? School of Psychology and Learning Sciences Research Institute. University of Nottingham, Nottingham (2008)
2. Alves, M.M.: Design of educational animation: recommendations of content, graphical presentation and motivation for learning. Master's Thesis. PPGDesign. UFPR, Curitiba (2012)
3. Barbosa Jr., A.L.: Art of Animation, 2nd edn. Senac, São Paulo (2005)
4. Baer, K.: Information design workbook. Rock Port Publishers, Inc., USA (2008)
5. Baranauskas, M.C.C., Martins, M.C., Valente, J.A.: Codesign de redes digitais: tecnologias e educação a service da inclusão social. Penso, Porto Alegre (2013)
6. Bertin, J.: The Neográfica and information processing. Editora da UFPR, Curitiba (1986)
7. Clark, R.C., Lyons, C.: Graphics for learning: proven guidelines for planning, designing and evaluating visuals in training materials. John Wiley & Sons, New Jersey (2010)
8. Csikszentmihalyi, M.: Flow: the psychology of optimal experience. Harper Perennial Modern Classics Edition, USA (1990)
9. Elbers, B.F.: Designing innovative business models: A methodology for structured business model innovation (Master's thesis) (2010), Retrieved from
   `http://alexandria.tue.nl/extra2/afstversl/`
   `tm/Elbers%20F.A.%202010.pdf` (accessed October 2013)
10. Filatro, A.: Instructional Design in practice. Pearson Education do Brasil, São Paulo (2008)
11. Furniss, M.: The Animation Bible: a guide to everything – from flipbooks to flash. Laurence King Publishing, London (2008)
12. Laybourne, K.: The Animation Book: A Complete Guide to Animated Filmmaking-From Flip-Books to Sound Cartoons to 3- D Animation. Three Rivers Press, New York (1998)
13. Löbach, B.: Bases for configuration of industrial products. Blucher, São Paulo (2001)
14. Lowe, R.: Beyond "eye-candy": improving learning with animation. Curtin University of Technology, USA (2001)
15. Lowe, R., Schnotz, W.: Learning with animation: research implications for design. Cambridge University Press, New York (2008)
16. Mackinlay, J.D.: Automating the design of graphical presentation of relational information (1986), `http://www.google.com.br/`
    `#hl=pt-BR&source=hp&q=%22Automating+the+design+of+graphical+`
    `presentations+of+relational+information%22&aq=`
    `f&aqi=&aql=&oq=&gs_rfai=&fp=90b51830697d5712`
    (accessed in May 10, 2010)
17. Malone, T.W.: What makes computer games fun? In: ACM, pp. 162–169 (1980)
18. Malone, T., Lepper, M.: Making learning fun: A taxonomy of intrinsic motivations for learning. In: Snow, R., Farr, M. (eds.) Aptitude, Learning, and Instruction: III. Conative and Affective Process Analyses, pp. 223–253. Erlbaum, Hillsdale (1987)
19. Malone, T.: Heuristics for designing enjoyable user interfaces: lessons from computer games. Xerox Palo Alto Research Center (1981)
20. Marx, C.: Writing for animation, comics and games. Focal Press, UK (2007)
21. Mayer, R.E.: Multimedia learning, 2nd edn. Cambridge University Press: Library of Congress (2007)

22. Mijksenaar, P.: Visual function: an introduction to information design. Princenton Architectural Press, New York (1997)
23. Ministry of Education. Notice of public call 2 of 26 February 2010. Diário oficial da União, seção 3, no 39 (2010)
24. Muller, M.J., Haslwanter, J.H., Dayton, T.: Participatory Practices in the software lifecycle. In: Handbook of Human-Computer Interaction, Elsevier Science B. V. (1997)
25. Osterwalder, A., Pigneur, Y.: Business model generation: A handbook for visionaries, game changers, and challengers. Wiley, Hoboken (2010)
26. Osterwalder, A., Pigneur, Y., Tucci, C.L.: Clarifying business models: Origins, present and future of the concept. Commnications of the Association for Information Systems (2005)
27. Pixar studio. Production process, http://www.pixar.com/behind_the_scenes (acesso em September 19, 2010)
28. Preece, et al.: Interation design: beyond human-computer interaction. Bookman, Porto Alegre (2005)
29. Taylor, R.: Enciclopedia de técnicas de animación, 2nd edn. Acanto, Barcelona (2004)
30. Thomas, F., Johnston, O.: The illusion of life: Disney animation (1995)
31. Weiss, R.E., Knowlton, D.S., Morrison, G.R.: Principles for using animation in computer-based instruction: theoretical heuristics for effective design. Computer in Human Behavior (2002)
32. Willians, R.: The animators survival kit. A manual of methods. Faber and Faber Limited, London (2009)
33. Zabala, A.: The educational practice: how to teach. Artmed, Porto Alegre (1998)

Investigating Heuristic Evaluation as a Methodology for Evaluating Pedagogical Software: An Analysis Employing Three Case Studies

Mike Brayshaw, Neil Gordon, Julius Nganji, Lipeng Wen, and Adele Butterfield

Department of Computer Science, University of Hull,
Hull, HU6 7RX, United Kingdom
{m.brayshaw,n.a.gordon}@hull.ac.uk

Abstract. This paper looks specifically at how to develop light weight methods of evaluating pedagogically motivated software. Whilst we value traditional usability testing methods this paper will look at how Heuristic Evaluation can be used as both a driving force of Software Engineering Iterative Refinement and end of project Evaluation. We present three case studies in the area of Pedagogical Software and show how we have used this technique in a variety of ways. The paper presents results and reflections on what we have learned. We conclude with a discussion on how this technique might inform on the latest developments on delivery of distance learning.

Keywords: Heuristic evaluation, pedagogy, pedagogical software, disability, technology enhanced learning, flexible learning.

1 Introduction

This paper addresses practical concerns about evaluation methods and techniques in the context of educational software. In it we discuss methods of evaluating software and pragmatic approaches about how this can be done in practice. We note that whilst this is often hard to do, it is a vital part of the software development lifecycle. Formal experimental empirical studies can be difficult to set up, organise and run. This paper discusses our experiences with a lightweight alternative. What this paper does is reflect on issues we have found and provides details through case studies to demonstrate the application of Heuristic Evaluation as an alternative possible solution route. Heuristic evaluation is a well established method for quickly evaluating the efficacy of new media solutions to interface issues [12-14]. One type of new media is that pertaining to pedagogy and educationally motivated software. Squires and Preece [16] first proposed using heuristic evaluation as a way of measuring quality, learning potential, and usability in educationally motivated applications. Albion [1] and Benson et al [3] are examples of this methodology being applied.

In this paper we will reflect on three case studies that have used this evaluation technique and the value and insight that it has afforded. The heuristics used here were developed from Squires and Preece [16] so all three studies used the same questions.

P. Zaphiris and A. Ioannou (Eds.): LCT 2014, Part I, LNCS 8523, pp. 25–35, 2014.

The first was a Semantic Web motivated Virtual Learning Environment, proposed as a general learning architecture, but instanced here as a computer science tutor [17].

This case study used heuristic evaluation at the end of a long software build to evaluate the usability and learnability of the final product. The second case study [8-9] looked at ontology-driven personalisation of services in the context of university students with disabilities. Thus the context and nature of the subjects of the evaluation was notably different from that of the first approach. Heuristic evaluation was carried out by both subjects with disabilities and without. The task was to locate resources and manage the learning packages in the context of a university using a specially designed software help and navigation tool. The third case study used heuristic evaluation to gain an understanding of the usability of a rolling prototype tutoring system for C# [4]. The prototype was evaluated by a group of experts who had established experience in teaching programming at First Year University level to an introductory computer science cohort. The technique was thus used not as an end user evaluation but as part of a rolling software development to get expert input into the evolving software tutoring tool.

This paper will report results from all three studies. In all the cases reported heuristic evaluation was found to be an effective tool and one that was easy and fairly fast to use. An evaluation of the effectiveness of all three case studies will be given and we will give individual examples of some of the outcomes and effectiveness of this type of activity. We will conclude with a discussion about what we have learnt about employing this technique and compare the type of outputs achieved from the approach taken here to that which we might have got from more formal or traditional evaluation methods. Indeed where we aim to turn next is to carry out a traditional empirical evaluation experiment with one of our case studies to compare the results. We look forward to being able to report on that in the future.

2   Case Study: A Schema-Driven Flexible Virtual Learning Environment

2.1   The Schema-Driven Approach

This case study is based on the evaluation of a system that was designed to provide a software platform for the provision of personalised content for virtual learning environments [17]. The system was designed to use a schema - that is machine-readable versions of instances of an educational process - providing a management system to allow the system to provide flexibility to the user in terms of building a personalised learning schema based on the users' needs. For this approach, semantic web concepts were utilised so that the users would be able to make their choices in terms of options such as the style of learning, and then the system would compile – i.e. combine and build – a suitable overall learning schema for the user.

2.2   Evaluation of the System

Once the prototype system was developed, the issue remained of how to evaluate its effectiveness. It was thus decided to develop an evaluation based around a set of usability elements, considered against the user's context i.e. the usability of the e-learning software, considering the designer/learner models, learner control, teacher customisation, and pedagogy. The heuristic evaluation approach in this case study was based around comparing the prototype against the perceived effectiveness of 3 other existing systems (for details of this see [17]).

In terms of Human-Computer Interaction, the system usability of the prototype was assessed as part of the overall heuristic evaluation, with regards to Nielsen's heuristics, for example "user control and freedom" , "flexibility and efficiency of use" and "help users recognize, diagnose, and recover from errors" [14]. Further, the prototype was considered against the assessment criteria for eLearning systems designed by Squires and Preece [16] that was developed from Nielsen's [14] heuristics. These criteria included "learner control", "teacher customisation" and "pedagogy".

For the prototype eLearning system in this case study, the participants were provided with information at least 3 days before the evaluation, which consisted of a hand-out with instructions, identifying the goals of the study, a set of definitions used in the evaluation and what they would be expected to do. The evaluation focussed on the typical use of the system – i.e. as users within the context of eLearning – not on general usage. To be specific, the study concerned the usability regarding flexibility of the selected eLearning tool around, for example, learner control, teacher customisation and pedagogy.

The participants were provided with instructions on using the different systems to carry out the requisite tasks, e.g. to select learning units, to collect these together to develop an overall learning process, and to review how they were able to manage that process. The study itself had 10 participants, ranging from 3 professors to a range of computer science PhD students. Interaction was constrained with the use of scripts to try to constrain the range of actions so that each system could be compared in a systematic way.

After each participant had used each system, there was a heuristic evaluation session to gather data on their use and perceptions of the system. There was also an opportunity to provide views on the overall process.

2.3   Results of the Evaluation

The evaluation produced data on the participants' views of using all 4 systems – that is the prototype system and the 3 comparison systems. The participants used the same evaluation heuristics enabling comparison across the systems. By collating data into Agree, Disagree or Maybe the different systems could be compared, especially in terms of the usability of the different systems. This enabled the ease of use of the prototype to be evaluated against the other systems. This provided a good indicator of the usability of the system, with 70% agreeing the prototype enabled the user to develop a suitable learning schema for them (with only 10%, 20% and 10% agreeing this for the comparison systems). All 4 systems received positive (70% or more) agreement on the question of whether the software provided multiple views and representation. For full details of the evaluation see [17]. The use of heuristic evaluation for the flexible virtual learning environment enabled the system to be compared against 3 other systems. The evaluation showed the benefits and some limitations in the prototype system.

The participants in the evaluation were asked to comment on the evaluation methodology itself. The results from this showed that 90% felt the evaluation did show differences between the 4 systems, and the limitations of each, and 80% agreed that the evaluation results provided useful statistics by which to compare the systems.

3   Case Study: The ONTODAPS e-Learning System

3.1   What is ONTODAPS?

To respond to the current need for inclusive blended learning in contemporary education which is greatly driven by information and communication technologies (ICTs), a disability-aware e-learning system needed to be designed, implemented and evaluated. The Ontology-Driven Disability-Aware Personalized E-Learning System (ONTODAPS) responds to that need and personalizes learning resources for students (both disabled and non-disabled) based on their disability type and severity whilst considering their learning goals and the preference of the formats in which learning resources should be presented.

3.2   The Need for a Disability-Aware e-Learning System

Although ICTs greatly facilitate learning for students without disabilities, it could pose a significant challenge to disabled students when the technologies are not accessible. With the success of the Web, learning is now being delivered online and numerous e-learning systems have been developed to facilitate learning. Nevertheless, some of these learning systems are not accessible to learners with disabilities. This problem could arise when the developers of the systems do not adhere to guidelines for accessible design such as WCAG 2.0 and do not consider the needs of disabled learners during the design process [9]. By engaging with disabled students at the University of Hull, directly in lectures and through mentoring sessions, we have been able to understand the difficulties these students face with using existing e-learning environments and to obtain their recommendations for increased accessibility in e-learning systems.

Over the past decade, our research has focused on how we deliver learning to students using educational software. With increasing awareness on the challenges faced by the increasing numbers of disabled students while trying to use blended learning technologies, we spread our tentacles into inclusive education, seeking novel ways to deliver courses in an inclusive way. From searching literature, we have found that very little research is being done to improve the learning of disabled students from a personalization approach particularly employing semantic web technologies and considering the needs of students with multiple disabilities. This response conforms to contemporary legislations in various countries that call for service providers to include the needs of disabled people through accessible systems. Such is the case with the Special Educational Needs and Disability Act, 2001 in the UK, the Accessibility for Ontarians with Disabilities ACT, 2005 and the Americans with Disabilities Act, 1990 just to mention these. The design process through which experts in disability and disabled students and other stakeholders are involved in designing inclusive and accessible blended learning systems adopted in the ONTODAPS design is in accordance with the disability-aware design approach [11].

3.3   Main Functionalities of the ONTODAPS System

ONTODAPS functions as a multi-agent e-learning system that is driven by the ADOOLES (Abilities and Disabilities Ontology for Online LEarning and Services) ontology. The architecture of ONTODAPS is presented in Fig. 1.

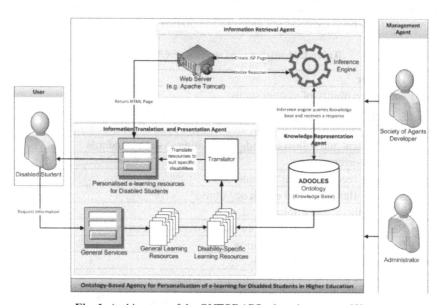

Fig. 1. Architecture of the ONTODAPS e-learning system [8]

As ONTODAPS currently employs an interface technology, a student seeking personalized learning resources interacts with the system through a visual interface implemented with Java. The student identifies himself through an authentication mechanism involving a username and password and the system then recognizes the student's disability type based on information stored in his profile. The student selects his learning goals and an indication of the severity of his disability. The ADOOLES ontology which represents knowledge about the student and the learning resources and goals is queried and information is passed onto the information retrieval agent which makes inference and then presents information to the information translation and presentation agent. The outcome is learning resource presented to the student in a format that is compatible with his disability and also meets his learning needs. If a student is visually impaired for instance, learning resources could be presented as audio or text and the text in the interface is also read out to the student through an inbuilt screen reader.

It is noteworthy that ONTODAPS has an administrative interface where administrators could manage the learning of the students and upload learning resources, setting up goals and also adding users to the system. There is also the possibility of a new user to register on the system and thence to manage their profile.

3.4   Heuristic Evaluation of ONTODAPS

Heuristic evaluation, fundamentally based on Nielsen's ten heuristics [14], is a cost effective evaluation method used in finding problems with the design of a piece of software before its release. The aim of this is to fix the problems found before users can use the system. Heuristic evaluation can also be used to evaluate educational software and has been successfully employed to do this.

Table 1. Heuristics used to evaluate ONTODAPS

No	Heuristic
1	Ensures visibility of system status
2	Provides match between the system and the real world
3	Flexible enough to provide the user enough control and freedom
4	Is consistent and follows common operating system standards
5	Prevents errors
6	Supports recognition rather than recall
7	Supports flexibility and efficiency of use
8	Uses aesthetic and minimalist design
9	Helps users recognise, diagnose and recover from errors
10	Provides help and documentation
11	Has clear goals and objectives
12	Context is meaningful to domain and learner
13	Content clearly and multiply represented and multiply navigable
14	Provides navigational fidelity
15	Provides appropriate levels of learner control
16	Supports personally significant approaches to learning

We evaluated ONTODAPS after *learning with software heuristics* [16], also incorporating some *educational design heuristics* [15] in a similar manner to [1] and [5]. To heuristically evaluate ONTODAPS, we used ten experts in pedagogy at the University of Hull who had at least three years' experience in evaluating educational software and in human-computer interaction.

Before the evaluation, the experts were given a guide to ONTODAPS which was presented in three formats: audio, video and text format. The experts could choose the format they preferred. After going through the guide, they were asked to interact with the system at least twice and then to perform specific tasks before evaluating the system based on specific heuristics as shown in Table 1.

3.5   Results of Heuristic Evaluation of ONTODAPS

For each heuristic presented in Table 1, evaluators were asked to rate the software on a scale of 10. The mean scores for each heuristic obtained from the ten expert heuristic evaluators are presented in Fig.2.

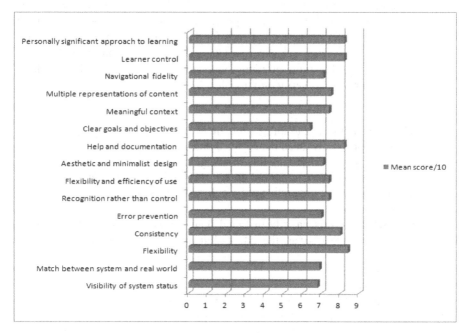

Fig. 2. Results of heuristic evaluation of ONTODAPS

Generally, ONTODAPS was seen to follow common operating system standards with its menus following platform standards. It provided appropriate levels of learner control by allowing learners to self-direct their learning through personalizing learning resources and allowing them to choose the format in which the resources are presented to them. Nevertheless, there were some usability problems in the area of system visibility status, needing much improvement in keeping users informed of what is going on through appropriate and timely feedback. Heuristic evaluation also helped find the need to fully grant keyboard only users access to the system by activating keyboard functionality. Thus, by carrying out a heuristic evaluation of the software, various usability problems categorized into major, minor and cosmetic problems were found and the system improved upon. By employing specific heuristics suitable for educational software, we ensured that the evaluated system meets the standards of educational software and focusing on special educational needs, we also ensured that the software is fully inclusive, meeting the needs of disabled users.

4   Case Study: An Inquiry-Based C# Tutor

The third case study was an Inquiry based tutoring system for C#. Inquiry based learning [7] aims to put the user as the centre of the learning process and through their exploration acquire, at their own pace, through their own efforts, and in their own language acquire the desired skills. The overall make of the tutoring system is heavily influenced by Anderson [2]. The novel thing in this case study is that the approach taken here was one of iterative refinement of the prototype. We engaged with the experts as soon as the first robust prototype was available. So instead of using heuristic evaluation as an end evaluation technique, we embedded it into the very body of the development process. The target audience for the tutoring system was novice programmers but the aim was to get expert teachers evaluating the interface from the start. Every usability and learning problem found should be recorded and the violated heuristic found and given a severity rating scale.

Severity Scale
0) I don't agree that this is a usability problem at all
1) Cosmetic problem only; need not be fixed unless extra time is available
2) Minor usability problem; fixing this should be given low priority
3) Major usability problem; important to fix; so should be given a high priority
4) Usability catastrophe; imperative to fix before this product is released

Once the usability errors have been found then the expert will need to go back through the C# tutorial to ascertain the extent of the problem by applying a scale [3].

Extensiveness Scale
1) This is a single case
2) This problem occurs in several places in the program
3) This problem is widespread throughout the program

The Heuristic evaluation proved to be successful and led to significant updates in the software at each iteration. When initially carrying out the evaluation it was believed that the software was almost at a stage of completion. Luckily the software evaluation was started early enough so from the feedback given, there was enough time for a significant amount of updates to take place.

An alpha study was carried out using PhD students which led to initial important modifications. The updated software was then sent to seven experts (who have at least 5 years teaching programming experience), in order to carry out the heuristic evaluation. After four evaluators replied, the collated results were extremely interesting and found some issues that had not been considered in the development of the project. The experts really tested the extremities of the program by not following set paths or reading the instructions: - an oversight which had been taken for granted. From the feedback given it led to more software updates to try and improve the system based on the comments provided.

This led to the completion of prototype 6. This version was then sent out to the same seven evaluators asking if they had time to carry out a heuristic evaluation on the current prototype. One of the evaluators responded promptly and their feedback pointed out some fundamental issues which needed to be dealt with immediately. The updates were duly carried out and led to the completion of prototype 7. This prototype was sent to five of the evaluators who had already been sent the previous versions and a new external (to the University) evaluator who also has had at least 5 years experience teaching programming. Thus heuristic evaluation informed an iterating evolution of prototypes. Some experts commented on a single version but others were involved over the whole process and were able to give insights into the evolution of the whole. Heuristic evaluation provided a key role in a rolling evolution of a software project.

To summarise the changes heuristic evaluation made overall for this process important revisions were made as follows:

- Important HCI navigational changes
- HCI Conformity and Consistency Changes
- Important Changes to Wording
- Updates to Pedagogic Issues
- Tutorial Learning Content

5 Evaluation, Discussion and Conclusion

The paper has considered some of the practical concerns about evaluation methods and techniques for educational software. It is not our intention to find a substitute for classical empirical studies. In an ideal world it would be great to be able to run full empirical evaluations of our target software using large numbers of subjects in a balance empirical design. Indeed this assumes that sufficient numbers of suitable users are available. The design of these studies is not a trivial task in addition to pragmatic issues. In the rapidly changing world of computing, technology functionality, interaction model, and the continuing evolution of the affordances of the technology, we need to evaluate the artifacts that we create. Indeed the emergence of things like ubicomp (Ubiquitous Computing, [18]) and how we interact with technology may well be on the move and we need a way of evaluating the effectiveness as we move to new delivery surfaces. Thus a quick and light touch way of being able to evaluate the pedagogical software is a timely thing. As time is an essence heuristic evaluation has here provided us with a way to answer these questions. We saw how this could be done in Case Studies 1 and 2 as a way of evaluating the pedagogic tool that was produced at the end of the project. Case Study 3 does demonstrate how it can be used actively to drive the very design process so that the output of the expert study feeds directly into the next generation of prototype, demonstrating how this approach could be deployed in a fast changing interface design.

There has been criticism in the past that heuristic evaluation just tests the opinion of those who are carrying out the evaluation [12]. It may not actually spot any real interface issues or problems, but just instead the preferences of the experts employed. Care has been taken in all these studies to choose experienced computer scientists in all these, students who we hope can be relied on to make expert judgement about HCI and pedagogy judgments. Indeed all three of the studies took place in a university context so the experts were in a position to comment on their effectiveness. Furthermore the use of the set series of questions [16] would act to focus the dialog onto the matter in hand.

Another issue that raised concerns was false alarm – where the expert identifies an interface issue which is actually of no concern to the user. Now it can be argued that false alarms are actually good things if it leads to more rigorous testing and investigation. As the audiences for online courses increases so may the range of users – possibly cutting down on false alarms by increasing varieties of behaviour.

One area that we are currently keen to compute is to compare our results that we have got from these quick and light evaluations with the types of results that would be obtained from a traditional empirical evaluation in the context of pedagogically motivated software (as opposed to more generally in HCI, e.g. [6]. We are currently in the process of designing and running such a study for Case Study 2 to see how closely these two results match or otherwise.

The move to learning online and therefore by computer mediated means we are accelerating even at the time of writing. In the past year or so we have seen a vast explosion in the use of MOOCs (Multiple Open Online Communities). These are now offered by a very large number of universities from all over the world offering courses, where student numbers are measured in their 100 000s, offering distance education for users in many different countries. Now trying to evaluate these systems, based on student experience, would present a problem, both due to the logistics of organising a multi-continent study, but also of issues of the extremely variable skill sets/life experiences of those who sign up for such courses. Anyone can sign up irrespective of whether these courses are appropriate given their study level. Thus any study would have to work who was being evaluated, how they were doing their study, and balance for such things in any study undertaken. However to extend the approach taken here will be an appropriate use of our light weight pedagogical evaluation developed here. Rather than casting around in the wide diaspora of users instead we can focus on the education material itself and carry out the evaluation by heuristic evaluation using a college of experts. Thus heuristic evaluation of pedagogic software has the potential to allow us to evaluate brand new ways of learning.

References

1. Albion, P.: Heuristic evaluation of educational multimedia: from theory to practice. In: ASCILITE 1999: 16th Annual Conference of the Australasian Society for Computers in Learning in Tertiary Education: Responding to Diversity, Brisbane, Australia (1999)
2. Anderson, J.R.: The expert module. In: Foundations of Intelligent Tutoring Systems, pp. 21–53 (1988)
3. Benson, L., Elliott, D., Grant, M., Holschuh, D., Kim, B., Kim, H., Lauber, E., Loh, S., Reeves, T.: Heuristic Evaluation Instrument and Protocol for E-Learning Programs (2001), http://it.coe.uga.edu/~treeves/edit8350/HEIPEP.html (accessed October 31, 2013)

4. Butterfield, A., Brayshaw, M.: A Pedagogically Motivated Guided Enquiry Based Tutor for C#, Submitted Article (2014)
5. Granic, A., Cukusic, M.: Usability Testing and Expert Inspections Complemented by Educational Evaluation: A Case Study of an e-Learning Platform. Educational Technology & Society 14, 107–123 (2011)
6. Jeffries, R., Desurvire, H.: Usability Test versus Heuristic Evaluation. SIGCHI Bulletin 24(4) (October 1992)
7. Kahn, P., O'Rourke, K.: Guide to curriculum design: enquiry-based learning. Higher Education Academy (2004) (March 30)
8. Nganji, J.T., Brayshaw, M., Tompsett, B.C.: Ontology-Based E-Learning Personalisation for Disabled Students in Higher Education. Italics 9(4) (2011) ISSN 1473-7507
9. Nganji, J.T., Brayshaw, M., Tompsett, B.: Ontology-Driven Disability-Aware E-Learning Personalisation with ONTODAPS. Campus Wide Information Systems 30(1), 17–34 (2013)
10. Nganji, J.T., Brayshaw, M.: Designing Personalised Learning Resources for Disabled Students Using an Ontology-Driven Community of Agents. In: Isaias, P., Baptista Nunes, M. (eds.) Information Systems Research and Exploring Social Artefacts: Approaches and Methodologies, pp. 81–102. Information Science Reference, Hershey (2013), doi:10.4018/978-1-4666-2491-7.ch005
11. Nganji, J.T., Nggada, S.H.: Disability-Aware Software Engineering for Improved System Accessibility and Usability. International Journal of Software Engineering and Its Applications (IJSEIA) 5(3), 47–62 (2011)
12. Nielsen, J., Molich, R.: Heuristic evaluation of user interfaces. In: Proc. ACM CHI 1990 Conf., Seattle, WA, April 1-5, pp. 249–256 (1990)
13. Nielsen, J., Mack, R.: Usability Inspection Methods. John Wiley, New York (1994) ISBN 0-471-01877-5
14. Nilesen, J., Mack, R. (eds.): Usability Inspection Methods. John Wiley, New York (1994)
15. Quinn, C.N.: Pragmatic evaluation: lessons from usability. In: Christie, A., Vaughan, B. (eds.) 13th Annual Conference of the Australasian Society for Computers in Learning in Tertiary Education (ASCILITE 1996). Australia Society for Computers in Learning in Tertiary Education, Adelaide (1996)
16. Squires, D., Preece, J.: Predicting quality in educational software: Evaluating for learning, usability and the synergy between them. Interacting with Computers 11, 467–483 (1999)
17. Wen, L., Brayshaw, M., Gordon, N.: Personalized Content Provision for Virtual Learning Environments via the Semantic Web. Italics (2012) ISSN 1473-7507
18. Weiser, M., Gold, R., Brown, J.S.: The origins of ubiquitous computing research at PARC in the late 1980s. IBM Systems Journal 38(4), 693–696 (1999)

A Narrative Research Approach: The Experiences of Social Media Support in Higher Education

Alev Elçi[1] and Begüm Çubukçuoğlu Devran[2]

[1] Aksaray University, Department of Management Information Systems, Aksaray, Turkey
alevelci@aksaray.edu.tr
[2] Eastern Mediterranean University, Department of Elementary Education, Famagusta, Cyprus
begum.cubukcuoglu@emu.edu.tr

Abstract. Narrative research is started to be used in educational context recently. This article focuses on a discussion of the reasons for choosing narrative research approach in discovering the experiences of social media usage in higher education. Moreover, the preliminary information of ongoing study is provided. The authors use this method to convey their experiences about using social media for supporting their teaching and learning outside the classroom. The increasing trend in social media usage among new generations is being used as an advantage to interact and communicate with students in 'their way'.

Keywords: narrative, narrative research, social media, collaboration, learning, storytelling.

1 Introduction

Once upon a time there was no social media support in education whereas these days there is a torrent of using technology and social media in higher education with the trend of increased usage of mobile devices, tablets and games among learners. Use of technology from younger ages challenges traditional teaching and learning approaches, where students seem reluctant to read books and write reports even not motivated to participate in the classroom. These changes necessitate efficient use of computers and communication technologies in education. Thus, the social media which already entered in student lives should be injected in the educational environments for efficient and demanding daily use. In this way surfing, sharing, and networking facilities of social media may be used more intensely for educational purpose. These will also support the innovative constructivist, active and social learning strategies.

One of the authors has been using social media in various courses since 2007 while the other one 2008 onwards. This paper is a narrative account of their experience. A brief review of social media usage in education domain is being introduced in sections 2-3 together with a literature review focused more on narrative research. The frame of this study in terms of the reason for selecting narrative and the methodology followed is taken up in subsequent sections. Since it is an ongoing study, in this paper it is aimed to discuss the narrative research and the reasons for using it, the findings of the

P. Zaphiris and A. Ioannou (Eds.): LCT 2014, Part I, LNCS 8523, pp. 36–42, 2014.

research study will be provided in another work. Conclusions are drawn at the end and suggestions are offered.

2   History of Social Media Usage

Social media and social networking are the communication tools/technologies where people interact for sharing information and having discussions in addition to exchanging content. "They appear in many forms including blogs and microblogs, forums and message boards, social networks, wikis, virtual worlds, social bookmarking, tagging and news, writing communities, digital storytelling and scrapbooking, and data, content, image and video sharing, podcast portals, and collective intelligence" [1]. These different forms of social media enable virtual practice of interaction. Research results revealed that, mostly for first year students, interactive media creates an opportunity to collaborate with their peers and faculty members [2]. Social media such as Facebook, Twitter, YouTube and Wikipedia are widely held emerging technologies within young generation.

Summarizing the history of social media is beneficial to see how it was drawn and how it is now. 'Friends Reunited' is stated as the first online social media founded in Great Britain by year 1999, followed by 'Friendster' (2002), 'MySpace' (2003) and 'Facebook' (2004) in USA [1]. Open membership was allowed for everyone in Facebook (2006), where the number of users around the globe hit 200 million in 2009 and recently 1.11 billion in 2013. In addition, Australian survey results claim that 13 percent of social media users were logged on at school.

3   Social Media for Education

Many research and practices investigate the use social media as an extension to class learning environment [4], [5]. Even some universities, such as Victoria University in Australia, created their own social networks for students and prepared best practice guidelines for the use of social media for faculty members' use. Victoria University Social Media Registry [6] shows that they allow institutional social media tools for some purposes, such as record keeping of student participation for assessment, creating "authenticated, equitable, secure, accessible and safe" virtual environment for students.

There are many researches which claim the use of social media by the students for educational purposes. However, some other research [2] shows that higher education students significantly prefer use of social media for social purposes than academic purposes. A similar study conducted by student researchers in New Hampshire show that 96% of students use Facebook where majority of students use it for social (89%) and entertainment (79%) where educational (26%) and professional (16%) use is less [7].

Another remarkable research is the use of blogs in Taiwan [5] where pre-service teachers doing master's degree were investigated. Outcomes of this study, in terms of pre-service teachers' professional development on the blogs, the difficulties they have encountered, problem solving strategies employed, and the students' perception of blogging were documented. The results have showed that blogging helped pre-service teachers to share their reflections of theories and practices, besides developing online interaction with the readers with active engagement.

Social media offers many opportunities for the higher education faculty members as well as learners. According to a recent research, it is found that nearly 90% of faculty members have been using social media for the courses they teach and for their professional development outside the class [8]. They also reported that there are no major differences between different groups (online teaching, tenure status, full-time, etc.) of faculty members in social media usage.

Besides using popular social media sites such as Facebook, Twitter, YouTube and Wikipedia, users create their own social websites and social networks for specific interest groups. For example Ning, Netlog, Weebly and Xing networks can all be used both in social life and as an educational learning environment. By being aware of these opportunities, higher education students may wish their faculty members to adopt such new educational opportunities in their teaching.

Since there is an increasing trend in social media use, the authors of this work experimented with using this as an advantage to interact and communicate with their students in 'their way' outside the classroom. As mentioned above, the authors have started using social media to support the teaching and learning in classes since 2008.

The aim of this study is to create a framework to narrate positive and negative experiences of two higher education faculty members in using social media; pros and cons of using social media are offered from the faculty perspective. The narrative research was adopted to discover both personal life experiences. In other words, both narrators tell their stories regarding the use of social media in higher education. This is ongoing study, so in this paper only the groundwork of the research process is provided.

4   The Narrative

A synonym of the term 'narrative' is 'story' or 'history'. Narrative is defined [9] as "a vital human activity which structures experience and gives it meaning". The process and the product features of narrative and the mode of inquiry differentiate them from each other. Narrative can be seen as a way of structuring and organizing new experiences and knowledge by constructing knowledge and making it more learnable [10].

Studying narrative is a way of studying the ways humans experience the world [11]. There cannot be any person who does not have narratives [12]. Whereas [13] argues that life itself could be seen as a narrative that consists of many other stories. Narrative research is gradually used in studies of education. Teachers and learners are the main touchstone in education and they are the storytellers 'in their own and other's stories' [11].

Narrative inquiry is both a phenomenon and a method where people tell their stories; narrative researchers explain such experiences by collecting stories and writing narratives of them [11]. Narrative inquiry provides an opportunity to the researcher access to the personal experiences of the participant, the storyteller. Storyteller speaks and declares life as experiences in a narrative form that is called story [9]. Thus, the researcher has an opportunity to study the subjects in their natural setting and understand the behavior, actions and feelings in a whole context.

5   The Reason and Context for Using Narrative

Usually narrative research is used in such diverse domains as sociology, anthropology, history, nursing, psychology, and communication studies [14]. Recently narrative research has been used in educational practices, especially in exploring experiences of teachers' and students' lives. However, there is not that much research conducted on the use of Web 2.0 technologies, and Social media by faculty members and their life stories.

We believe that while there is an intensive use of Web 2.0 and social media in education especially in higher education, there is a need to discover and understand lecturers' stories regarding integration of social media into their way of teaching and their students learning outside the classroom walls. One such research conducted [15] aimed to understand faculty reflections during the process of adapting digital technologies by listening to their life stories.

We the authors of this paper, and narrators, have had positive and negative experiences, and in some good and bad examples in practice. However, we wanted to bring a different point of view and carry out personal experiences in different social and disciplinary settings through a longer timeframe. We wanted to better understand our experiences and attitudes as faculty, behaviors to social media by telling our own stories. We chose storytelling because we believed that by doing so our colleagues and even we as storytellers may better learn pros and cons of using social media in higher education. Telling and hearing our own and each other's stories which are self-reflections of experiences may help to estimate our weaknesses. As [14] mentions, narrating may also engage and convince the readers. Indeed, some people prefer listening to storytelling for better learning. Thus, you will read our stories straight from us; not in the way other researchers molded it [16], exempted from intervention of other professionals [17].

6   Methodology

The purpose of this study can be identified with the following research questions:

- How do social media get used in higher education to support learning?
- What kinds of problems are faced while using social media in higher education?

This study is a qualitative research study that used narrative research as a strategy of inquiry. The qualitative research enables the researcher to reach detailed data in its natural setting and since it is interpretative it gives an opportunity to the researcher to interpret the data. It also focuses on participant's experiences and ideas [18]. As a strategy of inquiry, a narrative research aims at understating "the outcome of interpretation rather than explanations" by providing an opportunity to gather data from real life and lived experiences [9]. Narratives are related with life stories. [13] defines "a narrative is a story that tells a sequence of events that is significant for the narrator or audience or her or his audience" (p.60). Narrative research gives us stories about lived experiences that are not forgotten and the way of experiencing them [13]. In our case, the narrative approach highlighted the way that we integrated the social media into our courses as an educational tool outside the classroom.

Storytelling method was used to collect data in this study which includes the stories of two higher education faculty members who have been using social media as an educational tool in their teacher education since 2008 and information technology courses since 2007. The stories are about participants' use of social media in supporting their teaching. Stories explained how and why the participants started to use social media, the aims of using social media, the ways of using it. Moreover, the causes of using social media and the difficulties experienced, pros and cons of using social media in educational setting are all told.

In this study we have told our individual stories, which included our detailed experiences of what is done, how it is done, why it is done and our point of views. In the analysis we re-read our stories and reorganized them regarding to the aim of the research. In other words, the participant's stories [19] were restoried.

In narrative study, the cases that told their stories are a typical rather than representative of population [20]. We believed that since participants and researchers are the same persons so the bias is more or less disappeared from the aspect of researcher. There was not a direct interview so at the first hand there was no direct interaction with the researcher and participant.

Validity of the research was ensured as follows:

- After restorying the stories of others we took them back to story owner in order to confirm accuracy.
- We used 'peer debriefing to enhance the accuracy of account', [18] (p.196)
- Actions and applications that were done through the social media was controlled and compared with the stories.

Moreover, since the narrative inquiry provides an opportunity to researcher and participant work collaboratively in understanding behavior and discovering explanations, validity of the participant may be obtained [21].

7   Findings and Discussion

The aim of this research study is to understand and share the experiences of two university faculty members integrating social media into their courses. Since this is an ongoing study we may only provide preliminary findings and information regarding to the research results. The preliminary findings of the research show that both narrators have started to use social media in order to provide students an opportunity to connect and interact with their peers and lecturer outside the classroom. Another reason both the participants preferred to use specific social media is that they believed that their students use this social media very commonly for socialization with their friends. The instructors wanted to take advantage of this fact for their courses. Furthermore, they aimed to motivate students with different learning styles to participate in course related activities online for some might prefer virtual learning environments. However, one of the participants stated that "unfortunately, there are still students who do not participate even in Facebook group".

8   Conclusion

Social media is one of the important communication technologies that new generation students use commonly in communicating with their friends in their social life. They are using this technology very commonly within their daily life for socialization. Since they spend a long time with this technology it might be beneficial to use it in lessons in order to enhance teaching and learning in the classroom. The participants of this research study shared their experiences in using social media as part of their course work.

With this research study it is aimed to understand the difference and similarities in social media usage from different points of view of faculty members. Moreover, this paper is expected to review the narrative research and its applicability in technology enhanced learning. The results of this study will enlighten various types of using social media, weaknesses of using it, solutions to strengthen the use of social media as an educational tool in higher education rising from the recorded stories of two faculty members. The real stories that took place may help or guide the others who are willing to go through the process of preparing and using social media learning spaces as educational environments.

Moreover, the studying of life stories of researchers encourages self-reflection which should help participant researchers in understanding their weaknesses of the use of social media for learning purposes, so develop a refined strategy for future application and even may decide that they may need support. Since two researchers who are also participants working collaboratively, their active, collaborative and engaged participation to the research in constructing stories of past experiences may help them to develop new experiences.

We wanted to share our personal experience stories with academia with the belief in storytelling. Having in mind that, as [14] points out, we can engage and convince the readers to for experiencing innovative use of social media in education. Emphasizing that narrative applications are extended "beyond lived experience and worlds 'behind' the author" moving towards "human interaction in relationship" [14] (p.392).

References

1. Curtis, A.: The brief history of Social Media. Mass Communication Department, University of North Carolina at Pembroke (2013), http://www.uncp.edu/home/acurtis/NewMedia/SocialMedia/SocialMediaHistory.html (retrieved January 19, 2014)
2. BrckaLorenz, A., Cervera, Y., Garver, A.: Interactive technology and effective educational practices. Paper presented in Association for Institutional Research (AIR) in Atlanta, Georgia (2010), http://cpr.iub.edu/uploads/AIR2010%20Interactive%20Tech%20FINAL.pdf (retrieved January 19, 2014)

3. Abdelraheem, A.Y.: University students' use of social networks sites and their relation with some variables. In: WEI International Academic Conference Proceedings, Antalya, Turkey (2013)
4. Madge, C., Meek, J., Wellens, J., Hooley, T.: Facebook, social integration and informal learning at university: "It is more for socialising and talking to friends about work than for actually doing work". Learning, Media and Technology 34(2), 141–155 (2009)
5. Sun, Y.-C.: Developing reflective cyber communities in the blogosphere: a case study in Taiwan higher education. Teaching in Higher Education 15(4), 369–381 (2010)
6. Victoria University Social Media Registry. Using social media for teaching and learning – Staff Guide (2009), http://learningandteaching.vu.edu.au/teaching_practice/blended_learning/social_media/Resources/Using_social_media_for_learning_and_teaching.pdf (retrieved December 10, 2013)
7. Martin, C., et al.: Social networking usage and grades among college students. UNHSocial media report (2009), http://www.unh.edu/news/docs/UNHsocialmedia.pdf (retrieved December 1, 2013)
8. Moran, M., Seaman, J., Tinti-Kane, H.: Teaching, learning, and sharing: how today's higher education faculty use Social Media. ERIC database ED535130. Pearson Learning Solutions and Babson Survey Research Group, MA (2011)
9. Kramp, M.K.: Exploring life and experience through narrative inquiry. In: de Marris, K., Lapan, S. (eds.) Foundations of Research: Methods of Inquiry in Education and the Social Sciences, pp. 103–122. Lawrence Erlbaum, NJ (2004)
10. Pachler, N., Daly, C.: Narrative and learning with Web 2.0 technologies? Towards a research agenda. Journal of Computer Assisted Learning 25, 6–18 (2009)
11. Connelly, F.M., Clandinin, D.J.: Stories of experience and narrative inquiry. Educational Researcher 19(2) (1990)
12. Polkinghorne, D.E.: Narrative knowing and human sciences. State University of New York Press, New York (1988)
13. Moen, T.: Reflections on the narrative research approach. International Journal of Qualitative Methodology 5(4), article 5 (2006)
14. Riessman, C.K., Quinney, L.: Narrative in Social Work: A Critical Review. Qualitative Social Work 4, 391–412 (2005)
15. Cousins, S., Bissar, D.: Adapting to the digital age: a narrative approach. Research in Learning Technologies, 20 (2012)
16. Meadows, M.S.: Pause & effect: the art of interactive narrative. New Riders, Indianapolis (2003)
17. Watkins, J., Russo, A.: Beyond individual expression: working with cultural institution. In: Hartley, J., McWilliam, K. (eds.) Story Cycle: Digital Storytelling around the World. Wiley-Blackwell, Malden (2009)
18. Cresswell, J.W.: Research design: qualitative, quantitative and mixed methods approaches. Sage Publications, Thousand Oaks (2003)
19. Cresswell, J.W.: Qualitative inquiry and research design: choosing among five approaches. Sage Publications, Thousand Oaks (2006)
20. Cohen, L., Manion, L., Morrison, K.: Research methods in education. Routledge Falmer, London (2001)
21. Goodson, I., Sikes, P.: Life history research in educational settings: learning from lives. Open University Press, Buckingham (2001)

An Interactive Installation for the Architectural Analysis of Space and Form in Historical Buildings

Luis Antonio Hernández Ibáñez and Viviana Barneche Naya

VideaLAB. Universidade da Coruña. Spain
{luis.hernandez,viviana.barneche}@udc.es

Abstract. This paper describes a methodology for the development of a didactic installation intended to explore the spatial, volumetric and formal relationships that, being present in any architectural work, are basic to understand the compositive and stylistic aspects that define some historical key buildings as paradigms of the history of Architecture. Such an exploration can only be done by providing the user with the ability to inspect the exterior and interior spaces from all angles and distances and perform cross-sections through any meaningful plane.

One of the main challenges of that kind of interactive visualization resides in the geometrical complexity that is present in many historical examples, especially if there is a certain level of detail involved. The use of forms of illumination that reproduce indirect lighting and diffuse reflection, which are needed to properly simulate many interior lighting conditions also increments the difficulty to achieve a fluent simulation. Hence, one of the issues to solve is that of applying a methodology intended to maximize the efficiency of the model in terms of rendering computational cost.

The authors chose the Cathedral of Santiago de Compostela as a case of application. The temple was modeled with a high level of geometrical detail and lit using global illumination, creating a model valid for real-time presentation in order to be examined, explored and manipulated using natural interaction.

Keywords: Real-time architectural visualization, Multitactile interaction, Natural Interfaces, Cross-section, Cathedral of Santiago, Radiosity.

1 Introduction

The techniques used in architectural visualization have always been linked to the historical, technical and cultural moment in which they develop. The great paradigm shift in the techniques of architectural representation which took place in the late eighties was enabled by the development of Computer Aided Design. The development of these new systems allowed an evolution from the classical representation modes based in plans, elevations and cross-sections, perspectives and physical models to a new, more complete, three dimensional form existing in virtual space which can provide almost unlimited views of a design.

P. Zaphiris and A. Ioannou (Eds.): LCT 2014, Part I, LNCS 8523, pp. 43–52, 2014.

There is little doubt of the excellent visual quality of renderings and animations which can be achieved from a three dimensional model of a building. Rendering algorithms allow the modeler to attain a level of hyperrealism so that the digital image can be indistinguishable from the real.

In recent years, many experiences can be found that make use of visualization software such as Lumión [1], WorldViz [2] and videogame engines such as UDK [3 4, 5, and 6], Unity [7, 8] o CryEngine [9, 10] which provide with high visual quality and the capability of making architectural walkthroughs in the interior space of a building.

On the other hand, several authors have worked on navigation and camera control using multitouch interaction for three-dimensional user interfaces [11, 12, 13, and 14]

Additionally, there are several examples of software that permits users to make single cross-sections interactively on 3D models, such as Sketchup [15, 16] or Constructor SDK [17, 18] inside a CAD editor.

This paper presents a combination of the aforementioned features, in an application suitable to perform the spatial, volumetric, and sectional analysis of any building. Being especially suitable for complex historical buildings such as the case presented of the Cathedral of Santiago de Compostela by means of a natural interaction scheme implemented on a multitouch device that makes use of common gestures to interactively manipulate, examine and cross-section the model.

The analysis of the architectural form is a process that surpasses the simple contemplation of the building since it involves semantic factors which define the composition of the built object. Mass, space and function blend together materializing constructive elements which have relations that have to be understood to obtain an adequate interpretation of the building.

In all times, Architecture has searched for formal solutions that could satisfy the formal requirements of the building, adhering to the structural and constructive limitations of the techniques of its time by means of invention and design. The form of the building and its components then emerge from a mix of the techniques and aesthetics of a precise historical and cultural moment which defines a style.

The Cathedral of Santiago de Compostela constitutes a good example of the concurrence of stylistic features from different epochs living together. The initial Romanesque layout, frequently used as a paradigm to describe the characteristics of this style, was modified throughout the centuries with multiple additions and refurbishments. Those changes transformed parts and added new elements, sometimes in a subtle manner but sometimes in a spectacular way, like in the case of the façade of Obradoiro, designed by architect Casas y Novoa in mid-18th century.

The making of a digital model of a building intended to permit and interactive examination for such a formal analysis requires consequently the recreation of each and every constituent element with a level of detail adequate to a correct and complete visual description.

It is well known that the creation of a digital model for real time interactive visualization needs to fulfill very hard requisites in the making of the model in order to obtain a highly efficient geometry in terms of visual information versus rendering time. In this sense, the presence of geometry very profuse of elements to be represented constitutes a major obstacle for computational efficiency. This is especially true if the model has to display computer costly visual features that are considered important such as projected shadows and diffuse illumination

The following lines will explain the criteria and methodology used in this case.

2   Objectives

The main goal of this work is to obtain a methodology to develop virtual models of complex historical buildings for their architectural analysis using natural interaction techniques. Such models should fulfill the following requirements:

- The model should be manipulated by means of rotation, zoom to any of its elements, and interactive cross-section through any horizontal, transverse or longitudinal plane.
- The virtual reconstruction should reflect faithfully the geometry of the building in its architectonical aspects to preserve the formal accuracy. Simplifications should be avoided in all constructive elements and the use of techniques of emulation of geometry with the use of textures would not be permitted. Only sculptural elements should be allowed to be substituted by a simpler equivalent.
- Visual quality should be high enough to guarantee the presence of cast shadows and diffuse lighting effects.
- The model could be handled using natural interaction criteria.
- Only architectural shapes would be reproduced. Non-architectural elements such as sculptures, furniture, etc. could be simplified or discarded. The reconstruction would be limited to the main temple, excluding the museum, crypt, and the side chapel of Corticela.

3   Methodology

3.1   Project Design

The fulfillment of the aforementioned objectives imposed strong restrictions to obtain a highly efficient model, in spite of its geometrical complexity, that could be interactively manipulated using a common personal computer.

Global illumination was a necessary requisite to visualize adequately both the nuances of the volumes in shadow areas and the diffuse illumination of the interior. As of today, the calculation of global illumination in real time is something out of the capacities of the common computers. Although there are interesting works [19] in this direction, the characteristics of this case made necessary to utilize an approach based on the pre- calculation of the illumination. Current technologies implement this approach assigning a light map to each of the model's surfaces. However, the expected complexity of the model did not permit a solution of this kind due to the high number of texture files needed and the amount of memory required to host them within an acceptable resolution range.

Nevertheless, the high level of polygonalization of the model is just a concept affine to one of the algorithms used to calculate global illumination: the progressive refinement radiosity. This approach, although is not frequently used today in standard visualization software, permits to obtain and store illumination data in the vertices of a secondary mesh which is associated to the model, called energetic mesh. The calculation and further use of distinct energetic meshes on the interior and the exterior would allow combining two very dissimilar lighting states which correspond to the interior, lit with artificial light and the exterior, lit with solar light.

In order to permit the inspection of the spatial structure of the temple and the relations between inner and outer spaces, the application incorporates an interactive cross-sectioning system along three orthogonal axis, allowing the user to obtain any combination of longitudinal, transversal or horizontal section. This system coordinates with a natural interaction model based in the zoom, pan and rotate actions that can be found today in many multitouch device applications.

3.2   Documentation

The information needed to build the digital model was extracted from existing publications related to the planimetry of the temple [20, 21, 22], together with high resolution photographic documentation made specifically for this project. The final application also includes a mechanism to access those images.

3.3   Modelling

The model was made using AutoCAD, praying special attention in the architectural formal syntax for the creation of all of its elements, and attending to the stylistic rules of generation of every shape, that is, considering a column for instance, as the sum of base, shaft and capital, not as the simple replica of a solid volume of given dimensions. This approach permitted the generation of many reusable elements and the enhancement of the regularity, modulation and canonic appearance of the temple.

3.4   Illumination

The calculation of the global illumination was made using Lightscape, a software capable to generate a radiosity energetic mesh where every vertex stores an illumination value. The calculation used the progressive refinement radiosity approach, that is, the subdivision of each and every surface in smaller parts. The quantity of subdivisions is based on the gradient of illumination along the surface. Here is where the complexity of the model played favorably for the calculation, since the presence of the myriad of small elements that constitute every part of the model permitted that, in most cases, the surface subdivision could be very small or null.

The final radiosity mesh finally contained 3.8 million polygons for the exterior model and 2.1 million polygons for the interior, resulting a subdivision ratio with respect to the original meshes of 4.7 and 8.0. That is a result well under the common ratios which result from the application of this technique. Thus, similar visual results are obtained with significantly less computational cost.

Fig. 1. External view: main façade

Fig. 2. External view: Northwest façade

By means of this method, the illumination obtained displays adequately the diffuse reflection of light, both in the interior and in the shadow areas of the exterior. The contour of the shape of the cast shadows is also shown correctly.

Radiosity meshes were imported in 3DS Max and processed to be exported in OSG format using the corresponding plug-in after the application of LSColor, LSMesh and VertexColor modifiers.

3.5   Interactive Application

3.5.1   Engine

The model of the cathedral can be examined using an application developed ad hoc. Real-time rendering is done by means of Open Scene Graph graphic engine [23], based on the OpenGL standard.

Since the radiosity mesh stores the illumination in all of its vertices, there is no need of further lighting calculation during the real-time rendering. Hence, standard lighting can be deactivated with an enormous saving in rendering time, critical for the real-time visualization of a model of this complexity.

Colors among vertices are calculated by bilinear interpolation of the vertices values using Gouraud shading [24], hence avoiding abrupt illumination changes which could produce visual artifacts.

3.5.2   Cross-Section Planes

The cross section effect is done by using two planes in every axis which divide the space of the scene discarding the geometry located in the direction of one of its normal vectors

Since all surfaces in the models are polygons without any topological relation among them, it is extremely complex to obtain the surface of the cross section of the building through a given plane in real time. Instead of calculating this cross section,

Fig. 3. Combined longitudinal and transversal cross sections with interactor axes in green

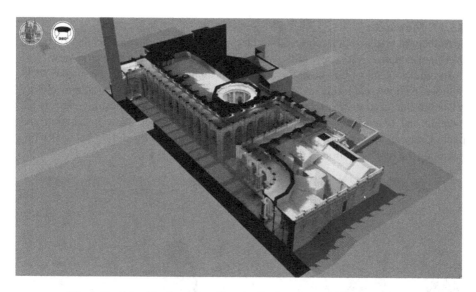

Fig. 4. Combined horizontal and longitudinal sections and interactor axes

Fig. 5. Double plane transversal cross-section

we used a much simpler approach consisting in applying a flat black color to every visible backface of a polygon. This way, the space between the interior and the exterior models becomes black revealing the shape of cross-section through the desired plane very clearly.

3.5.3   Movement

Architectural visualization requires interfaces with which both common and specialist users can examine every view of the model, from a close detail to a general view.

In order to achieve this goal, the application implements multitactile display technology. It allows exploring the building using a gesture tracking paradigm closely related to that used in smartphones and other devices. One touch gesture controls the panning and two touch gestures control zoom-in, zoom-out, view orientation and pitch. User can also define the location of the section planes by sliding his or her finger along the representation of the XYZ axes.

Fig. 6. User interacting with the application using hand-gestures

Fig. 7. Gesture based controls of the application

4   Results

The result of this work was an installation that accomplished all objectives and became part of the *Loci Iacobi* exhibition in Santiago de Compostela.

The resulting model is adequate for the architectural formal analysis both for the non-expert user, who could be only interested in general aspects of the architecture of the cathedral, and for the expert and the specialist, who can analyze the temple using this formally rigorous virtual model.

This digital model also constitutes another new source of documentation of this Romanesque building, which has been developed and can be reused in those CAD working environments that are commonly utilized in the making of architectural planimetric documentation.

5   Conclusions

This paper investigates the use of progressive refinement radiosity, combined with the use of highly geometrically detailed models. The methodology explained here allows obtaining highly efficient models, which can be used in real time with the realism provided by global illumination.

The application of natural interaction and gesture based criteria; combined with such a representation constitutes a very efficient tool for the inspection, and analysis of historical buildings in a fluent and intuitive way.

The use of these types of tools can be of great support in the study of the history of Architecture, and for the comprehension of architectural compositive concepts since it provides a unique experience in the examination of the building, being especially helpful for the volumetrical, spatial and formal analysis.

References

1. Lumion. Architectural visualization, http://lumion3d.com/
2. Architecture Interactive. Showcases, http://architecture-interactive.com/case-studies/hks-architects/
3. Epic Games. Unreal Engine, http://www.unrealengine.com/udk/
4. Gaudiosi, J.: Cowboys Stadium. Unreal Engine 3 Brings Architecture to Life, http://www.unrealengine.com/en/showcase/visualization/cowboys_stadium
5. Jacobson, J.H., Hwang, Z.: Unreal Tournament for Immersive Interactive Theater. Communications of the ACM 45(1), 39–42 (2002), doi:10.1145/502269.502292
6. Johns, R.L.: Unreal Editor as a virtual design instrument in Landscape Architecture Studio. In: 6th International Conference for Information Technologies in Landscape, Dessau, Alemania, pp. 330–336 (2005)
7. Unity Technologies, http://unity3d.com/unity
8. Indraprastha, A.S.: Constructing Virtual Urban Environment Using Game Technology. A Case Study of Tokyo Yaesu Downtown Development Plan. In: 26th eCAADe Proceedings, Antwerpen, Bélgica, pp. 359–366 (2008)
9. Crytek, Visuals, http://www.myCryEngine.com
10. Enodo, S.A.S.: Interactive Virtual Model of the Cluny Abbey, http://mycryengine.com/index.php?conid=69&id=12
11. Lu, K., Hsin-Hou, L., Ting-Han, C., Chi-Fa, F.: Finding the vital houses information using immersive multi-touch interface. In: Proc. 17th International Conference on Computer-Aided Architectural Design Research in Asia, CAADRIA, Hong Kong, pp. 379–386 (2012)
12. Chen, R.I., Schnabel, M.A.: Multi-touch: the future of design interaction. In: Leclereq, P., et al. (eds.) Proc. 14th CAAD Futures Conference, Liège, pp. 557–572 (2011)

13. Edelmann, et al.: The DABR–A Multitouch System for intuitive 3D scene navigation. In: Proc. 3DTV Conference, pp. 1–4 (2009)
14. Hancock, M., Carpendale, S., Cockburn, A.: Shallow-depth 3d interaction: design and evaluation of one, two-and three-touch. In: Proc. CHI 2007, pp. 1147–1156 (2007)
15. Google. Sketchup, http://www.sketchup.com
16. Wall, J.: Recovering Lost Acoustic Spaces: St. Paul's Cathedral and Paul's Churchyard in 1622, http://www.digitalstudies.org/ojs/index.php/digital_studies/article/view/251/310
17. NGrain 3D. Constructor SDK, http://www.ngrain.com/portfolio/constructor-sdk/
18. NGrain 3D. How to cross-section 3D model with Constructor 5, NGRAIN's 3D visualization SDK, http://www.youtube.com/watch?v=RFfTezucHSw
19. Martin, S., Einarsson, P.: Real Time Radiosity Architecture. Advances in Real-Time Rendering. In: SIGGRAPH 2010 (2010), http://dice.se/publications/a-real-time-radiosity-architecture/
20. Conant, K.J.: Arquitectura románica da Catedral de Santiago de Compostela. Ed. Colexio Oficial de Arquitectos de Galicia, Vigo (1983)
21. Franco Taboada, J.A., Tarrio Carrodeguas, S.: As Catedrais de Galicia. Descrición Gráfica. Departamento de Representación e Teoría Arquitectónicas. Ed. Xunta de Galicia, Santiago de Compostela (1999)
22. Taín Guzmán, M.: Trazas, Planos y Proyectos del Archivo de la Catedral de Santiago. Ed. Diputación Provincial de A Coruña (1999)
23. Kuehne, B., Marktz, P. (eds.): OpenSceneGraph Reference Manual v2.2, http://www.osgbooks.com/books/osg_refman22.html
24. Gouraud, H.: Continuous shading of curved surfaces. IEEE Transactions on Computers C-20(6), 623–629 (1971)

Introducing a Challenging Teachable Agent

Camilla Kirkegaard, Agneta Gulz, and Annika Silvervarg

Department of Computer and Information Science
Linköping University
{camilla.kirkegaard,agneta.gulz,annika.silvervarg}@liu.se

Abstract. This paper explores the potentials of a new type of pedagogical agent – a Challenger Teachable Agent. The aim of such a pedagogical agent is to increase engagement and motivation, and challenge students into deeper learning and metacognitive reasoning. It is based on the successful implementation of the Learning by Teaching approach in Teacheable Agents, and in addition it draws on previous work that has shown the potential of resistance or challenge as means to improve learning. In this paper we discuss how these two bases can be combined and realized through new types of behaviours in a Teachable Agent.

Keywords: teachable agents, challenging agents, self-efficacy, educational technology.

1 Introduction

More than 2000 years ago Seneca the Younger wrote dicendo discimus, which is latin for "by teaching, we learn", in a letter to Lucilius. Thus, the idea that one learns by teaching someone else has been around for a long time. In more recent years this idea has been realized in pedagogical approaches in classrooms. Studies have shown many advantages of the Learning by Teaching (LBT) approach, for instance, that people who learn in order to teach others to pass a test learn better than those who learn in order to pass the test themselves (Bargh & Schul, 1980).

There are many aspects of LBT that contribute to improved learning. Leelawong and Biswas (2008) mentions structuring, taking responsibility and reflecting. To be able to present and explain a material to someone else, the teacher needs to be responsible for what material to include and for the structuring of it. Leelawong and Biswas (ibid) showed that doing this leads to a deeper understanding of the material and better organization of ideas. Schneider (2008) also showed that meta-memory functions are supported and trained when the teacher is checking whether s/he has a sufficient understanding of the material to be able to explain it to others. Thus there are many advantages concerning the preparation phase of teaching. When moving on to the phase of actual teaching, other mechanisms come into play, for example what Leelawong and Biswas (ibid) refer to as reflection, that the teacher ponders on how the information presented was understood and used. The teacher has to compare his or her expectations with the actual outcome, to see if there is material that needs to be

P. Zaphiris and A. Ioannou (Eds.): LCT 2014, Part I, LNCS 8523, pp. 53–62, 2014.

explained in a different or more elaborate way. This may also lead to the teacher reflecting on his or her own understanding of the material and perhaps the teacher must revise his or her own ideas of the domain. Chin et al. (2010) describe how the three phases of teaching, result and repair, are repeated and how that results in a self-regulated learning cycle for the teacher.

In other words, the pedagogy of LBT can be powerful and involve several kinds of benefits. However, to implement fruitful LBT situations is not unproblematic. For example, when students teach other students, some students may find it hard to take a teacher role since they are not so knowledgeable or do not believe sufficiently in their own knowledge and competence. Also, if a student does a poor job as a teacher the students being taught are negatively affected. Moving to the digital arena is a way to keep the benefits of LBT and at the same time avoid the mentioned drawbacks.

The LBT approach can be implemented in virtual learning environments where the real student teaches a digital tutee, often referred to as a Teachable Agent (TA). AI techniques guide the TA's behaviour based on what it is taught (Brophy et al., 1999). This makes it possible for every student to have his or her own tutee to be a teacher for, and if the student fails at teaching no real person comes to harm. It is also possible to match the agent's knowledge to the level of the student to provide a reasonable challenge. The digitalization also adds the possibility to introduce game characteristics and other variables to support learning processes and emotional and motivational aspects. A further advantage with a digital learning environment is that it makes it possible to reach a larger audience.

More details on teachable agents and the benefits of using them are provided in the next section. The reminder on the paper then explores the idea of a new type of teachable agent, a Challenging Teachable Agent (CTA). We present some current ideas of why challenging behaviour of pedagogical agents is desirable, and how this can be integrated with teachable agents. Finally we give some examples from ongoing work with implementation of a challenging teachable agent in a virtual learning environment for history.

2   Teachable Agents

There are many learning environments that make use of pedagogical agents, but most of these are tutors, i.e. the agent is the expert teacher. A teachable agent is the total opposite, an agent that is to be taught by the student. The teachable agent therefore should exhibit a behaviour that invites and motivates the user to teach. In this section we present results from studies that illustrate the positive effects teachable agents can have on motivation and also other aspects of learning, such as metacognition.

2.1   Motivation and Effort

Effort is an essential aspect when aiming for more and deeper learning. Students often prefer pedagogical methods that results in surface learning, since deep learning requires more effort and it is more hard work (D'Mello et al., 2012). To aid the learning process, the student therefore needs to be motivated to make more effort and to strategically direct that effort.

In the LBT domain a central motivational factor that is often mentioned with respect to TAs is the *protégée effect*; i.e. "students make greater effort to learn for their TAs than they do for themselves" (s. 2). This effect was shown in a study where the alternatives were to either learn a material for a future test or to teach a TA (Chase et al., 2009).

According to Chase et al. (ibid) the protégée effect is attributed to a synergy of different contributing effects: i) *ego-protective buffer*, which means that a possible failure would be assigned to the TA, and not the student directly, thereby reducing failure anxiety in the student. ii) *responsibility*, in that the student treat his or her TA as a social entity and shows concern and responsibility for its academic success. By taking that responsibility the student is motivated to revisit learning material, rethink his or her own understanding and try to come up with new and better ways of helping the TA to understand the material. iii) *incrementalist theory*. To world as a teacher, the student appear to accept the idea of incremental knowledge, i.e. that TAs could perform academically better after being taught by the student.

2.2   Metacognitive Reasoning

One way to reach deeper learning is to increase metacognitive reasoning in the student. To stimulate metacognitive reasoning, we need to raise the students' awareness of the causality between learning choices and the results of those choices. This can be illustrated using teachable agents since the choices made during teaching of the agent are reflected in the understanding and knowledge the agent has as a result. In this way the learning process is made more visible. The positive effects do not appear only when the digital learning environment is being used, but also in transfer situations (Schwartz & Martin, 2006).

Letting students work with a TA that expresses its metacognitive reasoning, might stimulate the student to incorporate some of the learning strategies on herself. This was termed metacognition by proxy and was showed to be successful by Chin et al. (2010).

A learning environment could further aid the metacognitive processes by giving the students directions and letting the TA be a model of "productive learning behaviour" (Blair et al., 2007). This could be realized by designing a TA that demonstrates useful learning strategies, in addition to direct instructions from the TA or learning environment. A student that has a higher level of awareness for the causality between learning choices and their result, i.e. metacognition about learning strategies, will have a higher ability to take responsibility and further on direct effort strategically in his or her learning process.

3   The Power of Challenge

It can be tiresome and boring to interact with an agent that is always positive, compliant and cheerful – and such agents are weak in believability (Cassell & Thórisson, 1999). The TAs developed so far does not have much of a personality and usually accept all information provided by their teacher without questioning it. Although one of the seminal papers on TAs, (Brophy et al., 1999), proposed an agent that "may be impetuous, not listen or collaborate well", this has to our knowledge hitherto never been realized nor evaluated. In this section we explore positive aspects of agents that do not collaborate well but rather challenge the user in different ways, and other aspects of challenges during learning.

There have been approaches to experiment with characteristics as impetuousness within related fields with other types of pedagogical agents. Within the area of peer learning, Aïmeur et al (1997) describe a troublemaker agent in a virtual learning environment that also includes a tutor agent. The troublemaker peer may suggest a correct or faulty solution and ask the student if she agrees or not. If the student does not agree, the troublemaker will debate about its solution until the student either agrees or the troublemaker runs out of arguments. If the student agrees, the troublemaker solution will be presented to the tutor for feedback. In a study conducted by Frasson and Aïmeur (1999), it was found that the use of the troublemaker agent "encourages the learner to question his own knowledge" and thereby motivates the learner. However, the troublemaker agent and the teaching strategy "learning by disturbing" implied academic improvement primarily for high achieving students.

The learning by disturbing teaching strategy basically uses the intrinsic motivation that comes from not understanding each other, which sometimes, can be just what is needed. Dissonance theory proposes that when an individual experiences a conflict between her own and someone else's understanding, the individual also experiences a motivational drive to resolve the conflict (Aïmeur et al., 1997). To not understand one another might even be "an ignition to learn together" (Schwartz, 1999). An individual in a state of cognitive dissonance will get motivated to revise or defend his position to solve the mental conflict.

In a LBT condition it could therefore be meaningful for the teachable agent to cause dissonance or small conflicts, by for example introducing errors in the same manner as the troublemaker agent. This can manifest itself in productive learning behaviours if the teacher needs to revise or defend his/her position. This can in turn lead to the teacher having to revisit information material or formulate arguments about why his/her position is more correct.

Another way a teachable agent can challenge the student is in the choice of learning activities and the difficulty level of these activities. To facilitate learning the distance between the task difficulty and the student´s current level of mastery should be such that it creates a challenge. Clifford (2009) points out that a task needs to have a "moderate probability of success", in order to generate intrinsic motivation. She rates a 50% probability of success to be moderate. Clifford also writes about "the privilege of learning by mistakes", by encouraging students to try out task on a higher level than they master. An easy mastered task will not affect the intrinsic motivation since it is considered under the student's level of performance. A mastered task that was considered too difficult would be considered "out of luck" and would also not affect the intrinsic motivation. (Clifford, 2009). Thus, a teachable agent can push the teacher towards tasks of a challenging difficulty level.

4   Designing a Challenging Teachable Agents

Based on the theories and results from previous studies, which we have presented in the previous sections, we see a considerable potential in the combination of two potent teaching techniques; learning by teaching and troublemaking. We choose the name "challenger" TA (CTA) since we experienced that the word troublemaker in our contacts with schools had negative connotations, a troublemaker would be somebody who wants to make trouble – whereas a CTA would be a TA that wants to challenge the student in a positive way.

We suggest that a CTA should be designed to address two qualitatively different tasks; i) to help the student add effort to the learning process, and ii) to help the student direct his or her effort in the learning process.

4.1   Increase Motivation and Effort

Overrating Own Knowledge. An aspect that can fit an impetuous agent personality is a tendency to misjudge, and overrate its own knowledge. In line with this the CTA may insist on choosing learning and testing activities at a higher level than actually mastered. This would increase the level of challenge and may have positive effects on the level of intrinsic motivation (Clifford, 2009).

Varying Willingness to Learn. True collaborative work is based on the precondition that the individuals enter a relationship with free wills and their own goals/intentions with the collaboration (Schwartz D. 1999). Therefore we choose to simulate that the CTA has its own will and sometimes questions why a certain activities should be done or express reluctance to do some activities. This will accentuate that it has its own agency and strengthen the student's experience of responsibility towards, and also motivation for teaching, the CTA. Being questioned by the CTA about the task relevance can also spark metacognitive reflections within the student, as she has to find good arguments for persuading the CTA.

4.2   Improve Learning Strategies

Debating solutions in Learning Activities. "The desire to understand and be understood -- to share meaning -- is a strong motivator of human behaviour" (Schwartz, 1999, p. 8). The CTA can at times ask for explanations and clarifications before, perhaps, accepting a solution to a task in a learning activity. Designing the CTA not to readily accept everything the student tries to teach, is a possible way of promoting deep learning. A task oriented dialogue would also give the student an opportunity to train to use the domain specific concepts, relations and facts.

Introducing Errors. This strategy was used by Frasson & Aimeur (1996) for their troublemaking learning companion. The idea is to provoke the student to react and justify his/her answer, and thus become more certain of it and its bases. Training to distinguish between right and wrong solutions is also a mean to achieve higher confidence in the student with respect to the study material (i.e. self-efficacy).

Inducing Confusion. Confusion or cognitive disequilibrium can be induced by e.g. contradicting information and can provide deeper learning in a controlled setting for learning. When conflicting information is perceived, the individual heightens its attention towards the new information and tries to resolve the conflict through e.g. visiting informational material. The purpose is to provoke the student to reflect, deliberate, and decide on what is true, thereby processing the material at a deeper level. (D'Mello et al., 2012).

4.3   Individual Differences and Timing

While we believe a Challenger Teachable Agent can have many positive effects on students learning, we hypothesize that student variables like self-efficacy, goal-orientation and achievement will interact with different types of challenging behaviour and produce different learning outcomes and user experiences for different groups of users. For example, challenging tasks are viewed differently depending on a student's goal orientation, since challenging tasks present the risk of failure, but also offer opportunities for learning (Ames & Archer, 1988). A performance oriented student is more likely than a competence oriented student to try to avoid challenging tasks. Furthermore, students with high self-efficacy, may profit more from a CTA than students with low self-efficacy.

Another important factor to pay attention to is the time-relation between challenging behaviours and student variables. We hypothesize that some challenging behaviours are preferably introduced at a certain progression-level and some others would be a consistent feature. We suspect that the behaviours should be gradually phased in or out. How often the different behaviours should be occurring, and when, may also interact with student variables.

5   Realizing a CTA in a History Learning Environment

The CTA is currently being implemented in a digital learning environment for history where the target users are 10-12 year olds. To our knowledge this is the first TA system outside the STEM area. In the game narrative the old Guardian of History is about to retire and searches for a successor among his helpers. A potential successor

Fig. 1. The picture shows a historical setting with Galileo Galilee

has to show extensive knowledge of history, and in order to gain such knowledge the helpers have a time machine at their disposal. The helper Timy is very eager to learn about history, but unfortunately gets motion sickness in the time machine. Therefore the student is asked to use the time machine to learn about history in order to thereafter teach Timy. Thus the narrative introduces the TA in a natural way that can encourage the protégé effect. The main character Timy is gender neutral, since our earlier studies showed that it decreases negative gender-effects that sometimes appear in interactions with virtual agents (Silvervarg et al 2012, Silvervarg et al 2013).

The information gathering activities are performed with a time machine. During travels to the past the student can visit different historical settings and interact with people, documents and artefacts. Se Fig. 1 for the historical setting where the student is visiting Galileo Galilee in Pisa.

When the student return from the time travels s/he shall try to teach Timy what s/he has learnt. A learning activity is a game-like task which is performed by the student and Timy. Typically the student can choose if Timy should watch when the student plays or if they should play together. The system includes various learning activities, and the activities can be performed at different difficulty levels.

During a learning activity Timy will add new knowledge to his memory or grow more certain or uncertain about previous known facts that are included in the learning activity. Facts can be correct or incorrect, more or less certain, and typically reflect the student's own knowledge of the domain. Different learning activities promote different kinds of facts. For example, the learning activity in Fig. 2 uses a time line to

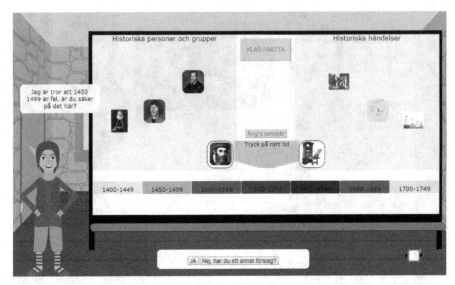

Fig. 2. A learning activity where the user is teaching the digital tutee Timy by doing a Timeline activity together

visualize facts about persons, events and time periods. In this example the student is doing the activity together with Timy. Timy questions that the student's proposed fact is correct, stating that he thinks that the time period is not correct. The student can now insist that he or she is correct or ask Timy what he thinks is correct, and in the next step either accept or reject Timy's suggestion.

A testing activity will be unlocked when a sufficient amount of learning activities has been carried out. Timy will then by himself answer the questions using the knowledge he has been taught by the student teacher. If Timy was taught well, s/he will get a good grade and also grow more certain of the answers s/he provided. The results of the test give the student feedback on how well s/he has taught Timy and hint at information gathering and/or learning activities s/he may have to redo in case of uncertainty or errors.

5.1   Challenging Behaviour during Learning Activities

The challenging behaviours of the CTA are realised in the choice of learning tasks and the performance of the learning activities, where agent will interact with the user through multiple choice dialogue, as illustrated in Fig. 2. This are the first challenging behaviours to be implemented in our CTA:

Varying Willingness to Learn. We implement this by letting the CTA sometimes question the learning activities the student chooses. During an activity the agent might express that the activity is too boring, too hard or that it would be more fun to do some other activity not directly related to learning. At such occasions the student will get a dialogue prompt to answer or motivate the agent to continue the activity.

Overrating Own Knowledge. The CTA knows nothing from the beginning, but learns from the user. A traditional TA learns rather slowly and needs to repeat a fact many times before s/he is confident that s/he "knows" it. The CTA puts much more confidence in what it has learnt, and can suggest that the student teacher moves on to learning activities and tests at higher difficulty level more quickly.

Learning more quickly and overrating own knowledge can also lead to the agent being certain of erroneous facts that has only been presented once, and it can use these to contradict the student teacher when the correct facts are introduced, and resist replacing erroneous with correct facts.

Debating Solutions in Learning Activities. When the student shows the CTA a fact or a solution, it will sometimes debate whether it is correct or not. In the "do together" activity mode, the agent might question the user's choices, e.g. "Are you sure?" or state "I don't agree" more often than a traditional TA would.

Introducing Errors and Inducing Confusion. Even if the student teacher only teaches the CTA correct facts, the agent may on purpose "misremember" and propose incorrect facts when it is doing a learning activity together with the student teacher. E.g. the agent may substitute Galileo Galilei as the author of the book "Dialogue Concerning the Two Chief World Systems" with Tycho Brahe.

6   Summary and Future Work

Teachable agents have been proven to work well as an implementation of the Learning by teaching approach, providing many advantages such as increasing motivation, depth of learning, effort, etc. Challenge in the learning process has also been shown to have positive effects on learning processes. In this paper we propose the combination of these two in a Challenging Teachable Agent. We believe that the addition of challenging behaviour in a TA can further strengthen the positive effects. However, this need to be further explored with regard to various user groups to make sure we build educational systems that can benefit all students.

We intend to evaluate the proposed CTA and compare it to a traditional TA as well as a system without an agent, with regard to student variables such as self-efficacy and goal-orientation. Based on findings from such a study, a future research goal is to develop and evaluate algorithms for adequate combinations of agent behaviours. When is it advantageous to use them; which of them and in which combinations – and with respect to which student variables?

References

1. Aïmeur, E., Dufort, H., Leibu, D., Frasson, C.: Some justifications for the learning by disturbing strategy. In: Proceedings of the Eighth World Conference on Artificial Intelligence in Education, pp. 1–14 (1997)

2. Ames, C., Archer, J.: Achievement goals in the classroom: Students' learning strategies and motivation processes. Journal of Educational Psychology 80(3), 260 (1988)
3. Bargh, J.A., Schul, Y.: On the cognitive benefits of teaching. Journal of Educational Psychology 72, 593–604 (1980)
4. Blair, K., Schwartz, D., Biswas, G., Leelawong, K.: Pedagogical Agents for Learning by Teaching. Educational Technology Special Issue 47, 56–61 (2007)
5. Blair, K., Schwartz, D., Biswas, G., Leelawong, K.: Pedagogical agents for learning by teaching: Teachable agents. Educational Technology & Society, Special Issue on Pedagogical Agents 47(1), 56 (2007)
6. Brophy, S., Biswas, G., Katzlberger, T., Bransford, J., Schwartz, D.: Teachable agents: Combining insights from learning theory and computer science. Artificial Intelligence in Education 50, 21–28 (1999)
7. Cassell, J., Thórisson, K.R.: The Power of a Nod and a Glance: Envelope vs. Emotional Feedback in Animated Conversational Agents. Applied Artificial Intelligence 13, 519–538 (1999)
8. Chase, C., Chin, D., Oppezzo, M., Schwartz, D.: Teachable Agents and the Protégé Effect: Increasing the Effort Towards Learning. Journal of Science Education and Technology, 334–352 (2009)
9. Chin, D.B., Dohmen, I.M., Cheng, B.H., Oppezzo, M.A., Chase, C.C., Schwartz, D.L.: Preparing students for future learning with Teachable Agents. Educational Technology Research and Development 58(6), 649–669 (2010)
10. Clifford, M.M.: Students need challenge - not easy success. Kaleidoscope (2009)
11. D'Mello, S., Lehman, B., Pekrun, R., Graesser, A.: Confusion can be beneficial for learning. Learning and Instruction (2012)
12. Frasson, C., Aïmeur, E.: A Comparison of Three Learning Strategies in Intelligent Tutoring Systems. Journal of Educational Computing Research 14, 371–383 (1996)
13. Leelawong, K., Biswas, G.: Designing learning by teaching agents: The Betty's Brain system. International Journal of Artificial Intelligence in Education 18(3), 181–208 (2008)
14. Schneider, W.: The Development of Metacognitive Knowledge in Children and Adolescents: Major Trends and Implications for Education. Mind, Brain, and Education 2(3), 114–121 (2008)
15. Schwartz, D.: The productive agency that drives collaborative learning. In: Collaborative Learning: Cognitive and Computational Approaches, pp. 197–218 (1999)
16. Schwartz, D.L., Martin, T.: Distributed learning and mutual adaptation. Pragmatics & Cognition, 1–29 (2006)
17. Schwartz, D., Chase, C., Chin, D., Oppezzo, M., Kwong, H., Okita, S., Wagster, J.: Interactive metacognition: Monitoring and regulating a teachable agent. In: Hacker, D.J., Dunlosky, J., Graesser, A.C. (eds.) Handbook of Metacognition in Education, pp. 340–358 (2009)
18. Silvervarg, A., Raukola, K., Haake, M., Gulz, A.: The Effect of Visual Gender on Abuse in Conversation with ECAs. In: Nakano, Y., Neff, M., Paiva, A., Walker, M. (eds.) IVA 2012. LNCS, vol. 7502, pp. 153–160. Springer, Heidelberg (2012)
19. Silvervarg, A., Haake, M., Gulz, A.: Educational Potentials in Visually Androgynous Pedagogical Agents. In: Lane, H.C., Yacef, K., Mostow, J., Pavlik, P. (eds.) AIED 2013. LNCS, vol. 7926, pp. 599–602. Springer, Heidelberg (2013)

File Formats Security – Proprietary vs. Open-Source

Edmund Laugasson[1] and Kaido Kikkas[1,2]

[1] Tallinn University, Institute of Informatics, Narva Road 25, 10120 Tallinn, Estonia
[2] Estonian Information Technology College, Raja St 4c, 12616 Tallinn, Estonia
{Edmund.Laugasson,Kaido.Kikkas}@tlu.ee

Abstract. Privacy and confidentiality are important components of digital literacy. Yet nowadays documents can be found online, which apparently consist only of one or two pages yet have huge file size - even several megabytes. Such documents may contain sensitive data that has been deleted but actually is still there. Our study provides an analysis of such cases in public sector of Estonia. Based on experiments and public sector web page analysis we describe security threats and features of different file formats and offer suggestions for their use, e.g. we found that using open-source formats like OpenDocument may help prevention of accidental disclosure of data.

Keywords: privacy, confidentiality, file format, proprietary, open-source, vendor lock-in.

1 Background

Privacy is often considered an area of digital literacy that is in danger of being overlooked, compared with other, more "marketable" ICT skills [1]. Yet, as seen below, even official documents on public networks have privacy shortcoming - this paper looks at privacy issues surfacing due to widespread use of proprietary file formats.

Based on Estonian Interoperability Framework 2011 [2] only OpenDocument formats like ODT, ODS, ODP can be recommended for editing by both sides [3]. OpenDocument is also a standard in other countries [4]. EIF 2011 suggests to use PDF file format when editing by both sides is not needed – this is also common standard in the world [5].

Additionally, file sharing must not be based on import-export. For example, using DOCX means using MS Word, as trying to open it with LibreOffice Writer actually means importing it. Saving DOCX with LibreOffice Writer is possible but strongly not suggested as it is not native format for LibreOffice Writer and therefore problems may occur [6].

Also important is the version of MS Word – for example, editing DOCX file with MS Word 2013 and trying to open it with MS Word 2010 will run into incompatibility problems; some formatting may be lost and even some data (e.g. graphics).

We subscribe to the notion that using open file formats like OpenDocument is strongly suggested, as is creating them with LibreOffice as native editor. When using DOC or DOCX file formats then an appropriate MS Word version should be used.

P. Zaphiris and A. Ioannou (Eds.): LCT 2014, Part I, LNCS 8523, pp. 63–72, 2014.

When sharing files, the same office suite at both sides should be used. Mixing office suites will run into compatibility problems [7]. Keeping the same version with LibreOffice is not expensive as it is free and open-source software. But keeping MS Office on the same version across institutions might be too expensive and overwhelming for users.

OpenDocument adoption in the world has also begun already since OpenOffice.org times but now LibreOffice gives better user experience.

It has been suggested that when saving information as DOC, RTF or some other proprietary file format (e.g. OOXML - Office Open XML – docx, xlsx, pptx, etc), it will store deleted information [8]. It can be seen when something is deleted from such a file, the file then saved and closed - after reopening, the deleted data is still there and can be discovered using some plain text editor (e.g. Notepad2, Notepad++ in Windows or Kate, Geany etc in Linux). However, saving the same file in ODF format (odt, ods, odp etc) will reduce file size and remove hidden parts.

There is a recurring pattern in file handling, especially visible in public sector - users open an file, delete (some of) its content, add new elements and save the file under a new name. These results in document files having just one or two pages but the file size can be in megabytes. Also, large document template files can be found from public sector web pages - and these files can contain sensitive data.

Saving the same file into OpenDocument may reduce the file size for 10 or even more times. The file will still contain the same information but not any ballast data. Proprietary formats do also have problems with revisioning. Finally, there is the ever-visible vendor lock-in problem.

2   Methods

We analyzed documents originating from public sector web pages and carried out experiments. We used Google search by file type to download five random DOC files, five DOCX files and five RTF files from Estonian public sector web sites. DOC and RTF files were opened with MS Word 2003, all content were deleted and replaced with a single word "Hello", the file was then saved and closed. Afterwards, the files were studied using a text editor, searching for deleted text. We used the same process for DOCX files, with the exception of using MS Word 2010 as likely the most used version at the moment (note: as of the time of writing, MS Word 2013 is not widely used in Estonia yet, so the assumption was that most DOCX files available from public sector websites are still created using older - 2007 and 2010 - versions of MS Word).

After this, the files were renamed for indexing. File sizes were registered for both original and changed files and the results compared (see the section "File size comparison" below).

Ubuntu 12.04 LTS 64-bit was used as the main testing platform (using separately added 64-bit kernel version 3.12.5) and file sizes were detected using bash command line and command ls -l. MS Word 2003 (11.5604.5606) and MS Word 2010 (14.0.7015.1000) were installed onto separate virtual machines using VirtualBox

4.3.4 r91027 with guest additions of the same version. The virtual machines used MS Windows XP Pro SP3 as operating system. All Microsoft software used was 32-bit.

For the file content investigation we used Emacs[1] 23.3.1, Midnight Commander[2] 4.8.1 - all available through regular repositories for Ubuntu 12.04 LTS (thus they were not of the latest versions but nevertheless rather up-to-date). For screen capturing Shutter[3] 0.90.1 was used.

Also text editors like Kate, Geany, gEdit, Vim, Cream (modern Vim), wxHexEditor were tested, but Emacs was seen to give the best results in our case.

After using Word to delete the original content and replace it with "Hello", the file was saved into the original format and the latter opened with LibreOffice Writer (LibreOffice version 4.1.3.2 64-bit was used). We then saved the document into ODT-format and repeated the content analysis.

3 Results and Discussion

We started with two hypotheses: The first one was that deleted information is still available in the files and can cause leaks of sensitive information. The second hypothesis was saving DOC, DOCX, RTF file into ODT format will reduce file size. The results of the experiments are described below.

3.1 Used Files

Below is a brief overview of the files tested. The files were indexed for faster investigation and to test their integrity.

In experiment were three different filetypes used – DOC, DOCX, RTF – they were markes as described also in Table 1.

Files used in experiment is available here -
http://url.zeroconf.ee//hcii2014experiment

3.2 File Size Comparison

Table 1 (below) shows the results of file investigation.

The new size and amount of characters were registered after deleting all content, replacing it by just one word: „Hello" (5 characters) and then saving the file. Negative values in Table 1 mean file size increase when saving to ODT format - thus we see that a significant reduction of file size can be obtained with DOC and DOCX files by merely saving them in OpenDocument. Saving the RTF as ODT, however, resulted in file size increase in some cases (but the change was smaller than in other cases). This is described in more detail below.

---

[1] http://www.gnu.org/software/emacs/
[2] http://www.midnight-commander.org/
[3] http://shutter-project.org/

Table 1. File size comparizon

File index	Original size, bytes	Original number of characters with spaces	New size, bytes (5 cha-racters)	New size in ODT, bytes	Difference with new size saved into ODT, bytes	Difference with new size saved into ODT, %
DOC1	50688	1594	19968	8340	11628	41,77%
DOC2	32768	867	19968	8348	11620	41,81%
DOC3	28672	2028	19968	8365	11603	41,89%
DOC4	28672	8128	19968	8744	11224	43,79%
DOC5	30208	1767	20480	9006	11474	43,97%
RTF1	10899	4319	4696	8117	-3421	-57,85%
RTF2	8676	801	3651	7964	-4313	-45,84%
RTF3	82970	2122	4811	8259	-3448	-58,25%
RTF4	141610	3381	12471	9099	3372	72,96%
RTF5	53631	1232	5063	8347	-3284	-60,66%
DOCX1	19837	2139	15966	8706	7260	54,53%
DOCX2	21748	527	14836	8660	6176	58,37%
DOCX3	19876	810	15816	8388	7428	53,03%
DOCX4	25957	3454	19311	8827	10484	45,71%
DOCX5	40935	1512	17055	9153	7902	53,67%

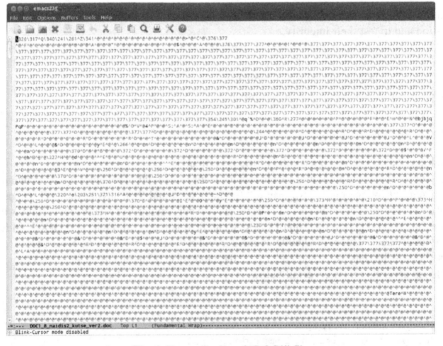

Fig. 1. Emacs display of "DOC1" file

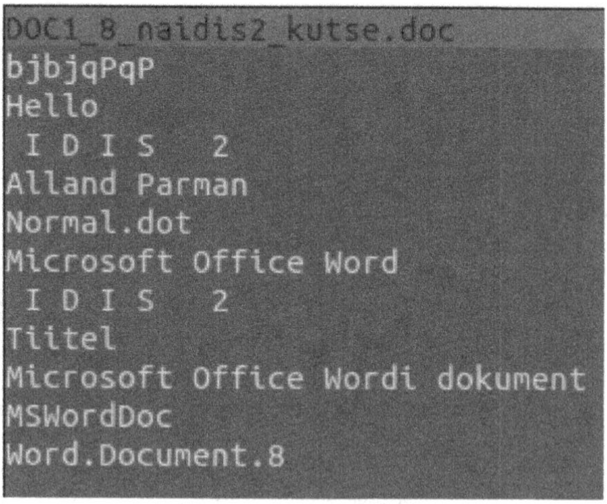

```
DOC1_8_naidis2_kutse.doc
bjbjqPqP
Hello
 I D I S   2
Alland Parman
Normal.dot
Microsoft Office Word
 I D I S   2
Tiitel
Microsoft Office Wordi dokument
MSWordDoc
Word.Document.8
```

Fig. 2. Midnight Commander view of "DOC2"

Experiments with „DOC1", „DOCX1", „RTF1" Files.

After opening „DOC1" file with MS Word 2003, replacing everything with „Hello" and saving it, the file size was 19 968 bytes. Using the text editor Emacs on the file still shows a lot of content (Figure 1). We got similar results with other DOC files.

Due DOC being binary format, the text is unreadable. But Midnight Commander shows the content as more legible (Figure 2).

As we can see, there are some more information visible in the Midnight Commander view than might be expected. This is one point where sensitive data may leak.

When opening DOCX file with Emacs, it shows archived XML-files at the beginning - these can be opened directly like hyperlinks (Figure 3).

```
M Filemode        Length  Date         Time      File
- ----------      --------  -----------  --------  ----------------------------
  -rw-rw-rw-        1819  1-Jan-1980   00:00:00  [Content_Types].xml
  -rw-rw-rw-         590  1-Jan-1980   00:00:00  _rels/.rels
  -rw-rw-rw-        1350  1-Jan-1980   00:00:00  word/_rels/document.xml.rels
  -rw-rw-rw-        1628  1-Jan-1980   00:00:00  word/document.xml
  -rw-rw-rw-        1466  1-Jan-1980   00:00:00  word/endnotes.xml
  -rw-rw-rw-        1472  1-Jan-1980   00:00:00  word/footnotes.xml
  -rw-rw-rw-        6992  1-Jan-1980   00:00:00  word/theme/theme1.xml
  -rw-rw-rw-        3313  1-Jan-1980   00:00:00  word/settings.xml
  -rw-rw-rw-        1451  1-Jan-1980   00:00:00  word/fontTable.xml
  -rw-rw-rw-       19000  1-Jan-1980   00:00:00  word/styles.xml
  -rw-rw-rw-       15713  1-Jan-1980   00:00:00  word/stylesWithEffects.xml
  -rw-rw-rw-         986  1-Jan-1980   00:00:00  docProps/app.xml
  -rw-rw-rw-         630  1-Jan-1980   00:00:00  docProps/core.xml
  -rw-rw-rw-        5686  1-Jan-1980   00:00:00  word/webSettings.xml
  -rw-rw-rw-        1639  1-Jan-1980   00:00:00  word/numbering.xml
- ----------      --------  -----------  --------  ----------------------------|
                  63735                            15 files
```

Fig. 3. Emacs view of "DOCX1" file structure

```xml
<?xml version="1.0" encoding="UTF-8" standalone="yes"?>
<w:document xmlns:wpc="http://schemas.microsoft.com/office/word/2010/wordprocessingCanvas"
xmlns:mc="http://schemas.openxmlformats.org/markup-compatibility/2006"
xmlns:o="urn:schemas-microsoft-com:office:office"
xmlns:r="http://schemas.openxmlformats.org/officeDocument/2006/relationships"
xmlns:m="http://schemas.openxmlformats.org/officeDocument/2006/math" xmlns:v="urn:schemas-microsoft-com:vml"
xmlns:wp14="http://schemas.microsoft.com/office/word/2010/wordprocessingDrawing"
xmlns:wp="http://schemas.openxmlformats.org/drawingml/2006/wordprocessingDrawing"
xmlns:w10="urn:schemas-microsoft-com:office:word"
xmlns:w="http://schemas.openxmlformats.org/wordprocessingml/2006/main"
xmlns:w14="http://schemas.microsoft.com/office/word/2010/wordml"
xmlns:wpg="http://schemas.microsoft.com/office/word/2010/wordprocessingGroup"
xmlns:wpi="http://schemas.microsoft.com/office/word/2010/wordprocessingInk"
xmlns:wne="http://schemas.microsoft.com/office/word/2010/wordml"
xmlns:wps="http://schemas.microsoft.com/office/word/2010/wordprocessingShape" mc:Ignorable="w14 wp14"><w:body><w:p
w:rsidR="00B66A88" w:rsidRPr="00374D62" w:rsidRDefault="00374D62"
w:rsidP="00374D62"><w:r><w:t>Hello</w:t></w:r><w:bookmarkStart w:id="0" w:name="_GoBack"/><w:bookmarkEnd
w:id="0"/></w:p><w:sectPr w:rsidR="00B66A88" w:rsidRPr="00374D62" w:rsidSect="00FB3C63"><w:pgSz w:w="11906"
w:h="16838"/><w:pgMar w:top="1417" w:right="1417" w:bottom="1417" w:left="1417" w:header="708" w:footer="708"
w:gutter="0"/><w:cols w:space="708"/><w:docGrid w:linePitch="360"/></w:sectPr></w:body></w:document>
```

Fig. 4. Emacs view of "DOCX1" file component "document.xml"

```
{\rtf1\ansi\ansicpg1257\uc1\deff0\stshfdbch0\stshfloch0\stshfhich0\stshfbi0\deflang1061\deflangfe1061{\fonttbl{\f0\froman\fcha
rset186\fprq2{\*\panose 02020603050405020304}Times New Roman{\*\falt Times New Roman};}
{\f35\fswiss\fcharset186\fprq2{\*\panose 020b0604030504040204}Tahoma{\*\falt Lucidasans};}{\f39\froman\fcharset0\fprq2 Times
New Roman{\*\falt Times New Roman};}{\f37\froman\fcharset238\fprq2 Times New Roman CE{\*\falt Times New Roman};}
{\f38\froman\fcharset204\fprq2 Times New Roman Cyr{\*\falt Times New Roman};}{\f40\froman\fcharset161\fprq2 Times New Roman
Greek{\*\falt Times New Roman};}{\f41\froman\fcharset162\fprq2 Times New Roman Tur{\*\falt Times New Roman};}
{\f42\froman\fcharset177\fprq2 Times New Roman (Hebrew){\*\falt Times New Roman};}{\f43\froman\fcharset178\fprq2 Times New
Roman (Arabic){\*\falt Times New Roman};}{\f45\froman\fcharset163\fprq2 Times New Roman (Vietnamese){\*\falt Times New
Roman};}
{\f389\fswiss\fcharset0\fprq2 Tahoma{\*\falt Lucidasans};}{\f387\fswiss\fcharset238\fprq2 Tahoma CE{\*\falt
Lucidasans};}{\f388\fswiss\fcharset204\fprq2 Tahoma Cyr{\*\falt Lucidasans};}{\f390\fswiss\fcharset161\fprq2 Tahoma
Greek{\*\falt Lucidasans};}
{\f391\fswiss\fcharset162\fprq2 Tahoma Tur{\*\falt Lucidasans};}{\f392\fswiss\fcharset177\fprq2 Tahoma (Hebrew){\*\falt
Lucidasans};}{\f393\fswiss\fcharset178\fprq2 Tahoma (Arabic){\*\falt Lucidasans};}
{\f395\fswiss\fcharset163\fprq2 Tahoma (Vietnamese){\*\falt Lucidasans};}}{\f396\fswiss\fcharset222\fprq2 Tahoma
(Thai){\*\falt Lucidasans};}}{\colortbl;\red0\green0\blue0;\red0\green0\blue255;\red0\green255\blue255;\red0\green255\blue0;
\red255\green0\blue255;\red255\green0\blue0;\red255\green255\blue0;\red255\green255\blue255;\red0\green0\blue128;\red0\green12
8\blue128;\red0\green128\blue0;\red128\green0\blue128;\red128\green0\blue0;\red128\green128\blue0;\red128\green128\blue128;
\red192\green192\blue192;}{\stylesheet{\ql \li0\ri0\widctlpar\aspalpha\aspnum\faauto\adjustright\rin0\lin0\itap0
\fs24\lang1061\langfe1061\cgrid\langnp1061\langfenp1061 \snext0 Normal;}{\*\cs10 \additive \ssemihidden Default Paragraph
Font;}{\*
\ts11\tsrowd\trftsWidthB3\trpaddl108\trpaddr108\trpaddfl3\trpaddft3\trpaddfb3\trpaddfr3\tscellwidthfts0\tsvertalt\tsbrdrt\tsbr
drl\tsbrdrb\tsbrdrr\tsbrdrdgl\tsbrdrdgr\tsbrdrh\tsbrdrv
\ql \li0\ri0\widctlpar\aspalpha\aspnum\faauto\adjustright\rin0\lin0\itap0
\fs20\lang1024\langfe1024\cgrid\langnp1024\langfenp1024 \snext11 \ssemihidden Normal Table;}{\s15\ql
\li0\ri0\widctlpar\aspalpha\aspnum\faauto\adjustright\rin0\lin0\itap0
\f35\fs16\lang1061\langfe1061\cgrid\langnp1061\langfenp1061 \sbasedon0 \snext15 \ssemihidden \styrsid2979352 Balloon
Text;}}{\*\latentstyles\lsdstimax156\lsdlockeddef0}{\*\rsidtbl
\rsid1641128\rsid1773162\rsid2979352\rsid3227400\rsid3434205\rsid4196462
\rsid9713028\rsid9911056\rsid11364192\rsid1232571\rsid12877287\rsid13580229}{\*\generator Microsoft Word
11.0.5604;}{\info{\title V\'f5ru Linnavalitsuse sotsiaalt\'f6\'f6osakonnale}{\author Eve.Tsegurov}{\operator
.}{\creatim\yr2008\mo3\dy4\hr14\min36}
{\revtim\yr2013\mo12\dy15\hr18\min21}{\printim\yr2007\mo5\dy4\hr14\min19}{\version4}{\edmins0}{\nofpages1}{\nofwords0}{\nofcha
rs5}{\*\company VLV}{\nofcharsws5}{\vern24689}}\paperw11906\paperh16838\margl1417\margr1417\margt1417\margb1417
\deftab708\widowctrl\ftnbj\aenddoc\hyphhotz425\noxlattoyen\expshrtn\noultrlspc\dntblnsbdb\nospaceforul\hyphcaps0\formshade\hor
zdoc\dgmargin\dghspace180\dgvspace180\dghorigin1417\dgvorigin1417\dghshow1\dgvshow1
\jexpand\viewkind1\viewscale100\pgbrdrhead\pgbrdrfoot\splytwnine\ftnlytwnine\htmautsp\nolnhtadjtbl\useltbaln\alntblind\lytcalc
tblwd\lyttblrtgr\lnbrkrule\nobrkwrptbl\snaptogridincell\allowfieldendsel\wrppunct\asianbrkrule\rsidroot11364192 \fet0\sectd
\linex0\headery708\footery708\colsx708\endnhere\sectlinegrid360\sectdefaultcl\sftnbj
{\*\pnseclvl1\pnucrm\pnstart1\pnindent720\pnhang {\pntxta .}}{\*\pnseclvl2\pnucltr\pnstart1\pnindent720\pnhang {\pntxta
.}}{\*\pnseclvl3\pndec\pnstart1\pnindent720\pnhang
{\pntxta .}}{\*\pnseclvl4\pnlcltr\pnstart1\pnindent720\pnhang {\pntxta )}}{\*\pnseclvl5\pndec\pnstart1\pnindent720\pnhang
{\pntxtb (}{\pntxta )}}{\*\pnseclvl6\pnlcltr\pnstart1\pnindent720\pnhang {\pntxtb (}{\pntxta )}}{\*\pnseclvl7
\pnlcrm\pnstart1\pnindent720\pnhang {\pntxtb (}{\pntxta )}}{\*\pnseclvl8\pnlcltr\pnstart1\pnindent720\pnhang {\pntxtb
(}{\pntxta )}}{\*\pnseclvl9\pnlcrm\pnstart1\pnindent720\pnhang {\pntxtb (}{\pntxta )}}\pard\plain
\ql \li0\ri0\widctlpar\aspalpha\aspnum\faauto\adjustright\rin0\lin0\itap0\pararsid4196462
\fs24\lang1061\langfe1061\cgrid\langnp1061\langfenp1061 {\insrsid4196462 Hello}{\insrsid13580229\charrsid4196462
\par }}
```

Fig. 5. Emacs view of "RTF1" file

Each of these XML files does contain data about formatting and also content. The most important component is document.xml, which contains the content of document (Figure 4).

Note: we can also rename DOCX file to ZIP and uncompress it but Emacs does it on the fly, which is much more comfortable. Emacs is available for all popular operating systems and is free software.

When looking inside the RTF-file we can finally read the content (Figure 5). It contains a lot of information but only one word entered by the user – the word „Hello" seen at the end of RTF block.

After saving the previously modified RTF-files into ODT-format, the situation changed. Some RTF-files were even bigger in ODT than in RTF-format itself but this is not always so as the „RTF4" got smaller when saved into ODT format (the result of file content comparison is shown in Appendix 1). Saving „RTF4" into ODT format saves a lot of file size. This also depends on the MS Word version that was used previously to modify the RTF-file. Each MS Word will leave its additions into file and the file gets bigger. All these additions will be removed when saving into ODT format.

Even if usually RTF comes smaller than ODT, it is not a good idea for use as a document format – usually it cannot support more complex formatting like ODT, DOC or DOCX does.

```
M Filemode       Length  Date         Time      File
- ----------     -------- -----------  --------  --------------------------------------------
  -rw-rw-rw-          39  15-Dec-2013  17:51:38  mimetype
  -rw-rw-rw-        1143  15-Dec-2013  17:51:38  meta.xml
  -rw-rw-rw-        9878  15-Dec-2013  17:51:38  settings.xml
  -rw-rw-rw-        5710  15-Dec-2013  17:51:38  content.xml
  -rw-rw-rw-         851  15-Dec-2013  17:51:38  Thumbnails/thumbnail.png
  -rw-rw-rw-         899  15-Dec-2013  17:51:38  manifest.rdf
  drwxrwxrwx          0  15-Dec-2013  17:51:38  Configurations2/images/Bitmaps/
  -rw-rw-rw-          0  15-Dec-2013  17:51:38  Configurations2/accelerator/current.xml
  -rw-rw-rw-       23270  15-Dec-2013  17:51:38  styles.xml
  -rw-rw-rw-        1086  15-Dec-2013  17:51:38  META-INF/manifest.xml
- ----------     -------- -----------  --------  --------------------------------------------
-                 42876                           10 files
```

Fig. 6. Emacs view of "RTF4" in ODT format

In ODT file the „content.xml" contains the file content itself (Figure 6).

4   Conclusion

The experiments revealed some problems with the files. The DOCX files were sometimes opened in compatibility mode, which suggests an earlier version of DOCX than MS Word 2010 (usually MS Word 2007). This means that DOC and DOCX files stored at Estonian public sector websites were created using earlier versions of MS Word than the current 2010 used for our experiment. The same situation is seen with MS Word 2010 and 2013 – the 2010 does not support all features available in 2013, so the compatibility mode will be used and some data may be lost due to this.

The first hypothesis – deleted information will be stored inside the file – was not completely confirmed. We may say that at least MS Word 2010 will permanently delete almost all content. There might be remain some small parts but these are not noticeable. But as Chinese researchers suggest: „Experiments show that 0.44 bit is embedded into each word and 1/151 bit is embedded into each bit of the document on average, which is higher than contemporary linguistic steganography approaches" then still we may say that MS Word is not cleanly deleting all the data [8]. Even Microsoft gives suggestions how to discover [9] and remove unnecessary parts of file

[10]. Considering all this, Estonian public sector shows similar vulnerabilities like those described by van Hamel [1] and should likewise strive towards an established set of privacy competencies to maintain confidential information online.

The second hypothesis – RTF, DOC, DOCX file sizes will be reduced when saving into ODT – were completely confirmed in part of DOC, DOCX files. Even if RTF-files were smaller than ODT-files, there is not recommended to use it due to lack of support more complex functions available nowadays modern office suites.

Using correct file formats with appropriate programs when working collaboratively – this all makes an important part of nowadays digital literacy. Using importing-exporting documents in foreign programs may run into incompatibility issues and even security leaks. Therefore interoperability frameworks are created and strongly suggested to follow to ensure hassle free collaboration between people.

Acknowledgements. This research was supported by the Tiger University Program of the Information Technology Foundation for Education.

References

1. van Hamel, A.: The Privacy Piece: Report on Privacy Competencies in Digital Literacy Programs in Canada, Britain, Australia, America, and Brazil. University of Ottawa (November 2011), https://www.priv.gc.ca/information/research-recherche/2011/hamel_201111_e.asp (retrieved)
2. RISO. Estonian Interoperability Framework (2011), http://www.riso.ee/en/estonian-interoperability-framework (retrieved)
3. RISO. Estonian state it architecture (2007), http://www.riso.ee/et/koosvoime/arhitektuur (retrieved)
4. Weir, R.: OpenDocument Format: The Standard for Office Documents. IEEE Internet Computing 13(2), 83 (2009)
5. PC Magazine. PDF File Format to Become Open Standard (2007); PC Magazine Online (2007), http://www.pcmag.com/article2/0,2817,2088283,00.asp (retrieved)
6. Park, E.G., Oh, S.: Examining Attributes of Open Standard File Formats for Long-term Preservation and Open Access. Information Technology & Libraries 31(4), 44–65 (2012)
7. Microsoft, 3. Differences between the opendocument text (.odt) format and the word (.docx) format (2013), http://office.microsoft.com/en-ca/word-help/differences-between-the-opendocument-text-odt-format-and-.the-word-docx-format-HA010355788.aspx (retrieved)
8. Fu, Z., Liu, Y., Li, B., Sun, X.: Text split-based steganography in OOXML format documents for covert communication. Security and Communication Networks 5(9), 957–968 (2012), doi:10.1002/sec.378
9. Microsoft, 1. Inspect documents for hidden data and personal information (2013), http://office.microsoft.com/en-us/word-help/inspect-documents-for-hidden-data-and-personal-information-HA010074435.aspx (retrieved)
10. Microsoft, 2. Remove hidden data and personal information by inspecting documents (2013), http://office.microsoft.com/en-us/word-help/remove-hidden-data-and-personal-information-by-inspecting-documents-HA010354329.aspx (retrieved)

APPENDIX 1

Here is the „RTF4" content compared with RTF and ODT format (Figure 7).

RTF4 Content

Fig. 7. „RTF4" content compared with RTF and ODT format

ODT Content of „RTF4" File

```
<?xml version="1.0" encoding="UTF-8"?>
<office:document-content xmlns:office="urn:oasis:names:tc:opendocument:xmlns:office:1.0"
xmlns:style="urn:oasis:names:tc:opendocument:xmlns:style:1.0" xmlns:text="urn:oasis:names:tc:opendocument:xmlns:text:1.0"
xmlns:table="urn:oasis:names:tc:opendocument:xmlns:table:1.0" xmlns:draw="urn:oasis:names:tc:opendocument:xmlns:drawing:1.0"
xmlns:fo="urn:oasis:names:tc:opendocument:xmlns:xsl-fo-compatible:1.0" xmlns:xlink="http://www.w3.org/1999/xlink"
xmlns:dc="http://purl.org/dc/elements/1.1/" xmlns:meta="urn:oasis:names:tc:opendocument:xmlns:meta:1.0"
xmlns:number="urn:oasis:names:tc:opendocument:xmlns:datastyle:1.0" xmlns:svg="urn:oasis:names:tc:opendocument:xmlns:svg-compatible:1.0"
xmlns:chart="urn:oasis:names:tc:opendocument:xmlns:chart:1.0" xmlns:dr3d="urn:oasis:names:tc:opendocument:xmlns:dr3d:1.0"
xmlns:math="http://www.w3.org/1998/Math/MathML" xmlns:form="urn:oasis:names:tc:opendocument:xmlns:form:1.0"
xmlns:script="urn:oasis:names:tc:opendocument:xmlns:script:1.0" xmlns:ooo="http://openoffice.org/2004/office"
xmlns:ooow="http://openoffice.org/2004/writer" xmlns:oooc="http://openoffice.org/2004/calc" xmlns:dom="http://www.w3.org/2001/xml-events"
xmlns:xforms="http://www.w3.org/2002/xforms" xmlns:xsd="http://www.w3.org/2001/XMLSchema"
xmlns:xsi="http://www.w3.org/2001/XMLSchema-instance" xmlns:rpt="http://openoffice.org/2005/report"
xmlns:of="urn:oasis:names:tc:opendocument:xmlns:of:1.2" xmlns:xhtml="http://www.w3.org/1999/xhtml"
xmlns:grddl="http://www.w3.org/2003/g/data-view#" xmlns:officeooo="http://openoffice.org/2009/office"
xmlns:tableooo="http://openoffice.org/2009/table" xmlns:drawooo="http://openoffice.org/2010/draw"
xmlns:calcext="urn:org:documentfoundation:names:experimental:calc:calcext:1.0"
xmlns:field="urn:openoffice:names:experimental:ooo-ms-interop:xmlns:field:1.0"
xmlns:formx="urn:openoffice:names:experimental:ooxml-odf-interop:xmlns:form:1.0" xmlns:css3t="http://www.w3.org/TR/css3-text/"
office:version="1.2"><office:scripts/><office:font-face-decls><style:font-face style:name="Lohit Hindi1" svg:font-family="&apos;Lohit
Hindi&apos;"/><style:font-face style:name="Arial" svg:font-family="Arial" style:font-family-generic="swiss"/><style:font-face
style:name="Arial Unicode MS" svg:font-family="&apos;Arial Unicode MS&apos;" style:font-family-generic="swiss"/><style:font-face
style:name="Tahoma" svg:font-family="Tahoma" style:font-family-generic="swiss"/><style:font-face style:name="Times New Roman"
svg:font-family="&apos;Times New Roman&apos;" style:font-family-generic="swiss"/><style:font-face style:name="Tahoma Greek"
svg:font-family="&apos;Tahoma Greek&apos;" style:font-family-generic="system"/><style:font-face style:name="Arial1" svg:font-family="Arial"
style:font-family-generic="swiss" style:font-pitch="variable"/><style:font-face style:name="Droid Sans" svg:font-family="&apos;Droid
Sans&apos;" style:font-family-generic="system" style:font-pitch="variable"/><style:font-face style:name="Lohit Hindi"
svg:font-family="&apos;Lohit Hindi&apos;" style:font-family-generic="system"
style:font-pitch="variable"/></office:font-face-decls><office:automatic-styles><style:style style:name="P1" style:family="paragraph"
style:parent-style-name="Standard" style:master-page-name="Standard"><style:paragraph-properties fo:margin-left="0cm" fo:margin-right="0cm"
fo:text-align="start" style:justify-single-word="false" fo:orphans="2" fo:widows="2" fo:text-indent="0cm" style:auto-text-indent="false"
style:page-number="auto" style:vertical-align="auto"/></style:style><style:style style:name="P2" style:family="paragraph"
style:parent-style-name="Footer"><style:paragraph-properties fo:margin-left="0cm" fo:margin-right="0cm" fo:text-align="end"
style:justify-single-word="false" fo:orphans="2" fo:widows="2" fo:text-indent="0cm" style:auto-text-indent="false"
style:vertical-align="auto"><style:tab-stops><style:tab-stop style:position="8.001cm" style:type="center"/></style:tab-stop
style:position="16.002cm" style:type="right"/></style:tab-stops></style:paragraph-properties></style:style><style:style style:name="P3"
style:family="paragraph" style:parent-style-name="Footer"><style:paragraph-properties fo:margin-left="0cm" fo:margin-right="0cm"
fo:text-align="center" style:justify-single-word="false" fo:orphans="2" fo:widows="2" fo:text-indent="0cm" style:auto-text-indent="false"
style:vertical-align="auto"><style:tab-stops><style:tab-stop style:position="8.001cm" style:type="center"/><style:tab-stop
style:position="16.002cm" style:type="right"/></style:tab-stops></style:paragraph-properties><style:style><style:text-properties style:font-name="Times
New Roman" fo:font-size="12pt" fo:language="et" fo:country="EE" style:font-size-asian="12pt" style:language-asian="et"
style:country-asian="EE"/></style:style><style:style style:name="T1" style:family="text"><style:text-properties style:font-name="Times New
Roman" fo:font-size="12pt" fo:language="et" fo:country="EE" style:font-size-asian="12pt" style:language-asian="et"
style:country-asian="EE"/></style:style><style:style style:name="T2" style:family="text"><style:text-properties fo:language="et"
fo:country="EE"/></style:style></office:automatic-styles><office:body><office:text><text:sequence-decls><text:sequence-decl
text:display-outline-level="0" text:name="Illustration"/><text:sequence-decl text:display-outline-level="0"
text:name="Table"/><text:sequence-decl text:display-outline-level="0" text:name="Text"/><text:sequence-decl text:display-outline-level="0"
text:name="Drawing"/></text:sequence-decls><text:p text:style-name="P1"><text:span
text:style-name="T1">Hello</text:span></text:p></office:text></office:body></office:document-content>
```

Fig. 8. ODT content of "RTF4" file

A Review of Storyboard Tools, Concepts and Frameworks

Nor'ain Mohd Yusoff[1] and Siti Salwah Salim[2]

[1] Faculty of Computing and Informatics, Multimedia University,
63100 Cyberjaya, Selangor, Malaysia
[2] Faculty of Computer Science and Information Technology, University of Malaya,
50603 Kuala Lumpur, Malaysia
norain.yusoff@mmu.edu.my, salwa@um.edu.my

Abstract. This paper describes and analyses storyboard tools, concepts and frameworks. It aims to identify gaps in storyboard works in an attempt to extend support for establishing a common ground between instruction designers and subject-matter experts as a distributed instructional design team. Twenty-four storyboard tools, concepts and frameworks are described according to the two classifications of domain applications, domain-independent and domain-dependent. They are reviewed and analysed with regard to three aspects of e-learning storyboard requirements: collaborative design environment, iterative process methodology and designer-centredness support. The finding shows that much less research has been done on collaborative environments and iterative processes than on supporting designers' work. It is also found that storyboard systems have some limitations in terms of giving the distributed instructional design team opportunity to engage in these cognitive task-related activities.

Keywords: storyboard tools, storyboard systems, distributed instructional design team.

1 Introduction

Instructional design teams in communities of practice recognise the importance of establishing a common ground with the people they work with. In an extended and distributed design project, experts from different domains must coordinate their efforts despite the limitations of time and distance. The application of storyboarding techniques has been a useful approach in distance learning development to support interaction between instructional designers and subject-matter experts in communicating the design of an e-learning course. A substantial amount of time and effort is required however to reach a shared understanding of the coordinated tasks and activities. The purpose of this paper is to review and analyse existing storyboard tools, concepts and frameworks. It begins by describing 16 storyboard systems and groups them into two types of software classification tools and models. The next section focuses on eight storyboarding concepts and frameworks which have the potential to become functional tools in future. This is followed by analysis of the storyboard tools, concepts and frameworks whose design implications have fostered an approach to support instructional designers and subject-matter experts' interaction as a distributed instructional design team.

P. Zaphiris and A. Ioannou (Eds.): LCT 2014, Part I, LNCS 8523, pp. 73–82, 2014.
© Springer International Publishing Switzerland 2014

2   Storyboard Tools and Concepts

Following Wang, Shen, Xie, Neelamkavil, and Pardasani (2002), these tools are classified into domain- independent and domain-dependent tools. These software classification tools and storyboard models are not confined to any particular domain and cover a wide spectrum.

2.1   Domain-Independent Tools

The domain-independent tools of storyboards are tools that support specific but general-purpose tasks. They are divided into three sub-categories: the sketch-based approach, authoring approach, and SCORM approach.

The sketch design approach is treated as a domain-independent tool as it can provide functionalities to assist designers to sketch user interfaces and web pages. Landay and Myers (2001) developed SILK (Sketching Interfaces Like Krazy), a storyboard that allows designers to sketch user interfaces easily by recognising the designer's ink strokes. Bailey, Konstan, and Carlis (2001) developed DEMAIS (Designing Multimedia Applications with Interactive Storyboards), a sketch-based, interactive multimedia storyboard tool that uses a designer's ink strokes and textual annotations as an input design vocabulary. Newman, Lin, Hong, and Landay (2003) developed DENIM (Design Environment for Navigation and Information Models), an informal website design tool that supports designers in sketching input, allows design at different levels of granularity, and unifies the levels through zooming.

In the context of instructional design, an authoring tool supports non-programmers in assembling media objects and preconstructed scripting code to build instructional learning applications (Chapman, 2008). The authoring approach is treated as a domain-independent tool to support users or designers in authoring any aspects of objects and processes required to reach a specific objective. Harada, Tanaka, Ogawa, and Hara (1996) developed ANECDOTE to support designers to edit the different aspects of the scenario using multiple editing views, and help them to create the final application seamlessly from the prototype scenario. Midieum, Byung-soo, and Jun (2005) developed the AR storyboard (augmented reality-based interactive storyboard authoring tool) to support intuitive interfaces for scene composition and camera pose/motion control. Thronesbery, Molin, and Schreckenghost (2007) developed the ConOps (Concept of Operation) storyboard to help designers to create, communicate, and refine concepts of operation information.

SCORM (Sharable Content Object Reference Model) is a technical specification that governs e-learning content creation and delivery (Bohl, Scheuhase, Sengler, & Winand, 2002). The SCORM approach is treated as a domain- independent tool as it helps designers to create e-learning content that complies with SCORM specifications. Ting et al. (2005) developed the eStoryboard authoring tool which is intended to provide designers with functionalities such as creation of HTML documents, Flash editing, and inserting images and, at the same time, generating outputs in flash format to produce a SCORM-compliant document. Yang, Chiung-Hui, Chun-Yen, and Tsung-Hsien (2004) developed the Visualized Online Simple Sequencing Authoring

Tool (VOSSAT) to help designers to edit existing SCORM-compliant content packages which can be embedded as a module on the Content Repository Management System (CRMS).

Table 1 shows a summary of domain-independent tools and their implementation technologies.

2.2 Domain-Dependent Tools

The domain-dependent tools of storyboards are tools that are hard-wired with theories and models in an instructional design that cannot be altered. These tools use underlying philosophical models and theoretical underpinnings (Gustafson, 2002). They can perform various functions for different kinds of learning solutions. They are divided into two sub-categories: the learning theories approach and instructional design model approach.

The learning theory approach is treated as a domain-dependent tool as it supports the intended application of learning theories which inform the designer about the flow of the modules and ensures that all aspects of the intended course have been covered. Hundhausen and Douglas (2000) developed SALSA (Spatial Algorithmic Language for StoryboArding) as a teaching approach in which students use the simple art supplied to construct and present the algorithm to their instructor and peers for feedback and discussion. Lee and Chong (2005) developed OntoID (Automated Eclectic Instructional Design) to support the design phase through the explication of different techniques in the learning theory categories. Deacon, Morrison, and Stadler (2005) developed Director's Cut to support students as designers in the production of multimodal texts which enable the understanding of conventions and processes. Mustaro, Silveira, Omar, and Stump (2007) developed a schematic storyboard for learning object development to support the instructional design (ID) team throughout the model schemes moulded in a linear process according to the five processes in ID: analysis, design, development, implementation and evaluation. Igbrue and Pathak (2008) developed the Multiple Intelligence Informed tool to support both novice and experienced IDs in designing storyboard assessments suitable for multiple intelligences in e-learning.

The instructional design model approach is treated as a domain-dependent tool as it supports the design of a particular instruction. Hodis, Schreiber, Rother, and Sussman (2007) developed eMovie to support designers in making molecular movies in 3D structures. Furini, Geraci, Montangero, and Pellegrini (2010) developed STIMO (STIll and MOving storyboard) to help designers to produce on-the-fly, still and moving storyboards.

Table 2 shows a summary of domain-independent tools and their implementation technologies.

3 Storyboard Frameworks

In addition to the above domain-independent and domain-dependent tools, the following storyboarding concepts and framework have the potential to become functional tools in future. Baek (1998) developed a KMS-based environment to support the knowledge management activities of multimedia designers. Jakkilinki, Sharda, and Ahmad (2006) developed the MUDPY (multimedia design and planning pyramid) to guide designers through the various phases of a multimedia project in a systematic fashion by allowing them to create a project proposal, specify the functional requirements, decide on the navigational structure and create a storyboard. Dohi, Sakurai, Tsuruta, and Knauf (2006) developed the Dynamic Learning Needs Reflection System (DLNRS) storyboard tool to support the formal process of representing, processing, evaluating and refining didactic knowledge. Choo Wou (2007) developed the ILC-CMAS Model (Intuitive Life Cycle-CMAS Model) to assist the process of content development and the storyboarding management process for multimedia software development. Bulterman (2007) developed a framework to support user-centered control of media within a collection of objects that are structured into a multimedia presentation. Kleinberger, Holzinger, and Müller (2008) developed MEMORY (Multimedia Module Repository) to provide designers with a technological base for implementing e-learning applications that make extensive use of continuous media, especially video. Wan (2007) developed the Content Storyboard Application System Framework to monitor subject-matter experts in performing storyboarding activities. Wahid, Branham, Harrison, and McCrickard (2009) developed the concept of Collaborative Storyboarding to help in aggregating designers' expertise in the storyboarding process, and it offers the opportunity for a group of designers to make progress toward creating a visual narrative for a new interface or technology.

Table 3 shows a summary of conceptual models and frameworks and their implementation technologies.

4   Design Implications: Storyboarding Approach

This section discusses three requirements of an e-learning storyboard which support instructional designers and subject-matter experts' interaction; the relationship of instructional designers and subject-matter experts, which is recognised as collaborative in nature, the importance of iterative process in design, and the importance of designer-centredness support. The storyboarding tools, concepts and frameworks are discussed in that context.

4.1   Collaborative vs. Non-Collaborative Design Environments

The literature contains no description of collaborative effort by tools from the domain-independent category and only one tool, i.e. Director's Cut (Deacon et al., 2005) from the domain-dependent category mentions this collaborative environment. The collaborative design environment has been identified in many conceptual models and framework research: Baek (1998) describes the KMS-based environment, Choo Wou (2007) the ILC-CMAS model, Wan (2007) the Content Storyboard Application System Framework, and Wahid et al. (2009) the concept of collaborative storyboarding.

Table 1. Summary of domain-independent tools and their implementation technologies

Name of System/Tool	Key Features	Implementation Technologies
SILK (Landay & Myers, 2001)	To support sketching for user interfaces.	Common Lisp. The Garnet toolkit.
DEMAIS (Bailey, Konstan, & Carlis, 2001)	To support the early stages of multimedia design.	Java language, Java Media Framework (JMF) and Java Speech Markup Language
DENIM (Newman, Lin, Hong, & Landay, 2003)	To support early-phase information and navigation design of websites.	Java 2. The SATIN toolkit
ANECDOTE (Harada, Tanaka, Ogawa, & Hara, 1996)	To support the early-design phase and the whole development process of multimedia applications.	-unspecified -
AR Storyboard (Midieum, Byung-soo, & Jun, 2005)	To support non-experienced designers using interfaces in real environments at the pre-production stage of film-making.	- unspecified -
ConOps (Thronesbery, Molin, & Schreckenghost, 2007)	To provide effective task that can support the difficulties of designer to understand end user tasks and software engineering principles.	- unspecified -
eStoryboard (Ting et al., 2005)	To create SCORM learning contents, generate multiple lesson plans, and predict learner performance from the generated lesson plans.	Artificial Intelligence Planning and Bayesian Reasoning.
VOSSAT (Yang, Chiung-Hui, Chun-Yen, & Tsung-Hsien, 2004)	To assist designers in editing the existing SCORM-compliant content packages for learning processes.	- unspecified -

Table 2. Summary of domain-dependent tools and their implementation technologies

Name of System/Tool	Key Features	Implementation Technologies
SALSA (Hundhausen & Douglas, 2000)	To support designers in constructing rough and unpolished low-fidelity visualisations.	spatial algorithmic language
OntoID (Lee & Chong, 2005)	To provide strong pedagogical guidance through the provision of educational models and techniques founded on learning philosophy.	XML technology
Director's Cut (Deacon, Morrison, & Stadler, 2005)	To support students in creating their own video sequences from a set of clips in order to promote creativity.	- unspecified -

Table 2. (*continued*)

Schematic Storyboard tool (Mustaro, Silveira, Omar, & Stump, 2007)	To support the instructional design team throughout the model scheme development and production of learning objects in storyboard.	- unspecified -
Multiple Intelligence In-formed tool (Igbrue & Pathak, 2008)	To guide IDs in creating the multiple intelligences informed e-learning con-tent	- unspecified -
e-Movie (Hodis, Schreiber, Rother, & Sussman, 2007)	To support designers with guidance and direction in the form of structures and conformation changes in filming.	open-source molecular graphics pro-gram
STIMO (Furini, Geraci, Montangero, & Pellegrini, 2010)	To support the production of on-the-fly video storyboards.	Farthest Point-First (FPF) clustering algorithm

Table 3. Summary of conceptual models and frameworks and their implementation technologies

Name of System/Tool	Key Features	Implementation Technologies
KMS-based environment (Baek, 1998)	To support multimedia designers in sharing their knowledge on the web.	Java script and Cold Fusion
MUDPY (Jakkilinki, Sharda, & Ahmad, 2006)	To streamline the process of creating a multimedia sys-tem by providing a clear pathway for planning, de-sign and development.	Protégé 2000
DLNRS storyboard tool (Dohi, Sakurai, Tsuruta, & Knauf, 2006)	To support the didactic knowledge that can be represented by storyboards and used for supporting dynamic learning activities of students.	- unspecified -
ILC-CMAS Model (Choo Wou, 2007)	To support experts of Smart Schools, organisations and universities involved in the development of multimedia software and courseware.	- unspecified -
User-centred multimedia control. (Bulterman, 2007)	To support user-centred control of multimedia that assist in locating or recom-mending media objects.	- unspecified -

Table 3. (*continued*)

MEMORY (Kleinberger, Holzinger, & Müller, 2008)	To support continuous media with adaptive multi-media processes in order to achieve efficiency in search, selection, rating and usage.	Python programming language, C++, Java, CORBA
Content Storyboard Application System Framework. (Wan Adli Ridzwan, 2007)	To support SME in con-structing e-learning content storyboards based on Gagne's Nine Learning Events.	PHP, MySQL
Collaborative story-boarding (Wahid, Branham, Harrison, & McCrickard, 2009)	To facilitate shared under-standing among designers.	- unspecified -

4.2 Linear vs. Iterative Process Methodology

The literature identifies only one tool from the domain independent category which implemented iterative process whereas none is identified from the domain-dependent category. The ConOps tool which is developed by Thronesbery et al., (2007) describes a concept of operations that requires iteration to support creative design activity. Researchers such as Dohi et al. (2006), Choo Wou (2007), and Bulterman (2007) implement an iterative process method in their conceptual models and frameworks.

4.3 Designer-Centredness vs. Learner-Centredness Support

In the literature, many researchers have concentrated on the designer-centred approach. All the sketch-based tools (Landay & Myers, 2001; Bailey et al., 2001; Newman et al., 2003) were designed to support designers. An authoring tool that supports designers' work was demonstrated by Harada et al. (1996), and both Midieum et al. (2005) and Thronesbery et al. (2007) designed tools for authoring storyboards to support learners.

All the SCORM-compliant based tools (Ting et al. 2005; Yang et al., 2004) support designers in developing learning content which is compliant with SCORM requirements. The same support can be found in the e-learning theory-based tools (Hundhausen & Douglas, 2000; Lee & Chong, 2005; Deacon et al., 2005). Mustaro et al. (2007) produced a schematic storyboard for learning object development and Igbrue and Pathak (2008) developed a multiple intelligence tool.

Instructional model-based tools (Hodis et al., 2007; Furini et al., 2010) are designed purposely for learners, however. Researchers such as Jakkilinki et al. (2006), Choo Wou (2007), Wan (2007) and Wahid et al. (2009) demonstrated storyboarding concepts and frameworks which are intended to support designers' work.

Figure 1 shows the classification of the available storyboard tools and frameworks in several categories for quick reference.

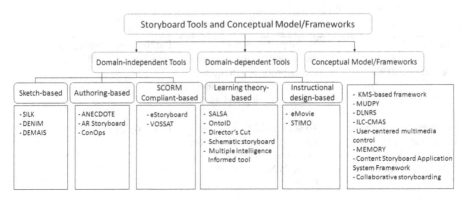

Fig. 1. Storyboard tools, conceptual models and framework

5 Conclusion

This paper discusses and analyses the available storyboard tools which are categorised in two types: domain-independent and domain-dependent tools. Existing conceptual models and frameworks have also been identified and presented. From the analysis of all the tools, concepts and frameworks, it can be concluded that less research has been done on collaborative environments and iterative processes, but much has focused on supporting designers at work. It is also evident that the existing storyboard systems have some limitations in terms of giving the distributed instructional design team opportunity to engage in these cognitive task-related activities.

This study sheds light on the storyboarding systems about the importance to handle the designers in performing their storyboarding task, as well as the cognitive effort that is needed by the designers in performing storyboarding activities. An empirical study has been carried out in order to understand the cognitive difficulties of designers during storyboarding (Yusoff & Salim, 2012). This study explores problem aspects of the cognitive task and the skills required of subject-matter experts by applying a cognitive task analysis approach from the expert perspective, and have consequently identified subject matter experts' difficulties in making decisions on three elements during e-learning course development: the storyboard templates, prescriptive interactive components, and review process.

On the other hand, a storyboard system that can work in a distributed and collaborative environment would be needed in order to support people's interaction, user communication and the iterative process. More necessary, however, for a distributed instructional design team is the functionality to adapt to changes and work towards shared mental model. Future works which incorporate collaborative tasks for the instructional design team should be able to function as a communication tool as well as perform design instruction rather than focusing on the process and tool development.

Acknowledgements. The research was funded by the Ministry of Higher Education, Malaysia (EP20120612006) and Multimedia University Malaysia Research Funding (IP20110707004 and IP20110707004).

References

1. Baek, S.L.: Knowledge management for multimedia systems design: toward intelligent web-based collaboration (Doctoral dissertation). George Washington University, Washington D.C. (1998)
2. Bailey, B.P., Konstan, J.A., Carlis, J.V.: DEMAIS: designing multimedia applications with interactive storyboards. Paper presented at the Proceedings of the Ninth ACM International Conference on Multimedia, Ottawa, Canada (2001)
3. Bohl, O., Scheuhase, J., Sengler, R., Winand, U.: The sharable content object reference model (SCORM) - a critical review. Paper presented at the Proceedings of the International Conference on Computers in Education (ICCE 2002), Auckland, New Zealand, December 3-6 (2002)
4. Bulterman, D.: User-centered control within multimedia presentations. Multimedia Systems 12(4), 423–438 (2007), doi:10.1007/s00530-006-0065-6
5. Chapman, B.L.: Tools for design and development of online instruction. In: Spector, J.M., Merrill, M.D., van Merrienboer, J., Driscoll, M.P. (eds.) Handbook of Research on Educational Communications and Technology, pp. 671–684. Lawrence Erlbaum, New York (2008)
6. Choo Wou, O.: Sistem pembangunan dan pengurusan kandungan automasi web (CMAS): pendekatan kolaborasi multimedia (Content development and management automated web system: multimedia collaborative approach) (Doctoral dissertation). Universiti Kebangsaan Malaysia, Bangi, Selangor Darul Ehsan, Malaysia (2007)
7. Deacon, A.E., Morrison, A., Stadler, J.: Designing for learning through multimodal production: Film narrative and spectatorship in Director's Cut. International Journal of Education and Development using ICT 1(1) (2005), doi:http://ijedict.dec.uwi.edu/viewarticle.php?id=26
8. Dohi, S., Sakurai, Y., Tsuruta, S., Knauf, R.: Managing academic education through dynamic storyboarding. Paper presented at the World Conference on E-Learning in Corporate, Government, Healthcare, and Higher Education, Honolulu, Hawaii, USA (2006)
9. Furini, M., Geraci, F., Montangero, M., Pellegrini, M.: STIMO: STIll and MOving video storyboard for the web scenario. Multimedia Tools and Applications 46(1), 47–69 (2010), doi:10.1007/s11042-009-0307-7
10. Gustafson, K.: Instructional design tools: A critique and projections for the future. Educational Technology Research and Development 50(4), 59–66 (2002), doi:10.1007/bf02504985
11. Harada, K., Tanaka, E., Ogawa, R., Hara, Y.: Anecdote: A multimedia storyboarding system with seamless authoring support. Paper presented at the Proceedings of the Fourth ACM International Conference on Multimedia, Boston, Massachusetts, USA (1996)
12. Hodis, E., Schreiber, G., Rother, K., Sussman, J.L.: eMovie: A storyboard-based tool for making molecular movies. Trends in Biochemical Sciences 32(5), 199–204 (2007), doi:http://dx.doi.org/10.1016/j.tibs.2007.03.008
13. Hundhausen, C., Douglas, S.: SALSA and ALVIS: a language and system for constructing and presenting low fidelity algorithm visualizations. Paper presented at the IEEE International Symposium on Visual Languages, Seattle, WA (2000)
14. Igbrue, C., Pathak, P.: A framework for creating multiple intelligences informed content for e-learning. Paper presented at the World Conference on E-Learning in Corporate, Government, Healthcare, and Higher Education, Las Vegas, Nevada, USA (2008), http://www.editlib.org/p/29876

15. Jakkilinki, R., Sharda, N., Ahmad, I.: MUDPY ontology: a tool for multimedia project planning, design and development. Journal of Enterprise Information Management 19(2), 165–174 (2006), doi:10.1108/17410390610645067
16. Kleinberger, T., Holzinger, A., Müller, P.: Adaptive multimedia presentations enabling universal access in technology enhanced situational learning. Universal Access in the Information Society 7(4), 223–245 (2008), doi:10.1007/s10209-008-0122-3
17. Landay, J.A., Myers, B.A.: Sketching interfaces: toward more human interface design. Computer 34(3), 56–64 (2001)
18. Lee, C.-S., Chong, H.-R.: Automated eclectic instructional design: design factors. Paper presented at the Proceedings of the 5th WSEAS International Conference on Distance Learning and Web Engineering, Corfu, Greece (2005)
19. Midieum, S., Byung-Soo, K., Jun, P.: AR storyboard: an augmented reality based interactive storyboard authoring tool. Paper presented at the the Fourth IEEE and ACM International Symposium on Mixed and Augmented Reality (ISMAR 2005), University of California in Santa Barbara, USA (2005)
20. Mustaro, P.N., Silveira, I.F., Omar, N., Stump, S.M.D.: Structure of storyboard for interactive learning objects development. In: Koohang, A., Harman, K. (eds.) Learning Objects and Instructional Design, p. 253. Informing Science Press, Santa Rosa (2007)
21. Newman, M.W., Lin, J., Hong, J.I., Landay, J.A.: DENIM: an informal web site design tool inspired by observations of practice. Hum.-Comput. Interact. 18(3), 259–324 (2003), doi:10.1207/s15327051hci1803_3
22. Thronesbery, C., Molin, A., Schreckenghost, D.L.: A storyboard tool to assist concept of operations development. Paper presented at the IEEE Aerospace Conference, Big Sky, MT (2007)
23. Ting, C.-Y., Chong, Y.-K., Ooi, W.-F., Tan, B.-S., Chuah, S.-J., Saw, K.-L.: eStoryBoard: an intelligent SCROM compliant authoring tool. Malaysian Online Journal of Instructional Technology 2, 1–16 (2005)
24. Wahid, S., Branham, S., Harrison, S., McCrickard, S.: Collaborative storyboarding: Artifact-driven construction of shared understanding. Computer Science Technical Report TR-09-02. University of Southampton, England (2009)
25. Wan, A.R., Wan, H.: An application for creating e-learning content storyboards based on instructional design principles (Master's dissertation). University Malaya, Kuala Lumpur (2007)
26. Wang, L., Shen, W., Xie, H., Neelamkavil, J., Pardasani, A.: Collaborative conceptual design–state of the art and future trends. Computer-Aided Design 34(13), 981–996 (2002), doi:10.1016/s0010-4485(01)00157-9
27. Yang, J.T.D., Chiung-Hui, C., Chun-Yen, T., Tsung-Hsien, W.: Visualized online simple sequencing authoring tool for SCORM-compliant content package. Paper presented at the IEEE International Conference on Advanced Learning Technologies (ICALT 2004), Joensuu, Finland, August 30-September 1 (2004)
28. Yusoff, N.M., Salim, S.S.: Investigating cognitive task difficulties and expert skills in e-learning storyboards using a cognitive task analysis technique. Computers & Education 58(1), 652–665 (2012), doi:10.1016/j.compedu.2011.09.009

Designing Learning Tools: The Case of a Competence Assessment Tool

Enric Mor[1], Ana-Elena Guerrero-Roldán[1],
Enosha Hettiarachchi[2], and M. Antonia Huertas[1]

[1] Computer Science, Multimedia and Telecommunication Studies,
Universitat Oberta de Catalunya, Barcelona, Spain
[2] Internet Interdisciplinary Institute (IN3)
Universitat Oberta de Catalunya, Barcelona, Spain
{emor,aguerreror,mhuertass}@uoc.edu,
khettiarachchi@uoc.edu

Abstract. Advancements in technology offer new challenges and opportunities for online education. The interaction design of digital learning and assessment tools directly influence the learning experience. The aim of this work is to show the process of user-centered design and development of an online assessment tool that allows setting, monitoring and displaying the achievements of educational skills and competences. The main challenges addressed were: dealing with a rich and complex educational context; researching the actual needs of the actors involved and managing the different requirements for the tool; the process to generate design solutions and the evaluation of the tool. It was evaluated in a real case scenario in a virtual learning environment of a fully online higher education institution.

Keywords: User-Centered Design, Learning Tools, Assessment Tools, Competence Assessment, Virtual Learning Environment.

1 Introduction

Online education is reshaping the way we teach and learn. Technological advancements, computer devices and interaction styles provide new opportunities for teaching and learning [1]. Online and distance teachers and learners need digital tools to communicate, interact, share contents and practice skills. Every day, innovative and specific solutions appear with the goal to address concrete online teaching and learning needs [2 -3].

There is a need for adequate processes, methodologies and techniques for conceptualizing, designing and evaluating digital learning tools and environments. The design of virtual learning environments has a deep impact in the way people learn. For instance, the time and effort students save on trying to use digital learning tools can be spent on learning content and skills. Therefore, instructional and UX designers and developers have a great responsibility around digital learning tools [4]. Consequently,

P. Zaphiris and A. Ioannou (Eds.): LCT 2014, Part I, LNCS 8523, pp. 83–94, 2014.

online education can be positively affected by Human-Computer Interaction (HCI), User eXperience (UX) and User-Centered Design (UCD) [5].

The impact of digital products and devices are causing changes on people's habits and behavior. In particular, learners demand educational institutions to continuously evaluate their pedagogical approaches to the learning and teaching process, both in face-to-face and virtual classrooms, taking advantage of the technologies. There is a large sample of digital tools for learning and assessment. These tools facilitate learning through interactivity, provide guidance and feedback and increase learner's engagement [6 -7].

In Europe, the whole educational scenario is changing according to the European Higher Education Area (EHEA) [8] and the use of information and communication tools. Higher education institutions are introducing a competence model centered on learners and activities. Learners have to interact with learning resources and tools in order to show competence performance. Competences tend to convey meaning in reference to what a person is capable or competent of, the degree of preparation, sufficiency and/or responsibility for certain tasks. These elements constitute a combination of attributes (with respect to knowledge and its application, attitudes, skills and responsibilities) that describe the level or degree to which a person is capable of performing them [9].

Learning objectives differ from competences because competences describe how learners gradually acquire a dynamic combination of knowledge, understanding, skills and abilities that can be applied to a variety of jobs, situations or tasks. In general, competence assessment is a complex educational process. The concept of competence is hard to understand especially from the learners' point of view. In addition to that, from the teachers' perspective, it is difficult to measure and quantify the learners' competence acquisition level.

In such a situation, digital learning tools offer new opportunities for learners to deal with the concept of competence. However, there are few tools that support competence assessment, and the existing ones have some issues to be addressed: very specific (not usable in different educational contexts), complex to use and understand and incomplete in terms of facilitating assessment. Everything results in a limited learning experience. All this motivates the need for designing and creating a tool that can reduce the problems associated with competences in learning environments, approaching competences to students and helping teachers on competence assessment.

The purpose of this paper is to present the user-centered design and development of an online assessment tool that allows setting, monitoring and displaying achievements of educational skills and competences. The tool is designed to be used in a fully virtual learning environment, but it is also useful for blended educational systems.

The paper is organized as follows: section 2 introduces the competences and the challenges associated with designing competences in education, while section 3 describes the context and the development of the competence assessment tool following a user-centered design process. In section 4, evaluation of the tool and the results are explained and finally, in section 5, conclusions and discussion are presented.

2   Competences as a Challenge for Design in Education

Based on the EHEA approach, teachers have to design courses taking into account a set of competences. Also, activities should be designed in order to provide learners with a specific level of these competences and learner's performance in activities is essential for competence achievement. Therefore, activities can be understood as a means for learners to achieve new competences improving their performance and skills. Nevertheless, the learning process through competences is not as easy as teachers and learners expected. Learners are assessed by competences (processes) and not just by content (knowledge).

Competences are usually assessed across rubrics [10]. A rubric is defined as "an assessment tool that identifies criteria for a work which includes different quality scales for each work". Rubrics are based on a table with criteria for the assessment and the associate mark for each one. This table can be paper based or embedded in a digital tool. The rubric associated to a competence allows providing assessment criteria based on established levels and/or qualification sections based only on marks. Teachers are using rubrics in a wide range of courses [11 -13]. Despite this, these experiences are centered on typifying the assessment criteria with the objective of establishing the level of achievement of the objectives and a mark [14]. In most cases, the relationship between the specific competences of the course, the mark and their visibility in the proposed activities is scarce. Establishing the appropriate links and relationships between the previous elements is essential to ensure both consistency and good teaching-learning process focused on the acquisition of competences. In particular, competences, activities and the criteria used by teachers in the assessment of the activities must be considered [15]. Then learners will be provided with a report based on their competence acquisition through activities.

Dealing with a competence-based learning model requires that, in the context of a course, teachers carry out a reflection, revision and analysis process. This process consists of 3 main steps: 1) Identification and definition of competences. 2) Design of course activities that conforms the assessment. 3) Make competences and the level acquisition, as clear as possible for learners.

For competence definition, it is needed to identify the set of general competences (at the Bachelor degree level) that are related to the course. Following this, specific competences must be defined at the course level. This can be done by a refinement process that arises competence hierarchies. In each hierarchy, intermediate and leaf nodes represent the specific competences attached to the course at different levels of description. Also, in a given hierarchy, each root node represents the specific competence (at the Bachelor degree level) that has been refined.

The design of activities that conforms the assessment must be guided by the specific course competences to be acquired by learners. Therefore, it is required to establish appropriate mappings between the activities and the specific competences (thus, the alignment with the Bachelor degree specific competences is also guaranteed). It is important to note that one activity can deal with several specific competences. In a similar way, a specific competence can be practiced in several activities. For each competence that is being assessed in every activity, its expected acquisition level should be defined.

When the teaching and learning process takes place in a fully virtual learning environment, this process is even more challenging. Different users are interacting with educational purposes for teaching and learning competences. Then the virtual scenario has to be simplified for working with different levels of competence acquisition and for making it clear for learners but also teachers. The virtual environment provides learners full access to knowledge, above and beyond the usual scheduling and location constraints. Courses take place in virtual classrooms which include learning resources, activities, but also competences are evaluated there by teachers. In this context, the key challenge is to find an appropriate way to store and visualize competence information in a simple but useful way for all users. The challenge we address consists of a solution to facilitate teachers' tasks and provide learners significant feedback about their competences acquisition.

3   Design and Creation of a Competence Assessment Tool

This work takes place in a virtual learning environment of a fully online higher education institution, Universitat Oberta de Catalunya (UOC)[1], a very rich environment for both users and stakeholders in terms of collecting requirements and designing interactions. The UOC is a fully online university with more than 53,242 students and 3,666 teachers. The university offers more than 16 degrees and 36 masters. Taking into account these numbers, it is clear that the design of the tools and learning environments are a strategic issue for the university since the learning experience will be strongly affected by the interaction design. In addition to that, in this kind of environments, technology plays a strategic role, specially affecting educational tools and their users (students and teachers). Therefore, interaction between tools and users should be carefully designed.

The UOC has a user-centered educational model based on activities. The whole learning process takes place through its virtual learning environment composed of a Learning Management System (LMS), learning materials, digital syllabus and assessment tools. UOC students have a specific profile since they are not full time students. Students choose UOC to update their skills and competences because they can overcome time and space constraints.

According to the EHEA, each UOC course provides learners with a set of cross curricular competences as well as a set of specific competences. Competences tend to be a non intuitive concept for students when they are doing activities. Thus, competences have to be clearly defined and teachers should be able to communicate them easily.

Currently, learners obtain a mark for each assignment activity with no explicit connection with the competences. Our proposal mainly focuses on creating a tool that teachers can link competences with activities and students can easily visualize it. For

---

[1]   http://www.uoc.edu

teachers, the tool should allow them to introduce and edit the competences related to each subject and to make explicit how each competence is achieved through the assignment activities. For learners, the tool should provide a general view about the competence acquirement progress.

3.1   The Design Process

The design process of this work followed the principles of ISO 13407 [16]: the active involvement of users and a clear understanding of the user and task requirements, an appropriate allocation of functions between users and technology, iteration of design solutions and multi-disciplinary design. Following these principles, a user centered design approach [5] was taken. In order to identify detailed requirements of the tool, user research techniques were carried-out throughout the project lifecycle to better understand users and their behaviors [17]. Also, these techniques were used to identify user groups that should be of highest priority during the project and their needs. Basic steps of user research include defining primary user groups, planning for user involvement, conducting research through data collection methods such as user interviews, validating user group definitions and as a result generating user requirements [4]. Two main types of requirements and user needs were identified: educational and technological. Educational requirements came from three main actors; educational institutions, teachers and students.

The purpose of studying the educational requirements is to understand the need for a competence assessment and how it can be adapted to the actual context. To obtain educational requirements, interviews with the teachers and coordinators, and observations in the actual context were carried-out.

Educational institutions received regulations for the administration on how to organize teaching, especially in relation to the acquisition of skills and competences. Teachers received instructions from their educational institution, making them add the concept of competence acquisition on each course and fit it into specific educational plans for each course. Finally, students are the third actor who is the end users of everything. Therefore, they should understand the concept of work and acquire skills and competences while progressing in the courses they are enrolled. Teacher and student requirements are user defined and were obtained through the interviews and UOC databases.

When it comes to learner profile, most of the students are following an online educational course for the first time and out of that 23% of students had a previous university degree. Average age of students is 32 years and 85% are male and 15% are female. Also, 91% of the students have a full time job, whereas the rest are full time students. In addition to that, students mostly use the virtual learning environment to complete assignment activities, mainly in weekdays evenings and at night. They prefer to have clearly defined learning goals and work on activities that require looking for contents rather than just reading learning contents.

The purpose of analyzing the technological requirements is to understand the technical issues associated with the competence assessment tool and how they can be solved [5]. The most appropriate technologies, tools, standards, web services and protocols that can be used to design and develop an appropriate competence assessment tool are also analyzed. Requirements such as security, interoperability, reliability, user-friendliness and consistency of the tool have to be considered. More consideration was given for security and interoperability. Technological requirements were mainly established by the technological architecture of the virtual learning environment of the university.

To obtain technological requirements, interviews with the system experts and administrators helped to identify the appropriate standards and protocols that can be used. At the same time, study of the relevant literature was also carried-out. In this research, when it comes to development, the existing marking tool used at the UOC for all courses were also studied. However, this tool only provided marks and direct feedback about the marks. The competences achieved by the students were not displayed. Considering this, the main concern was to design and develop a generic competence assessment tool which can be easily adapted to any subject and organization. Also, characteristics such as reliability, consistency, usability, interoperability and security are needed to be considered while designing and developing the tool.

The definition of the competence assessment tool included several functionalities which were really important for improving the students' experience in terms of skills and competences outputs. From the teachers' point of view, the competence tool should allow to register competences, but also to establish some relationships between learners-competences-activities on a course. It means that general competences have to be included in the tool as well as the specific ones. At the same time, these competences need to be related to each activity including the expected level of acquisition. From the students' point of view, the tool should be able to visualize when a competence is acquired. Therefore, when teachers introduce acquired competences students will be able to see them. As students advance in the course and activities are carried out, a competence progress bar may indicate their situation regarding the final competences to be reached. It can be noted, the marks are not included in the competence assessment tool because they are included in the university's register, which is an independent module.

Once the requirements were collected and analyzed, first the conceptual design of the system was finalized with the assistance of user profiles and scenarios. Conceptual design was understood as a description of the proposed system in terms of a set of integrated ideas and concepts about what it should do, behave, and look like, that will be understandable by the users in the manner intended [18]. User profiles describe the characteristics of typical target users and it helps to provide a clear representation of the person who is using the system, and potentially how they are using it [4]. Furthermore, creating user profiles helps to focus on representative users by providing insight into "real" behaviors of "real" users. This helps to resolve conflicts that arise when taking design and development decisions [4 -5]. Data about user profiles were obtained from interviews, UOC databases and questionnaires.

A scenario is a plausible description of the future based on a coherent set of assumptions. Scenarios are among the most powerful tools in product and service design, with uses ranging from developing requirements for ensuring that a design accounts for the full range of possible interactions [5]. User scenarios associated with each user profile are defined to understand how they interact with the system. A goal-directed scenario is a textual description of a user's interaction with the system. Each scenario begins with a specific situation, and then describes the interaction between user and system from the beginning of a task or session through its completion [5].

Based on the three main actors of the tool, three profiles were created. For each profile, three scenarios were created to depict the interaction between the user and the tool. Then the structure and the navigation of the system was designed based on the tasks identified through the scenarios. This is a visual way to display how content has been organized in the web application according to a hierarchical structure in order to aid the development process [4]. After designing the structure of the system as a visual hierarchy, interaction flow diagrams were constructed which identify the paths or processes that users or systems will take as they progress through the web application [4].

3.2   Prototyping and Developing the Tool

The user interfaces were first designed as prototypes for the competence assessment tool which was later used for the development. The main challenge for the prototype was to provide a simple design solution that took into account the rich and complex requirements. The prototype was improved by some design iterations, through the evaluations carried-out with the users, before coming up with the final design of the tool for the development.

The competence assessment tool was developed as a module for Moodle [19]. One of the reasons is that Moodle provided user management facilities and therefore the main consideration was needed for the tool. Another reason is that Moodle is one of the most commonly used LMS and any educational institution who doesn't have their own LMS can use it as their own. Finally, Moodle is a standardized tool and the modules should also be developed according to e-learning standards. Therefore, by developing the competence tool as a module with the Moodle LMS, it is possible to maintain the required technological requirements such as security and interoperability.

For the development, a predefined module [20] was selected and later modified according to the requirements and the given activities. The tool required to include taxonomy, which consisted of the competences and subcompetences that should be achieved by students. Overall, the tool was developed using PHP and it stores only the essential information needed for this research work. Thus, the tool consists of only main functionalities as tabs: "Module configuration", "Subjects & topics", "Assign activities", "Overview of competences" and "Assessment of competences".

Taxonomy for a particular subject is uploaded to the competence module using the "Module configuration" tab. Through the module configuration tab, it is possible to select the taxonomy for a particular degree program or a course by making appropriate changes to the XML file. Therefore, this tool is developed in a general way which can easily be adapted to any subject or degree program only by changing the taxonomy through the XML file.

"Subjects & topics" tab allows selecting the appropriate subject and the topics based on the subjects available through the uploaded XML file. Here, it was also necessary to add the new activity types, quizzes and tests from an external tool based on the activities given in the UOC classroom. Therefore, a link was added to display both quizzes and the tests from the external tool which directed teachers to a page consisting of marks. Also, some developments were made in order to display the marks

of the tests from the external tool, when teachers use the mouse over facility. Additionally, some changes were made to the look and feel of the module to suit the requirements.

After carrying out the required modifications and after the selection of the required subject, the related competences were displayed in the "Assign activities" tab. Then, teachers had to select appropriate competences related to each activity by marking a tick in the appropriate box. Here the activities were displayed horizontally and competences were displayed vertically as a grid.

In the "Overview of competences" tab, a table of competences and students of the course was generated. The names of the students were displayed in a row and the marks they had obtained for each activity were visible by hovering over the given icon. The attainment of a competences was assessed on the level of individual activities. Based on the marks, if the students had acquired the competences, the teacher could mark a tick next to the competence. For all students, the competences can be ticked off as a whole. The "Overview of competences" tab can be displayed as shown in Fig. 1.

In the competence module, the tabs including "Module configuration", "Subjects & topics", "Assign activities" and "Overview of competences" were only visible to teachers and administrators. Only tab that was visible to students was the "Assessment of competences" tab.

Then finally, in the "Assessment of competences", students could view the competences they had achieved as a progress bar as well as a list of tables. The assessment of competences for a particular student can be displayed as shown in Fig. 2.

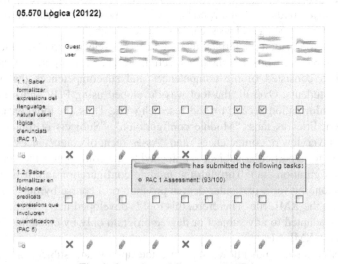

Fig. 1. Overview of Competences Tab

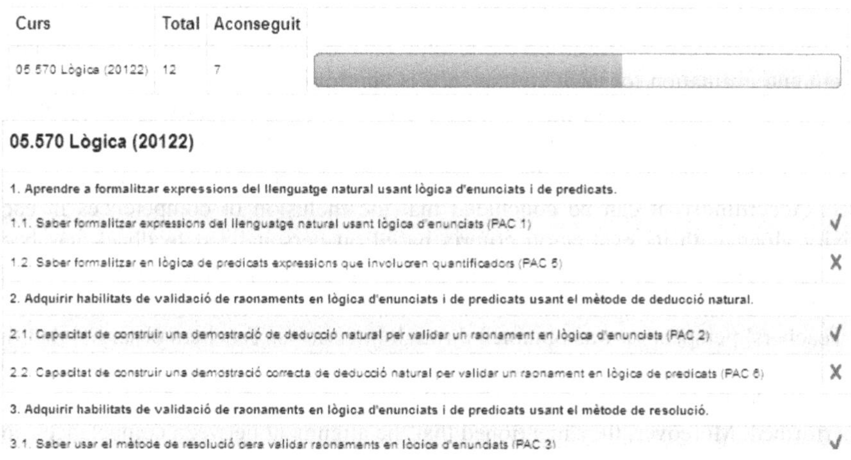

Curs	Total	Aconseguit
05.570 Lògica (20122)	12	7	

05.570 Lògica (20122)

1. Aprendre a formalitzar expressions del llenguatge natural usant lògica d'enunciats i de predicats.

1.1. Saber formalitzar expressions del llenguatge natural usant lògica d'enunciats (PAC 1)   √

1.2 Saber formalitzar en lògica de predicats expressions que involucren quantificadors (PAC 5)   X

2. Adquirir habilitats de validació de raonaments en lògica d'enunciats i de predicats usant el mètode de deducció natural.

2.1. Capacitat de construir una demostració de deducció natural per validar un raonament en lògica d'enunciats (PAC 2)   √

2.2. Capacitat de construir una demostració correcta de deducció natural per validar un raonament en lògica de predicats (PAC 6)   X

3. Adquirir habilitats de validació de raonaments en lògica d'enunciats i de predicats usant el mètode de resolució.

3.1. Saber usar el mètode de resolució cera validar raonaments en lògica d'enunciats (PAC 3)   √

Fig. 2. Assessment of competences for a particular student

4   Evaluation and Results

The competence assessment tool was introduced in an online learning scenario in order to assure the interoperability and usability during the teaching and learning process. A pilot study with teachers and students was carried out. It was a first year Logic course of a Computing Engineering Bachelor at UOC. The Logic course is based on Propositional and Predicate Logic. It is a fundamental course in the whole area of programming languages because of its relevance in formal verification and the derivation of algorithms. It is also essential for the study of databases following the relational data model, because the standard language is based on predicate logic. The skills and abilities needed to formalize and to validate or refute arguments in the logic formal language are essentially the same as detecting the problems of an incorrect specification that requires a high-order skills acquisition. This course was selected as it is a subject which requires a higher-level of skills in order to qualify in the subject. Therefore, competence based assessment plays an important role in this subject.

This pilot study took place during 14 weeks and involved more than 80 students. Student and teacher interaction and perceptions were collected through observations, interviews and questionnaires. The results showed that both teachers and students were satisfied with the competence assessment process and the ease of use of the tool.

Using the tool, teachers were able to track students' progress throughout the whole duration of the course. Overall, the activities of the Logic course were allocated with 12 competences. Based on the student performance in the continuous assessment activities, the progress of competences achieved for each activity was calculated. In order to obtain a particular competence, students had to obtain a minimum of 50 marks for each test. Based on the statistics stored within the tool, it showed that, overall, students had performed well in the Logic course with an average of 62% progress for all competences. Even for the individual competences, students were able to obtain a progress of more than 50%.

At the end of the course, students were given a questionnaire, to obtain their feedback regarding the tool. Based on the results, 86% of students think that the grading system and evaluation for each competence is appropriate and it allowed them to see how they are progressing in the course on a weekly basis. Regarding the feedback, 80% of the students appreciated it. They further mentioned that it also helped them to advance in the acquisition of skills and understand what it meant to acquire a competence. Accordingly, it can be concluded that the inclusion of competences in each activity along with its evaluation criteria based on personalized feedback has been well appreciated by the students and it helps them to understand the process of acquiring competences.

Teachers' perspective was obtained through interviews. Teachers observed that the process of establishing the relationships between specific competences, the activities and the students' assessment process is a laborious process, especially the first time it is performed. Moreover, they mentioned that the alignment between competences and activities required a continuous analysis to adjust and clarify issues regarding how competences have to be acquired and evaluated. However, teachers believe that such work is required in order to improve a teaching-learning model based on competences. Finally, in regard to the feedback, teachers think that setting the assessment criteria for each activity facilitates the students' evaluation process as well as the feedback to be provided. That is, a clear assessment criteria helps each student understand which competences have been acquired continuously.

5   Conclusions and Discussion

The main contribution of this paper is related to the process for designing and developing an educational tool for competence assessment. This tool summarizes the acquisition of learning competences in a visual and simple way. Also, the tool helps teachers to easily incorporate assessment based on competences and at the same time, learners are provided with a diagnostic profile related to the competences developed.

In addition to that, some interesting conclusions can be considered. A first consequence of the introduction of the tool in the real case scenario is that competence assessment based on activities through the tool can be done. Besides, teachers mentioned that the work of linking activities with competences through the tool has allowed them to adjust activities and competences in an accurate way. From learners side, they have understood the assessment process based on competences as well as the use of clearly specified evaluation criteria and feedback. In summary, the approach and the tool facilitated the overall process of assessing learners.

Also, it is interesting to remark that following a user-centered design process helped to match teachers and learners needs. In our opinion, the conceptualization, design, development and evaluation in a real case scenario have been essential to obtain a simple and efficient tool. The definition of the tool would not have been possible without previously carrying out a requisite analysis and a detailed, reflective process, revision and analysis about the implications and consequences of dealing with a competence-based learning model. Therefore, this work sketches a methodological approach which offer guidelines that can help teachers to structure an assessment model based on competences. Furthermore, using the tool in a real case scenario has shown that it provided enough support to this process, from both teachers and learners perspective.

Regarding the future work, we consider two main issues to be investigated. On the one hand, it is necessary to progressively extend the use of the tool to different kind of courses, to make it as general as possible but adaptable to different learning needs. On the other hand, it is necessary to study how to capture the students' global progress regarding to the acquisition of the whole specific competences associated with the degree, because one specific competence should be acquired and assessed (probably at different levels) in several (related) courses. This implies, at least two different objectives: firstly, to represent new data in the competence assessment tool, in order to keep track of the learners' competence progress in the different courses; secondly, to define new functionalities to be added to the tool. For instance, from the learners' perspective, the tool should show their progress about the whole degree where they are enrolled. Moreover, this functionality should be available outside of the context of a specific course, probably attached to their academic information.

Acknowledgements. This paper has been partially supported by Spanish Ministry of Science and Innovation funded Project MAVSEL (ref. TIN2010-21715-C02-02) and the Internet Interdisciplinary Institute (IN3) of the Universitat Oberta de Catalunya.

References

1. Beldarrain, Y.: Distance education trends: Integrating new technologies to foster student interaction and collaboration. Distance Education 27(2), 139–153 (2006)
2. Kim, K., Bonk, C.J.: The future of online teaching and learning in higher education: The survey says. Educause Quarterly 29(4), 22 (2006)
3. Keengwe, J., Kidd, T.T.: Towards best practices in online learning and teaching in higher education. MERLOT Journal of Online Learning and Teaching 6(2), 533–541 (2010)
4. Unger, R., Chandler, C.: A Project Guide to UX Design: For User Experience Designers in the Field or in the Making. New Riders (2009)
5. Goodwin, K.: Designing for the digital age: How to create human-centered products and services. Wiley (2011)
6. JISC, Learning in a Digital Age Extending higher education opportunities for lifelong learning (2012), http://www.jisc.ac.uk/media/documents/programmes/elearning/Digilifelong/Lifelong%20Learning%20accessible%20PDF.pdf
7. Peters, O.: Digital learning environments: New possibilities and opportunities. The International Review of Research in Open and Distance Learning 1(1) (2000)
8. European Higher Education Area, http://www.ehea.info/
9. Gonzales, J., Wagenaar, R.: Tuning Educational Structures in Europe (2003), http://www.unideusto.org/tuningeu/images/stories/Publications/Tuning_phase1_full.document.pdf
10. Moskal, B.M.: Scoring rubrics: what, when and how? Practical Assessment. Research & Evaluation 7(3) (2000), http://PAREonline.net/getvn.asp?v=7&n=3

11. Cooper, B.S., Gargan, A.: Rubrics in Education Old Term, New Meanings. Phi Delta Kappan 91(1), 54–55 (2009)
12. Reddy, Y.M., Andrade, H.: A review of rubric use in higher education. Assessment & Evaluation in Higher Education 35(4), 435–448 (2010)
13. Gezie, A., Khaja, K., Chang, V.N., Adamek, M.E., Johnsen, M.B.: Rubrics as a Tool for Learning and Assessment: What Do Baccalaureate Students Think? Journal of Teaching in Social Work 32(4), 421–437 (2012)
14. Tierney, R., Simon, M.: What's still wrong with rubrics: focusing on the consistency of performance criteria across scale levels. Practical Assessment, Research & Evaluation 9(2) (2004), http://PAREonline.net/getvn.asp?v=9&n=2
15. Richey, R.C., Fields, D.C., Foxon, M.: Instructional design competences: The standards. ERIC Clearinghouse on Information & Technology, Syracuse University, NY (2001)
16. ISO/IEC.: 13407 Human-Centred Design Processes for Interactive Systems, ISO/IEC 13407: 1999 (E) (1999)
17. Lazar, J., Feng, J.H., Hochheiser, H.: Research methods in human-computer interaction. Wiley (2010)
18. Rogers, Y., Sharp, H., Preece, J.: Interaction Design: Beyond Human-Computer Interaction, 3rd edn. Wiley Publishing, Inc. (2011)
19. Moodle.org: Open-Source Community-based Tools for Learning, http://moodle.org/
20. Moodle Blocks: Exabis Competences, https://moodle.org/plugins/view.php?plugin=block_exacomp

Blogging Revisited: The Use of Blogs in ESAP Courses

Anna Nicolaou and Elis Kakoulli Constantinou

Language Centre, Cyprus University of Technology, Limassol, Cyprus
{anna.nicolaou,elis.constantinou}@cut.ac.cy

Abstract. The technological innovations of the last decades and the appearance of the Web 2.0 have triggered various advancements in the field of education in general and language teaching and learning in particular. The weblog or blog is nowadays one of the most popular Information Communication Technology (ICT) tools used for educational purposes, thus research on the use of blogs in education has seen increasing interest. This paper examines blogging as a learning tool in the instruction of English for Specific Academic Purposes (ESAP) in tertiary education. It explores the possibilities and pedagogical value offered by using weblogs in language learning, as well as university students' attitudes towards the use of blogs in their language courses.

Keywords: blogs, language learning, language teaching, ESAP, ICT, CMC, BALL, New Technologies.

1 Introduction

Developments in Information and Communication Technologies (ICT) have had an impact on every facet of our lives including language education. Since the initiation of Web 2.0 at the beginning of the new millennium, interpersonal interaction through technology has been enhanced transforming all aspects of the teaching and learning process (Dudeney & Hockly, 2012). Terms such as Computer-mediated Communication (CMC) have evolved changing the role of both the language instructor and the language learner in the classroom.

In this era of vast technological advancements the weblog or blog constitutes one of the most widely embraced and easy-to-use 'Internet publishing tools' (Richardson, 2009: 2) as well as one of the most popular pedagogical applications. A blog 'can be thought of as an online journal that an individual can continuously update with his or her own words, ideas, and thoughts through software that enables one to easily do so' (Campell, 2003). It is a type of website the entries of which appear in reverse chronological order, a 'web diary' as Wu (2006: 69) characterizes it. Amongst the main features of blogs are that they are easy to use, they are interactive, since they allow readers to send comments, and they can combine text, podcasts, pictures, music, videos and many other types of visual design.

The ways in which blogs can be incorporated in the language teaching and learning process are various. Throughout the years blogging has been used either as an occasional activity supplementing the teaching and learning process or as a tool with a principal role

P. Zaphiris and A. Ioannou (Eds.): LCT 2014, Part I, LNCS 8523, pp. 95–106, 2014.

in the educational experience. Campbell (2003) has suggested three types of blogs that have been widely adopted by language educators: the tutor blog, the learner blog and the class blog. According to Campbell, the tutor blog, a blog created and run by the tutor, can serve as a means for the tutor to send entries to the learners providing them with the opportunity for daily reading practice. Through the tutor blog, the learner is encouraged to explore other English websites and therefore their confidence in using English websites is increased. Furthermore, the tutor blog provides the opportunity for online verbal communication to be encouraged since blogs allow readers to send comments, and it can also serve as a means for the tutor to provide learners with useful information about the course or the syllabus. Finally, it can be a resource of links for self-study. The learner blog, on the other hand, is the blog which is created and run by either one learner or a collaborative group of learners. Campbell claims that this type of blog encourages the use of search engines and internet surfing in English. Such blogs can be used as journals for writing practice and personal expression and they help the learners to develop a 'sense of ownership'. In addition, the fact that the blog can be read by anyone provides learners with the opportunity for authentic communication in the target language. Lastly, the third type of blog, the class blog, refers to the blogs which are created and run collaboratively by a whole class. In this case, blogs can serve as a 'free-form bulletin board' for learners to communicate and post their thoughts. They can also prove useful in cases where learners want to develop online resources for other people. Additionally, class blogs could be used for language exchange between learners from different countries who have publishing rights to the blog.

The widespread use of blogs in language education has inaugurated the development of an innovative research field, the area of Blog Assisted Language Learning (BALL), as Ward (2004) names it. Several research studies have been conducted on the use of blogs in language teaching and learning which demonstrate how language educators have utilized this tool to facilitate the learning process. The majority of these studies concentrate on the integration of blogging in the development of writing skills (Arslan and Sahin-Kizil, 2010; Fageeh, 2011; Kashani, Mahmud & Kalajahi, 2013; Lou et al., 2010; Sayed, 2010; Sun, 2010). Apart from improving writing skills however, the weblog also appears to be supportive for oral practice as well. Sun (2009), investigated the use of voice blogs for extensive study of learners' speaking skills and found that the nature of blogs allowed learners to express themselves freely in the target language promoting thus the development of fluency.

Various other studies have demonstrated that blogging can be very beneficial for language learning in general (Arena & Jefferson, 2008; Bartlett-Bragg, 2004; Baturay & Daloglu, 2010; Galien & Bowcher, 2010; Kavaliauskiene, 2007; Liou, 2011; Miceli, Murray & Kennedy, 2010; Richardson, 2009; Seitzinger, 2006). According to these studies, blogging in English language learning is a very enjoyable activity that raises language awareness, enhances learners' motivation, and promotes collaborative and autonomous learning. Most importantly, due to the journal nature of blogs, learners are engaged in contextualized and meaningful use of language and furthermore they are exposed to situations of authentic language use. Moreover, running a blog provides learners with the opportunity for reflection on their performance. Arena (2008, p.3) claims that blogging also promotes higher order thinking skills since in order to establish a conversation and to construct knowledge collectively, learners and instructors will have to 'go beyond superficialities, posting entries that increase reflection, analysis, discussion and synthesis'. Furthermore, blogging allows interaction with an international audience and thus the classroom expands breaking the physical constraints of a limited room. The use of blogs also develops a strong sense of community among the learners (Miceli, Murray & Kennedy, 2010). Seitzinger (2006) as well as Richardson (2009) additionally state that blogs enhance constructivist learning according to which learning should be active and manipulative, constructive and reflective, intentional, authentic and cooperative. Previous research also shows that blogging is an excellent way to develop listening or reading skills and it is also a tool that allows for each learner to keep an individual record of their work, to create an e-portfolio in other words. Finally, it is generally accepted that running a blog provides the learner with the opportunity to cater for their own learning style following their own learning pace.

The disadvantages reported in the literature mostly concentrate on practical and technical aspects such as difficulties in creating a blog account especially in cases where students do not possess sufficient technological literacy. Forgotten usernames and passwords and failure to keep the blog updated are some other weaknesses of blogs spotted by research conducted in the field (Kavaliauskiene, 2007). Nevertheless, whatever the shortcomings, apparently they are incapable of surmounting the benefits deriving from the use of blogs in the language teaching and learning process.

2   Research Objectives

The purpose of the study was to explore the possibilities and the pedagogical value offered by using weblogs in language learning, as well as to examine university students' attitudes towards the use of blogs in their English for Specific Academic Purposes (ESAP) courses. The study was a research initiative aiming at improving ESAP language course instruction through the use of a Web 2.0 tool that would help develop students' language skills, and increase interaction, collaboration and learner autonomy through asynchronous communication and exposure to various task-based activities.

3   Context

The research was carried out at the Language Centre of the Cyprus University of Technology (CUT) and it involved undergraduate students attending English for Specific Academic Purposes courses during their first academic year of study. The CUT is a newly founded university aspiring to become a pioneering, high-tech institution. The Language Centre of the CUT offers to its students the opportunity to learn foreign languages in a very friendly environment and with the use of the latest theories, methods and materials that are used in the teaching and learning of languages, including New Technologies. Language classes take place in the university's classrooms, most of which are equipped with computers and other technologies allowing access to the Internet at all times. ESAP courses are mandatory for all first-year students.

The blogs constructed for the ESAP courses were class blogs run by the researchers who were also the language instructors. All of the learners were invited to the class blog and they were encouraged to contribute to it. The class blogs were created using the Blogger.com platform and they were mainly used for writing practice even though they were employed for the completion of listening and reading tasks as well. They also served as a useful tool for the organization of the course and for posting material, announcements and useful links. Furthermore, the class blogs provided space on the Web for learners to upload their assignments and to communicate with their peers and the instructor offering and receiving feedback on the posted work. The class blog finally provided opportunities for reflection and introspection.

4   Participants

A total of one hundred and three (103) undergraduate students from four different university departments of the Cyprus University of Technology participated in the study. Twenty-eight students majored in Hotel and Tourism Management, sixteen students studied Agricultural Sciences, Biotechnology and Food Science, thirty-one students studied Commerce, Finance and Shipping, and twenty-eight students studied in the Mechanical Engineering, Materials Science and Engineering Department. The vast majority of students (93.2%) were of Cypriot origin. Gender was equally represented in the sample with 47.6% male and 52.4% female students. Most students (78.6%) were novices in the use of blogs and only 21.4% of them had experienced blogging before using the particular blog for their English course. However, participants exhibited experience with and exposure to other technologies, such as Facebook, Skype, Oovoo, Google+, and YouTube, amongst others. Most students indicated that they spent approximately five to twenty hours per week on the Internet.

5   Measure

For the purposes of the study a questionnaire was designed by the researchers in order to explore the affordances and the pedagogical value offered by using weblogs in language learning, as well as to measure the university students' attitudes towards the use of blogs in their ESAP courses. The questionnaires were administered at the end of the semester and requested the voluntary participation of students in order to yield useful information regarding blogging in English for Specific Purposes (ESP) courses. The questionnaires were anonymous and included mostly Likert-type questions pertaining to the usage of blogs, benefits and challenges of the particular Web 2.0 tool, as well as motivating and demotivating factors in using blogging for learning purposes. Some open-ended questions that allowed for reflection and further expression on the students' part were also included in the questionnaire. After receiving the completed questionnaires, data were entered in SPSS for statistical analysis. Quantitative data analyses were performed using frequencies and t-test analysis for differences between groups.

6   Results

Results that emerged from the analysis of the questionnaires indicated that, overall, students seemed to have a positive attitude towards blogging in a language class and considered the blog to be a user-friendly tool that could be easily navigated. The vast majority of the students indicated that they found the class blog easy to use (79.3%), and that they felt comfortable participating in the activities undertaken on the blog (91%). It is important to note that the language instructors provided students with instructions on how to use the class blogs at the beginning of the semester, and continued providing guidance throughout the whole semester. Most students (93%) indicated that they found their teachers' instructors easy to follow and considered their guidance very helpful.

6.1   Use of Blogs

Most students (85.4%) indicated that they spent approximately two hours per week on their language class blog, and fewer students (13.6%) used the blogs for around three to five hours per week. As an asynchronous tool, the blog allowed students to visit it both from class but also from home. Students mostly engaged in the blog activities during the class with the instructors facilitating the whole process. However, they were given the opportunity to revisit the content after class time in order to reflect on it, revise it, or look at the comments made either by peers or the teacher. A big percentage of the participants (71.6%) appeared to have enjoyed using the blog as part of their language class, and considered it to be a useful part of the course (86.1%). Furthermore, the vast majority of the sample indicated that they would like to use the blog again in the future as a learning tool both for a language class (73.8%) and for other university courses (79.6%).

The class blogs were incorporated in the specific language courses from the first weeks of the semester and activities to be undertaken on them were assigned throughout the whole semester. Students' participation in the blogs was constantly evaluated, reviewed and assessed, and part of the students' overall final grade in the course depended on their contribution to the class blog. Therefore, students realized that the blog constituted an integral part of the course early on and valued it as a learning and assessment tool that would have a determining role in their learning, but also in their achievement grade. This finding emerges from the way the students carried out the various blog activities. Based on their responses on the questionnaire, students appear to have engaged in certain practices typical of the ones they engage in when employing more traditional ways of learning, such as writing a draft, using the dictionary, checking the spelling, and searching the internet. Specifically, 21.6% of the respondents indicated that they wrote a draft of their blog post before they submitted it, and a higher percentage (48%) used the dictionary while they were writing their blog post. Moreover, 44.0% of the students indicated that they used the spell check before they submitted their blog post, and 68.0% of the sample searched the internet for information in order to complete a task on the blog. Such practices demonstrate that students valued their work on the blog, and they considered their contribution to it important and determining for their learning and assessment.

6.2   Attitudes Towards the Class Blogs

The study yielded interesting results with regard to the students' attitudes to the use of blogs for language learning purposes. Most of the respondents appear to have had a positive reaction to the class blog and felt that the activities that were carried out on the blog helped them develop their skills in English (78.3%). The blogs also seem to have developed the students' confidence in undertaking writing tasks as 87.3% of the respondents indicated that blogging increased their determination and desire to express their thoughts in writing. Additionally, a big part of the sample (71.8%) felt that their interaction with the teachers and peers increased through the various blog tasks, and 69.6% of the students indicated that contributing to the class blog made them feel as part of a network or a community.

6.3   Motivation and Blogging

Another interesting finding that emerged from the study was the positive impact of the language class blogs on the students' engagement with and motivation for the course. A big percentage of the participants (61.7%) indicated that they were more motivated to work on assignments on the blog compared to other writing assignments that were carried out in more traditional ways. Similarly, a large number of the respondents (62.7%) said that they looked forward to a new task on the blog during the semester. The study looked into the aspect of motivation more closely to identify the factors that motivated students to use the blogs in class. The figure below ranks the various factors that motivated students to use the class blog as they were identified by the respondents.

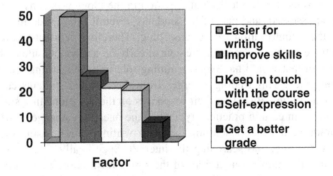

Fig. 1. Factors that motivated the students to use the class blog

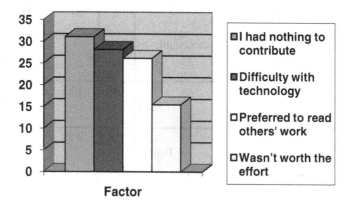

Fig. 2. Factors that demotivated the students to use the class blog

Since not all respondents maintained high levels of participation in the blog, the study also explored the factors that discouraged students from taking part in the blogging experience. Figure 2 presents the demotivating factors in contributing to the blog as these were ranked by the respondents.

6.4   Concerns in Using the Blogs and Gender Differences

Apart from the factors that demotivated the students to use their language class blog, the study identified certain concerns as these were put forward by the respondents. These concerns are related to some students' inhibitions in writing things that were accessible by their peers. In addition, using the blog in class seems to have overwhelmed certain students as they indicated that they felt pressure when they used the blog because it was a new experience for them on the one hand, and because it increased their workload, on the other.

Further exploration of these concerns yielded interesting results pertaining to gender differences when it comes to issues of privacy on the net and exposure to new classroom experiences. The t-test analysis that was computed to identify mean differences between male and female students indicated that female students felt more embarrassed because other students were able to read their blog posts, compared to the male students. Additionally, female students felt greater pressure when using the blog as a new learning tool as opposed to their male peers, and they also felt that their workload increased because of the blog to a greater extent than male fellow students.

Table 1. Gender differences regarding students' concerns about the class blog

Concerns/University	n	M	SD	P
Embarrassment because blogs were accessible by peers				
Male	48	1.85	,825	.018
Female	51	2.20	,800	
Pressure because of the new experience				
Male	48	2.00	,851	.023
Female	54	2.33	,727	
Increase in workload because of the blog				
Male	48	2.21	,743	.060
Female	54	2,56	,718	

Notes: Questionnaire scale responses were as follows: 1: strongly disagree; 2: disagree; 3: agree; 4: strongly agree.

The P value is below .05 level of significance.

6.5   Benefits of the Class Blogs

The study explored students' attitudes towards blogging in specific learning areas and practices. Overall, students considered the class blogs to be very beneficial in multiple ways. Table 2 indicates the areas and practices benefitted by the blogs as these were identified by the sample. The table shows that a big part of the sample feels that blogs were beneficial in a number of learning areas and practices. However, the study yielded interesting results with regard to differences in attitudes towards the benefits of blogs between experienced bloggers and novice users. The analysis of the students' responses indicated that the students who had tried blogging prior to their participation in the specific blog appear to feel more benefitted from their language blog

Table 2. Areas and practices benefitted by the blogs as identified by the students

Reasons	Percent
Receiving constructive feedback from the teacher	77.4
Communicating with the teacher	77.2
Completing writing assignments	76.5
Archiving my work and using the blog as a portfolio	73.5
Increasing my motivation for class activities	73.5
Reading important announcements	73.2
Working together with my fellow students	72.7
Expressing my thoughts and ideas	72.0
Being creative with my assignments	71.7
Sharing ideas with my fellow students	69.6
Keeping up-to-date with the course material	69.6
Working by myself outside the class	53.9

compared to the students who had never blogged before. Specifically, beginners in the blogosphere felt benefitted by the blogs to a lesser extent in the areas of learner autonomy and collaboration with peers. Finally, further examination of differences among groups indicated that attitudes towards the benefits of blogs in the areas of learner autonomy, collaboration with peers, as well as in the area of creativity seem to be informed by students' overall achievement and performance in the course.

7   Discussion

This study yielded interesting findings that are in line with other research findings pertaining to the possibilities and the pedagogical value offered by using blogs in language learning, as well as with regard to the students' attitudes towards the use of blogs in their university ESAP courses. The results that emerged from the questionnaires indicated that, overall, students appear to have had a positive reaction towards blogging as part of their language course, and considered this tool to be beneficial in multiple ways.

The use of blogs in the specific ESAP courses was well received by the vast majority of the participants who found this tool very user friendly and felt happy carrying out activities in this learning environment. Students were allowed access and sharing of information from any location and this gave them the opportunity to interact and collaborate through asynchronous communication outside the class and beyond the strict class hours.

The blog was considered as an integral part of the course and it was recognized as an additional learning tool that would facilitate language learning and that would determine students' overall assessment in the course. For this reason, most participants were found to have engaged in typical practices that are usually employed in traditional modes of learning, such as writing a draft, using the dictionary, checking spelling, and searching the internet whenever a task was assigned on the blog. Students felt that the blog provided them with a supplementary educational context where learning occurred either individually or collaboratively with constant facilitation on behalf of the instructor.

Students' attitudes towards their blogging experience were explored through the questionnaires. The vast majority of the respondents appears to have had positive attitudes towards the class blog and seems to have recognized that this tool produced unique educational affordances for them. Specifically, students indicated that with their active participation in the blog, their skills in English were developed, focusing on their improvement in expressing themselves in writing. Students also highlighted the increase of interaction between themselves and their instructor and among their fellow students through the assigned blog tasks. Interestingly, they indicated that being part of the class blog, they set up a community where collaboration and interaction were promoted.

Another important finding that emerged from the study related to students' motivation which seems to have been at high levels when undertaking activities on the class blog. Students exhibited willingness and interest, and sometimes even excitement about the various blog tasks. Further exploration in what motivated students to actively participate in the blogs indicated that the most motivating factor was that writing on the blog was considered to be easier than writing on paper, followed by the students' view that through the blog they felt their skills in English were improved. At the same time, an examination of the factors that discouraged students from actively contributing to the blog indicated that students would have liked to participate more, but they weren't sure they would have anything valuable to contribute. Also, some students were interested in participating, but they had difficulty coming to terms with the new technology.

The study also yielded interesting results with regards to gender differences in students' attitudes towards blogging in class. Specifically, female students appear to have felt more embarrassed than their male peers when they published their posts on the blog as everybody could read them and criticize their performance. In addition, female students appear to have been overwhelmed with the new technology that was added to the course to a greater extent than male students and indicated that they felt pressure and that their workload had increased. This finding is in line with other research findings that show female students to be more concerned with issues of privacy when writing on the net, as well as with regard to confidence in using ICT and handling new experiences with technology tools.

Other differences that emerged from the research centre on students' perceived attitudes towards the benefits of blogs in certain areas and practices in language learning. Specifically, beginners in the blogosphere felt benefitted by the blogs to a lesser extent in the areas of learner autonomy and collaboration with peers, compared to more experienced users. Finally, attitudes towards the benefits of blogs in the areas of learner autonomy, collaboration with peers, as well as creativity were also affected by the students' overall achievement and performance in the course. High achieving students appeared to feel much benefitted by blogs when working by themselves outside the class and when working together with their fellow students in collaborative assignments. They also seemed to value the class blogs in the area of creativity in the assigned tasks. Medium achieving students and low achieving ones appeared to feel benefitted in these specific areas and practices as well but to a lesser extent.

However, an overall examination of the students' perceived benefits of blogs in their ESAP courses indicated that various areas may be afforded by this Web 2.0 tool. As identified by the respondents, blogs can be very beneficial for receiving constructive feedback from and communicating with the language instructor. Moreover, students focused on the benefits of blogs in helping them develop their writing competencies, as well as in being creative with their assignments, and in enhancing learner autonomy and collaboration with peers. Finally, respondents viewed the class blog as a useful course management tool that allowed them to archive their work and stay in touch with the course material.

8   Conclusion

Technology seems to have become an integral part of teaching and learning in the recent years. Some students are willing to engage and participate in new ways of learning, while others are more reluctant to move from the traditional learning mode to which they are accustomed. Participants in this study appear to have developed positive attitudes towards the language class blogs and viewed this tool as an educational space where they learned, they interacted, they collaborated, and they belonged together. More in-depth research could point to a further understanding of the pedagogical value of blogs in language learning. All in all, the insights gained from the research help take the discussion of using Web 2.0 for learning purposes forward and could assist language instructors in developing a better strategy for incorporating this type of tool in language courses.

References

1. Arena, C., Jefferson, C.T.: Blogging in the Language Classroom: It Doesn't "Simply Happen". TESL-EJ 11(4), 1–7 (2008)
2. Arslan, R.S., Sahin-Kizil, A.: How can the use of blog software facilitate the writing process of English language learners? Computer Assisted Language Learning 23(3), 183–197 (2010)

3. Bartlett-Bragg, A.: Blogging to Learn. The Knowledge Tree (2003), http://www.csus.edu/indiv/s/stonerm/blogging_to_learn.pdf (retrieved May 25, 2011)
4. Baturay, M.H., Daloglu, A.: E-portfolio Assessment in an Online English Language Course. Computer Assisted Language Learning 23(5), 413–428 (2010)
5. Campbell, A.P.: Weblogs for Use with ESL Classes. The Internet TESL Journal IX(2) (2003), http://iteslj.org/Techniques/Campbell-Weblogs.html (retrieved May 25, 2011)
6. Dudeney, G., Hockly, N.: ICT in ELT: how did we get here and where are we going? ELT Journal 66(4), 533–542 (2012), http://eltj.oxfordjournals.org/content/66/4/533.abstract (retrieved January 30, 2014)
7. Fageeh, A.I.: EFL Learners' Use of Blogging for Developing Writing Skills and Enhancing Attitudes Towards English Learning: An Exploratory Research. Journal of Language and Literature 2(1), 31–48 (2011)
8. Galien, P., Bowcher, W.L.: Using Blogs in ESL/EFL Teaching and Teacher-Training. Asian EFL Journal. Professional Teaching Articles 42, 4–23 (2010)
9. Kashani, H., Mahmud, R.B., Kalajahi, S.A.R.: Comparing the Effect of Blogging as well as Pen-and Paper on the Essay Writing Performance of Iranian Graduate Students. English Language Teaching 6(10), 202–218 (2013)
10. Kavaliauskiene, G.: Weblogs in Language Teaching and Learning. The Journal of Teaching English with Technology 7(1) (2007), http://www.tewtjournal.org/VOL%207/ISSUE%201/03_WEBLOGSINLANGUAGE.pdf (retrieved May 10, 2011)
11. Liou, H.: Blogging, Collaborative Writing, and Multimodal Literacy in an EFL Context. In: Levy, M., Blin, F., Siskin, C.B., Takeuchi, O. (eds.) WorldCALL International Perspectives on Computer-Assisted Language Learning, pp. 3–18. Routledge, New York (2011)
12. Lou, S.J., Wu, S.C., Shih, R.C., Tseng, K.H.: Adoption of blogging by a Chinese language composition class in a vocational high school in Taiwan. Australasian Journal of Educational Technolog 26(6), 898–916 (2010)
13. Miceli, T., Murray, S.V., Kennedy, C.: Using an L2 Blog to Enhance Learners' Participation and Sense of Community. Computer Assisted Language Learning 23(4), 321–341 (2010)
14. Richardson, W.: Blogs, Wikis, Podcasts and Other Powerful Tools for Classrooms. Corwin Press, California (2009)
15. Sayed, O.H.: Developing Business Management Students' Persuasive Writing Through Blog-based Peer-Feedback. English Language Teaching 3(3), 54–66 (2010)
16. Seitsinger, J.: Be Constructive: Blogs, Podcasts, and Wikis as Constructivists Learning Tools. The eLearning Guild's Learning Solutions, 1–15 (July 31, 2006)
17. Sun, Y.: Voice Blog: An Exploratory Study of Language Learning. Language Learning and Technology 13(2), 88–103 (2009)
18. Sun, Y.C.: Extensive writing in foreign-language classrooms: a blogging approach. Innovations in Education and Teaching International 47(3), 327–339 (2010)
19. Ward, J.M.: Blog Assisted Language Learning (BALL): Push button publishing for the pupils. TEFL Web Journal 3(1) (2004), http://www.esp-world.info/articles_26/push%20button%20publishing%20ward%202004.pdf (retrieved February 18, 2014)
20. Wu, C.: Blogs in TEFL: A New Promising Vehicle. US-China Education Review 3(5), 69–73 (2006)

Learner Engagement in Computer-Supported Collaborative Learning Activities: Natural or Nurtured?

Andriani Piki

P.A. College, Larnaca, Cyprus
`a.piki@faculty.pacollege.ac.cy`

Abstract. Drawing on a mixed-methods study this paper aims to investigate what constitutes learner engagement and how postgraduate students engage in computer-supported collaborative learning (CSCL) activities (such as video-conferencing and blogging) in a real-life setting. This research contributes to current literature by proposing the WISE Taxonomy of Learner Engagement Archetypes which portrays the most universal engagement approaches that emerged within the studied context. The findings show that CSCL activities may engage postgraduate students irrespective of their perceived preference over individual or social learning. The findings also suggest that given certain conditions students may strategically disengage from CSCL activities and as a result they may fail to appreciate CSCL as an authentic activity which leverages the opportunity to learn from and with each other, as well as from the wide range of digital resources openly available to them.

Keywords: learner engagement, computer-supported collaborative learning, collaborative technologies, postgraduate education.

1 Introduction

Living, working, and learning in todays' knowledge society one cannot escape from the vast amount of information openly available online. Furthermore, innovations in technology use have transformed the way we interact throughout all facets of our lives. Consequently, learners in educational, professional, and social contexts are no longer mere receivers of information; collaborative educational technology allows them to act, react, and interact yielding new forms of knowledge which is in turn shared and made available to others. Hence, the question is no longer whether technology should be employed in education or not; the question is how we can engage students to assertively share, manage, and acquire new knowledge as well as develop their digital competences within computer-supported collaborative learning (CSCL) environments. Accordingly, the role of higher education in the digital age goes beyond equipping students with subject-oriented knowledge and skills. While educators need to instigate student interest towards a specific subject matter, at the same time they need to activate their engagement towards all aspects of learning (Piki 2010).

P. Zaphiris and A. Ioannou (Eds.): LCT 2014, Part I, LNCS 8523, pp. 107–118, 2014.
© Springer International Publishing Switzerland 2014

One of the main arguments put forward by proponents of CSCL is the 'engaging' nature of collaborative technologies (CTs). It has been argued that CTs provide tremendous potential for promoting learner engagement and collaboration, providing creative mechanisms for teaching and learning, and improving the learning outcomes (Clarke et al. 2008; Stahl et al. 2006). However, despite the profound benefits of emerging CTs and CSCL practices, there seems to be limited evidence contributing to our understanding of how – and indeed whether – learners naturally engage with CSCL tasks. There seems to be a persistent belief that the integration of technology in the curriculum will automatically transform the ways learners engage and collaborate with each other as part of their learning. Still, the varied assumptions that exist on the nature of learner engagement in CSCL activities are yet not fully empirically explored. Hence, the focus of this paper is not on learning per se; rather it is on how learners engage with learning activities which are mediated by technology. Furthermore, while many studies have explored the benefits and challenges inherent in CSCL in both formal and informal settings, its application at postgraduate education has yet to be broadly investigated. Therefore the selected milieu for this study was situated within postgraduate education.

The research presented here seeks to explore whether learner engagement is something that comes naturally due to the presence of CTs in teaching and learning practices, whether it is a skill or competence that can be nurtured, or indeed, whether it reflects an even more multifaceted concept. The paper draws on a mixed-methods study which aims to investigate the ways in which postgraduate students engage in knowledge sharing and collaborative activities through technology. More specifically, the focus is on how postgraduate learners engage in real-life CSCL activities, such as blogging and participating in video-conferencing group discussions.

The paper first sets the background to the research and then discusses the methodology and research design employed in the study. The analytical framework and the key findings are presented next followed by a discussion of the findings and the implications for practice. The study limitations and suggestions for further research are also discussed.

2   Background

CSCL is a robust interdisciplinary field with strong foundations in previous theory and research. Its roots can be traced back to the social-constructivist paradigm which is based on the tenet that individuals learn as they verify and improve their mental models through discussion, information sharing, and negotiating meanings with others (Dillenbourg 1999; Grabinger et al. 2007; Stahl et al. 2006). Key scholars in the field suggest that collaborative learning goes beyond an aggregation of individual efforts arguing that "collaborative learning involves individual learning, but is not reducible to it" (Stahl et al. 2006, p. 3). Dillenbourg (1999) also emphasizes that interactions among peers generate higher order mental processes which are conducive to learning.

Unquestionably, the applicability of CTs in education holds voluminous opportunities for generating novel ways of knowing, learning, and collaborating and for offering "creative activities of intellectual exploration and social interaction" (Stahl et al. 2006, p. 2). Notwithstanding the continuous developments in CTs, the foundation of CSCL research remains to be "centrally concerned with meaning and the practices of meaning making in the context of joint activity, and the ways in which these practices are mediated through designed artifacts" (Koschmann, 2002, p. 18). Towards this end, the main challenge facing educators is making an effective and impactful use of the available CTs in order to facilitate learner engagement, en route for enhanced learner achievement and improved learning outcomes. Yet, to exploit the proclaimed benefits of CTs it is necessary to explore and understand how students are likely to engage in real-life CSCL settings and the plausible mechanisms that underpin their ongoing interactions – both with each other and with the learning content. The current research attempts to address these issues. Although the value of collaborative learning has been advocated for decades, it is argued that new pedagogical models are needed in order to address the complex issues involved in collaborative learning practices when these are mediated by technology (Jaques & Salmon 2007; Piki 2010).

In recent educational research, the importance of student motivation and engagement has shifted from peripheral to central (Murphy & Alexander 2000; Pintrich 2003). In the very broadest sense, learner engagement refers to a "student's willingness, need, desire and compulsion to participate in, and be successful in, the learning process promoting higher level thinking for enduring understanding" (Bomia et al. 1997, p. 294). Engagement occurs when the student is involved in "active cognitive processes such as creating, problem-solving, reasoning, decision-making, and evaluation" (Kearsley & Shneiderman 1999, p. 1). It is also argued that "while in principle, such engagement could occur without the use of technology, [...] technology can facilitate engagement in ways which are difficult to achieve otherwise" (Kearsley and Shneiderman 1999, p.1).

Motivational literature is closely related with the study of academic achievement and development (Murphy & Alexander 2000), and appears to be central to research in learning and teaching contexts (Pintrich 2003). The studied literature seems to suggest that engagement is a complex and multifaceted concept (Ainley 2004; Murphy & Alexander 2000) with behavioral, affective and reflective facets. However, no existing theory seems to collectively consider all these dimensions of learner engagement with CSCL. This presents a need for models which explicitly address the complexity and dynamics embedded in learner engagement in – real-life rather than laboratory-based – CSCL activities. Therefore, in the context of this study a holistic view of learner engagement is taken in an attempt to capture the most prominent patterns of engagement that emerged within the real-life CSCL setting under investigation.

3   Methodology and Research Design

3.1   Research Setting and Participants

The chosen milieu for conducting the study is a postgraduate degree in the interdisciplinary field of Business Information Systems undertaken at a Higher Education Institution (HEI) in the UK. The choice of postgraduate education was triggered by the observation that within CSCL literature there seems to be a limited number of empirical studies conducted at postgraduate level. This observation coupled with the fact that HEIs are experiencing a rise in the number of students undertaking postgraduate degrees – a situation linked closely with the current critical financial situation – made the particular setting a favorable choice.

The participants were the students registered in two consecutive cohorts of the degree (approximately 45 students per year). The student cohorts were far from homogeneous in terms of age, nationality, academic background, and previous work experience. Each cohort included graduates from various degrees including Computer Science, Engineering, Business Administration, Accounting, and Marketing amongst others. Students were in the age range of early twenties to mid-forties. More than two thirds of the students had previous work experience or were working in conjunction with their studies. Furthermore, the participants formed a multicultural group including students from 23 different countries across Asia, Europe, Africa, and America.

The students were participating in CSCL activities such as blogging and discussions through video-conferencing. The learning objective of the video-conferencing tasks was to enhance their understanding of the course material by discussing it with peers while also gain hands-on experience with technology-mediated collaboration. Students were assigned into groups by the lecturer. The participating groups were located in different rooms but within the same building for practical reasons. Learning tasks included case study analysis, decision making, and creation of joint artifacts (such as reports, flow charts, or diagrams). Students reconvened after each video-conference and a discussions session followed where the lecturer as well as other students provided feedback and suggestions to the participating groups. Each student group also had to create and maintain a blog. The learning objective of the blogging tasks was to encourage students to reflect on their understanding and report on their learning experiences and the skills and competences they developed during the lecture, the workshops, and through their subject-related reading. Students were encouraged to read other groups' blogs and comment on their peers' posts but the frequency of blogging was neither strictly prescribed by the lecturer nor formally assessed.

The students' behavior was observed both in the classroom and online. Due to the numerous variables and the complexity of the real-life setting being studied, the focus was not on differentiating on how individuals from different countries, academic backgrounds, or age groups engage; rather the aim was to identify the different forms of engagement which are prominent across individuals within the studied setting. More specifically, the focus was on the nature of the observed engagement behaviors and on the students' self-reports on how they engage and why.

3.2 Research Methods and Data Collection Methods

The research method employed is a collective (Stake 1995), ethnographic case study. Philosophically, middle-range, mixed-methods research approaches value both qualitative and quantitative data collection methods. In this study, prolonged participant observation was enriched with additional data collected through in-depth, semi-structured focus groups; examination of students' blogs; photographic material and video-recordings of students while participating in video-conferencing sessions, as well as student questionnaires. Follow-up interviews and informal discussions (with both students and lecturers) also complemented the collected evidence and helped to validate initial patterns emerging in the course of the research. Many scholars promote the knowledge produced by mixed-methods research approaches (Creswell & Plano Clark 2011; Johnson & Onwuegbuzie 2004; Tashakkori & Teddlie 2003, 2010).

The research design adopted in the study involved a number of iterations between inductive and deductive reasoning towards devising a coherent set of theoretical ideas (Onwuegbuzie & Teddlie 2003). Indeed, theoretical ideas and empirical insights were constantly informing each other in a stimulating and illuminating way. This iterative process is central to grounded theorizing whereby data are used to form tentative ideas or propositions which in turn inform further data collection, interpretation, and sense making (Hammersley & Atkisnon 2007). For instance, while some students said they usually prefer to learn in groups and that they learn best when working with others, their contribution on the blogs was limited. This observation motivated deeper investigation into what might create a discrepancy between what students say they prefer and what they actually do, rather than taking any of the two sources of evidence at face value. The opportunity to present divergent views would not be possible without the collection of diverse types of data (Tashakkori & Teddlie 2003). The selected research design permitted a deeper understanding of which combinations of factors or characteristics lead to different types of engagement with CSCL activities.

4   Data Analysis and Key Findings

4.1   Analytical Framework

Analyzing data in mixed-methods research is one of the most challenging steps of the research process (Onwuegbuzie & Combs 2010). The multiplicity of the data sources used in the study, coupled with the longitudinal nature of the research, has generated a great amount of rich data in different formats (words, numbers, photographic and video-recorded material). Therefore an analytical framework was devised for guiding data analysis. In this respect, NVivo® was a useful tool not only for coding data but also for managing ongoing analytical steps. Data analysis involved data reduction techniques (Creswell 2002; Namey et al. 2007) aiming at identifying the most dominant themes inherent in the data related to learner engagement. This approach intended to make sense of the actions and perceptions of the informants (Hammersley & Atkinson 2007). Specifically, the ways students reasoned about their engagement were compared and contrasted with the observed patterns of student engagement to strengthen the interpretation and description of the phenomenon of learner engagement. The emphasis was placed on understanding social action 'in context' that is, what learners do, how, and why within the selected milieu. Emergent themes were then classified into thematic categories and relationships between them were explored (Miles & Huberman 1994). The purpose of analyzing the collected data was to gain a deeper understanding of learner engagement in CSCL activities.

4.2   WISE Taxonomy of Learner Engagement Archetypes

The themes that emerged from the study can contribute to our understanding of how postgraduate students engage in CSCL activities. Learner engagement emerged as a three-dimensional concept which incorporates the ways in which postgraduate students (i) approach, participate in, or act upon a CSCL task (behavioral dimension), (ii) think about the task or reflect about the way in which they approach the task (intellectual dimension), (iii) feel when participating in the task (affective dimension).

During the higher-order analytical stages of the research, an attempt was made to evaluate and select a set of variables which could collectively help to operationalize the level of engagement across each of the three dimensions. This was deemed necessary following the prominent observation that an individual student may engage differently within each dimension. For example, a student may be emotionally neutral, appear to be deeply engaged intellectually, yet contribute moderately on the actual CSCL task. However, the process of defragmenting each dimension of learner engagement was by no means a straightforward endeavor. Following extensive analysis a total of nine variables (both subjective and objective) were selected in an attempt to capture the varying degrees of engagement in each dimension. The objective measures were collected quantitatively (e.g. counting the number of blog posts) or through questionnaires (e.g. ASSIST (CRLI 1997; Tait et al. 1998) and AMS (Vallerand et al. 1992)), while the subjective variables were based on students' self-reported data and observation of student behavior. Behavioral engagement was characterized by three attributes: one objective (total number of blog posts, comments, and replies) and two subjective (level of contribution in video-conferencing CSCL tasks, and level of involvement in supportive, back-end collaboration and coordination activities). Intellectual engagement was also characterized by three attributes: two objective (academic motivation and approach to studying) and one subjective (degree of self-awareness regarding the relation between learner engagement and learning outcomes). Finally, affective engagement was measured using a single subjective variable (student's expressed feelings). Two additional independent variables (learning preference and assignment mark) were also included based on the observation that they were helpful in discriminating between different patterns of engagement. Table 1 below summarizes the set of variables used for each dimension of learner engagement.

Table 1. Variables measuring behavioral, intellectual, and affective engagement

	Variable
Behavioral	1. Contribution on the blogs [passive (0-1 posts), moderate (2-5), active (>=6)]
	2. Contribution in video-conferencing tasks [passive, moderate, active]
	3. Involvement in back-end activities [passive, moderate, active]
Intellectual	4. Academic motivation (AMS) [amotivated, extrinsically or intrinsically motivated]
	5. Approach to studying (ASSIST) [surface apathetic, strategic, deep]
	6. Degree of student self-awareness [unaware, ignored awareness, consciously aware]
Affective	7. Expressed feelings [negative, neutral, positive]
Additional	8. Learning preference [solo, mixed, social]
	9. Assignment mark [fail (<50%), pass (50-64.9%), distinction (>=65%)]

Data analysis yielded illuminating insights and helped to cluster individual learners based on how they engaged behaviorally, intellectually, and emotionally. This clustering process revealed four distinct ways in which learners may engage with CSCL activities. These constitute the four engagement archetypes labeled 'Withdrawn', 'Impulsive', 'Strategic', and 'Enthusiastic – hence the taxonomy is entitled 'WISE Taxonomy of Learner Engagement Archetypes'. The chosen labels for the four archetypes are believed to be broadly representative of the students grouped under each category. The archetypes and their inherent characteristics are discussed below.

Withdrawn Learner Engagement. This archetype characterizes those students whose overall behavioral, intellectual, and affective engagement was low. These students demonstrated an overall passive behavior towards all CSCL activities. They also appeared to lack intrinsic motivation to learn and followed a surface, apathetic approach to studying. The fact that almost one in every four students (22%) appeared to be genuinely disengaged is definitely not an encouraging outcome especially given the fact that these are postgraduate students preparing for a professional career. Findings revealed that students in this category generally prefer to learn and study on their own. They seemed to consider CSCL tasks as requiring too much time and effort, and therefore failed to see the true value of CSCL activities towards their learning as postgraduate students and upcoming professionals alike. This was also reflected in their assignment marks which were significantly lower compared to all other learner engagement archetypes. Additionally, the expressed feelings coming from this group of students were predominantly negative, the most common of which included feelings such as of apathy, boredom, and cynicism.

Impulsive Learner Engagement. Although this was an unexpected profile, it emerged prominently in the studied context (19%). The reason it was unexpected relates to the fact that in general, solo learners have a natural inclination towards studying on their own rather than getting involved in collaborative learning tasks. Nevertheless, half of the students who considered themselves solo learners were actually active both on the blogs and in supportive collaborative activities. Although impulsive students appeared to be shy in face-to-face discussions and contributed moderately in video-conferencing tasks, they were generally active on the blogs and in back-end activities involving the coordination of group tasks or negotiation of intra-group roles. Blogging was considered by impulsive learners as an opportunity to contribute to the group, to be heard, to share their ideas. The web-based, asynchronous nature of blogs allowed students to take their time before contributing. It was these opportunities that motivated impulsive students to leave their comfort zone and actually start collaborating. In doing so they started appreciating the importance of CSCL in their learning and progressively became more aware of how collaborative learning can enhance their self-confidence and their learning experience. These findings also suggest that if blogging was not a part of their education it is quite likely that these students may have failed to share their ideas and get engaged with the learning content and their peers alike. This emphasizes the significance of CSCL activities and the role of social and situational factors affecting their engagement.

Strategic Learner Engagement. Although the majority of students in this category expressed a preference towards social learning, their overall engagement was moderate to low. Strategic learners appeared to be active in face-to-face discussions yet they tended to disregard and devalue CSCL tasks on the basis that these tasks did not count towards their overall assessment. Although some strategic learners posted some content on the blogs they did not engage actively neither they replied to comments from their peers or the lecturer. This indicates that their strategic/achieving approach to learning and studying interfered with their engagement. In a way, the assessment strategy was conducive towards disengagement. In some cases, their assessment-oriented approach forced them to withhold information which was obstructing collaborative learning. From a pedagogical point of view, this illuminates both the importance of selecting appropriate assessment strategies in the context of CSCL and the value that postgraduate students often assign to extrinsic motives. It also re-emphasizes how personal (e.g. approach to learning) and situational (e.g. pedagogical practices) aspects may affect engagement. This was the second most prominent profile (27%) that emerged in the study, following enthusiastic learners.

Enthusiastic Learner Engagement. Enthusiastic learners demonstrated the highest level of overall engagement and they constitute the most prominent archetype in the studied context (32%). In terms of their behavioral engagement, enthusiastic learners were not only regularly contributing new content on the blogs, but they also engaged in web-based discussions with their peers and their lecturer. Their natural enthusiasm and excitement was also evident during the video-conferences. Their classmates confirmed their eagerness to coordinate the group activities and encourage other group members. Intellectually, they appeared to be motivated to learn and share their views with others. They also associated their experiences with CSCL with feelings of excitement, enthusiasm, and satisfaction and made clear, explicit connections between their learning experiences with CSCL tasks and their expected learning outcomes.

5   Discussion and Implications for Practice

The study findings have a number of implications for the design of 'engaging' CSCL pedagogies. Initially, the findings reinforce what has been previously argued in the literature: the fact that engagement is a complex and multifaceted concept (Ainley 2004; Murphy & Alexander 2000). Furthermore, the findings suggest that in conceptualizing learner engagement in CSCL we need a set of constructs that have the capacity to encapsulate what students 'do' when they are engaged but also how they 'feel' and 'think' when they are engaged. Thus, theorizing learner engagement as a three-dimensional concept defined by behavioral, intellectual, and affective constructs is useful for two main reasons. Firstly, for understanding the ways in which postgraduate students engage in CSCL tasks and secondly, for appreciating that students engage at a different extend within each dimension. The three-dimensional conceptualization of learner engagement alongside the WISE Taxonomy of Learner Engagement Archetypes provide a set of ideas which can help to make sense of how it is that postgraduate students engage with real-life CSCL activities and may, in turn, guide the design of pedagogical models for CSCL.

The findings seem to suggest that student engagement rests upon students' aptitude to intellectually, emotionally, and actively engage in the learning task but also illuminate the influence that personal and situational factors may have on students' actual engagement. Specifically, the taxonomy shows that some students may enthusiastically engage with a CSCL activity even if it does not constitute part of their assessed work, simply because it is itself a fulfilling activity. The taxonomy also reveals that students may be engaged or disengaged irrespective of their learning preference towards individual or social learning practices. Interestingly, however, many students may appear to strategically disengage from CSCL activities and as a result they may fail to appreciate CSCL as an authentic activity which leverages the opportunity to learn from and with each other, as well as from the wide range of digital resources openly available to them. Hence, in many ways, learner engagement appears to be analogous to the digital competences learners should acquire or cultivate through their education, such as the ability to learn and adapt quickly in the digital world, the confidence to effectively communicate and share information, and the ability to critically evaluate the vast amount of information available online. Viewing learner engagement with CSCL as a competence has implications for curriculum design indicating the importance of carefully selecting appropriate learning activities which are designed in a way that promotes collaboration and inspires students to learn how to approach learning tasks and how to engage with the learning content and with each other – through technology. All these constitute key elements towards cultivating learner engagement and developing the employability skills sought after in the modern workplace.

Furthermore, although lecturers usually expect postgraduate students to be highly self-motivated and self-directed, the intensity of most postgraduate degrees and the ever-increasing competition for jobs switches students' focus towards gaining higher grades. Apparently, adult learners are likely to "read, write papers, and discuss issues as long as they believe that these activities will help them achieve their goals" (Grabinger et al. 2007, p. 13). These findings have implications for student inclusivity suggesting that educators need to accommodate diverse types of engagement in their CSCL practices, not just diverse learning styles. They also highlight the fact that lecturers should consider students' ultimate goals and should not underestimate the importance of external triggers and incentives (Grabinger et al. 2007).

From a pedagogical perspective, the findings suggest that the adoption of CSCL practices will not automatically engage all learners. Various conditions or situational factors may enable or hinder learner engagement, such as the type of learning tasks, the assessment criteria assigned to them, the presence or absence of continuous feedback from the lecturer, the flexibility and openness in the learning process, and the dynamics in the student groups amongst others (Piki 2010). Understanding learner engagement from a holistic viewpoint – taking into consideration not only what students do, but also how they feel and think when approaching a CSCL activity – can be a challenging-yet-illuminating exercise that can help both students and educators to envisage the benefits of CSCL.

6   Limitations and Further Research

One potential limitation of the study may be the fact that it draws heavily on subjective measures such as observations of students' behaviors and students' self-perceptions. Future research may address the degree to which objective measures (e.g. age, gender, academic or cultural background) are correlated with the engagement strategies adopted by postgraduate students. Furthermore, the elicited archetypes of learner engagement were identified in a specific CSCL context, with a particular group of participants registered in a particular postgraduate course in the UK. While it is possible that instances of these archetypes may be present in other contexts (educational and/or vocational), this remains to be further explored. Another potential extension to this research would be to validate the proposed taxonomy across different CSCL contexts which employ different CTs (such as wikis, electronic forums, online argumentation tools, and social networking sites). Further research is also needed to better understand the multitude of personal, social, and situational factors that may enable or hinder learner engagement – in higher education and in the workplace alike.

7   Conclusion

The findings from this mixed-methods study suggest that although some students may naturally and enthusiastically engage in CSCL activities, learner engagement should not be taken for granted. Put differently, learner engagement should not be considered as an inherent feature of CTs. A more beneficial approach would be to consider learner engagement as a competence which can be nurtured through the application of coherent pedagogical models and assessment strategies taking into consideration not only how students prefer to learn but also how students are likely to engage in CSCL activities, and why. Although the value of CSCL practices is widely established, ensuring high quality learning outcomes are achieved requires empowering student engagement with the CSCL tasks and developing their skills and competencies through collaboration and knowledge sharing. This can be an attempt towards more engaging computer-supported collaborative learning journeys.

Acknowledgements. The author would like to express her gratitude to Prof. Duska Rosenberg for her invaluable input and suggestions throughout this research.

References

1. Piki, A.: Towards a holistic conceptual framework of learner engagement in CSCL environments. In: The Proceedings of the 9th European Conference on e-Learning, ECEL 2010 (2010)
2. Clarke, J., Hunter, J., Wells, M.: Enhancing the Student Experience Using Web 2.0 Technologies (Wikis, Blogs and Webcam Recordings) to Encourage Student Engagement and to Develop Collaborative Learning: a Case Study. Paper presented at the 7th European Conference on e-Learning (ECEL 2008), Cyprus (2008)

3. Stahl, G., Koschmann, T., Suthers, D.: Computer-supported collaborative learning: An historical perspective. In: Sawyer, R.K. (ed.) Cambridge Handbook of the Learning Sciences, pp. 409–426. Cambridge University Press, Cambridge (2006), http://GerryStahl.net/cscl/CSCL_English.pdf

4. Dillenbourg, P.: What do you mean by 'collaborative learning'? In: Dillenbourg, P. (ed.) Collaborative-Learning: Cognitive and Computational Approaches, pp. 1–15. Elsevier, Oxford (1999)

5. Grabinger, S., Aplin, C., Ponnappa-Brenner, G.: Instructional Design for Sociocultural Learning Environments. e-Journal of Instructional Science and Technology (e-JIST) 10(1) (2007)

6. Koschmann, T.: Dewey's contribution to the foundations of CSCL research. In: Stahl, G. (ed.) Computer Support for Collaborative Learning: Foundations for a CSCL Community: Proceedings of CSCL 2002, pp. 17–22. Lawrence Erlbaum Associates, Boulder (2002)

7. Jaques, D., Salmon, G.: Learning in groups: a handbook for face-to-face and online environments, 4th edn. Routledge, New York (2007)

8. Murphy, K., Alexander, P.: A motivated exploration of motivation terminology. Contemporary Educational Psychology 25 (2000)

9. Pintrich, P.R.: A motivational science perspective on the role of student motivation in learning and teaching contexts. Journal of Educational Psychology 95, 667–686 (2003)

10. Bomia, L., Beluzo, L., Demeester, D., Elander, K., Johnson, M., Sheldon, B.: The impact of teaching strategies on intrinsic motivation. ERIC Clearinghouse on Elementary and Early Childhood Education, Champaign (1997)

11. Kearsley, G., Shneiderman, B.: Engagement Theory: A framework for technology-based teaching and learning (1999), http://home.sprynet.com/~gkearsley/engage.htm

12. Pintrich, P.R.: A motivational science perspective on the role of student motivation in learning and teaching contexts. Journal of Educational Psychology 95, 667–686 (2003)

13. Ainley, M.: What do we know about student motivation and engagement? Paper presented at the annual meeting of the Australian Association for Research in Education, Melbourne (2004)

14. Stake, R.E.: The art of case study research. Sage, Thousand Oaks (1995)

15. Creswell, J.W., Plano Clark, V.L.: Designing and conducting mixed methods research, 2nd edn. Sage, Thousand Oaks (2011)

16. Johnson, R.B., Onwuegbuzie, A.J.: Mixed methods research: A research paradigm whose time has come. Educational Researcher 33(7), 14–26 (2004)

17. Tashakkori, A., Teddlie, C. (eds.): Handbook of Mixed Methods in Social and Behavioural Research. Sage, Thousand Oaks (2003)

18. Tashakkori, A., Teddlie, C. (eds.): Sage Handbook of Mixed Methods in Social and Behavioural Research, 2nd edn. Sage, Thousand Oaks (2010)

19. Onwuegbuzie, A., Teddlie, C.: A framework for analyzing data in mixed methods research. In: Tashakkori, A., Teddlie, C. (eds.) Handbook of Mixed Methods in Social & Behavioural Research, pp. 351–384. Sage, Thousand Oaks (2003)

20. Hammersley, M., Atkinson, P.: Ethnography: Principles in Practice, 3rd edn. Routledge, New York (2007)

21. Onwuegbuzie, A.J., Combs, J.P.: Emergent data analysis techniques in mixed methods research: A synthesis. In: Tashakkori, A., Teddlie, C. (eds.) Sage Handbook of Mixed Methods in Social & Behavioural Research, pp. 397–430. Sage, Thousand Oaks (2010)

22. Creswell, J.W.: Educational research: Planning, conducting, and evaluating quantitative and qualitative approaches to research. Pearson Education, Upper Saddle River (2002)

23. Namey, E., Guest, G., Thairy, L., Johnson, L.: Data Reduction Techniques for Large Qualitative Data Sets. In: Guest, G., MacQueen, K.M. (eds.) Handbook for Team-based Qualitative Research, pp. 137–162. Rowman Altamira (2007)
24. Miles, M.B., Huberman, M.: Qualitative Data Analysis: An Expanded Sourcebook. Sage (1994)
25. CRLI (Centre for Research on Learning and Instruction), Scoring key for the approaches and study skills inventory for students (1997),
    http://www.ed.ac.uk/etl/questionnaires/ASSIST.pdf
26. Tait, H., Entwistle, N.J., McCune, V.: ASSIST: A re-conceptualization of the Approaches to Studying Inventory. In: Rust, C. (ed.) Improving Students as Learners, pp. 262–271. Oxford Brookes University, Center for Staff and Learning Development, Oxford (1998)
27. Vallerand, R.J., Pelletier, L.G., Blais, M.R., Brière, N.M., Senécal, C.B., Vallières, E.F.: Academic Motivation Scale (AMS-C 28): College (CEGEP) Version. Educational and Psychological Measurement 52 (1992)

Digital Literacy for All Through Integrative STEM

Leo A. Siiman, Carlos Manuel Pacheco Cortés, and Margus Pedaste

Institute of Education, University of Tartu, Salme 1a, 50103 Tartu, Estonia
margus.pedaste@ut.ee

Abstract. The ever growing importance of digital literacy requires an effective educational strategy to introduce it into K-12 education. We propose teaching digital competences within the context of an integrative STEM framework. An overview of integrative STEM, its two core components (design from the context of technology education and inquiry from science education), and the natural connections to digital literacy are discussed. Two examples are given— robotics and 3-D computer software—as promising digital platforms to implement this strategy. Including digital literacy in integrative STEM offers all K-12 students the opportunity to acquire digital competences.

Keywords: Digital literacy, technology education, integrative STEM, design, inquiry, robotics, 3-D technology.

1 Introduction

The rapid development and widespread proliferation of digital technologies has brought greater conveniences to people in the 21st century. A mobile phone can now instantly retrieve the latest news across the globe or deliver multimedia entertainment experiences. But simply consuming the affordances of technology, without an awareness or understanding of how technology is created or applied, may leave many people unprepared for future challenges and opportunities. New technologies have shown an uncanny ability to automate tasks and replace humans at many jobs. In order to prepare people for the future workplace and improve their capabilities as citizens in daily life, technological and digital literacy must be emphasized in the educational curriculum. But how to include these literacies in today's educational framework while reaching a broad and inclusive audience is not obvious.

In Estonia, it is assumed that digital literacy is acquired through learning in all the different subjects, and a separate subject for learning computing, computers and software, or programming is only optional. However, the results – i.e. the average level of digital literacy in society and students interest to relate their career to ICT in different areas – are still not satisfying, and therefore digital competencies have been declared one out of five strategic goals of the Estonian educational strategy for 2020. Digital competencies are the core of digital literacy and thus there is a need to find new effective approaches to increase digital literacy. We assume that similar problems are faced by many other countries and an approach to acquiring digital literacy where subject-related specific aims are integrated could offer a beneficial solution.

P. Zaphiris and A. Ioannou (Eds.): LCT 2014, Part I, LNCS 8523, pp. 119–127, 2014.

One solution is to integrate digital literacy with STEM education where the inquiry approach has been widely used [1-3], but often not acknowledged by teachers. European level documents have stressed the importance of inquiry based education and regard it as one of the key aims in the future [4]. The current science classroom learning environment is often a mixture of divergent pedagogies and diverse students' orientations or preferences [5, 6]. There is a mismatch between opportunity and action in most education systems today. This revolves around the meaning of 'science education', a term that is often misappropriated in the current school practice, where rather than learning how to think scientifically, students are generally being lectured about science and asked to remember facts [7].

In this contribution we propose embedding digital literacy within an integrative STEM model. The STEM (science, technology, engineering, mathematics) disciplines are regarded as essential for ensuring future economic prosperity [4]. An integrative STEM model attempts to align science and mathematics education with technology and engineering education. Sanders (2009) [8] describes integrative STEM as intentionally combining two approaches: the design approach in technology/engineering education with the inquiry approach in science. We argue that digital literacy fits naturally within the integrative STEM program. Our research question is to investigate how digital literacy can be achieved in integrating inquiry related to science education with design related to technology education. To justify our position we organized this paper as follows. First we consider definitions of digital literacy to identify its key features. Next, the features of inquiry and design are separately summarized and compared to digital literacy. Then a discussion of integrative STEM is given to show its advantages and current challenges. Finally, the inclusion of digital literacy in integrative STEM is explored and two examples—robotics and 3-D computer software—are considered as potential practical implementations.

2   Digital Literacy

One definition of digital literacy comes from a list of recommendations on key competences for lifelong learning by the European Parliament and of the Council of the European Union, where it is stated that

Digital competence involves the confident and critical use of Information Society Technology (IST) for work, leisure and communication. It is underpinned by basic skills in ICT: the use of computers to retrieve, assess, store, produce, present and exchange information, and to communicate and participate in collaborative networks via the Internet. (European Union, 2006, p.15 [9])

At present the use of computers and the internet are the key enabling technologies for digital literacy. But in terms of characterizing digital literacy from a wider perspective, Hobbs (2011) [10] offers a list of five essential features to describe digital competencies:

- **Access** – use digital tools and technologies to access information
- **Analyze & Evaluate** – apply higher order thinking skills to process information
- **Create** – practice creative expression with digital technologies

- **Reflect** – engage in reflective thinking
- **Act** – participate and communicate in a social community

This list of competencies shows that digital literacy involves more than technical competency with digital tools. The *Reflect* competency describes a metacognitive process, *Create* implies originality and innovativeness, and *Act* requires social collaboration. Interestingly, many of these descriptions overlap with processes described by the inquiry and design. The inquiry and design approaches are the foundations for integrative STEM. Therefore integrating digital literacy with integrative STEM appears feasible and promising.

At this point it is useful to review the inquiry and design approaches separately before looking at how they merge with each other in integrative STEM.

3   Inquiry

Inquiry-based education is a teaching and learning strategy that promotes engagement and active participation of a learner to discovery knowledge. Recent meta-analysis studies show that inquiry-based instruction results in more beneficial learning than direct forms of instruction like lecturing [11, 12]. In inquiry, students ask questions and generate hypotheses, plan and conduct experiments, interact directly with investigative tools to explore phenomena, and communicate results. Computer-based learning environments have been shown to be especially effective ways to implement inquiry [13].

The inquiry process can be broken down into steps (usually called inquiry phases) to better explain the distinct reasoning processes that comprise inquiry. Inquiry phases originate from the steps found in the scientific method. Even though the scientific method is not a rigidly prescriptive sequence of steps it offers a useful basis for structuring inquiry in education. Mäeots, Pedaste, & Sarapuu (2011) [14] applied a typical list of inquiry phases to research student development of inquiry skills in a computer-based learning environment. The inquiry phases included transformative and regulative activities that should be applied not linearly but in integration:

Phases related to transformative processes:
- **Question** – generate research questions based on a problem
- **Hypothesis** – propose explanations and predictions that can be empirically tested
- **Experiment** – perform tests and collect data to confirm or refute a hypothesis
- **Data analysis** – synthesize new knowledge from experimental outcomes
- **Conclusion** –summarize and communicate results; contemplate future research
Phases related to regulative processes:
- **Planning** – design and schedule the learning process; set performance goals
- **Monitoring** –observe and record the study process
- **Evaluation** – verify that learning goals are achieved; reflect on the process

Comparing inquiry phases with features of digital literacy shows several similarities; such as applying higher order thinking skills, communicating, and reflective thinking. But inquiry sometimes does not explicitly emphasize features such as creativity, mentioned by Hobbs (2011) [10] as an important characteristic of digital literacy. Often the goal of inquiry is to ask a question about a scientific topic that leads to a single correct answer. Although students are challenged to actively discover the answer on their own, the final correct outcome is common to all investigators. In contrast, the design approach allows for open-ended problems where the outcomes can vary between students, yet still solve the original design problem. The design approach is useful for stimulating creativity in students.

4   Design

Design involves solving a practical problem while conforming to a certain set of constraints [15]. It is an iterative process that permits a multitude of solutions. Finding the optimal solution often requires creativity on the part of the designer.

The United Kingdom has a national curriculum in design & technology to prepare students for creative design and technological innovation. A recent report by the UK Department for Education [16] lists the key features of the curriculum as

- **Design** – identify user needs and practical problems; devise possible solutions
- **Make** – choose a solution and select the tools and materials to create a product
- **Evaluate** – test, evaluate, and critique the product against a set of specifications
- **Technical Knowledge** – understand the scientific and engineering principles governing the product or system

Often design has been seen too narrowly in the context of subjects as Design & Technology Education or even in Craft Education. Our aim is to show that the competencies in this field can be applied in many areas of peoples' everyday life. In this context we see design-based approach as strategy for solving one of a very complex type of problems – design problems. Design problems are introduced by Jonassen (2000) [17] as problems where problem solvers have to act on goals to produce artifacts even if there is only a vague goal with few guiding constraints. It assumes the problem solver to structure work, to set multiple undefined criteria for the expected solution in a context of a particular situation. Thus, it is a very ill-structured problem but very common in real life.

Comparing design to digital literacy reveals the strongest similarity in terms of making and creating. Hands-on, playful design work appeals to young people and can motivate increased enthusiasm and engagement for learning science [18, 19]. However, a criticism of design is that students can frequently use a trial-and-error strategy to solve a design problem and thereby avoid learning underlying science and mathematics principles that are actually responsible for the working solution [20]. Therefore, combining aspects of design and inquiry, such as in integrative STEM, offers potentially rewarding advantages while avoiding the potential disadvantages of either approach individually.

5   Integrative STEM

The importance of both inquiry and design for science education was recently made explicit in a new framework issued by the National Research Council in the United States [21]. It stated that

... learning about science and engineering involves integration of the knowledge of scientific explanations (i.e., content knowledge) and the practices needed to engage in scientific inquiry and engineering design. (National Research Council, 2012, p. 11 [21])

Lewis (2006) [22] argued that inquiry and design are conceptual parallels based on the unescapable interdependencies between science and engineering; and that integration offers greater prospects for learning in addition to increasing interest in science careers. Sanders (2009) [8] suggested that an integrated curriculum that "purposefully combines technological design with scientific inquiry" will help technology education become more relevant to society.

An integrative STEM graduate education program at Virginia Tech has been specifically created to embed technology/engineering design approaches into teaching science and mathematics content [23]. The goal of the program is to educate teachers with methods for implementing integrative STEM teaching practices. However, teachers still encounter challenges in implementing integrative STEM in practice [20]. There is a need for examples to illustrate effective implementations of integrative STEM in practice. Furthermore, the relevance of digital literacy for today's students is of great importance and should be included as part of integrative STEM instruction.

6   Digital Literacy through Integrative STEM

The features of digital literacy overlap with both inquiry and design and therefore integrative STEM is a suitable framework to facilitate digital competences. Moreover, teaching aspects of digital literacy in mandatory science and mathematics classes at the K-12 level guarantees that learning digital competencies is available to all students.

In the integrative STEM context, digital literacy could be implemented using innovative digital technologies. Two modern digital platforms that we consider promising are robotics and 3-D computer software. These digital platforms have been used in design approaches to motivate enthusiasm and interest in technology. But we contend that they can also be beneficially adapted for teaching science and mathematics, and hence appropriate in an integrative STEM context.

6.1   Robotics

Educational robotics provides a tangible and interactive learning platform for engaging students. But typical robot activities are mostly design based rather than inquiry-based and therefore using robotics to explore STEM concepts has not yet reached its full potential [24]. However, implementing an integrative STEM approach including digital literacy appears possible.

Improving mathematics learning with robotics is one promising start. Mathematical principles can be taught and motivated with robotics activities in the context of computer programming. The control and behavior of robots occurs through digital software instructions that must be programmed into a robot. The process of formulating an algorithm and writing code to program a robot requires mathematical sophistication. An effective program requires utilizing mathematical operators and manipulating variables (skills directly related to learning algebra). Robotics offers an opportunity to make abstract math concepts concrete. Design activities with robots can engage and motivate student learning.

In terms of science education, robotics can provide a systems-level model for learning a science topic. A system in the natural sciences is studied by breaking into separate parts, studying the parts individually, and then studying the interactions between the parts to see how the system as a whole behaves. Likewise, robots represent systems since they separate into parts with different functions; e.g. sensors collect input data, microprocessors process data, and electro-mechanical parts respond to output data sent from the microprocessors. The systems analogy between robotics and science therefore allows for an integrative STEM approach. Building and testing a systems model of a science topic using robotic parts is a promising way to implement a digital literacy based integrative STEM activity.

The digital competency benefits of robotics can include developing skills in electro-mechanics and computational thinking. In addition, working together in teams to design, build, and test a robot helps students learn to manage a project and work collaboratively.

6.2   3-D Computer Software

The growing popularity of 3-D printing has opened up a discussion about the potential of 3-D technology to improve learning. A recent pilot project by the UK Department for Education [25] explored the prospects of 3-D printers to enrich STEM education and found that

Feedback from this exploratory project confirms that 3D printers have significant potential as a teaching resource and can have a positive impact on pupil engagement and learning if schools can master how to use the printers in an effective and meaningful way. (UK Department for Education, 2013b, p. 23 [25]).

Therefore 3-D technology has promise but requires examples showing how to adapt the design-based use of 3-D technology with scientific inquiry. Siiman and Pedaste (2013) [26] proposed new ways of applying 3-D computer software to fulfill the complementary aim of learning science. They note that the structure and function of objects in nature, as well as their scale and proportion, are crucial elements to understand in science. But many objects are not accessible to direct observation or convenient to explore with traditional methods. Siiman and Pedaste (2013) [26] demonstrated interactive activities with digital 3-D models to teach the basic scientific fundamentals of structure, function, scale, and proportion. Practice with three-dimensional skills is also beneficial to science education because longitudinal studies have shown that 3-D spatial ability correlates strongly to success and achievement in science [27].

With respect to learning mathematics, 3-D software shares intrinsic links to the subject of geometry and the study of three-dimensional shapes. However, the animation features of 3-D software also allow for visualizing the motion of objects and studying concepts such as rate of change, a basic concept in calculus. Thus the potential of 3-D software extends across a range of mathematical topics and affords a diversity of learning options.

Although technology educators have extensively used 3-D computer assisted design (CAD) software to design and manufacture products, CAD software tends to be narrowly focused drafting technical drawings in engineering. In contrast, Siiman and Pedaste (2013) [26] chose an open-source 3-D software package mainly used by professionals and hobbyists in the arts & entertainment industries, but adapted it for educational purposes. The prospect of creating visually stunning visuals with 3-D software or designing 3-D models to manufacture using a 3-D printer is likely to stimulate the interest of students. Thus 3-D computer software promises new ways to motivate learning in an integrative STEM model that includes digital literacy.

7   Conclusion

Digital literacy can be facilitated through alignment with integrative STEM so that all K-12 students have the opportunity to acquire digital competences. Integrative STEM is a new educational strategy that attempts to merge the best features of scientific inquiry and technological/engineering design. At present more empirical data is necessary to find the most effective implementations of integrative STEM, but the aims and principles of the strategy are supported by a number of recent documents by national governmental organizations across the globe. Including digital literacy within integrative STEM follows naturally from technology designed-based approaches, but requires additional considerations for implementation with scientific inquiry or mathematics learning. We proposed robotics and 3-D computer software as two examples of digital platforms for implementing integrative STEM. Future work necessitates empirical testing to identify the practical effect with teachers and students.

References

1. de Jong, T., van Joolingen, W., Giemza, A., Girault, I., Hoppe, U., Kindermann, J., Kluge, A., Lazonder, A., Vold, V., Weinberger, A., Weinbrenner, S., Wichmann, A., Anjewierden, A., Bodin, M., Bollen, L., d'Ham, C., Dolonen, J., Engler, J., Geraedts, C., Grosskreutz, H., Hovardas, T., Julien, R., Lechner, J., Ludvigsen, S., Matteman, Y., Meistadt, Ø., Næss, B., Ney, M., Pedaste, M., Perritano, A., Rinket, M., von Schlanbusch, H., Sarapuu, T., Schulz, F., Sikken, J., Slotta, J., Toussaint, J., Verkade, A., Wajeman, C., Wasson, B., Zacharia, Z., van der Zanden, M.: Learning by creating and exchanging objects: The SCY experience. British Journal of Educational Technology 41(6), 909–921 (2010)

2. de Jong, T., Weinberger, A., Girault, I., Kluge, A., Lazonder, A.W., Pedaste, M., Ludvigsen, S., Ney, M., Wasson, B., Wichmann, A., Geraedts, C., Giemza, A., Hovardas, A., Julien, R., van Joolingen, W.R., Lejeune, A., Manoli, C., Matteman, Y., Sarapuu, T., Verkade, A., Vold, V., Wanders, B., Zacharia, Z.C.: Using scenarios to design complex technology-enhanced learning environments. Educational Technology Research & Development 60(5), 883–901 (2012)

3. Pedaste, M., de Jong, T., Sarapuu, T., Piksööt, J., van Joolingen, W.R., Giemza, A.: Investigating ecosystems as a blended learning experience. Science 340(6140), 1537–1538 (2013)

4. Rocard, M., Csermely, P., Jorde, D., Lenzen, D., Walberg-Henrikson, H., Hemmo, V.: Science education now: A renewed pedagogy for the future of Europe. European Commission: Directorate-General for Research, Brussels (2007)

5. Chang, C.-Y., Tsai, C.-C.: The interplay between different forms of CAI and students' preferences of learning environment in the secondary science class. Science Education 89(5), 707–724 (2005)

6. Chang, C., Hsiao, C., Barufaldi, J.-P.: Preferred-actual learning environment "spaces" and earth science outcomes in Taiwan. Learning Environment Spaces 90(3), 420–433 (2006)

7. Alberts, B.: Restoring science to science education. Issues in Science and Technology. A Publication of National Academy of Sciences, National Academy of Engineering, Institute of Medicine, University of Texas at Dallas (2009), http://www.issues.org/25.4/alberts.html (retrieved December 14, 2013)

8. Sanders, M.: STEM, STEM education, STEMmania. The Technology Teacher 68(4), 20–26 (2009)

9. European Union. Recommendation of the European Parliament and of the Council of 18 December 2006 on key competences for lifelong learning. Journal of the European Union, L394 (2006), http://eur-lex.europa.eu/LexUriServ/site/en/oj/2006/l_394/l_39420061230en00100018.pdf (retrieved)

10. Hobbs, R.: Empowering Learners with Digital and Media Literacy. Knowledge Quest 39(5), 12–17 (2011)

11. Alfieri, L., Brooks, P.J., Aldrich, N.J., Tenenbaum, H.R.: Does discovery-based instruction enhance learning? Journal of Educational Psychology 103, 1–18 (2011)

12. Furtak, E.M., Seidel, T., Iverson, H., Briggs, D.C.: Experimental and quasiexperimental studies of inquiry-based science teaching. Review of Educational Research 82, 300–329 (2012)

13. de Jong, T.: Computer simulations: Technological advances in inquiry learning. Science 312, 532–533 (2006)

14. Mäeots, M., Pedaste, M., Sarapuu, T.: Interactions between Inquiry Processes in a Web-Based Learning Environment. Paper presented at the Advanced Learning Technologies (ICALT), 2011 11th IEEE International Conference on Advanced Learning Technologies, Athens, USA (2011)

15. Brophy, S., Klein, S., Portsmore, M., Rogers, C.: Advancing engineering education in P-12 classrooms. Journal of Engineering Education 97(3), 369–387 (2008)

16. UK Department for Education. National curriculum in England: design and technology programmes of study (2013), https://www.gov.uk/government/publications/national-curriculum-in-england-design-and-technology-programmes-of-study (retrieved)

17. Jonassen, D.H.: Toward a design theory of problem solving. Educational Technology Research and Development 48, 63–85 (2000)

18. Cantrell, P., Pekcan, G., Itani, A., Velasquez-Bryant, N.: The effects of engineering modules on student learning in middle school science classrooms. Journal of Engineering Education 95(4), 301–309 (2006)
19. Cejka, E., Rogers, C., Portsmore, M.: Kindergarten robotics: Using robotics to motivate math, science, and engineering literacy in elementary school. International Journal of Engineering Education 22(4), 711–722 (2006)
20. Roehrig, G.H., Moore, T.J., Wang, H.H., Park, M.S.: Is Adding the E Enough? Investigating the Impact of K-12 Engineering Standards on the Implementation of STEM Integration. School Science and Mathematics 112(1), 31–44 (2012)
21. National Research Council. A Framework for K-12 Science Education: Practices, Crosscutting Concepts, and Core Ideas. Committee on a Conceptual Framework for New K-12 Science Education Standards. Board on Science Education, Division of Behavioral and Social Sciences and Education. The National Academies Press, Washington, DC (2012)
22. Lewis, T.: Design and inquiry: Basis for an accommodation between science and technology education in the curriculum? Journal of Research in Science Teaching 43, 255–281 (2006)
23. Wells, J.G.: Integrative STEM education at Virginia Tech: Graduate preparation for tomorrow's leaders. Technology & Engineering Teacher 72(5), 28–34 (2013)
24. Altin, H., Pedaste, M.: Learning approaches to applying robotics in science education. Journal of Baltic Science Education 12(3), 365–377 (2013)
25. UK Department for Education. 3D printers in schools: uses in the curriculum (2013), https://www.gov.uk/government/uploads/system/uploads/attachment_data/file/251439/3D_printers_in_schools.pdf (retrieved)
26. Siiman, L.A., Pedaste, M.: Towards a pedagogy for using digital 3-D content in science education. In: 6th International Conference of Education, Research and Innovation (ICERI 2013), Seville, Spain, November 18-20, pp. 5992–5999 (2013)
27. Wai, J., Lubinski, D., Benbow, C.P.: Spatial Ability for STEM Domains: Aligning Over 50 Years of Cumulative Psychological Knowledge Solidifies Its Importance. Journal of Educational Psychology 101, 817–835 (2009)

A Model for Human-Computer Trust
Contributions Towards Leveraging User Engagement

Sonia Sousa[1], David Lamas[2], and Paulo Dias[1]

Universidade Aberta, Tallinn University
Palcio de Ceia, Narva mnt 25
Lisboa, Tallinn
Portugal, Estonia
{scsousa,pdias}@uab.pt, david.lamas@tlu.ee

Abstract. Trusting is a rather complex phenomena and this complexity has been increasing with the pervasiveness of computing systems. In this virtual realms, Human-computer trust represents a key issue in today's organizations, and it has a significative role in leveraging interactions and mediating interrelationships and auto-regulate knowledge sharing processes.

This paper reports an research framework, which aims to facilitate the use of the acquired understanding of the role of trust in (A) Human Computer Interaction; and in (B) Computer mediated Interaction.

Results situate the model as a key contribute for leveraging people's interactions and their technological artefacts.

Keywords: Human-computer Trust, User experience, Trusted interactions, Social engagement, Collaborative Learning.

1 Introduction

Computing is at one of its most exciting moments, playing an essential role in supporting human activities, facilitated by the growing availability of services, devices and interaction modalities. With the evolution from the large-scale computing to the contemporary pervasive and ubiquitous computing interaction paradigms, users were brought from the periphery to the successive waves of the personal, networked, collaborative, mobile, augmented and virtual reality interaction paradigms.

This article describes a research framework that builds on the previously body of knowledge on Trust and uses it to contribute towards leverage higher levels of engagement and overall systems sustainability.

The first part come in line with authors attempt to situate Trust as a contribute to better understanding of the role of trust in Human Computer Interaction; and in Computer mediated Interaction. This part provides a comprehensive introduction to Human-computer trust conceptualisation and it address it dynamics. The following parts addresses authors' conceptual contribution on Human-computer trust, then it ends by provide possible future directions.

P. Zaphiris and A. Ioannou (Eds.): LCT 2014, Part I, LNCS 8523, pp. 128–137, 2014.

2   Human-Computer Trust

Everyday, and often without any reflection, we place our trust in people and in services those people provide. We trust our friends will not betray our confidence; that our food will not be poison; we trust our teacher and parents to tell us the truth and teach us well; trust our country; the list here is practically endless and staggeringly broad. Trust was always a topic, which is of ubiquitous importance to people.

Trust is referred in a relatively broad set of constructs. Is a topic that has been attracting research from many fields like sociology, economics, psychology, cognitive sciences and lately from computer science. Yet, Trust is a topic, rather complex to address, making it difficult to compare or to provide clear insights about the nature of trusting relations (e.g. Rotenberg, 2005; Mayer et al., 1995; Goudge, 2005; Fukuyama, 1995; Lewis and Weigert, 1985).

Trust's cross-disciplinary nature has originated a considerable debate about what trust is, how it is influenced, and how it is represented; makes it difficult to be defined in a narrow definition, or just as a "single static" concept; trust per si, carry's many meanings and play a role in divergent contexts.

While sociologists tend to see trust as structural in nature (e.g., Garfinkel, 1967; Lewis & Weigert, 1985; Shapiro, 1987), or in terms of behavior (e.g. James S. Coleman, 1996;) or even as a moral choice (e.g. Francis Fukuyama, 1995; Tyler and Degoey, 1996).

Psychologists examines it as a personal attribute (e.g., Erikson, 1968; Rotter, 1967) and analysis trust as behavioral intention (relates to the predict acceptance of behaviors by others). (e.g. Erikson, 1968; Rotter, 1971)

Social psychologists tend to view trust as an interpersonal phenomenon (e.g., Deutsch, 1973; Holmes, 1991; Mishra 1996; Weber 2003; Meyerson, 1996), a social structure to provides interpersonal relationships, known as institution-based trust or willingness to trust if within a more social physiological perspective.

Economists are more inclined to view trust as a rational choice mechanism, as a game (the game theory) (e.g. Levy and Razin, 2003; McKnight, D., H., Chervany, N. L., 2001).

The philosophic perspective sees trust and distrust attitudes as something that affects our feelings and the way we think and act (e.g. Baier, A. 1986; McLeod, C., 2006).

Computer scientists on the other hand, tend to approach the Trust topic from two distinct perspectives. One that reflects the tendency to examine Trust from a more deterministic approach; observing it as a sort of rational choices vs a measurable risk. Examples can be found in literature that addresses issues like Trust management or computational trust associated with security, reputation and privacy (e.g. Kini, 1998; Abdul, 1999; Walter, 2008).

Another, point of view relates Trust to the human cognitive and affective aspects. An approach that focus on qualifying the trust attributes and in understand the potential Trust implications among human users. Examples can be found in literature that addresses issues like computer supported collaborative work, communities of practice, design for trustful interactions, social capital,

Table 1. Trust conceptualisation framework

Sociologist's	Trust is a reflection of behaviours, choices and decisions	Represents a intention
Psychologist's	Trust is an attitude or intention	Represents a personal attribute; an observable behaviour.
Socio-psychologist's	Trust is an interpersonal phenomenon	Represent a social structure
Economist's	Trust is a rational choice mechanism	Represent a rational decision
Computer science	Trust is user's confidence in a system and their willingness to act	represents a cognition and affect based perceptions of another person or group and an artifact.

Organizational Trust, Technology-Mediated Social Participation (e.g. Bachrach, 2001, Mcknight 1996, McKnight, 2002, Constantine, 2006; Weber, 2003; Yan, 2006).

3   Measuring Human Computer Trust

Human-computer trust is defined in this study to be a measurable risk, represented by a deterministic quality (measured during a snapshot in time) or a observable attitude, represented by more subjective and hedonic quality (measured during an episode in time).

Both tendencies are invariable reflected throughout and within the trust social dynamics; and this dynamics represents, not just, the interaction between individuals constituent of society or organisation and their communication artifacts, but also represents the interaction between a user or a group of users and their artifacts.

Trust within and interactive processes, represents users predisposition to interact (based on a calculative orientation toward the risky) ; i.e. by trusting we assume a potential gain, while by distrust we are avoiding a potential loss [1,5]. Trusting, also represents a reinsurance elements, which often helps users to support their intended behaviours.

This reinsurance mechanisms can be combine through a set of measurable observable behaviours that emerge from social and technical categorizations, e.g. group or individual's political, economic and social orientation [4], or from institution-base properties [6,10]; or even from certain social qualities like honesty, benevolency or reciprocity [?].

This reinsurance mechanisms give party's the structural assurance or confidence that support individuals' trusting predisposition, that further in time takes a form of trusting stance, i.e. belief in others.

In sum, Trust is a reflection of a a state of mind a confidence and one's predisposition to trust another. This based on a set of perceptions of other (a society, a person, and or a technological artifact) as 'trustworthy' [3, 9, 11]. Formed by a combination of observable behaviours which includes perceived affect and cognition based behaviours [2]. And, a violation of trust usually lies not in a simple isolated interpersonal event, but rather it is a significant event that is likely to have impact on the parties and on the relationship [12].

Trust dynamic, then contemplates a subtlety decision that lies on the complexity of the game that he or she find herself playing as Bacharach [1] describes it. Within this 'game' trust comes associated with a time anchor proprietary, represented by an initial trust moment (trust exist or not) and an ongoing trust moment (trust can be weaken or strengthen over time) [8].

More, the identification of trustworthy making qualities (what underlies people's trust beliefs) is not enough to induce trust, it is needed also to understand if this signs of trust are to be trusted (confidence) [1]. What addressees the question of the reliability of trustworthy making qualities, especially in a virtual environments where there is an increased omnipresence of social network services and communities.

Thus, this paper contribute towards the identification of possible trustworthy making qualities and signs that support user's predisposition to trust. It proposes a model, a model of Human-computer Trust and uses it to perceive how it can contribute to leveraging user's engagement with and through their technological artefacts.

This works herein presents aims in the future to contribute to the development of strategies for support interdisciplinary teams when assessing, designing and creating trust-fostering interactive systems; and or to support the design, development and evaluating of a toolset to monitor Human-computer trust levels, thus facilitating the deployment of trust level regulation interventions.

4   A Model of Human-Computer Trust

This model depict trust as a construct informed by individual attributes qualities such as, motivation, willingness, reciprocity, predictability, honesty, benevolence, and competence, and determined the extent to which one relates with one?s social and technical environment [14, 17].

This model was used as a research lens to establish relations that linked trust online interactive processes qualities, e.g. to openness [13], to sharing [18], to privacy [7] and to collaboration [15]

This model was achieved by an extensive literature review on trust and was complemented by a participatory design procedure, that resulted in

- the Identification of most common trust notions (design a concept map);
- An personal unified view of possible trust implications in today?s online communities structures (participatory design session with experts and users) [16];

This was complemented by a personal unified view of trust dynamics (see section 3) and Davis and Venkatesh Technology acceptance views [3] [19].

This model takes into consideration seven trust observable warranty qualities, that help users to categorize their trust beliefs towards a system or another individual or even a third party. Those trust belief's support a set of constructed intentions, predispositions to trust that facilitates the interaction process (e.g. share, communicate and or relate online).

This is a iterative process, that evolves through time, see figure 2.

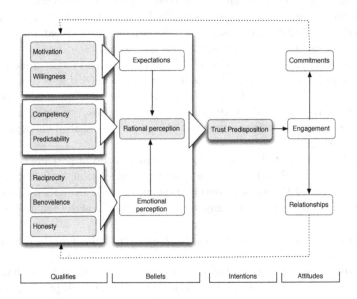

Fig. 1. A model of Human-computer Trust

Further section present the results on the validation of this model, its uses a mixed method study and it procedure is described in the following section 4.1.

4.1   Model Validation Process

Above presented model of Human-computer Trust aims to contribute to leverage higher levels of user engagement with other users and artifacts. This validation was achieved through mixed method studies, combining divergent research approaches over a period of time. During each validation process the set of constructs attributes underwent in a series of refinements to eliminate or refine the above presented model, see figure 2.

4.2   Attitudes Towards Others, Sharing and Communicate Online

This first research iteration aimed to determined the extent to which one is predispose to relate online in a specific social and technical environment.

To achieved above aims a survey was randomly conducted among 480 individuals, who interact online frequently for education purpose. From those three-hundred and forty (340) individuals were consider for analysis, the remaining where either incomplete or where consider biased. Participants where portuguese teachers 53.5 % or portuguese higher education students 46.5%).

A confirmatory factor analysis was applied to test if the empirical data was conform the proposed model. This factorial analysis process included question that assessed (1) individuals' trust towards others; (2) their expectations to engage in give and take actions, and (3) their predisposition to engage in online relationships. This analysis toked into consideration the proposed Human-computer trust warranty qualities addressed in the instrument and intercept those with the divergent nature of the online relationships (ranging from more close and intimate relations (e.g. friends, family, colleague), to open (e.g. acquaintance, strangers).

Results of the principal components analysis strongly support the relationship between users perceived trust and their intentions and attitudes towards others.

In sum, achieved results also stress a need for a clear understand this trust elements as a key factor for leveraging user engagement with and through interactive systems [18].

4.3   Attitudes towards Openness and Sharing Knowledge

This second study aimed to establish a relation between the proposed Human-computer trust warranty qualities and users believes towards using openness and open sharing knowledge systems.

This study included two main contexts of use:

- Estonian Higher education students (32), with experience in using open-base blogging systems; and
- Estonian Secondary education students (53), with no or little experience with open-base blogging systems.

Estonia is consider to be a peculiar country in terms of ICT use, as at the high school level the new National Curricula states an obligation for every school to have an e-learning environment. At the level of universities and vocational schools there are a lot of choices of open and non-open solutions to choose from, e.g. Wikiversity, Moodle, Blackboard, IVA, LeMill, WordPress, etc.

Results revealed that user's attitudes towards openness and sharing depends on the information they share and with who they share that information.

For example uses that are more aware of potential threats of privacy tend to stress more for being assured that their open activities are protected from potential threats [7].

Also, in both cases users indicated they don't mind to share learning information openly with everyone (if they feel control on what they share in open environments). In fact as for example 37.93% of the Higher education students claim that this could contribute to increase the learning processes reliability and credibility [13]. But, given the choice, they prefer to share personal information and comments with their friends; family and co-workers only.

Strong concerns where shown special on the need to have control with whom they share their grading, assignment comments and teacher's feedback information. They claim that should remain private by default.

Regarding the intention to share in open environments attributes like: honesty (48,28%), other users reputation (37,93%), respect and affinity attitudes (31,03%); as well as empathy and sympathy (41,38%) are consider very important qualities to be willing to share information and to trust online. Same regards to friendly and transparent attitudes (44,83%); Honesty (44,83%); sense of belonging (27,59%) and mutual respect (37,93%) are consider very important qualities for communicate online.

4.4   Human-Computer Trust and Collaboration

In this case study we focus on using the teacher role as lens to observe possible relations between Human-computer trust and collaborative activity patterns like:

- Individual commitments and group bound;
- Group support and articulation; and
- Social dynamic activity.

The observed course "Technology Enhanced Learning TEL course, was part of a European project called CoCreat — "Enabling Creative Collaboration through Supportive Technologies" (http://let.oulu.fi/cocreat). The course, was deployed by four (4) partners from eight (4) different European countries, Finland (University of Oulu); Norway (Norwegian University of Science and Technology Trondheim); Romania (Valahia University of Targoviste); and Estonia (Tallinn University).

Project main purpose was to find new solutions for promoting creative collaboration in terms of new and innovative learning models based on social media and mobile technology. Most activities performed in the course involve collaborative tasks, collaborative thinking and reflection. In the course students were initially divided into small groups (from 4 to 9 students maximum) and different tutors were assigned to the groups. All learning activities were design and coordinated by a teacher who coordinate overall group activities.

Be willing towards fulfilling a common goal (predisposition to interact) is consider to be an important key to establishing group collaboration and to ensure it success. The results indicated that those who were more predispose to interact (easily engaged in online activities) had more sucess in perform collaborative activities and in foster groups collaboration.

On the other hand, individuals competency and their appetency to be engaged in online relationships aren't always related (this was clearly reflected during group synchronous communications). The less social engaged, committed students tend to follow group and contribute punctually when requested.

Contradictory to what was expected open or close activities seamed less important for ensure the success of the group support and articulation. On the other hand qualities like reciprocity, kindness and benevolence were important attributes to ensure students bound and work articulation.

Overall group-working methods differentiated from group to group, though in the end the majority of the groups achieved pretended results. Groups first activities were relevant to set the work climate and to establish future working actions (know how to behave and to observe other intentions and attitudes). Major group concerns regarded the previsibility, e.g. predict what actions will be need to be taken to ensure a successful collaboration. In return, system predictability and and it perceived competency were important attributes for selection of artefacts to communicate and use in their collaborative activities.

5   Final Considerations

Our contribution towards perceiving Human-computer Trust enabled to better understand the Human Computer Trust role in,

- providing effective social human relations;
- create, develop and maintain working, organisational, or networking relationships; and
- create, develop and maintain a learning environment which eventually could lead to sustainable online engagements.

As well this model future contribution is towards perceiving Trust as an interaction facilitator construct. Contributing to the development of strategies for support interdisciplinary teams when assessing, designing and creating trust-fostering interactive systems; and or to support the design, development and evaluating of a toolset to monitor Human-computer trust levels, thus facilitating the deployment of trust level regulation interventions.

The underlying hypotheses for this future aim is that real time monitoring of self and third party trust levels can in fact be used to trigger interventions designed to regulate (moderate, improve, recover) trust levels to adequate standings.

Thus, as on the design, development and evaluation of tools to monitor trust levels based on the current understanding of the construct, the proposed research questions are:

- What data can be used to monitor trust?
- How often should data be sampled to generate robust trust indicators?
- How should data samples be collected taking into account that the impact of the sampling process in the generation of confidence indicators should be minimized?
- What metrics should be used to express trust levels?
- How should trust indicators be interpreted?

References

1. Bachrach, M., Guerra, G., Zizzo, D.: The self-fulfilling property of trust: an experimental study. Theory and Decision, 349–388 (2007)
2. Bromiley, P., Cummings, L.L.: Transaction costs in organizations with trust. In: Robert, J., Bies, R.J., Lewicki, B.L.S. (eds.) Research on Negotiations in Organizations, pp. 219–247. JAI Press, Greenwich (1995)
3. Davis, F.D.: Perceived usefulness, perceived ease of use, and user acceptance of information technology. MIS Quartely 13(3), 319–340 (1989)
4. Fukuyama, F. (ed.): Trust: The social virtues and the creation of prosperity. Free Press, New York (1995)
5. Gambetta, D.: Trust making and breaking co-operative relations. In: Gambetta, D. (ed.) Can We Trust Trust?, pp. 213–237. Basil Blackwell (1998)
6. Kramer, R.M.: & Brewer, M.B.H.B.A.: Collective trust and collective action: The decision to trust as a social decision. In: Kramer, R., Tyler, T. (eds.) Trust in Organisations: Frontiers of Theory and Research, pp. 357–389. SAGE Publications Inc., California (1996)
7. Lorenz, B., Sousa, S., Tomberg, V.: Privacy awareness of students and its impact on online learning participation – A case study. In: Ley, T., Ruohonen, M., Laanpere, M., Tatnall, A. (eds.) OST 2012. IFIP AICT, vol. 395, pp. 189–192. Springer, Heidelberg (2013)
8. Luhmann, N.: Familiarity, confidence, trust: Problems and alternatives. In: Gameta, D., Blackwell, B. (eds.) Trust: Making and Breaking Co-operative Relations. Basil Blackwell, Oxford (2000)
9. Mayer, R.C., Davis, J.H., Schoorman, F.D.: An integrative model of organizational trust. The Academy of Management Review 20(3), 709–734 (1995)
10. Mishra, A.K.: Organizational responses to crisis: The centrality of trust. In: Kramer, R., Tyler, T. (eds.) Trust in Organizations: Frontiers of Theory and Research, pp. 261–287. SAGE Publications Inc., California (1996)
11. Preece, J., Shneiderman, B.: The reader-to-leader framework: Motivating technology-mediated social participation. AIS Transactions on Human-Computer Interaction 1(1), 13–32 (2009)
12. Ries, S.: Certain trust: a trust model for users and agents. In: SAC 2007: Proceedings of the 2007 ACM Symposium on Applied Computing, pp. 1599–1604. ACM, New York (2007)
13. Sousa, S.C., Tomberg, V., Lamas, D.R., Laanpere, M.: Interrelation between trust and sharing attitudes in distributed personal learning environments: The case study of lepress ple. In: Leung, H., Popescu, E., Cao, Y., Lau, R.W.H., Nejdl, W. (eds.) ICWL 2011. LNCS, vol. 7048, pp. 72–81. Springer, Heidelberg (2011)
14. Sousa, S., Lamas, D.: Emerging trust patterns in online communities. In: CPSCom 2011: The 4th IEEE International Conference on Cyber, Physical and Social Computing. IEEE Computer Society (2011)
15. Sousa, S., Lamas, D.: Leveraging trust to support online learning creativity–a case study. eLearning Papers 30(Special Issue), 1–10 (2012)
16. Sousa, S., Lamas, D., Dias, P.: A framework for understanding online learning communities. In: Leung, H., Popescu, E., Cao, Y., Lau, R., Nejdl, W. (eds.) ECEL 2011 - 7th International Conference on e-Learning, pp. 1000–1004. Academic Publishers (2011)

17. Sousa, S., Lamas, D., Dias, P.: The interrelation between communities, trust and their online social patterns. In: Xia, F., Chen, Z., Pan, G., Yang, L.T., Ma, J. (eds.) SCA2011 - International conference on Social Computing and its Applications, pp. 980–986. IEEE Computer Society (2011)

18. Sousa, S., Lamas, D., Dias, P.: The implications of trust on moderating learner's online interactions - a socio-technical model of trust. In: Martins, M.J., Cordeiro, J., Helfert, M. (eds.) CSEDU 2012 - Proceedings of the 4th International Conference on Computer Supported Education, vol. 2, pp. 258–264. SciTePress (2012)

19. Venkatesh, V., Morris, M.G., Davis, G.B., Davis, F.D.: Perceived usefulness, perceived ease of use, and user acceptance of information technology. MIS Quarterly 27(3), 425–478 (2003)

Going Digital: Literature Review on E-textbooks

Terje Väljataga and Sebastian H.D. Fiedler

Centre for Educational Technology, Tallinn University, Tallinn, Estonia
{terje.valjataga,fiedler}@tlu.ee

Abstract. Digitising textbooks is becoming an increasingly important practice in formal education. While higher education has been the main focus of research on e-textbooks so far, the topic is also gaining attention in other areas of formal education. This paper reports on an initial attempt to review and synthesise research and development literature on e-textbooks - mainly in the context of K-12 education. While the project is still work in progress, some provisional findings, main demarcation lines, and visible directions in the field are reported and discussed.

Keywords: e-textbooks, literature review, digitisation, K-12 education.

1 Introduction

Digitising textbooks is becoming an increasingly important practice in formal education. While higher education has been the main focus of research on e-textbooks so far, the topic is also gaining attention in K-12 education. In recent years academic and educational publishers have started to follow the phenomenon of extensive digitisation by converting printed textbooks into digital formats that can be read on a computer screen, a special e-book reader, a personal digital assistant (PDA), or even a mobile phone [1].

This paper reports on an initial attempt to review and synthesise research and development literature on the use of e-textbooks mainly in K-12 education. In the literature the terms e-textbook, digital textbook, electronic textbook are used interchangeably and were thus included into the search and selection of material for our literature base. While collecting literature we noticed that some authors have used the more general term e-book to refer to instructional materials in educational settings. Literature in which e-book is clearly used in the sense of "textbook" in an educational setting was included in our literature base. For consistency and clarification we have decided to use one term - e-textbook throughout this paper. We attempt to provide an overview of what are considered to be the main research problems related to e-textbooks in the context of formal education and to delineate the evolution of research trends in this field. It must be noted here that the majority of contributions deals with problems and challenges related to e-textbooks in higher education. Though our current interest is primarily in the context of K-12 education, we found it useful and informative to also include literature into our review that reports on challenges and empirical findings regarding the use of e-textbooks in

P. Zaphiris and A. Ioannou (Eds.): LCT 2014, Part I, LNCS 8523, pp. 138–148, 2014.

higher education. While our review project is still work in progress, we want to take the opportunity to report and discuss some provisional findings and insights in the following paragraphs.

2   The Role of Textbooks

Textbooks have been used and still are used as the main reference tool and primary means of delivering course content in K-12 education since the widespread availability of the printing press [2]. Textbooks are often seen as the central tool in instructional settings providing input into classroom lessons in the form of texts, activities, explanations, and so on [3]. Many proponents of the textbook culture in education believe that "no teaching-learning situation, it seems, is complete until it has its relevant textbook" [3, p. 315]. For teachers textbooks are an instructional aid. They save time, give direction to lessons, guide discussion, facilitate homework assignments, thus making teaching practice better organized and somewhat more convenient and easier to handle. For students textbooks in their traditional sense are meant to be as a framework or guide that helps them organising and supporting their learning activity in the classroom and at home. Most of all the role of the textbook is to provide structure, confidence and security [3]. Textbooks reflect the academic standards, specific objectives, and ideologies commonly found in public curricula. Thus, problems of availability of up-to-date, governmentally approved, textbooks are generally considered to severely impair teaching practice. Without a doubt, textbooks have played, and still play, an enormous role in K-12 education as the most convenient means for providing structure for guiding through an instructional event.

3   Rationale for Going Digital

It is of little surprise that the ever-growing expansion of digitisation in different spheres of our society shows an increasing impact on educational practice in recent years. Digitising textbooks has become – and appears to remain for the foreseeable future - one of the popular issues of research, debate and discussion. How should an e-textbook look like in the first place? What is the added value and challenges of implementing an e-textbook? are typical questions raised in this context. Maynard and Cheyne [4], for example, simply define e-textbooks as "educational materials that have been electronically published to assist both teaching and learning methods" (p.104). This general and commonly accepted definition has been taken as a basis for many e-textbook implementation initiatives in K-12 education. The aforementioned definition reflects a basic replication of a printed textbook within a different medium. It is quite likely that this type of understanding is somewhat nurtured by the commercially successful and constantly growing market for "e-books" in general.

E-books have been around for quite some years by now and educational publishing companies have started to follow the same road, carrying the assumption that the added-value of e-textbooks is in principle perceived along very similar lines. The mere digital re-production of formally printed textbooks allows for the continuation of educational practices that had developed around printed texts [5]. In addition to its presentation as an innovative medium in education, the e-textbook is very often demonstrated as an entertainment technology or an instrument to raise students' motivation of digital age. The current status of our ongoing literature review seems to indicate that the main driver for "going digital" with textbooks is regularly purely economical considerations. Although, most of the studies we reviewed refer to cost reductions through the introduction of e-textbooks in higher education, it seems reasonable to assume that a similar claim should be also valid in the context of K-12 systems. For those interested in numbers and cost models we recommend for example the following papers: [6-11].

There is little doubt that digitisation is transforming a wide range of human activity systems. While this inevitably creates tensions and contradictions, it also provides a wide variety of new potentials for action and interaction and its mediation. In fact, the potential for increased levels of interaction has been acknowledged and promoted as one key added-value of digital textbooks. It is becoming a rather common belief among publishing companies, educators, instructional designers and policy makers that e-textbooks need to (and can) be redesigned in a way that enables somewhat richer and more variable opportunities for interaction with their content. McFall [2], for example, claims that "in order for electronic textbooks to be widely accepted, they must be designed with a goal of transforming the way students interact with a textbook to significantly enhance student learning" (p. 74). In a similar vein Tezak [12] offers an interactive model of an e-textbook supplemented with a workbook. It contains inner and outer links providing access to additional resources on the Web. Severin and Capota [13] report on a South Korean initiative to replace traditional textbooks with interactive e-textbooks. These interactive and customisable e-textbooks include the content of existing textbooks, reference books, workbooks, glossaries, and so forth, and integrate them with additional digital audio-video material such as video clips, animations, and elements of virtual reality.

Turning e-textbooks more interactive in comparison to their printed counterparts is a step further in terms of technical and conceptual development. However, the bulk of e-textbook solutions and implementations models currently available are not making use of the full potential of digital media and technology in educational use contexts.

4   Students' Performance and Experiences with E-textbooks

Aside from research on economical and interactivity issues, another prominent strand in the field of e-textbook research is related to students' experiences, perceptions and performance with e-textbooks. This research strand is dominant in higher education settings (see for example 14-21], however, a few studies can be found also in the context of K-12 education (see for instance [22-24]).

Typical research questions in this strand are for instance: *How do students experience and perceive e-textbooks in comparison to their printed versions? Do e-textbooks enhance or influence students' performance and overall learning activity? ... and so forth*. The findings are mixed. Shepperd et al. [17], for example, found that students using e-textbooks spent less time on reading for class compared to students using printed texts. In addition, they were not interested in a continued use of e-textbooks (as a replication of the printed version). Similar conclusions are made by McGowan et al. [14] who claim that an overwhelming number of students prefer paper based textbooks.

While some authors emphasise that the experience of reading e-books is not equivalent to reading e-textbooks [25], studies on reading capability and behavior in respect to e-textbooks demonstrate that students do not prefer them over printed textbooks regardless of their gender, level of computer use, or comfort with computers. E-textbooks are regularly perceived as even more time consuming than working with paper based texts (see for example [26, 27]. Thus, some authors conclude that paper based textbooks should not be readily abandoned. Simon's [18] study, however, demonstrates quite the opposite. He explored students' e-reading habits and reported that students who volunteered using e-textbooks were happy about the experience, mainly because e-textbooks allowed some additional functions such as glossary look-up and bookmarking features to be used [18].

With respect to improved student performance there are rather incompatible research results reported. They range from claims that learners do not perform differently, or significantly better, with current e-textbooks (e.g. [27]) to claims that students who engage with e-textbooks show higher motivation and better learning outcomes (e.g. [4]).

Sun et al. [19] studied how an e-textbook can facilitate college students' learning, how well it promotes student's involvement in learning, and how much it improves learning outcomes. Their results indicate that e-textbooks are perceived as enhancers of student learning outcomes and involvement. Positive findings were also demonstrated by [16] who claim that textbooks can be extremely popular and widely used - mainly for obtaining snippets of information and for fact-finding. The main reason for using e-textbooks among the students apparently was ease of access and convenience [16].

In the context of K-12 education system, Luik and Mikk [23] designed a study that explored which characteristics of electronic textbooks correlated with knowledge acquisition by learners of different achievement levels. They concluded that not only the content of e-textbooks but also the design of the e-textbook software should be adapted according to the different achievement levels of students [23]. Lau [22] reports that e-textbooks should be seen as an extension of printed textbooks - not a replacement but an enhancement. Lau also suggests that younger students adopt e-textbooks a lot easier, while adult learners seem to be more reluctant.

5   The Limited Popularity of E-textbooks

Whenever a new tool or technology comes along there is the potential for disruption to the existing order of activity and practice [28]. According to Smith et al. [28] disruption comes mainly in two forms: "e-[text]books can enable us to do the same things but in different ways, but they can also enable us to do different things – things that we were not able to easily do before they arrived or even do at all" (p. 50). While we are not denying the importance of economical considerations and the examination of new affordances for interaction that e-textbooks provide, we want to suggest that it seems crucial to raise some fundamental questions regarding educational practices mediated by digital texts and their further development:

In what ways is digitisation transforming our current teaching and learning practices and the use of textual artefacts?

How can we re-conceptualise the textbook and textbook-like procedures in the context of the ongoing digital transformation?

What kind of digital artefacts might be betters suited to mediate individual and collaborative knowledge construction in an increasingly networked environment?... and so forth.

From our perspective, not addressing these type of questions and issues constitutes the main underlying weakness of the current use of e-textbooks in education. The continuous attempt to replace printed textbooks with their digital copies - without rethinking the educational practices that underpin the use of these resources – seems to be an important reason why electronic textbooks have not grown in popularity so far [2]. Resnick [29], among many others, believes that "teachers will continue to look for and use print materials because they like to teach with books, and books still do work when used correctly" (p. 176). On the other hand, contrary to Resnick [29], Warlick [30] and others suspect that in some cases teachers are dropping their traditional textbooks and exclusively use their digital materials that they curate or design themselves. Salpeter [31] even claims that good teachers stopped using textbooks years ago. In addition, as lessons and subjects become more and more interdisciplinary in nature - a demand that is explicitly formulated in some contemporary curricula - it is increasingly difficult to find a textbook that effectively covers all topics for a particular lesson. Many teachers already supplement or entirely replace their lessons with informational resources found and customised from the Internet.

To conclude this section, e-textbooks in their current form have not made a proper entrance into K-12 education. What seems to be missing is an examination of current and evolving educational practices and their mediation with digital texts [28]. What seems to work in the context of general e-book consumption, for example, does not necessarily work for using e-textbooks in an educational setting. While simply turning traditional books into e-books has been a relatively successful practice, there is some evidence that this might not hold true for e-textbooks. After all, textbooks provide specific types of content and structure, and cater to different purposes.

6   Re-conceptualising E-textbooks

The textbook is an evolving instrument: from papyrus scrolls to illuminated texts of monastic libraries to mass-produced, richly appointed books [30]. In the midst of the unfolding digital transformation the textbook will most likely go through more thorough changes over time. After all "...the textbook is constantly updated right before our eyes" [30, p. 29]. Our literature review has produced so far only a small number of contributions that attempt to re-conceptualise the e-textbook altogether. Park et al. [32], for example, propose a digital textbook, which is built on a problem-based learning model. Smith et al. [28], on the other hand, propose that e-[text]books can be (re-)conceptualised in numerous ways:

- As stand-alone resources to be consulted by individual learners, for convenience or for reasons of preference;
- As part of an ecology or abundance of resources;
- As a bridge between informal and formal learning;
- As new cognitive tools that exploit multimedia capabilities to engage and reinforce learning;
- As social tools enabling community-building through sharing or collaborative annotation;
- As a further step towards greater inclusion and accessibility;
- As part of an emerging industry of self-publishing and disaggregated content.

Their conceptualisations of e-textbooks are seemingly close to the notion of *open (-access) e-textbooks* – a concept that has gained attention and popularity in recent years. Although this strand of thinking carries a strong economical connotation, it also opens up some new pedagogical opportunities. Some hold the view that open e-textbooks are indeed the future [33] and hold the potential to change the way textbooks are used, produced, and sold. Kanter et al. [34] define an open textbook very generally, and somewhat medium-independent, as "a body of educational content made openly available via the Internet, by mail, or in a bookstore with a copyright license that permits reproduction and distribution by the user" (p. 2). Among other characteristics, open textbooks are "protected by the creative commons license by which content may be copied, shared, or changed so long as the original author is attributed; they are developed by a community of authors or users and intended for educational purposes; and they are free" [35, p. 69]. Some authors maintain that being "open" makes it possible to keep content current, timely, and fresh; personalise, customise and localise it for a lesson [36]; marry the content with pedagogy and curriculum for a richer experience; break the textbook into granular pieces for instructors to bring in local context; and make the content portable and adaptable [35].

There are many initiatives for open-access textbooks (see for instance [35]). One good example comes from the CK 12 Foundation (http://ckI2.org) which provides open-access content through what they call FlexBooks, allowing teachers to author, modify, customize, and assemble existing content into books that fit the needs of the classroom or an individual student. They have established a community of educators and students who create, access, share, rate, recommend and publish. Subject matter experts and practitioners review the content produced. In addition it is ensured that the content is aligned to state and national curriculum standards. "The collaborating experience introduces an element of peer-review and in that way contributes to the authority of the information presented" [33, p. 3].

This type of e-textbook approach is a step further in the overall e-textbook evolution in an economical and pedagogical sense because open-access textbooks emphasise a crowd-based co-authoring approach and the formation of a community enabling anyone to contribute and modify the textbook. This type of "model" stresses the teacher as an important and necessary contributor to the creation of e-textbooks. It demonstrates the fact that textbook authors and publishing companies cannot expect to be anymore the sole authors and owners of content. Open e-textbooks allow teachers the freedom to choose and compile their own resources to cater to particular curriculum objectives [33].

Warlick [30] pondered already in 2006: "If teachers are beginning to construct the online digital textbook for their students, might there be some value in asking students to assemble their own textbooks? Is there some relevance in the 21st century to make students producers of their learning resources rather than mere consumers?" (p. 29). He continued his line of thinking in the following words:

"…Think for a minute about learning environments where one of the jobs of the student is to research, select, collect, organise, and adapt content from various resources and assemble that information into a growing and evolving digital textbook, supervised both directly and digitally by the teacher. The student's textbook would be crafted for his or her learning style, special interests, and personal sense of visual preference. Teachers would monitor their students' textbooks by suggesting additional resources, questioning others, and supporting the ongoing assembly" [30 p. 29].

A few years later Rampell [37] talks about online, peer-reviewed, interactive, user-editable e-textbooks as "social learning" sites, where students can chat and share notes while reading and instructors can edit the authors' words without permission. A similar vision (students as textbook generators) is proposed also by Smith et al. [28] and Sharples et al. [38]. They continue that "a logical extension to this mass sharing of comments is for students to write additions to textbooks, offering their own interpretations, explanations and examples, which they can then publish alongside pages of the book. Book publishers would need to set up a simple system of publishing and reward for such 'book extensions" [38 p. 9]. Because of the emergence of e-textbooks Moorefield-Lang [39] imagines students to become contributors of knowledge. They can read the book, take notes, add and share those notes, and contribute to the body of knowledge at large [39]. Her ideas are aligned with Scardamalia and Bereiter [40], who see students as a resource that has been largely wasted and that can be brought into play through pervasive technology. Students can construct and build their own knowledge by incorporating artifacts, which are professionally developed by instructional designers, teachers, and others. Students as creators are expected to gain more profound knowledge and become part of the collective intelligence [39]. In that way, e-textbooks are not anymore only representations of political, cultural, economic and political battles and compromises of small expert groups, but interlaced with students views, artifacts and knowledge. From this perspective the next generation e-textbooks will become information artefacts that need to be explored and co-created, rather than a road to be walked [30].

7   Breaking Down the Textbook and Textbook Procedure

While going through the current e-textbook literature we have also come across a few position papers that argue for a more drastic kind of change. Their authors want to do away with textbooks and the "all done by the textbook"-approach entirely - no matter if based on printed or digital material. They claim that textbooks are becoming less and less useful, both to students and instructors [2]. They see it as increasingly problematic that both textbooks and e-textbooks are generally designed to be read from beginning to end [41] as a coherent and predefined whole that learners and teachers need to work through in a linear fashion. For instance, Salpeter [31] in her article refers to Matt Federoff, director of technology for the Vail School District (Arizona), who claims that "the textbook delivery model is out of gas. No job in the world says read the chapter and answer the questions at the end of the book... Why should we take pre-packaged bulky content and try to shoehorn it into what we need to teach?" The possible alternative could be "the iTunes model" which allows for buying individual songs rather than the whole album. Similarly, instead of acquiring the whole textbook, a teacher might want to access only a small part of it. Since such a system of provision is already available for video and music content, some think it could easily be transferred to the field of learning and teaching [39].

A rather similar stance is also taken by Davy [42], a progressive publisher who suggests to cluster professionally authored content items around a specific learning objective, rather than providing a complete textbook. In this model the textbook becomes a resource, which is broken down into its components that can be accessed in a number of different ways. Butler [41] envisions a practice in which teachers can customise e-textbooks as aggregations of various materials, not just what a single publisher has already aggregated in a particular textbook. However, the report delivered by MindCET [43] warns us that we are running "the risk of taking the digital textbook to become a collection of digital items, missing the main educational message of offering a meaningful educational learning environment" [43, p. 2].

8   Conclusions

We are well aware of the limitations that go along with reporting from an analytical work in progress, however, we were able to identify some initial strands and concerns related to the current state of e-textbook research. So far the evolution of the textbook is predominantly driven by economic considerations - from the printing press to digital production, and from digital production to digital distribution - often leaving untouched issues of educational practice in the context of a wider socio-technological landscape that is increasingly dominated by digitisation and networking. Our literature review has shown so far that despite of some occasional, positive results in terms of student performance, current e-textbooks mimicking their print counterparts do not seem to be an attractive proposition for students, regardless of the economic benefits, flexibility, accessibility, and alleged attractiveness that has been attributed to them (see [26, 44-46]. The simple content digitisation that forms the basis for many contemporary e-textbook initiatives might serve as yet another example for the rather restricted and uninspired ways in which ICT is used in today's classrooms and schools, basically recreating traditional teaching and studying approaches with some digital means [47]. While we have found some promising examples of work that explicitly focuses on a more ambitious re-conceptualisation of the notion e-textbooks in formal education, the majority of published research doesn't seem to share such a progressive agenda. Apparently, it rather follows what Fischer and Scharff [48] had so aptly called the "gift wrapping approach" in which digital technology is merely wrapped around old frameworks for education. To overcome this state of affairs we need more analytically driven efforts that follow a research rationale that is based on a notion of systemic intervention into current educational practice (see for example, [49, 50]). While we are trying to develop our own project work (Learnmix) into this direction, we will continue our ongoing review project and hope to report a more differentiated analysis of our still expanding literature base in the near future. Up to now we have only been able to draw some main demarcation lines and to highlight visible directions in the field.

Acknowledgement. This research has been produced in the context of LEARNMIX project (No RU/3013) funded by Archimedes Foundation.

References

1. Nelson, M.: E-books in higher education: Nearing the end of the era of hype? Educase Review 43(2) (2008)
2. McFall, R.: Electronic textbooks that transform how textbooks are used. The Electronic Library 23(1), 72–81 (2005)
3. Hutchinson, T., Torres, E.: The textbook as agent of change. ELT Journal 48(4), 315–328 (1994)
4. Maynard, S., Cheyne, E.: Electronic textbooks help children to learn? The Electronic Library 23(1), 103–115 (2005)
5. Warren, J.W.: Innovation and the future of e-books. The International Journal of the Book 6(1), 83–93 (2009)
6. Bell, S.: Textbook turmoil: Library's role in the textbook revolution. Library Issues 31(1) (2010)
7. Schuetze, C.F.: Textbooks finally take a big leap to digital. The New York Times (2011), http://www.nytimes.com/2011/11/24/world/americas/schoolwork-gets-swept-up-in-rush-to-go-digital.html
8. Tomassini, J.: Educators weigh e-textbook cost comparisons. Education Week 31(30), 17–19 (2012)
9. Young, J.R.: Format war heats up among publishers of electronic textbooks. The Chronicle of Higher Education (2010), http://chronicle.com/article/Format-War-Heats-Up-Among/64323/
10. Young, J.R.: How Kindle could change the textbook market. Chronicle of Higher Education 55(36) (2009)
11. Vasileiou, M., Hartley, R., Rowley, J.: An overview of the e-book marketplace. Online Information Review 33(1), 173–192 (2009)

12. Tezak, D.: Digital textbooks with workbooks for elementary and secondary education. In: Cohen, E., Boyd, E. (eds.) Proceedings of the IS 2003 Informing Science + IT Education Conference, pp. 1509–1512. Turku School of Economics and Business Administration Pori Unit, Pori (2003)

13. Severin, E., Capota, C.: The use of technology in education: lessons from South Korea. IDB Education 10, 1–8 (2011)

14. McGowan, M.K., Stephens, P.R., West, C.: Students perceptions of electronic textbooks. Issues in Information Systems 10(2), 459–465 (2009)

15. Nicholas, A.J., Lewis, J.K.: The net generation and e-textbooks. Faculty and Staff - Articles & Papers, Paper 17 (2009)

16. Nicholas, D., Rowlands, I., Jamail, H.R.: E-textbook use, information seeking behaviour and it impact: Case study business and management. Journal of Information Science 36(2), 263–280 (2010)

17. Shepperd, J.A., Grace, J.L., Koch, E.J.: Evaluating the electronic textbook: Is it time to dispense with the paper text? Teaching of Psychology 35(1), 2–5 (2008)

18. Simon, E.J.: Electronic textbooks: A pilot study of student e-reading habits. Future of Print Media Journal Winter 2001, 1–5 (2001)

19. Sun, J., Floers, J., Tanguma, J.: E-textbooks and students' learning experiences. Decision Sciences Journal of Innovative Education 10(1), 63–77 (2012)

20. Vernon, R.F.: Teaching notes. Paper of pixels? An inquiry into how students adapt to online textbooks. Journal of Sociai Work Education 42(2), 417–427 (2010)

21. Weisberg, M.: Student attitudes and behaviors towards digital textbooks. Publishing Research Quarterly 27(2), 188–196 (2011)

22. Lau, J.: Students' experience of using electronic textbooks in different levels of education. SCROLL. Essays on the Design of Electronic Text 1(1) (2008)

23. Luik, P., Mikk, J.: What is important in electronic textbooks for students of different achievement levels? Computers & Education 50, 1483–1494 (2008)

24. Seo, Y., Lee, Y.: Meta analysis on the digital textbook's effectiveness on learning attitude. In: Wong, S.L., et al. (eds.) Proceedings of the 18th International Conference on Computers in Education. Asia-Pacific Society for Computers in Education, Malaysia (2010)

25. Woody, W.D., Daniel, D.B., Baker, C.A.: E-books or textbooks: Students prefer textbooks. Computers & Education 55, 945–948 (2011)

26. Clyde, L.A.: Electronic books. Teacher Librarian 32(5), 45–47 (2005)

27. Daniel, D.B., Woody, W.D.: E-textbooks at what cost? Performance and use of electronic v. print text. Computers & Education 62, 18–23 (2013)

28. Smith, M., Kukulska-Hulme, A., Page, A.: Educational use cases from a shared exploration of e-books and iPads. In: Goh, T.-T. (ed.) E-Books and E-Readers for E-Learning, pp. 25–53. Victoria Business School, Victoria University of Wellington, Wellington (2012)

29. Resnick, R.M.: School market size, growth and the shift to digital resources in K-12 Classrooms. Publishing Research Quarterly 27(2), 169–177 (2011)

30. Warlick, D.: Textbooks of the future. It's time the textbook industry redefined what they do and how they do it. Technology & Learning, 28–29 (May 2004)

31. Salpeter, J.: Textbook deathwatch. Technology & Learning 30(1), 26–30 (2009)

32. Park, C.-S., Kim, M., Yoo, K.-H.: Design and implementation of a problem-based digital textbook. International Journal of Software Engineering and Its Applications 6(4), 213–222 (2012)

33. Szeto, H.: Open source digital textbooks for secondary schools. Access to Knowledge: A Course Journal 1(2), 1–8 (2009)
34. Kanter, M., Baker, J.: Sustainability models for community college open textbooks (2008), http://cosl.usu.edu/events/opened2008/full_papers/Sustainabi lity_Models_baker_thierstein_kanter_forte.doc
35. Polanka, S.: Exploring open access e-textbooks. Booklist 106(16), 69 (2010)
36. Matkin, G.: Open learning: What do open textbooks tell us about the revolution in education? Research & Occasional Paper Series: CSHE 1.09 (2009), http:// cshe.berkeley.edu/publications/docs/ ROPs-Matkin-OpenLearning-03-31-09.pdf
37. Rampell, C.: Free textbooks: An online company tries a controversial publishing model. Chronicle of Higher Education 54(34), 1–2 (2008)
38. Sharples, M., McAndrew, P., Weller, M., Ferguson, R., Fitzgerald, E., Hirst, T., Mor, Y., Gaved, M., Whitelock, D.: Innovating pedagogy 2012: Open University Innovation Report 1. The Open University, Milton Keynes (2012)
39. Moorefield-Lang, H.: An exploration of e-textbooks. Library Media Connection, 18–19 (May/June 2013)
40. Scardamalia, M., Bereiter, C.: Higher levels of agency for children in knowledge-building: A challenge for the design of new knowledge media. The Journal of the Learning Sciences 1(1), 37–68 (1991)
41. Butler, D.: The textbook of the future. Nature 458(2) (2009)
42. Davy, T.: E-textbooks: opportunities, innovations, distractions and dilemmas. Serials 20(2), 98–102 (2007)
43. MindCET: The future of digital textbooks (2012), http://www.mindcet.org/ wp-content/uploads/2012/10/ Digital-Textbooks.-A-literature-review1.pdf
44. Coleman, G.: E-books and academics: An ongoing experiment. Canadian Library Association Feliciter 4, 124–125 (2004)
45. Long, S.A.: The case for e-books: An introduction. New World Library 104(1/2), 29–32 (2003)
46. Myers, D.G.: Using new interactive media to enhance the teaching of psychology (and other disciplines) in developing countries. Perspectives on Psychological Science 4(1), 99–100 (2009)
47. Hedberg, J.G., Chang, C.H.: G-Portal: Supporting argumentation and multimodality in student solutions to geographical problems. In: Kommers, P., Richards, G. (eds.) Proceedings of ED-MEDIA 2005 World Conference on Educational Multimedia, Hypermedia and Telecommunications, pp. 4242–4247. Association for the Advancement of Computing in Education, Norfolk (2005)
48. Fischer, G., Scharff, E.: Learning technologies in support of self-directed learning. Journal of Interactive Media in Education 98(4) (1998)
49. Fiedler, S.H.D.: Emancipating and developing learning activity: Systemic intervention and re-instrumentation in higher education. Painosalama, Turku (2012)
50. Fiedler, S., Väljataga, T.: Interventions for second-order change in higher education: Challenges and barriers. Electronic Journal of e-Learning 8(2), 85–92 (2010)

Novel Approaches in eLearning

HIP – A Technology-Rich and Interactive Multimedia Pedagogical Platform

Ali Shariq Imran and Stewart James Kowalski

Norwegian Information Security Lab, Gjøvik University College, Norway
{ali.imran,stewart.kowalski}@hig.no

Abstract. Technology enhanced learning is a key part of learning and teaching in most of the higher education. It not only provides easy access to pedagogical content of interest with few clicks, but it is a great way to acquire knowledge at ones doorstep. Many universities are providing distance and blended education programs through eLearning platforms, learning management systems (LMS) and smart tools, along side traditional lectures for on campus students. The use of recorded lecture videos and audios, lecture notes, presentation slides, handouts, etc., are commonly used to disseminate knowledge via various eLearning platforms. While these platforms are a good way to reach out to off-campus students, they often lack a two-way communication between a student and a teacher, and the interactivity with the content. The lack of real-time interactivity and right communication channel make online courses less effective. To address this problem we propose the use of an intelligent pedagogical media called hyper interactive presenter (HIP).

Keywords: eLearning, pedagogical platforms, hyper media, interactive media, intelligent chat bot.

1 Introduction

Numerous eLearning platforms, educational tools, learning management systems (LMS), and open educational video resources have emerged in the last decade with rapid development in eLearning technology. These include Fronter [1], ATutor [2], Moodle [3], Khan academy [4], Coursea [5], edX [6] etc. These eLearning platforms and tools provide useful mechanism of delivering educational resources for distance and blended education. The resources normally comprise of recorded lecture videos, PowerPoint presentation slides, audio transcripts, and related documents. They are stored locally on the server or in learning object repository (LOR) such as MERLOT [7] , either centrally or distributed. Learning objectives are defined and meta-data is associated with these resources before they are distributed to masses as learning objects (LO) [8], via eLearning platforms.

Despite successfully delivering the LOs, existing LMS and other eLearning platforms still have not succeeded in capturing the real essence of a LO i.e. interoperability, reusability, and most importantly the interactivity. Users may be able to browse, locate and view the content in existing systems but they often

P. Zaphiris and A. Ioannou (Eds.): LCT 2014, Part I, LNCS 8523, pp. 151–160, 2014.

cannot navigate to certain portion within the text, audio or video content. The associated meta-data is often used only to search, store, and index educational resources. It hasn't been used to train and teach the system to adapt itself based on users' learning needs.

Theories like learning styles should also be taken into consideration. Learning styles is a theory developed based on the fact that the ability of every individual to process information differs during the learning process. In other words, every individual learns in a different way [9]. Although studies showed no concrete evidence that learning styles can improve the knowledge acquisition process of students in classroom environment, they nevertheless remained significant and resulted in different models in order to categorize learning style [10].

With the evolution of eLearning, more studies were conducted in order to see if the learning styles affect the quality of learning through eLearning platforms and if there is any difference between the way of learning through the classroom and the eLearning platforms. The findings of studies like the one performed by Manochehr [11], showed that learning styles although they are irrelevant when the students are in a classroom, they had statistically significant value according to the knowledge performance in a web-based eLearning environment.

There are possibly many ways to transfer knowledge to individuals based on their learning style [12]. The success of a learning process is depended upon two factors – users' learning style or preferences and the way the knowledge is presented to the user. Fleming's VARK model [13] has grouped learners into four categories: visual, audio, read/write and kinesthetic. To aid the learning process, we need to deliver the educational resources adhering to users' preferences based on their learning style [14]. Existing eLearning platforms mostly rely only lecture videos, which tend to be oriented towards visual learners. In addition, lecture videos are often quite large, lacks interactivity, and are normally non-structured. This makes it difficult for the learners to keep their interest level high.

In this paper, we propose a technology-rich pedagogical media platform called hyper interactive presenter (HIP). The aim of HIP is to provide an interactive learning environment to users by incorporating the concept of nano-learning [15], and to address the above stated issues by creating effective multimedia learning objects (MLO); a platform where users can interact with educational content comprising of structured multimedia. The platform is in development stage and is currently being used for research purpose only.

The rest of the paper is organized as follows. In section 2, we present the proposed platform. Section 3 presents the initial experimental results on the evaluation of HIP, while section 4 concludes our paper.

2   Hyper Interactive Presenter

HIP is an eLearning platform that provides technology-rich pedagogical media for continuous education and connected learning. It combines four media modalities to suit ones learning styles. These include text documents such as wiki pages and pdf documents, PowerPoint presentations, lecture videos (visual/aural), and

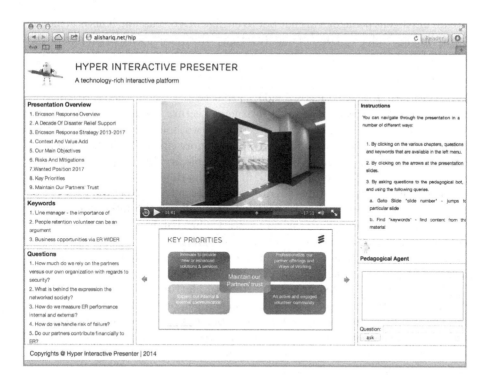

Fig. 1. A sample screen shot of hyper interactive presenter (HIP)

an interactive dialogue (intelligent pedagogical agent) along with navigational links, tagged keywords, and frequently asked questions (FAQ). HIP supports nano-learning by creating smaller chunks of video learning objects (VLOs), and hyperlinking similar LOs across different media.

HIP comprises of many media elements, which are assembled in different sections (components), and are bundled (interlinked) together to form a HIP page. These components are designed to support different types of learning styles. Figure 1 shows an example of a HIP page layout with different components.

2.1   HIP Components

HIP comprises of four main components. The components are designed to present the knowledge in number of ways, utilizing all the available media modalities. These include hyper-video, PowerPoint presentation slides, documents, and a pedagogical agent. We use these different media modalities in HIP to map the VARK model, in order to support variety of learning styles.

It is a well-established fact that about approximately 65% of the population are visual learners while others are textual learners [16], and 90 percent of information that comes to the brain is visual [17]. HIP therefore, supports different learning styles by combining visual information with the text, and by providing users with an intelligent pedagogical chat bot to engage in a discussion. This is achieved by interlinking different components together, which are briefly explained in the following section.

Hyper-Video. Recorded lecture videos are used as an educational resource to primarily assist visual and auditory learners. Lecture videos are usually very long. A lecture video can often last for one to two hours and it can contain a variety of different information, covering one or more subjects. For these reasons lecture videos are very rich media with high complexity. Even though numerous lecture videos are available on the web, most of the time they lack the necessary supporting information and metadata; they are usually unstructured, unedited, and non-scripted. This makes it extremely difficult for the interested student to find relevant information easy and fast. Taking bandwidth limitations into account the process becomes even more challenging.

HIP on the other hand, provides a hyper-video; segmented, structured and edited VLO, based on the concept of nano-learning. A lecture video undergoes a series of image and video processing steps to identify area of interest (AOI). The AOI could be a start of a question, a new topic, or a pause during a lecture etc. The identified AOIs are used as index points to create a smaller segment of a video called VLO from the full-length instructional video. The index points are used to create hyperlinks to jump to particular timestamps in the video for quick navigation.

PowerPoint Presentations. The second main component that defines HIP consists of PowerPoint slides. The use of slides caters to visual as well as textual learners. PowerPoint presentations are processed independently to create images of slides that are used in the HIP. The images are synchronized with corresponding lecture video via presentation overview. A presentation overview provides navigational links to jump directly to a desired slide and to corresponding timestamp in a video. Each slide title is automatically extracted to create a presentation overview.

Semantic keywords are also extracted from presentation slides to create navigational links and tag clouds. A tag cloud represents important words used in the instructional content. The more important a word is in the given context the bigger its size in a tag cloud. The importance of a word is computed based on its frequency, its font size in PowerPoint slides, and the amount of time it was visible in a particular shot in the corresponding video. Tag clouds are used to provide a time-aligned navigation to hyper-video, PowerPoint presentation slides, and text documents. Figure 3 shows an example of a tag cloud.

Documents. The document section is aimed at textual learners, learners who prefer to read and go through details rather than watching and listening to videos and to slides. The document section primarily constitutes lecture notes, handouts, and/or wiki pages. These documents provide detailed content and

Fig. 2. An example of a 3-dimensional tag cloud for HIP.

additional references to presented material in lecture videos and PowerPoint slides.

Pedagogical Agent. The pedagogical agent is an artificial intelligent markup language (AIML) based chat bot that act as the brain of the HIP. It is primarily intended for a variety of different learning styles. For instance, it can benefit learners that like to read and write. It is also very useful for auditory learners that learn better through discussion.

The pedagogical agent provides interactivity to the user, responds to their queries, find relevant material and concepts from within the lecture material including lecture videos, PowerPoint slides, and documents, and it communicates with users. The pedagogical agent has to be fed with the course domain knowledge to be able to interact intelligently, and engage in a discussion with users. The chat bot is a great way to interact with the user in real-time in absence of a teacher, as is normally the case with existing eLearning platforms. This will most likely keep users interest level optimal, and will help speed up the learning activity.

In addition, the relevant meta-data information is also extracted for each segment of a LO. The meta-data partially comes from videos such as the timestamps i.e. start time and the end time of a particular segment, and partially from accompanying material such as PowerPoint slides, audio transcripts and other textual documents. The meta-data is used for creating hyperlinks among different media components of same LOs, and for segmentation and structuring of MLOs.

2.2 HIP in Action

HIP provides two-way synchronization between PowerPoint slides and corresponding lecture videos. For instance, if someone browse presentation slides, the video automatically jumps to start of a segment in video that contains that particular slide and vice versa. At the same time, corresponding content from the document would appear in the document section. If it were a wiki document, the page containing the corresponding information would appear. Similarly, the presentation outline, extracted keywords and/or key phrases along with FAQ are all linked to their corresponding VLOs, PowerPoint presentation slides, and to accompanying documents/wiki pages.

For example, if one clicks a keyword about 'eLearning', appropriate video segment would appear which talks about the given topic i.e. eLearning in this case, and the corresponding slide would appear that was used during the talk, along with wiki page containing information about eLearning. In addition, it is possible to query the system via pedagogical agent to navigate to a particular topic simultaneously across different media.

2.3 Case Senario

A simple case scenario would be that a user logs into his profile and navigate to weekly lectures of the course he has registered. In weekly lectures the user is provided with synchronized and structured HIP page.

Being a visual learner a user can play a video from start and watch it till end. At the same time the PowerPoint slides automatically changes as the user progress through the video, and the corresponding document will show up. If at any stage a user feels like going through the slide for better understanding, he can pause the video and look at the corresponding slide. Likewise, he can refer to the document for even detailed information. A user can also query the pedagogical agent to inquire about a particular topic or a concept if it is not elaborated enough in the material. The agent will answer to user questions, and will find requested information. The user can then engage in a discussion with the pedagogical agent as if he is corresponding to a course instructor.

Contrary to visual learners, the textual learners can directly go through the text document or PowerPoint slides. If they do not understand any concept or topic, they can play the synchronized video from the point where they are in the slide and/or document, and listen to the explanation provided by the teacher in the video.

3 Experiment and Results

We conducted an experiment to evaluate the usefulness of HIP. The experiment is divided into two parts. The first part of the experiment group students into four categories based on their learning preferences. A standard VARK questionnaire was used to differentiate students' learning style and to group them as visual,

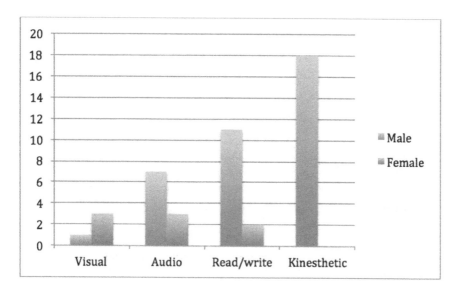

Fig. 3. Grouping of students based on VARK learning model

audio, text and kinesthetic learners [10]. The questionnaire was distributed to 55 students comprising of bachelor and master level at Gjøvik university college (GUC). The students were grouped into their respective category based on their learning style, to have an equal distribution for the second part of the experiment. The distribution of students is shown in Figure 3.

In second part of the experiment, the students were asked to go through the HIP and non-HIP version of recorded lectures and to give their appreciation on a Likert scale from 1 to 5, where 1 corresponds to strongly disagree while 5 corresponds to strongly agree.

The first four questions were aimed towards usability study of HIP in comparison to existing system *(fronter)* at GUC. The questions were:

1. Covering material through HIP is more useful?
2. It is easy to cover material through HIP?
3. Finding material in HIP is less time consuming?
4. Reviewing the material is easier than existing system?

The initial feedback was encouraging. 80% of the participants agree in response to first question, whereas, 5% responded neutral and 15% against it. For the second question, 85% students find it easy to cover the material through HIP, while 15% disagree. Similar trend were observed for other questions. The results are shown in Figure 4. Mostly students responded in favor of HIP when asked if they would recommend a fellow student to use HIP, and if they will prefer to use such a system to prepare for the exams. The results are depicted in Figure 5.

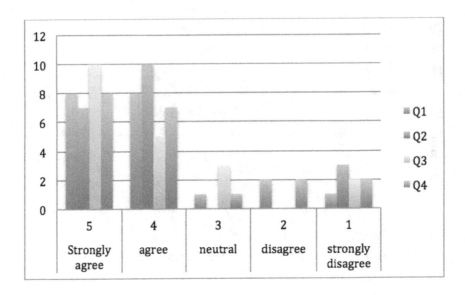

Fig. 4. Students' response on a Likert scale of 1-5 for first four questions

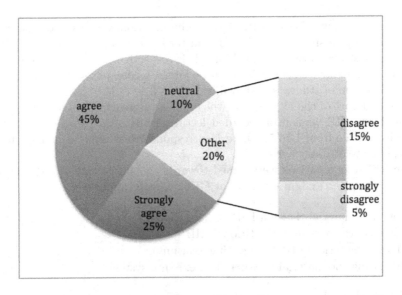

Fig. 5. Students' response to recommend and use HIP for preparation for exams

The findings of our initial experiment suggests that about 80% of the students would prefer HIP compared to the existing system in use at GUC. This is due to the fact that many students find it easy to navigate and jump through the material without browsing the full video and presentation slides. On the contrary, few students were reluctant to adapt to the new environment, as they were comfortable using the old one and would not like to switch.

4   Conclusion

HIP provides technology-rich and interactive pedagogical hypermedia that supports multiple media modalities for fast and easy navigation of instructional content. It combines text, audio/video, and PowerPoint presentation slides to best suit individual's learning style. It also provides interactive tools such as pedagogical chat bot to engage the user in the learning process. HIP provides the users with the option to use the medium they are best adapted to. Thus maximizing the learning outcome and reducing the time one spend on learning activity. From initial empirical analysis, it is safe to conclude that such a system would prove beneficial for keeping the learners interest level high and attention span longer, ultimately maximizing the learning outcome. As a future work, subjective experiments are underway to evaluate the learning outcome experience of the users and the effectiveness of such a platform.

References

1. Pearson, Fronter, http://www.com.fronter.info (last accessed January 25, 2014)
2. ATutor, http://atutor.ca (last accessed January 26, 2014)
3. Moodle Trust, Moodle, http://moodle.org (last accessed January 26, 2014)
4. Khan Academy (2014), http://www.khanacademy.org (last accessed January 26, 2014)
5. Coursera, http://www.coursera.org (last accessed February 1, 2014)
6. edX, http://www.edx.org (last accessed February 1, 2014)
7. California State University, MERLOT II, http://www.merlot.org (last accessed February 1, 2014)
8. Northrup, P.T.: Learning objects for instruction: design and evaluation, pp. 1–348. IGI Global (2007)
9. Tuan, L.: Matching and stretching learners learning styles. Journal of Language Teaching and Research 2(2) (2011)
10. De Bello, T.C.: Comparison of eleven major learning styles models: Variables, appropriate populations, validity of instrumentation, and the research behind them. Journal of Reading, Writing, and Learning Disabilities International 6(3), 203–222 (1990)
11. Manochehr, N.-N.: The Influence of Learning Styles on Learners in E-Learning Environments: An Empirical Study 18, 10–14 (1999)
12. Felder, R.M., Silverman, L.K.: Learning and teaching styles in engineering education. Engineering Education 78(7), 674–681 (1988)
13. Fleming, N.: VARK a guide to learning styles. Wired (2001), http://www.vark-learn.com/english/page.asp?p=questionnaire (last accessed January 10, 2014)

14. Franzoni, A.L., Assar, S., Defude, B., Rojas, J.: Student learning styles adaptation method based on teaching strategies and electronic media. In: Eighth IEEE International Conference on Advanced Learning Technologies, ICALT 2008, pp. 778–782 (2008)
15. Masie, E.: Nano-Learning: Miniaturization of Design, Chief Learning Officer, http://clomedia.com/articles/view/nano_learning_miniaturization_of_design (last accessed February 4, 2014)
16. Jonassen, D.H., Carr, C., Yueh, H.P.: Computers as mindtools for engaging learners in critical thiking. TechTrends 43(2), 24–32 (1998)
17. Hyerle, D.: Visual Tools for Transforming Information into Knowledge, 2nd edn. Corwin (2009)

Cloud Storage Services in Higher Education – Results of a Preliminary Study in the Context of the Sync&Share-Project in Germany

Christian Meske[1], Stefan Stieglitz[1], Raimund Vogl[2],
Dominik Rudolph[2], and Ayten Öksüz[1]

[1] University of Muenster, Department of Information Systems, Germany
{christian.meske,stefan.stieglitz,ayten.oeksuez}@uni-muenster.de
[2] University of Muenster, ZIV-Centre for Applied Information Technology, Germany
{r.vogl,d.rudolph}@uni-muenster.de

Abstract. In recent years, a growing number of institutions in higher education is in progress to adopt cloud storage services. This paper describes the Sync&Share NRW-project in North Rhine-Westphalia (Germany) with a target audience of up to 500,000 users and presents the main results of a preliminary large-scale survey at the University of Muenster with more than 3,000 participants. The results of the analysis indicates a very high demand for an on-premise cloud service solution in German higher education with mobile access, a storage volume comparable to commercial offerings, collaborative features such as simultaneous work on text documents and, above all, high data protection standards.

Keywords: cloud storage services, higher education, technology adoption, trust.

1 Introduction

Cloud storage services like Dropbox allow users to store files remotely and to synchronize them over multiple devices. This approach has gained increasing attention during the last years. Beside the ubiquitous availability of personal files through mobile devices like smartphones and tablets, enhanced collaboration possibilities also contribute to the arguments for the use of such services. However, a still unsolved problem is the legal framework for governing cloud solutions. Until now, there exists no international legislation regarding data protection. Furthermore, national laws are rarely equivalent and can be even conflicting on a global level. The situation is aggravated by the fact that all major public cloud storage providers like Dropbox, Google, Amazon, Microsoft or Apple are located in the US. Latest revelations on the mass surveillance undertaken by the NSA caused a further loss of trust in public cloud services. In the academic community, the utilization of cloud services, free or paid, is not uncommon, even for storing sensible research and teaching data. This creates substantial data privacy and confidentiality issues.

P. Zaphiris and A. Ioannou (Eds.): LCT 2014, Part I, LNCS 8523, pp. 161–171, 2014.

Against this background, the leading IT managers of the majority of the research universities in North Rhine Westphalia (NRW) have launched the "Sync&Share NRW"-project with the aim to set up a cooperatively operated cloud storage platform for researchers and students. A consortium of research and applied science universities, headed by the University of Muenster and covering approx. 60 percent of the academic community in NRW, has been formed to design a system for possibly up to 500,000 users. In this paper, we describe and discuss the results of a large-scale survey conducted at the University of Muenster, which includes more than 3,000 responses.

This article is structured as follows. In the next section we provide a general introduction into cloud computing and cloud storage services in higher education. Afterwards, the design and structure of the survey as well as main facts regarding the group of participants will be described. In the subsequent section we present the main survey results. The paper concludes with a summary and some implications of the results as well as an outlook for further research and next steps of the Sync&Share-project.

2   Theoretical Background

2.1   Cloud Computing

As a new emerging technology and due to its considerable benefits for companies [1], cloud computing has gained a lot of attention in recent years. According to the definition of the National Institute of Standards and Technology (NIST), cloud computing is "a model for enabling ubiquitous, convenient, on-demand network access to a shared pool of configurable computing resources (e.g., networks, servers, storage, applications, and services) that can be rapidly provisioned and released with a minimal effort or service provider interaction as a pool of computing resources" [2]. There are three types of cloud computing service models: Software as a service (SaaS), platform as a service (PaaS), and infrastructure as a service (IaaS) [2-4]. In the case of SaaS, access to software is provided remotely as a web-based service [2]. PaaS provides a computing platform to allow users, mostly developers, to build applications and services over the internet [2]. In the case of IaaS, computing resources such as storage is provided through the internet [4]. Regarding the deployment models, four types can be distinguished: A private cloud is exclusively used by a single institution whereas a public cloud is used by the general public [2]. A community cloud is exclusively used by a community of users from institutions that have the same concerns (e.g. security or compliance requirements) [2]. A hybrid cloud is a composition of two or more cloud infrastructures. The physical location of the cloud infrastructure can be either off premise or on premise (except in the case of public clouds) [2].

2.2   Cloud Computing in Higher Education

Cloud computing is not only used in the business community. Educational establishments have also recognized the various benefits of using cloud computing services

[5]. As is the case with organizations, cloud computing can help to reduce universities' IT complexity and costs by replacing software installation on campus computers with applications delivered via the Internet [6]. Furthermore, due to web-based access, university teachers, students and staff can access educational tools or files saved in the cloud from almost any internet-capable device [7]. Especially in case of hardware failures, cloud computing can serve as an effective backup and recovery solution [8] for study related materials such as theses or research papers. In addition, cloud computing can be used to facilitate collaboration among working groups as well as between universities and their partner organizations [9, 10]. For example, a researcher team working on a paper can collectively create a temporary shared workspace and thus ease the joint work on this paper [10]. Since more and more researchers are working with team members from different universities and countries, this kind of virtual teamwork could gain in importance.

Statistics show that the use of cloud computing in educational institutions is on the rise. The CDW 2011 Cloud Computing Tracking Poll[1] for example reported that 34% of higher education institutions use some form of cloud computing [5]. A number of universities, such as the University of Westminster or the New York University, for example, use Google Apps for education which provides email and collaboration tools [11]. In the next years, higher education institutions even plan to spend more on cloud resources.

However, the use of public cloud at universities also entails certain risks such as privacy invasion or data security breaches [10]. For example, researchers storing research data in a public cloud could lose the copyright of their research work. Furthermore, universities could face regulatory compliance problems [12]. Employees of the university administration are working with very sensitive personal data of their students. When they store personal data of the students on the servers of a cloud provider, they lose a degree of control over these sensitive data [12]. The cloud provider then has to protect that data from hackers and internal data breaches rather than the university [12]. Nevertheless, the university has to comply with relevant regulatory laws as well as information security standards (e.g. ISO27001) and thus is still ultimately responsible for that data [12]. Due to certain characteristics of cloud computing, to fulfill this responsibility becomes a very challenging matter. In most cases for example, the storage location of the data is obscure and it is also unclear, who has accessed the data [13]. In addition, the university often does not exactly know which security measures the provider has implemented to secure the data [12]. These mentioned concerns indicate that a cloud computing system specifically for university purposes is needed. There are very few practical examples showing that this concept can succeed. The Oxford University together with VMware e.g. created a database-as-a-service (DBaaS) in a hybrid cloud for use by its researchers [15]. With this service,

---

[1] The CDW 2011 Cloud Computing Tracking Poll surveyed 1,200 IT professionals in U.S. organizations: small, medium, and large businesses, local government agencies, health care organizations as well as K-12 and higher education institutions.

researchers are able to securely store their research materials for easy access. In the following sections, we want to contribute to the discussion of cloud services in higher education on a large-scale basis.

3   Survey Structure and Participants

To study user expectations as well as acceptance on a broad basis, the Research Group for Communication and Collaboration Management (CCM) at the University of Muenster, which represents the headquarter of the European Research Center for Information Systems (ERCIS), conducted an online survey in cooperation with the Centre for Applied Information Technology (ZIV) at the University of Muenster. Established in 1780 and with 40,800 students as well as 6,650 employees (2013), the University of Muenster is one of the oldest and biggest universities in Germany, located in the federal state of North Rhine-Westphalia. All students and employees of the University of Muenster were invited to participate in the survey; 4,830 of them started and overall 3,774 (2,704 students and 1,070 employees) completed the questionnaire. Each of these participant groups, students and employees, were asked up to 27 questions, dependent on their replies to specific filter questions. Four topics were assessed in total. In the first section the respondent was assigned to a participant group (student or employee) and also to a specific area of studies (e.g. economic sciences). The second section served the goal of raising the status quo, by enquiring i.e. the actual memory storage requirements and gathered experience with other cloud storage services (e.g. Dropbox). In the third section the Sync&Share project was described in detail. Following, the relevance of certain properties, features and functionalities as well as the participant's willingness to use the service were surveyed. The last section included the sampling of demographic and additional personal data (age, gender, used devices and operating systems, etc.), that could be voluntarily provided by the respondents. The posed questions predominantly consisted of multiple choice questions that allowed both single and multiple selections of predefined answers. At some points, the participants were also able to leave comments, additions and specify their responses with regard to certain aspects, by using the provided text fields.

With regards to the group of participants in the collected data set, the majority of the students is between 20 and 30 years old (84%). 36% of the employees is between 20 and 30 and 32% between 31 and 40 years old. Furthermore, 57% of the students and 64% of the employees are male. 65% of the students (employees: 67%) rank their computer knowledge as "good" and 22% (employee: 26%) see themselves as experts. The majority of the surveyed students is enrolled in economic sciences (13%) respectively mathematics and informatics (11%), while the largest share of the participating employees works in the areas of medicine (17%) respectively chemistry and pharmacy (9%). With regard to the deployed operating systems on their PC/laptop, both user groups mainly use Windows (students: 76%; employees: 73%), followed by Mac OS (16% respectively 17%) and Linux (7% respectively 8%). Students use Android smartphones more frequently than employees (62% versus 52%), while the latter is more frequently in the possession of an iPhone (32% versus 40%).

4   Survey Results

4.1   Current Use of Cloud Services and Reasons for Rejection

85% of the students currently use at least one cloud service (employees: 73%). Most of them use Dropbox (79%; employees: 65%) and Google Drive (each 17%), as can be seen in fig. 1. The majority of the participants started to take notice of cloud services due to recommendations from their closer social environment like friends, relatives or colleagues (students: 81%; employees: 76%).

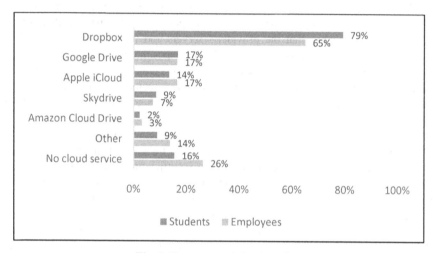

Fig. 1. Current use of cloud services

Students currently use cloud services for project work (83%) and teaching material (78%). Furthermore, cloud services are used for private pictures (54%) and other personal data (58%). Employees use cloud services mainly for work-related material (78%), private pictures (52%) and other private data (62%). The majority of the students states to use a study related data volume between 1,1 to 4,9 GB (30%). Others (21%) indicate a volume ranging from 5 to 10 GB. Only 3,3% utilize a volume from 21 to 30 GB and 5% more than 30 GB. By comparison, employees specify a considerably higher data volume. Here, the most frequently stated storage volume is more than 30 GB (20%). Another 19% claim a volume ranging from 5 to 9,9 GB and 17% a volume of 1,1 to 4,9 GB.

The most important reason for rejecting cloud storage services (multiple selections) is a low confidence in the data protection of commercial providers (students: 64%; employees: 62%). Based on a first analysis of answers on an open-ended question, answered by 1,636 (43%) of the survey participants, we were able to identify factors that are important for the trustworthiness of a provider. In this regard, data privacy and data protection are of top priority. Approximately 45% of all participants state that the provider has to consider certain technical aspects in order to be evaluated as trustworthy: the provider needs to implement measures for data privacy and protection, to comply with high security standards, to be certified by independent institutions, to ensure a high availability of the system, to use data encryption techniques also during data transmission and to realize access restrictions. In addition, 18% state that high transparency is an important criterion for establishing trust. The participants want to know, for example, who has access to their personal data, where the data is being stored, and which security measures are being implemented in order to ensure data protection and security. Furthermore, the comprehensiveness of the terms of conditions (AGB) and the privacy policy are mentioned. 42% of the respondents express that the provider should not only act in his own interest but also in the interest of the users. In addition, the data should not only be protected against the access of third parties, but also against the provider itself. Another aspect is legal compliance. The respondents, who mention this aspect, emphasize the importance that the provider's servers and jurisdiction are located in Germany. Furthermore, a closed-ended question indicates that universities per se enjoy a high level of trust. 81% of the students and 74% of the employees would trust a cloud provider more if it was a university rather than a private sector company.. The personal contact to the provider is named by 10% of the participants as another criterion for trust establishment.

The second most important reason for students' reluctance to use cloud services is "no current need" (41%), while this is only the case for 25% of the employees (see fig. 2). For the latter group of participants the insufficient presence of information (36%) is the second most important reason (students: 35%). For the majority of the participants, it is very or rather important that the provider gives them information regarding implemented security and privacy measures (students: 77%, employees: 82%), skills and responsibilities of their staff (students: 56%, employees: 69%), general information about their organization (students: 77%, employees: 75%) and descriptions of users' rights (students: 71%, employees: 67%). The fear of data loss is for both students (32%) and employees (28%) of comparatively low relevance.

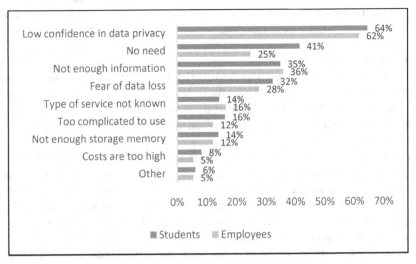

Fig. 2. Reasons for the disuse of cloud services

In an open text field, 24 participants give further indications for the disuse. In doing so, 29% again express their concern for data privacy concerns. 25% prefer other methods to share or backup data (e.g. "USB sticks are safer"; "I own a network drive (NAS)"). 17% state that there is a lack of motivation and time to deal with the topic.

4.2   Expectations Towards a Cloud Storage Service at the University

The expectations towards the features and functions of a university cloud storage service are quite homogenous among students and employees (see fig. 3).

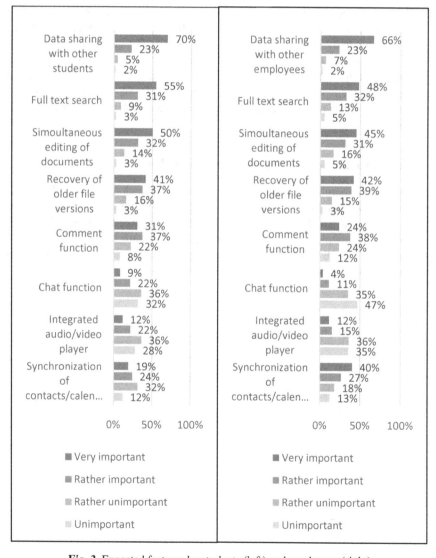

Fig. 3. Expected features by students (left) and employees (right)

The majority of both participant groups considers the possibility of flexible data sharing with other students/employees (students: 70%; employees: 66%), a full text search function (55% respectively 48%) and the simultaneous and collaborative editing of electronic documents as most important features.

With regard to the required properties and attributes, 74% of the students consider a constant availability on different devices very important (employees: 80%). Furthermore, 65% of the students agree on the high importance of the encryption of data (employees: 64%). The storage of the data on German server sites is regarded as very important by 41% of the students and 53% of the employees. With regard to the integration of existing learning systems, this is the case for 29% of the students and 44% of the employees. Concerning the preferred devices deployed for the use of the services, students would mainly use PCs/laptops (98%), followed by computers provided by the university (63%), and smartphones (59%). The employees specified to use their professional (95%) respectively private (79%) PC/laptop, followed by the private smartphone (48%). Moreover, 33% of the students and 37% of the employees consider their personal relationship to the provider of the service important. To have a local contact person is important for 67% of the students and for 76% of the employees.

4.3   Demanded Storage Volume and Intention to Use

With regard to the required memory storage offered by the cloud service, the participant groups show deviating volume needs (see fig. 4). While the surveyed students are predominantly satisfied with 1,1 to 4,9 GB (29%) respectively 5 to 9,9 GB (25%), the majority of the employees specifies a required data volume of 10 to 20 GB (25%) respectively 5 to 9,9 GB (20%). 12% of the employees state a required data volume of more than 40 GB what is only for 4% of the students the case.

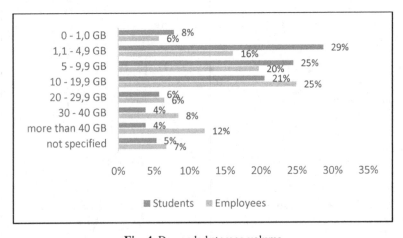

Fig. 4. Demanded storage volume

93% (employees: 90%) of all respondents have the intention to use the university cloud storage service. For the students who have already used cloud services in the past or present, the willingness to use the Sync&Share service (97%) is 22% higher than for students without any cloud experience (75%). Regarding the employees, the results are similar. 97% of the employees with cloud experience but only 76% of those without experiences with such kind of technology signalize an intention to use. 54% of the students and 45% of the employees that state to have the intention to use the cloud service would like to continue to use it even after their studies respectively employment ended. If the university does not facilitate continuous usage, 41% of the students would appreciate a transition period of three to six months (employees: 37%) and 38% of more than six months (employees: 36%).

Besides the descriptive statistics, we also searched in the data for factors influencing the willingness to use the university cloud service. Some results indicate that there might be few influencing factors especially with regard to students' willingness to use the cloud service.. For example, students who already use Dropbox, have a 13% lower willingness to change the provider and exclusively use the cloud service of the university. The more important the information regarding the data security, the higher is the willingness to solely use the service. Furthermore, 22% of the respondents who consider provided information regarding data security as "rather important" state that they would exclusively use the university cloud service while 28% of the participants who consider these information as "very important" give this response. The consideration of a German server site seems to have equal impact on the intention to use. The more a storage location in Germany is considered as important,, the higher is the willingness to exclusively use the university cloud service. 22% are among the participants who consider this as "rather important", while 33% select "very important" as their response.

5   Conclusion and Outlook

For the success of the described Sync&Share NRW-project, it is important to gain indications on how the cloud service should be designed to be attractive for the target audience. In this regard, identifying factors which positively impact the intension to use such a university cloud computing service is of high relevance. Furthermore, these results can contribute to knowledge regarding the use of cloud services in higher education in general. The survey shows that most of the survey participants already use or used cloud services for private or professional purposes. This is important, as the Sync&Share cloud storage service will not be a new technology to these persons, what in turn increases the chance of their cloud adoption compared to people without any cloud experience. The possibility of sharing data with other cloud users, a full text search function and the simultaneous editing of text documents are seen as the most relevant cloud service functions. Moreover, the students and employees emphasize the need for data access through different mobile devices such as laptops, tablets and smartphones.

Another crucial aspect has a high impact both on the design of the planned cloud service as well as on the willingness of the users to adopt it: data security. The survey reflects the awareness for data security issues, e.g. caused by the NSA scandal. At the moment, the majority of the participants uses cloud services such as Dropbox or Google Drive that store their data primarily on servers in the US. The survey indicates a significant distrust towards these commercial providers, while public academic institutions are seen as far more trustworthy. The high percentage of current cloud users and simultaneous distrust towards their provider shows that students and employees lack of alternatives to existing commercial cloud solutions. An on-premise solution, hosted by educational institutions with the academic community as the target group, would represent such an alternative. If such a cloud service provides storage volume comparable to current commercial offerings and comprises functions and features that meet the demand for data protection as well as the progression of work in mobile, interdisciplinary and distributed dimensions, it will be an important tool for future collaboration in higher education.

The next step of the research agenda will be the analysis of further survey data that were recently collected from other universities in North Rhine-Westphalia (altogether over 10,000 participants). Regarding the project management, the objective is not only to compare the results on a cross-university basis but also to derive conclusions regarding the cloud service adoption rate and required average storage volume of the target user groups. In aspects of science, the goal is to contribute by additional publications regarding the diffusion of large-scale cloud storage services in higher education, identification of valuable use-cases and impact factors on the technology acceptance. In addition, an in-depth analysis of the open-ended question (factors influencing users' trust in cloud computing providers) would help to develop a general concept of users trust in cloud computing providers. It is also needed to investigate what kind of additional services (e.g. social media applications, mobile access) could be offered to the users [17, 18]. Furthermore, the Sync&Share NRW project may also serve as a teaching case in order to educate students about cloud computing in the context of higher education, as well as entailed aspects such as trust building.

References

1. Catteddu, D.: Cloud Computing: benefits, risks and recommendations for information security. In: Serrão, C., Aguilera Díaz, V., Cerullo, F. (eds.) IBWAS 2009. CCIS, vol. 72, pp. 17–17. Springer, Heidelberg (2010)
2. Mell, P., Grance, T.: The NIST Definition of Cloud Computing (Draft) Recommendations of the National Institute of Standards and Technology. The National Institute of Standards and Technology (NIST), Gaithersburg (2011)
3. Armbrust, M., Stoica, I., Zaharia, M., Fox, A., Griffith, R., Joseph, A.D.: A view of cloud computing. Communications of the ACM 53, 50–58 (2010)
4. Vaquero, L.M., Rodero-Merino, L., Caceres, J., Lindner, M.: A break in the clouds: towards a cloud definition. SIGCOMM Comput. Commun. Rev. 39, 50–55 (2008)

5. CDW, From Tactic To Strategy: The CDW 2011 Cloud Computing Tracking Poll, `http://webobjects.cdw.com/webobjects/media/pdf/Newsroom/CDW-Cloud-Tracking-Poll-Report-0511.pdf` (last access on December 30, 2013)

6. Sasikala, S., Prema, S.: Massive Centralized Cloud Computing (MCCC) Exploration in Higher Education (2011)

7. Siegle, D.: Cloud Computing: A Free Technology Option to Promote Collaborative Learning. Gifted Child Today 33, 41–45 (2010)

8. Marston, S., Li, Z., Bandyopadhyay, S., Zhang, J., Ghalsasi, A.: Cloud computing — The business perspective. Decision Support Systems 51, 176–189 (2011)

9. Erkoç, M.F., Kert, S.B.: Cloud Computing For Distributed University Campus: A Prototype Suggestion. In: International Conference on Future of Education, Firenze (2011)

10. Sultan, N.: Cloud computing for education: A new dawn? International Journal of Information Management 30, 109–116 (2010)

11. New York University, NYU Google Apps for Education, `http://www.nyu.edu/its/google/` (last access on December 31, 2013)

12. JUCC IS Task Force, Cloud Computing - A newsletter for IT Professionals, `http://www.istf.jucc.edu.hk/newsletter/IT_03/IT-3_Cloud_Computing.pdf` (last access on December 31, 2013)

13. Zissis, D., Lekkas, D.: Addressing cloud computing security issues. Futur. Gener. Comp. Syst. 28, 583–592 (2012)

14. Vogl, R., Angenent, H., Bockholt, R., Rudolph, D., Stieglitz, S., Meske, C.: Designing a Large Scale Cooperative Sync& Share Cloud Storage Plattform for the Academic Community in Northrhine-Westfalia. In: 19th European University Information Systems — EUNIS 2013 Congress Proceedings, pp. 205–208 (2013)

15. Curtis, S.: Oxford University Builds VMware Private Cloud, `http://www.techweekeurope.co.uk/news/oxford-university-builds-vmware-private-cloud-43123` (last access on December 31, 2013)

16. Davis, F.D.: Perceived usefulness, perceived ease of use, and user acceptance of information technology. MIS Quarterly, 319–340 (1989)

17. Schneider, A.-M., Stieglitz, S., Lattemann, C.: Social Software as an Instrument of CSR, ICT. In: Transparency and Social Responsibility Conference 2007, Lisbon, pp. 1–10 (2007)

18. Steiner, M., Götz, O., Stieglitz, S.: The Influence of Learning Management System Components on Learners' Motivation in a Large-Scale Social Learning Environment. In: Proceedings of the 34th International Conference on Information Systems (ICIS), Milan, Italy (2013)

An HTML5-Based Online Editor for Creating Annotated Learning Videos

Jan-Torsten Milde

Hochschule Fulda, Computer Science Department, Germany
milde@hs-fulda.de

Abstract. Creating multi media learning resources has become a common standard in university level teaching. We present an online video annotation editor, allowing to create time aligned annotations of video material. The editor is implemented using HTML5-technology and runs in a standard web browser. The annotations are used to generate searchable indexes, making it easy to quickly navigate in the video.

Keywords: online video annotation, learning videos, time aligned annotations.

1 Introduction

Creating multi media learning resources has become a common standard in university level teaching. Large amounts of video data are created as video recordings of standard classroom lectures, as screencasts produced to introduce into software systems, or as dedicated learning resources produced in professional tv studios. One of the central drawbacks of such recordings is their lack of accessible internal structure. When learning with electronic resources, students need to have access to the presented content, especially when preparing for exams. An automatic processing of the video content is still very limited, providing results that are far from satisfactory.

In our approach we developed an online video annotation tool allowing to annotate video content based on timing information. The annotations are stored in a separate XML-file. Based on this data, structural navigation and search can be perfomed by the students. From the XML-file we are generating specific HTML5-based online views that provide the students with a content outline, search menus and also generate an alphabetic index. These ressources are all linked to the original video data, making it easy to identify the relevant content.

2 TASX-Corpora

Over the last decade multiple tools for the creation of multimodal annotated media resources have been realized (see [1], [2], [3], [4], [5]). Especially the creation of multi level annotated data sets has been under investigation here. Our work so far has been focusing on the development of tools for the creation of multimodal

P. Zaphiris and A. Ioannou (Eds.): LCT 2014, Part I, LNCS 8523, pp. 172–179, 2014.

corpora (TASX-Annotator, later the Eclipse-Annotator, see [8], [10]), followed by a tool for the creation of parallel text corpora (SAM, see[11]). The TASX-Annotator has been used to create annotated language recordings, including annotated corpora of video recordings of german sign language (see [9]).

From the collected data an XML-annotated multimodal corpus has been set up. The XSL-T based transformation of the data allows to generate multiple output formats from a single data source. The TASX-environment supports the complete corpus setup procedure: XML-based annotation of raw video data, the transformation of non XML-data and the analysis and dissemination of the corpus.

2.1 The TASX Format

A central aspect of our research ist to explore up which point standard XML technology (XML, XSL-T, XSL-FO, XPath, SVG, XQuery) can be used to model multi media corpora, to transform, query and distribute the content of such corpora and to perform adequate search and usage analysis. As a result all annotation data in our system ist stored in an XML-based format called TASX: the *T*ime *A*ligned *S*ignal data e*X*change format. A TASX-annotated corpus consists of a set of sessions, each one holding an arbitrary number of descriptive tiers, called layers. Each layer consists of a set of separated events. Each event stores some textual information (e.g. explanations form the teacher, question of the students) and is linked to the pimary video data of the classroom recording. This is realized by defining two time stamps per event, denoting the interval the event. Events may also carry non speech data, including slide changing marks, pointing directions, mode changes, external references. Relations between events on different tiers can be encoded by defining links using the ID/IDREFS mechanism of XML. This approach is comparable to using stand-off markup in the creation of multimodal corpora. Finally, arbitray meta-data can be assigned to the complete corpus, each session, each layer and each event. It might be necessaryto extend the meta data description in a way, that tree structured data can immediatly be described by XML-annotaitons. Currently we rather use the simpler version describing meta data in a linear structure. The following DTD formalizes the structutre of the TASX format:

```
<!-- corpus data -->
<!ELEMENT tasx (meta*,session+)>
<!ELEMENT session (meta*,layer+)>
<!ELEMENT layer (meta*,event+)>
<!ELEMENT event (#PCDATA,meta*)>
<!-- meta data -->
<!ELEMENT meta (desc*)>
<!ELEMENT desc (name,val)>
<!ELEMENT name (#PCDATA)>
<!ELEMENT val (#PCDATA)>
```

```
<!-- atributes -->
<!ATTLIST session
  s-id CDATA #REQUIRED
  day CDATA #REQUIRED
  ref IDREF #IMPLIED
  month CDATA #REQUIRED
  year CDATA #REQUIRED>
<!ATTLIST layer
  l-id CDATA #REQUIRED
  ref IDREF #IMPLIED>
<!ATTLIST event
  e-id CDATA #REQUIRED
  start CDATA #REQUIRED
  end CDATA #REQUIRED
  ref IDREF #IMPLIED
  mid CDATA #IMPLIED
  len CDATA #IMPLIED>
<!ATTLIST meta
  m-id CDATA #REQUIRED
  ref IDREF #IMPLIED
  access CDATA #IMPLIED
  level CDATA #IMPLIED>
```

Despite of it's simplicity,the TASX-format is powerful enough to encode most of the corpus annotation formats currently in use. Indeed a number of format transformation programms have been implemented. For example, in order to reconstruct the equivalent annotation graphs representation of a TASX annotated corpus, one only has to collect the time stamps encoded in the start and end attributes of the event tags, sort them and then produce the timeline. Finally the time stamps of the events have to be replaced by references to the timeline.

2.2   The TASX-Annotator

In order to create TASX-annotated corpora the TASX-annotator has been developed. The programm is very user friendly and can be used without a high level of computer skills. It is possible to completely control the tool by either mouse or by keyboard shortcuts. Video and audio playback can be controlled by a foot switch. Different data views are programmed (time-aligned partiture, word-aligned partiture, sequential text view) to make annotation as effective as possible. The time aligned view is organized as a two dimensinal grid of infinite size.

A layer is presented as a horizontal tier of events. The order of the layers is arbitrary and can be changed instantly. The user is able to define time intervals by dragging the mouse. Each time interval represents an ev ent. The event is displayed as a graphical box which can be selected and moved with the mouse. The content of an event is entered in an additional text field.

Fig. 1. A screenshot of the TASX-annotator. In the bottom half, the main panel is visible, where the time aligned tier view has been selected. On top of the main window, the font selection panel is visible (showing some IPA characters) and above it the find tool. In the upper left corner the video display can been seen.

Any (unicode) font (e.g. IPA fonts, HamNoSys fonts etc.) available for the operating system can be used for the transcription. The user can choose font and fontpage from a table displaying all characters of the selected font. It is also possible to define a virtual keyboard which maps the given keystrokes to arbitrary characters of the target font.

A separate video playback window will open up for each video file making it possible to e.g. display multiple perspectives of the same scene. The video playback is synchronized with the transcription. For audio transcriptions an oszillogram is calculated and is displayed inside the main window. In the text view the data can be manipulated in a standard text editor panel.

The content of the editor represents the layer and each line represents an event. A list selection box allows switching between different layers. It is possible to transfer text from standard text editors, e.g. Microsoft Word, by cut and paste operations. In order to additionally speed up the transcription process, a word completion function has been implemented for the text view. Entering the initial letter of a word will bring up all words starting with this letter. Once the text is tranferred into the TASX-annotator, the events still have to be aligned with the primary audio and video data.

Switching back to the time aligned view and moving the events with the mouse makes this task quite simple. In the partiture vie w the data cannot be edited. In practice this means that the data is transformed into an HTML table and then displayed to the user. A number of different HTML formatted views have been designed. The views can also be saved to external files and loaded into standard web browsers. One potential strength of the TASX-annotator is its manner of handling the export/import of XML based information. A standard way of solving this problem would be the implementation of a set of format specific XMLparsers which construct the internal representation of the XMLfile. While powerful integrated development systems make the design of such XML handlers simpler, it still remains a complex task to implement such a parser. In the TASX-annotatorwe follow a different approach. The system integrates an XSL-T processor (saxon), making it easy to perform on the fly data transformations. The import of an XML-file is split into two steps: first an XSL-T stylesheet transforms the XML file into TASX, second another XSL-T stylesheet will transform the TASX file into a simple text oriented format. This format can be loaded efficiently.

2.3   Pause Tracker

To speed up the annotation process a pause tracking programm has been developed. The programm separates speech from pauses and generates a TASX annotated XML document with two tiers, one holding all pause events, the other one holding all speech events. The tracker uses Praat to perform the actual speech analysis. It simply calculates the pitch curve of the audio signal. If no pitch is detected, then non-speech is assumed, otherwise speech. In a second step, the results of this classification are combined to continuous stretches of pauses/speech. Finally the TASX conformant output is generated. The pause tracker has shown to work quite reliably on a set of recording in different languages (Japanese, English, German, Saterfriesisch, French, Ega).

Even if tracking is far from perfect, the annotator gets a good pre-segmentation of the signal. This allows to move very quickly through the file, possibly performing minor adjustments to the boundaries or combining a set of separated events of one speaker . While the pause tracker gives good results when processing lecture recordings it is not of much help overlapping speech.

3   VAT: The Video Annotation Tool

Currently a large number of course recordings are created at the university. Students use these recordings as part of the preparation for the final exams. A big drawback of such recordings is their (long) duration and the lack of direct access to the content. Searching for slides, finding explanation of specific topics or keywords across all recordings is not possible.

In order to create more effective video learning ressources we have started to develop an online annotation editor for the creation of multi level annotated learning videos. The development is part of a cooperation between central elearning laboratory and the computer science department of Fulda University of Applied Sciences.

The annotation levels are synchronously linked to the video, each level containing an arbitrary number of events, holding a level specific description of the associated part of the video content. Events may overlap inside the levels and across levels.

The annotation data is stored in the XML-based format TASX (Time Aligned Signal data eXchange format). The TASX files eventually carry all information

Fig. 2. A short video annotated with the video annotation tool. The user is able to load video and annotation from separate files. The event list is presented to the user. A simple click moves the video to the corresponding position in the video. The complete system is realised as a HTML5 application, running in standard browsers on almost any platform.

Browser	MP4	WebM	Ogg
9+	YES	NO	NO
5+	YES	YES	YES
3.6+	NO	YES	YES
5+	YES	NO	NO
10.6+	NO	YES	YES

- MP4 = MPEG 4 files with H264 video codec and AAC audio codec
- WebM = WebM files with VP8 video codec and Vorbis audio codec
- Ogg = Ogg files with Theora video codec and Vorbis audio codec

Fig. 3. The video annotation editor supports a number of different video formats. These depend on the support of the underlying web browser.

about a specific digital artifact, including the video file meta data, the level structure and of course all description events with their respective temporal information.

The implementation of the tool is based on HTML5 technologies. As such, it runs in most of the current web browsers and is therefore platform independent. The video material is streamed by the central video server of the university.

We tried to make the user interaction with the annotation editor as simple and effective as possible. Moving through the video data, adding layers and events and entering annotations is straight forward and fast. Upon key press, the editor will generate the XML-file, which can be stored locally or put onto the central elearning server.

Once the annotations are completed, the TASX file can used to generate various elearning resources. A linked index of all annotation is automatically created, making it possible to directly jump to specific topics. Further processing of both video and annotation data is realized with XSL-T programs. We have implemented programs to generate book like HTML structures out of the video

Fig. 4. Inserting an annotation with video annotation tool is simple. The annotator is moving to video to a definite position and enters the describing text. This also works, while the video is running. As soon, as text is entered, an annotation event is created and stored.

content. This process combines the textual annotation with screenshots of the slides and at same time provides the relevant (small) parts of the video. The students love these enhanced video view and use it very effectively during the exam prepration.

We have started to experiment with speech recognition and OCR in order to automatically extract annotations from the video. Results are promising, but further tests have to be performed.

4   Conclusions

We presented the development of a video annotation tool used for the creation of annotated learning videos. The underlying data is stored in an XML-file using the TASX-format. TASX provides a general format for the exchange of time aligned data, thus being specifically useful in the context of lecture annotations. While already powerful annotation tools existed, we chose to create a simple to learn online video annotation tool. Using standard HTML5-technology makes it possible to quickly create annotated version of lectures, both by students and teachers.

References

[1] Kipp, M.: Anvil - A Generic Annotation Tool for Multimodal Dialogue. In: Proceedings of the 7th European Conference on Speech Communication and Technology (Eurospeech), pp. 1367–1370 (2001)
[2] Schmidt, T.: Transcribing and annotating spoken language with EXMARaLDA. In: Proceedings of the LREC-Workshop on XML Based Richly Annotated Corpora, Lisbon. ELRA, Paris (2004)

[3] Sasaki, F., Wegener, C., Witt, A., Metzing, D., Pönninghaus, J.: Co-reference annotation and resources: A multilingual corpus of typologically diverse languages. In: Proceedings of the 3nd International Conference on Language Resources and Evaluation (LREC 2002), Las Palmas (2002)

[4] Broeder, D., Offenga, F., Willems, D., Wittenburg, P.: The IMDI Metadata set, its Tools and accessible Linguistic databases. In: IRCS Workshop, Philadelphia (2001)

[5] Bird, S., Liberman, M.: A Formal Framework for Linguistic Annotation. Speech Communication 33(1-2), 23–60

[6] Milde, J.-T., Gut, U.: The TASX environment: an XML-based toolset for time aligned speech corpora. In: Proceedings of the third International Conference on Language Resources and Evaluation, Las Palmas, pp. 1922–1927 (2002b)

[7] Milde, J.-T., Gut, U.: A Prosodic Corpus of Non-Native Speech. In: Bel, B., Marlien, I. (eds.) Proceedings of the Speech Prosody Conference, pp. 503–506. LPL, Aix-en-Provence (2002a)

[8] Behrens, F., Milde, J.: The Eclipse Annotator: an extensible system for multi-modal corpus creation. In: Proceedings of the Fifth International Conference on Language Resources and Evaluation, Genova (2006)

[9] Geilfuss, M., Milde, J.-T.: SAM - ein Annotationseditor für parallele Texte. In: Berliner XML Tage, pp. 71–78 (2005)

[10] Sippel, T.: Eine Anwendung zur touchgesteuerten Annotation elektronischer METS/MODS-Dokumente in Silverlight C#. Masterthesis. Hochschule Fulda (2011)

From Information Systems to
e-Learning 3.0 Systems's Critical Success Factors:
A Framework Proposal

Paula Miranda[1], Pedro Isaias[2], and Carlos J. Costa[3]

[1] Escola Superior de Tecnologia de Setúbal, IPS
Campus do IPS, Estefanilha 2910-761 Setúbal - Portugal
paula.miranda@estsetubal.ips.pt
[2] Universidade Aberta,
Palácio Ceia, Rua da Escola Politécnica, nº 141-147,
1269-001 Lisboa, Portugal
pisaias@uab.pt
[3] University Institute of Lisbon (ISCTE-IUL), Adetti-IUL
Avenida Forças Armadas,
1649-026 Lisboa, Portugal
carlos.costa@iscte.pt

Abstract. This paper seeks to identity and provides Critical Success Factors (CSFs) that affect the decision of adoption of e-Learning 3.0 systems. The study begins with a literature review related to the CSFs for information systems, followed by a literature review for e-Learning systems CSFs. The paper introduces an initial framework for understanding of which factors can influence successfully the adoption of an e-Learning 3.0 system. The framework is composed of five main dimensions, such as: technology, content, students, professors and educational institutions, as well of its influencing factors, and characterizes the factors in each dimension. This study can assist the stakeholders, i.e. students, professors and organization, in their intension to adopt an e-Learning 3.0 system

Keywords: Information Systems, e-Learning, Web 3.0, e-Learning 3.0, Critical Success Factors (CSFs), higher education.

1   Introduction

The exponential deployment of information technology, along with new developments in education, launched excellent opportunities for new learning methods. In the last decade, the e-Learning concept had a growing recognition and is currently one of the most prominent developments in the information systems industry.Today, e-learning has evolved into a model widely adopted in academic institutions [1].The first version of e-Learning, e-Learning 1.0, was pioneer in the online distribution of educational contents. Learning materials transposed the walls of the classroom. However, as the internet was in its early stage of development, these

P. Zaphiris and A. Ioannou (Eds.): LCT 2014, Part I, LNCS 8523, pp. 180–191, 2014.

contents were read only. The information was available, but it was static, and could not be edited. With e-Learning 1.0, students had freedom in terms of space and time, allowing them to organize their learning processes and at their own rhythm. However, the learning process remained pre-established.The content was organized into units and modules. Learning Management Systems (LMS) were introduced to assist the process of administration content and didactic tools to enhance learning [2]. With the evolution of the Web and the great popularity of Web 2.0, e-Learning took the technology behind "read/write web" and addressed itself more to the student and to the collaborative environment. Collaboration, information exchange, social learning, content generation, are the pillars of e-Learning 2.0 [3].Education faces many challenges such as budget constraints, rising costs and increasing demand for e-learning platforms [4]. The response to these challenges, by educational institutions, has led those to reassess how the teaching is being carried out. In this perspective, the added value that Web 3.0 brings to e-Learning has been questioned as well. As with other technologies and pedagogical tools [69] [70], the first step to implement Web 3.0 on e-Learning is to decide whether, in fact, it is a valuable resource. It is believed that Web 3.0 can be a powerful pedagogical tool that has the potential to improve the construction of knowledge and personalize the learning experience of students. At the same time, it is expected that it facilitates some aspects from the teachers' responsibilities (i.e. support the development, assessment and student support) [5].Web 3.0, called Semantic Web or Web of data, is the new generation of the Web, with features and technologies such as collaborative filtering, cloud computing, big data repositories, mobility, etc.. If Web 2.0 is a social network where predominates the collaboration between creator and user, then Web 3.0 is the intelligent Web applications. If we want a more intelligent Web, with tools that enable us to find the information we need and when we need it, it is necessary to give more meaning to the information found therein. The information must be structured in such a way that the devices can read and understand as humans do, without ambiguity. Despite many uncertainties, educational institutions have followed this whole evolution of e-Learning. However, it is necessary to focus on what is really essential for the success of e-learning programs. Nowadays it is necessary a total understanding of the critical factors that contribute to the success of an e-Learning system. Institutions need to identify which factors actually contribute to that success. However, there are no studies that identify these critical factors for e-Learning 3.0. Thus proven the gap, it is intended with this study propose a framework for the critical success factors in e-Learning 3.0 adoption. With the integration of e-learning in most educational institutions, there are several factors that should be considered when it is decided to adopt an e-Learning 3.0 system, so that its application can succeed in institutions currently very demanding.

2   Critical Success Factors

It is recognized the importance of identifying the critical success factors for the organizations when there is an intention in adopt a new system.Being the focus of this research to identify the CSF that affect the decision of the adoption of e-Learning 3.0, the study began with a literature review on critical success factors of information systems in general and in e-learning systems in particular. These literature review, and the study of Web 3.0 and e-Learning 3.0, supported the development of an initial framework of critical success factors of e-Learning 3.0.The critical success factors are seen as activities and constituents that must be addressed to ensure the success of your compliance. They can also be seen as what should be done if an organization wants to succeed. The critical success factors should be few in number, measurable and controllable [6].

2.1   Critical Success Factors for Information Systems

The critical success factors for the implementation of information systems are addressed by several authors. In reviewing the literature we can find researchers that

Table 1. Critical success factors for information systems implementation

Dimensions	Critical Success Factors	Authors
Organisational	- Top management support and commitment - Culture (collaborative, innovative) - Communication (involvement of all in sharing information and opportunity for expression) - Clear strategic goals - Interdepartmental collaboration - Motivation	[8], [9], [10], [11], [12], [13], [14], [15], [16], [66]
Technology	. New technologies - Equipment conditions - System complexity and lack of interoperability - Hardware, Software	[8], [9], [10], [13]
Education and training	- Continuous monitoring - Training	[8], [10], [12], [13], [14], [15], [66]
Evaluation	- Impact of the new system - Monitoring and evaluating performance	[10], [12], [13], [15]
People	- Team capacity (high competence and expertise of the team) - Specialization - Project Manager	[9], [10], [11], [13]
Data accuracy	- Reliable data from both internal and external sources - Maintenance and integrity - Confidence in the information provided by the system	[7], [9], [13]

discuss about the importance of commitment from the management in order to invest time and effort guiding the project, clear link to the strategic goals, management of organisational resistance to challenges, appropriate technology, the quality of the staff with technical knowledge, reliable data from both internal and external sources [7].Table 1 summarizes the critical success factors for information systems implementation, grouped in six dimensions, according to their similarities. The organisational dimension includes factors related to leadership, management support, communication, strategy, culture, motivation. Other dimension, technology, focuses on issues related to the technological challenges and equipment conditions. Education and training (training of users and staff), evaluation, people (enough management and technical skills) and data are the others dimensions considered in this study.

2.2   Critical Success Factors for e-Learning

The critical success factors for e-Learning emerge from the existing literature. A literature review was performed to collect the CSFs identified by several authors.

Table 2. Critical success factors for e-Learning

Dimensions	Critical Success Factors	Authors
Technology (infrastructure)	- Broadband (internet speed) - Equipment quality - Network security - System backup - Equipment availability - Appropriate equipment	[17], [18], [19], [20], [21], [22], [24]
Environment (Learning)	- Accessibility - Interface design - Interaction among participats - Usability - Being according to the objectives	[17], [18], [19], [20], [21], [22], [23], [24], [26]
Professor	- Learning facilitator - Technical competence - Interaction with the class - Clarification of objectives - Attitude toward the students	[17], [18], [19], [20] , [24], [26]
Student	- Motivation - Commitment and responsibility - Student content interaction - Student-student interaction - Confidence - Knowledge technology	[17], [18], [19], [20], [23], [24], [26]
Institutional support	- Training - Help desk - Technical support	[17], [19], [22], [24], [25]
Leadership	- Being an expert	[21]

These CSFs can be considered critical to the success of an e-Learning system. The most prominent are mentioned in the next table. According to the research study, six dimensions were considered: technology, learning environment, professor, student, institutional support and leadership. Each dimension included several factors.

2.3   Critical Success Factors for e-Learning 3.0

2.3.1   Expectations and Challenges

The notion of e-Learning 3.0 emerged from the increasing popularity of Web 3.0 as an educational asset. E-learning has been taking advantage of Web 3.0's innovations. In general terms, Web 3.0 has become an appealing tool for education due to its promise of increased personalisation, effective knowledge management and improved interactive and collaborative instruments. The use of the Semantic Web is expected to maximise the resources that are already in place and to address its main challenges.

There are three main components in Web 3.0's definition: Semantic, Mobile and Immersive [67]. The semantic aspect relates to the precept of a personalised Internet, using each user's profile to customise their experience online. This is supported by software that has the ability of "utilizing natural language searches" and of "understanding the meaning of data". In terms of mobility, Web 3.0 offers the opportunity of using several devices with increasingly advanced features that enable a richer internet navigation, regardless of the device that users employ. The notion of an immersive internet concerns virtual and augmented reality and 3D settings. Web 3.0 "encompasses efforts to build a new WWW architecture that enhances content with formal semantics, which enables better possibilities for navigating through the cyberspace and accessing its contents" [58]. Also, Web 3.0 can be classified as a variety "of Internet-based services and technologies that include components such as natural language search, forms of artificial intelligence, software agents that make recommendations to users and the application of context to content" [67]. Web 3.0 envisions the internet as a database, it seeks to transform it into an organised data source. It uses Web 2.0 tools as enablers. This stage of the web unites both We1.0 and Web 2.0, but it takes the concept of the Web forward to include semantics, intelligent agents, personalisation, increased mobility and a more focused experience for each user [68].The panoply of benefits emerging from the use of Web 3.0 in e-Learning have been made clearer by the pioneers of its application, but as with any innovation, e-Learning 3.0 needs to be accepted and employed. The majority of the challenges deriving from e-Learning 3.0 are common to its predecessors' versions. Since the beginning of the electronic delivery of learning there have been aspects that concern the education community and impede a wider acceptance of e-Learning. In order to fully comprehend the hazards of e-Learning 3.0 it is paramount to understand that some of these challenges are common to all versions of e-Learning and that others are specific to the use of Web 3.0.Innovative technologies have several advantages, but while they can be a valuable ally for learning it is overwhelming to accompany the speed at which they are developed and evolve. Institutions and professionals are yet in the process of trying to harness web based learning and research shows that great part of Web 2.0's tools and precepts have not been completely embraced. Hence, when artificial intelligence, mobile interfaces or immersive virtual environments start to appear as potential educational instruments, some scepticism and confusion is expected [67].The fact the e-Learning 3.0 is invested in the development of information as a resource that is accessible without time, space and interface constraints, poses a challenge in terms of interoperability. To achieve this goal, it becomes necessary to enable several types of applications and interfaces to interact to facilitate a more proficient setting for users [27].The challenges of using ontologies relate, namely, to their creation, to the way they are build. While it is possible to find a variety of approaches to create ontologies, none of these approaches is regarded has being a standard method [32]. Additionally, ontologies of superior quality require substantial monetary means and significant time allocation. Financial resources and time are two of the main obstacles for the development of superior quality ontologies [53].Despite the many advantages that cloud computing presents it still has some challenges namely repercussions in terms of performance due to internet connection velocity; a higher cost that the hardware itself, when considering a long term subscription of the data centre; and the key effect that service quality and backups have when considering the security of the data [47].To move forward into a fully functional E-Learning 3.0, the aforementioned challenges must be considered and addressed. Online education can benefit greatly from the pioneering precepts of the Web 3.0 but for its advantages to be truly enjoyed, it is essential that the educational institutions evaluate all these issues.

2.3.2   The Framework

In order to identity the CSFs for e-Learning 3.0 systems it was carried out a literature review on the topics evolution of the Web and evolution of the e-Learning followed by a detailed review of Web 3.0 and e-Learning 3.0. These, combined with the information systems and e-Learning CSFs, contributed to design an initial framework.Based on all this work it was identified a list of potential CSFs to adopt when an institution intend to adopt an e-Learning 3.0 system. During this process some CFSs from the informations systems and e-Learning systems were refined (added or removed), and new dimensions and factors were added.This framework organized the CSFs into five dimensions (table 3).

Table 3. Critical success factors for e-Learning

Dimensions	Critical Success Factors	Authors
Technology	Smart mobile technology	[27]
	Web 3.0	[27], [28]; [29], [30]
	Semantic features	[28], [29], [31], [32]
	Video games	[33]
	High power graphics	[34]
	3D and immersive web	[34]
	Ontology-based tools	[29], [31], [36], [39]
	3D visualization and interaction	[35]
	Intelligent Search Engines	[34]
	Cloud computing	[29], [36], [37]
	Independency from centralized institutional web-sites	[37]
	Service-oriented infrastructures	[41]
	User-friendly interfaces	[30], [38], [40]
	User profiling techniques	[42]
	Artificial intelligence	[43], [45]
	Ontology creation	[30],[44],[46]
	Ontology maintenance	[44], [46]
	Hardware equipment (computers, laptops, mobile phones, etc.)	[47]
	Fast internet connection	[47]
	Semantic interoperability	[31]
	Interoperability of web-based educational systems	[48]
	Easy to use end-user applications	[30]
	Mobile Apps	[49]
Content	Widely spread ontology structure	[41], [50]
	Personalised content	[51], [52]
	Machine-understandable learning material	[47]
	Semantic homogeneity	[39], [50]
	Development of domain ontologies	[31] [53];
	User generated	[54]
	Dynamic	[54]
	Semantic markup	[31], [56]
	Metadata	[41], [52], [57], [58];
	Semantic web ready content	[30], [46], [50], [59]
	Open data	[60]

Table 3. *(continued)*

Students	Collaborative learning	[35]
	Self-organization	[37]
	Real-time learning and real-time collaboration	[35]
	Personalized learning	[43]
	Trust	[55]
	Tagging resources	[61]
	e-Skills	[62]
	Feedback on content	[52]
	Add information to learning systems	[46]
Teachers	Basic understanding of Web 3.0	[63]
	Trust	[55]
	ICT training	[62]
Educational Institutions	Creation of learning value systems	[55]
	Policy-aware infrastructure–Interoperability/Standards	[55]
	Training for e-learning Tutors	[64]
	Inter-connectedness among institutions	[65]
	Development of learning methods based on real experience	[57]
	Data integration platforms	[50]
	Infrastructural semantic tools and services	[50]
	Large repositories of linked data	[50]
	Educational servers	[29]

3   Conclusions and Future Work

There is no doubt related to the integration e-Learning 1.0 systems and its successor, e-Learning 2.0, in the majority of higher education institutions [70]. Therefore, an evaluation to the factors that determine the success of this adoption need to be done.

Several studies were carried out by different researchers on CSFs of information systems and e-learning and also frameworks were proposed [69]. However, no specific study was done for e-Learning 3.0.

This paper, in line with what have been done for the IS and e-Learning systems, illustrates the CSFs which need to be considered when decide to adopt and e-Learning 3.0 system.

The idea of identifying CSFs as a basis for determining the adoption of e-Learning 3.0 follows the sense that the CSFs represents the main issues without which a project stands little chance of success [14].An initial framework for CFS in adoption of e-Learning systems is proposed in this paper. Despite some obstacles (i.e. financial, organizational, people), e-learning seems to be recognized as an important support for education. In order to facilitate the decision to adopt an e-learning 3.0 system, a framework was proposed to support the decision of adoption.Future research should be conducted to validate this framework by collecting opinions from a group of experts, and the resultant framework will be also assessed by a survey.

References

1. Wang, Y.: Assessment of Learner Satisfaction with Asynchronous Electronic Learning Systems. Information & Management 41(1), 75–86 (2003)
2. Rubens, N., Kaplan, D., Okamoto, T.: E-Learning 3.0: anyone, anywhere, anytime, and AI. In: International Workshop on Social and Personal Computing for Web-Supported Learning Communities (2011)
3. Virtič, M.P.: The Role of Internet in Education. In: DIVAI-International Scientific Conference on Distance Learning in Applied Informatics (2012)
4. Wagner, N.L., Hassanein, K., Head, M.M.: Who is Responsible for E-Learning Success in Higher Education? A Stakeholders' Analysis. Educational Technology & Society 11(3), 26–36 (2008)
5. Morris, R.D.: Web 3.0: Implications for online learning. TechTrends 55(1), 42–46 (2011)
6. Masrom, M., Zainon, O., Rahiman, R.: Critical success in e-learning: an examination of technological and institutional support factors. International Journal of Cyber Society and Education 1, 131–142 (2008)
7. Poon, P., Wagner, C.: Critical success factors revisited: success and failure cases of information systems for senior executives. Decision Support Systems 30(4), 393–418 (2001)
8. Nam, T., Pardo, T.: Identifying Success Factors and Challenges of 311-Driven Service Integration: A Comparative Case Study of NYC311 and Philly311. In: Proceedings of the 46th Hawaii International Conference on System Sciences, vol. 2013 (2013)
9. Catersels, R., Helms, R.W., Batenburg, R.S.: Exploring the gap between the practical and theoretical world of ERP implementations: results of a global survey. In: Proceedings of IV IFIP International Conference on Research and Practical Issues of Enterprise Information Systems, Rio Grande Do Norte, Brazil (2010)
10. Trkman, P.: The critical success factors of business process management. International Journal of Information Management 30(2), 125–134 (2010)
11. Chow, T., Cao, D.B.: A Survey Study of Critical Success Factors in Agile Software Projects. Journal of Systems and Software 81(6), 961–971 (2008)
12. Wong, K.Y.: Critical success factors for implementing knowledge management in small and medium enterprises. Industrial Management & Data Systems 105(3), 261–279 (2005)
13. Umble, E.J., Haft, R.R., Umble, M.M.: Enterprise resource planning: Implementation procedures and critical success factors. European Journal of Operational Research 146(2), 241–257 (2003)
14. Coronado, R.B., Antony, J.: Critical success factors for the successful implementation of six sigma projects in organisations. The TQM magazine 14(2), 92–99 (2002)
15. Al-Mashari, M., Al-Mudimigh, A., Zairi, M.: Enterprise resource planning: a taxonomy of critical factors. European Journal of Operational Research 146(2), 352–364 (2003)
16. Wong, B., Tein, D.: Critical Success Factors for ERP Projects. Journal of the Australian Institute of Project Management 24(1), 28–31 (2004)
17. Puri, G.: Critical success Factors in e-Learning – An empirical study. International Journal of Multidisciplinary Research 2(1), 149–161 (2012)

18. Bhuasiri, W., Xaymoungkhoun, O., Zo, H., Rho, J.J., Ciganek, A.: Critical success factors for e-learning in developing countries: A comparative analysis between ICT experts and faculty. Computers & Education 58(2), 843–855 (2012)
19. Cheawjindakarn, B., Suwannatthachote, P., Theeraroungchaisri, A.: Critical Success Factors for Online Distance Learning in Higher Education: A Review of the Literature. Creative Education 3, 61–66 (2012), doi:10.4236/ce.2012.38B014
20. Musa, M.A., Othman, M.S.: Critical success factor in e-Learning: an examination of technology and student factors. International Journal of Advances in Engineering & Technology 3(2), 140–148 (2012)
21. Borotis, S., Poulymenakou, A.: Critical Success Factors for E-Learning Adoption. In: Handbook of Research on Instructional Systems and Technology, pp. 496–511. IGI Global, Greece (2008)
22. Masrom, M., Zainon, O., Rahiman, R.: Critical success in e-learning: an examination of technological and institutional support factors. International Journal of Cyber Society and Education 1, 131–142 (2008)
23. Salmeron, J.L.: Augmented fuzzy cognitive maps for modelling LMS critical success factors. Knowledge-Based Systems 22, 275–278 (2009)
24. Selim, H.M.: Critical success factors for e-learning acceptance: Confirmatory factor models. Computers & Education 49(2), 396–413 (2007)
25. Govindasamy, T.: Successful implementation of e-Learning; Pedagogical considerations. The Internet and Higher Education 4(3-4), 287–299 (2002)
26. Volery, T., Lord, D.: Critical success factors in online education. The International Journal of Educational Management 14(5), 216–223 (2000)
27. Rego, H., Moreira, T., Morales, E., Garcia, F.: Metadata and Knowledge Management Driven Web-Based Learning Information System Towards Web/E-Learning 3.0. International Journal of Emerging Technologies in Learning (iJET) 5(2) (2010)
28. Sheeba, T., Begum, S.H., Bernard, M.J.: Semantic Web to E-Learning Content. International Journal 2(10), 58–66 (2012)
29. Devedžić, V.: Web intelligence and artificial intelligence in education. Educational Technology & Society 7(4), 29–39 (2004)
30. Devedžić, V.: The Setting for Semantic Web-Based Education. In: Semantic Web and Education, vol. 12, pp. 71–99. Springer US (2006)
31. Ivanova, M., Ivanova, T.: Web 2.0 and web 3.0 environments: Possibilities for authoring and knowledge representation. Revista de Informatica Sociala 12(7), 7–21 (2009)
32. Gladun, A., Rogushina, J., García-Sanchez, F., Martínez-Béjar, R., Fernández-Breis, J.T.: An application of intelligent techniques and semantic web technologies in e-learning environments. Expert Systems with Applications 36 (2009)
33. Bidarra, J., Cardoso, V.: The emergence of the exciting new Web 3.0 and the future of Open Educational Resources. Paper presented at the Proceedings of the EADTU's 20th Anniversary Conference (2007)
34. Rajiv, M.L.: Web 3.0 in Education & Research. BVICAM's International Journal of Information Technology 3 (2011)
35. Banciu, D., Florea, M.: Information Quality–A Challenge for e-Learning 3.0. Revista Română de Informatică şi Automatică 21(3), 75 (2011)
36. Holohan, E., Melia, M., McMullen, D., Pahl, C.: Adaptive e-learning content generation based on semantic web technology (2005)
37. Goroshko, O.I., Samoilenko, S.A.: Twitter as a Conversation through e-Learning Context. Revista de Informatica Sociala 15 (2011)

38. Hsu, I.-C.: Intelligent Discovery for Learning Objects Using Semantic Web Technologies. Educational Technology & Society 15(1), 298–312 (2012)
39. del Mar Sánchez Vera, M., Breis, J.T.F., Serrano, J.L., Sánchez, M., Espinosa, P.P.: Practical Experiences for the Development of Educational Systems in the Semantic Web. NAER: Journal of New Approaches in Educational Research 2(1), 23–31 (2013)
40. Wang, J.: Education 3.0: Effect learning style and method of instruction on user satisfaction. European Academic Research I(5) (2013)
41. Sheeba, T., Begum, S.H., Bernard, M.J.: Semantic Web to E-Learning Content. International Journal of Advanced Research in Computer Science and Software Engineering 2(10), 58–66 (2012)
42. Giannakos, M., Lapatas, V.: Towards Web 3.0 Concept for Collaborative E-Learning. In: Proceedings of the Multi-Conference on Innovative Developments in ICT. ICTEL (2010)
43. Padma, S.: Maximum Spanning Tree Model on Personalized Web Based Collaborative Learning in Web 3.0. International Journal of Computer Science, Engineering and Information Technology 1(5), 51–61 (2011), doi:10.5121/ijcseit.2011.1505
44. Torniai, C., Jovanovic, J., Gasevic, D., Bateman, S., Hatala, M.: E-learning meets the social semantic web. In: ICALT 2008 - Eighth IEEE International Conference on the Advanced Learning Technologies (2008)
45. Rubens, N., Kaplan, D., Okamoto, T.: E-Learning 3.0: anyone, anywhere, anytime, and AI. In: The International Workshop on Social and Personal Computing for Web-Supported Learning Communities (2011)
46. Ciravegna, F., Chapman, S., Dingli, A., Wilks, Y.: Learning to Harvest Information for the Semantic Web. In: Bussler, C.J., Davies, J., Fensel, D., Studer, R. (eds.) ESWS 2004. LNCS, vol. 3053, pp. 312–326. Springer, Heidelberg (2004)
47. Pocatilu, P., Alecu, F., Vetrici, M.: Using cloud computing for E-learning systems. Paper presented at the Proceedings of the 8th WSEAS International Conference on Data Networks, Communications, Computers, DNCOCO 2009 (2009)
48. Aroyo, L., Dicheva, D.: The New Challenges for E-learning: The Educational Semantic Web. Educational Technology & Society 7(4), 59–69 (2004)
49. Armstrong, K.: From IA Richards to Web 3.0: Preparing Our Students for Tomorrow's World. World Academy of Science, Engineering and Technology 58, 954–961 (2009)
50. Tiropanis, T., Davis, H., Millard, D., Weal, M.: Semantic technologies for learning and teaching in the web 2.0 era: a survey of uk higher education. In: Proceedings of the Web Science 2009 Conference, WebSci (2009)
51. Kurilovas, E., Serikoviene, S., Vuorikari, R.: Expert centred vs learner centred approach for evaluating quality and reusability of learning objects. Computers in Human Behavior (2014)
52. Wang, T.I., Tsai, K.H., Lee, M.-C., Chiu, T.K.: Personalized learning objects recommendation based on the semantic-aware discovery and the learner preference pattern. Educational Technology & Society 10(3), 84–105 (2007)
53. Karadimce, A.: Quality Estimation of E-learning Semantic Web Ontology. In: ICT Innovations 2013 Web Proceedings (2013)
54. Shah, N.K.: E-Learning and Semantic Web. International Journal of e-Education, e-Business, e-Management and e-Learning 2(2) (2012)
55. Naeve, A., Lytras, M., Nejdl, W., Balacheff, N., Hardin, J.: Advances of the Semantic Web for e-learning: expanding learning frontiers. British Journal of Educational Technology 37(3), 321–330 (2006)

56. Ghaleb, F., Daoud, S., Hasna, A., ALJa'am, J.M., El-Seoud, S.A., El-Sofany, H.: E-learning model based on semantic web technology. International Journal of Computing & Information Sciences 4(2), 63–71 (2006)

57. Alsultanny, Y.A.: E-learning system overview based on semantic web. The Electronic Journal of e-Learning 4(2), 111–118 (2006)

58. Stojanovic, L., Staab, S., Studer, R.: eLearning based on the Semantic Web. In: WebNet 2001-World Conference on the WWW and Internet (2001)

59. Tresp, V., Bundschus, M., Rettinger, A., Huang, Y.: Towards Machine Learning on the Semantic Web. In: da Costa, P.C.G., d'Amato, C., Fanizzi, N., Laskey, K.B., Laskey, K.J., Lukasiewicz, T., Nickles, M., Pool, M. (eds.) URSW 2005 - 2007. LNCS (LNAI), vol. 5327, pp. 282–314. Springer, Heidelberg (2008)

60. Powell, M., Davies, T., Taylor, K.C.: ICT For or Against Development_an intro to Web 3.0. IKM Working Paper (16), 1–34 (2012)

61. Halimi, K., Seridi-Bouchelaghem, H., Faron-Zucker, C.: An enhanced personal learning environment using social semantic web technologies. Interactive Learning Environments (ahead-of-print), pp. 1–23 (2013)

62. Loureiro, A., Messias, I., Barbas, M.: Embracing Web 2.0 & 3.0 Tools to Support Lifelong Learning - Let Learners Connect. Procedia - Social and Behavioral Sciences 46, 532–537 (2012), doi:10.1016/j.sbspro.2012.05.155

63. Morris, R.D.: Web 3.0: Implications for online learning. TechTrends 55(1), 42–46 (2011)

64. Paechter, M., Maier, B., Macher, D.: Students' expectations of, and experiences in e-learning: Their relation to learning achievements and course satisfaction. Computers & Education 54(1), 222–229 (2010)

65. Ohler, J.: The semantic web in education. Educause Quarterly 31(4), 7–9 (2008)

66. Kaur, B., Aggrawal, H.: Exploration of Success Factors of Information System. International Journal of Computer Science Issues (IJCSI) 10(1), 226–235, 10 p. (2013)

67. Oakes, K.: Web 3.0: Transforming Learning. Training Industry Quarterly, 38–39 (2011)

68. Singh, K., Gulati, D.: Technological March from Web 1.0 to Web 3.0: A Comparative Study. Library Herald (2011)

69. Isaías, P., Miranda, P., Pífano, S.: Critical Success Factors for Web 2.0 – A Reference Framework. In: Ozok, A.A., Zaphiris, P. (eds.) OCSC 2009. LNCS, vol. 5621, pp. 354–363. Springer, Heidelberg (2009), http://dx.doi.org/10.1007/978-3-642-02774-1_39

70. Miranda, P., Isaias, P., Costa, C., Pifano, S.: WEB 2.0 Technologies Supporting Students and Scholars in Higher Education. In: Ozok, A.A., Zaphiris, P. (eds.) OCSC 2013. LNCS, vol. 8029, pp. 191–200. Springer, Heidelberg (2013)

Exploring the Validity of an Instrument to Measure the Perceived Quality in Use of Web 2.0 Applications with Educational Potential

Tihomir Orehovački[1], Snježana Babić[2], and Mario Jadrić[3]

[1] University of Zagreb, Faculty of Organization and Informatics
Pavlinska 2, 42000 Varaždin, Croatia
tihomir.orehovacki@foi.hr
[2] Polytechnic of Rijeka
Trpimirova 2/V, 51000 Rijeka, Croatia
snjezana.babic@veleri.hr
[3] University of Split, Faculty of Economics
Cvite Fiskovića 5, 21000 Split, Croatia
mario.jadric@efst.hr

Abstract. The aim of the work presented in this paper was to examine to what extent the subjective measuring instrument supports the assessment of all relevant facets of the quality in use in the context of Web 2.0 applications. For that purpose, two scenario-based studies were conducted. In both studies users were observed during their interactions with two Web 2.0 applications that are widely used in educational settings. Data analysis has verified the validity of the post-use questionnaire at various levels of the conceptual model. Findings of empirical studies together with implications for researchers and practitioners are presented and discussed.

Keywords: Web 2.0 Applications, Perceived Quality in Use, Post-use Questionnaire, Empirical Findings.

1 Introduction

Web 2.0 [19] refers to the novel generation of web applications which enable users to actively participate in the development of online resources. The support for different kinds of interaction among users has found its application in numerous fields including education. Under the influence of social and technological trends, the traditional forms of computer-supported learning have evolved into e-learning 2.0 [6]. The implementation of Web 2.0 applications into educational ecosystem brings lots of advantages for both teachers (in terms of enhanced communication with students and facilitated monitoring of their progress) and students (through the development of personal learning environments and educational artefacts that are adapted to their learning styles) [14]. Drawing on harnessing the power of the crowd and network effects, Web 2.0 applications encourage the development of innovative pedagogical

P. Zaphiris and A. Ioannou (Eds.): LCT 2014, Part I, LNCS 8523, pp. 192–203, 2014.

approaches that have the potential to improve students' educational experiences [22]. In addition, Bennett et al. [1] stated that content creation and sharing by means of Web 2.0 applications results in learning benefits for students. Finally, Den Exter et al. [5] emphasized that Web 2.0 applications due to their flexibility and ease of use offer various learning opportunities for distance education students. In order to gain benefits from the implementation of technology into learning process, special attention should be paid to finding and selecting applications with sufficient level of educational potential. In that respect, Orehovački et al. [15] developed a taxonomy of Web 2.0 applications which consist of following three dimensions: the type of Web 2.0 application, their function, and cognitive processes that are part of the revised Bloom's taxonomy. Although Web 2.0 applications are widely employed in various fields of education, sound measuring instrument meant for subjective assessment of their quality in use is still not available. The set forth motivated us to initiate a research on the development of a post-use questionnaire that would enable the evaluation of the perceived quality in use of Web 2.0 applications. The remainder of the paper is structured as follows. Next section offers a brief literature review together with the description of an enhanced version of the conceptual model. Details on employed research methodology are provided in the third section. Findings of two experimental studies are presented in the fourth section. Conclusions and future research directions are contained in the last section.

2   Background to the Research

2.1   Literature Review

Recent research related to the assessment of Web 2.0 applications was predominantly focused on exploring diverse aspects of quality, usability, quality in use, and adoption. For instance, Bubaš et al. [2] created a post-use questionnaire meant for evaluating navigability, ease of use, understandability, and reliability of Web 2.0 applications with educational potential. Sassano et al. [21] suggested the extension of the software quality model that was introduced in international standard ISO/IEC 25010 [10] with a characteristic that would enable the assessment of content accuracy, suitability, accessibility, and legal compliance. As a result of an in-depth literature review on website evaluation, Pang et al. [20] proposed a set of five first-order and twenty-five second-order dimensions meant for measuring the quality of Web 2.0 applications. Orehovački and Žajdela Hrustek [18] designed an online questionnaire that enables the assessment of six technical and five pedagogical usability aspects of educational artifacts created with Web 2.0 applications. García-Martín and García-Sánchez [8] found that gender, educational level, and age define patterns of Web 2.0 applications use. Hartshorne and Ajjan [9] revealed that students' attitudes and subjective norms significantly influence their decisions to adopt Web 2.0 applications. Finally, Dwivedi et al. [7] discovered that usefulness and ease of use are strong predictors of users' intentions to adopt Web 2.0 applications. Our journey to the comprehensive methodology that would enable the evaluation of all relevant aspects of the quality in use of Web 2.0 applications started with the initial set of attributes which significantly contribute to the success of Web 2.0 applications [13]. As a follow up, a conceptual model and measuring instruments that support the assessment of Web 2.0 applications from both subjective and objective perspective were developed [11]. The psychometric characteristics of the aforementioned model and measuring instruments were validated on the representative sample of Web 2.0 applications meant for collaborative writing [12], mind mapping [17], and diagramming [16]. Since the outcomes of the set forth studies have suggested that the model and the post-use questionnaire do not encompass all relevant dimensions of the quality in use of Web 2.0 applications, they were both revised.

2.2   Novel Categorization of Quality in Use Attributes

The enhanced version of the conceptual model is comprised of six categories which are further decomposed into 43 quality in use attributes. System quality refers to attributes that measure the extent to which Web 2.0 application: provides various navigation mechanisms (navigability); has uniform interface structure, design, and terminology (consistency); is similar to previously used applications (familiarity); can be customized to meet users' needs (customizability); has implemented mechanisms that protect created artefacts from unauthorized use (security); operates properly with different types of devices and among different environments (compatibility); can exchange files with other applications and use files that were exchanged (interoperability); offers accurate and efficient internal search engine (searchability). Service quality relates to attributes aimed for evaluating the degree to which Web 2.0 application: provides various forms of help to users (helpfulness); is available every time users need it (availability); facilitates management of created artefacts (artefacts management); contains mechanisms that prevent errors to emerge (error prevention); is dependable, stable, and bug-free (reliability); can quickly recover from errors and operational interruptions (recoverability); notifies users with appropriate and useful messages (feedback); supports teamwork and data sharing (collaborativity); enables different types of communication among users (communicativity).

Content quality consists of attributes meant for the assessment of the extent to which artefacts created by means of the Web 2.0 application are: error-free, valid, and precise (correctness); complete, displayed clearly, and appropriately represented (coverage); unbiased, trustworthy, and verifiable (credibility); supplementable, modifiable, and updatable (timeliness); advantageous and impact users' decisions (value-added). Performance refers to attributes that measure the extent to which the use of Web 2.0 application: enables users to execute tasks accurately and completely (effectiveness); enables users to quickly perform tasks (efficiency); responds promptly to users' actions (responsiveness); is capable to operate under an increased or expanding workload (scalability); is usable within and beyond initially intended contexts of use (context coverage).

Effort relates to attributes dealing with the evaluation of the degree to which: the interaction with Web 2.0 application requires small amount of keyboard and mouse usage (minimal action); the use of Web 2.0 application requires small amount of mental and perceptive activities (minimal memory load); Web 2.0 application is usable to people with the widest range of characteristics and capabilities (accessibility); users have full freedom in executing tasks by means of the Web 2.0 application (controllability); is simple to operate the Web 2.0 application (ease of use); is easy to become proficient in interacting with the Web 2.0 application (learnability); is simple to memorize how the Web 2.0 application is used (memorability); the interaction with Web 2.0 application is unambiguous (understandability). Acceptability refers to attributes meant for measuring the extent to which: the Web 2.0 application has visually appealing user interface (aesthetics); the Web 2.0 application is beneficial in the context of tasks execution (usefulness); the interaction with the Web 2.0 application holds the users' attention and stimulates their imagination (playfulness); users have positive perception about the use of Web 2.0 application (attitude towards use); the Web 2.0 application has met users' expectations (satisfaction); the Web 2.0 application arouses users' emotional responses (pleasure); the Web 2.0 application is distinctive among applications with the same purpose (uniqueness); users have the intention to continue to use the Web 2.0 application and recommend it to others (loyalty).

3   Methodology

The aim of this paper is to examine the validity of the enhanced version of subjective measuring instrument. For that purpose, two studies were carried out. In the first study, the participants were observed during their interactions with two Web 2.0 applications aimed for collaborative writing (Zoho Writer and Microsoft Word Web App), and in the second with two Web 2.0 applications meant for mind mapping (Mindomo and Wise Mapping). The reason why we have selected these two types of Web 2.0 applications as a representative sample in our research relies on the fact that there are a number of examples how they can be employed in educational settings (for more information see e.g. [3], [15], and [23]). Research subjects in both studies were students from three Croatian higher education institutions. Both studies adopted a repeated measures design comparing evaluated Web 2.0 applications that have the same purpose. Studies were conducted during winter semester of the academic year 2012/2013. To ensure accuracy of the collected data, students were given detailed oral and written instructions related to the implementation of the study in which they were involved. Firstly, students had to complete predefined scenario that was composed of representative assignments (45 in the case of Web 2.0 applications meant for collaborative writing and 43 in the context of Web 2.0 applications aimed for mind mapping). After students have completed the scenario with both Web 2.0 applications, they were asked to fill out the post-use questionnaire and in that way evaluate diverse facets of their quality in use. The questionnaire consisted of 244 statements where each quality in use attribute was assessed with between 3 reflective items and 16 formative indicators. The responses were modulated on a five-point Likert scale (1 – strongly agree, 5 – strongly disagree). A sum of responses yielded a single number that represents a composite measure of the perceived quality in use of evaluated Web 2.0 applications at different levels of granularity in the conceptual model. The findings extracted from the conducted empirical studies are presented and discussed in more detail in the following section.

4   Results

In order to examine differences between evaluated Web 2.0 applications, Wilcoxon Signed-Rank Tests were applied. The reason why we have employed this non-parametric equivalent of the dependent t-test is because results of Shapiro-Wilk Tests revealed that at least one of the variables in a pairwise comparison significantly deviates from a normal distribution ($p < .05$). Consequently, all the reported results are expressed as the median values.

4.1   First study

Participants. A total of 209 respondents were involved in the first study. The sample was composed of 62.68% male and 37.32% female participants. Most of them (44.98%) were students at Polytechnic of Rijeka, 43.54% were enrolled in Faculty of Organization and Informatics in Varaždin while 11.48% of them studied at Faculty of Economics in Split. At the time when the study was carried out, the majority of participants (45%) were first-year undergraduate students. They ranged in age from 18 to 30 years ($M = 20.18$, $SD = 1.594$). More than half of respondents (62.68%) had at least good knowledge of using Web 2.0 applications. All study participants had been loyal users of the social networking site Facebook and video podcasting service YouTube (73.21% and 67.47%, respectively, used those applications at least between once to twice a day).

Findings. The participants perceived the overall quality in use of Zoho Writer ($Mdn = 587$) as significantly higher ($Z = -4.934$, $p = .000$, $r = -.24$) than those of Microsoft Word Web App ($Mdn = 622$). More specifically, it appeared that Microsoft Word Web App ($Mdn = 159$) has significantly lower level of the perceived system quality ($Z = -2.290$, $p < .05$, $r = -.11$) than Zoho Writer ($Mdn = 152$). The analysis of collected data also revealed that Zoho Writer ($Mdn = 32$) has significantly better navigation mechanisms ($Z = -2.336$, $p < .05$, $r = -.11$) than Microsoft Word Web App ($Mdn = 34$). On the other hand, results of the analysis indicate that Microsoft Word Web App ($Mdn = 11$) has significantly less consistent structure and design of interface elements ($Z = -2.210$, $p < .05$, $r = -.11$) than Zoho Writer ($Mdn = 10$). Pairwise comparisons discovered that users perceived interaction with Microsoft Word Web App ($Mdn = 10$) as significantly more similar to previously used applications ($Z = -2.834$, $p < .01$, $r = -.14$) than interaction with Zoho Writer ($Mdn = 11$). Wilcoxon signed ranks test implies that Zoho Writer ($Mdn = 27$) can be customized to suit users' needs to the significantly higher degree ($Z = -2.725$, $p < .01$, $r = -.13$) than Microsoft Word Web App ($Mdn = 28$). Compared to Zoho Writer ($Mdn = 40$), Microsoft Word Web App ($Mdn = 39$) has significantly better mechanisms aimed for protecting created artefacts from unauthorized use ($Z = -4.651$, $p < .001$, r = -.23). The evaluated Web 2.0 applications (Mdn = 12) do not differ significantly (Z = -.915, p = .360) in terms of their operating in diverse browsers and at different devices. However, Wilcoxon signed ranks test indicates that search engine implemented in Microsoft Word Web App (Mdn = 13) is significantly less accurate and efficient (Z = -3.698, p = .000, r = -.18) than those integrated in Zoho Writer (Mdn = 11). Concerning the quality of artefacts being exchanged with other desktop, web, or mobile applications, Zoho Writer (Mdn = 8) presents significantly better solution (Z = -7.875, p = .000, r = -.39) than Microsoft Word Web App (Mdn = 11).

The perceived service quality of Zoho Writer (Mdn = 141) is significantly higher (Z = -7.110, p = .000, r = -.35) than those of Microsoft Word Web App (Mdn = 153). According to the results of data analysis, the quality of help resources provided by Microsoft Word Web App (Mdn = 18) is significantly lower (Z = -3.735, p < .001, r = -.18) than those offered by Zoho Writer (Mdn = 16). In addition, it appeared that Zoho Writer (Mdn = 14) is significantly more readily available to users (Z = -5.629, p = .000, r = -.28) than Microsoft Word Web App (Mdn = 16). Microsoft Word Web App (Mdn = 40) provides significantly less functionalities that facilitate management of created artefacts (Z = -4.907, p = .000, r = -.24) than Zoho Writer (Mdn = 38) offers. There was no significant difference between Web 2.0 applications meant for collaborative writing (Mdn = 9) in terms of the quality of mechanisms that prevent users from committing errors (Z = -.264, p = .792). On contrary, Zoho Writer (Mdn = 9) has significantly less bugs (Z = -2.518, p < .05, r = -.12) than Microsoft Word Web App (Mdn = 10). Furthermore, Microsoft Word Web App (Mdn = 11) is significantly less successful in recovering from errors (Z = -3.294, p = .001, r = -.16) than Zoho Writer (Mdn = 10). Nevertheless, the quality of displayed messages was not significantly affected by the Web 2.0 application (Mdn = 20) that was used while performing steps of the scenario (Z = -1.180, p = .238). Finally, Zoho Writer (Mdn = 18 and 8, respectively) offers significantly better support for teamwork (Z = -5.133, p = .000, r = -.25) and communication (Z = -7.586, p = .000, r = -.37) among users than Microsoft Word Web App (Mdn = 19 and 9, respectively) does.

According to the results of data analysis, quality of artefacts created with Zoho Writer (Mdn = 50) is significantly higher (Z = -3.025, p < .005, r = -.15) than quality of artefacts generated by means of Microsoft Word Web App (Mdn = 50). Artefacts created by employing Microsoft Word Web App (Mdn = 13) are significantly less accurate (Z = -2.141, p < .05, r = -.10) than artefacts derived from the use of Zoho Writer (Mdn = 13). However, there was no significant difference between evaluated Web 2.0 applications (Mdn = 8 and 13, respectively) in terms of completeness (Z = -1.485, p = .137) and credibility (Z = -1.042, p = .298) of generated artefacts. The quality of user interface functionalities for altering created artefacts was significantly higher (Z = -2.175, p < .05, r = -.11) in the case of Zoho Writer (Mdn = 4) than in the context of Microsoft Word Web App (Mdn = 5). Finally, artefacts created by means of Microsoft Word Web App (Mdn = 10) are significantly less advantageous (Z = -2.207, p < .05, r = -.11) than artefacts generated with Zoho Writer (Mdn = 10).

Results of the analysis indicate that interaction with Microsoft Word Web App (Mdn = 54) enhances users' performance in executing task to significantly lower extent (Z = -5.077, p = .000, r = -.25) than the use of Zoho Writer (Mdn = 50) does.

Namely, when interacting with Zoho Writer (Mdn = 12), users are significantly more effective in executing tasks (Z = -6.584, p = .000, r = -.32) than when they are using Microsoft Word Web App (Mdn = 15). On the other hand, results of data analysis imply that evaluated Web 2.0 applications for collaborative writing (Mdn = 10) do not differ significantly from the perspective of users' efficiency in completing the scenario (Z = -.006, p = .238). Microsoft Word Web App (Mdn = 10) is significantly slower in responding to users' actions (Z = -3.348, p = .001, r = -.16) than Zoho Writer (Mdn = 9). In addition, Zoho Writer (Mdn = 9) has significantly higher level of scalability (Z = -5.419, p = .000, r = -.27) than Microsoft Word Web App (Mdn = 11). Finally, there is no significant difference (Z = -.941, p = .346) between Zoho Writer (Mdn = 9) and Microsoft Word Web App (Mdn = 10) regarding the flexibility in the scope of their use.

The analysis of collected data suggests that Zoho Writer (Mdn = 80) and Microsoft Word Web App (Mdn = 81) do not differ significantly in terms of the overall perceived effort needed for the completion of the scenario steps (Z = -1.480, p = .139). Although there was no significant difference between evaluated Web 2.0 applications (Mdn = 12) in terms of the amount of mental effort required to execute steps of the scenario (Z = -1.910, p = .056), users reported that they had to invest significantly more physical effort to complete the scenario (Z = -2.044, p < .05, r = -.10) when they used Microsoft Word Web App (Mdn = 10) than when they applied Zoho Writer (Mdn = 10). Results of data analysis also revealed that Zoho Writer (Mdn = 17) is significantly more accessible to users with different capabilities and characteristics (Z = -2.676, p < .01, r = -.13) than Microsoft Word Web App (Mdn = 18). Furthermore, it was discovered that users have significantly less freedom (Z = -2.084, p < .005, r = -.10) in interaction with Microsoft Word Web App (Mdn = 7) than when they use Zoho Writer (Mdn = 6). Besides, it is significantly easier to memorize (Z = -2.944, p < .005, r = -.14) how to use Microsoft Word Web App (Mdn = 6) than to remember where interface functionalities of Zoho Writer (Mdn = 6) are located. Nevertheless, there is no significant difference between Zoho Writer (Mdn = 11, 8, and 8, respectively) and Microsoft Word Web App (Mdn = 10, 8, and 8, respectively) in terms of their ease of use (Z = -.927, p = .354), learnability (Z = -.796, p = .354), and understandability (Z = -1.086, p = .278). According to the results of gathered data, Zoho Writer (Mdn = 113) has significantly higher level of perceived acceptability (Z = -3.539, p = .000, r = -.17) than Microsoft Word Web App (Mdn = 117). No significant difference was found between evaluated Web 2.0 applications (Mdn = 11) in terms of the user interface attractiveness (Z = -.093, p = .926). However, Microsoft Word Web App (Mdn = 14) was perceived by users as less beneficial Web 2.0 application for completion of scenario tasks (Z = -4.998, p = .000, r = -.24) than Zoho Writer (Mdn = 13). In addition, there was no significant difference between Web 2.0 applications aimed for collaborative writing (Mdn = 18) in terms of their playfulness (Z = -1.540, p = .124). It was also found that users have a significantly more positive attitude (Z = -3.558, p = .000, r = -.17) towards using Zoho Writer (Mdn = 11) than towards the interaction with Microsoft Word Web App (Mdn = 12). Besides, participants reported that Zoho Writer (Mdn = 12) made significantly better impression on them (Z = -4.601, p = .000, r = -.23) than Microsoft

Word Web App (Mdn = 14) did. However, the level of pleasure perceived by respondents do not differ significantly between evaluated Web 2.0 applications for collaborative writing (Mdn = 12, Z = -1.507, p = .132). Results of data analysis also uncovered that Microsoft Word Web App (Mdn = 12) is significantly less distinctive among web application with the same purpose (Z = -3.067, p < .005, r = -.15) than Zoho Writer (Mdn = 12). Finally, significantly more participants (Z = -2.826, p = .005, r = -.14) is willing to continue to use Zoho Writer (Mdn = 20) than to employ Microsoft Word Web App (Mdn = 22) regularly.

4.2   Second Study

Participants. A total of 213 respondents (61.03% male, 38.97% female), aged 20.18 years (SD = 1.627) on average, took part in the second study. All of them had been using Facebook and YouTube on a regular basis (75.58% and 70.42%, respectively, had been using those popular Web 2.0 applications at least between once and twice a day). More than half of students (62.91%) reported that they have at least good knowledge of using Web 2.0 applications. At the time the study took place, the majority of participants (44.60%) were first-year undergraduate students. Most of them (45.07%) studied at Polytechnic of Rijeka, 42.72% were enrolled in Faculty of Organization and Informatics in Varaždin while 12.21% of them were students at Faculty of Economics in Split.

Findings. According to the results of data analysis, Mindomo (Mdn = 552) has significantly higher (Z = -11.812, p = .000, r = -.57) level of the perceived quality in use than Wise Mapping (Mdn = 635). More specifically, it appeared that the system quality of Wise Mapping (Mdn = 170) was perceived as significantly lower (Z = -9.948, p = .000, r = -.48) than those of Mindomo (Mdn = 155). It was also found that navigational mechanisms offered by Mindomo (Mdn = 32) are significantly better organized and deployed (Z = -7.309, p = .000, r = -.35) than those provided by Wise Mapping (Mdn = 34). Moreover, participants reported that Wise Mapping (Mdn = 11) employs significantly less uniform interface functionalities, design, and terminology (Z = -6.036, p = .000, r = -.29) than Mindomo (Mdn = 10) does. In addition, data analysis uncovered that Mindomo (Mdn = 11) is significantly more similar to web applications respondents normally use (Z = -4.031, p = .000, r = -.20) than Wise Mapping (Mdn = 12). Besides, Wise Mapping (Mdn = 30) is significantly less customizable (Z = -10.158, p = .000, r = -.49) than Mindomo (Mdn = 26). However, Web 2.0 applications meant for mind mapping (Mdn = 42) do not differ significantly in terms of the quality of mechanisms that protect security of created artefacts (Z = -.699, p = .485). Results of data analysis indicate that Mindomo (Mdn = 13) is significantly more compatible with diverse web browsers and devices that can be connected to the Internet (Z = -4.920, p = .000, r = -.24) than Wise Mapping (Mdn = 13). In the context of the support for the exchange of created artefacts and quality of artefacts that have been exchanged, Mindomo (Mdn = 8) presents significantly better solution (Z = -5.111, p = .000, r = -.25) than Wise Mapping (Mdn = 10). Search results provided by internal search engine implemented in Wise Mapping (Mdn = 15) are significantly less accurate and relevant (Z = -7.751, p = .000, r = -.38) than those of internal search engine integrated in Mindomo (Mdn = 11).

Results of data analysis suggest that Mindomo (Mdn = 137) has significantly higher degree of perceived service quality (Z = -11.554, p = .000, r = -.56) than Wise Mapping (Mdn = 160). Namely, help resources that are implemented in Wise Mapping (Mdn = 21) are of significantly lower quality (Z = -9.135, p = .000, r = -.44) than those integrated in Mindomo (Mdn = 16). In addition, Mindomo (Mdn = 14) has significantly higher level of perceived availability (Z = -6.994, p = .000, r = -.34) than Wise Mapping (Mdn = 16). On the other hand, Wise Mapping (Mdn = 41) contains significantly less functionalities meant for artefacts management (Z = -8.692, p = .000, r = -.42) than Mindomo (Mdn = 36). The quality of functionalities that disable users from committing errors is significantly higher (Z = -4.856, p = .000, r = -.24) in the case of Mindomo (Mdn = 8) than in the context of Wise Mapping (Mdn = 9). Drawing on the results of data analysis, Wise Mapping (Mdn = 9) is significantly less dependable and stable mind mapping Web 2.0 application (Z = -3.779, p = .000, r = -.18) than Mindomo (Mdn = 8). It was also discovered that Mindomo (Mdn = 8) is significantly more efficient and effective in recovering from errors and operational interruptions (Z = -5.320, p = .000, r = -.26) than Wise Mapping (Mdn = 9). Besides, messages displayed by Wise Mapping (Mdn = 22) are significantly less useful and precise (Z = -5.791, p = .000, r = -.28) than messages shown by Mindomo (Mdn = 20). Finally, analysis of collected data revealed that Mindomo (Mdn = 17 and 8, respectively) provides better support for collaboration (Z = -8.413, p = .000, r = -.41) and communication (Z = -9.876, p = .000, r = -.48) among users than Wise Mapping (Mdn = 19 and 12, respectively) does. The quality of mind maps created by means of Mindomo (Mdn = 48) is significantly better (Z = -7.628, p = .000, r = -.22) than quality of mind maps generated with Wise Mapping (Mdn = 51). Artefacts derived from the use of Wise Mapping (Mdn = 13, 8, 13, 4, and 10, respectively) are significantly less correct (Z = -4.591, p = .000, r = -.22), complete (Z = -6.413, p = .000, r = -.31), trustworthy (Z = -5.106, p = .000, r = -.25), modifiable (Z = -3.426, p = .001, r = -.17), and beneficial (Z = -5.311, p = .000, r = -.26) than those generated by means of Mindomo (Mdn = 12, 8, 12, 4, and 10, respectively).

Results of data analysis indicate that users' performance in completing tasks is significantly lower (Z = -6.699, p = .000, r = -.32) when they use Wise Mapping (Mdn = 52) than when they employ Mindomo (Mdn = 48) for the same purpose. It was also found that interaction with Mindomo (Mdn = 10) enhances users' effectiveness in generating mind maps to significantly greater extent (Z = -7.167, p = .000, r = -.37) than the use of Wise Mapping (Mdn = 12) does. When interacting with Mindomo (Mdn = 9), users can complete tasks significantly much quicker (Z = -5.052, p = .000, r = -.24) than when they apply Wise Mapping (Mdn = 10). The perceived responsiveness of Wise Mapping (Mdn = 9) to users' actions is significantly lower (Z = -2.822, p = .005, r = -.14) than those of Mindomo (Mdn = 8). Nevertheless, Web 2.0 applications (Mdn = 11) aimed for mind mapping do not differ significantly in terms of their capability to retain performance under an increased workload (Z = -1.332, p = .183). Finally, the analysis of collected data revealed that

Mindomo (Mdn = 10) has significantly wider range of uses (Z = -5.529, p = .000, r = -.27) than Wise Mapping (Mdn = 10). Perceived overall effort needed for executing tasks is significantly higher (Z = -11.509, p = .000, r = -.56) in the case of Wise Mapping (Mdn = 83) than in the context of Mindomo (Mdn = 72). There was no significant difference between evaluated mind mapping Web 2.0 applications (Mdn = 10 and 12, respectively) in terms of perceived amount of physical (Z = -1.922, p = .055) and mental (Z = -.234, p = .815) effort needed to complete the scenario steps. On the other hand, it was found that Mindomo (Mdn = 15) is significantly more usable to users with diverse capabilities and characteristics (Z = -9.858, p = -.48) than Wise Mapping (Mdn = 18). Furthermore, users stated that the way of carrying out tasks by means of Wise Mapping (Mdn = 7) is significantly less flexible (Z = -6.138, p = .000, r = -.30) than using Mindomo (Mdn = 6) for the same purpose. Results of data analysis also indicate that is significantly easier for users to operate (Z = -11.915, p = .000, r = -.58) Mindomo (Mdn = 8) than to execute tasks by means of Wise Mapping (Mdn = 11). Users reported that is significantly harder (Z = -4.453, p = .000, r = -.22) to become proficient in using Wise Mapping (Mdn = 8) than to learn how to use Mindomo (Mdn = 8). Besides, the analysis of collected data uncovered that is significantly easier (Z = -4.443, p = .000, r = -.22) to memorize how Mindomo (Mdn = 6) is used than to remember how to interact with Wise Mapping (Mdn = 6). Finally, interface functionalities provided by Wise Mapping (Mdn = 8) are significantly less comprehensible (Z = -5.504, p = .000, r = -.27) than those offered by Mindomo (Mdn = 8). Considering results of data analysis, Mindomo (Mdn = 96) is significantly better accepted by users (Z = -10.710, p = .000, r = -.52) than Wise Mapping (Mdn = 120). More specifically, interface design of Mindomo (Mdn = 9) is significantly more pleasant to the eye (Z = -10.537, p = .000, r = -.51) than those of Wise Mapping (Mdn = 15). Moreover, users believe that Wise Mapping (Mdn = 13) is significantly less advantageous in the context of creating mind maps (Z = -7.171, p = .000, r = -.35) than Mindomo (Mdn = 10). Respondents reported that using Mindomo (Mdn = 16) can successfully hold their attention for significantly longer period of time (Z = -7.380, p = .000, r = -.36) than interaction with Wise Mapping (Mdn = 18). Results of the analysis also imply that users have significantly less positive attitude (Z = -8.484, p = .000, r = -.41) towards using Wise Mapping (Mdn = 13) than towards interaction with Mindomo (Mdn = 11). Besides, Wise Mapping (Mdn = 14) has met users' expectations to significantly lower degree (Z = -8.387, p = .000, r = -.41) than Mindomo (Mdn = 10) has. Furthermore, users reported that they had significantly less fun (Z = -7.605, p = .000, r = -.37) when they have been creating mind maps with Wise Mapping (Mdn = 12) than when they have been using Mindomo (Mdn = 10) for the same purpose. Mindomo (Mdn = 9) is also significantly more unique among applications meant for mind mapping (Z = -8.980, p = .000, r = -.44) than Wise Mapping (Mdn = 12). Finally, significantly more respondents are willing to use Mindomo (Mdn = 17) frequently (Z = -8.040, p = .000, r = -.39) than to employ Wise Mapping (Mdn = 23) on regular basis.

5   Concluding Remarks

With an objective to examine the validity of the post-use questionnaire aimed for evaluating the quality in use of Web 2.0 applications, two empirical studies were carried out. The analysis of collected data uncovered statistically significant differences between evaluated Web 2.0 applications in both conducted studies. More specifically, composite measures which represent a sum of responses at different levels of granularity in the conceptual model have shown small (.10), medium (.30), and large (.50) effects in size (as proposed in [3]) which indicate that post-use questionnaire has a high level of validity and can be therefore employed for the assessment of all relevant aspects of the perceived quality in use of Web 2.0 applications. In that respect, the work presented in this paper provides implications for both researchers and practitioners. Given that proposed enhancement of the conceptual model adds to the current body of knowledge, researcher can use it as a framework for future advances in the context of evaluating the quality in use of Web 2.0 applications. On the other hand, practitioners can apply the post-use questionnaire to measure and improve the quality in use of Web 2.0 applications. Taking into account that reported findings are a constituent part of an ongoing research, our future work will be focused on the assessment of psychometric characteristics of the conceptual model that will reflect interplay among specified quality in use attributes.

References

1. Bennett, S., Bishop, A., Dalgarno, B., Waycott, J., Kennedy, G.: Implementing Web 2.0 technologies in higher education: A collective case study. Computers & Education 59(2), 524–534 (2012)
2. Bubaš, G., Orehovački, T., Balaban, I., Ćorić, A.: Evaluation of Web 2.0 Tools in the e-Learning Context: Case Studies Related to Pedagogy and Usability. In: Rudak, L., Diks, K., Madey, J. (eds.) University Information Systems - Selected Problems, pp. 259–277. Difin SA, Warsaw (2010)
3. Buisine, S., Besacier, G., Najm, M., Aoussat, A., Vernier, F.: Computer-supported creativity: Evaluation of a tabletop mind-map application. In: Harris, D. (ed.) HCII 2007 and EPCE 2007. LNCS (LNAI), vol. 4562, pp. 22–31. Springer, Heidelberg (2007)
4. Cohen, J.: A power primer. Psychological Bulletin 112(1), 155–159 (1992)
5. Den Exter, K., Rowe, S., Boyd, W., Lloyd, D.: Using Web 2.0 Technologies for Collaborative Learning in Distance Education - Case Studies from an Australian University. Future Internet 4(1), 216–237 (2012)
6. Downes, S.: E-learning 2.0. eLearn Magazine – Education and Technology in Perspective (2005), http://www.elearnmag.org/subpage.cfm?section=articles&article=29-1
7. Dwivedi, Y.K., Ramdani, B., Williams, M.D., Mitra, A., Williams, J., Niranjan, S.: Factors influencing user adoption of Web 2.0 applications. International Journal of Indian Culture and Business Management 7(1), 53–71 (2013)
8. García-Martín, J., García-Sánchez, J.-N.: Patterns of Web 2.0 tool use among young Spanish people. Computers & Education 67, 105–120 (2013)

9. Hartshorne, R., Ajjan, H.: Examining student decisions to adopt Web 2.0 technologies: theory and empirical tests. Journal of Computing in Higher Education 21(3), 183–198 (2009)

10. ISO/IEC 25010:2011. Systems and software engineering - Systems and software Quality Requirements and Evaluation (SQuaRE) - System and software quality models (2011)

11. Orehovački, T.: Development of a Methodology for Evaluating the Quality in Use of Web 2.0 Applications. In: Campos, P., Graham, N., Jorge, J., Nunes, N., Palanque, P., Winckler, M. (eds.) INTERACT 2011, Part IV. LNCS, vol. 6949, pp. 382–385. Springer, Heidelberg (2011)

12. Orehovački, T.: Perceived Quality of Cloud Based Applications for Collaborative Writing. In: Pokorny, J., et al. (eds.) Information Systems Development – Business Systems and Services: Modeling and Development, pp. 575–586. Springer, Heidelberg (2011)

13. Orehovački, T.: Proposal for a Set of Quality Attributes Relevant for Web 2.0 Application Success. In: Proceedings of the 32nd International Conference on Information Technology Interfaces, pp. 319–326. IEEE Press, Cavtat (2010)

14. Orehovački, T., Bubaš, G., Konecki, M.: Web 2.0 in Education and Potential Factors of Web 2.0 Use by Students of Information Systems. In: Proceedings of the 31st International Conference on Information Technology Interfaces, pp. 443–448. IEEE Press, Cavtat (2009)

15. Orehovački, T., Bubaš, G., Kovačić, A.: Taxonomy of Web 2.0 Applications with Educational Potential. In: Cheal, C., Coughlin, J., Moore, S. (eds.) Transformation in Teaching: Social Media Strategies in Higher Education, pp. 43–72. Informing Science Press, Santa Rosa (2012)

16. Orehovački, T., Granić, A., Kermek, D.: Evaluating the Perceived and Estimated Quality in Use of Web 2. 0 Applications. The Journal of Systems and Software 86(12), 3039–3059 (2013)

17. Orehovački, T., Granić, A., Kermek, D.: Exploring the Quality in Use of Web 2.0 Applications: The Case of Mind Mapping Services. In: Harth, A., Koch, N. (eds.) ICWE 2011. LNCS, vol. 7059, pp. 266–277. Springer, Heidelberg (2012)

18. Orehovački, T., Žajdela Hrustek, N.: Development and Validation of an Instrument to Measure the Usability of Educational Artifacts Created with Web 2.0 Applications. In: Marcus, A. (ed.) DUXU 2013, Part I. LNCS, vol. 8012, pp. 369–378. Springer, Heidelberg (2013)

19. O'Reilly, T.: What is Web 2.0: Design patterns and business models for the next generation of software (2005), http://oreilly.com/web2/archive/what-is-web-20.html

20. Pang, M., Suh, W., Hong, J., Kim, J., Lee, H.: A New Web Site Quality Assessment Model for the Web 2.0 Era. In: Murugesan, S. (ed.) Handbook of Research on Web 2.0, 3.0, and X.0: Technologies, Business, and Social Applications, pp. 387–410. IGI Global, Hershey (2010)

21. Sassano, R., Olsina, L., Mich, L.: Modeling Content Quality for the Web 2.0 and Follow-on Applications. In: Murugesan, S. (ed.) Handbook of Research on Web 2.0, 3.0, and X.0: Technologies, Business, and Social Applications, pp. 371–386. IGI Global, Hershey (2010)

22. Simões, L., Gouveia, L.B.: Web 2.0 and Higher Education: Pedagogical Implications. In: 4th International Barcelona Conference on Higher Education (2008), http://www2.ufp.pt/~lmbg/com/lsimoes_guni08.pdf

23. Vallance, M., Towndrow, P.A., Wiz, C.: Conditions for Successful Online Document Collaboration. TechTrends 54(1), 20–24 (2010)

Promoting Distributed Cognition at MOOC Ecosystems

Kai Pata and Emanuele Bardone

Centre for Educational Technology, Tallinn University, Tallinn Estonia
{kpata,bardone}@tlu.ee

Abstract. The paper proposes describing connectivist MOOCs as a learning ecosystem. We highlight two aspects of distributed cognition epistemic and collective – that MOOCs promote and relate these with learning by chance-seeking and learning from ecological enculturation. Finally we outline some design aspects for supporting chance-seeking and learning from an encultured environment in connectivist MOOC ecosystems.

1 Introduction

Connectivist MOOCs may be viewed as self-organised ecosystems of learners and digital contents and services, which have good potential for supporting distributed cognition. In this theoretical paper we explain how some of the learning behaviours related with distributed cognition – learning as chance-seeking and ecological enculturation – may be promoted by building on the ecological principles that guide MOOC ecosystems. We outline some design aspects of MOOC ecosystems for supporting chance-seeking and learning from an encultured environment.

2 MOOC Ecosystems as Distributed Cognitive Systems

2.1 Characteristics of MOOCs as Learning Ecosystems

We define a MOOC as a unit of learning with specified institutional affiliation, schedule, content and learning tasks which engages self-directed and self-organised learners and leading practitioners in the field by fostering open enrollment, open curriculum, open and partially learner-defined learning goals and outcomes, the usage of open resources and open learning environment, and the enabled open monitoring of learning activities (see [1][2]) with the aim of facilitating learning as a process of navigating, growing and pruning connections and interactions within distributed networks, and generating coherence, resonance and synchronisation in knowledge [3]. There is a diversity among MOOC designs – some focus on supporting the development of learners' domain-related knowledge and self-directed learning competences [4,5], whereas others, inspired by Connectivism [6], target rather the emergence of the distributed connective

P. Zaphiris and A. Ioannou (Eds.): LCT 2014, Part I, LNCS 8523, pp. 204–215, 2014.

knowledge networks among learners which should sustain after the end of the course [1,7,2,8]. We see our contribution in proposing the distributed cognitive learning behaviours that are particularly promoted by connectivist MOOCs because of their ecosystem-like functioning.

The MOOC is a learning ecosystem in which we may consider three types of "organisms": 1) producers, 2) digital "organisms" (such as digital learning contents created by various MOOC users, digital learning tools and services activated as part of PLEs and the big MOOC ecosystem), and c) the digital learning services of MOOCs. In accordance with the 'produsage' concept introduced by Bruns [9] we may assume that all users (learners, experts, facilitators) provide the MOOC with some services that enhance learning. 'Produsage concept combines learners production and consumption as inseparable from each other in the surrounding environment. The learning services may be considered as the digital organisms that exist as the symbiosis of digital components and produsers. Since different produsers target learning differently, they populate the MOOC with particular kind of learning services for their own and their communitys benefit.

Knowledge in MOOCs is operated by as well as is incorporated into the different learning services that the produsers activate. Knowledge can flow and become aggregated as a distributed structure in the learning ecosystem, creating new opportunities for 'produsers' who can remix it repurpose it, feed it forward, or create new knowledge [6,10] and new learning services of it. An example of such learning services is scaffolding services that are created by other learners and facilitators, or that emerge as a result of the accumulation of MOOC participants learning and support activities [11]. For example, the socially annotated and aggregated contents may provide learning support [12]. MOOC learners' motivation appears as a formation of intention and attention of the resources available in the MOOC in an ongoing coupling between learner's goals and the affordances they perceive from the environment [13,14]. Considering and using learning services that are currently available in the MOOC ecosystem causes some ecosystem services to compete with each other and others to form alliances, some services increase in numbers while others perish. User attention fuels the knowledge flows through the services, which defines the productivity of learning ecosystems. Abundance and variety of mutually communicating learning services in MOOC ecosystems provided by all MOOC participants facilitates their mutual awareness and participatory surveillance [15,5] which in turn contributes to social embeddedness as a motivating factor of learning [16,17].

2.2 Distributed Cognition in MOOCs

MOOCs have a similarity to natural ecosystems also at a distributed cognition level – while in a natural ecosystem the flow and transformation of energy and matter are operated by the trophic network of species, the MOOCs as distributed cognitive networks facilitate knowledge transformations. In a distributed cognition approach Hollan, Hutchins, and Kirsh [18] explain interactions and the coordination of activities between people and technologies assuming that people form a tightly coupled system with their environments, and the latter serves as one's partner or cognitive ally in the struggle to control the activity. Social organisation is therefore seen as a form of cognitive architecture that determines the way information flows in the context of activity [18].

There are two main ways in which, distributed cognition may be fruitfully framed in MOOCs – epistemic distributed cognition that we relate with chance-seeking, and collective distributed cognition that we relate with learning from ecological enculturation. It is important to note that chance-seeking and learning from ecological enculturation complement each other in the MOOC ecosystem.

Epistemic Distributed Cognition. The word "distributed" refers to the fact that humans drastically lean on external resources in solving problems and making decisions. MOOC takes place in a digital (but also a hybrid) distributed learning environment, which is co-constructed by users with different backgrounds, but shared interests. From the user's point of view the emerging infrastructure can be a temporally extended personal learning environment (PLE), which allows the sharing of learning resources (people, artifacts, practices) and goals openly among the MOOCs learning networks. This distributed cognitive system serves as a partially external and uncontrollable locus of control [18] both from the point of view of learners as well as facilitators, and course organisers. In this case, distributed cognition refers to the assumption that one's performance cannot only be confined to what happens within his or her own skull. Conversely, humans continuously offload some of their cognitive functions onto external objects and artifacts, which can just be found out-there or designed for accomplishing specific goals and tasks. In this respect, human cognition functions in an opportunistic way, that is, by seeking out chances to make the most of body and (social) environment [19] and integrating them into unified systems of distributed problem-solving [20]. Distributed cognition considers the interactions of people and the resources in the environment as an emergent distributed cognitive system [18] where internal resources memory, attention, executive function and external resources the objects, artifacts, and at-hand materials and software are temporally integrated into goal-based affordance networks [21] that support actions. This kind of distribution is eminently epistemic, because it deals with the very activity of knowing and understanding the world one lives in. Giere [22] refers to this kind of distribution as "locally distributed" cognition. We prefer to call it epistemic distributed cognition (hereafter EDC), because we want to stress the epistemic dimension involved. Characteristic to EDC is that it can only be attributed to individual agents (produsers) who are the only ones that are endowed with attributes such as intentions, beliefs, consciousness, and so on. EDC is based on a tacit dimension of knowledge that is different for everyone and influences different chances to be found, creating diversity and variability of using external resources as part of the distributed cognitive system.

Collective Distributed Cognition. The second type of distributed cognition may be called collective distributed cognition (hereafter CDC). In this concept the word "distributed" may be applied to cognition where the output of a certain cognitive process cannot be attributed or tracked back to the effort of a single agent, but it is the product of collective effort. For example, a connectivist knowledge creation is the result of a number of MOOC produsers plus various digital artifacts and tools. CDC targets ecological enculturation. Traditionally, enculturation refers to the process by which a person becomes acquainted with a given culture (or community of practice) [23], which may be related with EDC. In our approach, enculturation refers to the fact that part of the environment can be encultured, that is, modified so that it becomes potentially meaningful for certain purposes rather than others. Bardone [19] suggests that human beings act as an integral part of their environment while at the same time actively modifying and constructing this environment. Enculturation brings the traces of previous activities available in some form for future use. We can distinguish between emergent and purposeful enculturation. While emergent enculturation occurs as a product of self-organised system behaviour from the interactions between various types of produsers such as in connectivist MOOCs, the purposeful enculturation can be related to pre-designed learning environments and instructional designs.

3 Learning Behaviours Related to Distributed Cognition

3.1 Learning as a Chance-Seeker

Many participants of MOOCs do not come to the course with certain objectives in mind, but rather discover them while learning at the MOOC [2]. Learning lies outside the realm of regular expectations and involves a forward-looking attitude. We tend to treat learning as a linear process that can somehow be "directed" and would imply to assume something we do not know yet. This gives the illusion that we can actually control and therefore direct the whole process, when in fact our understanding is based on a mere selection of those past events that help to create a coherent and therefore compelling story. We can easily come up with a causal explanation about how and why learning has occurred. However, that can only happen retrospectively – by looking backward at the process after it came to an end, as many MOOC participants have reported [2]. Incoherence and messiness cannot fit into the linear learning model. We are unable to predict learning events because there is nothing in the past that may reasonably hint at their happening. As Shackle [24] brilliantly noted that all we know about the future is nothing but an inference drawn from the past. We can rely on the past, if we can reasonably assume that the future will resemble the past, but that is never the case. Past events can never be a solid bases for predicting what is going to happen next.

We tend to think that the distribution of cognition in MOOCs, and the subsequent extension of 'produsers ability to solve problems, can only be with regards to the interaction with specific objects, tools and services available at learning environment allowing them for extending their specific abilities. However, little attention has been given precisely to situations in which it is the unanticipatedness of MOOC ecosystem that provides a fundamental aid. We posit that MOOC participants dynamically evolve the ecosystem producing its unanticipatedness. The idea of environmental unanticipatedness posits that the environment plays an active role in a given course of action, since unanticipated and unexpected events potentially open up the way to new knowledge or information we would not be able to acquire otherwise. Chinese general Sun Tzu in The Art of War pointed out that "if we do not know what we need to know, then everything looks like important information". This means that under conditions of ignorance and inexperience, we can only turn to our environment as a provider of unanticipated and potentially helpful events. We lean on something external to us, something that we basically lack for we must entrust ourselves to something we do not fully or partly control. There is however a crucial difference between environmental unanticipatedness and virtually all other forms of cognitive distribution: we make use of our ignorance and turn to environmental unanticipatedness, when we just do not know; while when we are have a precise intent in mind, we can turn to certain patterns detectable in the ecosystem (which we will explain further on).

Learning implies chance-seeking that we introduce here as one of the fruitful distributed cognitive behaviours in MOOCs. Chance-seeking is about how people may come to utilise chance to their advantage and tentatively amplify the unanticipated, yet positive potential, until they create a useful pattern, a potentially replicable solution to the problem for themselves. In this case the learner can identify that he has learned something. In our definition, a chance is any unanticipated event that falls outside of one's control. Such an event conveys an opportunity for action that appears to have some strategic value in pursuing one's learning goal. This definition contains three elements that need clarification. Unanticipatedness is related to our inability to guess and predict what is going to happen on the basis of what we know, so as to be prepared beforehand to face the possible consequences. Not all unanticipated events in MOOCs that lead to learning are necessarily chances, but only those, which convey an opportunity for learning. Chance must somehow appear meaningful to the person. One has to identify in a chance event purposiveness and positive significance with respect to personal learning goals. Chance may be of no immediate relevancy for one's goal, but it may be conceived as strategically useful, because it projects the problem-solving process towards further chances. So, the identification of a chance implies a sense of purposiveness, it is a form of knowing as one goes rather than knowing before one goes [25]. What a MOOC participant actually identifies as a chance is a subjective matter, and its identification depends on several different factors specific to the individual, including his or her knowledge, attitude, personality, and other more contingent and transitory factors like moods or feelings. It is also important to note that a chance is not necessarily a new or surprising happening, because what counts is the way a person makes sense of it in relation to his or her learning goals.

We cannot anticipate that certain happenings in our ecosystem may turn out to be a resource when we are facing an adapting challenge like in the case of learning. We cannot entirely rely on what happened in the past, but we must inevitably look forward, projecting ourselves onto the future, which is by definition unknown. If we cannot anticipate what is going to happen, we may try to amplify the positive potential of those chance encounters that happen to appear somehow meaningful to us. This process, which is at the heart of chance-seeking, can be characterised as a "deviation-amplifying mutual causal process". This concept was introduced by Magoroh Maruyama [26] to refer to the fact that the outcome of a process is initiated by an insignificant or accidental "kick" and is then built upon its subsequent amplifications and so diverging from the initial condition. The environmental feedback is so that deviations (in the form of unanticipated/unexpected events) are not counteracting the learner's work as in the case of following a predefined and planned course of action. Conversely, deviations become a source of mutual positive feedback, which expose the learner to subsequent and potentially positive unanticipated events.

Once a chance is recognised, an action is taken to amplify the potentials of positive significance. This is indeed entirely conjectural and tentative. The action taken on the basis of inevitably marginal, unassorted and apparently irrelevant resources may uncover new possibilities in terms of subsequent chances or novel observations. This process involves iterative circularity. Which means that the amplification of the positive potentials of chance encounters is reiterated until a satisfying solution is reached, if it is reached. By that the learner forms a personally defined distributed space - a cognitive niche. We see chance amplification as the main way of cognitive niche formation. The chance amplification enables to optimize the results of chance-seeking by testing the fitness of each chance encounter in the ecosystem. As an example of chance amplification we can consider a help-seeking service created by the produser in MOOC: he sends to different spaces (Twitter, blog, forum) the same request, modifies the request content etc. until discovering the viable solution how the requests get answered in this ecosystem.

The whole process of chance amplification can be described in terms of tinkering (or *bricolage*). Planning learning mostly relies on knowledge that necessarily must be held in stock before one starts, one may reasonably design for and aim at optimised solutions. What the chance-seeker does is to tinker with chance encounters. In the case of tinkering, it is not possible to identify beforehand that the body of knowledge will turn out to be relevant: one must act flexibly, and be ready to adjust his or her strategy according to contextual elements as they arise. Tinkering with chance events implies that "we only know what we know when we need to know it", as Snowden [27, p. 110] put it. The process of tinkering with chance encounters is driven by the absence of a plan. The chance-seeker as a tinkerer in MOOC does not subordinate a course of action for making a list of resources one should necessarily have. Tinkering is immediate and contingent upon past events, but with no view to the future [28]. In this respect, creativity emerges by recombining pre-existing resources resonating with chance encounters, as we have noted above. Siemens and Downes [10] have high-lighted repurposing – creating something of their own – as activity learners do at Connectivist MOOCs. They describe at MOOCs the connectivist learning practices of remixing and reflecting on the resources and relating them to what people already know. In our paper we extend repurposing concept also to the learning services that the learners create as producers. We assume that it is important to emphasise that such repurposing has to involve the element of chance, rather than being purposeful action that leads to linear learning. It is worth noting here that those pre-existing resources used in tinkering and repurposing are never the result of a linear process. Conversely, they are bound to contingent happenings. In the case of tinkering with chance events, solutions are never optimised solutions, but always workable and provisional ones, which may serve more as a springboard to subsequent ones than as end-points and definitive results.

3.2   Learning as an Ecological Enculturation

By chance-seeking, the learner can detect one's learning as a personally useful pattern – the solution to his problem. He explores the fitness of this pattern in this eco-system through the process of chance amplification. The result of many chance-seekers self-organised cognitive activities however contributes to ecological enculturation. It is increasing the anticipatedness of the environment by pattern formation. In this chapter we want to discuss patterns from the distributed cognition angle – how they are formed and perceived as part of the encultured environment, and how patterns may influence learning. We want to highlight ecological enculturation and pattern appropriation as second type of distributed cognitive behaviours that are common to MOOC learners.

When we interact with cues in the environment or see the others interacting with it we can recognise the patterns. By definition, a pattern is any regularity that organises what we see in a consistent, regular manner. Alexander and associates [29] define design patterns as the visible/explicit part of a solution to a problem in a field of interest. They assume that patterns tend to focus on the interactions between the physical form of the built environment, and the way in which that inhibits or facilitates various sorts of personal and social behaviour within it [29]. Culture propagates itself with patterns and pattern systems. The patterns are loosely connected across scales: any given pattern typically points to smaller scale patterns which can support it, and larger scale patterns in which it may participate [29].

Several MOOCs designs have incorporated learning analytic elements as part of the course design. It was done with the intention to learn about learning analytics but also with the aim of using learning analytics for making MOOCs more effective, creating the environmental feedback channel for visualizing patterns to the learners. Such learning patterns are apt to guide learners in dynamically making informed decisions and adaptively changing their learning behaviours.

From the CDC point of view, patterns are easily recognisable generalisations of solutions for a problem, that emerge as the contingent result of all the occasions there have been to renew or enrich, or to maintain the stock of this problems solutions, using the remains of previous constructions or destructions from individuals. Culturally, each pattern exists as an emergent niche in the ecosystem in which the environment becomes anticipated and ecologically encultured due to many learners activities. Patterns can appear like visible macro-structures of processes or structures: i) event sequences in distributed systems (e.g. learning paths), ii) semantic knowledge structures (e.g. tag clouds), or as iii) functional (e.g. design solutions as collective phenomena) or iv) behavioural (social network visualisations of interaction) compositions. In MOOCs, mainly the structural patterns of resources and behavioural patterns of users have been visualised with learning analytics tools that have been incorporated to the courses, while recognising processual patterns (e.g. transformative knowledge flows in the ecosystem operated by and incorporated into learning services by producers), and functional patterns (e.g. design structures of the ecosystem services, their abundance and interrelations) is not well supported with visualisations. Neither were such patterns dynamically fed back to the learners. One might anticipate that interacting with the environment having a specific learning goal, the appropriation of patterns would decrease the need to seek chances, since the ecologically encultured environment can lead you with patterns that might do the job effectively. The trivial understanding of pattern usage is, that taking a pattern it can be used as a template for repeating the pattern. However that view of pattern-replication is misleading, since there are no defined patterns one can "take" but patterns exist in an abstract way as effective niches in the encultured environment, which are evolving constantly. These niches emerge as abstract spaces and the range for the pattern niches is created as the fitness of many similar individual patterns is tested in the cultures ecosystem. Alexander et al. [29] calls such niches the pattern prototypes. The embodiment of pattern prototypes has person-dependent and culture-dependent components and variability, therefore at every juncture patterns are perceived and accommodated as part of the chance-seeking process. They are the raw material for bricolage and tinkering. Since learning is a prospective form of cognition that is projected onto and into the future, it is only known by the learner that a collectively formed pattern facilitates something and encapsules the potential of eculturation as some kind of "niche" of this culture that has sorted out some solutions. But he does not know whether any collectively defined pattern helps him in his learning. So we may claim that there can be no learners who are pattern-replicators – using patterns is always related with deviations within the pattern niche. And this pattern niche may be extended or shifted radically by chance-seeking, when totally new solutions are tinkered with as part of learning.

Patterns can be found because they are cognitively afforded partially internal and partially culture defined multi-dimensional spaces [30]. The discoverability of patterns of the culture is related with the cultural belonging as well as the EDC of individuals. The patterns exist as pattern systems, the overlapping niches in the ecosystem from which the chance-seeker may discover and tinker with. An option for finding dimensions incorporated into cultural patterns is aligning one's attention in MOOCs with crowded places, looking for the traces left by others, or mimicking and uptaking others' behaviours in the environment. This is mostly what is happening in current MOOCs that do not comprise sufficient pattern visualizing methods to accumulate learner's behaviours and feedback to them. Another limitation of supporting learning from encultured environment is that the art of creating emergent visualisations that support learners in MOOCs is still not sufficiently advanced. Not much is known about how learners use such visualisations to orient or reorient their learning activities.

4   Designing MOOC Ecosystems to Support Distributed Cognition

In the design approach we suggest considering MOOCs as ecosystems where producers use and also create learning services. Learning services are incorporated into distributed cognitive systems of learners as well as operate the transformative learning flows in their personal and shared distributed cognitive system. The abundance, diversity and variability of the learning services, their interconnections, aggregation and interaction in the MOOC learning ecosystem become the important design considerations that enable distributed cognition for MOOC participants. We posit that dynamically maintaining the emerging learning services in MOOCs as well as promoting distributed cognitive learning behaviors – chance seeking and pattern appropriation – may be done effectively using principles that govern natural ecosystems. Evolving MOOCs as productive distributed cognitive systems presumes promoting the productive loops of pattern appropriation, chance-seeking and ecological enculturation (see Figure 1).

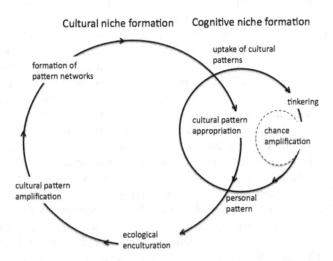

Fig. 1. The distributed cognition – pattern-finding, chance-seeking and ecological enculturation loops

We can relate the two types of distributed cognition to cognitive and cultural niche formation. The epistemic distributed cognition comprises two loops of cognitive niche formation – the creative loop of chance-seeking uses the ecosystem unanticipatedness for chance-seeking, tinkering with chances and chance amplification and results with personal patterns as cognitive niches; the accommodating loop of pattern appropriation builds on cultural anticipatedness and results with validating and amplifying some cultural patterns. The collective distributed cognition and the formation of cultural niches as optimal collectively selected solution paths is fed by the personal patterns. Personal patterns as cognitive niches are incorporated to the cultural patterns and cultural niches of these patterns. The chance-seekers create cognitive niches that may extend or shift the cultural pattern niches evolving the ecosystem, whereas pattern appropriation activity validates cultural pattern niches and stabilizes the ecosystem.

The design approach employed in MOOC ecosystems to promote epistemic and collective distributed cognition is twofold. On the one hand the connectivist MOOCs should be built so that they facilitate the self-organisation of learning ecosystems, which promotes environmental unanticipatedness for chance-seekers. On the other hand, for promoting pattern appropriation and increasing ecological enculturation different means of learning-analytics should be used that make patterns in the shared cultural niche visible for learners.

5   Conclusions

In this paper we discuss what makes MOOCs ideal environment for being incorporated into distributed cognitive processes of learning. Our main contribution is to introduce learning behaviours in MOOC ecosystems from the distributed cognition point of view. We propose chance-seeking, pattern appropriation and ecological enculturation concepts to generalise some learning phenomena that MOOC learning design should target.

We assume that learning involves a forward-looking attitude. The learner as a chance-seeker engages the environment in a series of trial and error and, in so doing, benefits from the feedback and modifies the environment. Chance-seeking does not happen in a vacuum but is environmentally and culturally mediated. Chance-seeking is based on environmental unanticipatedness – the idea that the environment plays an active role in a given course of action, since unanticipated and unexpected events potentially open up the way to new knowledge or information we would not be able to acquire otherwise. Chance-seeking is defined as tinkering with events that fall out of one's control and the amplification of their potential positive significance for learning. The product of chance-seeking is the formation of one's personal cognitive niche that is not immediately available to other learners. However, as long as it leaves traces in a shared environment, it may be re-interpreted and re-enacted by others depending on their knowledge, goals, and the interaction with other cognitive niches present in the cultural niche. The result of many chance-seekers self-organised cognitive activities is ecological enculturation. Cognitive niches from learners epistemic distributed cognition may be accumulated as emergent shared collective niches and enculture the environment ecologically. It is increasing the anticipatedness of the environment by pattern formation and pattern finding that are forms of Collective Distributed Cognition. Learning from the ecologically encultured patterns may help the learner, since one can try to replicate and or/exploit what other learners have already done, and it may be easier to achieve the learning flows determined by the culture.

The individuals' self-directed learning behaviour, personal learning environment (PLE) and – network (PLN) creation, accompanied with open publishing and sharing practices cause MOOCs to be open, dynamic, self-regulated and evolving learning ecosystems. The ecosystem architecture of MOOCs as communities of learning services that produsers activate from digital components allows considering the ecosystem principles to be used for designing productive MOOCs that can promote chance-seeking and learning from ecological enculturation. The nature of interrelations between the learning ecosystem organisms – producers, digital components and digital learning services – allows the emergence of distributed cognitive systems. Our future studies are directed towards exploring the potential of utilizing ecosystem principles in designing learning ecosystems that make use of how we conceptualize learning as the distributed cognitive process.

Acknowledgments. This research was supported by the Estonian Science Foundation and co-funded by the European Union through Marie Curie Actions, ERMOS72.

References

1. McAuley, A., Stewart, B., Siemens, G., Cormier, D.: The mooc model for digital practice (2010)
2. Kop, R.: The challenges to connectivist learning on open online networks: Learning experiences during a massive open online course irrodl (2011)
3. Siemens, G.: What is the theory that underpins our moocs? (2012)
4. Rodriguez, O.: Moocs and the ai-stanford like courses: Two successful and distinct course formats for massive open online courses
5. Pata, K., Merisalo, S.: Self-direction indicators for evaluating the design-based elearning course with social software. In: Multiple Perspectives on Problem Solving and Learning in the Digital Age, pp. 325–342. Springer (2011)
6. Siemens, G.: Knowing knowledge (2006)
7. Kop, R., Fournier, H.: New dimensions to self-directed learning in an open networked learning environment. International Journal of Self-Directed Learning 7(2) (2011)
8. Ostashewski, N., Reid, D.: Delivering a mooc using a social networking site: the smooc design model. In: Internet Technologies & Society (ITS 2012), pp. 217–221 (2012)
9. Bruns, A.: Blogs, Wikipedia, Second Life, and Beyond: From Production to Produsage. Peter Lang, Bern (2008)
10. Siemens, G., Downes, S.: Connectivism & connected knowledge (2006)

11. Tammets, K., Pata, K., Laanpere, M.: Promoting teachers' learning and knowledge-building in the socio-technical system. The International Review of Research in Open and Distance Learning 14(3), 251–272 (2013)
12. Lytras, M., Pouloudi, A.: Towards the development of a novel taxonomy of knowledge management systems from a learning perspective – an integrated approach to learning and knowledge infrastructures. Journal of Knowledge Management 10(6), 64–80 (2006)
13. Young, M.F.: An ecological psychology of instructional design: Learning and thinking by perceiving-acting systems. In: Jonassen, D.H. (ed.) Handbook of Research for Educational Communications and Technology. Erlbaum, Mahwah (2004)
14. Pata, K.: Modeling spaces for self-directed learning at university courses. Educational Technology & Society 12(3), 23–43 (2009)
15. Albrechtslund, A.: Online social networking as participatory surveillance. First Monday 13(3) (2006) (retrieved)
16. Zimmerman, B.J.: A social cognitive view of self-regulated academic learning. Journal of Educational Psychology 81(3), 329–339 (1989)
17. Siadaty, M., Gašević, D., Jovanović, J., Pata, K., Milikić, N., Holocher-Ertl, T., Jeremić, Z., Ali, L., Giljanović, A., Hatala, M.: Self-regulated workplace learning: A pedagogical framework and semantic web-based environment. Educational Technology & Society 4, 75–88 (2012)
18. Hollan, J., Hutchins, E., Kirsh, D.: Distributed cognition: Toward a new foundation for human-computer interaction research. ACM Transactions on Computer-Human Interaction 7(2), 174–196 (2000)
19. Bardone, E.: Seeking Chances. From Biased Rationality to Distributed Cognition. Springer, Heidelberg (2011)
20. Clark, J.: Models for Ecological Data: An Introduction. Princeton University Press, Princeton (2007)
21. Barab, S., Roth, W.M.: Intentionally-bound systems and curricular-based ecosystems: An ecological perspective on knowing. Educational Researcher 35(5), 3–13 (2006)
22. Giere, R.: Distributed cognition without distributed knowing. Social Epistemology 21(3), 313–320 (2007)
23. Wenger, E.: Communities of Practice: Learning, Meaning, and Identity. Cambridge University Press, Cambridge (1998)
24. Shackle, G.: Policy, poetry, and success. The Economic Journal 76(304), 755–767 (1996)
25. Ingold, T.: The Perception of the Environment: Essays in Livelihood, Dwelling and Skill. Routledge, London (2001)
26. Maruyama, M.: The second cybernetics: Deviation-amplifying mutual causal processes. American Scientist 5(2), 164–179 (1963)
27. Snowden, D.: Complex acts of knowing: paradox and descriptive self-awareness. Journal of Knowledge Management 2, 100–111 (2002)
28. Turner, J.S.: The Tinkerer's Accomplice: How Design Emerges from Life Itself. Harvard University Press, Cambridge (2007)
29. Alexander, C., Ishikawa, S., Silverstein, M., Jacobson, M., Friksdahl-King, I., Angel, S.: A Pattern Language: Towns, Buildings, Construction. Oxford University Press, Oxford (1977)
30. Zhang, J., Patel, V.L.: Distributed cognition, representation, and affordance. Pragmatics & Cognition 14(2), 333–341 (2006)

Layout Considered Harmful: On the Influence of Information Architecture on Dialogue

Peter Purgathofer and Naemi Luckner

Institute of Design and Assessment of Technology
Vienna University of Technology, Austria
{purg,naemi}@igw.tuwien.ac.at

Abstract. Discussions are an important tool for students to engage with new content, bring up new ideas and generate knowledge. This paper focuses on the representation of asynchronous online discussion forums in an e-learning context and how it influences the outcome of discussions. We compare the results of a traditional discussion visualisation - a vertically threaded comment system - to the two dimensional system *Discourse*, in which every new statement of the discussion opens a new subthread. We draw our conclusions from a qualitative analysis of pairs of discussions on the same topic conducted in both systems. Our findings suggest that discussions in *Discourse* are more focused and goal-oriented than in traditional threaded system.

1 Introduction

It has been found that discussion systems increase critical thinking skills [1], facilitate educational dialogue and provide a means for feedback between students and instructors [2]. Students can actively participating in debates, contribute and gain new knowledge from others [3]. In asynchronous discussions students have time to research and formulate their arguments, which leads to a high quality of the discussion [3]. Other projects have tapped into the wide range of possibilities posed to educational purposes by online discussions ([4], [5], [6]).

As of yet, there is not much literature on the topic of representations of collaborative learning discourse, and their impacts on the outcomes of discussions. Suthers [7] describes different forms of online discussions and compares their influences on the way discussions are lead. Popolov et al. [8] analyse existing discourse representations and point out their flaws, as well as suggests possible new designs. More generally, Wright has written about the psychology of layout [9]. She discusses how layout influences the effort it takes to use read information, the influence of layout on the willingness to read, on readers' assumptions and on reading strategies. Even though she is not referring to discourse layout in particular, her general observations apply to collaborative discussion interfaces as well. Dyson [10] generally describes the effect of typography and layout on reading from screens. Middlestadt and Barnhurst [11] found that different layout changes the perception of the content of newspaper articles and reader's attitude

P. Zaphiris and A. Ioannou (Eds.): LCT 2014, Part I, LNCS 8523, pp. 216–225, 2014.

towards them. The layout of the *Discourse* system has already been discussed in [12].

Discourse, the redesign for online discussions, derives its inspiration from the *Infinite Canvas* concept introduced by Scott McCloud [13]. Traditional representations of online discussion rely on one dominant dimension (in most cases the vertical dimension Y) to represent the flow of postings.

Discourse uses both available dimensions to structure and present information. Each new statement in the discussion is listed in a column to the left of the screen. Replies to these statements are arranged in columns to the right of the statement. As each of these replies can be replied to, each one can have a column of replies associated with it. The principal structure of the presentation of comments and replies can be seen in Figure 1.

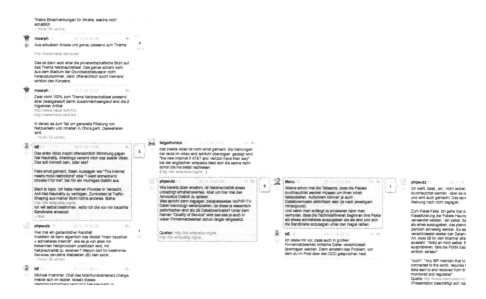

Fig. 1. Selected items have a dashed outline and are shown with a grey underlay, indicating that the column next to it displays replies to the selected item

In this paper, we are comparing two threaded discussion systems that were used in a university lecture in two consecutive years. The remainder of this paper is structured as follows: The next section 'Similar structure, different layout - two threaded discussion systems' offers a detailed description of both discussion systems. The section is followed by a 'Setting and method' chapter describing the approach and setting in which the data was collected and evaluated. In the chapter 'Evaluation and discussion', the quality of discussions across the two systems is compared using qualitative content analysis according to Mayring [14]. Comparisons are drawn between discussions held on identical lecture topics in the old system in the first year, and in the new system in the second year. The paper closes with a 'Conclusion' chapter, summarizing the findings.

2   Similar Structure, Different Layout – Two Threaded Discussion Systems

Both discussion systems are embedded in an online learning support system used at the Vienna University of Technology. The system is comprised of various modules like an organizational Newsfeed, a section for lecture slides and comments to the slides, as well as a portfolio section for each student. A detailed description of the system can be found in [15].

The system used in the first part of the evaluation was a one dimensional threaded discussion system embedded in the lecture slide view, that featured only one level of indentation (see Figure 2). Discussions were started with a top-level posting, outlining the topic and including statements or questions the students could reply to, all in the context of the respective slide. Students could either respond directly to the top-level posting, or start a new thread beneath it. Replies were arranged vertically under each thread in their chronological order. Within threads, replies could be directed at the first posting of the thread as well as at other replies. To convey the affiliation of a reply to another persons post, students could refer to it, using tags like *@username*. Hence, the whole discussion was represented vertically on two levels: top-level postings, and indented replies, notwithstanding more complex relations between the content of postings.

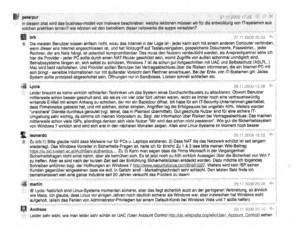

Fig. 2. A one dimensional threaded discussion with one indentation level. Referring to other postings within the indentation level is done by mentioning the other persons username at the start of the reply.

The second system, *Discourse*, was not integrated in the slides section but worked as an independent module of the online learning support system. Students could either navigate to the *Discourse* section directly, or via the discussion starter that was still attached to a slide in the slides section, but now only serving as a link to the *Discourse* module. The link lead directly to the chosen discussion, while navigating to the discourse section showed only an overview of currently running discussions. The overview provides students with information about currently running discussions and also if there have been new, unread postings in discussions the student is currently involved in.

The multi-threaded discussions are represented in two dimensions. Students are encouraged to post new thoughts and ideas that have not been discussed yet as new top-level postings in the discussion. All top-level postings are represented as a vertical list in the second column on the page, with the first column consisting of a thumbnail of the slide, and the discussion starter. Whenever a students logs into a discussion, these two columns are visible. If replies to a posting exist, an information box appears next to the comment, containing the amount of replies that exist in this thread; how many of these replies the participant has not read yet; and a spark-line representation of the further structure of the thread. Each element in the spark-line represents one level of responses to a comment, with the amount of bars showing how many replies postings are in this level on average.

To read a thread, it can be unfolded by clicking the information box. Students can either unfold the whole thread at once, or navigate through it, layer by layer. All postings, including replies, can be replied to. Each reply is displayed in the column immediately to the right of the posting. For example, a thread that started with a top-level posting followed by an interplay of single replies is represented as a horizontal string of postings. Only one thread of the discussion can be open at the same time. To keep track of which comment thread is open at the moment, the active comments have a grey background for accentuation. A more detailed description of the *Discourse* system can be found in [16].

3   Setting and Method

We had the suspicion that a layout differing in key characteristics from the traditional format could influence the way discussions are held online. In order to evaluate the impact of such a design, we used different systems in two successive years to facilitate participant discussions in a university course in the area of 'Informatics and Society'. In both years, we asked the respective students to participate in identical discussions, against the background of an identical lecture [1] held by one of the authors of this article, Peter Purgathofer. The course is offered as part of the Informatics Bachelor programs at the Vienna University of Technology, and is mandatory for all first-year students in the second semester. Participation in the discussion was voluntary, and general discussion was welcome. To promote substantial participation, students were offered points toward their grade for individual contributions of high quality.

In the research discussed in this article, we focussed on evaluating the interaction between students as well as the discussion as a whole, rather than e.g.

---

[1] 'identical' - Of course, the content of a lecture in 'Informatics and Society' has to reflect current events and trends; Still, for the purpose of this comparison, the lectures can be assumed sufficiently identical

collaboration or community structure within our system. In her paper, Meyer discusses different methods of discussion evaluation: content analysis; rubrics; and frameworks [17]. The analysis of the presented system was done using qualitative content analysis, following the approach laid out in Mayring [14]. While we also applied some quantitative criteria to more directly compare the differences, we think that the qualitative analysis makes the influence of the different systems much more explicit.

Coding and categorizing the postings was done by the two authors independently, and in a second step the evaluations were compared. Since the interpretation of meaning in latent content is a subjective process, bias cannot fully be avoided. This two-step process was chosen in order to produce reliable results and lessen inaccuracies of the evaluation introduced by subjective interpretation of the postings. In the first step, all postings were read, and a classification was developed based on the content of the postings and the relation of the postings to each other. This classification is shown in table 1. In a second pass, we coded all postings following this classification, and additionally asserted in which way they related to the respective preceding posting, i.e., supportive, oppositional, or neutral . Finally, the structure of the discussion was visualized in a directed graph with type of each posting instead of the text in order to better understand the flow of discourse.

Table 1. Coding: This table shows a list of possible posting types and their explanation

Category	Semantic	Example
Statement	A posting where facts are stated and/or external sources are quoted.	'Bill Buxton states that?'
Opinion	A posting where the author gives her opinion on the matter, without specifying sources.	'I believe we have to?'
Question	In such a posting, the author openly poses a question into the discussion.	'Can it really happen that?'
Answer	Such a posting can answer an explicit question, or refer to issues left open implicitly in a statement or opinion positing.	'Yes, it is indeed possible that?'
Materials	Such a posting adds sources and/or other materials relevant to the discussion.	'You can find more information at?'
Example	The author introduces an example into the discussion.	'Where I work, people usually?'
Clarification	In such a posting, the author tries to clarify an unclear or open issue in the preceding positing.	'To sum it up, I would say?'
Insight	Here, the author expresses a realization of something that was hitherto unknown to her.	'Ok, i see your point.'

The posting types themselves are more or less self-explanatory, and are described in Table 3. In the structural visualizations, each posting is represented by its respective posting type. To visualise the argumentative relation of postings, we use an arrow, pointing either upwards or downwards. Posting supporting the preceding posting are indicated by an upwards arrow; postings contradicting the preceding posting are indicated by a downwards arrow. Some postings are neutral, which usually means that they don't really respond to the preceding posting and can be considered a non sequitur.

Finally, we color-coded postings by author and posting frequency. For the printed version, all postings of the author who contributed most to the discussion in terms of quantity are indicated using white type on a darker gray background; postings by authors who contributed more than once to the discussion have a light gray background; and postings by authors with only a single contribution are shown with a white background. Also, the discussion starter is highlighted with white text on a black background. This makes any differences in repeated participation between the two representations quite obvious[2].

4   Evaluation and Discussion

We applied this evaluation on five discussions held both in the traditional forum format in the first year and *Discourse* in the second year. Due to practical constraints, we can only show the results of one evaluation in this article in detail. All five evaluations can be examined in detail in the complimentary online section[3] of this article.

Figure 3 shows the structure of a discussion on *net neutrality*, facilitated with the old forum system. In the discussion starter (labelled 'initial statement + questions' in the visualizsations), participants were asked to watch an anti-net-neutrality commercial from the National Cable & Telecommunications Association[4] and a pro-net neutrality ad from Google[5], and read a (then recent) online document[6]. Participants were then asked a couple of questions, initiating a discussion of the theoretical value and the reality of net neutrality.

Using the plain forum format, the resulting discussion comprised of 35 replies, submitted by 34 students, an average of just 1.03 posting per participant. A single student wrote two postings, whereas everybody else stopped after posting a single entry into the discussion. Interaction was the exception rather than the norm; only 10 postings, less than 30%, were written in response to what somebody else wrote. 21 postings are completely isolated, meaning they don't

---

[2] For the complementary online version of the same visualizations, the postings of each author are shown in different colors

[3] http://igw.tuwien.ac.at/designlehren/discourse_evaluation.html

[4] http://www.youtube.com/watch?v=oPIYxtjLFeI

[5] http://www.youtube.com/watch?v=o9Dv8OnIwmc

[6] The Verizon-Google Legislative Framework Proposal,
http://www.scribd.com/doc/35599242/
Verizon-Google-Legislative-Framework-Proposal

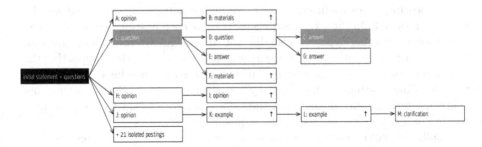

Fig. 3. Discussion on net neutrality using the plain forum format. The black discussion starter was posted be the course instructor. Posts from the user with most contributions are dark gray. All posts from users with more than one contribution are light gray.

refer to any posting other than the 'initial statement + questions' posting, and are not referred to by another posting. The distribution of the 14 non-isolated postings is shown in Figure 5.

Counting the links, the single longest chain of discussion is 4, while the average length is 2.6. 50% of all postings within these discussion threads and 80% of all postings are end points in the graph, that is, they are not replied to.

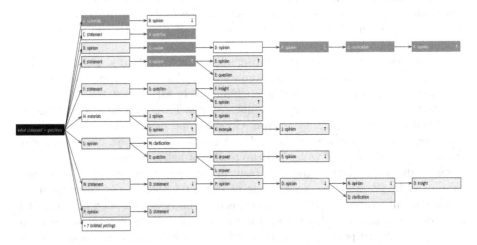

Fig. 4. Discussion on net neutrality using the *Discourse* system. The black discussion starter was posted be the course instructor. Posts from the user with most contributions are dark gray. All posts from users with more than one contribution are light gray. Please note that due to recent changes in html/css rendering, some elements are slightly misplaced from their intended position.

Using *Discourse* a year later, 20 students participated in the discussions, writing 46 contributions. This constitutes an average of 2.3 postings per participant - much more than in plain forum version. Of these, only 7 postings were isolated, while 39 postings were either replies to other comments, or being replied to by somebody else. This alone constitutes a much higher rate of interaction between the participants. 30 comments, or 65%, were written as a response to another posting.

The longest chain of discussion is 6 postings, with the average length being 3.31 postings. 41% of all postings within these discussion threads and 50% of all postings are end points.

Figure 5 shows the difference in the frequency of the types of comments in each system. Using this approach, three differences become evident.

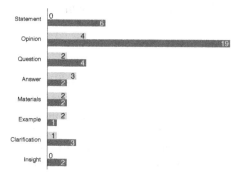

Fig. 5. Occurrence of posting types in both the traditional forum system and *Discourse*

- 6 statements were posted (as compared to 0 in the plain forum version); writing a statement is more work than writing an opinion, this implies a higher rate of engagement than in the plain forum.
- At the same time, 19 of the 39 non-isolated comments were opinions, 16 of which were written as a reaction to other postings. While writing an opinion as a response is much less work than writing one of the more substantial posting types, it indicates a higher rate of reading and involvement than the plain forum version.
- 3 comments were categorized as insight in *Discourse*, versus 0 in the traditional system. A possible explanation for this is that it is a direct consequence of the longer chains of discussion in *Discourse*, which in turn can be seen as an indicator for more involvement in the discussion.

The visualisations of the discussions using the codified posting types invites a number of further observations:

- In the discussion using the traditional forum system, participants never openly oppose each other, while in *Discourse*, we can identify multiple singular instances of opposition. Even more, we can see participants answering to these oppositional stances, even leading to insight in the end. One could argue that this is what open discussions are about: critically reflect and reconsider one's point of view.

- The large number of isolated posts in the traditional view suggests that many participants coming late to the discussion had no incentive to read through the discussion so far, and ended up posting their own opinion or statement without regard for what other participants wrote. The much more structured *Discourse* system invited people to first read what others wrote before posting something.
- While most participants in the traditional forum system posted only a single contribution, most postings in *Discourse* came from students who wrote more than one contribution. This again shows that the rate of interaction with the discussion was higher than in the traditional system. The results of the analysis of the other four discussions confirm these results.

5   Conclusion

Our evaluations show that the discussions facilitated with *Discourse* display improvements in a number of essential qualities compared to the discussions done in the admittedly quite simple, but still very common single-thread system. While we cannot really shed light on why this is the case, we can formulate a number of hypothesis to explain the effect. Whatever the real reasons might be, we think that all of these hypothesis point to advantages of *Discourse* over traditional online discussion layouts.

- The much higher demand for interactivity in *Discourse* leads to a feeling of more agency. For example, *Discourse* forces participants to make a decision whether to follow a thread further, or to ignore it; this choice fosters involvement.
- Traditional forum layouts suffer from 'context blur'. For example, a feud between two participants pushes all prior replies away from it's 'parent', making more substantial replies much harder to find. Often, when reading long discussions in a traditional threaded format, it is challenging to remember which posting a reply refers to. In *Discourse*, it is much easier to see and understand the local context of a postings, i.e. it's 'parent' and 'siblings'. A feud is simply a long horizontal chain of postings, and can be ignored much easier. This overview gives participants a better chance to find the place and posting they want to respond to.
- The relatively low number of first-level-postings in *Discourse* makes it easier to catch on with an ongoing discussion. This in turn motivates participants to find a place to respond, rather than just deposit their opinion.

This list is neither exhaustive nor sufficient to explain the reasons why online discussions can be elevated simply by layout and interaction alone. Still, we think that our observations support the assumption that the role of information architecture and interaction design of ICT systems goes way beyond the mapping of functionality onto a simple to use interface.

References

1. Wilson, M., Fairchild, C.: Collaborative Learning and the Importance of the Discussion Board. Journal of Diagnostic Medical Sonography 27(1), 45–51 (2010)
2. Comer, D.R., Lenaghan, J.A.: Enhancing Discussions in the Asynchronous Online Classroom: The Lack of Face-to-Face Interaction Does Not Lessen the Lesson. Journal of Management Education 37(2), 261–294 (2012)
3. Nandi, D., Hamilton, M.: How active are students in online discussion forums? In: Proceedings of the Thirteenth Australasian Computing Education Conference (ACE), pp. 125–134 (2011)
4. Caswell, B., Bielaczyc, K.: Knowledge Forum: altering the relationship between students and scientific knowledge. Education, Communication & Information, 37–41 (2012)
5. Scardamalia, M.: CSILE / Knowledge Forum. In: Education and Technology: An Encyclopedia, pp. 183–192 (2004)
6. Cheng, C.K., Paré, D.E., Collimore, L.M., Joordens, S.: Assessing the effectiveness of a voluntary online discussion forum on improving students' course performance. Computers & Education 56(1), 253–261 (2011)
7. Suthers, D.D.: Effects of Alternate Representations of Evidential Relations on Collaborative Learning Discourse. In: Proceedings of the 1999 Conference on Computer Support for Collaborative Learning, CSCL 1999. International Society of the Learning Sciences (1999)
8. Popolov, D., Callaghan, M., Luker, P.: Conversation Space: Visualising Multi-threaded Conversation. In: Proceedings of the Working Conference on Advanced Visual Interfaces, AVI 2000, pp. 246–249. ACM, New York (2000)
9. Wright, P.: The psychology of layout: Consequences of the visual structure of documents. American Association for Artificial Intelligence Technical Report (1999)
10. Dyson, M.C.: How physical text layout affects reading from screen. Behaviour & Information Technology 23(6), 377–393 (2004)
11. Middlestadt, S.E., Barnhurst, K.G.: The influence of layout on the perceived tone of news articles. Journalism & Mass Communication Quaterly 76(2), 264–276 (1999)
12. Purgathofer, P.: Visuelle Repräsentation und Interaktion im Diskurs: zum Zusammenhang von Form und Inhalt von Online-Diskussionen. FIfF-Kommunikation 3, 53–57 (2012)
13. McCloud, S.: Reinventing Comics: How Imagination and Technology Are Revolutionizing an Art Form. William Morrow Paperbacks (2000)
14. Mayring, P.: Qualitative Inhaltsanalyse, Grundlagen und Techniken, 8th edn. Beltz, Weinheim (2003)
15. Purgathofer, P., Luckner, N.: Aurora - Exploring Social Online Learning Tools Through Design. In: TBP: Proceedings of The Seventh International Conference on Advances in Computer-Human Interactions, ACHI 2014, Barcelona (2014)
16. Holzkorn, P.: Discuss. New designs for asynchronous online discussion for e-learning in higher education. PhD thesis, Vienna University of Technology (2011)
17. Meyer, K.: The method (and madness) of evaluating online discussions. Journal of Asynchronous Learning Networks, 83–97 (2006)

Analyzing Interactivity in Asynchronous Video Discussions

Hannes Rothe, Janina Sundermeier, and Martin Gersch

Department Business Information Systems, Freie Universität Berlin, Germany
{hannes.rothe,janina.sundermeier,martin.gersch}@fu-berlin.de

Abstract. Evaluating online discussions is a complex task for educators. Information systems may support instructors and course designers to assess the quality of an asynchronous online discussion tool. Interactivity on a human-to-human, human-to-computer or human-to-content level are focal elements of such quality assessment. Nevertheless existing indicators used to measure interactivity oftentimes rely on manual data collection. One major contribution of this paper is an updated overview about indicators which are ready for automatic data collection and processing. Following a design science research approach we introduce measures for a consumer side of interactivity and contrast them with a producer's perspective. For this purpose we contrast two ratio measures 'viewed posts prior to a statement' and 'viewed posts after a statement' created by a student. In order to evaluate these indicators, we apply them to Pinio, an innovative asynchronous video discussion tool, used in a virtual seminar.

Keywords: Online discussion, asynchronous video discussion, educational data mining, interactivity, higher education.

1 Introduction

The development and spread of information and communication technologies as well as the increasing number of participants per course in higher education are only two reasons why the use of and the demand for technology-enhanced education tools are rising steadily [1]. Besides, the demand on peer-to-peer learning concepts and the integration of virtual communities into online learning environments is growing [2–4]. Especially the implementation and encouragement of asynchronous online discussions within technology-enhanced education are of wide interest in higher education [5]. Asynchronous online discussions favor the realization of Massive Open Online Courses (MOOCs) and many other types of online courses that allow students to study online at their own pace at different times (e.g. in different time zones) [6, 7].

Although the utilization of online discussions is of high interest for research on and practice of technology enhanced education, a research gap has been identified. Existing research on the evaluation of these applications only partially reflects the actual interactivity of students within asynchronous online discussions. Especially with the rise of learning analytics in general and educational data mining (EDM) in particular quantitative indicators for the interactivity of students for educational purposes are of

P. Zaphiris and A. Ioannou (Eds.): LCT 2014, Part I, LNCS 8523, pp. 226–237, 2014.

increasing interest. Most approaches in research on EDM related to asynchronous online discussions make use of 'active' indicators such as the 'number of posts per students' or 'number of reviews per student' in order to determine the interactivity and to evaluate the expected learning outcome [7, 8]. The role of 'passive' indicators, such as reading the posts and learning from it without actively taking part in a debate [9, 6], is only partially considered yet. Prior experiments and qualitative research showed that acquiring and assimilating information from peers by reading or watching contributions from other students has positive outcomes on the learning outcome [10, 6].

Hence, the intensity with which a student interacts with information from their peers should be included into proper interactivity evaluation. Following the approach of [11] we discern between two roles a student impersonates in online discussion - consumers and producers. Based on this differentiation, the central question of this paper is: *How can we use data mining to evaluate online discussions against the background of a multifaceted view on interactivity?* Thus, the purposes of this paper are to contribute to the ongoing debate on indicators for online discussions in two ways. First of all, we update the suggestions from Dringus and Ellis [12] about indicators used to evaluate online discussions which can be applied to EDM. Moreover, we introduce measures for the consumer's side and contrast them with the producer's perspective.

Following a design science research approach [13], we use an asynchronous video discussion tool to introduce extended indicators for the analysis of a consumer- and a producer dimension alike. Our research design starts by clarifying the problem field. We introduce current sets of indicators for online discussions within research on learning analytics and EDM. Afterwards we demonstrate the use of our indicators for assessing Pinio, an asynchronous (video) discussion application. The pertaining application was applied to the course Net Economy. Net Economy is an online course with 140 students from six institutes in higher education who engaged in several online discussions in 2013. The demonstration is supplemented by an explorative correlation study to assess the additional information gain from both indicators.

2   Objectives of a Solution

2.1   Online Discussion

Discussions in higher education, whether online or offline, should encourage debates among students as well as between students and course instructors [14]. Typically we distinguish between synchronous and asynchronous discussions that mainly differ in terms of presence of the participants. The focus of this paper lies on asynchronous online discussions. Within these debates participants do not necessarily need to be present in a discussion forum at the same time. New entries within the online discussion are recorded and can be accessed at any time without a direct need to respond immediately [5, 15]. Thus, participants can decide when and where they take part in the online discussion. Hence they can flexibly integrate the online discussion into their schedules [16]. Moreover, online discussions are an important element to trigger extensive and helpful dialogues between students [2, 17]. Several authors find that sufficient time to develop own thoughts and to prepare an appropriate statement are further benefits of online discussions [14, 18, 8, 15]. It has been shown that active participation in online discussions oftentimes lead to effective learning outcomes [7]. Especially students who feel less comfortable in face-to-face discussions profit from an anonymous discussion environment [14, 8]. Furthermore, students are able to prepare their answers and responses according to their own pace; they do not necessarily follow the pace of a learning group [19]. Apart from the before mentioned advantages, several authors identified also a couple of disadvantages related to online discussions. One of which is the unpredictable amount of time participants have to wait for replies to their former posts [20]. The authors Dringus and Ellis [12] found that participants might even be discouraged when facing an over proportional long waiting time. Moreover, the structure of the online discussion forum is an important factor influencing whether some post remains unread and unanswered because participants lose track of what has been written.

The role of the educator, namely instructor or course designer, is to moderate online discussions in a manner that irrelevant or even wrong contributions are clarified. Additionally instructors keep track of a discussion to ensure relevance of postings for the course topics, reduce off-topic and support a positive debate culture. In order to do so, the course instructors need to evaluate the quality of a discussion. Following the brief introduction on factors influencing online discussion, this is a complex task. In the following we will discuss, whether this process of quality assessment can be supported by information technology and measures from the field of educational data mining.

2.2   Educational Data Mining in Online Discussions

Considering the fact, that educators in e- or blended learning settings mostly interact through (web-based) technology with students, potential transparency of student's actions mostly decreases. Lecturers who give their presentation via video streams can only guess if students are watching them at home or switch to another browser tab. Also online discussions may quickly become either very complex or stay hardly initiated; as a result educators can either hardly review the amount of data or stay unclear why a discussion does not thrive [8]. Educators giving traditional lectures may be able to recognize a distracted audience and intervene promptly, for instance by cold-calling. Nevertheless web-based technologies impede this strategy at a first glance. A few years ago Learning Analytics gained common recognition as a field of research that may resolve these issues. The general attention on Learning Analytics within research on educational technology grew tremendously since the publication of the Horizon Report 2020 by the European Union [21]. Following the literature on Learning Analytics its main task lies within the collection, processing and evaluation of usage data in the educational sector [22–24]. A recently developing branch within the field Learning Analytics is called Educational Data Mining. EDM uses techniques from Business Intelligence and Data Mining to transform data into information using algorithms to support decision making processes [25]. For example text mining, clustering or rule setting methods can be used to help educators interpret large amounts of data which are mostly collected by web services, like web-based trainings, course management systems and also online discussion tools. For this purpose key indicators need to be created to find answers for hypotheses regarding educational technologies in general and online discussion tools in particular. Following this initial step these indicators may be directly collected or processed using raw data. Sources of data are diverse. To test hypotheses regarding educational technologies we need to advance the data mining process. Subsequently manual data collection is an obstacle. We need to use data that can be collected machine-aided to enable automatic data analysis. Within educational technology server-sided data (like log files) as well as client-sided data (like client-triggered events via javascript) are common [25]. Therefore our main task to evaluate the quality of an online discussion tool is finding relevant and quantifiable indicators that could be collected automatically.

To assess the quality of online discussion within a course, we ask for the interactivity of students with other students, the educator and the learning content [26–28]. Dringus & Ellis [12] were not able to identify 'the' key indicators for participation in online discussions, even though they presented a list of indicators based on a thorough literature review. They subsume that relevant constructs and 'the associated indicators are found in the literature, but only in piecemail'. Their study nevertheless contains many indicators that are collected manually. Additionally they propose indicators that could be of use for data mining. Prominent indicators which measure interactivity between humans (student-to-student as well as student-to-educator) within online discussion boards are the amount of replies or posts per user. Other indicators, like the amount of accesses to a discussion board, are used to assess the level of human-computer or human-to-content interaction [7]. These indicators nevertheless only partially reflect the interaction of students and the online discussion. 'Lurking' or content 'consumption' are not directly assessed.

Interactivity in online discussions is embodied by active participation - or knowledge 'production' - as well as passive 'consumption'. Active participants post answers to existing contributions or initiate new discussion streams. Passive consumption of online discussions involves reading of central contributions and finding relevant information without contributing or answering to an existing discussion [7]. In literature, the term "lurker" is often adopted in this context to describe students who are only observing the ongoing discussion and who remain themselves silent [7, 8]. The passive consumption in contrast reflects to a type of interactivity that may be linked to a prior or following content production.

Research mostly argues about indicators for active types of interactivity in the context of online discussions. Several authors measure the access to online discussions boards as well as the number of posts or reviews per students in order to determine the effectiveness of online discussions in terms of learning outcomes [29–31, 7, 9]. [6] examined in experiments the number of views per user and posting. The results of this approach show that a combination of active posting within discussion forums and passive consumption – like reading of posts – contribute to the learning process. Even though the authors Jyothi et al. [8] acknowledge that lurking has some kind of contribution to the learning process they focus on indicators for active participation, such as access to the discussion forum. In order to gain further insights related to the passive consumption of asynchronous online discussions, Wise et al. [9] intend to operational-ize the passive consumption of online discussions in terms of reading. For this pur-pose, the authors measure time difference between two activities and assume that the students dedicate a certain amount of the mean time to read prior posts. In a similar manner, [31] observes the number of website hits per student in order to determine the passive consumption of the discussions. These indicators are based on the assumption, that students visit the web page to read thoroughly through postings, which may lead to a biased interpretation. Students may dedicate their time spent on a site with activi-ties unrelated to the actual discussion, e.g. switching the browser tab without closing the discussion. Another approach, adopted by several authors, is to count the number of posts that are marked as 'read' or 'important' [32, 29, 33]. Instead of measuring passive consumption they observe manual or automatic 'ticking' of a checkbox. These indicators may be biased by students who do not mark every single post.

In contrast to [12] we present a list of indicators which were used for machinable data collection and data processing (see table 1). The displayed results follow a litera-ture review of peer-reviewed articles regarding data-mining and online discussion for educational purposes.[1] Our overview shows that most conducted research makes use of indicators for 'active' participation such as the access to the discussion forum and the number of posts per user in order to enhance existing research. Indicators 'pas-sive' interactivity are less often determined. In the following we develop and demon-strate indicators to determine passive indicators of asynchronous online discussions ready for data mining techniques.

Table 1. A list of indicators that can be collected and processed automatically

	Indicator	Operationalization	Reference, cf.
	amount of posts created	-	[7, 9, 12, 29, 30, 34, 35]
	Time difference between two posts	-	[12, 36]
	amount of words / sentences	amount of text elements (regular expres-sions)	[33]
active	amount of reviews / edits	-	[9, 29]
	change in subject	change in title/subtitle of post	[8]
	response	reply to a post with and without mentioning a prior author within this post	[8, 12]
	detect key words, phrases related to topic	text mining for keywords and phrases	[12]

---

[1]   Databases: ScienceDirect, EBSCO, ERIC, IEEE Xplore

Table 1. (*continued*)

detect genre of posting using text mining	cascade classification model for detecting a "discussion, comment, reflection, information sharing and scaffolding"	[37]
centrality measures	network analytical approach on a micro level: Degree, Betweenness, Closeness, Auth/Hub Centrality	[8, 32, 33]
density of the discussion	network analytical approach on a macro level	[8]
amount of reads	action 'read' estimated by time spent on a page	[9, 35]
amount of website hits	amount of page hits	[31, 38]
amount of 'scans'	action 'scan' estimated by time below 6.5 seconds per word	[9]
marked as "read"	amount of posts that are marked as "read" or "important" by students	[29, 32, 33]

passive (row label applied to the lower group of the table)

3   Assessing the 'Consumer' Perspective

3.1   Institutional Context

We build upon our findings from the literature review to evaluate an asynchronous video discussion tool which was used in the course 'Net Economy'. 'Net Economy' is a virtual seminar that is offered in collaboration across several locations. The setting targets participants with heterogeneous educational backgrounds in the fields of business and economics, business information systems, and educational sciences. Besides teaching about Entrepreneurship in the Net Economy the virtual collaborative learning setting focusses on spanning across different cultural backgrounds from Germany (Bochum, Berlin, Clausthal, Soest), Ukraine (Simferipol), and Indonesia (Jakarta). 140 students participated in the course in 2013.

Every Net Economy class is divided into three phases: 'preparation phase, knowledge development phase' and 'case study phase'. Throughout the course, project work is conducted in small teams of six students and across locations, both in terms of team composition as well as presentation and discussion of findings. By separating these phases, learning and working processes are structured as a project with the use of predefined milestones. Preparation phase consists of a team building process, where students get in touch with each other. For this purpose we integrated a virtual social network into the seminar [3]. The following knowledge development phase consists of pre-recorded video lectures and team assignments regarding the course topics. During the final case study phase every team applies what they learned before. Every finding is documented and discussed in steering committees and team websites following phase-specific assignments. Steering committees and final presentations are held at each location and are merged together through synchronous video conferencing.

Besides the virtual social network the course is complemented by an innovative, asynchronous video discussion tool called Pinio. Pinio[2] is a web tool that contains video statements of lecturers and students. Each statement takes up to thirty seconds and usually contains a key argument of a discussant. In contrast to traditional text-based asynchronous discussion tools the video tool reduces anonymity. As a result every argument is complemented by facial expression and gestures. Every participant of the class was allowed to start and reply to discussions. During Knowledge Development Phase we had two initial discussion threads in the first week. Participation in at least one of these discussions was mandatory. In the following weeks starting a discussion or replying to a post was completely voluntary. During Case Study Phase each of the 23 teams had to start a discussion containing their first idea for a new business model. Additionally each team had to reply to at least two discussions from other teams to give them feedback for their ideas.

3.2   Indicators for an Asynchronous Video Discussion

To assess the interactivity of students in online discussion we need to incorporate passive consumption and active participation. While active participation could be easily measured by the amount of video comments of a student, the influence of passive consumption can be manifold. First of all we need to gather data on consumption. While merely capturing the duration spent on a web site has been used to assess 'reading', this measure may be difficult. The duration is indirectly measured by the time difference between two hits or events on a website [9]. Depending on the online discussion software it is difficult to distinguish between reading one or multiple posts.

In Pinio every video post has a maximum duration of 30 seconds. A video is measured as being played when a student clicks on the pertaining button and keeps playing it until the end unless the browser tab is changed or closed. Once a video is finished, an event is triggered that sends data for a complete video presentation to the database. Therefore viewing a discussion post is more reliably logged, then merely guessing the amount of time spent on a web site. Based on the received data we aggregated indicators for the consumption of a video statement.

We distinguish between two sets of indicators that refer to the process perspective of learning. On the one hand we processed the amount of viewed comments (v) in a discussion (D) prior to a statement (p_x) at time (t). We call it *viewPrior*. While watching comments beforehand we might get insights into the intensity with which a student prepares his or her comment. Additionally watching prior comments is necessary for linking an argument to the overall discussion. On the other hand we measured *viewAfter* as the amount of comments that have been watched after a student contributed to a discussion. We assume that following a discussion after posting a statement signals engagement and an involvement in the learning content that reaches beyond

---

[2]   see also www.pinio.me

an explicitly or implicitly created need within a course. The absolute number of views depends on the moment a statement is made by a student. If he or she contributes lately to a debate, there are many videos posted beforehand and less videos will be stated afterwards. Hence, to compare results of viewAfter or viewPrior we need to standardize both indicators (see eq. 1 and 2 for both ratio variables).

$$\text{Ratio of viewPrior:} \quad rvp_x = \frac{\sum_{t_o}^{t_x-1} v_{D,t}}{\sum_{t_o}^{t_x-1} p_{D,t}} \tag{1}$$

$$\text{Ratio of viewAfter:} \quad rva_x = \frac{\sum_{t_x+1}^{T} v_{D,t}}{\sum_{t_x+1}^{T} p_{D,t}} \tag{2}$$

For this purpose we designed the ratio of consumed or watched videos posted before or after a statement in relation to the amount of existing and following statements at that time ($p_{D,t}$). Therefore we are able to assess the percentage of viewed videos prior and after contributing to a discussion.

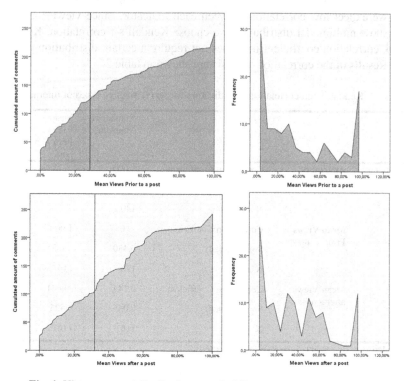

Fig. 1. Histograms and distributions, vertical lines represent median views

During the course 270 video statements were created. In sum, 6.483 videos have been watched. Hence students watched by far more videos then they recorded, which is in line to the findings of [38] for text-based online discussions. Figure 1 presents the distribution of mean ratios for viewPrior and viewAfter of every student within the class Net Economy. Additionally we present the distribution of the pertaining variables in contrast to the cumulated amount of comments. As we can see for both variables, the distributions of viewPrior and viewAfter are multimodal. Apparently both indicators are skewed towards each end of the scale (0% and 100%). As we relate these distributions to the amount of comments, we gain insights into the relationship between the active and passive type of interactivity. A large amount of comments is made without watching prior posts at all. There are also many students who only state their argument and do not track the following dispute. Nevertheless, we see a higher median as well as comparably greater marginal values for the upper 50-percentile for viewAfter in comparision to viewPrior. Subsequently there are some students who show involvement above the level of what they are asked for within the given task.

To assess the added value of both indicators in terms of information gain, we measure correlation between indicators for passive and active interactivity. We assume an information gain, if indicators quantify different dimensions of interactivity. Hence, we expect low correlation between each indicator. Since viewPrior and viewAfter show multimodal distribution we choose Kendall's-τ correlation. Kendall's-τ is a rank correlation coefficient that does not require a certain distribution of the variables. Results of the correlation analysis are shown in table 2.

Table 2. Kendall's tau correlation of indicators for active/passive types of interactivity

			Number of comments	Mean Views Prior to a post	Mean Views after a post
Kendall's tau correlation	Amount of Comments	Correlation Coefficient	1.000		
		Sig. (2-tailed)			
		N	140		
	Mean Views Prior to a post	Correlation Coefficient	-0.057	1.000	
		Sig. (2-tailed)	0.430		
		N	116	116	
	Mean Views after a post	Correlation Coefficient	0.144[*]	-0.041	1.000
		Sig. (2-tailed)	0.045	0.525	
		N	116	116	116

*. Correlation is significant at the 0.05 level (2-tailed).

As we can see, the only significantly positive relationship exists between viewAfter and the amount of comments. We assume that higher involvement and motivation in the pertaining debate or the learning content are positively associated to the amount of viewed comments after adding a statement. Hence, both indicators may be related to the same construct. A following qualitative study or an experiment may research the causation behind this occasion. Nevertheless, we see that viewPrior and viewAfter as well as viewPrior and amount of comments are not correlated. Subsequently we gain more information about the passive type of interactivity within an online discussion.

4   Conclusion

Our literature review showed that some studies built upon the work of Dringus and Ellis [12] meanwhile. The strengthened focus on educational data mining within technology enhanced learning had a positive effect on research about quality assessment of online discussions in higher education. Nonetheless, we see that assessing how effective an application for online discussion actually is, remains a complex task. Many indicators are still only partially validated and there is still a lot of room for enhancing these indicators. In contrast to many indicators for the active 'producer perspective', we found that the passive 'consumer perspective' is weakly considered in EDM. Nevertheless this perspective promises valuable insights into the interactivity between students and the discussion technology. For this purpose we demonstrated the use of two variables, 'mean views prior to a student's statement' and 'mean views after a student's statement'. As a matter of machine-aided routine we may now differentiate between a student who posted two videos and watched none of the former comments, and a student who posted only one video, but followed the whole discussion.

Our research calls for a multitude of follow up questions. First of all, behavioristic research could validate the relationship between the active and passive dimensions of interactivity within online discussion. Furthermore the presented indicators were weakly correlated, but contain valuable information about the student's interactivity with the online discussion system. Hence, applying these indicators in a cluster analysis for discussant types may lead to more insights. In his research [39] argued for a typical distribution in the dichotomy between very active and rather passive students, who use web 2.0 tools in educational settings. Further research may ask whether we'll also find a normal distribution between those types of students in online discussion. Furthermore we might examine the influence of deviations from a typical distribution for learning success and learner's satisfaction.

The results of this paper are limited to some extent. The study focused solely on EDM. Qualitative research on online discussion was widely neglected. Combining quantitative and qualitative approaches would be beneficial to gain further insights [31, 9]. Additionally qualitative methods or experiments are fundamental to test assumptions on causality. In contrast to former research we applied our indicators to a new type of online discussion: asynchronous videos. Further research should investigate the difference between the progress of online discussions in traditional discussion boards compared to asynchronous video discussions. We suggest applying an experiment to test the causality of the associated hypotheses.

References

1. Bures, E.M., Abrami, P.C., Amundsen, C.: Student motivation to learn via computer conferencing. Research in higher Education 41(5), 593–621 (2000)
2. Swan, K., Shea, P.: The development of virtual learning communities. In: Learning Together Online: Research on Asynchronous Learning Networks, pp. 239–260 (2005)
3. Weber, P., Rothe, H.: Social networking services in e-learning. In: Bastiaens, T., Marks, G. (eds.) Education and Information Technology 2013: A Selection of AACE Award Papers, AACE, vol. 1, pp. 89–99. Chesapeake (2013)
4. Kear, K.: Peer learning using asynchronous discussion systems in distance education. Open Learning: The Journal of Open, Distance and e-Learning 19(2), 151–164 (2004)
5. Hammond, M.: A review of recent papers on online discussion in teaching and learning in higher education. Journal of Asynchronous Learning Networks 9(3), 9–23 (2005)
6. Cheng, C.K., Paré, D.E., Collimore, L., et al.: Assessing the effectiveness of a voluntary online discussion forum on improving students' course performance. Computers & Education 56(1), 253–261 (2011)
7. Webb, E., Jones, A., Barker, P., et al.: Using e-learning dialogues in higher education. Innovations in Education and Teaching International 41(1), 93–103 (2004)
8. Jyothi, S., McAvinia, C., Keating, J.: A visualisation tool to aid exploration of students' interactions in asynchronous online communication. Computers & Education 58(1), 30–42 (2012)
9. Wise, A.F., Perera, N., Hsiao, Y., et al.: Microanalytic case studies of individual participation patterns in an asynchronous online discussion in an undergraduate blended course. The Internet and Higher Education 15(2), 108–117 (2012)
10. Beaudoin, M.F.: Learning or lurking?: Tracking the "invisible" online student. The Internet and Higher Education 5(2), 147–155 (2002)
11. Tobarra, L., Robles-Gómez, A., Ros, S., et al.: Analyzing the students' behavior and relevant topics in virtual learning communities. Computers in Human Behavior 31, 659–669 (2014)
12. Dringus, L.P., Ellis, T.: Using data mining as a strategy for assessing asynchronous discussion forums. Computers & Education 45(1), 141–160 (2005)
13. Peffers, K., Tuunanen, T., Rothenberger, M.A., et al.: A design science research methodology for information systems research. Journal of management information systems 24(3), 45–77 (2007)
14. Harasim, L.: Shift happens: Online education as a new paradigm in learning. The Internet and Higher Education 3(1), 41–61 (2000)
15. Kaye, A.: Computer-mediated communication and distance education. In: Mason, R., Kaye, A. (eds.) Mindweave: Communication, Computers, and Distance Education. Pergamon, New York (1989)
16. Gibbs, W., Simpson, L.D., Bernas, R.S.: An analysis of temporal norms in online discussions. International Journal of Instructional Media 35(1), 63 (2008)
17. Woo, Y., Reeves, T.C.: Meaningful interaction in web-based learning: A social constructivist interpretation. The Internet and Higher Education 10(1), 15–25 (2007)
18. Jonassen, D.H., Kwon II, H.: Communication patterns in computer mediated versus face-to-face group problem solving. Educational Technology Research and Development 49(1), 35–51 (2001)
19. Prestera, G.E., Moller, L.A.: Exploiting opportunities for knowledge-building in asynchronous distance learning environments. Quarterly Review of Distance Education 2(2), 93–104 (2001)

20. Peters, V.L., Hewitt, J.: An investigation of student practices in asynchronous computer conferencing courses. Computers & Education 54(4), 951–961 (2010)
21. Johnson, L., Adams Becker, S., Cummins, M., Estrada, V., Freeman, A., Ludgate, H.: NMC Horizon Report: 2013 Higher Education Edition (2013), http://www.nmc.org/publications/2013-horizon-report-higher-ed (accessed February 15, 2013)
22. Campbell, J.P., DeBlois, P.B., Oblinger, D.G.: Academic Analytics. Educause Review 42(4), 40–57 (2007)
23. Elias, T.: Learning Analytics: Definitions, Processes and Potential (2011), http://learninganalytics.net/LearningAnalyticsDefinitionsProcessesPotential.pdf
24. Siemens, G., Long, P.: Penetrating the fog: Analytics in learning and education. Educause Review 46(5), 30–32 (2011)
25. Romero, C., Ventura, S.: Educational data mining: A survey from 1995 to 2005. Expert Systems with Applications 33(1), 135–146 (2007)
26. Romero-Zaldivar, V., Pardo, A., Burgos, D., et al.: Monitoring student progress using virtual appliances: A case study. Computers & Education 58(4), 1058–1067 (2012)
27. Bernard, R.M., Abrami, P.C., Borokhovski, E., et al.: A meta-analysis of three types of interaction treatments in distance education. Review of Educational Research 79(3), 1243–1289 (2009)
28. Moore, M.G.: Editorial: Three types of interaction. American Journal of Distance Education 3(2), 86–89 (1989)
29. Hamuy, E., Galaz, M.: Information versus communication in course management system participation. Computers & Education 54(1), 169–177 (2010)
30. Mazzolini, M., Maddison, S.: When to jump in: The role of the instructor in online discussion forums. Computers & Education 49(2), 193–213 (2007)
31. Thomas, M.J.W.: Learning within incoherent structures: The space of online discussion forums. Journal of Computer Assisted Learning 18(3), 351–366 (2002)
32. Bayer, J., Bydzovská, H., Géryk, J., Obšivac, T., Popelínský, L.: Predicting drop-out from social behaviour of students. In: Proceedings of the 5th International Conference on Educational Data Mining (2012)
33. Romero, C., López, M., Luna, J., et al.: Predicting students' final performance from participation in on-line discussion forums. Computers & Education 68(0), 458–472 (2013), doi:10.1016/j.compedu.2013.06.009
34. Thomas, M.J.W.: Learning within incoherent structures: The space of online discussion forums. Journal of Computer Assisted Learning 18(3), 351–366 (2002)
35. Hung, J., Zhang, K.: Revealing online learning behaviors and activity patterns and making predictions with data mining techniques in online teaching. MERLOT Journal of Online Learning and Teaching (2008)
36. Kumar, V., Chadha, A.: An Empirical Study of the Applications of Data Mining Techniques in Higher Education. International Journal of Advanced Computer Science and Applications 2(3), 80–84 (2011)
37. Lin, F., Hsieh, L., Chuang, F.: Discovering genres of online discussion threads via text mining. Computers & Education 52(2), 481–495 (2009)
38. Ebner, M., Holzinger, A., Catarci, T.: Lurking: An underestimated human-computer phenomenon. IEEE Multimedia 12(4), 70–75 (2005)
39. Lehr, C.: Web 2.0 in der universitären Lehre (2011), http://www.diss.fu-berlin.de/diss/receive/FUDISS_thesis_000000035056 (received at February 2, 2014)

Assessing the Need of Augmenting Video Lectures with Supporting Information

Gaurav Kumar Singh, Abhay Doke, Varun Kumar,
Savita Bhat, and Niranjan Pedanekar

Systems Research Lab, Tata Research Development and Design Centre,
Tata Consultancy Services, Pune, India
{gauravk.singh2,abhay.doke,kumar.varun1,
savita.bhat,n.pedanekar}@tcs.com

Abstract. Massively Online Open Courses (MOOCs) consist of online video lectures delivered by experts. Learner drop-out is a major concern for MOOCs. Early drop-outs are often associated with cognitive overload partially caused by unfamiliarity of concepts being taught. In such cases, the course can be augmented with supporting information such as definition and explanation for concepts. In this paper, we propose a metric quantifying the need for augmentation of individual concepts as a course progresses. We examine the metric using a MOOC course. We also present a preliminary experiment with 36 undergraduate students on using such augmentation.

Keywords: MOOCs, Education, Augmentation, Metric, e-learning.

1   Introduction

Over the last decade, Massively Online Open Courses (MOOCs) have gained popularity amongst learners. MOOCs typically consist of a number of video lectures of varying length grouped according to topics and arranged in an appropriate sequence. In a MOOC, the learners see a teacher, typically an expert in the field, delivering a lecture in front of a camera. The teacher can also present slides on the topic or write on a blackboard or pose questions which need to be answered by the learner. The learners can rewind, fast-forward or pause the videos according to their need.

However, MOOCs have failed to deliver on their disruptive promise mainly due to high attrition rates [1]. Studies indicate that over 90% of learners registering for MOOCs drop out without completing the course [2]. A study of the edX Circuits and Electronics course reported an attrition of 95% with almost 50% taking place in the early stages of the course [3].

One can argue that if the drop-outs could be prevented, MOOCs could have more business and social impact. In a review of the factors contributing to early drop-outs of learners in e-learning, Tyler-Smith [4] argued that the early drop-outs typically occurred due to a cognitive overload experienced by the learners. First-time learners deal with multiple tasks contributing to the cognitive load: being able to adopt tech-

P. Zaphiris and A. Ioannou (Eds.): LCT 2014, Part I, LNCS 8523, pp. 238–249, 2014.

nology, using the learning interface, taking on new concepts and interacting with other learners. In another work on MOOCs, Adamapoulos [5] reported that the conceptual difficulty experienced by a learner has a negative effect on the course completion rate.

Cognitive load may also be caused by a phenomenon known as the 'Curse of Knowledge' (COK) [6]. Due to COK, experts often tend to overlook the perspective of the novice and end up using unfamiliar or unrelated terms while teaching the main concept. For example, if a teacher expert in Unix/Linux casually says that 'information retrieval is a little like the *grep* command' in an information retrieval course, some learners may not understand what she wants to say. In an online setting, since the learners cannot ask questions, they have to pause the lecture and look up the unfamiliar term on the Internet. This involves hunting for information and trying to make sense of it in the context of what is being taught. This may further add to the learner's cognitive load.

Agrawal et al used various spatial and semantic characteristics of the learning material to propose a method for assessing comprehension burden in a textbook [7]. In another work, Agrawal et al [8] proposed augmenting textbooks with supporting information to ease the comprehension burden. One can argue that just like textbooks, if MOOC learners are provided supporting information for simplification of unfamiliar or important concepts at early stages of learning, they can counter the cognitive load to some extent. In fact, some studies [9] advocate the use of additional information from online resources while learning from MOOCs.

In a typical MOOC, thousands of concepts appear throughout the course. But which of these concepts should one augment? There seems to be no prior work on prescribing when augmentation should be provided during a MOOC to ease the burden on the learner. In this paper, we present, to our knowledge, the first attempt **to measure the augmentation need (AN) for concepts in a MOOC**. We specifically choose the familiarity of a concept to the learner as a basis for evaluating this need. We propose a metric for quantifying the augmentation need to determine whether a concept being mentioned needs to be augmented with supporting learning material at a given time during the course. In the proposed augmentation need metric, we incorporate the effects of the learner's familiarity with the concept, the importance of the concept in a particular lecture and the progress through the course. We report an analysis of a MOOC for Computer Architecture using this metric.

But does augmentation with additional information work towards reducing the cognitive load? We present a preliminary controlled experiment with undergraduate students in an attempt to answer the following questions:

1. Do learners of MOOCs need augmentation?
2. From a Human Computer Interface (HCI) perspective, how do first time learners receive such augmentation?
3. What effect does such augmentation have on the learner's understanding?

2   Augmenting MOOCs

One can imagine several dimensions of augmentation when it comes to MOOCs. We argue that a MOOC could be augmented with additional information such as: definitions to make learners familiar with a concept, explanations to make them understand concepts, complementary information (*e.g.* practical examples when theory is being explained), engagement mechanisms (*e.g.* rewards and challenges) when the lecture sounds monotonous, and assessment questions when a concept has been explained. In this paper, we focused only on the familiarity of a concept when assessing the augmentation need. For example, when a concept such as *grep* appears in an information retrieval course, it may not be very familiar to most learners. Perhaps a definition and an example of *grep* would help in making the learner understand the concept.

We make three main observations related to the need for augmentation of a concept during a lecture.

2.1   The Effect of Familiarity of a Concept

There are certain concepts in the domain of computer science that are more familiar to learners. A concept such as *Microsoft Windows* being mentioned by an instructor hardly needs any supporting information. A concept such as *bit* perhaps needs some introduction to the uninitiated. Advanced concepts such as *Re-order Buffer* need much more supporting information.

2.2   The Effect of Progress in a Course

As a course progresses, the learner is likely to know more about a concept. The need of the learner to make use of explanatory material may diminish over time. As the concept is mentioned more number of times, the augmentation need goes down.

2.3   The Effect of Importance of a Concept

A concept such as *sparse matrix* is important when describing the data structures used for information retrieval. But the concept may not even appear in other lectures of the course. So the need for supporting information for such concepts may be localized. A concept such as *corpus* may appear in many places in a natural language processing course and needs to be understood clearly.

3   Augmentation Need (AN) Metric

MOOC video lectures typically have subtitles. These are provided by the instructor or are available through crowdsourcing. We used these subtitles as the base for finding out what concepts are being mentioned by the instructor. We extracted the concepts from the course subtitles that have a corresponding Wikipedia page using the Wikipedia Miner [10] which allowed an accuracy of 75% in identifying Wikipedia links for given text [11]. The extracted concepts formed a set of augmentation candidate concepts.

Based on the three observations in previous section, we proposed a metric to quantify the need for augmentation of any given concept at any point during a course. We proposed that for a given concept c_i appearing in the course in lecture l, AN is a weighted average of the three effects mentioned above as

$$AN_{i,l} = \begin{cases} w_1 F_i + w_2 P_{i,l} + w_3 I_{i,l}, & c_i \text{ appears in } l \\ 0, & c_i \text{ does not appear in } l \end{cases}$$

where w_1, w_2 and w_3 are weights of the familiarity, progress and importance effects.

3.1   Familiarity Effect

For representing the familiarity of a concept, we proposed a metric based on the number of pages that refer to the concept's page in Wikipedia. For this, we formed a graph of all Wikipedia pages. We calculated the Global Familiarity (GF) for a concept c_i as

$$GF(i) = \log \frac{w_i}{W}$$

where w_i is the number of pages that link to the Wikipedia page for c_i and W is the total number of links in Wikipedia. A larger value of GF indicates a more familiar concept. For example, GF(*Microsoft Windows*) is -7.03, while GF(*Re-order Buffer*) is -14.11.

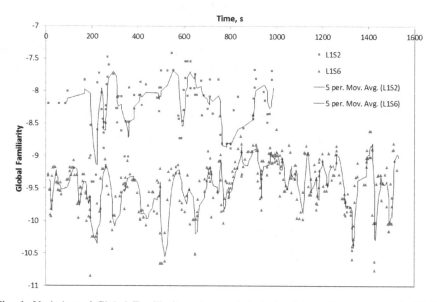

Fig. 1. Variation of Global Familiarity values and their 5-point moving averages for L1S2 (introductory) and L1S6 (advanced) lectures in the CA course

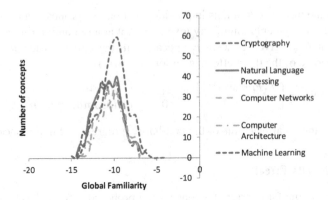

Fig. 2. Distribution of global familiarity over 5 MOOCs from Coursera

Figure 1 shows higher GF values for concepts occurring in an introductory lecture as compared to those in a more advanced lecture. We found GF scores for concept terms in 5 MOOCs from Coursera [12-16] and observed that the GF values are distributed in a similar way for all the courses as shown in Figure 2. From this we concluded that GF values are a consistent measure of familiarity of concepts. We normalized the GF for the concept c_i as

$$\overline{GF}(i) = \frac{GF(i) - GF_{min}}{GF_{max} - GF_{min}}$$

where GF_{max} and GF_{min} are GF values of the most familiar and the least familiar concepts in the course, respectively. We observed that very familiar terms do not need augmentation and they need to be given less importance in the metric. So we further shaped the normalized values as an inverted sigmoid curve as shown in Figure 3 for obtaining the global familiarity effect F_i for a concept c_i in a course using

$$F_i = \left(\frac{e^{-v}}{1 + e^{-v}}\right) \ where \ v = 10(\overline{GF}(i) - 0.5)$$

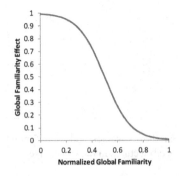

Fig. 3. Variation of familiarity effect F_i with the normalized global familiarity scores

3.2   Progress Effect

For representing progress through the course, we considered the fraction of a concept that remained to be talked about at a given point in the course. We proposed a metric to denote the progress effect P_i for a concept c_i as

$$P_i = 1 - \frac{n_{i,l-1}}{N_i}$$

where $n_{i,l-1}$ is the number of occurrences of c_i till the beginning of the lecture l and N_i is the number of occurrences of c_i in the whole course. The metric has an automatic value of 1 for the first lecture as no concept has been talked about yet. Figure 4 shows the variation of the progress effect with the frequency of a concept recorded over 8 lectures.

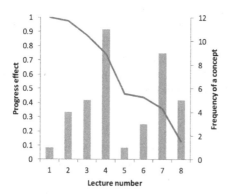

Fig. 4. Variation of the progress effect over lectures (shown as the line) for a given distribution of concept occurrences in those lectures (shown as bars)

3.3   Importance Effect

For incorporating the importance of concepts in a given lecture, we used the Term Frequency-Inverse Document Frequency measure (TF-IDF) as it is the standard measure of importance used in information retrieval [17]. We first calculated the importance $imp_{i,l}$ of a concept c_i in a given lecture l as

$$imp_{i,l} = f_{i,l} * log\left(\frac{L}{L_i}\right)$$

where $f_{i,l}$ is the frequency of occurrences of the concept c_i in a lecture l, L_i is the number of lectures in which the concept c_i appears and L is the total number of lectures.

We further normalized the importance values over each lecture to get the importance effect $I_{i,l}$ for a concept c_i in a lecture l as

$$I_{i,l} = \frac{imp_{i,l} - imp_{l,min}}{imp_{l,max} - imp_{l,min}}$$

where $imp_{l,min}$ and $imp_{l,max}$ are the minimum and maximum values of importance in lecture l, respectively.

4   Analyzing MOOCs Using the AN Metric

We analyzed a part of the Computer Architecture MOOC course offered by Prof. David Wentzlaff at Coursera [12] using the AN metric. This part has 27 lectures prescribed for a period of 6 weeks. Using the subtitles of the videos, we found 235 augmentation candidate concepts using Wikipedia Miner. We also recorded the time at which these concepts appeared in each lecture. We calculated the AN metric for each of these concepts in each lecture. We used equal weights in the weighted average in the AN metric equation ($w_1 = 0.33$, $w_2 = 0.33$ and $w_3 = 0.33$). We recommended candidate concept terms with AN values higher than a threshold of 0.33 amounting to at least one effect fully contributing to the AN value. This was done in order to suppress the number of augmentation candidate terms.

4.1   Observations

Figure 5 shows a partial visualization of the AN values for all 27 lectures in the Computer Architecture (CA) course. This visualization shows the top 10 concepts used in the course based on the average of their AN values over all lectures. Each column represents a lecture and each row represents a concept. The darker the cell colour, the greater is the augmentation need. The line graph at the end shows the variation of the AN value over the lectures. We observed that not all concepts are prescribed augmentation for all lectures. Some concepts such as *register file* are important throughout the course. These may need augmentation relevant to the context as the course proceeds. Concepts such as *Computer Architecture* appear early on, but are not prescribed for augmentation during later lectures. Concepts such as *Microsoft Windows*, *Linux* and *Java* (not seen in the figure) are not at all prescribed for augmentation.

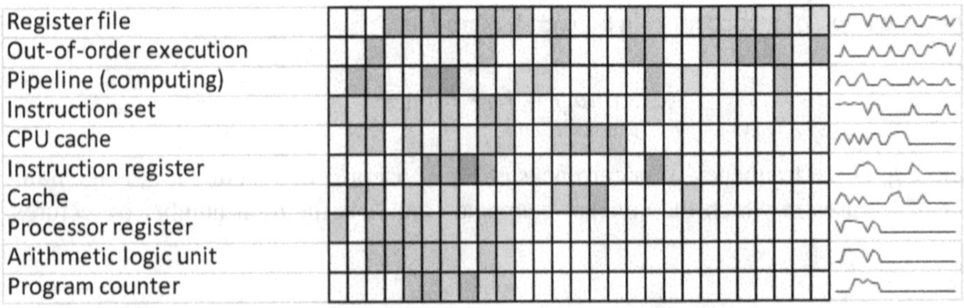

Fig. 5. Concepts with highest average AN values over the whole course

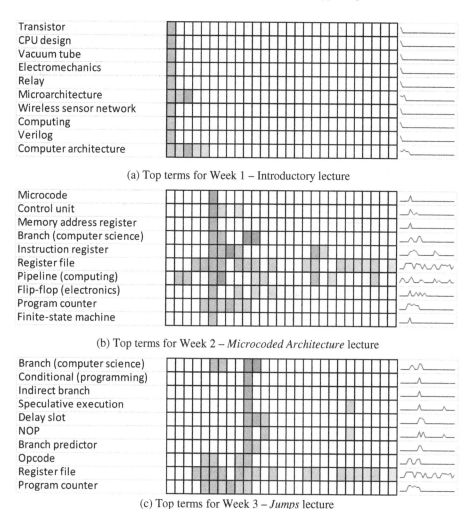

(a) Top terms for Week 1 – Introductory lecture

(b) Top terms for Week 2 – *Microcoded Architecture* lecture

(c) Top terms for Week 3 – *Jumps* lecture

Fig. 6. Variation in the AN of concepts according to specific lectures

Also, for a given lecture the augmentation plan can be different than other lectures. For example, as seen in Figure 6(a), concepts such as *Moore's law* are prescribed for augmentation in the first introductory lecture. Most of these concepts may not be revisited later, but can cause discomfort early on if not familiarized. Figure 6(b) shows the top concepts in the first lecture of Week 2 about Microcoded Architecture of the CPU. Concepts such as *microcode* and *control unit* are important to this lecture and are not very familiar concepts. Therefore, they need to be augmented. Similarly, as seen in Figure 6(c), concepts such as *branching* and *conditional branching* are central to the first lecture in Week 3 about Jumps, and need to be augmented.

We also analyzed the relative contribution of the three effects on the AN value. As seen in Figure 7(a), a concept such as *pipelining* is not very familiar, but is very important in certain lectures. Though the progress effect diminishes later, the importance of the concept in the later lectures as well as the relative unfamiliarity of the concept are high. This causes the augmentation need to increase above the threshold for all lectures where *pipelining* appears. As seen in Figure (b), *bit* is not very important in lectures and is relatively familiar. So its augmentation need is below threshold for most lectures.

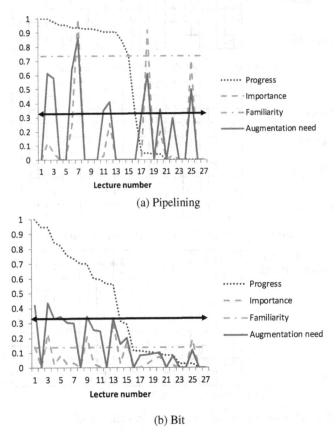

(a) Pipelining

(b) Bit

Fig. 7. Contribution of the three effects to the AN metric over the entire MOOC

5   A Preliminary Experiment with Augmentation

In earlier sections, we described the need for augmentation and proposed a metric for augmentation need specifically to avoid discomfort owing to unfamiliarity with concepts. In order to test whether such augmentation works in practice, we carried out a preliminary experiment with 36 undergraduate students studying Information Technology. We designed an augmentation web interface for one of the video lectures in the Natural Language Processing course by Jurafsky and Manning [13], which described the concept of term-document matrices used in information retrieval. The augmentation interface consisted of the video lecture accompanied by clickable buttons with concept names as shown in Figure 8.

Fig. 8. Augmentation interface for a MOOC lecture used for the experiment

The buttons appeared in the side frame as a concept was mentioned, stayed for 10 seconds and faded away. Clicking the button paused the video and brought up preliminary information such as definition and links for explanation. The learner could use it if required and get back to the video by un-pausing it. We gave the augmented video to a test group of 19 students and the non-augmented video to a control group of 17 students. At the end of the 10-minute lecture, the learners appeared for a quiz consisting of 6 questions. They also answered survey questions about the need for, the usefulness and interestingness of, and the distraction due to augmentation. They also stated which concepts they found difficult. We also recorded the clicks of the learners as they used the augmentation information.

We found that there was no significant difference in the scores of the control and the test group. Also there was no significant difference in the perceived interestingness and degree of difficulty of the video between the control and the test group. 31% of the test group respondents said that they found the augmentation distracting, while 89% found it to be useful. 76% of the control group respondents said that they wanted additional information during the video. We also found that all the concepts which learners had stated to be difficult (*corpus, Caeser, grep, matrix, sparse matrix, Unix, data structure, string search, Boolean algebra*) were suggested as augmentation candidates using the AN metric. We observed that though learners in the test group had clicked on the buttons for definition, they did not extensively utilize the explanation links provided.

6   Discussion

Analysis of the Computer Architecture MOOC and the experimental results indicate that the AN metric works fairly well in identifying concepts needing supporting information. It captures the effects of familiarity, progress and importance on the augmentation need and reduces the set of candidate concepts to a manageable set for practical use. Due to the interplay of importance and progress effects, locally important terms which have to be understood well are given due importance. Globally importance terms also are recognized for augmentation, but the augmentation need diminishes over time. Very familiar terms do not receive augmentation, while the ones which are unfamiliar do get recommended for augmentation. One can vary the weights of the metric to suit the course needs, *e.g.* reduce the familiarity weight in an advanced course that contains difficult terms, so that even the terms which are less difficult get augmentation.

Among the main limitations of this approach, is the use of Wikipedia to estimate global familiarity. Concepts for which the global similarity value is not appropriate, the AN metric also does not make sense. We recommend using a more robust method for assigning global familiarity. Similarly, the use of Wikipedia Miner for recognizing concepts is another limitation as inaccurate recognition leads to redundant or incorrect concept candidates.

The results of the preliminary experiment suggest that learners needed augmentation, but did not specifically use the augmentation interface extensively to reduce their cognitive load. So despite the augmentation need being recognized, designing an interface that is intuitive to use and does not distract learners may be the key to reducing cognitive load.

7   Conclusion

In this paper, we presented, to our knowledge, the first attempt at assessing whether concepts being taught in a MOOC need supporting information. We proposed an augmentation need metric based on the effects of the familiarity of concepts, the progress in a course and the relative importance of a concept in a lecture. We also presented an analysis of applying the AN metric to a Computer Architecture MOOC. We reported experimental results on using augmentation interface with MOOCs. We believe that learners need augmentation during MOOCs and the AN metric provides MOOC instructors or designers a plan for using supporting information about concepts. We believe that we have demonstrated the utility of the AN metric, but a large scale validation is needed to assess it better. We plan to apply the AN metric to a large number of MOOCs in order to visualize, compare and contrast course characteristics.

References

1. Yang, D., Sinha, T., Adamson, D., Rose, C.P.: "Turn on, Tune in, Drop out": Anticipating student dropouts in Massive Open Online Courses. In: NIPS Workshop on Data Driven Education (2013)
2. Jordan, K.: MOOC Completion Rates: The Data, http://www.katyjordan.com/MOOCproject.html (retrieved February 21, 2014)
3. Breslow, L.B., Pritchard, D.E., DeBoer, J., Stump, G.S., Ho, A.D., Seaton, D.T.: Studying learning in the worldwide classroom: Research into edX's first MOOC. Research & Practice in Assessment 8, 13–25 (2013)

4. Tyler-Smith, K.: Early attrition among first time eLearners: A review of factors that contribute to drop-out, withdrawal and non-completion rates of adult learners undertaking eLearning programmes. Journal of Online learning and Teaching 2(2), 73–85 (2006)
5. Adamopoulos, P.: What Makes a Great MOOC? An Interdisciplinary Analysis of Student Retention in Online Courses. In: Proceedings of the 34th International Conference on Information Systems, ICIS, vol. 2013 (2013)
6. Wieman, C.E.: APS News–The back page. The "curse of knowledge" or why intuition about teaching often fails. American Physical Society News 16(10) (2007)
7. Agrawal, R., Chakraborty, S., Gollapudi, S., Kannan, A., Kenthapadi, K.: Empowering authors to diagnose comprehension burden in textbooks. In: Proceedings of the 18th ACM SIGKDD International Conference on Knowledge Discovery and Data Mining, pp. 967–975. ACM (2012)
8. Agrawal, R., Gollapudi, S., Kenthapadi, K., Srivastava, N., Velu, R.: Enriching textbooks through data mining. In: Proceedings of the First ACM Symposium on Computing for Development, vol. 19. ACM (December 2010)
9. Bruff, D.O., Fisher, D.H., McEwen, K.E., Smith, B.E.: Wrapping a MOOC: Student Perceptions of an Experiment in Blended Learning. Journal of Online Learning & Teaching 9(2) (2013)
10. Milne, D., Witten, I.H.: An open-source toolkit for mining Wikipedia. Artificial Intelligence (2012)
11. Milne, D., Witten, I.H.: Learning to link with wikipedia. In: Proceedings of the 17th ACM Conference on Information and Knowledge Management, pp. 509–518. ACM (2008)
12. Wentzlaff, D.: Computer Architecture, http://www.coursera.org/course/comparch
13. Jurafsky, D., Manning, C.: Natural Language Processing, http://www.coursera.org/course/nlp
14. Boneh, D.: Cryptography 1, http://www.coursera.org/course/crypto
15. Wetherall, D., Krishnamurthy, A., Zahorjan, J.: Computer Networks, http://www.coursera.org/course/comnetworks
16. Ng, A.: Machine Learning, http://www.coursera.org/course/ml
17. Salton, G., Yang, C.S.: On the specification of term values in automatic indexing. Journal of Documentation 29(4), 351–372 (1973)

Low-Achieving Students' Perceptions of Online Language Learning: A Case of English Proficiency Threshold

Ai-Ling Wang[1], Yuh-Chang Lin[2], and Shu-Fen Chang[3]

[1] T amkang University, English Department, New Taipei City, Taiwan
Wanga@mail.tku.edu.tw
[2] Aletheia University, Center for General Education, New Taipei City, Taiwan
Au1258@mail.au.edu.tw
[3] Kang-Ning Junior College of Medical Care and Management, Taipei, Taiwan
Fen587@webmail.knjc.edu.tw

Abstract. This study aims at exploring how low-achieving EFL learners perceive and make use of the instructional web site to fulfill part of the requirements for a college degree. Participants were college students who did not pass the threshold of the required level of English proficiency set by the college.

Online Tutorial English was a one-semester course offered for the above-mentioned students; they did not come to the class for onsite instruction except for the weeks before the mid-term and final exam. Students were provided with weekly reading articles and were required to do assignments online. At the end of the semester, students were asked to fill out a questionnaire and some students volunteered for an interview.

The researchers analyzed the qualitative data, using Grounded Theory Method. Findings of the study showed that low-achieving EFL learners could not really be motivated to learn and that the primary aim for those students to learn English as a foreign language was to pass the course and get their college diploma.

Keywords: English proficiency threshold, online language learning, low-achieving language learners, remedial English course.

1 Introduction

Modern technologies have made online learning more and more popular and feasible, especially in the field of language learning. People may learn different languages through communicating with people online. On the other hand, being able to communicate in the global community has become more and more important for people who wish to enrich their life. English has long been the lingua franca of the world. Although some people may claim that social, political, technological, and economical changes may alter the status of English as the lingua franca of the world, English is still the most widely used language in the global community [1].

Standardized English proficiency tests, such as Test of English as a Foreign Language (TOEFL), Test of English for International Communication (TOEIC), and The

P. Zaphiris and A. Ioannou (Eds.): LCT 2014, Part I, LNCS 8523, pp. 250–258, 2014.

International English Language Testing System (IELTS), have been developed to measure an individual's English proficiency. Achieving a certain level of English proficiency may be required for admission to a university, employment in a trading company or a travel agency, promotion to a higher level of position, and application of a scholarship [2].

In Taiwan, the government has urged college administers to set an English proficiency threshold for a college degree in the hope that college graduates can have basic skills to communicate in English and can participate in the global community freely and easily. Many colleges in Taiwan have set different levels of English proficiency threshold, depending on their students' general English proficiency and the levels of proficiency required in their professional studies and types of their future career. However, we may say that some students are not really apt to language learning. They may have excellent professional knowledge in a certain field; however, they have problems expressing themselves in an international context. For those low-achieving students, some colleges in Taiwan offer alternatives for them. It is a general practice that those who fail to step across the threshold are allowed to take an English course instead.

This study aims at exploring how low-achieving college students who took a remedial English course online to partially fulfill the requirements for a college degree perceive learning English online. On the other hand, how English proficiency threshold is practiced in Taiwan and how those students perceive the practice of English proficiency threshold.

2   Literature Review

In this section, the authors will review two domains of literature relevant the present study, namely English proficiency threshold and low-achieving language learners and distance learning.

2.1   English Proficiency Threshold

As mentioned earlier, in order to prepare students for their future career or further studies, the Ministry of Education (MOE) in Taiwan has urged college administers to set an English proficiency threshold as one of the requirements for a college degree and many colleges have done so. In some of the public and private sectors, achieving a certain level of English proficiency is a must before one can be hired. The tendency has revealed that the government in Taiwan is eager to actively participate in the global community and being proficient in English is the first step for its citizens to communicate with people from different countries.

Chun Shin Limited [2] reported that Japanese and Korean students outperformed Taiwanese students on TOEIC in the recent years. The government in Taiwan is aware of the importance of its citizens' being able to communicate and function in the global community. In this report, the authors reported some of the effective ways of language management practiced in Japanese and Korean educational institutions and private sectors. For example, the Rakuten Global Market in Japan, led by its CEO Hiroshi Mikitani, strictly practiced its Englishnization in the organization and had developed its language management system, which requires its employees to reach a certain level of English proficiency, depending on their position level and their chances of using English in their workplace. The government in Taiwan is eager to learn from those successful cases to advance its citizens to the global community.

For those students who have problems crossing the threshold of English proficiency test, many schools offer alternatives. Students may be allowed to take a remedial English course instead. Generally speaking, these students are low-achieving language learners and they are not motivated to learn English as a foreign language. They lack the confidence and the affective factors required to learn a second or foreign language. How to motivate low-achieving EFL learners to learn online is even more complicated than language teachers can expect, given the fact that teachers cannot really monitor students learning as they do in the traditional classroom context.

2.2   Distance Learning

Distance learning is definitely not new to educators and students. However, as White [3] mentioned, due to differences between traditional classroom and online language learning environment, learners will face new challenges when they move their language learning environment to an online one. These challenges include:

- There are some immediate demands to adjust to an online language learning environment, such as feeling being isolated, problems with motivation and self-discipline, and the need for effective time management.
- The absence of teacher mediation and real-time face-to-face interaction requires language learners to establish their own set of learning behaviors and manage the course of their own learning.
- Online learning is a self-instruction context and learners need to be more self-directed and better aware of the process of language learning and the need to manage their learning.
- Online language learning provides learners with a wide variety of learning opportunities to cross the border to interact and collaborate with physically apart learners. However, new technologies are constantly developing and new skills need to be developed in order to function within technology-mediated language learning environments.

Distance learners need to adjust their learning behaviors in an online learning context as mentioned above. The same is true for distance teachers. Chuah [4] urged distance teachers to re-design students' learning experience to attract, inform, and invoke students. He argued that, in order to ensure the design can provide students with an enjoyable e-learning experience, the design of an online course should be entertaining, educational, esthetic, and escapist. Chuah argued that the way distance teachers create the learning environment may be crucial to motivate students to learn and may contribute to the success of language learning.

From the literature reviewed above, we may conclude that online learning is different from traditional classroom learning. The present study aims at exploring how low-achieving language learners perceive online language learning and how they would say about their online language learning experience.

3   Methodology

In this section, the researchers will first introduce the research paradigm employed and the participants involved in the present study. Then they will go on to introduce the online language learning course. Finally, they authors will describe how the data were collected and analyzed.

3.1   Research Paradigm

The present study was developed under the qualitative research paradigm. The researchers followed the Grounded Theory Method (GTM) to collect and analyze data. Bryant and Charmaz [5] defined Grounded Theory Method as "a systematic inductive and comparative approach for conducting inquiry for the purpose of constructing theory....The method is designed to encourage researchers' persistent interaction with their data, while remaining constantly involved with their emerging analyses". That is, for grounded theorists, data are key to research, and researchers do not have predominant assumptions. Rather, they let patterns or theories emerge from data. As stated by Dick [6], grounded theorists do not test hypothesis; rather, they aim to discover the patterns and theories implicit in the data.

Approaches to grounded theory method may be slightly different among different grounded theorists. However, the principles of grounded theory remain the same. Dick [6] sketched the phases through which grounded theorists work:

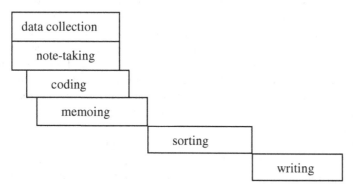

Fig. 1. Phases of Grounded Theory Method

In the entire process, researchers may do data collection, note-taking, and coding at the same time from the very beginning. After they look over all the data they have collected and assign each important part of the data a code, researchers may sort the data based on the similar categories or properties they address. Finally, researchers may write the research report up and present findings based on the patterns that have emerged from the data.

3.2   Participants

The researchers have been offering remedial English courses for those college students who failed to pass the English proficiency test required by the school. Participants of the present study were those students who took Tutorial English with the researchers as an alternative to an English proficiency test and they were in different academic fields. Students were required to take an official English proficiency test before they were allowed to enroll in the course as an alternative. It was because the school wanted to make sure that students did try and take an English proficiency test at least once. Only those who failed were allowed to take the remedial English course. It is obvious that the school was trying hard to encourage its students to take English proficiency tests and to improve their communicative skills in English. In order to secure the validity and reliability of the present study, the researchers collected data for three consecutive semesters. That is, participants of the study were from three different groups of students in three different semesters. With a larger group of participants, the researchers believe that they could better draw a picture of how low-achieving language learners perceive online language learning.

3.3   The Course

The remedial English course is termed Tutorial English. It is because this is an online course. Students did not have to physically attend the class for onsite instruction except for two or three designated days. Instructional websites, WebCT and Moodle, were organized especially for the course. At the beginning of the web page there was technical instruction as to how to register for the website, how to download articles, upload assignments, discuss with peer students, etc. Each week, the instructor would post articles of students' interest and challenge students with some questions or assignments. Students were required to read these articles and upload their assignments or responses to the questions to the website before the date due. Their assignments would then be graded and posted on the website and students could check their own scores. In order to help students read these articles on their own, the instructor also uploaded explanation of vocabulary words, sentences, and important grammatical points in PowerPoint files.

Students might also raise questions relevant to the required readings or ask for technical help on the discussion board, and the instructor, teaching assistants or even peer students would help answer these questions. Occasionally, words of encouragement, complaint or valuable information would appear on the discussion board. The instructor or teaching assistants would also make use of the discussion board to make announcements, explain some grammatical issues or share personal experiences of learning English as a foreign language with students.

3.4   Data Collection and Data Analysis

The researchers collected data for the present study from different sources, including: students' assignments uploaded to the website, students' postings on the discussion board, oral and written conversations between the instructor and the teaching assistants, open-ended questions responded by the students, interviews with students, and the researchers' field notes. These data were then analyzed, following the steps of grounded theory method. The researchers found some patterns emerged from the data, which will be discussed in the next section.

4   Findings and Discussion

Based on the patterns emerged from different sources of qualitative data, the researchers would like to present findings of the present study as follows.

4.1   Low-Achieving EFL Learners Are Aware of the Importance of English Proficiency in the Modern Society

From students' postings on the WebCT or Moodle website and in-depth interviews with students, the researchers found that most low-achieving EFL learners agree that having a certain level of English proficiency is quite important in the modern society even though they themselves have problems learning English. The key here is that they are aware that even though they can pass the required English proficiency threshold and graduate, there is still another English proficiency threshold waiting for them to attain in their job seeking and future career.

In the interview with students, most of the students claimed that definitely they think that attaining a certain degree of English proficiency is very important for them. A graduate student from the department of finance stated that even though they are not required to write their M.A. thesis in English, they feel an English version of thesis is more prestigious. He also felt it important that in his future career search, he may be required to submit his certificate of English proficiency and his level of English proficiency may affect his future promotion.

> *"I am graduating and I need to look for a job pretty soon. I understand that if I want a better job, I definitely need to improve my English."*

Another graduate student from the Department of Electrical Engineering expressed his frustration of not being able to publish an academic article in English even though his articles had considerable professional values. English proficiency has been his greatest barrier in his professional growth. It was quite common that his academic papers contributed to professional journals were rejected because of his poor expression in English.

"As a graduate student, I am required to publish my articles in professional journals in order to get my degree. However, my articles were always rejected with comments such as, poor English, a lot of grammatical errors, etc.

Students' comments on English proficiency mentioned above showed that students did feel a sense of urgency in terms of English proficiency despite that they felt frustrated in their learning process. However, feeling an urgency to improve their English proficiency is one thing; how they can do with their poor English is another. Generally speaking, students felt they could not get immediate reward even though they focus their attention on the study of English as a subject.

4.2   Online Learning Cannot Really Motivate Students to Learn

From students' postings on the discussion board, the researchers found that mostly students care about their grades, technical problems, and forthcoming exams. Although the researchers encouraged students to post whatever vocabulary words or grammatical problems they might have and share their language learning experiences with peer students, such kinds of postings were seldom found in the discussion board. Mostly students cared about whether or not they can pass the course and get their degree.

An overview of students' postings on the discussion board, the researchers found that almost 90% postings were relevant to technological problems, inquiries of assignments and assignment-related questions, grades assigned to them, texts to be covered on the exams, and excuses for being uploading assignment late.

"How come I didn't get my grade for the 3rd exercise?"
"I had problems uploading my assignment for this week. Can I turn in a hard-copy instead? Please!"
"Dear teacher: Please double check my grade for the mid-term. I felt I deserved more points."

Only about 10% of the postings were relevant to grammatical issues, vocabulary words, and language learning strategies. It is obvious from the phenomenon that being able to pass the course was students' upmost goal. Although online learning can provide learners with more freedom to learn, this alone is not sufficient to engage students in the learning environment. Students were seeking whatever may benefit them in their learning process. For example, they may hope they can develop friendship with learning partners and help each other with their learning of English.

4.3   Students Care More about Their Professional Study Than about Learning English

In the interview with students, the researchers found that students obviously prioritized their professional study. They felt that their professional knowledge can really help them in their future professional career. There are a lot of professional areas to be covered in their curricula and English is regarded as a plus to their academic achievement. This is most obvious in the science fields. The class roster showed that 70% of the students who took Tutorial English were science majors, and only 30% of the students were social science majors.

Science majors, especially, devoted most of their time to the study of their professional subjects. In the interview with students, most of the science majors mentioned that they have well-achieved their professional studies, such as computer science, physics, electrical engineering, etc. However, they have problems expressing themselves in English and have problems getting their articles published in professional journals. For them, reading professional textbooks written in Chinese is much easier than reading articles written in English. An electrical engineering major mentioned in an interview that, although it is not uncommon for college professors to assign English textbooks for students to read, students tend to buy a Chinese version of the textbook to help them understand the professional messages.

"Can anybody tell me what will be on the final exam? I am sorry I didn't attend the onsite final review class because I had an important meeting with my Chemistry professor."

"Dear teacher: I am sorry I will not be able to attend your review class tomorrow because I have an important exam on Physics tomorrow. Could you please let me know what will be covered on the final exam?"

It may be clear from here that professional subjects weigh heavily on students' mind, compared with English as a subject. It may be because students feel they can have considerable immediate rewards, such as higher grades and professional growth, if they focus on their professional subjects as mentioned earlier. For them, English is but an academic course and they have a lot of professional courses to take. Improving English proficiency may take time and require long-term planning. It is a great challenge for language teachers to heighten students' language awareness and to draw students' attention that English, as a lingua franca, can function in a variety of ways, such as helping professional growth.

5   Conclusion and Recommendations

From findings of the present study mentioned above, the researchers would like to conclude that low-achieving EFL learners are aware of the importance of English proficiency in their career. However, these same learners lack confidence required to improve their English proficiency. Some students may have considerable professional knowledge in a specific field, such as computer science, statistics, or chemistry; however, they feel they are not apt to language learning.

Another issue found in the present study was that online language learning is not necessarily effective for low-achieving language learners. Creating an enjoyable and effective online learning environment may be the key to motivating students to learn. An environment of learning community may provide students with a sense of participation. In the virtual community, students may help each other in their learning process and students will not feel alone and isolated. Wang [7] pointed out that online learning should be beneficial to all participants and distance teachers should create an optimal learning environment to ensure effective language learning to occur.

Findings of the present study showed that most of the students cared about their professional studies. The researchers would like to suggest that online language learning curricula may incorporate with English for Specific Purposes (ESP) to meet low-achieving students' needs. In this case, students may secure their professional studies, and improve their English proficiency at the same time and they may feel particularly rewarding to learn English online.

References

1. Crystal, D.: English as a Global Language, 2nd edn. Cambridge U. P., Cambridge (2003)
2. Chun Shih Limited: Global HRM & TOEIC. Taipei, Taiwan (2012)
3. White, C.: Language Learning in Distance Education. Cambridge U. P., Cambridge (2003)
4. Chuah, C.P.: Experience Redesign: A Conceptual Framework for Moving Teaching and Learning into a Flexible E-learning Environment. In: Tsang, P., Kwan, R., Fox, R. (eds.) Enhancing Learning Through Technology, pp. 37–50. World Scientific, Singapore (2007)
5. Bryant, A., Charmaz, K. (eds.): The Sage Handbook of Grounded Theory. Sage, U.K. (2007)
6. Dick, B.: Grounded Theory: A Thumbnail Sketch, http://www.scu.edu.au/schools/gcm/ar/arp/grounded.html
7. Wang, A.-L.: Engaging Students in Language Learning via Successful, Cross-cultural Video-conferencing. In: Hamada, M. (ed.) E-learning: New Technology, Applications and Future Trends, pp. 243–258. Nova Science Publishers, New York (2013)

Student Modeling and Learning Behaviour

Card Sorting Assessing User Attitude in E-Learning

Ghada R. El Said

Business Information Technology, Future University in Egypt (FUE),
90th street, Fifth settlement, New Cairo
Ghada.refaat@fue.edu.eg,
Ghadarefaat_04@hotmail.com

Abstract. Various undergraduate and post graduate educational bodies, now a day, employ blended learning systems to complement the face to face communication between educator and learner. While E-learning tools in general have been found to improve access to resources, these tools need to be reliable and usable; the ease of use of E-learning would have a meaningful impact on the learning experience.[1]

This paper investigates learners' perception of quality and willingness to use of E-learning environments. It also explores the attitude of users from two different cultural groups towards a number of E-learning sites. The paper aims to reveal some of the perception of quality for these groups of users in interacting with learning virtual communities.

In September/ October 2013, series of card sorting sessions were conducted with number of learners enrolled in a joint venture European-Arab Master Program. In the individual sessions, each participant was asked to look at card of selected E-Learning sites, and to choose a single criterion by which the E-learning main pages could be differentiated from one another. Cards were then sorted based on different categories under each criterion. Participants repeated sorting the cards according to criteria and categories they generated. A second round of sorting sessions were conducted by the same participants, where they sorted the same cards according to the Willingness to Use criterion, and provided a reason for the sorting decisions made.

The analysis of the card sorting sessions reveals some interesting findings concerning interface elements which seem to be salient for users in E-learning environment, such as: Interface Comprehensibility and Obviousness, Content Usefulness, and Site Affiliation and Reputation. Some differences in quality perception were also found between the two cultural groups.

This paper makes a contribution to universal access in HCI by describing the quality perception, preferences, and general attitude for different group of users in the context of E-learning environment.

Keywords: E-learning, Assessing User Attitude, Card Sorting.

1 Introduction

Recent E-learning environments employs Internet communication technology to add the feature of asynchronous learning activities, and customization of instruction and

P. Zaphiris and A. Ioannou (Eds.): LCT 2014, Part I, LNCS 8523, pp. 261–272, 2014.
© Springer International Publishing Switzerland 2014

assessment, it serves to facilitate a simultaneous independent and collaborative learning experience.[2] Bended learning environment can build an online community where forums can be held to better support the learning process.

Modern E- learning education programs enable learners to gain knowledge, at least in part, through online delivery of materials and instructions, while empowering learners with some components of individual control over time, path, and/or pace.[2]

Nevertheless, little study looked at learners' attitude and satisfaction in E-learning environments or their subsequent use. Additionally, while online communities are a suitable venue for assessing Multi-Cultural user attitudes, little research has looked into this issue in the learning context.

This paper looks at the case of a Multi-Cultural Blended Leaning community, a European-Arab Master's Program, jointly provided by an Educational Institute in central Europe and a faculty of Education in an Arab country. The purpose of the master program is to develop and to provide managerial skills as well as competencies for cross-cultural challenges in education management. The paper aims to unfold some general user attitude matters for different cultural groups of users in the context of E-learning environment.

2   Method

2.1   The Card Sorting Technique

Some researchers [3] suggested that studying human perception of information systems starts with exploratory studies to generate hypotheses based on authentic participants' preferences. Card sorting technique is a recommended method for investigating criteria by which users evaluate web pages; it discovers users' understanding of quality features and design of interactive web-based systems.[4]   Categories based on which cards are sorted highlight what seems to be significant for the users, hence generating mature research hypotheses.

Repeated Single Criterion Sort Sessions were conducted, where participants are asked to select a criterion by which the main page could be distinguished from one another, using the main page cards. Having named the sorting criterion, categories for this criterion are identified and cards are sorted accordingly. This sequence is repeated until the participants could think of no more criteria. Criteria and categories that are most frequently selected by the participants reveal which web site design features are most noticed, hence reflect participants' perception about web site evaluation.[5]

Forced Sort Sessions were conducted by the same participants, where they sorted the same cards according to the criterion: "I would/would not use this site". Having sorted the cards according to this criterion, participants were asked to provide a reason for the sorting decisions made.

2.2   The Participants

Card sorting techniques can result valuable insights with a relatively small sample.[6] Thirty educators (fifteen Egyptians and fifteen Germans) doing their post graduate studies using a Blended Learning joint program participated in card sorting sessions. Gender was equally distributed with fifty percent females in both groups. The sample age range varies from 30 to 45, with 50% under 40. All participants were regular Internet users, used the Internet for social networking, educational, and professional development purposes. All participants owned a very good English language, with which they communicate online, and use English language materials and web sites. English language proficiency is a requirement for joining the joint program, for both Germans and Egyptians.

2.3   The Instrument

In sorting techniques, working with higher hierarchy, such as site's main page, would generate more general categories.[6] In the current research, as general insights are acquired, pictures of main pages of educational sites were used for the sorting tasks. The main page illustrates major site's features and category of contents.

2.4   Selecting Educational Sites

Nine E-learning sites were chosen for the sorting study, this number complements the range of items, between eight and twenty, recommended in sorting sessions.[7] Selected E-learning sites includes Web 2.0 open access sites, such as: Khan Academy (khanacademy.org), UNESCO open training platform (opentraining.unesco-ci.org), and TrackStar4Teachers (http://trackstar.4teachers.org). Restricted access sites were also used, such as: Epsilen (corp.epsilen.com), AUC Blackboard+Learn (blackboard.aucegypt.edu). The nine sites included different options of materials categorization, search features, and different interface styles.

Images of the main page of selected sites were captured in November 2013, cropped on the same size and brightness, and high quality colored printed on A4 white paper. Pictures were numbered to make sorting results easier to record. Printed pictures were then covered with hard plastic covers. Participants are allowed to spread cards out wide on a large clear desk during the session.

2.5   Sorting Sessions Administration

During the months of November and December 2013, card sorting sessions were conducted by the researcher in individual sessions. Each session started with an orientation in which written instructions concerning the purpose, duration, and steps of the session were discussed with the participant. A short orientation on card sorting technique was introduced using cards from different domain. Each participant tried sorting until feeling comfortable to start the formal sorting session. Following, the nine E-learning main page cards were presented to the participant.

In the individual sessions, each participant was asked to look at the main page cards and to choose a single criterion by which the E-learning main pages could be differentiated from one another. Cards were then sorted based on different categories under each criterion. Participants repeated sorting the cards according to criteria and categories they generated, until they could think of no more criteria. This procedure was repeated until the participants could think of no more criteria. Sorting criteria, categories, as well as comments on the perception towards the site were all noted by the researcher during the session.

A second sorting session was conducted with the same participants, where they sorted the same cards according to the criterion: "I would/would not use this site". Participants were asked to provide a reason for the sorting decisions made.

3   Data Analysis

Card sorting result analysis was based on the examination of criteria count, textual analysis, as well as cluster analysis.

3.1   Frequency Analysis for the Repeated Single Criterion Sort

Commonality of criteria is the main source for data analysis in card sorting. Commonly selected criteria are recommended to be most salient interface elements for participants.[7] Frequency analysis looked at criteria communality, where criteria names of same meaning were grouped into a common single super-ordinate construct. **Table 1** below shows super-ordinate constructs sorted descending by selection frequency.

Table 1. Super-ordinate constructs sorted by selection frequency

Super-Ordinate Construct	German Participants (total: 15)	Egyptian Participants (total: 15)	All Participants (total: 30)
General Interface Appearance	13 – 87%	14 – 93%	27 – 90%
Content Usefulness	13 – 87%	12 – 80%	25 – 83%
Site Affiliation and Reputation	8 – 53%	14 – 93%	22 – 73%
Content Quality	11 – 73%	7 – 47%	18 – 60%
Familiarity with the Site	4 – 27%	8 – 53%	12 – 40%
Online Help	4 – 27%	6 – 40%	10 – 33%
Search method	4 – 27%	1 – 7%	5 – 17%

According to Table 1, for the overall participants of the sorting session, the most salient E-learning site features were *General Interface Appearance, Content Usefulness, Site Affiliation and Reputation, and Content Quality*.

The *General Interface Appearance* was the criterion selected by the highest majority (90%) of the overall participants (14 out of 15 Egyptians and 13 out of 15 Germans). This suggests that Interface is a highly salient feature for this group of users. In defining the *General Interface Appearance* criterion, most of the participants (21 out of 30) used two categories: *Comprehensive/ Straightforward/ Obvious* versus *Unclear/ Complicated/ Obscure*. Some participants (18 out of 30) used another two categories: *Neat/ Structured/ Organized* versus *Disordered/ Crowded/ Messy*. Few participants (6 out of 30) used three categories: *Appealing Interface/ Attractive* versus *Acceptable/ Somehow Attractive* and versus *Poor/ Un-Attractive*. Other Few participants (4 out of 30) used two categories: *Professional* versus *Non-Professional*.

Two criteria selected by the participants are concerning the content of the E-learning main page; those are *Content Usefulness* and *Content Quality*. While *Content Usefulness* ranked the second most frequently selected criterion (chosen by twenty five, 83%, of participants, and almost equality selected by the two cultural group); *Content Quality* was ranked the forth most frequently selected criterion (chosen by eighteen, 60%, of participants, and seems to be of more importance to the German participants as it was selected by 73% of Germans and only 47% of Egyptians).

According to participants, *Content Usefulness* criterion refers to the participants' perception of how relevant is the displayed material to their work/ interest as well as their professional development goals. Most of participants defined the *Content Usefulness* criteria by using two categories: *Relevant Material/ Helpful Content/ Useful Information,* versus *Of Little Relevance/ Not Sufficiently Helpful/ Barely Useful*.

On the other hand, for the participants, *Content Quality* criterion refers to the participants' perception of how updated, well structured is the content, as well as the amount of advertisement embedded within. Most of participants defined the *Content Quality* criteria by using three categories: *Updated/ Well-Structured Materials* versus *Barely Updated/ Somehow Structured*, and versus *Outdated/ Junk*. Few participants (4 out of 30) used two different categories concerning the advertisements load in the site, such as: *Advertisement Free* versus *Distracting Advertisements*. It could be argued that there is a substantial overlap between the two criteria: *Content Usefulness* and *Content Quality*, as they are both concerned with the perception of quality of materials included in the E-learning site, and its relevance to the participants need.

The *Site Affiliation and Reputation* was the third most frequently selected criterion (chosen by twenty two, 73%, of participants, and seems to be of more importance to the Egyptian participants as it was selected by 93% of Egyptians and only 53% of Germans); *Site Affiliation and Reputation* criterion refers to the participants' perception of site reputation and its affiliation name and recognition. Most of participants defined the *Site/Affiliation Reputation* criteria by using two categories: *Well Known Site/ Site maintained by a Reputable Affiliation-Institute/ Trustworthy,* versus *Unheard of Site/ Unknown Owner of the Site/ Untruthful*.

When looking at differences between the German and Egyptian participants in terms of criteria and categorizations generated, it could be suggested that the Egyptian participants give more weight to the affiliation of the site, as well as the degree of their familiarity with using the site before. While it could be suggested that German participants focus more on content quality and usefulness.

Rag Bag categories, such as "not sure" and "don't know" appear rarely, same for the categories of "not applicable". This suggests that the uncertainty of participant was relatively low.[3]

On the other hand, there was a significant absence of some expected criteria, such as: *Level of Interactivity, User Control,* and *Feedback* features; such features are suggested to affect the user attitude towards E-learning sites.[8] This absence is one of the limitations of static card sorting technique, where no interactive features can be explored by the participants during the session.

3.2   Frequency Analysis for the Forced Sort

In the forced session, participants were asked to sort the same cards based on the criterion: "Sites I am willing to use / Sites I am not willing to use", and to provide one or more reason(s) for their choice. Reasons of same meaning were grouped into a common title. Frequency and commonality of reasons provided by the participants for their sorting choices were analyzed, while distinguishing between the two cultural groups of participants.

As listed in Table 2 below, main page *Interface Obviousness and Comprehensibility* was the most common reason for willingness to use the site, for thirteen out of fifteen of Germans and for thirteen out of fifteen of Egyptians. In total, for 87% of the thirty participants, the obviousness and comprehensibility of the interface of the main page card, was the factor that generates a willingness to use the E-learning site.

Content Usefulness was ranked as the second highest reason for willingness to use, selected by 73% (twenty two out of thirty) of overall participants; followed by *Site Affiliation and Reputation*, selected by 67% (twenty out of thirty); While *Content Quality* was selected by only 57% (seventeen out of thirty) of overall participants.

Some differences were found while comparing the preference of use between the two cultural groups. For the German participants, *Content Usefulness* was ranked as the second highest reason for willingness to use, selected by 80% (twelve out of fifteen) German participants; Followed by *Content Quality*, selected by 67% (ten out of fifteen) participants of this cultural group; While *Site Affiliation and Reputation* was selected by only 53% (eight out of fifteen) German participants.

Table 2. Reasons for Willingness to Use

Stated Reasons for Willing to Use an E-Learning Site from a Site	German Participants (total: 15)	Egyptian Participants (total: 15)	All Participants (total: 30)
Interface Obviousness and Comprehensibility	13 – 87%	13 – 87%	26 – 87%
Content Usefulness	12 – 80%	10 – 67%	22 – 73%
Site Affiliation and Reputation	8 – 53%	12 – 80%	20 – 67%
Content Quality	10 – 67%	7 – 47%	17 – 57%

For the Egyptian participants, *Site Affiliation and Reputation* was ranked as the second highest reason for willingness to use, selected by 80% (twelve out of fifteen) Egyptian participants; Followed by *Content Usefulness*, selected by 67% (ten out of fifteen) participants of this cultural group; while *Content Quality* was selected by only 47% (seven out of fifteen) Egyptian participants.

3.3   Cluster Analysis

A complementary qualitative analysis technique for card sorting results was conducted using cluster analysis. Custer analysis establishes categories based on commonalities between categories selected by multiple participants.[7] In this research, cluster analysis was done using computer aided software that indicates the degree of category relatedness between items by a tree structure. The shorter the path traced between two items through the tree, the more likely the items are to belong to the same category. *This is done by providing a means of calculating the strength of the perceived relationship between pairs of cards based on how often members of each possible pair of cards are sorted into a common group by multiple participants.*[7]

Fig. 1 illustrates the cluster analysis of the forced sort "Willing/ Not Willing to Use". Each branch on the left hand side connecting two sites indicates that the majority participants grouped the sites together. The branch on the right hand side connecting groups of sites indicates that no participants grouped the items together. According to the current results, clusters are classified as following: *Cluster 1:* Khan Academy, UNESCO Open Training and Epsilen. *Cluster 2:* TrackStar, IEarn, AUC Learn+, Google for Educators, BCIT, and MIT OpenCourseWare.

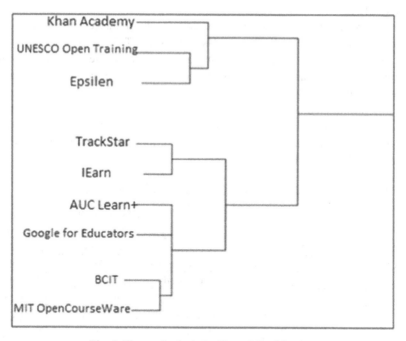

Fig. 1. Cluster Analysis for Forced Card Sorting

According to cluster analysis of the forced sorting session, three E-learning sites are more likely to be used. The remaining E-learning sites are less likely to be used. The following section examines the reasons provided by the participants for their willingness to use these three sites. The following section also analysis the results of the two sorting sessions together to investigate whether these three E-Learning sites, which are more likely to be used, share some categories and criteria in the first sorting session.

4   Results

Sorting results from both sessions were examined to investigate whether there were any features that distinguished the sites where participants were more likely to use, from those which participants were less likely to use. This is done by examining the commonality of categories and criteria associated with the three sites participants were more likely to use, and whether these three sites were categorized together according to any of the other sort criteria. As indicated in Table 3, the "Willing to Use" sites appeared to share a lot of the same salient features. These sites generally are Comprehensive, Organized, with Helpful Content and Well Known sites. Features such as Appealing Interface, Attractive, Professional, and Updated are shared in the "Willing to Use" and "Not Willing to Use" sites without any suggested effect on the willingness to use.

The *General Interface Appearance* criterion wholly predicted membership of the "Willing to Use" and "Not Willing to Use" category. This criterion correctly predicted the outcome for all sites. Participants were willing to use sites categorized as Comprehensive and organized, and they were unwilling to use any of the sites categorized as Unclear and Messy.

The *Site Affiliation and Reputation* criterion correctly predicted the outcome for all but one of the sites. Participants were willing to use all of the sites categorized as Well Known Site and Trustworthy, and they were unwilling to use any of the sites categorized as Unheard of Site, except one site.

Table 3. Analysis of the Site Willingness to Use versus Criteria and Categories

Site	Willing/ Not willing to use	General Inter-face Appearance	Site Affiliation/ Reputation	Content Usefulness
Khan Academy	Willing to Use	Comprehensive	Well known	Helpful
UNESCO Open Training	Willing to Use	Comprehensive	Well known	Helpful
Epsilen	Willing to Use	Organized	Trustworthy	Helpful
TrackStar	Not Willing to Use	Messy	Unheard of	Not Helpful
IEarn	Not Willing to Use	Unclear	Unheard of	Not Helpful
AUC Learn +	Not Willing to Use	Unclear	Unknown	Not Helpful
Google for Educators	Not Willing to Use	Messy	N/A	N/A
BCIT	Not Willing to Use	Messy	Unknown	Not Helpful
MIT OpenCourseWare	Not Willing to Use	Unclear	Unknown	Not Helpful

The *Content Usefulness* criterion correctly predicted the outcome for all but one of the sites. Participants were willing to use all of the sites categorized as Helpful Content, and they were unwilling to use any of the sites categorized as Not Sufficiently Helpful, except one site.

Although some differences were suggested between the German and Egyptian participants when analyzing the two sorting sessions separately, no differences was found when analyzing the results of the two sorting sessions together. Thus the systematic integration of the two sorting session results can not suggest any effect of participant's culture on the willingness to use. Still, such cultural difference is highlighted in Table 2, based on the reasons given by the participants themselves for their willingness to use an E-learning site.

5   Discussion

This paper explores the attitude of users from two different cultural groups towards E-learning environment. Two card sorting techniques were conducted to investigate criteria by which users evaluate web sites. First: Repeated Single Criterion Sort Sessions, where participants selected a criterion to differentiate between cards of main pages, categories for this criterion are identified and cards are sorted accordingly. Second: Forced Sort Sessions, where same participants sorted the same cards according to the criterion: "I would/would not use this site", reasons for this decision were given.

As reported in the previous sections of this paper, the analysis was done on four steps, while distinguishing between the two cultural groups of participants. First: Frequency analysis of commonly selected criteria as illustrated in Table 1. Second: Frequency analysis of commonly given reasons for willingness to use as illustrated in Table 2. Third: Cluster analysis to identify categories commonalities for cards where participants are willing to use as showed in Fig. 1. Forth: Analyzing the commonality of criteria associated with the sites more likely to be used as listed in Table 3.

The results of the four types of analysis consistently suggest that for the overall participants the most salient E-Learning site feature is *General Interface Appearance*, namely *Interface Obviousness and Comprehensibility*. The obviousness and comprehensibility of the interface are the factors generating a willingness to use an E-Learning site. Participants were willing to use all sites categorized as *Comprehensive* and *organized*, and they were unwilling to use any of the sites categorized as *Unclear* and *Messy*.

Content Usefulness is the second most salient feature, ranked as the second highest reason for willingness to use an E-Learning site. Participants are more willing to use sites with *Helpful Content*.

The *Site Affiliation and Reputation* was the third most frequently selected criterion, and the third most cited reason for using an E-Learning site. It refers to the participants' perception of site reputation and its affiliation name and recognition. Participants were willing to use all of the sites categorized as *Well Known Site* and *Trustworthy*.

These finding are consistent with one of the most influential and widely used model of IT adoption, the Technology Acceptance Model (TAM).[9] The model posits that perceived usefulness and perceived ease of use are significantly correlated with systems use. Where perceived ease of use is defined as *the degree to which a person believes that using a particular system would be free of effort* and perceived usefulness is *the degree to which a person believes that using a particular system would enhance his or her performance*.[9]

On a similar context, TAM was used to understand factors that lead to technology adoption in five Arab countries. [10] This research suggested that the two main variables of TAM, ease of use and perceived usefulness, might aid in the adoption of IT in the Arab world.

Other features were reported of importance to participants also affecting the willingness to use decisions, such as *Content Quality*, and *Familiarity* with the web site. Nevertheless, these two features were not consistently confirmed by the four types of results analysis.

On the other hand, some differences were found between the German and Egyptian respondents. While the Egyptian participants give more weight to the affiliation of the site, as well as the degree of their familiarity with using the site before; German participants focus more on Content quality and Usefulness. Still, these differences were not confirmed by the four types of results analysis, which contradicts with some previous research [11, 12] suggesting cross-cultural differences of systems use, especially within cultures from different cultural groups.[13]

6   Conclusion

The various analysis techniques employed in this study consistently suggest that the *Interface Obviousness and Comprehensibility*, followed by the *Content Usefulness*, and finally *the Site Affiliation and Reputation*, represent respectively the most salient features affecting the participants' attitude towards E-learning sites. These features, with the same order of importance, are suggested to be driving reasons for the participants' willingness to use the sites.

The fact that same findings have been acquired with different sorting sessions and with various analysis techniques, suggests that these features shape learners' attitude and satisfaction in E-learning environments and their subsequent use of such tools.

While some differences were highlighted concerning the preferences of participants from two cultural groups; nevertheless, the current study could not suggest a consistent effect of culture on user attitudes and preferences. Future research would like to address such important factor in the E-learning context.

In summary, the results of the current study suggest some important factors that tend to be associated with E-learning sites for the targeted group of participants. *Ease of Use*, *Content Usefulness* and *Site Reputation* are suggested as salient components of building positive attitude and willingness to use towards an E-learning site. Future research would build on these findings to investigate any possible inter-relationships between them.

7   Limitations

The use of static images of selected sites as sorting materials could be considered as limitation of card sorting technique in general. The use of images excludes many effects of the dynamic aspects of a web site such as Interactivity. Some interface features may only become important to users once they interact with the site. Some studies suggest an effect of Interactivity on user attitude and performance improvement in E-Learning context.[8] Therefore, a future research, allowing participants to interact with the E-learning sites, would complement the finding of the current study.

On the other hand, in this study, while cluster analysis was done using computer aided software; collecting participants' data during card sorting sessions were administered manually by the researchers. To eliminate bias, a computer program would be used by card sort participants to sort digital cards instead of physical cards. This computer program can also generate card list and enter existing card sort result from individual participants.

References

1. Garrison, D.R., Kanuka, H.: Blended learning: Uncovering its transformative potential in higher education. The Internet and Higher Education 7, 95–105 (2004)
2. Harel Caperton, I.: Learning to Make Games for Impact. The Journal of Media Literacy 59(1), 28–38 (2012)
3. Rugg, G., McGeorge, P.: The Sorting Techniques: A Tutorial Paper on Card Sorts, Picture Sorts and Item Sorts. Expert Systems 14(2), 80–93 (1997)
4. Giddens, A.: The Constitution of Society: Outline of the Theory of Structure. University California Press (1984) ISBN: 0520057287
5. Maiden, N., Rugg, G.: ACRE: A Framework for Acquisition of Requirements. Software Engineering 11(3), 68–86 (1996)
6. Upchurch, L., Rugg, G., Kitchenhan, B.: Using Card Sorts to Elicit Web Page Quality Attributes. IEEE Software 18(4), 84–89 (2001)
7. Eberts, R.E.: User Interface Design. Prentice Hall College Div. (1994) ISBN: 0131403281
8. Kettanurak, V., Ramamurthy, K., Haseman, W.D.: User attitude as a mediator of learning performance improvement in an interactive multimedia environment: an empirical investigation of the degree of interactivity and learning styles. International Journal of Human Computer Studies: Incorporating Knowledge Acquisition 54(4), 541–583 (2001)
9. Davis, F.D.: Perceived Usefulness, Perceived Ease of Use and User Acceptance of Information Technology. MIS Quarterly 13(3), 319–339 (1989)
10. Rose, G., Straub, D.: Predicting IT Use: Applying TAM to the Arabic World. Journal of Global Information Management 6(3), 39–46 (1998)
11. De la Cruz, T., Mandl, T., Womser-Hacker, C.: Cultural Dependency of Quality Perception and Web Page Evaluation Guidelines: Results from a Survey. In: Day, D., Evers, V., Del Galdo, E. (eds.) Designing for Global Markets 7: Bridging Cultural Differences: IWIPS 2005 Proceedings. The Seventh International Workshop on Internationalization of Products and Systems, Grafisch Centrum Amsterdam, Amsterdam, The Netherlands, July 7-9, vol. 5, pp. 15–27 (2005) ISBN: 0-9722184-7-5

12. Evers, V.: Cross-Cultural Applicability of the User Evaluation Methods: A Case Study amongst Japanese, North American, English and Dutch Users. In: Loren, T. (ed.) Changing the World, Changing Ourselves: CHI 2002 Proceedings. The CHI Conference on Human Factors in Computing Systems, Minneapolis, Minnesota, USA, April 20-25 (2002)
13. Hofstede, G.: Cultures and Organizations: Software of the Mind: Intercultural Cooperation and its Importance for Survival. McGraw-Hill International (1991) ISBN: 0-07-707474-2

Empirical Analysis of Changes in Human Creativity in People Who Work with Humanoid Robots and Their Avatars

Doori Jo[1], Jae-gil Lee[1], and Kun Chang Lee[2,*]

[1] Department of Interaction Science, Sungkyunkwan University,
Seoul, Republic of Korea
[2] Professor at SKKU Business School, Sungkyunkwan University,
Seoul 110-745, Republic of Korea
{jdl6427,kunchanglee}@gmail.com, firstmage@me.com

Abstract. This study presents results from an analysis of the relationship between humanoid robots and human creativity, which has not been demonstrated in the literature to date. To increase the academic rigor of our study, we adopted humanoid robots and their avatars in our experimental procedures. After participants engaged in experiments with humanoids and their avatars, we assessed the degree to which their levels of creativity changed. In experiments with 90 participants, we found that interactions with humanoid robots produced a statistically significant effect in increasing their creativity.

Keywords: Creativity, Creativity training, Human-robot interaction.

1 Introduction

In our competitive modern society, creativity has become an increasingly important factor in innovative development for individuals and society. For example, many researchers have shown that creative individuals were reported to be more productive and satisfied with their occupations [1]. Also, creativity within organizational and professional domains has been a popular subject of inquiry for managers and researchers. According to the research of Littleton et al., creativity enables workers to be more flexible and entrepreneurial within their organizations [2]. Thus, the presence and performance of creative people is essential to every organization, whether in the public or private sector, because their ability to invent, dream, problem solve, craft, and correspond in fresh, new ways is vital to organizational success [3]. Therefore, it is expected that enhancing an individual's creativity will enhance the performance of groups and organizations. If so, how can we improve individual creativity?

Training is one of the most common methods used to enhance creativity [4]. Creativity training tasks are based on the belief that creativity requires an environment that encourages risk taking and self-initiated projects and offers help and time for develop-

---

* Corresponding author.

P. Zaphiris and A. Ioannou (Eds.): LCT 2014, Part I, LNCS 8523, pp. 273–281, 2014.

ing ideas and individual effort. Previous studies have suggested several methods for enhancing creativity, among which are those intended especially for concrete problem-solving situations, including: brainstorming [5], verbal check-lists [6], picture stimulation and mind mapping [7]. Higgins [8] has also provided many methods to enhance creative problem solving. The purpose of many of these techniques is to generate ideas by using different types of games or tasks in order to suppress the common tendency to criticize or reject ideas.

Since evidence of the importance of creativity was first reported by researchers, many programs have been developed that use creativity training tasks to enhance individual creativity. Several researchers have reported the effectiveness of robot-mediated training in enhancing individual creativity, as well as the advantages of using robots in education [9, 10, 11, 12, 13]. According to Hwang and Lee [14], a dinosaur shaped robot had no significant effect on creativity enhancement, but the robot's avatar enhanced subjects' creativity. Likewise, in mediated creativity training, the level of creativity was found to be influenced by the type of mediator.

According to the research by Amabile [15], one more consideration in mediator-based creativity training is the fact that the presence of others can affect creativity. When the 'presence of others' is a mediator in the form of a robot, this can affect an individual's creativity. As Zhuo [16] reported, individuals who have high levels of creativity will be discouraged when they are with someone who is monitoring them, while the opposite occurs in the case of a person with low levels of creativity. Therefore, research should be conducted to understand the effects of the mediator's presence.

Until now, we have investigated the importance of individual creativity, tasks to improve creativity, mediator-based creativity training and the effect of another's presence on creativity. In this paper, we investigated the effects of the presence of a humanoid robot and its avatar on individual creativity in the performance of a task. The hypotheses developed in this research are:

— Hypothesis 1: A humanoid robot will enhance subjects' creativity in task performance.
— Hypothesis 2: A humanoid avatar will enhance subjects' creativity in task performance.
— Hypothesis 3: Enhanced creative task performance will differ between the humanoid and its avatar.
— Hypothesis 4: Highly creative people will be discouraged when they are with the robot or the avatar.
— Hypothesis 5: People with low creativity will be encouraged when they are with the robot or the avatar.

2   Literature Review

Creativity. Hennessey & Amabile [17] stated that: "Creativity involves the development of a novel product, idea, or problem solution that is of value to the individual and/or the larger social group". Creativity is also defined as the production of original, unexpected and useful work [18]. Following these definitions of creativity, it seems that creativity and creative skills have become regarded as highly important in almost every field of work and education, especially those fields focused on creativity enhancement.

It has been demonstrated that creativity can be enhanced, and training has been used to achieve this. According to meta-analyses, creativity training is generally effective. Many methods are used in the work and education fields, but before applying them, we need to know how creativity is enhanced.

Pioneers in creativity research have come to share similar views, that creativity requires certain components, one of which is intrinsic motivation [18, 19]. Intrinsic motivation is considered a well-established predictor of creativity [20], and is the extent to which an individual is interested in a task and engages in it for the sake of the task itself [21]. Therefore, in this research, we measured the results of training on creative task performance according to the degree of the subjects' intrinsic motivation. To control for differences in personal creativity, we measured subjects' creativity levels (high, low) before the experiment, then analyzed the effects of creativity training by changes in their post-experiment levels of creativity. We also assessed the effect on creativity of the type of mediator.

Mediator-Based Creativity Training. In this paper, we used two types of mediators (robot and avatar) in creativity training. Since technology was introduced into the field of education, robots have been adopted to promote individual creativity. Several previous studies have introduced robot- mediated creativity education and demonstrated its effectiveness. Research with the Thymo robot found that this robot partly fulfilled the goal of promoting creativity. Because of its flexible characteristics several other researchers have used Lego Mind Storms to investigate individual creativity [13, 14].

The majority of previous research has employed the concept of experimental learning, which is described as: "The process whereby knowledge is created through the transformation of experience" in [22]. Therefore, students were able to promote creativity while engaging in robot-related tasks.

This study builds on previous work, but we addressed several distinctive features by comparison to previous research. First, we used two types of mediators: a robot and the robot's avatar. We used avatars because they are well known mediators in education and creativity training and also because they have flexible characteristics. Thus, by using both robot and avatar mediators, we were able to investigate the effect of mediator type on creativity training; to focus on the effects of the presence of the two types of mediators, we chose to match the avatar's and robot's appearance. Finally, a control group that had no mediator was used to investigate the training effect itself.

3   Experiment

Participants. 94 student participants were recruited via online advertisements and 90 of those were accepted. There were 38 males and 52 females who ranged in age from 20-32 years (mean = 23.31, SD = 2.56).

All participants first completed the Epstein Creativity Competencies Inventory for Individuals (EEC-I) to measure self-assessed individual creativity. The EEC-I is composed of 28 Likert 5-scale items (lower is better), and we used the scores as a criterion to group the participants. First, we divided them into two groups based on their creativity scores (low, high). Second, we set three conditions (None-NAO-Avatar) in each group already divided according to creativity. Participants were placed in these three groups, with each group having similar creativity scores. Finally, we divided all participants into six groups on the basis of high and low creativity and the three experimental conditions.

Table 1. Participants Group

Participants groups	Experimental conditions		
	None	NAO	Avatar
High creativity score	14 participants Mean : 74.07 SD : 9.19	15 participants Mean : 74.47 SD : 8.65	15 participants Mean : 74.53 SD : 6.45
Low creativity score	16 participants Mean : 95.59 SD : 7.58	15 participants Mean : 95.8 SD : 7.20	15 participants Mean : 95.38 SD : 9.27

Measures. To verify the influence of another's presence on creative performance, we designed two tasks based on the Torrance Tests of Creative Thinking (TTCT) verbal task and Consensual Assessment Technique (CAT). TTCT is the most well-known and widely used test to measure creativity (Baer, 1993; Kim, 2006; Ferrando, 2006; Wechsler, 2002). TTCT has 4 indicators: fluency, flexibility, originality, and elaboration. CAT provides a method to judge the creative content of, for example, stories and poems. CAT is one of the most powerful tools in assessing creativity (Kaufman et al, 2006). We accepted and revised the TTCT and CAT to fit our purposes.

In the first task, we asked participants to create words by assembling letters in the Korean alphabet. A Korean word consists of a series of characters, and a single character is composed of assemblies of the Korean alphabet, which consists of 14 consonants and 10 vowels. We provided 14 basic alphabet cards to participants, and they created words by assembling these alphabets. The alphabet cards that we provided consisted of 8 single consonants and 6 single vowels that were surveyed as the most used alphabets by the National Institute of the Korean Language. These alphabets could combine consonants with vowels to make a single character, and consonants with consonants or vowels with vowels to create double consonants or diphthongs. We applied three criteria from the TTCT to evaluate participants' performance on the alphabet assembling task.

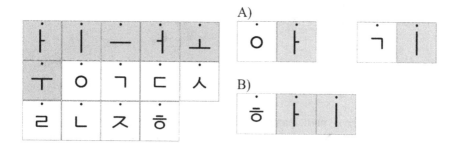

Fig. 1. Korean alphabet cards that used in word assembling task. Gray cards are vowels and white cards are consonants(Left), Example of assembled words. A) Baby, B) Sun. (Right)

- **Fluency** : Number of words participants created.
- **Originality** : The rarity of usage in words created.
- **Elaboration** : Number of alphabet cards used to create a single character.

We developed a program to analyze the results of the alphabet assembly task. Fluency was counted as the words that were assembled correctly. The National Institute of the Korean Language made a list of the frequency of word use, which we used to rate the originality of each word. As mentioned above, each alphabet could be combined in various ways. Thus, elaboration could be judged by counting the number of alphabet cards that were used to create a single character.

The second task was storytelling with the words created in the first task. The story-telling task is also used widely to measure creativity. The creative story products from the second task were evaluated by CAT using our revised TTCT criteria.

- **Fluency**: Number of characters in the story.
- **Originality**: Originality of the subject; creative usage of words.
- **Flexibility**: Number of words used in story that was created in first task.

The total number of words that was used in the stories represented fluency. Originality was rated by an expert who was a registered poet in a Korean writers' association. He rated the originality of the stories on a 100 point scale. We counted the number of words used in the story that were created in the first task and used that as our criterion of flexibility.

Finally, each task had three conditions, so a total of six criteria was used to measure creativity. We converted the results of all six indicators to a maximum 20 point score. The sum of the three criteria scores contained in each task represented the creative performance on that task. These two task performance scores were aggregated to assess comprehensive creative performance.

Fig. 2. Real robot NAO(Left), Avatar NAO(Right)

Procedure. Upon arrival, participants were ushered to separate rooms according to their experimental condition (None, NAO, Avatar). In the "None" control condition, there was only one participant in the room during the experiment. We introduced the minimum information necessary in order to conduct the experiment and stepped out of the room. In the NAO condition, participants conducted the experiment with an actual humanoid robot (NAO). In the Avatar condition, participants conducted the experiment with a virtual avatar on the screen. We used Webots for NAO that can also simulate NAO in a virtual environment. Thus, we could present the same appearance, behavior and feedback to participants between the two groups, NAO and Avatar.

- **None**: No feedback.
- **Nao**: Information and feedback about tasks from real robot NAO.
- **Avatar**: Information and feedback about tasks from virtual NAO Avatar.

Our ultimate goal was to find a way to enhance people's creative performance using a humanoid robot. Thus, we designed the behavior of and feedback from the NAO to enhance participants' creativity.

To begin, NAO said hello to the participant with an animated hand wave. When introducing the task, NAO usually gazed into the participant's eyes, sometimes nodding and shaking its head to indicate allowed and restricted actions. When each task began, NAO pointed its finger to the answer paper needed to conduct the tasks and explained how to use it. During the task, NAO gazed at the task field and gave feedback to the participants. First, NAO gave an example to which the participants could refer. Second, NAO gave a speech of encouragement about the participants' progress. Third, NAO counted the time remaining to increase motivation. For the first task, assembling the alphabet, 3 minutes were allowed, and for the second task, storytelling, 4 minutes were allowed.

4   Results

The analyses showed that the proposed hypotheses were supported in part. First, subjects who were in the NAO condition (m = 69.59, SD = 14.58) had significantly higher average creativity scores than those in the 'None' control condition (m = 58.80, SD = 13.32: t = -3.008, p = 0.005). Therefore, hypothesis 1 was supported. The NAO avatar also enhanced subjects' creativity levels (m = 65.11, SD = 15.36), but was not significantly different from the 'None' condition (t = -1.69, p = 0.10); thus, hypothesis 2 was not supported. Finally, NAO enhanced subjects' creativity levels more than the NAO avatar, but again, there was no significant difference between the two (t = 1.06, p = 0.30), indicating that hypothesis 3 was not supported.

Further, the highly creative group showed no significant differences when they were exposed to the NAO vs. the avatar. However, the low creativity group was affected only by NAO (t = -2.71, p = 0.02). Therefore, hypothesis 4 was not supported and hypothesis 5 was partially supported. According to these results, many of the hypotheses were nonsignificant statistically; however, other factors need to be considered in the interpretation of our results.

Table 2. The average score of the creative task

Condition	Creativity level	Score			
		Task1	Task2	Total	
Alone	High	26.48	34.30	60.78	58.80
	Low	25.17	31.66	56.84	
With Nao	High	31.06	37.93	69.00	69.59
	Low	31.85	38.33	70.19	
With Nao avatar	High	32.88	32.75	65.62	65.11
	Low	33.40	31.20	64.60	

5   Conclusion and Future Work

The goal of this study was to investigate the effect of the presence of a humanoid robot and its avatar on individuals' creative task performance. Therefore, 5 hypotheses were proposed based on previous studies. We expected all of the hypotheses to be supported, but most were not. However, there are some points to consider.

First, the effect of the robot in creativity training was verified statistically, which is consistent with previous research. Second, people with low creativity were more motivated by the type of mediator than highly creativity people. From this result, we obtained the useful information that when conducting creativity training for those with low creativity, it is better to use a mediator that has a high presence.

In the future, we will focus on improving the tasks and measurements and use a larger sample size before conducting the experiment again.

Acknowledgment. This work was supported by the National Research Foundation Grant funded by the Korean Government (NRF-2009-342-B00015).

References

1. Amabile, T.M.: The social psychology of creativity: A componential conceptualization. Journal of Personality and Social Psychology 45(2), 357–376 (1983)
2. Littleton, K., et al.: Special issue introduction: Creativity and creative work in contemporary working contexts. Vocations and Learning 5(1), 1–4 (2012)
3. Egan, T.M.: Factors influencing individual creativity in the workplace: An examination of quantitative empirical research. Advances in Developing Human Resources 7(2), 160–181 (2005)
4. Scott, S.G., Bruce, R.A.: Determinants of innovative behavior: A path model of individual innovation in the workplace. Academy of Management Journal 38, 483–503 (1994)
5. Osborn, A.F.: Applied imagination; principles and procedures of creative problem-solving. Scribner, New York (1963)
6. Eberle, R.F.: Scamper: Creative games and activities for imagination development. Prufrock Press, Inc., Waco (2008)
7. Buzan, T.: Use both sides of your brain: New Mind Mapping Techniques. Plume Books, New York (1991)
8. Higgins, J.M.: 101 creative problem solving techniques: The Handbook of New Ideas for Business. New Management Publishing (1994)
9. Jenyi, C.: The effects of LEGO Mindstorms on indigenous students' creativity in Taiwan—A case study of an Energy and Robotics Course. In: Proc. IEEE Int. Conf. Electrical and Control Engineering, pp. 5907–6910 (2011)
10. Riedo, F., Rétornaz, P., Bergeron, L., Nyffeler, N., Mondada, F.: A two years informal learning experience using the thymio robot. In: Rueckert, U., Joaquin, S., Felix, W. (eds.) Advances in Autonomous Mini Robots, vol. 101, pp. 37–48. Springer, Heidelberg (2012)
11. Kwak, S.S., Eun Ho, K., Jimyung, K., Youngbin, S., Inveom, K., Jun-Shin, P., Eun Wook, L.: Field trials of the block-shaped edutainment robot HangulBot. In: Proc. 7th ACM/IEEE Int. Conf. on Human-Robot Interaction, Boston, Massachusetts, USA, p. 403 (2012)
12. Bonani, M., Raemy, X., Pugh, J., Mondana, F., Cianci, C., Klaptocz, A., Magnenat, S., Zufferey, J.C., Floreano, D., Martinoli, A.: The e-puck, a Robot Designed for Education in Engineering. In: Proceedings of the 9th Conference on Autnomous Robot Systems and Competitions, May 7, vol. 1, pp. 59–65. IPCB, Castelo Branco (2009)
13. Xuemei, L., Gang, X.: Interdisciplinary innovative education based on modular robot platform. In: ISECS International Colloquium on Computing, Communication, Control, and Management, CCCM 2008, Guangzhou, China, August 3-4, pp. 66–69 (2008)
14. Hwang, J., Lee, K.C.: Examining the effect of short-term robot-mediated training for creativity education. Digital Creativity 32, 129–137 (2013)
15. Amabile, T.M., Goldfarb, P., Brackfleld, S.C.: Social influences on creativity: Evaluation, coaction, and surveillance. Creativity Research Journal 3(1), 6–21 (1990)
16. Zhuo, J.: When the presence of creative coworkers is related to creativity: Role of supervisor close monitoring, developmental feedback, and creative personality. Journal of Applied Psychology 88(3), 413–422 (2003)
17. Hennessey, B.A., Amabile, T.M.: Creativity. The Annual Review of Psychology, 569–598 (2010)
18. Sternberg, R., Lubart, T.: The Concept of Creativity: Prospects and Paradigms. In: Handbook of Creativity. Cambridge University Press (1999)

19. Torrance, E.P.: Insights about creativity: Questioned, rejected, ridiculed, ignored. Educational Psychology Review 7(1995), 313–322 (1995)
20. Amabile, T.M.: Creativity in context. Westview Press, Boulder (1996)
21. Utman, C.H.: Performance effects of motivational state: A meta-analysis. Personality and Social Psychology Review, 170–182 (1997)
22. Sawyer, R.K.: Group genius: The creative power of collaboration. Basic Books, New York (2007)

Empowering L&D Managers through Customisation of Inline Learning Analytics

Evangelos Kapros and Neil Peirce

Learnovate Centre, Trinity Technology & Enterprise Campus,
Dublin 2, Ireland
{evangelos.kapros,neil.peirce}@scss.tcd.ie
http://www.learnovatecentre.org/

Abstract. Popular learning management systems (LMS) often feature dashboards displaying various analytics. This dashboard display might be suboptimal for some learning and development managers (L&D). Moreover, the analytics presented are often based on standardised quizzes or semesters, which might be unsuitable (e.g., informal learning, corporate education, etc.). Finally, each LMS has its bespoke reporting solution, thus making it difficult for L&D managers to monitor the situation across various LMSs. We propose an interactive system where an L&D manager can customise the data source, queries, filters, and visualisations of their LMSs, and display them inline. To this end, we have built EVADE, a system that allows L&D managers to capture data from various LMSs, analyse them, and embed related visualisations in each LMS. In this instance, we have integrated EVADE with a Moodle instance for corporate education, and Almanac, a tablet application for informal learning. In this paper we present EVADE and discuss how it can improve the L&D manager-LMS interaction.

Keywords: Learning Analytics, Visualisation, Corporate Learning, LMS.

1 Introduction

The emerging field of Learning Analytics aims to measure, collect, analyse, and report on data about learners and their contexts, for the purposes of understanding and optimising learning and the environments in which it occurs [6]. A key component in realising Learning Analytics is the wealth of learner evidence that can be captured through Learning Management Systems (LMSs). LMSs are increasingly being used to administer, deliver, and assess learning in higher education and corporate training. Within a corporate training setting these systems are administered by Learning and Development (L&D) managers to deliver internal training, certification and compliance training, and Continuing Professional Development (CPD). Although these systems typically provide reporting to the L&D managers, there is often a lack of statistical reporting and visualisation to understand the effectiveness of the training [4]. Where visualisations of analytics are provided they are often restricted to a predefined set of metrics,

P. Zaphiris and A. Ioannou (Eds.): LCT 2014, Part I, LNCS 8523, pp. 282–291, 2014.

delivered through a separate application, or generated periodically in batch style reports [3]. A further challenge for a corporate L&D manager in understanding training effectiveness is the diversity of systems that contain valuable learner evidence. In addition to a LMS, a Human Resources Management (HRM) system will contain data on performance appraisal and attendance, whereas forums and wikis can also contain informal contributions to learning and training [2]. In order to gain a holistic understanding of a learners performance a learning analytics system is required that considers diverse sources of learner evidence. Such a system would also integrate the analytics into the day-to-day workflow of the L&D manager. This integration would contextualise the analytics whilst also facilitating real-time insights into training effectiveness. In this paper we begin with an introduction to the field of Learning Analytics with particular reference to the visualisation of analytics. This is followed by an explanation of the novel End-to-end Visualisation and Analytics of Data for E-Learning (EVADE) system. The design of the EVADE system is detailed including example workflows for IT managers and L&D managers. We conclude this paper with a discussion on the merits of the system and directions for future work in this area.

2   Related Work

Learning analytics state-of-art is quite diverse: the six largest corporate LMS products constitute approximately 50% of the market, and none of these six is popular in the education sector [5]. In a corporate setting one is more probable to encounter SumTotal [9] or Meridian [10], while in the education sector one is more probable to encounter Moodle [11], or Blackboard [12]. Apart from these traditional LMSs, MOOC platforms like Canvas [13] or OpenScholar [14] are gaining traction and are adding LMS functionality. All of these platforms include some reporting and visual analytics tools. Usually these tools follow the dashboard paradigm, and offer printer-friendly views for paper reports. For example, on the corporate end of the spectrum SumTotal offers visual analytics that can even contain HR-related operations, while on the academic side OpenScholar offers integration with project or class pages. However, there is often a lack of statistical reporting and visualisation of reports to understand the effectiveness of the training [6]. Where visualisations of analytics are provided they are often restricted to a predefined set of metrics, delivered through a separate application, or generated periodically in batch style reports [4]. Dashboard analytics is not a paradigm restricted to learning analytics; indeed, its predominant field is Business Intelligence (BI). A number of tools like Tableau, Crystal Reports, Data Hero, or Datawunder, can visualise data from various sources using copying-and-pasting of arbitrary data and offering the end user a choice of visualisations to choose from. More often than not, these tools offer static, though embeddable, views of data. This functionality creates the risk of a temporal mismatch between the state of the visualised data and the possibly updated state of the real data. To avoid such a mismatch, contemporary LMSs and their data analytics are tightly integrated [4],[6].

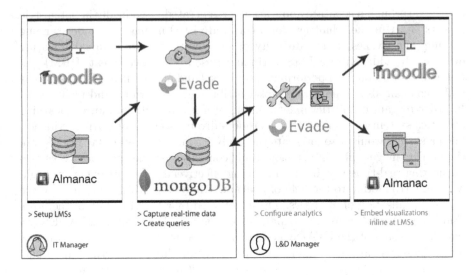

Fig. 1. Architecture diagram of EVADE

3 EVADE

The design of many Learning Analytics systems are influenced by established research in educational data mining [7] and the research emerging from focused conferences such as the International Learning Analytics and Knowledge Conference (LAK) [15]. Despite this research base the majority of Learning Analytics systems are focused on and developed around concerns in higher education. In the design of EVADE an alternative approach was taken, that is to engage with the more than 30 industry partners of the Learnovate Centre to collaboratively define the industry challenges in learning analytics. Through working closely with several suppliers and users of eLearning software we derived the following list of challenges faced by these companies.

Data Capture and Management

- Capturing learning events from diverse systems.
- Catering for evolving reporting and analytics requirements.
- Real-time analytics as opposed to periodic batch processed reports.

Data Analytics

- Continuous and dynamic performance management.
- Identification of meaningful learning events.

Visualisation and User Interaction

- Developing a data-driven decision making culture.
- Flexibility to cater for high-level and fine-grained analysis.
- Intuitive visual interfaces for configuration, reporting and display of analytical outputs.

Through discussions with industry partners it became apparent that the key users of the learning analytics, namely the L&D managers, have the insight as to how learning should be analysed and presented, yet typically lack the technical skills to capture and query the learner data. For this reason the EVADE system considers two key users, the non-technical L&D manager, and a technical IT manager who understands what data is being captured and how to setup queries over the data. The requirements for EVADE that are derived from these challenges are to:

- Enable IT administrators to create APIs to capture data from diverse sources, and to setup queries over the gathered data.
- Enable L&D managers to easily select the data sources and queries they deem appropriate for understanding the progress of their learners.
- Allow visualisations based on the selected analytics to be embedded within web-based LMSs so that the analytics are contextualised within the systems they relate to and are encountered during the day-to-day workflows.
- Generate visualisations based on the analytics that are considerate of the visual space constraints of LMSs, that can highlight anomalous data, and also encourage exploration of problematic learners or learning content.
- Accommodate the busy pace of modern-day businesses by saving the L&D manager from studying extensive reports and rather give indicators that might trigger exploration towards problematic areas for either learners or content.

3.1   System Architecture

The architecture of EVADE is built around two core components, the web-app that forms the interface for the IT manager and the L&D manager, and the database that allows the storage and querying of captured data.

The EVADE Web-app. The web-app component is built using the Groovy language and the Grails web application framework. The data capture APIs all receive JSON over HTTP. The rational behind standardising on JSON is based on its platform independence, its ease of integration with rich web-applications, and its usage in the Experience/Tin Can API [7]. The Tin Can API is an emerging standard for capturing evidence of learning activities, it is seen as a successor to the Sharable Content Object Reference Model (SCORM) [1] standard, and allows EVADE to act as a Learner Record Store (LRS) [7]. In order to collect data from diverse client side application EVADE supports both CORS and JSONP

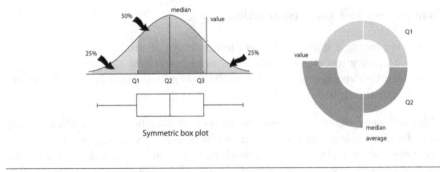

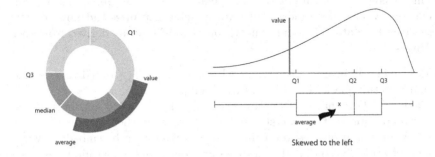

Fig. 2. Bi-level quartile doughnut charts

to cater for cross-domain requests. As an initial integration with a LMS, a plugin was developed for Moodle that captures events from both the PHP backend and through client-side JavaScript. The ALMANAC app is the second system integrated with EVADE and it is the outcome of project on informal mobile learning also being undertaken at the Learnovate Centre.

Data Storage. The database component of EVADE is separated from the webapp by a JSON API in order not to bind the system to one particular database technology. Due to the heterogeneous data sources that are collected by EVADE and the key-value nature of the data the initial database component is implemented using MongoDB (http://www.mongodb.org). As well as providing flexibility and scalability through sharding, MongoDB also provides powerful aggregation queries that can be applied across datasets with varying schemas.

Visualisations. The output of any data query within EVADE can be retrieved through a JSON API allowing flexibility in how the data is consumed for visualisation. One of the key requirements of EVADE is to embed visualisations within web-based LMSs. These visualisations will have limited space and must be indicative visualisations that warrant exploration, as opposed to prescriptive ones that require time consuming interpretation. Inline visualisations facilitate more usable interfaces, in the sense that drilling down through the content and displaying the visualisations inline means that one has to recognise the piece of content they want to explore rather than recall where it would be on a separate reports page. Moreover, inline visualisations can improve analytic reasoning by contextualising the analysis by content. They should use less working memory since end users can associate each item with its visualisation [2]. For example, a L&D manager working on a Learning Management System (LMS) could be navigating through the course structure as usual when viewing the content, and view inline visualisations while doing that (Fig. 3). That would give the benefit of viewing each course in context, instead of a ranked list of potentially irrelevant courses presented at a dashboard reporting page. To achieve this, we visualise distributions of learners data by applying the following steps. Firstly, we reduce the distribution graph to a one-dimensional chart of its quartilesthe result resembles a coloured box plot. Then we produce a circular version of the quartiles chart by converting its coordinates to a polar system with radius r and we subtract a circle with radius l so that the remaining doughnut has width $r - l$ (see Fig. 2). Moreover, we visualise the distance of a value to the median as a second level ring; it is calculated in the same way; that is, the distance of the value from the median is converted to polar coordinates with radius m. So, a box plot can be implemented so as to represent its box and whiskers (but not the outliers) in a limited space of just $(2 * m)^2$. The EVADE web-app currently supports embedding visualisations generated using D3.js (http://d3js.org/).

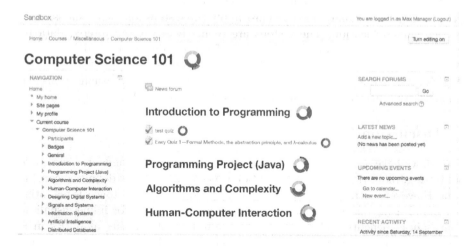

Fig. 3. A Learning Management System (LMS) using inline bi-level quartile doughnut charts

3.2   User Workflows

To illustrate a typical usage of the EVADE system the workflows of the two user types are presented.

IT Manager Workflow. As shown in Fig. 4 the IT manager firstly creates an API to capture data in the desired format (Fig. 4a) in this case from a Moodle Plugin. Each API receives JSON messages with a number of fields. A field has a data type as supported by the JSON format, namely Double, String, Boolean, Array, or nested JSON Object. Once fields have been added the API is live and can start receiving data.

The second step involves filtering the data in order to present only the relevant fields to the L&D manager (Fig. 4b). As well as including and excluding fields, basic conditions (e.g. *score* > 50) can be applied. The third step involves creating multiple queries on the filtered data using the query editor (Fig. 4c). An example query would be to calculate the average number of courses completed for each learner. These queries will subsequently used by the L&D manager. The final step in the workflow involves the creation of embed locations within the LMS. This is achieved by using a regular expressions to indicate which URLs the embed should be applied to, a jQuery selector to identify where in the DOM the visualisations should appear, and the number of visualisations that should appear in the embed location (Fig. 4d). Despite the sequential nature of this workflow data capture APIs, filters, queries, and embed locations can be created and modified at any time.

L&D Manager Workflow. In comparison to the IT manager the workflow of the L&D manager is intentionally simpler. To allow the user to quickly and easily configure the analytics they must apply three steps for each visualisation, in each embed location. These steps are to firstly select the filtered data to analyse (Fig. 5a), secondly to select one of the queries configured by the IT manager (Fig. 5b) and thirdly to select the time period to apply this query to (Fig. 5c). Once the configuration has been saved the updated visualisations are immediately reflected within the LMS as is shown in Fig. 2.

4   Discussion

Though we have implemented this solution for an LMS and conducted some initial testing, more rigorous user evaluation is necessary to draw definitive conclusions. However, both our initial testing and previous work hint towards potential benefits of using charts specifically designed and developed for inline visualisations. These benefits include the contextualisation of learning analytics in a potentially beneficial way for the L&D managers working memory. The broader issue to be addressed here is identifying issues in real time and intervening at a moment when it is more relevant for the learners and the organisation. The current alternative is to discover problems too late, that is, when the course is over and improvements can only be made at another offering of the same course. With regard to the data management aspect of the system, the current implementation is sufficiently fast, as the LMS loads the embedded visualisations at time $t < 200ms$, even though the code has not been optimised for speed. Please note that ongoing development of a "big-data" style database to enable scalability and speed is underway. It is/will be based on Apache HBase and Hadoop

Fig. 4. IT Manager Workflow using the EVADE Web App

Fig. 5. L&D Manager Workflow using the EVADE Visualisation Builder

databases in order to allow for a scalable implementation of EVADE. We expect that this "big data" infrastructure will increase the plugability of EVADE to various data sources, so that it will further reduce costs and increase the benefit of the learning analytics to L&D managers.

5   Future Work

With regard to the UI, in the future we plan to allow embeds to be configured directly from within the LMS, that is, where they are visible in the LMS. From the data management point of view, we anticipate that the use of HBase and Hadoop databases will facilitate querying using languages such as Splout SQL and even apply more advanced machine learning and data mining algorithms with tools like Apache Mahout. These tools would allow us to perform clustering and predictive analysis on the data of the learners to improve the understanding and possibly enhance intervention.

Finally, we have partnered with a corporate Banking education organisation to conduct a trial of EVADE with one of their courses. The learners are professionals in the Banking sector who participate in either continuing professional development (CPD) courses to improve their skills or compliance testing. The trial is scheduled to run for the duration of the whole semester when the course is offered, and a few hundred learners are scheduled to participate.

6   Conclusion

In conclusion, we present a learning analytics solution which incorporates actual requirements from industry partners. EVADE is an attempt to bridge the gap between academic learning analytics and business intelligence tools, and enhance their functionality to address the need for corporate and informal education analytics.

The main contribution of EVADE is twofold. Firstly, the ability to capture real-time data from various data sources, including corporate and informal LMSs, and secondly the affordance of inline visualisations, which facilitate the understanding of learning analytics by L&D managers.

A further implication of this project is that it allows the L&D manager to inspect both learner- or content-related problems at real time and intervene to address them and improve the learning outcome. Finally, a smaller contribution is the specific development of visualisations for inline use, and in particular the visualisation of distribution data in order to avoid problems of scale and size caused by the screen real estate use which derives from embedding visualisations inline.

Acknowledgments. This research is supported by the Learnovate Centre at Trinity College, the University of Dublin. The Learnovate Centre is funded under the Technology Centre Programme through the Government of Irelands state agencies Enterprise Ireland and IDA Ireland.

References

1. Advanced Distributed Learning. SCORM, http://www.adlnet.org/scorm/
2. Dix, A., Finlay, J., Abowd, G., Beale, R.: Human-Computer Interaction. Prentice-Hall, New Jersey (1998)
3. Macfadyen, L.P., Dawson, S., Mining, L.M.S.: data to develop an "early warning system" for educators: A proof of concept. Computers & Education 54(2), 588–599 (2010)
4. Mazza, R., Milani, C.: Exploring usage analysis in learning systems: Gaining insights from visualisations. In: AIED 2005 Workshop on Usage Analysis in Learning Systems, pp. 65–72 (2005)
5. O'Leonard, K.: The Corporate Learning Factbook 2009. Deloitte (2009)
6. Romero, C., Ventura, S., García, E.: Data mining in course management systems: Moodle case study and tutorial. Computers & Education 51(1), 368–384 (2008)
7. Romero, C., Ventura, S.: Educational data mining: A survey from 1995 to 2005. Expert Systems with Applications 33(1), 135–146 (2007)
8. SOLAR. Society for Learning Analytics Research | About (2013), http://www.solaresearch.org/mission/about/
9. SumTotal, http://www.sumtotalsystems.com
10. Meridian, http://www.meridianks.com
11. Moodle, https://moodle.org/
12. Blackboard, http://www.blackboard.com
13. Canvas, http://www.instructure.com/
14. OpenScholar, http://openscholar.harvard.edu/
15. Learning Analytics Conference, http://lakconference2013.wordpress.com/
16. Tin Can API, http://tincanapi.com/

Fuzzy Student Modeling for Personalization of e-Learning Courses

Carla Limongelli and Filippo Sciarrone

Roma Tre University - Engineering Department
Via della Vasca Navale, 79
00146 Rome
{limongel,sciarro}@dia.uniroma3.it

Abstract. In the context of e-learning courses, personalization is a more and more studied issue, being its advantage in terms of time and motivations widely proved. Course personalization basically means to understand student's needs: to this aim several Artificial Intelligence methodologies have been used to model students for tailoring e-learning courses and to provide didactic strategies, such as planning, case based reasoning, or fuzzy logic, just to cite some of them. Moreover, in order to disseminate personalised e-learning courses, the use of known and available Learning Management System is mandatory.

In this paper we propose a fine-grained student model, embedded into an Adaptive Educational Hypermedia, LS_Plan provided as plug-in for Moodle. In this way we satisfy the two most important requirements: a fine-grained personalization and a large diffusion. In particular, the substantial modification proposed in this contribution regards the methodology to evaluate the knowledge of the single student which currently has a low granularity level. The experiments showed that the new system has improved the evaluation mechanism by adding information that students and teachers can use to keep track of learning progress.

1 Introduction

Distance learning is a mode of teaching/learning more and more required, used in education and working contexts. Research in this field has dramatically increased in different directions: human-computer interfaces, design of Learning Management Systems (LMSs), social context [14], students' modeling [20], teachers' background and teaching styles [18].

In this context,the use of known and available LMSs is mandatory and essential to create and to spread content, but a LMS that provides all these features is difficult to find.

Moreover, the personalization of the learning experience is closely related to the efficiency and effectiveness of the learning process itself: personalized content is more easily assimilated and the learner is more motivated. However student diagnosis is uncertain, and a possible approach to face this problem is a fine-grained student modeling, that several researchers (e.g. [24]) assessed

P. Zaphiris and A. Ioannou (Eds.): LCT 2014, Part I, LNCS 8523, pp. 292–301, 2014.

as adequate to carry out the student's assessment and pedagogical strategies. Fuzzy logic techniques have been used to improve the performance of intelligent educational systems due to their ability to handle uncertain information, such as students actions, and to provide human descriptions of knowledge and of students cognitive abilities [11].

In this paper we focus on the definition of a fine grained student model, taking inspiration from the work reported in [20], that allows to create and customize courses basing on student's learning styles according to the Felder-Silverman model. We integrate into this model Kosba's studies ([11]) on the application of fuzzy logic for the description of the cognitive level of the students with respect to certain topics. We propose a plugin for the most world-widespread LMS: Moodle. In particular, our aim is to modify and improve the existing student model, that is the set of acquired information from student learning style and needs, and from the interactions with the system during her own personalized learning material fruition. The current student model provides a student adaptive component, and evaluates students' needs according to their knowledge and learning preferences. In this proposal, the substantial modification regards the knowledge representation of the student, which currently has a low granularity level. LS_Plan basically uses two values to estimate the knowledge: acquired or not acquired. We introduce in the new student model a fine-grained Cognitive State with four different levels of knowledge acquisition. This improvement brings a great advantage to the end user that has her personalized course carefully tailored on her personal knowledge and learning goals, avoiding waste of time and motivations in studying topics that could reveals trivial or too much difficult in a "one-size-fits-all" course, or in a course not carefully personalized.

In the following section we report about some meaningful related work, in Sec. 3 we describe the fine-grained Student Model. In Sec. 4 we show an example of application. Conclusions and future work are drawn in Sec. 5.

2   Related Work

Fuzzy approach is a widely applied technique in user modeling, in particular it is used to model different aspects of student's characteristics such as the degree of knowledge the student has or acquires in a given subject. It allows natural description of knowledge and inference in the form of imprecise concepts, operators, and rules.

For example in [24] is proposed BSS1 that is an ITS with a general fuzzy logic engine for supporting the intelligent features of the ITS. In [2], ABITS defines the domain knowledge where Learning Objects (LO) and related metadata are the basic elements of the system. Its student model is represented by Cognitive state, student's preferences, and curricula. Fuzzy logic is applied here to represent the uncertainty of the student's score that can be obtained by different kind of assessments and with different degree of reliability, as we also consider. Following a similar approach, in [12] the author presents TADV that is a famous framework for web distance education characterized by the Advice Generator that communicates with the student, during her didactic path, about results gained over time. Its student model is represented by four main aspects that, on the whole, contribute to the overall student evaluation. They are: general information, behaviour, preferences, knowledge. The last one is represented by fuzzy logic, where the knowledge of a student about a certain topic is modeled by the following variables: Certainty Factor (CF), Measure of Belief (MB), Measure of Disbelief (MD). The Certainty Factor is a variable that takes on values between −1 and 1, and is directly influenced by the other two variables MB and MD. MB and MD are variables extrapolated from the results of the assessment quiz that the student takes for each concept of a specific course. Both MD and MB range between 0 and 1. The first increases with each correct answer given by the student to a specific quiz. The second one is increased if the student responds incorrectly or skips the quiz. The result of the two values is combined giving the final value of CF. Kosba defines three levels of learning: completely learned, learned and unlearned. The CF is compared with the intervals that define the learning levels and stores the result obtained by the student for the specific concept. Not only quizzes modify the degree of understanding assigned to each student, but also the time variable that contributes to define the Belief Graph. On the other way TADV gives suggestion to students, but does not provide a personalized didactic strategy.

The work presented in [10] proposes an educational hypermedia where for each domain concept the user model saves a corresponding value using a linguistic variable concept knowledge, which takes three possible values which estimates user knowledge of that concept: unknown, known, and learned. More recently, [3] proposes an adaptive learning environment for computer programming based on hybrid student model, which combines an overlay model with stereotype and fuzzy logic techniques. In a perspective of technology enhanced learning, there is research work [5], [4], [6], [21] aiming to integrate more traditional individualized e-learning [23] and social-collaborative e-learning [22], [1] and [7]. Many personalized e-learning systems do not use fuzzy approach to model students. They rather insist to suitably represent student's learning styles, such as [9] or [20],[8], and also teachers' teaching styles ([13], [15], [17],[16]).

We start from the work presented in [20], [19] and improve it with some aspects of the student model that can be made more realistic by means fine-grained modeling. Being inspired by the work of Kosba, we integrate into LS_Plan a student model that will provide more realistic assessment of the students and the subsequent re-planning of the learning that the student must follow. Unlike other Adaptive Educational Systems like [10] and [3] that are "problem oriented", LS_Plan provides a personalization engine that can be plugged in any educational system being, therefore, problem independent.

3   The Student Model

In this section we present the Student Model (SM) and its relation with the adaptive system in which it is involved. Fig. 1 shows some relations among the

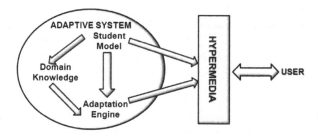

Fig. 1. Coarse-grained relations among components into Adaptive Systems. On the bases of a given SM, the Adaptation Engine configures a personalized course extracted from the Domain Knowledge. The course is presented to the student through a Hypermedia.

main components of an adaptive system. Before describing more in detail the characteristics of the new student model we will introduce some definitions about the elements we are going to work with, then we show new mechanisms defined in the Adaptation Engine, which exploit the new model.

Definition 1. (KNOWLEDGE ITEM). *A knowledge item KI is an atomic element of knowledge about a given topic. KI is a set: $KI = \{KI_K, KI_A, KI_E\}$ where KI_ℓ, with $\ell \in \{K, A, E\}$, represents a cognitive level taken from Bloom's Taxonomy: Knowledge, Application and Evaluation.*

We have chosen only three out of the six levels of Bloom's taxonomy: it is easy, but heavy, to provide the KI with all the six levels.

Definition 2. (LEARNING STYLE). *A Learning Style LS is a 4-tuple: $LS = \langle D_1, D_2, D_3, D_4 \rangle$, with $D_i \in [-11, +11]$, $i = 1, \ldots, 4$ where each D_i is a Felder and Silverman Learning Style Dimension, i.e., D_1: active-reflective, D_2: sensing-intuitive, D_3: visual-verbal, D_4: sequential-global.*

We used the range $[-11, +11]$ according to the Felder-Soloman ILS scale.

Definition 3. (COGNITIVE STATE). *The Cognitive State CS is the set of all the KI_ℓ possessed by the student with respect to the given topic: $CS \subseteq DK$.*

Definition 4. (STUDENT MODEL). *The student model SM is a pair: $SM = (CS, LS)$ where, CS is given in Definition 3 and LS is given in Definition 2.*

This is the original Student Model definition presented in [20]. In the following we will not consider LS, because they will stay unchanged. Rather, we refine KIs, which contribute to CS, with fuzzy aspects taking inspiration from the work reported in [11].

Definition 5. (FUZZY KNOWLEDGE ITEM). *A fuzzy knowledge item KI is an atomic element of knowledge about a given topic. KI is a set: $KI = \{KI_K, KI_A, KI_E\}$ where KI_ℓ, with $\ell \in \{K, A, E\}$ is a real number. Each $KI_\ell \in [0, \ldots, 1]$. The less the value, the less is the knowledge acquired for that item. KI is divided in four evaluation classes: $[0, 0.4)$ not sufficient, $[0.4, 0.6)$ sufficient, $[0.6, 0.8)$ good, $[0.8, 1]$ excellent.*

With this definitions we will represent always all the KI the student will deal with, even if they are equal to 0 (see the outcome of the two SM in Fig. 3). On the other hand in the previous SM in CS there were only KI (fully) acquired.

The use of fuzzy logic is highlighted in the evaluation mechanism, in particular when a student is assigned a score to the end of a quiz. In order to describe these mechanisms we have to introduce the Learning Node which is strictly related to the quiz.

Definition 6. (LEARNING NODE). *A Learning Node LN is a 5-tuple: $LN = \langle LM, AK, RK, LS, T \rangle$ where*

LM *is the Learning Material, i.e., any instructional digital resource.*

AK *Acquired Knowledge. It is a KI_ℓ that represents the knowledge that the student acquires at a given level as specified in Definition 1, after having passed the assessment test related to the KI_ℓ of the node. If such a test is not present in the node the AK is considered acquired anyway.*

RK *Required Knowledge. It is the set of KI_ℓ necessary for studying the material of the node, i.e., the cognitive prerequisites required by the AK associated to the node.*

LS *is given in Definition 2.*

T *is a pair of reals $T = (t_{min}, t_{max})$ that represents the estimated time interval for studying the material of the node, as prefixed by the teacher.*

Let us consider a quiz related to a given LN. The mechanism for computing scores related to quizzes are normalized, for each quiz, between 0 and 1. Let us consider a LN having N questions related to it. The set of all the questions $Q_{LN} = \{q_1, \ldots, q_N\}$ forms the quiz for that LN. Each q_i has a weight w associated to it, i.e. the score obtained in case of correct answer. The maximum score a student can get in a quiz is 1.

$$\sum_{k=1}^{N} w(q_i) = 1$$

In this way, the score is directly related to the degree of knowledge acquired for that LN. In case the teacher does not specify weights, the weight computation is given by

$$w(q_i) = \frac{1}{N}$$

In particular, the new aspects of the student model will be the following: new representation of the student's knowledge; new representation of the score tests; new management of time variable associated to quizzes.

According to it, the learner's knowledge will be classified within one of these four classes.

Timing are also considered in a different way: time computation is no more related to material fruition (that is difficult to estimate), but to the time the student needs to take the quiz at the end of each Learning Node. This is actually more realistic evaluation than the time spent for studying the lesson itself. Obviously it is not possible to know if the fruition time (t_f) of a Learning Node is actually spent on studying or if it is affected by other factors. However, the thresholds t_{min} and t_{max} that we consider, allow to eliminate at least two student behaviors: the so-called "coffee break" effect, when the fruition time t_f is greater than t_{max}, and a casual browsing of a given material, when t_f is less than t_{min}.

This kind of knowledge representation provides also more flexibility for the teacher that can fix different thresholds for different LN, depending on the importance that LN has in the context of a given course. For example if a LN explains a very important concept that the student must acquire, the teacher can fix threshold to 0.7 and if less that LN will be proposed again to the student.

4 Experiments with Moodle

The new student model and the related management has been implemented into LS_Plan and Moodle 1.9. The experimentation has been carried out with the purpose of verifying if the new student model is more refined than the previous one, highlighting the differences between the same two courses, the one running with improved LS_Plan and the other one with the original plug-in. The experimental course is very small, but enough to show the difference with the previous system. Fig.2 shows the platform and the conceptual map of the experimental course. In this experiment all the concepts are at the same level K.

We consider two courses with 5 Learning Nodes which represent the concepts related to the course on neorealist cinema: intro C_1, themes C_2, movies C_3, desica C_4, rossellini C_5. For the sake of readability in the table we show labels associated to the topics. 5 students attended the course. They first answered to the initial questionnaire. For each concept the system selected a number of questions between 3 and 6. The overall initial questionnaire was composed by 15 questions. The old system memorized the Cognitive State reported in the following table:

The new system memorized also the level of knowledge that students got for each concept in the KI Score section of the LS_Plan Data Base.

We follow the student $s2$ whose initial situation is depicted in Fig. 2. The figure is a snapshot of the system after the initial questionnaire. Let us note that only C_2, C_4 and C_5 are proposed to the student, because he proved to know already concepts C_1 and C_3 in the initial questionnaire. $s2$ studies the first lesson proposed by the system, $C_2 themes$, obtaining a score of 0.7 as reported in Tab. 3.

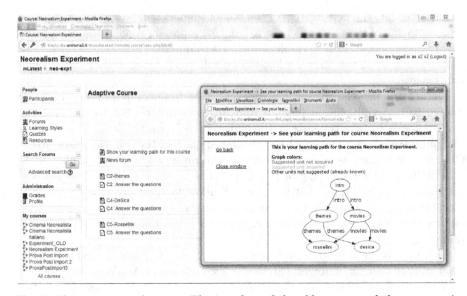

Fig. 2. The experimental course. The interface of the old system and the new one is exactly the same, the difference is in the internal user knowledge representation and in the adaptation mechanism at the initial stage.

Table 1. Cognitive state of the students after the initial questionnaire

Student	Course	Cognitive State	CS Level
s1	id1	C_1,C_2,C_5	K,K,K
s2	id1	C_1,C_3	K,K
s3	id1	C_2,C_4	K,K
s4	id1	C_2	K
s5	id1	C_2,C_3,C_5	K,K,K

Table 2. Cognitive state of the students after the initial questionnaire with the new student model. Bold numbers in the rightmost column represents the acquired concepts.

Student	Course	Cognitive State	CS Level	KI score $(C_1,\ldots,C_5)$
s1	id1	C_1,C_2,C_5	K,K,K	**0.5**, **0.4**, 0.2, 0, **0.5**
s2	id1	C_1,C_3	K,K	**0.5**, 0.1, **0.5**, 0.2, 0.2
s3	id1	C_2,C_4	K,K	0.2, **0.4**, 0.1, **0.5**, 0.2
s4	id1	C_2	K	0.1, **0.5**, 0.2, 0.2, 0.1
s5	id1	C_2,C_3,C_5	K,K,K	0.1, **0.4**, **0.4**, 0.2, **0.5**

The visible effect of the updating mechanism is an indication of the knowledge acquired during the course (together with the learning preference that can be tuned during the fruition of a course) as indicated by the system, like in Fig. 3.

Fig. 3. The outcome of the two advices. On the top there is an dialogue window that describe user's knowledge with the new model: all the KI are listed with their respective degree of acquisition. In the dialogue window below, the previous SM indicates only the list of acquired KI.

Table 3. KI score updating for concept C_2 of student $s2$

Student	Course	Cognitive State	CS Level	KI score $(C_1, \ldots, C_5)$
s2	id1	C_1, C_3, C_5	K,K	$\mathbf{0.5}, \mathbf{0.7}, \mathbf{0.5}, 0.2, 0.2$

5 Conclusions

In this work we adopted fuzzy representation for a student model used into the Adaptive Educational System LS_Plan. Starting form the student model proposed in [20] and taking inspiration from the work presented in [12] we introduced a fuzzy representation of the Cognitive State of the student model and, consequently, all the related adaptation rules. These rules act mainly at the quiz level, in particular fuzzy CS modeling allows to give a more fine grained evaluation about the knowledge acquired by the student and a consequent freedom for the teacher to apply possible different didactic strategies.

In fact, with this new personalization process, not only teachers can estimate in a more precise way how much a student knows about a given topic, but also the student can have more appropriate suggestions about her/his way of learning.

The adaptation has been carried out with a plug-in for Moodle 1.9. We are going to adapt it to Moodle 2.5 in order to perform wider experiments.

References

1. Biancalana, C., Flamini, A., Gasparetti, F., Micarelli, A., Millevolte, S., Sansonetti, G.: Enhancing traditional local search recommendations with context-awareness. In: Konstan, J.A., Conejo, R., Marzo, J.L., Oliver, N. (eds.) UMAP 2011. LNCS, vol. 6787, pp. 335–340. Springer, Heidelberg (2011)
2. Capuano, N., Marsella, M., Salerno, S.: Abits: An agent based intelligent tutoring system for distance learning. In: Proceedings of the International Workshop in Adaptative and Intelligent Web-based Educational Systems, pp. 17–28 (2000)
3. Chrysafiadi, K., Virvou, M.: Dynamically personalized e-training in computer programming and the language c. IEEE Transactions on Education 56(4), 385–392 (2013)
4. De Marsico, M., Sterbini, A., Temperini, M.: A strategy to join adaptive and reputation-based social-collaborative e-learning, through the zone of proximal development. International Journal of Distance Education Technologies 19(2), 105–121 (2012)
5. De Marsico, M., Sterbini, A., Temperini, M.: The definition of a tunneling strategy between adaptive learning and reputation-based group activities, pp. 498–500 (2011)
6. De Marsico, M., Temperini, M.: Average effort and average mastery in the identification of the zone of proximal development (2013)
7. Gasparetti, F., Micarelli, A., Sansonetti, G.: Exploiting web browsing activities for user needs identification. In: Proceedings of CSCI 2014. IEEE Computer Society, Conference Publishing Services (March 2014)
8. Gentili, G., Micarelli, A., Sciarrone, F.: Infoweb: An adaptive information filtering system for the cultural heritage domain. Applied Artificial Intelligence 17(8-9), 715–744 (2003)
9. Graf, S.: Kinshuk: Providing adaptive courses in learning management systems with respect to learning styles. In: e-Learn 2007 (2007)
10. Kavcic, A.: Fuzzy user modeling for adaptation in educational hypermedia. IEEE Transactions on Systems, Man, and Cybernetics, Part C: Applications and Reviews 34(4), 439–449 (2004)
11. Kosba, E.: Generating Computer-Based Advice in Web-Based Distance Education Environments. PhD thesis, University of Leeds School of Computing (2004)
12. Kosba, E., Dimitrova, V., Boyle, R.: Using fuzzy techniques to model students in web-based learning environments. In: Palade, V., Howlett, R.J., Jain, L. (eds.) KES 2003. LNCS, vol. 2774, pp. 222–229. Springer, Heidelberg (2003)

13. Limongelli, C., Lombardi, M., Marani, A., Sciarrone, F.: A teacher model to speed up the process of building courses. In: Kurosu, M. (ed.) HCII/HCI 2013, Part II. LNCS, vol. 8005, pp. 434–443. Springer, Heidelberg (2013)

14. Limongelli, C., Lombardi, M., Marani, A., Sciarrone, F.: A teaching-style based social network for didactic building and sharing. In: Lane, H.C., Yacef, K., Mostow, J., Pavlik, P. (eds.) AIED 2013. LNCS, vol. 7926, pp. 774–777. Springer, Heidelberg (2013)

15. Limongelli, C., Miola, A., Sciarrone, F., Temperini, M.: Supporting teachers to retrieve and select learning objects for personalized courses in the moodle-ls environment. In: Giovannella, C., Sampson, D.G., Aedo, I. (eds.) ICALT, pp. 518–520. IEEE (2012)

16. Limongelli, C., Mosiello, G., Panzieri, S., Sciarrone, F.: Virtual industrial training: Joining innovative interfaces with plant modeling. In: ITHET, pp. 1–6. IEEE (2012)

17. Limongelli, C., Sciarrone, F., Starace, P., Temperini, M.: An ontology-driven olap system to help teachers in the analysis of web learning object repositories. Information System Management 27(3), 198–206 (2010)

18. Limongelli, C., Sciarrone, F., Temperini, G., Vaste, M.: The lecomps5 framework for personalized web-based learning: A teacher's satisfaction perspective. Computers in Human Beaviour 27(4) (2011)

19. Limongelli, C., Sciarrone, F., Vaste, G.: LS-pLAN: An effective combination of dynamic courseware generation and learning styles in web-based education. In: Nejdl, W., Kay, J., Pu, P., Herder, E. (eds.) AH 2008. LNCS, vol. 5149, pp. 133–142. Springer, Heidelberg (2008)

20. Limongelli, C., Sciarrone, F., Vaste, G.: Personalized e-learning in moodle: The moodle_ls system. Journal of e-Learning and Knowledge Society 7(1), 49–58 (2011)

21. Sciarrone, F.: An extension of the q diversity metric for information processing in multiple classifier systems: a field evaluation. International Journal of Wavelets, Multiresolution and Information Processing, IJWMIP 11(6) (2013)

22. Sterbini, A., Temperini, M.: Collaborative projects and self evaluation within a social reputation-based exercise-sharing system, vol. 3, pp. 243–246 (2009)

23. Sterbini, A., Temperini, M.: Selection and sequencing constraints for personalized courses, pp. T2C1–T2C6 (2010); cited by (since 1996)

24. Warendorf, K., Tsao, S.J.: Application of fuzzy logic techniques in the bss1 tutoring system. J. Artif. Intell. Educ. 8(1), 113–146 (1997)

Slow Learner Children Profiling for Designing Personalized eBook

Marzita Mansor, Wan Adilah Wan Adnan, and Natrah Abdullah

Faculty of Computer and Mathematical Science,
Universiti Teknologi MARA (UiTM), Malaysia
marzita@fskik.upsi.edu.my,
{adilah,natrah}@tmsk.uitm.edu.my

Abstract. Advances in reading technology have created significant interest for young children to use eBook. But similar opportunity and enjoyable experience of using the eBook suit with slow learner needs seems to be impossible. This is due to the fact that the existing eBooks on the market are not designed to suit with the slow learner reading capability. This situation stimulates the desire to explore on the need to design a personalized eBook for slow learner children. This paper presents the findings of the interview session conducted on five slow learner children and a school teacher at one of the primary school in Malaysia in order to explore on the need to provide individual learning. It also presents an overview of the research approach and shares an initiative conducted to adapt Segmented Personalization and Scaffolding approach in the eBook application development. We do hope that this study able to provide an overview on the importance of providing personalized learning especially for individuals with learning disabilities.

Keywords: personalized, eBook, slow learner, reading.

1 Introduction

Personalization is found to have a great impact on education. In general, personalization of education aims at providing individualized learning which enables learners learn according to their uniquely identified personal, needs and learning content. However, the missing link in implementing the personalization dreams are due to heavy emphasizes on implementing personalization for normal students, but the individual needs and unique characteristic of students with special needs have been ignored. Motivated by this factor, this study aims to adapt the personalization touch in order to assist students with learning disabilities, the slow learners who have difficulties in reading by designing personalized eBook for their reading purposes. The reading difficulties of the slow learner children are chosen as one of the study phenomenon due to the fact that reading ability determine success or failure of the children (Musen, 2010) . Apart from that this study also chooses eBook application to be used as a learning tool embedded with the personalization touch and reliable principles

P. Zaphiris and A. Ioannou (Eds.): LCT 2014, Part I, LNCS 8523, pp. 302–311, 2014.

related to reading in order to cover the slow learner children's need and suit with their profile. In this study, we see the potential of eBook due to increasing on its usage on the net and its capability and availability at anytime are some of eBook potentials.

As other learning technology, eBook also required personalization touch embedded in its interface design in order to assist readers, especially in the context of this study, the slow learner, in a more convenient way of reading. EBook, the electronic version of the printed book with the enhancement of the electronic features able to provide easily accessed to the reading materials worldwide. Although there is a positive reaction (Roskos & Bruek (2009) on the eBook usage of young children, for one thing it could be argued that the studies on eBook is lack of discussion on design principles. Only several researchers see the importance of implementing book with design principles from theories (Barua, Kay, Kummerfeld, & Paris, 2011) or framework in the area of design. There is also lack of studies related to eBook (Mckay, 2011)and limited evidence on any guideline principles for development of existing eBook discusses by academic scholars especially for special need children as the slow learner. Other than that, previous research has indicated that despite from the comeback of the eBook as reading technology, there are some unanswered questions in the eBook designing area. A study by (Beer & Wagner, 2011) stated that eBook concepts also need some enhancement in the design process. Meanwhile, a study by (Colombo & Landoni, 2011) and a survey conducted by the researcher during the Malaysian International Book Fair 2013 at Putra World Trade Centre (PWTC) Kuala Lumpur have proven that eBook available on the Malaysia are poor copied of translation of book in printed format and require a new design in order to take full advantage of eBook potentials. This paper presents two aspects; the user profile of the slow learner in order to show the need of personalized learning and presents a research approach of the eBook design process with the adaptation of segmented personalization and scaffolding approach.

2   Related Works

2.1   The Implementation of eBook in Malaysia Context

Although the new concept is not widely discussed and the study concerning the eBook is so limited, the benefit that the eBook can provide is undeniable. Several studies have pointed out the main advantages of eBooks compared to printed books. Advantages of eBook are a capability of quick navigation, meaning that eBook allows easy to jump between chapters; it offers bookmarks or highlighting features; eBook can be translated to any preferred language set by individual users (Beer & Wagner, 2011) and also eBook found to be more responsive to user needs (McKay, 2011). Other than that, eBook provides a lot of benefit to its reader especially to slow learner children in term of language proficiency by improving children concentration, comprehension skills, increasing vocabulary and learning the eBook with the use of personal interaction and experience. Although the eBook is not widely used as an educational material in the classroom, the accessibility of the eBook which available across the border due to the availability to be purchased online be the most benefit to all. In Malaysia perspective, this new trend can be regarded as a positive impact to the slow learner children. The changing on the perspective of using the technology to fulfill children ample time with game activities may be shifted to the use of technology devices for reading purposes. IPad, laptop, handheld devices which are close to the heart of the generation Y children can be utilized to promote reading habits for slow learner children. In recent years, there has been an increasing interest in the eBook. It can be denied that an eBook has a lot of potentials. As mentioned before, the use of eBook in Malaysia environment is still new, especially related to learning materials for primary school children. A simple survey conducted by the researcher during the Malaysian International Book Fair 2013 at Putra World Trade Centre (PWTC) Kuala Lumpur, Malaysia has shown that although the price for eBook in Malaysia is not expensive compared to physical printed book of the same title, the eBook material is so limited. Most of the eBook offered in the exhibition is only for adult readers. The interface for eBook for children also has limited features and found to not be interactive. The interface only allows its user to change the font, the theme and adjust the screen size. Other that that the eBook promoted during this exhibition can only be considered as the direct translation of the printed book to the electronic version without any additional multimedia featured embedded in the eBook. During the informal interview that has been conducted, it is clearly stated by the eBook exhibitors, who are among the pioneers of the eBook industries in Malaysia, the implementation of the eBook is still limited. In addition to that, the researcher also questioned the exhibitor regarding the plain features of the eBook compared to the one that we can purchase from any other outside countries. The exhibitor honestly admitted the eBook is not widely used in Malaysia   and the reading materials for slow learner children is so limited and still under progress on converting original printed materials into an electronic format.

3   Research Approach

The development of personalized eBook design for slow learner children requires a clear understanding of the characteristics of slow learner profiles, the intervention strategy and relevant personalization strategy and principle to be adapted in the eBook design. This session will discuss a research approach that has been conducted in order to come out with the personalized design of the eBook.

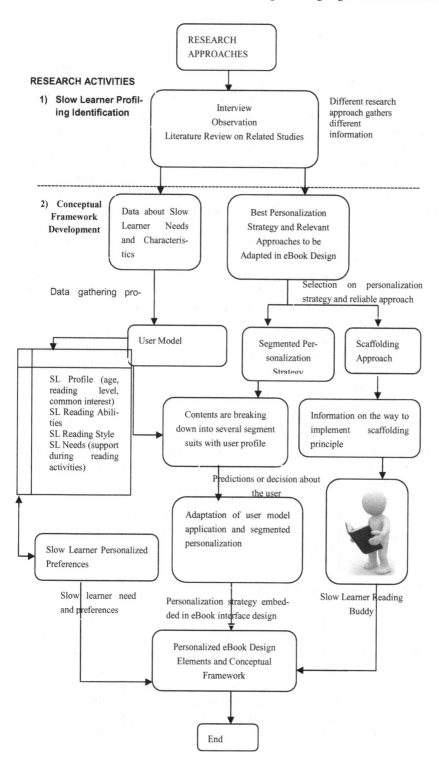

4   Analysis and Result

The slow learners are no longer a rare case in Malaysia and they are not categorized as people with special need. Being a slow learner means is that the student is unable to learn something in the amount of time assigned for the actual learning. (Vinci, 2009). Inability of slow learners to read also limits their capability to catch up with the learning process at school. Due to the inability of school authorities or even parent to recognize slow learner students at their early age, the slow learner students are allocated at the same classroom as normal students and both share the same syllabus, same teaching aids and approaches of teaching and learning style from the same teachers without considering their limited knowledge capability. Moreover, the standardization of learning material and learning content to every child in schools also do not give any privilege to slow learner children as the content of learning document provide a guideline of the learning content without looking at the individual differences in term of their cognitive ability and characteristics. The high level of knowledge which cannot be coped by their mental capability make a major problem to slow learner children as majority of slow learner children having difficulty in reading. Therefore, in order to cater the problem in providing the reading materials for the slow learner, the personalized eBook can be utilized as a learning tool which emphasizes on the individual need of each slow learner problems is introduced in this study. This study is undertaken with the specific intention to find the possible solution to slow learner children whom having difficulties in reading through the eBook personalization as a solution. By doing so, it is perhaps to ensure that the researcher fully understand whole aspects of these children before adapt the intervention solution with the introduction of personalized eBook application for the slow learner children. This study aims to involve slow learner children in exploring eBook as an alternative reading material which encompasses of interactive multimedia elements to attract their attention to learn reading through more engaging, usable and fun e-book interfaces for them. Thus, this study focuses on providing slow learner children with a new exposure of personalized eBook application setting and taking into account their reading ability and needs in a classroom. The respondents of the study consist of 5 slow learner children in a primary school in Malaysia and 2 slow learner teachers. The result of the data gathering process will be discussed in the next session presented in this paper.

5   Slow Learner User Profile

The preliminary investigation has been conducted twice in order for the researcher to have a look at the real problem happens in the classroom setting. With an intention to interact with the school teacher as well as the slow learner session, the researcher has sought permission from the school headmaster to see how the slow learner children at school learn. One hour session has been utilized with the interview, observation and interaction. The result learned from the investigation shows that the slow learner children who having difficulties in reading also have different characteristics. These results also illustrate the need to provide personalization approach as a solution that can cover the need of each individual user in reading aspect. Figure 1.0 shows the unique characteristics of each slow learner children in relation to their performance in reading.

Name	Age	SL Need	Reading Ability based on Construct (School Assessment)	Reading Ability Level	Reading Style
Nina	8 years old/ Girl/ Malay	Need repetition and reading companion	Construct 2	Able to read up to 2 syllables, able to read but do not able to understand what have been read.	Interested with reading exercise using toys and game instead of using book.
Tom	8 years old/ Boy/ Indian Muslim	Need repetition and reading companion	Construct 4	Able to sound closed syllables	Prefer an individual attention, prefer to learn using ICT
Adam	8 years old / Boy/ Indian Muslim	Need repetition and reading companion	Construct 6	Able to read and write words with 'ng' closed syllables.	Prefer to learn using ICT.
Jim	8 years old / Boy/ Chinese	Able to read with minimum supervision	Construct 12	Able to read and understand stimulation material	Prefer to learn using ICT.
Jenny	8 years old/ Girl/ Indian	Able to read with minimum supervision	Construct 12	Able to read and understand stimulation material	Prefer to learn using ICT.

*Pseudonyms have been used for the students' name mentioned in this paper.

6 Segmented Personalization Strategy for eBook Development

By definition, personalization is a process that has a potential to provide a solution on providing reading materials according to individual needs and preferences. The reading material which has its own target reader can be customized or represented into more understandable, attractive and able to increase user's motivation, especially for the beginning reader who has variation in learning style and unique characteristics as an individual. Personalization has proven to be an effective tool in education fields. A number of studies conducted by (Tsianos, Germanakos, & Lekkas, 2010)(Siadaty, 2008)(Brom, Bromová, Děchtěrenko, Buchtová, & Pergel, 2013) has shown the effective way in which the personalization proven to be an effective way to maximize the learning process in order to achieve the optimum way of learning. The one-size-fits-all approach in reading can be defined as a way of reading where by ignoring the uniqueness of individual characteristics, behavior, knowledge, experience, learning style and level of thinking, the same reading materials are used by everyone who looking at the subject or topics. This traditional way of reading do not focus on the individual needs, previous knowledge of the reader as long as the reading activity can be performed. Instead, the personalization process taken care of all aspects of reading, including the user or reader profile which consists of the readers demographic information, knowledge and ability; the categorization of the knowledge to be transferred to the reader according to readers need in order to ensure that the transformation of knowledge performed in an efficient and effective order. Personalization of reading activity that considers the variety of reader characteristics able to generate new knowledge in the readers' mind faster that the traditional reading materials which can be considered as one-size-fits-all approach. The outcome of the study is hoped able to provide a broad picture on the need to provide specific guidelines in order for us to understand the uniqueness of slow learner children and to provide a suitable personalized reading tool for them. By doing so, it will ensure that the material use of teaching and learning suit with the capability of slow learner children as an alternative for one-size-fits-all approach as implemented in the real classroom setting. Another possibility is that by providing an eBook as an extra alternative reading tool perhaps we will be able to cater slow learner problems in relation to reading difficulties as reading is a gateway to future success in school and in life (National Institute for Literacy, 2007). Again, the designing aspect of the user interface of an eBook is a part of the study, which concern on the personalization aspects that might be useful in helping slow learner children read better as it provides the solution based on the individual need of each young child.

According to Martinez (2011) Segmented Personalization is one type of personalization strategy that uses demographics, common attributes, or surveys to group or segment learning populations into smaller, identifiable and manageable groups. In the personalization, the users are being segmented into different group a common characteristic they have shared. This study proposes the use of the segmented personalization strategy in order to categorize the slow learner children into several suitable categories. Then after the categories have been identified, the personalization strategy will be adapted to the development of the personalized eBook for the slow learner children. . In a survey conducted and explained in figure 1.0, we can conclude that several segments have been categorized based on the slow learner common characteristics, ability and need as follows:

- Slow Learner Common characteristics: age, gender, preference on topic or subject
- Reading Ability Level (Determine by construct: Reading Achievement)

- Slow Learner Need (Repetition, Reading Style: read alone/ Scaffolds, Categories: Beginner, intermediate, advance Slow Learner)

7   Scaffolding Approach for Slow Learner Children

The Scaffolding Theory is the theory commonly uses in the education area. As the name implies scaffolding theory promotes the assistive learning for the children as an assistant that can help the children throughout the learning processes. The initial idea Of Scaffolding grew out of Vygotsky's work and then the concept then is expanded into the Scaffolding theory developed by the Psychologist, Jerome Bruner. The Scaffolding Theory is a theory implies the technique of assisting children to learn by providing the learning tools and then after the children master at a certain level, the assistance will be gradually withdrawn in order to allow the children learn language independently. In this study the concept of scaffolding is embedded in the artifacts developed in this study, not only in the instantiation in a form of eBook, but also in the proposed conceptual framework and guidelines. The Scaffolding Theory is chosen to be embedded in this research due to its capability in providing assistance to the special needs children who have difficulties in reading. The idea of scaffolding is consistent with the Zone of Proximal Development (ZPD) suggested by Vygotsky (1978) which describe the importance of achieving Zone of Proximal Development in the learning process. In general, the ZPD focus on understanding current level of a child's achievement and provide support (scaffold) in the learning process in order to enhance the child's potential in learning activities. The ZPD suggests that the learner can achieve an understanding of the knowledge beyond they expected with the use of scaffolding which describe the importance of providing support for the student in the learning process. The feel of boredom and anxiety can be minimized with the assistance of the scaffolding whether it relates to the existence of a human, tool or technology.

The concept of scaffolding allows the slow learner to learn reading based on their need. The scaffolding assists the slow learner during the reading activities until they have mastered certain level which shows they can learn reading on their own. At the first stage of the learning process, the reading activities begin when the teacher does the demonstration to the slow learner on how to read by introducing the read aloud activities. This process considers slow learner as a beginner. At this stage, the teacher chooses suitable material for teaching purpose. After the slow learner has shown their interest to learn and voluntarily want to participate in the reading activities, the teacher can change their role from a demonstrator to the reading partner by sharing reading material with the slow learner in an enjoyable manner. The process continues, and after the slow learner able to read on their own, the slow learner is allowed to learn independently and they also can choose their own reading materials. The scaffolding concepts indirectly guide and encourage the slow learner during the reading process, and after the slow learner has shown some improvement, they are allowed to perform an independent reading. The concept of scaffolding is suitable to be adapted in the reading technology as an eBook. The interactive reading buddy suggested by the scaffolding concept able to grasp the slow learners attention and perhaps able to provide an opportunity to make them learn reading in a most enjoyable manner.

8   Conclusion

In general, personalization idea promises to provide individual learning to each individual learner. Despite limited studies on the implementation of the personalization to learner with learning disabilities, we see that the concept of personalization is ideal to be implemented in the educational field, especially when dealing with the slow learner children who have limited abilities in literacy skills, especially in reading. This study reveals the difference characteristics of the slow learner from the preliminary investigation conducted. Other than that, the concept of the personalization also has a potential in assisting slow learner difference characteristics, variation in reading ability, reading style and needs. In conclusion, apart from that the exploration on the relevant principle, the scaffolding, this study also provides the benefit for the researcher in understanding in depth on the implementation of the personalization which not only require the information technology related strategy or approach, but also need more consideration beyond that which includes an adaptation of other related principles.

References

1. Barua, D., Kay, J., Kummerfeld, B., Paris, C.: Theoretical foundations for user-controlled forgetting inscrutable long term user models. Theoretical foundations for user-controlled forgetting inscrutable long term user models (2011),
   http://dl.acm.org/citation.cfm?id=2071541 (retrieved)
2. Beer, W., Wagner, A.: Smart Books – Adding context-awareness and interaction to electronic books, pp. 5–7 (2011)
3. Brom, C., Bromová, E., Děchtěrenko, F., Buchtová, M., Pergel, M.: Personalized Messages in a Brewery Educational Simulation: Is the Personalization Principle Less Robust than Previously Thought? Computers & Education (2013), doi:10.1016/j.compedu.2013.11.013
4. Colombo, L., Landoni, M.: Towards an engaging e-reading experience. In: Proceedings of the 4th ACM Workshop on Online Books, Complementary Social Media and Crowdsourcing - Books Online 2011, p. 61 (2011), doi:10.1145/2064058.2064074
5. Landoni, M.: Ebooks children would want to read and engage with. In: Proceedings of the Third Workshop on Research Advances in Large Digital Book Repositories and Complementary Media - BooksOnline 2010, p. 25 (2010), doi:10.1145/1871854.1871862
6. Mckay, D.: A jump to the left (and then a step to the right): Reading practices within academic ebooks (2011)
7. Musen, L.: I N D I C AT O R Early Reading Proficiency (May 2010)
8. National Institute for Literacy. Early Literacy: Leading the Way to Success (2007)
9. Siadaty, M.: E-Learning: From a Pedagogical Perspective 6(2), 99–117 (2008)

10. Tsianos, N., Germanakos, P., Lekkas, Z.: Working memory span and e-learning: The effect of personalization techniques on learners' performance. ..., and Personalization (2010),
    http://link.springer.com/chapter/10.1007/978-3-642-13470-8_8 (retrieved)
11. da Vinci, L.: Slow learners, pp. 1–8 (2009)
12. Vygotsky, L.: Thought and Language, trans. A. Kozulin. Harvard University Press, Cambridge (1934/1986)
13. Wilhelm, J., Baker, T., Dube, J.: Strategic Reading. Heinemann, Portsmouth (2001)

A Web Analytics and Visualization Tool to Understand Students' Behavior in an Adaptive E-Learning System

Barbara Moissa, Lucas Simões de Carvalho, and Isabela Gasparini

Department of Computer Science
University of Santa Catarina State (UDESC), Joinville, SC, Brazil
{barbara.moissa,lucas.scarvalho}@gmail.com,
isabela.gasparini@udesc.br

Abstract. Web analytics in the learning environment is the use of intelligent data, learner-produced data, and analysis models to discover information and social connections. This paper describes a web analytics and visualization tool
which collects, analyses and visually represents the data collected in an
e-learning environment. The goal of this tool is allow the teacher to better understand his students' behavior in front of the environment and support the decision making related to the pedagogical content adapted to the students' need.

Keywords: learning analytics, information visualization, adaptive e-learning
system.

1   Introduction

Web Analytics is the measurement, collection, analysis and reporting of internet data
for purposes of understanding and optimizing web usage [5]. It helps to identify popularity trends, to estimate how traffic to a website changes and also provides information about the numbers of visitors and the number of page views.

In the context of e-learning, it is usually named learning analytics, and it helps the
measurement, collection, analysis and reporting of data about learners and their contexts, for purposes of understanding and optimizing learning and the environments in
which it occurs. Web analytics in the learning environment is the use of intelligent
data, learner-produced data, and analysis models to discover information and social
connections. These gathered data can help teachers in discovery and understand students' behavior in their courses, in the collaborative tools provided by the system, and
the system could predict and advise people's learning [10].

One problem faced by teachers who use e-learning environments is to understand
the students' needs. One way to deal with this issue is to collect data about the students' actions and interactions with the e-learning environment and analyze it to gather useful information and to present the best contents adapted to students' needs and
profile.

Although web analytics tools can help teachers discovering students' behaviors and
trails, some tools are difficult to understand and to extract information, because their

P. Zaphiris and A. Ioannou (Eds.): LCT 2014, Part I, LNCS 8523, pp. 312–321, 2014.

diversity of the metrics or their poor usability. Visualization information techniques can be applied in these tools, helping user to understand the data generated. Information visualization (InfoVis) produces visual representations of abstract data to reinforce human cognition; thus enabling the viewer to gain knowledge about the internal structure of the data and causal relationships in it [6].

In this work, we describe a tool for mining and visualizing student's interaction to an adaptive web-based educational system that we have developed in order to help teachers/instructors to discover student's behavior.

This paper is structured as follows. In the section 2 we present the related works. Section 3 introduces the adaptive e-learning system where the tool was integrated. Section 4 presents the functionality of the tool to mine and analyze student's interaction and behavior, how the students' data is collected and the defined metrics. Section 5 describes the visualization tool, how the defined metrics are converted into a graphical and interactive visualization tool and how teachers can benefit from it. In section 6 experimental results obtained are then discussed, showing how the experiment was planned and conducted and also the interpreted results. Finally, in Section 7, conclusions and future work are presented.

2   Related Work

Learning Analytics intends to collect data about and produced by learners in order to use it to enhance education and learners' success. These data can be used in several ways and with several different reasons. The Open Learning Analytics platform [11], for example, is focused in four groups: learners, educators, administrators and researchers. While learners view data regarding their progress in the course, educators view information that can help them to know what has impacted on the learners' engagement; administrators view statistics about the courses and researchers can use this data to discover new information.

While the Open Learning Analytics platform has focus on four distinctive groups, the Student Activity Meter (SAM) [4] focuses only at the learner and the teacher. The tool aids learners to see how they spent their time and also recommend materials to them. In the other hand, teachers can see what and how students are doing, where they are spending more time and which are the most popular materials.

There are also tools as eLAT [1] that focuses only on the teachers and aims to process all the data quickly considering privacy aspects and individual interests. This tool enables teachers to explore and correlate the learning object usage, user character, user behavior and assessment results using a graphical interface and, by doing this, they can reflect and identify opportunities for improvement.

Our proposal has similarities with these works, since we focus on helping teachers to better understand their students' behavior in the system. In the future, we also intend to recommend some action to the teachers (e.g. improve their communication with the students, changes in his navigational paths, etc.) and to the students (e.g. recommendations about their engagement, works and tasks, etc.) based on the learning styles, patterns and behaviors discovered.

3   AdaptWeb

AdaptWeb (Adaptive Web-based learning Environment) is an adaptive e-learning environment whose purpose is to adapt the content, presentation and navigation in an educational Web course, according to the student's profile. Currently, it is an open source environment in operation in different universities. This adaptation is based in the student's profile, such as his knowledge about a certain concept, his navigational preferences and his background. Another feature of the environment is the ability to offer a discipline to more than one course. For example, the same Calculus discipline can be offered to the courses of Computer Science, Electrical Engineering and Civil Engineering with its content properly adapted.

In AdaptWeb, the student has access to three sections: Class Environment, Messages Board and Discussion Forums. Each one of these three sections is part of an offered discipline in a certain course. In other words, the system make available particular content to each profile, e.g., a Calculus student from Computer Science can see, in all the three sections, only the content available for Computer Science students', while an Electrical Engineering student will see only the content available to Electrical Engineering students'.

The discipline's content can be seen in the Class Environment. From this section, the student can obtain access to the concepts, examples, exercises and complementary materials. The student can access this section by two different ways: Tutorial mode or Free mode.

In the Tutorial mode (guided tour), prerequisites criteria among concepts determine the student's navigation, and navigation adaptation is based on the register of concepts studied: every time the same student accesses the web course, the colors of the menu links are restored. In the Free mode, the student can study any concept available in the navigation menu. The colors used follow the usability rules by Nielsen [9], that is, we adopted blue for links that were not accessed (but they are accessible to click), and purple for the accessed ones. For concepts that the student is not allowed to see (tutorial mode) the color of the link is black, and the mouse cannot click on them [2].

In the Messages Board section, the student can see the messages of his course/discipline from the last 30 days. These messages can be from another student or from the teacher, and they can be public or private. Beyond sending a message to the class (students and teacher), the student can also send a message only to the teacher.

Finally, the Discussion Forum section allows students to interact with each other. They can create discussions (topics) about some subject of their interest and get aid to accomplish the exercises or to understand a concept.

4   Collecting and Analyzing Data

Among several existing web analytics tools, the vast majority use the same mechanism for collection and storage of data, usually done through web logs [7]. The data capture is one of the most important web analytics processes. There are two main ways to collect data of user interactions on the sites. The methods are classified in web logs and page tagging [8].

The web logs files are the source of the data access of the sites. They were designed with the goal of recording errors generated by web servers and later evolved to capture data access enabling an analysis not only of technical failures but also of marketing data and user behavior [8].

The second method that collects data from users is the page tagging. The first techniques were to carry an invisible image along with the requested page of a site to detect whether the page had loaded successfully and thereafter send a message to the server with the user information. This technique is also described as page tagging web beacon [7]. The page tagging technique involves adding scripts on each page of the website to capture and log usage statistic of each page in question. These data are collected during page load and usage of the site by the browser. The page tagging approach provides more accurate and complete data for web analytics applications than web logs [5].

The web analytics tool proposed in this paper intends to complement the analysis of student behavior when using the environment. This proposal was implemented through the combination of different metrics, providing more specific analyzes for the teacher. The development of the tool in AdaptWeb was divided into three modules: i) data collection module, ii) data analysis module, and iii) data visualization tool.

The structure of the data collection module consists in the capture and storage of navigation data, clicks, downloaded files, and other forms of students' interactions with the environment. The method of data collection for this study is based on a hybrid model (as shown in Figure 1) using existing data on the environment in the log table in the database and the page tagging technique to capture the data from the student's browser. We had used Piwik page tagging tool for this technique.

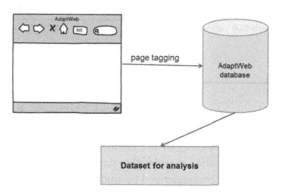

Fig. 1. Hybrid model of data collection

The module collects data from different sources. First it collects data from the AdaptWeb environment, where it reuses the existing logs of the database and then it includes an embodiment of Piwik, an open-source web analytics tool. Piwik helps the capture and storage through page tagging with a JavaScript code embedded in the source code of AdaptWeb' pages. Based on the data collected, the data analysis module was developed considering the metrics defined in Table 1:

Table 1. Metrics of the web analytics tool

Group	*Metric*	*Derived metrics*
General use	Total number of students visiting the e-learning system	Total Visits per student
	Individual access time in each discipline	Students' Average Access time
	Frequency of student access	Frequency of access
	Technological user data	Browsers
		Operation Systems
		Screen Resolutions
	Access time in each section	Total Hits to each section
Class environment	Access time in each section	Navigation Mode
	Concepts	Total Hits to Concepts
	Examples	Total Hits to Examples
	Complementary Materials	Total Hits to Complementary Materials
	Performance of tasks	Total Hits to Exercises
	Internal search	Total Use of The Search Engine
		Keywords searched
Discussion Forum	Participation in the discussion forums	Total Hits to Topics
		Total Topics Created
		Total Answers
Messages Board	Interaction via messages	Total Sent Messages
		Types of Sent Messages
		Total Views

The goal of the data analysis module was to provide metrics for the visualization module and also being flexible and extensible to future work. Its structure can easily be incorporated into other modules of the environment, delivering information in a standardized manner. The metrics are related to data from the environment where they were captured, which can be parameterized by student, teacher, discipline and course.

A total of 20 metrics, according to Table 1, were mapped into the system. These metrics can be queried via a generic function in the web analytics tool library. As a result of this data analysis module, we obtained a set of functions grouped by General Use, Class Environment, Discussion Forum and Messages Board.

5   Visualization Tool

Visualization is the process of transforming data, information and knowledge into visual form making use of humans' natural visual capabilities. In this way, with effective visual interfaces we can interact with large volumes of data rapidly and effectively to discover hidden characteristics, patterns and trends [3].

To provide a way for teachers to find the information they need in a quick and easy way, visualization techniques were also studied and used in the tool to represent the students' data collected according with the metrics established. By using these techniques not only teachers can see the data represented visually, but they can also interact with the tool, and change some aspects of the representation in order to find useful information.

The tool's interface is composed of four areas: (a) filters, (b) metrics selection, (c) chart and (d) detailed information table. In Figure 2 the filter and the metrics selection are shown.

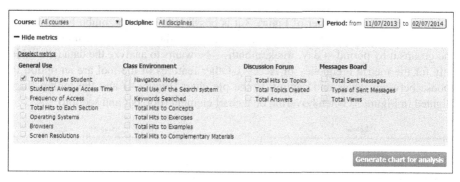

Fig. 2. Filter and metric selection areas

As can be seen in Figure 2, the teacher can filter the data by choosing a course, a discipline and defining a time period (initial and final date - which, if not defined, will be automatically set as the last three months). Another action the teacher can do is choosing the metric(s) he wants to analyze. The metrics available for analysis are listed in the blue area of Figure 2, organized in four categories: General Use, Class Environment, Discussion Forum and Messages Board.

The majority of these metrics can only be analyzed individually, but some metrics can be jointly analyzed: Total Hits to Concepts, Total Hits to Exercises, Total Hits to Examples and Total Hits to Complementary Materials from the Classroom Environment category can be analyzed together; and Total Hits to Topics and Total Answers from the Discussion Forum.

After selecting the metrics, the teacher must press the Generate chart for analysis button and the results will be shown according to Figure 3, below the filter and the metric selection areas.

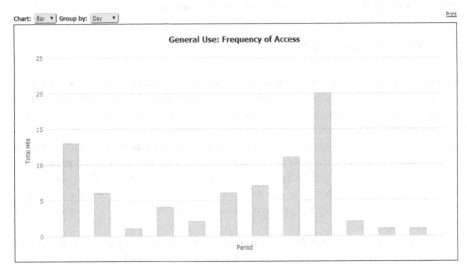

Fig. 3. Graphical results of metric *Frequency of Access*

In the left superior corner of Figure 3 it is possible to see two combo boxes where the teacher can select different graphical patterns for the chart — bar, line or pie — and groups it by period— day, week, month — he wants to analyze the data (available only for the metric Frequency of Access). Other features of the tool are an option to choose between labels and caption to the pie chart (Figure 4) and the tooltip (highlighted in Figure 5) when hovering on a chart element (dot, bar and section).

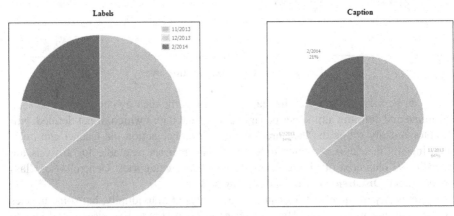

Fig. 4. Pie chart with labels and caption

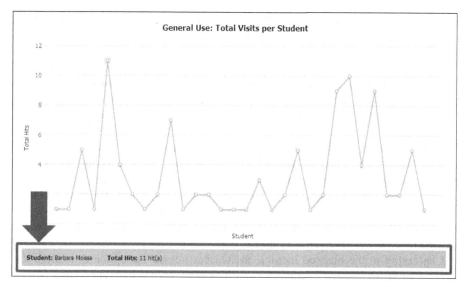

Fig. 5. Tooltip

Finally, the last area of the tool is the detailed information table. This table has a few useful features to help teachers to better understand the values represented such as being manageable and allowing the teacher to sort (ascending and descending) the lines according to the values of a column of his choice and having a filter by keyword to display only the lines that he is really interest. One interesting thing about this table, when analyzing the metric Access Frequency is that the data presented in it changes according to the grouping chosen (i.e. by month, week, or day), this way if it is organized by day, then the table will show the records grouped by day.

This visualization tool has a Help Section and three hyperlinks — located in three different positions of the tool (above the chart, between the chart and the table and below the table) — to redirect the teacher to a print page where he can choose which section he wants to print (i.e. chart, detailed information table or both).

The web analytic tool, composed by the data collection module, the data analysis module, and the data visualization module, was designed and implemented in a real and operational adaptive e-learning environment, namely AdaptWeb.

6   Case Study

We have conducted a case study with the web analytics tool based on a real dataset of undergraduate students of Computer Science and Information Technology. This study involved, at first, the inclusion of our tool in the AdaptWeb's environment placed in the server of University of Santa Catarina State.

After we installed and tested our tool, we invited two teachers to participate in a study case based on their large experience of using e-learning systems. Thus, the data collection tool began monitoring the interaction and behavior of their students.

After a month, we had sufficient data to support different analysis. We invited the teachers to participate in our first usability test. An experiment of observation and analysis with one of the teachers was conducted. In this experiment the developers presented the tool to the teacher and asked him to use it. The teacher could express himself anytime while he was interacting to the tool (beyond the observation, we had used the thinking aloud protocol). After the observation section, the developers discussed the tool with the teacher and understood the challenges and details of the visualization tool.

As the first results, the graphical representations of the metrics were easily understood by the teacher; however he had some difficulties while selecting the metrics because he could not visually distinguish which metrics could be analyzed together and which could not. The teacher needed to be guided to try features such as changing the type of frequency of the *Frequency of Access* (e.g. grouped by month, by week, by day) and the features of the detailed information table, however, after he used it for the first time, he considered it very useful.

Concerning to the mapped metrics, the teacher missed the option to analyze the metric *Frequency of Access* with others such as *Total Hits to Concepts*, *Total Hits to Examples*, *Total Hits to Exercises* and *Total Hits to Complementary Materials*. He also mentioned that a new metric, *Student's Path*, could also be interesting, to visually identify students trails and, perhaps, to change some of his discipline structure.

7   Conclusion and Future Works

In this paper we presented a web analytics and visualization tool to help teachers to understand student´s behavior in an adaptive e-learning environment. This tool consists of three modules: i) data collection module, ii) data analysis module, and iii) data visualization tool, which enables the teacher to visualize and interact to the generated analyzes. Our tool was integrated in the AdaptWeb environment, an adaptive e-learning system used in our university.

We have conducted a case study, tested with data collected from two courses — Computer Science and Information Technology, aiming to identify the prior usability problems related to the visualization tool, and to discover whether the metrics satisfy teacher's needs. The preliminary results demonstrated the importance of well described metrics and filters. Currently we are conducting other experiments, in order to improve our tool.

Future work will include the integration of our web analytic tool with more disciplines from different courses and areas of knowledge. We also plan to enhance our tool with intelligent recommendation support and evaluate its usefulness and usability.

References

1. Dyckhoff, A.L., Zielke, D., Bültmann, M., Chatti, M.A., Schroeder, U.: Design and Implementation of a Learning Analytics Toolkit for Teachers. Educational Technology & Society 15(3), 58–76 (2012)

2. Gasparini, I., Eyharabide, V., Schiaffino, S., Pimenta, M.S., Amandi, A., Palazzo, M., de Oliveira, J.: Improving user profiling for a richer personalization: modeling context in e-learning. In: Graf, S. (ed.), ch. 12, pp. 182–197. IGI Global (2012)
3. Gershon, N., Eick, S.G., Card, S.: Information visualization. Interactions 5(2), 9–15 (1998), http://doi.acm.org/10.1145/274430.274432
4. Govaerts, S., Verbert, K., Duval, E.: Evaluating the student activity meter: Two case studies. In: Leung, H., Popescu, E., Cao, Y., Lau, R.W.H., Nejdl, W. (eds.) ICWL 2011. LNCS, vol. 7048, pp. 188–197. Springer, Heidelberg (2011)
5. Hasan, L., Morris, A., Probets, S.: Using Google Analytics to evaluate the usability of e-commerce sites. In: Kurosu, M. (ed.) HCD 2009. LNCS, vol. 5619, pp. 697–706. Springer, Heidelberg (2009)
6. InfoVisWiki - Information Visualization community platform (2014), http://www.infovis-wiki.net/index.php/ Information_Visualization
7. Jansen, B.J.: Understanding User–Web Interactions via Web Analytics. Morgan & Claypool (2009)
8. Kaushik, A.: Web Analytics: An Hour a Day. Wiley Publishing Inc. (2007)
9. Nielsen, J.: Designing Web Usability: The Practice of Simplicity. New Riders Publishing, Indianapolis (2000)
10. Romero, C., Santos, S.G., Freire, M., Ventura, S.: Mining and Visualizing Visited Trails in Web-Based Educational Systems. In: EDM, pp. 182–196 (2008)
11. Siemens, G., Gasevic, D., Haythornthwaite, C., Dawson, S., Shum, S.B., Ferguson, R., Duval, E., Verbert, K., Baker, R.S.: Open Learning Analytics: an integrated & modularized platform. Proposal to design, implement and evaluate an open platform to integrate heterogeneous learning analytics techniques (2011)

Markov Chain and Classification of Difficulty Levels Enhances the Learning Path in One Digit Multiplication

Behnam Taraghi, Anna Saranti, Martin Ebner, and Martin Schön

Graz University of Technology, Münzgrabenstr. 35/I, 8010 Graz, Austria
{b.taraghi,martin.ebner}@tugraz.at,
s0473056@sbox.tugraz.at, mrtnschn@googlemail.com

Abstract. In this work we focus on a specific application named "1x1 trainer" that has been designed to assist children in primary school to learn one digit multiplications. We investigate the database of learners' answers to the asked questions by applying Markov chain and classification algorithms. The analysis identifies different clusters of one digit multiplication problems in respect to their difficulty for the learners. Next we present and discuss the outcomes of our analysis considering Markov chain of different orders for each question. The results of the analysis influence the learning path for every pupil and offer a personalized recommendation proposal that optimizes the way questions are asked to each pupil individually.

Keywords: Learning Analytics, One digit multiplication, Knowledge discovery, Math, Markov chain, Primary school.

1   Introduction

Generally, recommender algorithms use the implicit data generated through monitoring the users' interactions with the underlying system to understand better the hidden users' preferences. Once the users' interests are known, the system can provide personalized recommendations to the users that best suites their needs and interests.

Recommender systems in e-learning applications follow the same approach [1]. The analysis of chronological user activities or user traces (sometimes called user navigation) helps to provide personalized recommendations to the users [2].

Learning applications in particular can benefit from such an approach too. Duval [3] pointed out that we have to think about learners' traces and their learning efforts. Siemens and Baker [4] defined learning analytics as the measurement, collection, analysis and reporting of data about learners and their contexts, for purposes of understanding and optimizing learning as well as the environments in which it occurs.

Graz University of Technology has been developing math trainers since 2010 with the aim to improve the basic math education for primary schools [5]. First of all the 1x1 trainer [6] was implemented followed by the multi-math-coach [7] as well as the addition / subtraction trainer [8]. All applications can be used for free at the URL: http://mathe.tugraz.at.

P. Zaphiris and A. Ioannou (Eds.): LCT 2014, Part I, LNCS 8523, pp. 322–333, 2014.
© Springer International Publishing Switzerland 2014

In primary school, learning the one digit multiplication table is one of the major goals in the four-year lasting education. The learning problem seems to be trivial at first glance, but by studying the literature several difficulties unfold: Language implications in general [9], the role of math as first non-native language [10], pure "row learning" [11] etc.

Therefore a web-based application was developed which on the one side can assist the learning process of the pupils and on the other side can enhance the pedagogical intervention of the teachers. The full implementation, the intelligent algorithm and the first results are described in [6].

Several educational, pedagogical and psychological surveys classify various pupils' common errors in one digit multiplications. One common finding is the problem size effect [12][13]. Large multiplications such as 9*8 tend to have a higher error rate than smaller ones, such as 2*3. Therefore this set of questions is assumed to be more difficult to learn. [14], predict that errors in simple multiplication are more probable, if they contain the same digit as the correct result. Some studies investigated on easy and difficult groups of questions and denoted patterns of easy questions to learn, such as doubles, times five and square numbers [15, 16, 17]. However we could find no previous work dealing with the problem of one digit multiplication table computationally and analytically.

We have already made a first computational analysis on the provided dataset, using a Markov chain model and classification algorithms, to discover some common structures within the answers of the pupils. These structures help to better understand the pupils' behavior especially when they answer to the set of difficult questions. The results and the analysis are published in [18]. In this paper we present in more detail the clustering algorithm that is used to identify different difficulty classes in one digit multiplication problems. Furthermore, the outcomes of the analysis from our new Markov model are presented and discussed. The results are then used to influence the learning path within the application and hence provide a proposal for basic recommendation of the asked question's sequence.

2   Methodology – Markov Chains

Markov chains are used to model stochastic processes such as navigation models. There are many works investigating on Web navigation and human navigation patterns on World Wide Web such as [19, 20, 21]. Another example is the Random Surfer model in Google's PageRank algorithm that can be seen as a special case of a Markov chain [22], where Web pages are represented as states and hyperlinks as probabilities of navigating from one page to another. In our model the answer types to each question represent the states and the probabilities to the answer type of the subsequent same question in the sequence as transition links between states. In this section we introduce the Markov chains formally.

A finite discrete Markov chain of the first order is a sequence of random variables $X_1, X_2, X_3, \ldots, X_n$ for which the following Markov property holds:

$$P (X_{n+1} = x_{n+1} \mid X_1 = x_1, X_2 = x_2, \ldots, X_n = x_n) = P (X_{n+1} = x_{n+1} \mid X_n = x_n). \quad (1)$$

We assume that the probabilities do not change as a function of time, hence the Markov chains are time-homogeneous.

A Markov chain of order k is described formally as follows:

$$P (X_{n+1} = x_{n+1} \mid X_1 = x_1, X_2 = x_2, X_n = x_n) =$$
$$P (X_{n+1} = x_{n+1} \mid X_n = x_n, X_{n-1} = x_{n-1}, \ldots, X_{n-k+1} = x_{n-k+1}). \quad (2)$$

The Markov chain of first order is characterized as memoryless, meaning that the next state depends only on the current state. Considering the Markov chain of order k, the probability of the next state depends on the k previous states.

The Markov model is represented as a matrix P of all stochastic transition probabilities between the states. Hence for n states, the Matrix P is of size $n*n$. Each row in the matrix represents the stochastic transition probabilities from one state to all the other states. As a result the sum of probabilities within a row is always 1.0.

3   Answer Types

In this paper we perform our analysis on the dataset from the database of "1x1 trainer" application. The application puts each question to the pupils at least two times. Based on whether the submitted answers in the user history are correct or not, the answers for each question are classified into one of six different answer types. If a pupil answers a question for the first time correctly (answer type R that stands for RIGHT), the same question is asked once again later to ensure that the answer is truly known by the pupil. If a question is answered correctly for the second time (answer type RR), the application assumes that the user had already truly known the answer to the asked question. In contrast, if the pupil answers the question incorrectly in the second round (answer type RW) the application keeps asking the same question later on till the pupil answers it correctly (answer type WR). Answer type W (stands for WRONG) implies the first incorrect answer to a question. Answer type WW implies an incorrect answer to a question after a preceding wrong answer.

Table 1 lists these six defined answer types and their definitions. The following example illustrates how the answer types are assigned to each given answer. Assuming the application has asked a pupil the question 9*3 5 times in his history and the pupil's answers have been as follows: 27, 24, 26, 27, 27. The assigned answer types for this set of answers would be: R, RW, WW, WR, RR. The defined answer types build the states of the Markov chain model in our analysis.

Table 1. Six different answer types and their definitions. "R" stands for "Right" and "W" for "Wrong"

Answer type	Definition	Preceding answer	Current answer
R	First correct answer	-	R
W	First wrong answer	-	W
RR	Correct answer given a preceding correct answer	R	R
RW	Wrong answer given a preceding correct answer	R	W
WR	Correct answer given a preceding wrong answer	W	R
WW	Wrong answer given a preceding wrong answer	W	W

4   Difficult Questions

In this section we begin with the analysis of probabilities and reaction times to identify the questions that are most difficult for the pupils. The probabilities of the occurring answer types in the dataset reveal the most difficult questions. To identify the difficult questions most efficiently we divided the dataset to two subsets. The first subset includes only the R and W answer types. These are the questions that are put to the pupils by the application and answered by the pupils for the first time. The goal is to identify the questions that were mostly already known (hence easy) and those that were mostly already unknown (hence difficult) to the pupils before a learning process actually begins within this application. The second subset includes only RW, WR and WW answer types. These are the unknown questions answered by the pupils at least for the second time. The goal is to identify the most difficult as well as easiest questions within this subset of data. These are the questions that the pupils have repeated the most and least times till they got the correct answer.

4.1   Subset of R and W Answer Types

Figures 1 illustrates the questions that are quite easy (known by a high percentage of pupils) and the ones that are rather difficult (unknown by a high percentage of pupils). The 1x1 trainer application provides 90 multiplication problems (1*9 to 10*9), hence 10 rows and 9 columns in the heatmap. The heatmap illustrates that the multiplications where 1, 2, 5, and 10 occur as operands can be classified as easy or most known questions, whereas 3, 4, 6, 7, 8 and 9 as operands build multiplications that can be classified as difficult or most unknown. From the first view it could be inferred that the pupils knew most of the questions beforehand. 7*8 and 6*8 are the first two questions that the most number of pupils have difficulties.

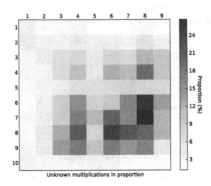

Fig. 1. Heatmap of the asked unknown questions (multiplications) proportionally within the subset of R and W answer types. The rows correspond to the first operand of the multiplication and the columns correspond to the second operand.

If we consider the reaction times consumed by the pupils - especially for the set of known (easy) answers (R answer type) - we can observe that the pupils need more time for the identified difficult unknown questions than for the identified easy ones. Figure 2 illustrates this result in a heatmap. It shows the average time consumption for each question individually from the set of known questions. This observation confirms our results about the identified difficult and easy questions.

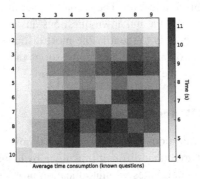

Fig. 2. Heatmap of the average time consumption from the set of asked known questions (multiplications) within the subset of R and W answer types. The rows correspond to the first ope and of the multiplication and the columns correspond to the second operand.

4.2   Subset of RW, WR and WW Answer Types

Figure 3 illustrates the histogram of the 30 most difficult questions within this subset. 6*8 and 7*8 are again the first two questions that have the highest probabilities. Figure 4 is a heatmap that illustrates the questions that are quite easy to learn (low probabilities) and the ones that are rather difficult (high probabilities). It is can be seen again that the multiplications where 1, 2, 5, and 10 occur as operands can be classified as easy to learn questions whereas 3, 4, 6, 7, 8 and 9 as operands build multiplications that can be classified as difficult.

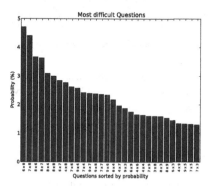

Fig. 3. Histogram of the most 30 difficult questions within the subset of RW, WR and WW answer types.

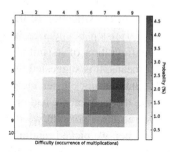

Fig. 4. Heatmap of the probabilities of questions (multiplications) within the subset of RW, WR and WW answer types. The rows correspond to the first operand of the multiplication and the columns correspond to the second operand.

Considering the reaction times within this subset for correct answers (WR answer types) we can observe the same results as we did in the first subset (R and W answer types). Figure 5 illustrates this result in a heatmap. It shows the average time consumption for each question individually from the set of correct answers (WR answer type). This observation reinforces our beliefs about the identified difficult and easy questions.

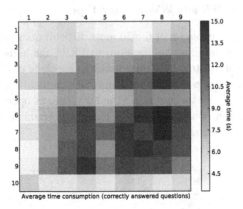

Average time consumption (correctly answered questions)

Fig. 5. Heatmap of the average time consumption from the set of correct answered question (multiplications) within the subset of RW, WR and WW answer types. The rows correspond to the first operand of the multiplication and the columns correspond to the second operand.

5   Classification of Questions

The goal is to classify the questions into different difficulty levels. The categorization bases on one dimensional data that represent the occurrence probabilities of answer types within the observed dataset. Beginning with the hypothesis that there are three difficulty levels, we used the k-means algorithm [23] to compute the three clusters.

Figure 6 shows one possible hard classification of the data. Each data point is assigned to a specific cluster; the decision boundaries between them are linear. The algorithm is sensitive to the configuration of its initial iteration i.e. the assumption about the position of the cluster means. It is suggested that one runs the k-means algorithms several times with different starting cluster means (usually randomly chosen samples from the dataset). Due to the fact that we had prior knowledge and interpretation for our data, each time we ran the algorithm we divided the sample's values in three equal intervals. In a second step we picked randomly a sample (that had a value in a particular interval) to be the initial mean point of its corresponding cluster. Different runs in our training data reveal that the number of questions that are classified as difficult varies between four to eight. Figure 6 shows the first difficulty level identified by 3-means algorithm. It contains eight questions that own the highest probabilities within the dataset. The second difficulty level contains twenty two questions. The biggest cluster contains the set of easiest questions involving sixty questions with the least probabilities.

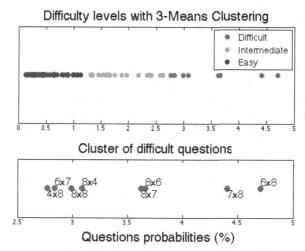

Fig. 6. Clusters representing the difficulties of questions as computed by the 3-means algorithm. The upper figure demonstrates the three identified difficulty levels. The lower figure shows the questions within the first level difficulty cluster.

In a second step we tried to identify the optimal number of clusters that best classifies one digit multiplication questions with respect to their difficulty. We ran the k-means algorithm using different number of clusters. The choice of the initial mean of each cluster was made in the same manner as in the three clusters case. Due to the fact that our training data contain only ninety samples and we don't have a test set, we used k-fold cross-validation to provide an estimate of the test error [24]. The quality measure that was used to indicate a potential improvement in our choice between different number of clusters was the averaged cumulative distance. The algorithm stops when the cumulative distance converges to prevent overfitting. The algorithm suggests that the optimal number of clusters is six. The cluster representing the most difficult problems contains 4 questions (level one) followed by 10 questions in level two.

Figure 7 illustrates the six identified difficulty levels.

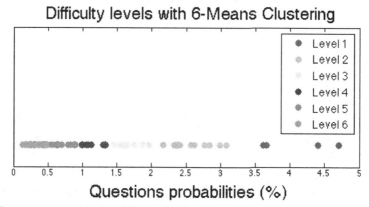

Fig. 7. Clusters representing the difficulty levels of questions as computed by the 6-means algorithm.

6   Markov Chain Analysis

In our Markov chain model the answer types to each question represent the states. The probability to the answer type of the subsequent same question in the sequence characterizes the transition link between these states. In other words, for each of the ninety questions we apply our Markov chain model individually.

Figure 8 illustrates the three dimensional plot of the Markov chain of six orders and all questions. For k >=2 the plots show the portion of each last (k-th) answer type for each question individually. As expected, most of the pupils answer the questions correctly once they get the questions for the first time. This can be observed in the first plot (high proportion of answer type R for k = 1). In the second round (k = 2) the majority of answer types are RR, which means that the pupils mostly answer correctly once they get the same question for the second time. The proportion of R and W answer types comes to 0% while k >=2. This is in accordance with our definition of R and W answer types. They imply the correct and wrong answers to a question for the first time (without any preceding answer). A common observation over all questions is that the proportion of answer type RW decreases whereas the proportion of answer types WR and WW increases in k >=4. This occurs because a question that is asked repeatedly (ascending k) has a higher probability of not being answered correctly in the past (preceding steps). Looking precisely to each question individually we can observe a remarkable difference in the proportion of k-th answer type in different difficulty levels. This proportion value acts as a measure in our recommendation proposal to weight each question depending on k (the step in which the application must decide which question to put as next).

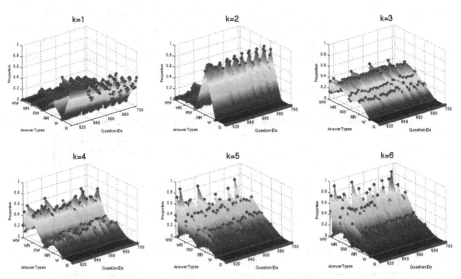

Fig. 8. Markov chains of all questions for k = 1 to 6. The x axis represents the question ids. The y axis represents the last (k-th) answer type within the chain of the length k. The z axis represents the proportion of last (k-th) answer type for each question and order k.

7   Future Work

The goal of our research was to develop applications for basic math education, which allow individualized learning. Each child should be assisted on its own and personal way. The data analyses presented in this publication will help to improve the application in two different ways: the current empirical estimated difficulties of the question have to be adapted to the difficulty levels we have identified through this work. Assuming a pupil answers the question X from the difficulty level n correctly. The next question (Y) should be selected from the difficulty level m whereas either m=n (the same) or m=n+1 (the next higher difficulty level n+1). If a pupil answers the question X from the difficulty level n incorrectly, the next question (Y) should be selected from the difficulty level m whereas either m=n (the same) or m=n-1 (the preceding lower difficulty level n-1). The proportion measure p from the analysis of Markov chains introduced in this work will be used as selection criterion from the set of new difficulty level m. For each candidate question Y within the set of difficulty level m and step k (the k-th time the pupil will answer to the question Y) the question Y that owns the highest proportion rate referring to answer type WR or RR will be selected. The chosen answer type depends on the preceding answer type (W or R for step k-1) to that question (Y).

8   Conclusion

In this work we analyzed the dataset from "1x1 trainer" application that was designed for primary school children to learn one-digit multiplications. We identified the easiest and the most difficult questions by looking through the probabilities of different answer types of the pupils in two different subsets. The reaction time of the pupils for answering the questions was also taken into consideration. The result from both data sets was almost the same. The multiplications where 1, 2, 5, and 10 occur as operands can be classified as easy to learn, whereas 3, 4, 6, 9, and especially 7, 8 operands build multiplications that can be classified as difficult. We classified the questions into three difficulty levels (difficult, intermediate and easy) using k-means algorithm. We gained eight difficult, twenty two intermediate and sixty easy questions totally. The identified class of difficult questions contains the following eight multiplications: 6*8, 7*8, 8*6, 8*7, 8*4, 8*8, 6*7 and 4*8. As can be seen, the difficult set is characterized mainly by the operand 8.

Next we identified an optimal number of clusters that best classifies one digit multiplication questions in respect to their difficulty. The algorithm suggests that six clusters can optimally represent the different difficulty levels of the questions.

Our Markov model analysis for each question leads to a measure that can be used in the recommendation proposal to improve the question selection algorithm in the application.

References

1. Linton, F., Schaefer, H.P.: Recommender systems for learning: Building user and expert models through long-term observation of application use. User Modeling and User-Adapted Interaction 10, 181–207 (2000)
2. Taraghi, B., Grossegger, M., Ebner, M., Holzinger, A.: Web Analytics of user path tracing and a novel algorithm for generating recommendations in Open Journal Systems. Online Information Review 37(5), 672–691 (2013)
3. Duval, E.: Attention Please! Learning Analytics for Visualization and Recommendation. In: Proceedings of LAK 2011: 1st International Conference on Learning Analytics and Knowledge (2011)
4. Siemens, G., Baker, R.S.J.: Learning Analytics and Educational Data Mining: Towards Communication and Collaboration. In: LAK 2012 Proceedings of the 2nd International Conference on Learning Analytics and Knowledge, pp. 252–254 (2012)
5. Ebner, M., Schön, M.: Why Learning Analytics in Primary Education Matters! Bulletin of the Technical Committee on Learning Technology 15(2), 14–17 (2013); Karagiannidis, C., Graf, S. (eds.)
6. Schön, M., Ebner, M., Kothmeier, G.: It's Just About Learning the Multiplication Table. In: Shum, S.B., Gasevic, D., Ferguson, R. (eds.) Proceedings of the 2nd International Conference on Learning Analytics and Knowledge (LAK 2012), pp. 73–81. ACM, New York (2012), doi:10.1145/2330601.2330624
7. Ebner, M., Schön, M., Taraghi, B., Steyrer, M.: Teachers Little Helper: Multi-Math-Coach. In: Nunes, M.B., McPherson, M. (eds.) Proceedings of the IADIS International Conference e-Learning 2013, pp. 183–190. IADIS Press, Prague (2013)
8. Ebner, M., Schön, M., Neuhold, B.: Learning Analytics in basic math education – first results from the field. eLearning Papers 36, 24–27 (2014)
9. Gerster, H.D.: Schwierigkeiten bei der Entwicklung arithmetischer Konzepte im Zahlenraum bis 100. In: Fritz, A., Ricken, G., Schmidt, S. (eds.) Rechenschwäche. Lernwege, Schwierigkeiten und Hilfen bei Dyskalkulie, pp. 248–268. Beltz, Weinheim (2009)
10. Landerl, K., Butterworth, B., Lorenz, J.H., Möderl, K.: Rechenschwäche - Rechenstörung - Dyskalkulie: Erkennung - Prävention – Förderung. Leykam, Graz (2003)
11. Fuson, K.C.: Using a base-ten blocks learning/teaching approach for first- and second-grade- place-value and multidigit addition and subtraction. Journal for Research in Mathematics Education 21(3), 180–206 (1990),
    http://webschoolpro.com/home/projectlead/Research%
    20Articles%20and%20links/Base%20Ten%20Blocks.pdf
12. Geary, D.C., Widaman, K.F., Little, T.D.: Cognitive addition and multiplication: Evidence for a single memory network. Memory & Cognition 14, 478–487 (1986)
13. Stazyk, E.H., Ashcraft, M.H., Hamann, M.S.: A network approach to mental multiplication. Journal of Experimental Psychology: Learning, Memory, & Cognition 8, 320–335 (1982)
14. Verguts, T., Fias, W.: Neighbourhood effects in mental arithmetic. Psychology Science 47, 132–140 (2005)
15. Chambers, D.: Direct modeling and invented procedures: Building on children's informal strategies. Teaching Children Mathematics 3, 92–95 (1996)
16. Garnett, K.: Developing fluency with basic number facts: Intervention for students with learning disabilities. Learning Disabilities Research & Practice 7, 210–216 (1992)
17. Thornton, C.: Strategies for the basic facts. In: Payne, J. (ed.) Mathematics for the Young Child, pp. 133–151. National Council of Teachers of Mathematics, Reston (1990)

18. Taraghi, B., Ebner, M., Saranti, A., Schön, M.: On Using Markov Chain to Evidence the Learning Structures and Difficulty Levels of One Digit Multiplication. In: Proceedings of the 4nd International Conference on Learning Analytics and Knowledge, Indianapolis, USA, pp. 68–72 (in print, 2014)

19. Brin, S., Page, L.: The anatomy of a large-scale hypertextual web search engine. In: Proceedings of the Seventh International Conference on World Wide Web 7, WWW7, pp. 107–117. Elsevier Science Publishers B. V., Amsterdam (1998)

20. Deshpande, M., Karypis, G.: Selective Markov models for predicting web page accesses. ACM Trans. Internet Technol. 4(2), 163–184 (2004)

21. Lempel, R., Moran, S.: The stochastic approach for link-structure analysis (salsa) and the tkc effect. Comput. Netw. 33(1-6), 387–401 (2000)

22. Borges, J., Levene, M.: Evaluating variable-length Markov chain models for analysis of user web navigation sessions. IEEE Trans. on Knowl. And Data Eng. 19(4), 441–452 (2007)

23. Bishop, C.: Pattern Recognition and Machine Learning, pp. 424–430. Springer Science and Business Media, LLC, New York (2006)

24. Bishop, C.: Pattern Recognition and Machine Learning, pp. 32–33. Springer Science and Business Media, LLC, New York (2006)

The Emotion Component on Usability Testing Human Computer Interface of an Inclusive Learning Management System

Vânia R. Ulbricht, Carlos Henrique Berg, Luciane Fadel, and Silvia R.P. Quevedo

Campus Universitário Reitor João David Ferreira Lima
Florianópolis, Santa Catarina, Brasil, 88040-900
{vrulbricht,liefadel}@gmail.com, henrique.berg@terra.com.br,
silviareginaquevedo@hotmail.com

Abstract. Learning Management Systems –LMS supported by the Information and Communication Technologies to distribute knowledge at any time and to any place, to most different kind of people with different backgrounds. Human Computer Interface – HCI, use known metaphors that makes the mediation between human and machine. Because humans define the metaphors, final users can find some barriers to the comprehension of them. To evaluate LMS's HCI, there are few paradigms available, but the only one who uses final users is the Usability Test – UT. These tests focus on evaluate the efficiency and efficacy of an interface, but seldom evaluate the user's emotions. In order to do that, new researches point out the importance of having the emotions evaluated. This paper aims to describe methods and techniques used to evaluate HCI using Usability Tests UT with emotions and validate one of them in the WebGD LMS at http://egc.ufsc.br/webgd/login/index.php.

Keywords: Learning Management System, Human Computer Interface, Usability Tests with Emotion.

1 Introduction

1.1 Research Problem

Communities of people with some kind of impairment use the Word Wide Web – WWW for information, knowledge, education, leisure and so on, and these impairments must be considered during the designing of an LMS. To allow these communities to use the WWW, and its benefits the Human Computer Interface - HCI must be accessible, and identifying barriers to the accessibility is an important issue. For that purpose the HCI Evaluations can be used.

Some authors argue that are four mainly evaluation paradigms. Nielsen and other researches (1990, 1993, 1995, 2007) [7, 8, 9, 4], establish these four paradigms as Computing Procedures, Heuristic Evaluations, Inspections with Experts and Usability Tests. The Usability Tests – UT are the only one that can beapplied with users and

P. Zaphiris and A. Ioannou (Eds.): LCT 2014, Part I, LNCS 8523, pp. 334–345, 2014.

can be a powerful tool to find more about the possible problems of the interface and lead? to new findings.

Traditional UT are based on techniques of measurement with timing and errors logs to establish the performance of an user. In addition, concomitantly, researchers apply satisfaction queries and take notes during the evaluation. The results from a traditional UT are statistics evaluation from the measure of timing and errors which can be analyzed by a subjective human focus. Furthermore, analyze the query and researcher notes are made with the same subjective focus.

In a Systematic Review of Literature (BERG, 2013) [3], Agarwal and Meyer [1] show that the emotions have important issues in the central questions for HCI. For example, these authors claim that the human being is more efficient and creative in solve a problem when they are happy. Sauer e Sonderegger (2008) [12] add to the discourse the concepts of joy, pleasure, fun and the satisfaction of the finished task, which also must be included in the HCI issues. Tzvetanova, Tang, e Justice (2007) [16] declare that positive emotions affect the memory, motivation and the feeling with the commitment.

These findings lead the researchers to theorize that using emotions to evaluate HCIs can improve its accessibility. Then, in another Systematic Review of Literature (BERG, DATA) [3], seeking for UTs that use emotions found some methods and technics in which can evaluate HCI, as the section 1.2 Methodology explains.

1.2   Methodology

This paper uses a Mixed Method approach (quantitative and qualitative research methods) as recommended by Creswell (2003). This approach considers using a combination of the two techniques to support reliance to the research, as the result of one might validates the second group of results and vice versa. In order to do so, the research will use systematic reviews as recommended by Cochrane Collaboration, (COCHRANE COLLABORATION, 2013) [14]. The systematic review allows identifying the most relevant articles about some theme using indexed articles data banks. The articles data banks used were Scopus and Web of Knowledge.

The results of the review lead to the second step which is to choose one UT This was done by evaluating and comparing each UT to the other. The selection focused on the cheaper and faster method. This was necessary because of a low budget and just few researchers were available.

The research was planned using the DECIDE framework (PREECE, ROGERS and SHARP, 2002) [11] which is a helpful tool to plan Social Science researche. After the planning, the UT will be applied in the WebGD LMS with deaf and hearing subjects to validate the UT and evaluate the LMS

The results of the validation of the UT and the HCI evaluation will be present using descriptive narratives and with the support of a data miner, to cluster using a K-Means algorithm and with graphic representations by density. The final regards will trace two conclusions: if the UT works, if the HCI of the LMS WebGD is accessible.

1.3   WebGD Learning Management System Accessible

There are needs to allow the access of the blind and deaf people in the internet. Then, researchers from the Federal University of Santa Catarina – Brazil, are developing a Learning Management System accessible to blind, deaf and hearing people. Named WebGD the LMS has contents of Descriptive Geometry and is supported by Moodle (moodle.org, 2013) [6]. The LMS was created using the Universal Design, and by using rules and recommendations following the W3C (w3c.org, 2014) [18]. Fig. 1 shows the WebGD home page.

Fig. 1. Print Screen from the WebGD main entrance
egc.ufsc.br/webgd, 2013

The environment WebGD was positive evaluated by different evaluation paradigms, by expert inspections, computing procedures and traditional usability test. The results of the evaluations could identify some barriers, and the researches could fix them. The next step is to improve accessibility.

2   Systematic Review

Considered with great scientific importance, a systematic review is one of the methods used in most publications of a scientific nature in different areas (SCIVERSE SCOPUS, 2012) [13]. Then, to make the systematic review in Scopus and Web of Knowledge (THOMSON REUTERS, 2013) [15] the review use five words combinations: usability, "emotional design", "human computer interface", "interface usability" and "emotional design".

The constrictions that were made were two: articles with CAPES imprint and by relevancy. In Brazil, there is the CAPES (Coordination for the Improvement of Stricto Sensus High Grade Personal) which has an agreement with international publications to give free access to the Brazilian researchers. By this way, a research done with this endorsement can be traceable and is possible to confirm the research. Choosing the articles signed by CAPES, the result is 19 papers.

The second is to rank the results from the most relevant to less relevant, by the newest to the oldest and by number of citations and extract the five first one from relevancy, date and citations, resulting in eight most relevant articles. The table 1 shows the title, first author and year of publication.

Table 1. Titles, first author and publication year

Title	#1 author	Year
Beyond usability: Evaluating emotional response as an integral part of the user experience	Anshu Agarwal	2009
Designers of different cognitive styles editing e-learning materials studied by monitoring physiological and other data simultaneously	Károly Hercegf	2009
How is it for you? (A case for recognizing user motivation in the design process)	Shane Walker	2008
Interactive graphics for expressing health risks: Development and qualitative evaluation	Jessica S. Ancker	2009
Mobility, emotion, and universality in future collaboration	Thomas Kleinberger	2007
Participatory design with children in the development of a support system for patient centered care in pediatric oncology	Cornelia M. Ruland	2008
Virtual reality exposure therapy: 150-Degree screen to desktop PC	Jennifer Tichon	2006
Emotional Web Usability Evaluation	Sylvia Tzvetanova	2007

Font: BERG, 2013

2.1   The Influence of the Emotion on Usability

By reviewing the articles, it was possible to identify some concepts about the influence of the emotions on usability. From Agarwal [1], they affirm that humans have qualitative emotions experiences when they use a product or an interface. These emotions are central when users judge the totality of the experience and this can affect the perception of the usability [1]. Researches demonstrate that the motivated users have less anxiety, more perception of your self-efficacy and have more positive attitude when using software (WALKER; PRYTHERCH, 2008) [17].

Developing interfaces with more positive emotional responses is a necessity to the accessibility and achieving this requires that models must bring more friendly interface, becoming as near as humans communicate with each other (TZVETANOVA; TANG; JUSTICE, 2007) [16]. The cognitive theory proposed by Ortony, Clore e Collins (in TZVETANOVA; TANG; JUSTICE, 2007) [16] define emotions as reactions with positive and negative valences to situations as events, actors and objects. Similarly, Ancker, Chan e Kukafka (2012) [2] describe emotional responses as positive, negative or mixed valences (ANCKER; CHAN, e KUKAFKA, 2012) [2]. Tzvetanova; Tang; Justice (2007) [16], affirm that the adaptive interfaces has more positive emotions valence then others.

This research identifies also, some usability test to evaluate interfaces with emotion component. The usability test include verbal and nonverbal technics and psychological metrics (AGARWAL; MEYER, 2009) [1]. Verbal methods consist of self-report, notes from testimonies (AGARWAL; MEYER, 2009) [1] and questionnaires in which the users give personal impressions with their own words (TZVETANOVA; TANG; JUSTICE, 2007) [16]. Just Agarwal e Meyer (2009) [1] do not use questionnaires, the rest of authors cited the questionnaires as use full tool. These techniques have a limitation: the dependence of the language, detain a transcultural use (AGARWAL; MEYER, 2009) [1].

More common nonverbal metrics include visual representation of the emotions that characterize feelings, like for example facial expressions. (AGARWAL; MEYER, 2009) [1]. Psychological metrics compare heartbeats with skin resistivity. (HERCEGFI et al., 2009) [5]. The advantage of this nonverbal approach is that the user do not need to use cognitive effort, and the responses can be more near to user though. The table 2 show the identified tests for HCI evaluation with emotions.

Table 2. Tests, resume, kind and authors identified

Test	Description	Type	Authors
PAD Semantic Scale	measure three important emotion aspects: pleasure, excitation and domain	Verbal	Agarwal e Meyer, 2009
Emocard	consist in the selection of *emoticons* using two different emotions dimensions	Nonverbal	Agarwal e Meyer, 2009
INTERFACE	investigate simultaneously heartbeats and skin resistivity when changing moods	Psychological	Hercegfi et al., 2009
SISOM	self-reporting on symptoms and management	Verbal	Ruland, Starren e Vatne, 2007
VRET	allow the recreation of an anxiety situation, which evocate a similar emotional response as the in live therapy	Verbal	Tichon e Banks, 2006

BERG, 2013

The next section, DECIDE Framework, the work will define which one will be used in the research.

3   DECIDE Framework

As proposed in the methodology, this research will use the DECIDE framework, a helpful tool to plan social researches. DECIDE was suggested by Preece, Rogers e Sharp (2002) [11], and is the acronyms of Determinate, Explore, Choose, Identify, Decide and Evaluate.

Determinate Goals. The goal is test the WebGD LMS with deaf and hearing people using Usability Test (UT) with emotion component to identify for accessibility barriers.

Explore the Questions. The Web Accessibility Initiative (WAI, 2013) defines four characteristics of a website: perceptible, operable, understandable and robust. This paper will try to identify the perceptible characteristic of the WebGD LMS. The main question to evaluate is related to the emotional valences from WebGD's interface, and the questions of this research is about design and colors. The questions are:

- *What did you feel about the colors of the environment?*
- *What did you feel about the design of the environment?*

3.1   Choose the Evaluation Paradigm

The PAD Semantic Differential Scale, SISOM and VRET tests use verbal approaches (BERG, 2013) [3]. Verbal approaches means that a language is used, and language is one of the form that humans can try to represent one idea. In addition, languages imply in observe some codes, rules, and it is embodied of moral and ethics. Throughout this, to use language implies in some cognitive effort, to convert ideas to language, the human must search in your mind the rules, codes, moral and ethics to express yourself.

By the other hand, the EMOCARD and the INTERFACE (Integrated Evaluation and Research e Facilities for Assessing Computer-users' Efficiency) are nonverbal methods. EMOCARD consist in the selection of one emoticon in a chart, with two important emotions aspects: „pleasantness" and „arousal". The INTERFACE investigate psycho physiologic behavior by crossing heartbeats and skin resistivity on line to identify mental efforts. This nonverbal approach don't uses verbal constructions and by this way, it avoids the cognitive effort on translating the idea in language, bringing up a more internal response, without rules, codes, morals and ethics.

Then, in the research, it would be used the nonverbal approach, to allow to the user to express. The INTERFACE require specific and expansive equipment, and an expert to do the investigation process. As the research has low budget and a few participants, this tool could not be used. Otherwise, the EMOCARD tool offer simplicity, do not need any expensive cost, and can be done with two or three experts. Because of that, the research will use the EMOCARD to evaluate the WebGD LMS.

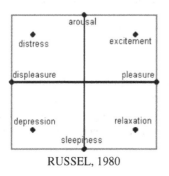 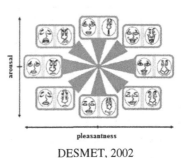

RUSSEL, 1980   DESMET, 2002

Fig. 2. Russell's Circumflex of Affect   **Fig. 3.** EMOCARD

Emocard. The EMOCARD, was developed by Desmet (2003) [4] and consist in the selections of drawing faces expressing emotions between two emotional aspects: „pleasantness" and „arousal" (AGARWAL; MEYER, 2009) [1], allowing nonverbal evaluation. The EMOCARD was developed based on 1980 Russell's circumflex of affect, in Fig 2. Desmet (2003) [4] developed a nonverbal self-report method in the aim to identify emotions in products or interfaces and call them EMOCARD. This method is based in a chart, with drawings of eight human faces, each one representing one emotion. The drawings allow evaluating the valences felt during a HCI use, Fig. 3 shows the Desmet's EMOCARD. At this point, the research has defined the Usability

Test EMOCARD that uses emotion to evaluate Human Computer Interface in Learning Management System accessible WebGD. The decision afetr identifying methods using a systematic review, selecting nonverbal methods to avoid cognitive effort and, finally, selecting in accordance to the restrictions of research the EMOCARD DESMET, 2003 [4].

3.2   Identify the Practical Issues

Two practical issues will be considered here, the first one is related to the timing and de second one is define the research subjects.

Timing. The timing will use five weeks since the subject definition to the results. The table 3 shows the stages and the dates of the research

Research Subjects. To choose the research subjects, the characteristics shall be balanced as in gender, as deaf and hearing people to make reliable comparisons. The deaf people selected must know the LIBRAS (Brazilian Sign Language) because the LMS has LIBRAS contents, and this have to be evaluated.

Table 3. Timing chart

Action	2013				
	JAN		FEV		
	15 – 22	23 – 31	1 – 7	8 – 15	16 – 23
Identification of the research subjects	X				
Scheduling the research subjects	X				
Research		X	X		
Data tabulation			X		
Data analyses				X	
Results					X

BERG, 2013

About the skills of the research subjects, all of them, must be experienced in internet navigation, as Nielsen e Loranger (2007) [10] premises. This is the use of the internet for more than four years, more than ten hours by week and have a third of internet advanced behaviors: chat use, change favorite names, update browsers, create their own homepages and follow technologies trends.

Table 4. Research Subjects

Type	Gender	
	Man	Woman
Deaf	3	3
Hearing	3	3

BERG 2013

To determinate the amount of research subjects it was considered the recommendations from several authors. Preece, Rogers e Sharp (2002) [11], recommended six or seven subjects. Dumas e Redish (1999) [8], claim the ideal amount varies since five to twelve subjects. The reasons to choose this amount is the low budget (NIELSEN e LORANGER, 2007) [10], timing (PREECE, ROGERS e SHARP, 2007) [11], as well as avoid repeating of the results (NIELSEN e LORANGER, 2007) [5]. Because of these recommendations, twelve research subjects was choose as table 4 show.

Then, it was choose twelve research subjects, six deaf and six hearing people, from the both genders and with high internet skills.

3.3   Deciding How to Deal with the Ethics

The first ethic issue is about the anonymity of the subjects. No one was identified by personal data or social questions as religion, ethnics or political affiliation, just by the profile. The second issue, researchers make the subjects know that is the environment is in evaluation and not them. The third issue is that the answers could not identify the subject.

3.4   Evaluating

The last DECIDE step is to apply the research. To evaluate the Human Computer Interface - HCI of the Learning Management System - WebGD LMS accessible the subjects could navigate in the environment to do be familiar with. After this familiarization it was asked to answer the two questions. The answers should be signed in the EMOCARD. At the end of the research, the EMOCARD was collected and the subjects were dismissed. The EMOCARDS with the answers are tabulated and prepared for analysis.

4   Results and Comments

After the evaluation, the tabulation was made and in this section the data will be analyzed. The questions "What did you feel about the colors of the environment?" and "What did you feel about the design of the environment?" was answered signing in the EMOCARD the emotion felt. All twelve-research subjects had answered the two questions. The first analyze is the general results, in which the figure 4 show.

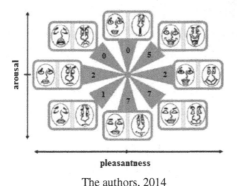

The authors, 2014

Fig. 4. General Results of the reseach

The two emotions more signed was relaxation and sleepiness, both with seven signs (29%). The excitement was five times signed (20%), pleasure and displeasure was two times signed (9%) and depression was one time signed (4%). No one of the subjects has signed arousal and distress emotions. As general result, the positive valences domain the WebGD HCI.

4.1   Analyzing Questions

The analysis of each question shows different results. To do this analysis it was used The Rapid Miner to process the data and generate a specific kind of representation. The data was tabulated in the Microsoft Excel and mining to do a clusterization of them. This clusterization allows to generate a nonusual graphic representation and was elaborated using three steps, using the following tools: Read Excel, Select Attribute and Clustering with K-Means. In this paper the authors will not try to explain all functions of the Rapider Miner, just the procedures.

After the execution of the clustering process it was chosen the density graphic representation. This density graphic representation allows the visualization of the clusters and the inter-relationship among the results. This algorithm uses color density and it is quite simple: each data point contributes to all pixels depending on the distance of the pixel data point. The color is calculated as distance – average weight of all points of each pixel, showing the dependency between the three dimensions of a cluster.

Color Results Analyzes. The answers of the question "What did you feel about the colors of the environment?" were analyzed and identified the most signed emotion as the sleepiness. Relaxation and excitement was three times signed, depression and displeasure was signed once. None of the research subjects has signed distress, arousal and pleasure. The dominant emotions as suggest this result are neutral to positive balanced. Processing the data in the data miner, after clustering the results, was generating the color density graphic representation as shown in fig. 5.

The authors, 2014

Fig. 5. Color density graphic representation from the question "What did you feel about the colors of the environment?

This color density graphic representation can give new interpretation of the results. The process has allocated the answers valenced as positive, negative or neutral. The positive valences are the blue color, the red is neutral and the green color is negative. In this case, the predominant color is green, that represent the negative valences. As can be seen at the figure 5, the blue color (positive valences) and the red color (neutral valences) have smaller area then the green color. Therefore, the question about the colors from the WebGD, regarding this graphic representation using color density, lead to the conclusion that the Human Computer Interface of the Learning Management System has negative valences.

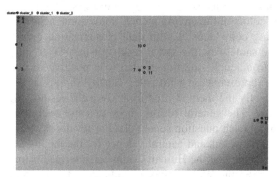

The authors, 2014

Fig. 6. Color density graphic representation from the question "What did you feel about the design of the environment?"

Feeling Result Analyzes. The answers for the question "What did you feel about the design of the environment" show the most signed emotion as the relaxation with four signs, de second one was sleepiness three times signed. Pleasure and excitation was signed two times and displeasure was signed once. None of the research subjects has signed distress, depress and arousal. this result suggest that the dominant emotions are positive to neutral balanced. After processing of the data, it was also generated the color density graphic representation as shown in figure 6.

In this turn, the clustering process and the color density graphic representation define different colors. The blue color is still representing the positive valences, but the green color concentrate now the neutral valences and the red area the negative valences. In this graphic representation, the predominant area is the green – neutral valences, and the smaller areas, blue and red, the negative and positive valences.

5   Final Regards

This paper has presented a research of Usability Test it's use to evaluate some designs questions from the WebGD LMS, an accessible Learning Management System, created to teach descriptive geometry to people with hearing and visual impairment, and people without impairment. The research identified, through a Systematic Review of the Literature, five Usability Tests that use emotional responses. To select one tool to do the evaluation, verbal methods was discarded because they require some cognitive effort. Then, the INTERFACE and the EMOCARD, as nonverbal methods, were examined and it was chosen the EMOCARD because it is fast to use and need few resources. The planning of the evaluation was made with the DECIDE framework following the Preece, Rogers and Sharp (2002) [11] recommendations, where was defined practical issues about the objective, questions, timing, research subjects, evaluation paradigm and ethical questions. The evaluation was performed and all of the twelve research subjects answered the two research questions about color and feelings from the WebGD's interface.

In the first moment the analysis the rough numbers from the question "What did you feel about the colors of the environment?" show some neutral – positive valences, but, the result using color density with data clusterization give a negative valence perspective. As the same way, the initial results of the "What did you feel about the design of the environment?" question leaded to a positive to neutral valences, but, again, the graphic representation with color density show that the LMS has neutral feelings. Independently the method used to analyze the results, the environment was valenced differently. The general results show that the overall HCI is positive valence, but, looking in each question separately, the results show that the environment is negative valance for colors and neutral valence for the feeling about the HCI. Then, it is possible to conclude that the Human Computer Interface from the Learning Management System accessible WebGD has some barriers to the accessibility in the colors with the negative valence and the feeling with neutral valence.

Detecting these barriers leaded the developers to create a new proposition, beyond the rules and recommendations. At this time the developers and designers considered the human emotion to build a new HCI. Figures 7 show the new lay out of the front page of the WebGD LMS.

Silvia Quevedo, 2013 (Videobes)

Fig. 7. New WebGD Interface

The developers of the WebGD LMS now are implementing this recomendations. This paper showed how evaluating a Human Computer Interface can give new solutions from HCI problems. In the next step of the research is to set a new evaluation process in the new interface in the aim to validate it.

References

1. Agarwal, A., Meyer, A.: Beyond Usability: Evaluating Emotional Response as an Integral Part of the User Experience. In: CHI 2009, pp. 2919–2930. ACM, Boston (2009)
2. Ancker, J.S., Chan, C., Kukafka, R.: Interactive Graphics for Expressing Health Risks: Development and Qualitative Evaluation. Journal of Health Communication: International Perspectives 5(14), 37–41 (2012)
3. Berg, C.H.: Avaliação De Ambientes Virtuais De Ensino Aprendizagem Acessíveis Através De Testes De Usabilidade Com Emoções. 2013. 80 f. Dissertação (Mestrado) - Curso de Mídia do Conhecimento, Departamento de Engenharia e Gestão do Conhecimento, Universidade Federal de Santa Catarina, Florianópolis, Cap. 6 (2013)
4. Desmet, P.M.A.: Measuring emotion: Development and application of an instrument to measure emotional responses to products. In: Blythe, M.A., Monk, A.F., Overbeeke, K., Wright, P.C. (eds.) Funology: From Usability to Enjoyment, pp. 111–123. Kluwer Academic Publishers, Dordrecht (2003)
5. Hercegfi, K., Csillik, O., Bodnár, É., Sass, J., Izsó, L.: Designers of Different Cognitive Styles Editing E-Learning Materials Studied by Monitoring Physiological and Other Data Simultaneously. In: Harris, D. (ed.) EPCE 2009, HCII 2009. LNCS (LNAI), vol. 5639, pp. 179–186. Springer, Heidelberg (2009)
6. MOODLE (Australia). Welcome to the Moodle community (2013), https://moodle.org/ (access in: March 10, 2013)
7. Nielsen, J., Mollich, R.: Heuristic evaluation of User interfaces. In: CHI 1990 Proceedings, pp. 249–256 (1990)
8. Nielsen, J., Mollich, R.: Usability Engineering. Academic Press Limited, London (1993)
9. Nielsen, J., Mollich, R.: Technology Transfer of Heuristic Evaluation and Usability Inspection. In: IFIP INTERACT 1995, Lillehammer, pp. 1–9 (1995)
10. Nielsen, J., Mollich, R., Loranger, H.: Usabilidade na Web: projetando websites com qualidade, 406 p. Elsiever, Rio de Janeiro (2007)
11. Preece, J., Rogers, Y., Sharp, H.: Interaction Design: Beyond Human- Computer Interaction, 552 p. Univ. of Maryland, Maryland (2002)
12. Sauer, J., Sonderegger, A.: The influence of prototype fidelity and aesthetics of design in usability tests: Effects on user behaviour, subjective evaluation and emotion. Applied Ergonomics (40), 670–677 (2008)
13. Scopus (Brazil) (Ed.). An eye on global research (2013), http://www.elsevier.com/online-tools/scopus (access in: March 10, 2013)
14. The Cochrane Collaboration (UK) (Ed.). Cochrane Review (2013), http://www.cochrane.org/cochrane-reviews (access in: March 10, 2013)
15. Thomson Reuters (Germany). Web of Science (2013), http://apps.webofknowledge.com (access in: March 10, 2013)
16. Tzvetanova, S., Tang, M.-X., Justice, L.: Emotional Web Usability Evaluation. In: Jacko, J.A. (ed.) HCI 2007. LNCS, vol. 4553, pp. 1039–1046. Springer, Heidelberg (2007)
17. Walker, S., Prytherch, D.: How Is It for You (A Case for Recognising User Motivation in the Design Process). In: Peter, C., Beale, R. (eds.) Affect and Emotion in HCI. LNCS, vol. 4868, pp. 130–141. Springer, Heidelberg (2008)
18. World Wide Web Consortium (Brazil). W3C Brasil (2013), http://www.w3c.br/Home/WebHome (access in: March 10, 2013)

Measuring Students' Flow Experience in a Multimodal Learning Environment: A Case Study

Christina Vasiliou, Andri Ioannou, and Panayiotis Zaphiris

Cyprus Interaction Lab, Department of Multimedia and Graphic Arts,
Cyprus University of Technology, Limassol, Cyprus
{c.vasiliou,andri.i.ioannou,panayiotis.zaphiris}@cut.ac.cy

Abstract. This research paper focuses on the relationship between flow experience and multimodal learning environments. Flow experience has been defined as the state in which an individual feels completely absorbed and fully engaged in an activity. This concentration and complete engagement can lead to optimal learning. Several scholars in the areas of distance learning [2] and game-based learning [3] highlighted the relationship between high levels of flow experience and the effectiveness of technology-enhanced learning environments. Yet, this theory has not been applied in the area of multimodal learning environments, were multiple forms of technologies are provided to collocated learners. The purpose of the present study was, by studying an HCI course, to explore learners' flow experience and to understand the affordances of that promote flow experience. Findings suggest that flow experience does exist in collaborative activities within a multimodal learning environments and that it offers a useful construct to understand the affordances of technology in similar learning environments.

Keywords: Flow experience, multimodal space, CSCL.

1 Introduction

Csikzsentmihalyi [1] defined flow experience as the state in which an individual feels completely absorbed and fully engaged in an activity. Flow experience (flow) is an extremely rewarding experience, balancing challenge and skill. It allows the individual to perform at an optimum level. It has been researched in many aspects of everyday life, from sports, to creative arts or work-related environments where this highly state of performance could be beneficial.

In the literature, one can find a large number of research projects which comment on experiencing flow during a learning activity. These investigations were based on the premise that such an experience can improve learners' motivation, interest and increase learning. More specifically, recent studies have investigated the relationship between flow and computer supported learning environments, in distance learning [2] and online game based learning [3]. Among their findings was the positive association between flow and effectiveness of these learning environments.

P. Zaphiris and A. Ioannou (Eds.): LCT 2014, Part I, LNCS 8523, pp. 346–357, 2014.

Nowadays, a wider palette of information technologies becomes available on our fingertips, promoting the use of multiple devices to assist us during every task. Tablets, digital gadgets and interactive surfaces are blended together [4] offering fascinating spaces that could foster learning activities. Yet, limited attention has been paid in learners' experiences within collocated learning settings where students blend different interaction styles and move away from being focused in front of a single screen. How does a group occupying a shared space experience the multiple digital and physical tools around them? How do these technologies allow a group to experience flow? Is there a need for particular design principles that could foster flow experience in these environments?

This research's aim is two-fold. First, to explore students' flow experience during problem based learning activities within a multimodal learning environment with authentic users and settings. Second aim of this study is to improve the multimodal learning environment by understanding the affordances of the environment that promote or hinder students' flow experience. The paper starts with a description of the multimodal learning environment and then presents the findings of our study, in terms of flow experience and technology. Finally, we discuss the implications of these findings and provide design principles to support flow experience and improve such multimodal learning environments.

2 Background

Csikszentmihalyi [5] described flow as the optimal experience, "the state in which individuals are so involved in an activity that nothing else seems to matter". Csikszentmihalyi [1] further annotated flow as the optimal experience, the state in which people feel totally involved and effortlessly engaged in an act. First experiments on flow included activities as diverse as creative arts, chess playing, dancing, rock climbing. What these experiences had in common was that participants in each activity lost the sense of time and their self-consciousness. Summarizing up his investigations on flow, Csikszentmihalyi [5] indicated that this experience consists of multiple dimensions; the balance between challenge and skill, clear goals and immediate feedback, the intense concentration, an emergence of action and awareness, the loss of self-consciousness, a sense of control, a feeling of time distortion, and experiencing the activity as intrinsically rewarding.

Subsequent research has revealed several affordances of computer systems that are positively associated with an increase in users' flow experience and in part to the effectiveness of a computer system. In Sicilia, Ruiz and Tomaseti [6], researchers measured consumers' flow experience in order to evaluate and improve the effectiveness of a website influencing marketing opportunities. Higher levels of flow experience can enhance online visits and consumers' enjoyment. Additionally, among the factors that have been associated with flow in computer systems is the different type of technology provided each time and user's technology efficacy [7]. Furthermore, it can be correlated with particular features of the computer system, such as interactivity [8], modifiability, and flexibility [9]. Since flow encloses effective dimensions of human behavior, it was revealed as an important aspect to be considered when designing effective computer systems.

From an educational perspective, the nature of flow experience as an intrinsically rewarding experience is what pushes people in flow to "higher levels of performance" [5], contributing to peak performance and learning. Researchers have largely invested their efforts in evaluating online learning systems and web-based instructional tools [2] [10]. Results by Liao [2] confirm that flow is a valuable element in distance learning environments and can support the engagement and commitment of students in the duration of an online course. In addition, identifying the importance of flow experience in game design, Kiili [11] used flow as a framework to facilitate positive user experience maximizing the impact of educational games. However, Pearce, Ainley and Howard [12] argue that the learning context raises new challenges in terms of producing highly engaged environments. We therefore understand that tested exemplars and design models are needed for particular technologies and specific learning activities.

As indicated by Csikszentmihalyi, Abuhamdeh and Nakamura [13], flow construct is a valuable strategy in technology-rich learning environments. Flow experience was able to assist in designing and improving the learning experience for online instructional tools and game based learning applications. Yet, limited attention has been paid in collocated learning contexts where students use multiple technologies, blending different interaction styles. As technology progresses, we are no longer limited within online systems and multimedia game environments. The vision Weiser [14] once described as ubiquitous computing is now partially a reality, with so many technologies available on our fingertips, such as smartphones, tablets, and interactive surfaces. There are much more possibilities of blending these technologies together into something unified instead of using them independently.

Therefore, the current study will approach the evaluation of a multimodal learning environment with everyday technologies by measuring learners' flow experience. More particularly the purpose of the present study is initially to explore students' flow experience within a multimodal learning environment, where their attention is no longer entirely focused on a single screen. Furthermore, we wish to understand the affordances of the multimodal learning environment that can promote or hinder learners' flow experience, based our evaluation with authentic users and settings.

3   Methods

3.1   Context

The study was part of a 13-week graduate-level course on Human Computer Interaction (HCI). The course aimed to provide to the students a comprehensive vision of the area and a hands-on experience of the user-centered design process. A Problem Based Learning (PBL) approach was employed, where groups of self-directed learners worked collaboratively to form a solution to an open-ended problem [15]. The 3 hour weekly sessions of the course, were organized in 1-hour mini-lectures and 2-hour group activities on solving a design problem. Mini lectures served as a triggering point for learners' understanding towards particular issues of the user-centered design process. Group activities were situated in a multimodal learning environment to provide a collaborative work space for the design procedure.

3.2   Setting

In this section we will describe the design of the multimodal learning environment, which provides a set of physical and digital tools to support collaborative problem-based learning activities. This technology rich workspace was developed for co-located learners to work together towards the solution of a design problem, and also for them to be able to interact with each other between physical meetings [16].

A large horizontal table surface with a downward pointing projection was chosen as the central focal point for the group activities. This table projection surface was powered by a Mac mini and controlled by a wireless keyboard and mouse. It was intended to provide a focal point for fertile discussion and support various collaborative activities, such as the presentation of digital artifacts (e.g. images, notes).

However, using a single surface to support the multitasking nature of the group was considered problematic. Therefore, portable devices, such as tablets, iPods, infrared pen and pen readers (IPPR) and laptops were provided to be used as needed. These devices aimed to support multitasking in web-browsing as well as record-keeping but also provided higher flexibility in the environment [9]. Tutors also encouraged learners to enrich the multimodal learning environment with their own portable devices, such as tablets and smart-phones, whenever they felt it was appropriate.

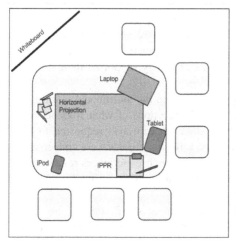
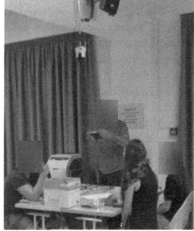

Fig. 1. Multimodal Learning Environment. Left: Space Layout. Right: An example set-up.

In addition to digital gadgets, a social network site[1] (SNS) was provided as a platform for sharing information, communication and coordination. The SNS was used with a two-fold purpose. Initially, the SNS provided a communication and sharing channel between the members of the group while away from the physical learning space. This was considered important to keep group members connected and with the ability to coordinate group progress. The second aim of the SNS was to support the communication and sharing of information between the devices available within the multimodal information space (e.g. handheld devices, horizontal projection). Finally, physical tools such as a whiteboard and stationery (e.g., pens, markers, post-it notes) were also provided for each group to use as appropriate. The aim was to provide materials used in traditional problem-based learning settings. The layout of the multimodal information space is demonstrated in Figure 1.

3.3   Participants

Two tutors and a total of 21 post-graduate students (8 male, 13 female) from varied backgrounds (e.g., computer science, graphic arts, multimedia, and education) participated in the study. Students were divided in 4 groups of 5 to 6 students each. For the allocation of students in groups, we kept in mind the aim of creating multidisciplinary groups thus the procedure of forming groups was in part based on each student's background. Therefore, each group was composed of members from different disciplines.

3.4   Data Collection

The ways to measure flow vary in literature based on the context and task under evaluation. For this study, we followed a mixed method approach to data collection and analysis to answer the questions posed. Both quantitative and qualitative data were gathered to measure student's flow experience, their perceptions of the multimodal learning environment, and the ways in which technology supported their flow experience.

At the end of each weekly laboratory session within the multimodal learning environment, the facilitators kept detailed notes and reflections of what students had encountered during the meetings. In addition, students were also requested to keep a reflection diary and submit it weekly. Students' reflective diaries were concerned with their overall learning experience but also referred to their experiences regarding flow. To support their reflections on flow as a holistic sensation we adapted a measure by Novak, Hoffman and Yung [17].

In order to understand flow experience as a process [12] during the 13-week course, a self-report questionnaire was administered three times during the course, at the beginning (Week 2), middle (Week 7) and end of the course (Week 12). This questionnaire aimed to assess students' flow experience within the multimodal learning environment and was adapted from Jackson and Marsh [18]. This measure

---

[1] In this case study the social network site in use was Facebook.

includes 36 Likert-type items with a 7-point agreement response scale (from 1: strongly disagree, to 7: strongly agree), designed to capture the nine dimensions of flow experience.

At the end of the course, four focus groups were conducted (one with each group) to explore student's flow experience within a multimodal learning environment and understand the affordances of this environment to promote students' flow experience. Each focus group lasted approximately 30 minutes and was facilitated by a researcher who aimed to uncover the opinions of the individual learners as well as the shared viewpoints of the group members.

4   Results

4.1   Questionnaire Results

A total of 20 students completed the questionnaire on flow during the three tasks. First the internal consistency for each subscale of flow was assessed using Cronbach's alpha; all 9 subscales had acceptable internal consistency (Cronbach's alphas > .60). Afterwards, all subscale mean scores were calculated and as demonstrated in Table 1 were all above the midpoint of the response scale suggesting that participants were in flow during their activities within the multimodal learning environment. More specifically, during the Task A participants were highly concentrated on the task at hand (M=4.12, SD=49) and felt that they lost track of time (M=3.98, SD=.68). During Task B, students reported increase in terms of the sense of control they had over the environment they were working (M=3.55, SD=.77) and the goals were clearer (M=3.48, SD=.65). Finally, towards Task C, participants reported clearer goals (M=3.98, SD=.65) and feedback (M=3.63, SD=.63), greater sense of control (M=3.87, SD=.70), while the balance between challenge and skills was higher (M=3.94, SD=.64).

Table 1. Subscales and Descriptive Statistics for Flow Questionnaires - (N=20)

Subscale	Items	Week 2 Means (SD)	Week 7 Means (SD)	Week 12 Means (SD)
1. Challenge-Skills Balance	4	3.65 (.61)	3.7 (.75)	3.94 (.64)
2. Action Awareness	4	3.21 (.81)	3.24 (.62)	3.88 (.67)
3. Clear Goals	4	3.21 (.81)	3.48 (.89)	3.98 (.65)
4. Unambiguous Feedback	4	3.07 (.68)	3.27 (.72)	3.63 (.63)
5. Concentration on task	4	4.12 (.49)	3.75 (.94)	3.99 (.86)
6. Sense of Control	4	3.38 (.80)	3.55 (.77)	3.87 (.70)
7. Loss of self-consciousness	4	3.46 (1.11)	3.56 (1.10)	3.98 (.87)
8. Transformation of time	4	3.98 (.68)	4 (.70)	3.60 (1.09)
9. Autotelic Experience	4	3.75 (.62)	3.43 (1.00)	3.55 (.99)

A graphical representation of the individual dimensions of flow per week is demonstrated in Figure 2. We can positively identify the change in all flow dimensions and can presume that the results from Week12 are slightly improved and more concise, compared to the sparse means from Week2.

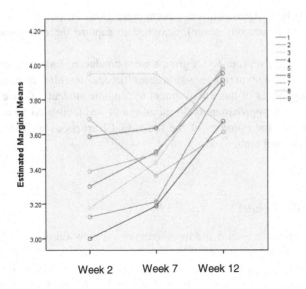

Fig. 1. Means of individual flow dimensions per week

4.2   Qualitative Data Analysis

The investigators conducted a thematic analysis of the focus group data to understand participants' flow experience within a multimodal learning environment and the affordances of this environment to promote students' flow experience. To improve the rigor and trustworthiness of the findings, the investigators used the observation field notes kept by the tutors and the reflective diaries kept by the students as a contrasting data source. The prominent themes found in learners' self-report were fully consistent with the impressions the tutors had gained and recorded through observation.

Next we discuss the core themes that emerged from the thematic analysis. Direct quotes are used throughout to provide evidence of the students' experiences and concerns raised during the focus groups.

Theme 1: Technology did not Enhance Flow, but Acted as a Supporting Role for Keeping us in Flow. This core theme revealed the supporting role of technology in flow experience and how the technological aspects of the multimodal learning environment affected their participation. Learners' reported that even though they experienced flow, technology did not play a significant role in their experience.

Group 1 participant: "I do believe that we could experience flow even without the technology. But I feel that technology was there to keep us in flow. We had too much information for record keeping that simple pen and paper would not be able to support us. The multimodal learning environment supported our activities."

Group 4 participant: "The whole atmosphere of the laboratory with the people working on the same tasks with the technology is something that helps experience this (flow). Technology gadgets and group work is a combination you cannot compete."

Group 3 participant: "We never felt interrupted because something was not there or it was at a distance place. I think that the proximity and immediate availability of the physical and digital items in the environment played an important role on keeping us in flow."

More specifically, participants reported that the downwards projection kept them closely together during the face to face sessions and provided a central focal point during their interactions. The shared surface was extensively used by all the groups brought the group members closer, keeping them all together in flow. For example,

Group 3 participant: "All my attention was focused around the projection on the table and nothing else seem to bother me outside the group activities. I was so focused on what we were doing that I could not even hear the rest of the class talking. It felt like we were the only team in the class."

Group1 participant: "The projection on the table was the most useful item within the environment [...]. I do prefer having the downwards projection rather than a single computer screen."

In addition, the SNS that was used as a communication and sharing tool to support in between session group activities, was considered an ideal tool for keeping the group motivated and in continuous contact with the project, keeping them in flow.

Group 1 participant: "I think what made this all more realistic and kept us motivated was the constant communication with my team through technology, for example Facebook and Google documents. The familiarity we had with Facebook and the immediate communications – getting notification on my smartphone all the time – kept me up to date and in that amazing group mood."

Group 3 participant: "Facebook actually got fire! Due to our busy schedules this tool was the thing that kept us together focused on the project between the face-to-face sessions."

Theme 2: I Felt Focused but not in Strong Flow while Working within the Multimodal Learning Environment. This core theme was equally important and included responses relevant to whether flow experience existed and how strong was this experience within the multimodal learning environment. Students supported that they were focused during the collaborative activities and that the multimodal learning environment promoted learners' flow experience but not in high intensity. For example,

Group 4 participant: "I don't believe that I experienced high levels of flow. Sometimes, mostly during the design process, I felt more focused and immersed in the activity. I think that my interest towards design supported this feeling."

Group 1 participant: "I have felt this (flow experience) during our group work. During the course, I felt absorbed [...] but not intensively."

Yet, in contrary to the collective opinion of the group about the low level of flow experience, one participant argued,

Group 1 participant: "I think I have experienced this (flow) 100%. I find it astonishing the extent to which I became so immersed in the project work. The learning experience has been unparalleled."

Theme 3: Feeling the Transformation of Time Within the Multimodal Learning Environment. The theme emerged from students' responses on describing moments where they felt in flow within the multimodal learning environment. More particularly participants identified that they were fully concentrated on the activities and that they lost track of time.

Group 3 participant: "I actually realized I was in flow from the way time flies during our activities."

Group 4 participant: "All the group members were totally focused and connected to each other producing high quality work. During those moments we completely lost track of time, it seemed to us that time was going really fast."

5   Discussion

To this end, we analyze our findings in terms of how measuring flow experience assisted on understanding the affordances of the multimodal learning environment and whether the technology supported or hindered this experience.

5.1   Learners' Flow Experience

Our analysis of learners' flow experience within the multimodal learning environment shows how learners' levels of flow experience were above the mid-point of the response scale on average, indicating medium flow experience. This finding also emerged as a core theme from the thematic analysis of focus groups and diaries (Theme 2), since students felt highly focused during group activities and experienced a transformation of time (Theme 3). However, students reported that this experience was not intensive but was rather kept at a medium to low level during the activities within the multimodal learning environment, with few exceptions of students with higher intrinsic motivation.

5.2   Flow Experience as a Design Strategy

An important finding in this study is that even though technology did not initiated learners' flow experience, results indicate that technology successfully maintained flow. When learners described instances of flow experience within the multimodal learning environment, technology was not an important aspect of their experience. For instance, one participant argued that the team would be able to experience flow even outside the multimodal learning environment. Nonetheless, based on the thematic analysis, the role of technology was identified as supporting, acting on the background of collaborative activities (Theme 1). For example, the downward projection was indicated as a common focal point and managed to concentrate group's attention on a particular task. Another example was the use of an SNS as a communication and interaction medium keeping motivation levels high. Therefore, technology within the multimodal learning environment maintained learners' flow experience longer than a simple pen and paper environment would do.

As described earlier in the paper (Section 3.2), we enriched the learning environment with multiple digital tools and gadgets in order to support the multitasking of group work and flexibility of the workspace [9]. Having this multiplicity of devices, one of our considerations was to negatively affect the groups' focused attention, and instead spread it across multiple devices. However, questionnaires' results indicated medium to high levels of concentration on task at hand and focused attention towards the activity (M=3.87). Verifying the quantitative results, students argued that they felt completely focused and absorbed with the activities within the multimodal learning environment. Additionally, one group indicated that the proximity of objects within the space was an important element. Even though they choose to use them as appropriate having them immediately available "at hand" was considered a major advantage for the learning environment. Therefore, the multimodal character of the learning space was able to maintain attention of the learners and their concentration on the activities, especially when the proximity between the multiple elements was high.

Furthermore, what emerged from the analysis was the power of the table surface screen, rising as a "focal character" attribute [4] for the multimodal learning environment. The majority of the participants argued that the shared screen on the table was an extremely useful element within the learning space and was used during every session. The shared surface managed to provide a focus spot fostering the collaborative activities of the team and bring the team closer together. Therefore, the proximity that surface table provided to the team is a necessary attribute to take into consideration when designing similar learning environments.

In addition, the SNS successfully kept each group in touch and active within the project work. Our findings are in agreement with results from the area of distance learning [2] where high motivation levels are required to reduce the drop-out rate of students from online learning systems. What the particular selection of the SNS adds is the increased levels of familiarity with the tools and the immediate feedback that it provided. For example, one member would post a particular argument for consideration on the group page and even though he exited the application, a notification would be sent directly on his smartphone. Thus, we identify that clear feedback and immediacy are important attributes in the design of such complex systems.

5.3   Limitations and Future Directions

One of the limitations of this research is the subjectivity in terms of the collected data. We understand that the fact that only self-reported and subjective data were collected may weaken the results of this research study. However, the systematic investigation of such complex environments with real users does not allow the use of more objective measures such as physiometric and psychometric elements. Through this exploratory study though, we have pinpointed that focus groups and reflective diaries were the most valuable tools providing a more holistic perspective of the flow experience of students. More specifically, in order to better understand the factors that allowed the students to experience flow, and to comprehend the affordances of the environment to support flow, qualitative approaches were more suitable. Still though, the mixed method approach to data collection was considered too intrusive, detecting the need for the development of new instruments to capture this new multimodal experience.

The literature would suggest that an increase in flow experience would positively affect learning and interaction within a learning environment [2]. In our investigation, this relationship was not explored within the multimodal learning environment to confirm previous findings. This association would be largely valuable for those teaching and designing a similar course. Therefore, we would further extend the current investigation of the multimodal learning environment by measuring and correlating flow experience to the learning performance of the participants or particular learning activities. Such an investigation is necessary to prove multimodal learning environments as successful learning spaces and provide further examples and cases on using such environments in real context.

Another issue identified in this research was the fluctuation of attention between weeks. Even though the multimodal character of the learning space was able to maintain their concentration on the activities, there was an unexplained fluctuation. This observation indicates that further investigation is needed towards understanding how is learners' attention scattered across elements in the learning environment and how are different tasks affecting their concentration on the activity.

6   Conclusion

As technology constantly becomes more affordable, students are now using their own smartphones, tablets and handheld devices serving all their needs. Each class now is becoming a multimodal learning environment on its own. The possibilities are countless. But the way to handle all this technology so that we keep focus on tasks and performance high is still unexplored. The importance of this research lies beneath this need. It is important that researchers that lead and support the design of educational environments have models to draw upon. In the context of educational games and online learning tools the concept of flow has been extensively researched to assist the design of such environments and several design principles and models have been proposed. However in multimodal learning environments there is lack of exemplars and models for educators to draw upon in their practice. Therefore, in this study we enriched a collaborative learning environment with multiple interactive, digital and physical items (e.g. projector, SNS, tablets and smartphones), to support collaborative PBL activities. Our aim was to understand students' flow experience and the affordances of the technology-rich learning environment. Our analysis of learners' flow experience within the multimodal learning environment provided important findings contributing to our understanding of learners' behavior within a multimodal learning environment, and importantly, to further improving the design of the multimodal learning environment.

Acknowledgement. This project is funded by the Cyprus Research Promotion Foundation (DESMI 2009-2010) and the Slovenian Research Agency (ARRS), under the "Bilateral Cooperation" between Slovenia and Cyprus (ΔΙΑΚΡΑΤΙΚΕΣ/ΚΥ-ΣΛΟ/0411). DESMI 2009-2010 is co-funded by the Republic of Cyprus and the European Regional Development Fund of the EU.

References

1. Csikszentmihalyi, M.: Beyond Boredom and Anxiety: Experiencing Flow in Work and Play. Jossey-Bass, San Francisco (1975)
2. Liao, L.: A Flow Theory Perspective on Learner Motivation and Behavior in Distance Education. Distance Education 27(1), 45–62 (2006)
3. Hwang, G.L., Wu, P.H., Chen, C.C.: An online game approach for improving students' learning performance in web-based problem-solving activities. Computers & Education 59(4), 1246–1256 (2012)
4. Coughlan, T., Collins, T.D., Adams, A., Rogers, Y., Haya, P.A., Martin, E.: The conceptual framing, design and evaluation of device ecologies for collaborative activities. International Journal of Human-Computer Studies 70(10), 765–779 (2012)
5. Csikszentmihalyi, M.: Flow: The Psychology of Optimal Experience. Harper and Row, New York (1990)
6. Sicilia, M., Ruiz, S., Tomaseti, E.: The Moderating Effect of Flow State on Web Site Effectiveness. In: Australian and New Zealand Marketing Academy Conference 2004, Wellington, New Zealand (2004)
7. Trevino, T.K., Webster, J.: Flow in Computer-Mediated Communication: Electronic Mail and Voice Mail Evaluation and Impacts. Communication Research 19(5), 539–573 (1992)
8. Hoffman, D.L., Novak, T.P.: Marketing in Hypermedia Computer-Mediated Environments: Conceptual Foundations. Journal of Marketing 60(3), 50–68 (1996)
9. Webster, J., Trevino, T.K., Ryan, L.: The dimensionality and correlates of flow in human computer interaction. Computers in Human Behavior 9(4), 411–426 (1993)
10. Choi, D.H., Kim, J., Kim, S.H.: ERP training with a web-based electronic learning system: The flow theory perspective. International Journal of Human-Computer Studies 65(3), 223–243 (2007)
11. Kiili, K.: Digital game-based learning: Towards and experiential gaming model. Internet and Higher Education 8(1), 13–24 (2005)
12. Pearce, J., Ainley, M., Howard, S.: The Ebb and Flow of Online Learning. Computers in Human Behavior 21(5), 745–771 (2005)
13. Csikszentmihalyi, M., Abuhamdeh, S., Nakamura, J.: Flow. In: Elliot, A.J., Dweck, C.S. (eds.) Handbook of Competence and Motivation, pp. 598–608. The Guilford Press, New York (2005)
14. Weiser, M.: The computer for the 21st century. Scientific American (September 1991)
15. Hmelo-Silver, C.E.: Problem-based learning: What and how do students learn? Educational Psychology Review 16(3), 235–266 (2004)
16. Vasiliou, C., Ioannou, A., Zaphiris, P.: Technology Enhanced PBL in HCI education: A Case Study. In: Kotzé, P., Marsden, G., Lindgaard, G., Wesson, J., Winckler, M. (eds.) INTERACT 2013, Part IV, vol. 8120, pp. 643–650. Springer, Heidelberg (2013)
17. Novak, T.P., Hoffman, D.L., Yung, Y.F.: Measuring the Customer Experience in Online Environments: A Structural Modeling Approach. Marketing Science 19(1), 22–42 (2000)
18. Jackson, S.A., Marsh, H.W.: Development and Validation of a Scale to Measure Optimal Experience: The Flow State Scale. Journal of Sport & Exercise Psychology 18, 17–35 (1996)

Attention Profiling Algorithm
for Video-Based Lectures

Josef Wachtler and Martin Ebner

Graz, University of Technology

Abstract. Due to the fact that students' attention is the most crucial
resource in a high-quality course it is from high importance to control
and analyze it. This could be done by using the interaction and the
communication because they are known as valuable influencing factors of
the attention. In this publication we introduce a web-based information
system which implements an attention-profiling algorithm for learning-
videos as well as live-broadcastings of lectures. For that different methods
of interaction are offered and analyzed. The evaluation points out that
the attention profiling algorithm delivers realistic values.

1 Introduction

It is a known fact that students are confronted with a growing quantity of information. Huge amounts of shapes, colors, and text are presented to them in many
different ways. Furthermore it is clear that they can handle and process only a
limited number of these information at the same time [1]. So most of them is
filtered out centrally [2]. It has been pointed out that a mechanism known as
selective attention is the most crucial resource for human learning [3]. This indicates that managing this attention enhances both, behavioral and neuronal
performance [4]. [5]

Further important influencing factors of students' attention are both, the
interaction and the communication. This means that they should be used in
many different forms (e.g. face-to-face, e-mail, live-chat or newsgroups) as well as
in all possible directions. So interaction and communication is not only important
from the lecturer to the students and vice versa. In addition the so-called student-
to-student communication and the interaction of the students with the content
itself are key factors of a high-quality learning process especially of a video-based
online-course. [6]

Furthermore the mentioned forms of interaction and communication should
be used to analyze the attention of the students. So the lecturer should be able
to gain more information about the students' understanding of the content. In
addition this analysis helps to evaluate if both, the way of presenting and the
content itself are suited for the target audience. [7]

So it is clear that human learning processes are strongly depending on the
attention of each single student. Furthermore a more detailed knowledge about

P. Zaphiris and A. Ioannou (Eds.): LCT 2014, Part I, LNCS 8523, pp. 358–367, 2014.
© Springer International Publishing Switzerland 2014

the progress of the attention of the students can help to adopt the lecture accordingly. Due to these facts any mechanism helping to analyze students' attention is from high importance.

Based on the mentioned facts regarding students' attention we like to introduce an attention profiling algorithm which operates on interactions. This algorithm is implemented by a web-application which provides different methods of interaction and communication to learning-videos as well as live-broadcastings of lectures. So this could be formulated as the following research-question: *implementing an attention profiling algorithm to fully analyze students' attention and evaluating it under realistic conditions.*

At first Section 2 presents some related work. After that Section 3 explains the functionalities of the web-application as well as the different parts of the attention profiling algorithm. Finally an evaluation is shown in Section 4 and discussed by Section 5.

2   Related Work

One possible solution to control and to analyze the attention is known as a so-called Audience-Response-System (ARS) which enables the lecturer to present questions to students during the lecture in a standard classroom situation. Furthermore it offers different features of analysis. [8]

Many studies claim that an ARS is a very powerful tool to enhance both, students' attention and participation [9]. So for instance an ARS was compared to other classroom communication methods (e.g. answering questions by cards) by [10]. They pointed out that answering questions with an ARS leads to the highest formal participation (100%). This is also confirmed by [11].

In addition Youtube[1] provides some mechanisms of interactivity to enrich the videos. So for instance it offers the possibility to add questions to videos. However there are not very much features to fully analyze the answers as well as the attention.

3   Implementation

This section explains the developed attention profiling algorithm in a detailed way. For that the main functionalities of the web-application called *LIVE*[2] are presented (see Section 3.1) to clarify the operating-context of the algorithm in question. This attention profiling algorithm is divided in two parts. The first one is responsible for a detailed recording of the joined timespans of each single user (see Section 3.2). The second part consists of the calculation of an attention-level which is based on the reaction-times of the attendees to the interactions (see Sections 3.3 and 3.4)

---

[1] https://www.youtube.com/video_questions_beta (last accessed December 2013)
[2] Short for *LIVE Interaction in Virtual learning Environments*.

3.1   Functionalities of LIVE

As mentioned above *LIVE* enriches learning-videos as well as live-broadcastings of lectures with different methods of interaction. For that it offers the video or the live-stream to the attendees and if an interaction occurs it displays them as an overlaying dialog (see Figure 1).

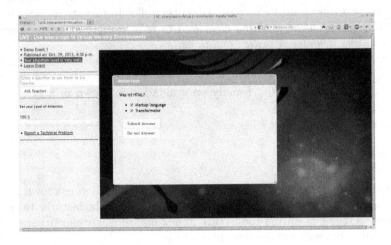

Fig. 1. An interaction occurs during a video

As a summarizing overview the following list presents the most important features of the web-application which implements the developed attention profiling algorithm:

- only available for registered and authenticated users
- different methods of interaction:
  - automatically asked questions and captchas[3]
  - asking questions to the lecturer
  - asking text-based questions to the attendees
  - multiple-choice questions at pre-defined positions
  - reporting technical problems
- many different forms of analysis (e.g. the attention profiling algorithm presented by the following sections)

3.2   Recording Joined Timespans

The first part of the attention profiling algorithm implements a detailed recording of the joined timespans of each single attendee. This means that for each

---

[3] Short for *Completely Automated Public Turing Test to Tell Computers and Humans Apart.*

attendee it is possible to say at which time he/she watched which part of the video or of the live-broadcasting.

For that two models are used (see Figure 2). If a user joins an event at the first time and becomes an attendee of this event an instance of the *JoinedUser*-model is created. Furthermore the method *join()* of this new instance is called to build the first instance of the *History*-model. This sets the fields *join_relative* as well as *join_absolute* and marks this *History*-object as active. So a *History* actually records a joined timespan. For that it holds all relevant data about it in relative as well as in absolute values.

While a user is joined the fields *leave_relative* and *leave_absolute* are updated every five seconds. If the attendee leaves the event the according method is called to mark the current *History*-object as non-active. On a further join it is required to call the according method of his/her *JoinedUser*-object again which leads to the construction of a further *History*-object. So it can be seen that there will be a set of *History*-objects for each joined user where every *History*-object represents a joined timespan.

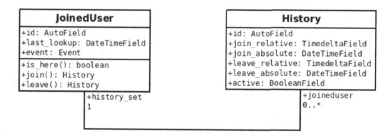

Fig. 2. The models to record the joined timespans of a user (simplified)

With these recordings it is possible to calculate different statistical values as for instance the shortest or the longest joined timespan as well as the average length of the joined timespans. In addition a timeline is drawn for each attendee. It shows the joined timespans by marking them with colored bars.

3.3   Interactions and Reaction-Times

As mentioned above the second part of the attention profiling algorithm consists of a calculation of an attention-level which is based on the reaction-times of the attendees to the interactions. For that it is required to log them.

The corresponding models are shown by Figure 3. It can be seen that the logging of the reaction-times works very similar to the recording of the joined timespans presented by the previous section. The interactions are represented by a model with its concrete sub-class models for each possible receiver of an interaction. This model holds a set of *CallHistory*-models to log every occurrence of the interaction in question. This is required because of the fact that in a video

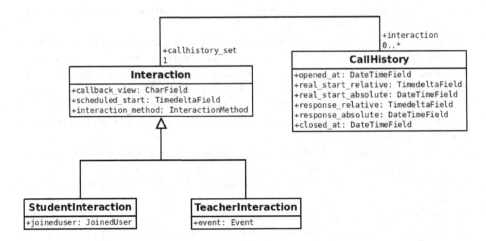

Fig. 3. The models of the interactions and their call-histories (simplified)

the attendee is able to watch it more often than once and so an interaction could also occur not only once.

The *CallHistory*-model logs all required times to compute the reaction-times of each single call of an interaction in relative and absolute values. For that the fields which contains the real start time and the response time are the most important ones because the difference between them is equal to the reaction-time. The other fields are used if the interaction is missed or not answered. With this values it is possible to state for each call of an interaction how the associated attendee reacted.

3.4   Calculating the Attention-Level

With the logged reaction-times presented by the section above now it is possible to calculate an attention-level for each joined timespan of each single attendee. As shown by Figure 4 the calculation is split in three rounds:

1. calculation of an attention-level based on the reaction-times for every call of an interaction (I) related to the joined timespan in question
2. grouping them to attention-levels (AL) of each interaction-methods (IM)
3. generalizing them to an attention-level of a joined timespan

It is clear that round one is the most crucial part of the calculation which operates under the following maxim: *if the attendee reacts slower the attention-level decreases.* Figure 5 visualizes this calculation. It can be seen that it is configured by two parameters which are different for every interaction-method:

1. *SUCCESS_UNTIL* states the time until an attention-level of 100% could be reached

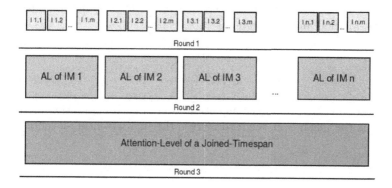

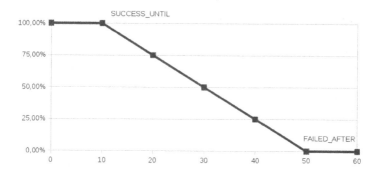

Fig. 4. The calculation of the attention-level is split in three rounds

Fig. 5. The calculation of the attention-level of a single interaction is controlled by two parameters

2. *FAILED_AFTER* indicates after which reaction-time an attention-level of 0% will be assumed

So the attention-level of the j-th interaction of the i-th interaction-method is calculated by the following formula if we assume that t_{ij} is the corresponding reaction-time:

$$f(t_{ij}) = \begin{cases} 100 & \text{if } t_{ij} \leq \text{SUCCESS\_UNTIL} \\ 0 & \text{if } t_{ij} > \text{FAILED\_AFTER} \\ g(t_{ij}) & \text{else} \end{cases} \quad (1)$$

Where $g(t_{ij})$ is

$$g(t_{ij}) = 100 - \left(\frac{t_{ij} - \text{SUCCESS\_UNTIL}}{\text{FAILED\_AFTER} - \text{SUCCESS\_UNTIL}} * 100 \right) \quad (2)$$

As mentioned above round two groups the attention-levels of round one to their corresponding interaction-methods. This is done by forming the mean of them which leads to this formula where a_i will be the attention level of the i-th interaction-method and m_i the number of its interactions:

$$a_i = \frac{\sum_{j=0}^{m_i} f(t_{ij})}{m_i} \tag{3}$$

Finally round three takes the attention-level of each interaction-method and again forms the mean over them to receive the final attention-level of a joined timespan:

$$attention = \frac{\sum_{i=0}^{n} a_i}{n} \tag{4}$$

4   Evaluation

The evaluation of the developed attention profiling algorithm in the context of the described web-application consists of three parts with individual goals:

1. gaining suitable parameters to force the algorithm to deliver realistic values
2. comparing the results of the algorithm with the feedback of the attendees to implement adoptions
3. evaluating the effects of the adoptions

To reach the first goal the web-application is used at two units of the lecture *Societal Aspects of Information Technology*[4] at Graz University of Technology to offer a live-broadcasting. This lecture consists of several presentations which are hold by guest-lecturers. To gain realistic values for the parameters of the second part of the attention profiling algorithm (see Section 3.4) the recorded reaction-times of the interactions are analyzed. This means that the average reaction-time of them is calculated to place the parameters around this point. Now the algorithm is able to reflect the attention of the attendees in a realistic way.

The second step of the evaluation is performed by using the web-application at the lecture *Introduction to Structured Programming*[5] at Graz University of Technology. This large freshman-course presents the basics of structured programming in six units. They are offered as live-broadcastings by *LIVE*. Figure 6 compares the complete number of attendees with the number of active ones. We assume an attendee to be active if he/she watched more than 75% with an attention-level of at least 50%. It can be seen that the number of active attendees is very low. The feedback provided by the attendees states that they

---

[4] https://online.tugraz.at/tug_online/lv.detail?sprache=1&clvnr=162241 (last accessed December 2012)

[5] https://online.tugraz.at/tug_online/lv.detail?sprache=1&clvnr=162268 (last accessed December 2012)

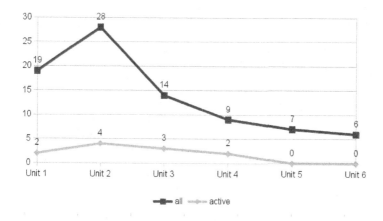

Fig. 6. Comparison of all attendees with active (watched $\geq$ 75% and attention-level $\geq$ 50%) attendees of the lecture *Introduction to Structured Programming*

felt very uncomfortable with their attention-level because they assumed a much higher one. Furthermore it was pointed out that it was impossible to answer faster to the interactions presenting difficult questions due to the fact that the live-stream did not stop if an interaction occurs. Additionally it was remarked that the number of interactions should not be very high.

Based on the gained feedback some adoptions are implemented. So for instance the video pauses if an interaction occurs now and it is declared that a lecturer has to pause his/her presentation at the occurrence of an interaction in the case of a live broadcasting. Furthermore the number of interaction is lowered to a maximum of three interactions in a period of ten minutes.

With this adoptions the web-application is used at the lecture *Learning in the Net: From possible and feasible things* [6] at the Karl-Franzens University of Graz. This lecture explains and discusses different technologies from the field of the so-called new medias in the context of teaching. The content of the lecture is provided by eight videos. Again the number of all attendees is compared to the number of active attendees (see Figure 7). Now these two numbers are not very different. This leads to the conclusion that the attention profiling algorithm is now able to reflect students' attention more realistically.

5   Discussion

The evaluation presented by the previous section points out that the selection of the parameters for the calculation of the attention-level is highly sensitive. Their accuracy depends on many different factors as for instance the difficulty of the

---

[6] https://online.uni-graz.at/kfu_online/
   lv.detail?cperson_nr=63360&clvnr=370548 (last accessed December 2013)

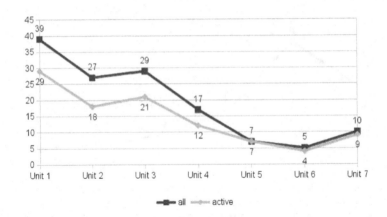

Fig. 7. Comparison of all attendees with active (watched $\geq$ 75% and attention-level $\geq$ 50%) attendees of the lecture *Learning in the Net: From possible and feasible things*

questions presented by the interactions as well as the content of the video or the live-broadcasting itself. Furthermore the timespan between the interactions should not be to small. This means that a phase between three and five minutes with no interactions is acceptable.

Furthermore it can be stated that the two parts of the attention profiling algorithm are only powerful in combination due to the fact that they have different goals:

- The detailed recording of all joined timespans for each attendee to state when which part was watched
- The reaction-time based attention-level to indicate how active the corresponding attendee was at a joined timespan

However the correctness of the calculated attention-level has various influencing issues (see above). This leads to the final statement that the attention-level delivers a first overview of the students' attention which could act as a starting point for a more detailed analysis.

6   Conclusion

With this publication an attention profiling algorithm is presented to analyze the attention of the students at learning-videos as well as live-broadcastings of lectures. This is done due the fact that students' attention is the most crucial resource in human learning.

This algorithm is implemented by a web-application which enriches the videos or the live-broadcastings with different methods of interaction. In addition the evaluation of the web-application indicates that the attention profiling algorithm delivers realistic values after some adoptions. So the defined research-question is answered finally.

References

1. Shiffrin, R.M., Gardner, G.T.: Visual processing capacity and attentional control. Journal of Experimental Psychology 93(1), 72–82 (1972)
2. Moran, J., Desimone, R.: Selective attention gates visual processing in the extrastriate cortex. Science 229, 782–784 (1985)
3. Heinze, H.J., Mangun, G.R., Burchert, W., Hinrichs, H., Scholz, M., Münte, T.F., Gös, A., Scherg, M., Johannes, S., Hundeshagen, H., Gazzaniga, M.S., Hillyard, S.A.: Combined spatial and temporal imaging of brain activity during visual selective attention in humans. Nature 372, 543–546 (1994)
4. Spitzer, H., Desimone, R., Moran, J.: Increased attention enhances both behavioral and neuronal performance. Science 240, 338–340 (1988)
5. Ebner, M., Wachtler, J., Holzinger, A.: Introducing an information system for successful support of selective attention in online courses. In: Stephanidis, C., Antona, M. (eds.) UAHCI 2013, Part III. LNCS, vol. 8011, pp. 153–162. Springer, Heidelberg (2013)
6. Carr-Chellman, A., Duchastel, P.: The ideal online course. British Journal of Educational Technology 31(3), 229–241 (2000)
7. Helmerich, J., Scherer, J.: Interaktion zwischen lehrenden und lernenden in medien unterstützten veranstaltungen. In: Breitner, M.H., Bruns, B., Lehner, F. (eds.) Neue Trends im E-Learning, pp. 197–210. Physica-Verlag HD (2007)
8. Tobin, B.: Audience response systems, stanford university school of medicine (2005), http://med.stanford.edu/irt/edtech/contacts/documents/2005-11_AAMC_tobin_audience_response_systems.pdf (online; accessed October 9, 2012)
9. Ebner, M.: Introducing live microblogging: how single presentations can be enhanced by the mass. Journal of Research in Innovative Teaching 2(1), 91–100 (2009)
10. Stowell, J.R., Nelson, J.M.: Benefits of electronic audience response systems on student participation, learning, and emotion. Teaching of Psychology 34(4), 253–258 (2007)
11. Latessa, R., Mouw, D.: Use of an audience response system to augment interactive learning. Family Medicine 37(1), 12–14 (2005)

Supporting Problem-Based, Inquiry-Based, Project-Based and Blended Learning

Promoting Students' Writing Skills in Science through an Educational Simulation: The GlobalEd 2 Project

Scott W. Brown[1] and Kimberly A. Lawless[2]

[1] University of Connecticut,
Educational Psychology Department,
249 Glenbrook Road, Storrs, CT 06269-3064, USA
[2] University of Illinois at Chicago,
1040 West Harrison Road, School of Education, Chicago, IL 60607, USA
scott.brown@uconn.edu, klawless@uic.edu

Abstract. Using a problem-based learning (PBL) approach, GlobalEd 2 (GE2) utilizes an interdisciplinary approach to learning writing, science, and social studies. Leveraging technologies commonly available in most middle grade classrooms (computers with Internet connections), GE2 engages classrooms of students as teams in simulated negotiations of international agreements on issues of global concern such as water resources and climate change. The impact of student interactions within the simulation on the writing self-efficacy and the ability to author evidenced-based arguments in science of 420 7th and 8th grade students across two states is presented. Results indicate that after participation in a GE2 simulation, students not only increased their writing self-efficacy, but also significantly increased the quality of their written scientific arguments.

Keywords: Writing, Problem-based Learning (PBL), Simulation, Self-Efficacy.

1   Introduction

It has been argued, that to develop a scientifically literate citizenry, science education needs to be grounded in meaningful socio-scientific contexts related to the world in which students live [1; 2]. Socio-scientific issues are complex in nature and often do not have a single clear-cut solution. Such issues confront students with situations in which they have to engage in formulating their own opinions based on data, their own experiences and values, and collaborative decision-making. They are regarded as real-world problems that afford students the opportunity to participate in the negotiation and development of meaning through scientific argumentation [3; 4; 5]. Argumentation includes any dialog that addresses "the coordination of evidence and theory to support or refute an explanatory conclusion, model, or prediction" [4, p. 995]. Research has shown that when students engage in scientific argumentation, they not only learn to develop valid arguments but also learn science concepts while they are arguing [e.g., 5; 6; 7; 8].

P. Zaphiris and A. Ioannou (Eds.): LCT 2014, Part I, LNCS 8523, pp. 371–379, 2014.
© Springer International Publishing Switzerland 2014

Unfortunately, inquiry-based approaches to teaching and learning science that involve socio-scientific issues are not often employed within typical science classrooms [3; 9; 10; 11]. The lack of socio-scientific inquiry tasks in science classrooms likely results from fact that the shift in the science standards towards scientific literacy and related pedagogical reform was set forth without commensurate alteration of the curricular space devoted to the teaching of science in the schools [12]. Inquiry-based curricula, especially programs that immerse learners in active investigations of contemporary issues, can consume significant chunks of classroom time. Given the standardized test-driven culture of today's educational system, the allocation of scarce instructional time and resources is a major concern for both teachers and administrators [13]. Further, research on science teachers has found that they feel under prepared and often lack the confidence necessary to implement and manage socio-scientific inquiry within the science classroom context [14; 15 16; 17]. So while it appears that we know what to do develop a scientifically literate citizenry and address dwindling science interest and participation among our students in STEM, we are simply not doing it as much as we should or could.

Rather than compete for the already overburdened curricular space devoted to science instruction, GE2 expands the curricular space afforded to the teaching of science by building upon the interdisciplinary nature of social studies. PBL researchers have illustrated that leveraging interdisciplinary contexts, like social studies, as a venue to engage in real world problem solving can deepen students' understanding, flexibility in application and transfer of knowledge [18 19; 20; 21]. Because problem-based learning (PBL) consists of a presentation of authentic problems as a starting point for learning, it increases student motivation and integration of knowledge [22] and when working cooperatively in groups within a PBL environment, students learn how to plan and determine what they need to solve problems, pose questions, and decide where they can get these answers as they make sense of the world around them [23].

There can be no doubt that recent USA policy initiatives across local, state and national levels have placed increased pressure on schools to improve student performance in the domains of literacy, mathematics and science. Problem-based learning (PBL) researchers have illustrated for decades that leveraging interdisciplinary contexts as a venue to engage in real world problem solving can deepen students' understanding, flexibility in application and transfer of knowledge [24; 25; 18; 19]. Recognizing this, the GlobalEd 2 Project (GE2) is an educational multi-team game that uses educational technologies currently available in most middle schools to build upon the interdisciplinary nature of social studies as an expanded curricular application aimed at increasing instructional time devoted to science and persuasive writing in a virtual environment [25].

The GE2 game operates within a middle school social studies class, focusing on an international science crisis. GE2 capitalizes on the interdisciplinary nature of social studies in order to expand the curricular space for additional opportunities to learn science and the use of educational technology, without sacrificing the curricular goals of the social studies curriculum. It works as a simulation environment in which classrooms of students work to reach an agreement on a critical global science issue, while representing a specific country over a period of 14 weeks.

The core of GE2 is the problem-based scenario. Interactions occur through a web-based system enabling email and real-time conferencing in a secure environment. Classrooms of students are assigned their country 4-6 weeks before the simulation, and are given analytical tasks to broad topical issue areas (i.e., human rights, economics, environment, health) presented in the scenario. Students are told that their country has to "stay in character" (e.g., remain consistent in policy positions and value systems of their country), while attempting to develop responses to problems within the issue areas. The scenario developed for the current simulation focused on Global Water Resources.

Students are instructed to learn about the values and customs of their respective countries prior to the simulation, so that they are prepared to make appropriate "in character" responses. Students did not know the name, race, sex or location of the students on other teams, only the name of the country, issue area and student's initials; there are generally 14-18 countries in a simulation.

There are three phases of the GlobalEd 2 Project: Research, Interactive and Debriefing (see Appendix A). The Research phase lasts six weeks, the Interactive phase lasts six weeks and the Debriefing phase lasts two weeks. The goal presented to the students is to negotiate an agreement on the science topic with at least one other country-team in the game.

2   Statement of the Research Problem

GE2's extensive use of written communications creates an invaluable venue for students to learn and practice written scientific argumentation in a real world context and to an authentic audience. Research illustrates that both instruction and authentic opportunities to write have been shown in the literature to improve writing skill [26; 27]. In addition, with more opportunities to experience success in writing there is a greater chance to positively impact their writing self-efficacy. Writing self-efficacy has been shown to mediate academic performance in writing [28]. As such, GE2 has the potential to impact not only the quality of students' written work within the simulation, but also has the opportunity impact longer-term performance.

The three research questions addressed are: 1) Is there a significant increase in middle grade students writing self-efficacy after participating a GE2 simulation?; 2) Is there a significant increase in the quality of students' written scientific argumentation after participating in a GE2 simulation?; and 3) Are there differences on the impact of GE2 with respect to the quality of written scientific argumentation across gender and socioeconomic status?

3   Methodology

A total of 420 student participated in a GE2 simulation; 312 of these students were from suburban schools located in New England, the remaining 118 students were from a large Midwestern city. All schools participating were public schools, with students drawn from both the 7th and 8th grades. Suburban schools were markedly higher with respect to socioeconomic status with fewer than 15% of participants receiving free/reduced lunches. Students from urban schools were significantly lower socio-economically, with over 80% of student receiving subsidies for lunches. IRBs were obtained for all students whose data was collected. Those students who did not have parental consent participated in the educational program but did not participate in the research component of GE2.

Prior to implementing the GE2 simulation in their classrooms, teachers from both sites were trained for the implementation of GE2, including writing and teaching scientific argumentation. Students complete a battery of pre-test instruments prior to being introduced to GE2 (see Appendix A for a breakdown of the three GE2 phases and timeline of assessment administration). Within this battery was a 5-item measure of writing self-efficacy (Likert scale format, 1 representing low efficacy and 5 representing high efficacy) and an open ended writing prompt patterned after prompts students receive as part of state mandated standardized tests. This writing prompt asked students to write a persuasive argument either for against the claim that the Earth is in danger of running out of fresh water. They were asked to clearly provide a claim, provide evidence for their claim as well as the reasoning they used to link that evidence to their claim. All assessments were administered using paper and pencil format. Students then began participation in the GE2 simulation that lasted for approximately 14 weeks. After completing the 14-week simulation portion of GE2, student were re-administered the same battery of assessments as post measures of performance. See Appendix B for a figure detailing the GE2 learning environment.

Writing self-efficacy items were summed to create one composite score pre and post for each student (possible range: 5-25). Student essays were scored by two trained independent raters - blinded to student identity and time of administration. An adapted version of the argumentation rubric developed by Midgette, Haria and MacAuthur [29] was used to rate essays for quality of argumentation. The basic structure of this rubric examines the presence of claims, evidence and reasoning, the completeness of these argumentation chains as well as whether they addressed the opposition in their arguments (possible range 0-5). Inter-rater agreement exceeded 85%. Where ratings differed, scores from each rater were averaged to yield a single argument score for each student's essay.

4   Results

To address the first research question, regarding writing self-efficacy of the overall sample, pre and post scores were analyzed using a dependent t-test. Results indicated a significant difference between pre and post scores $(t(415)=2.27, p<.05)$, with students indicating significantly greater writing self-efficacy after participation in GE2.This analysis was repeated for research question 2, examining the argumentation quality score derived from the open-ended essay responses provided by students. Results of this t-test also indicated a significant increase in scores from pre to post.

To further examine the impact of gender and socioeconomic status on student writing self-efficacy and argumentation quality over time, a series of ANCOVAs were conducted where pretest scores served as the covariates, post-tests as the dependent variables and gender and socioeconomic status as the independent factors. Results indicated significant differences between both gender and socioeconomic status with respect to writing self-efficacy at the time of the post-test after controlling for pre-test differences on this construct ($F(1,410) = 5.9$, $p < .05$; $F(1,416) = 3.97$, $p < .05$, respectively). The results show while that students representing each strata changed positively over time, females and students from the urban setting were significantly more self-efficacious with respect to writing than their counterparts at the time of the post-test, after controlling for pre-test differences. Regarding argument quality as measured by the open-ended essays, no differences in the amount of change by gender or socio economic status were noted, indicating that all groups improved their writing quality relatively equally ($ps > 05$).

5   Conclusions

There is much still to learn about GE2 and its impacts on student learning. However, we believe that the increased opportunities that GE2 affords students to construct written arguments in a real world context, the application of knowledge to solve problems rather than recall information and the authenticity of the audience to which students are writing are particularly salient affordances promoting positive change in academic performance. While this study does not provide a control group against which we can assess the changes in GE2 participants' performance compared to standard educational practice, the results presented here speak to the potential of GE2 as a meaningful context within which students can learn and practice their ability to construct written scientific argumentation. Students who participated in the simulation increased both their writing self-efficacy and their writing performance scores over the course of the curricular intervention, across gender and socioeconomic status. Further, the results of this study suggest very positive curricular implications of writing intensive, interdisciplinary, problem-based learning (PBL) approaches like GE2, while also suggesting future directions for PBL research.

Acknowledgements. This work was supported by the United States Department of Education's Institute for Education Science grant numbers Award # R305A080622 and R305A130195. The opinions and findings presented are those of the authors and do not necessarily reflect the position of the United States Department of Education.

The authors would like to thank Kamila Brodowinska Bruscianelli, Lisa Lynn, Mark Boyer, Greg Mullin, Mariya Yukhymenko Lescroart and Donalyn Maneggia for their assistance on this research project.

References

1. Anderson, R.D.: Reforming science teaching: What research says about inquiry. Journal of Science Teacher Education 13, 1–12 (2002)
2. Sadler, T.D. (ed.): Socio-scientific issues in the classroom. Springer, NY (2011)

3. Chinn, C.A., Malhotra, B.: Epistemologically authentic inquiry in schools: A theoretical framework for evaluating inquiry tasks. Science Education 86(2), 175–218 (2002)

4. Osborne, J.F., Erduran, S., Simon, S.: Ideas, Evidence and Argument in Science. In-service Training Pack, Resource Pack and Video. Nuffield Foundation, London (2004)

5. Schwarz, B.B., Neuman, Y., Gil, J., Ilya, M.: Construction of collective and individual knowledge in argumentative activity: An empirical study. The Journal of the Learning Sciences 12(2), 221–258 (2003)

6. Erduran, S., Simon, S., Osborne, J.: TAPping into argumentation: Developments in the application of Toulmin's argument pattern for studying science discourse. Science Education 88, 915–933 (2004)

7. Jiménez, A.M.P., Pereiro-Muños, C.: Knowledge producers or knowledge consumers? Argumentation and decision-making about environmental management. International Journal of Science Education 24, 1171–1190 (2002)

8. Osborne, J.F., Erduran, S., Simon, S., Monk, M.: Enhancing the quality of argument in school science. School Science Review 82(301), 63–70 (2001)

9. Driver, R., Leach, J., Millar, R., Scott, P.: Young people's images of science. Open University Press, Philadelphia (1996)

10. Taber, K.S.: Towards a curricular model of the nature of science. Science and Education 17(2-3), 179–218 (2008)

11. Turner, S.: School science and its controversies; or, whatever happened to scientific literacy? Public Understanding of Science 17(1), 55–72 (2008)

12. Sadler, T.D., Barab, S., Scott, B.: What do students gain by engaging in socioscientific inquiry? Research in Science Education 37(4), 371–391 (2007)

13. Sadler, T.D., Amirshokoohi, A., Kazempour, M., Allspaw, K.M.: Socioscience and ethics in science classrooms: Teacher perspectives and strategies. Journal of Research in Science Teaching 43(4), 353–376 (2006)

14. Alozie, N., Moje, E.B., Kracik, J.S.: An analysis of the supports and constraints for scientific discussion among high school project-based science. Science Education 94, 395–427 (2010)

15. Bartholomew, H., Osborne, J.F., Ratcliffe, M.: Teaching students 'Ideas-About-Science': five dimensions of effective practice. Science Education 88, 655–682 (2004)

16. Bennett, J., Lubben, F., Hogarth, S., Campbell, B.: Systematic review of research in science education: Rigour or rigidity. International Journal of Science Education 27(4), 387–406 (2005)

17. Levinson, R., Turner, S. (eds.): The teaching of social and ethical issues in the school curriculum, arising from developments in biomedical research: A research study of teachers. Institute of Education, London (2001)

18. Jonassen, D.H.: Assembling and analyzing the building blocks of problem-based learning environments. In: Silber, K.H., Foshay, W.R. (eds.) Handbook of Improving Performance in the Workplace, Volume One: Instructional Design and Training Delivery. John Wiley & Sons, Inc., Hoboken (2009)

19. Koschmann, T.D., Kelson, A.C., Feltovich, P.J., Barrows, H.S.: Computer-supported problem-based learning: A principled approach to the use of computers in collaborative learning. In: Koschmann, T. (ed.) CSCL: Theory and Practice of an Emerging Paradigm, pp. 83–124. Lawrence Erlbaum, Mahwah (1996)

20. Mergendoller, J.R., Bellisimo, Y., Maxwell, N.L.: Comparing problem-based learning and traditional instruction in high school economics. Journal of Educational Research 93(6), 374–383 (2000)

21. Strobel, J., van Barneveld, A.: When is PBL more effective? A meta-synthesis of meta-analyses comparing PBL to conventional classrooms. The Interdisciplinary Journal of Problem-based Learning 3(1), 4 (2009)
22. Bednar, A.K., Cunningham, D., Duffy, T.M., Perry, J.D.: Theory into practice: How do we link? In: Duffy, T.M., Jonassen, D.J. (eds.) Constructivism and the Technology of Instruction: A Conversation. Lawrence Erlbaum Associates, Publishers, Hillsdale (1992)
23. Brown, S.W., Lawless, K.A., Boyer, M.A.: Expanding the Science and Literacy Curricular Space: The GlobalEd II Project. US Department of Education: The Institute of Education Sciences, IES. # R305A080622 (2008-2012)
24. Bereiter, C., Scardamalia, M.: The psychology of written composition. Lawrence Erlbaum Associates, Hillsdale (1987)
25. Hayes, J.R.: A new framework for understanding cognition and affect in writing. In: Indrisano, R., Squire, J.R. (eds.) Perspectives on Writing: Research, Theory and Practice, pp. 6–44. International Reading Association, Newark (2000)
26. Pajares, F.: Self-efficacy beliefs in academic settings. Review of Educational Research 56, 543–578 (1996)
27. Midgette, E., Haria, P., MacArthur, C.: The effects of content and audience awareness goals for revision on the persuasive essays of fifth- and eighth-grade students. Reading and Writing 21(1-2), 131–151 (2008)

Appendix A.   The Three Phases of GlobalEd 2

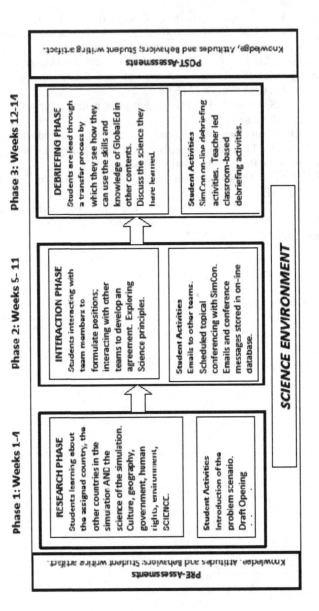

Appendix B. GlobalEd 2 Learning Environment

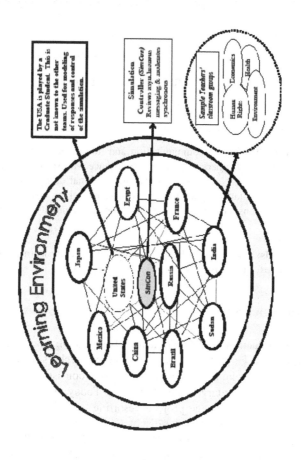

Distance Exchange Projects at Elementary School: A Focus on a Co-learning Process

Anne Choffat-Dürr

ATILF/CNRS, Université de Lorraine, France
anne.durr@univ-lorraine.fr

Abstract. The use of communication and information technology at primary school enables learners to interact at a distance with speakers of the target language. The article aims to show that international distance exchange projects between early-language learners contributes to making a shift in attitudes. The study questions a co-action process based on a reciprocity principle as a social construct.

Keywords: Computer mediated communication, early learning, collaboration, distance exchange projects .

1   Introduction

Before the introduction of technological tools at school, Alziary & Freinet (1947) and later Galisson and Puren (1999), among other researchers, had sceptical views about the capacity of early language learners to deliver consistent exchanges either in their own language or in the target one (ibid. 124). Today, we observe that when they are engaged in distance exchange projects resorting to various computer mediated communication tools, the link and the distance between their own and others' language and culture have to be considered differently (Choffat-Dürr, 2013).

Under the name of distance exchange projects (DEP) we understand that two or more people or groups of people are engaged in a partnership usually for a school year. The purpose is to make native speakers (or speakers of the target language) relate with other language learners in a crossed relation thanks to tools that enable distance interactions.

Our presentation at HCI international 2014 discusses these DEPs as change agents influencing conditions and methods in language teaching and learning at elementary school. It focusses on collaboration for the benefit of first and second language learning in the context of distance exchanges between peers of the same age (8- to 11-year-old learners).

2   Context of the Study

In the UK, the learning of a L2 is not statutory at Key Stage 2, but is tending in that direction (awaited in September 2014), except in Scotland where it is already compul-

P. Zaphiris and A. Ioannou (Eds.): LCT 2014, Part I, LNCS 8523, pp. 380–387, 2014.

sory like in France where learning a foreign language starts at the age of 7 with the aim of reaching level A1, the lowest level in the Common European Reference Framework for Languages (CEFR). According to this standard, at the end of elementary school a learner is expected to be able to:

- Recognise and use familiar words and simple phrases for concrete purposes;
- Introduce himself or someone else;
- Ask and answer basic questions about home, family, surroundings, etc.;
- Communicate in a basic way when the other person speaks slowly and clearly, and is ready to repeat or reformulate to help communication (CEFR, 2001, 24).

To reach this level, the main approach that has been resorted to so far is the communicative approach. However, research in the field of the didactics of languages is critical of it as it is observed in classrooms[1] where, according to theory, the accent should be brought to bear more on the dynamics of social interaction (Audin, 2005). Moreover, as Gaonac'h indicated as early as 1991, "observed practices force us to call into question the artificial character of interactions in a school context" (in French), since, "during language communication activities, systems for communication are indeed set up, but is there really any sense in communicating for communication's sake?" (in French, Bourguignon, 2007). And indeed, despite the principle announced by the CEFR, "While acts of speech occur within language activities, these activities form part of a wider social context, which alone is able to give them their full meaning" (CEFR, 2001, p.9), we can only observe that it is difficult to create such types of activities within the four walls of the classroom.

In this context however, the European commission through the eTwinning[2] platform or national institutions encourage school partnerships, to open the class to native speakers. To some extent they share a common consideration in calling for a socially-engaged perspective having classrooms connected to other parts of the world. Even though they are not numerous at elementary level, some teachers, however, answer positively. Showing a converging willingness to promote communicative competences including intercultural components through the medium of communication tools, some get involved into DEPs.

3   Research Question and Hypothesis

Our research questions the activities undertaken by young L2 (second language) learners with a minimal level in the target language (1 to 3 years of learning A1 level) when involved in DEPs. Hence the question: Does resorting to DEPs with young students help their learning process?

---

[1] The term "class" or "classroom" is used to refer to the body of students that are taught together for a school year.

[2] eTwinning is an online platform under the supervision of the European Commission. It enables schools across Europe to link online and engage in information and communication technology. It provides online tools such as a "TwinSpace", a safe controlled working environment, and other resources such as ready-made project kits.

More particularly, we suppose that with the influence of information and communication tools, young learners, who were previously excluded from any international correspondence because they could not deliver consistent exchanges, can now communicate. Language which was formerly viewed as a sole written code enabling penfriends to interact can now be considered in its more universal concept, namely the ability to communicate. Today, ICT offers a great range of tools that allow young students to show their creativity in finding alternative ways to communicate.

Consequently, we aim to identify variables and influences in classrooms where students are linked to speakers of the target language and in particular the communicative contexts in which action takes place. Besides, the importance of the pedagogical context is also under scrutiny, since we assume that it is one of the major factors of the dynamics that may occur. Indeed, the main hypothesis is that resorting to DEPs induces active pedagogy. We suppose that teachers cannot expose their pupils without consulting them on what they expect to do with their distant partners and how they imagine they will go about it. In other words, a socio-constructivist and interactionist approach is at stake. Therefore, the study seeks to show that the learning process is guided by intentions or communicative needs that are created and shared through the dynamics emerging between the two distant groups (reference to activity theory). As a consequence, the tasks or the activities would be central to the social action (Ollivier, 2009). Needless to say that the tools contributing to the action and the co-action process figures among the factors that are to be considered: Which ones are used? On which grounds are they selected? To what purpose? Etc.

4   Method

Our analysis is based on the observation of the activities undertaken for a school year by four partnerships between French and British primary schools. All partnerships were initiated by teachers who were not familiar with distance pedagogy. The data comes from classroom observations (audio and video recordings), interviews and questionnaires from participants in the DEPs. The entire e-mail correspondence between the distant teachers has also been gathered. This collection follows a preliminary survey among 121 French primary school teachers that we conducted to put instructional and pedagogical actions into context.

As Dillenbourg said as early as 2002, we have to keep in mind that this type of studies focussing on "the effectiveness of collaborative learning [to which we include DEPs] depends upon multiple conditions such as group composition (size, age, gender, heterogeneity, ...), task features and communication media" (ibid, 61). Since the conditions are numerous and diverse, and since they interact with each other in a complex way, our study has to be viewed more as case studies that make us enter the process and bring elements that help the understanding of what results from acting collectively at a distance. In particular, it is aimed at identifying some of the common variables that impact the social link (cf. social cognitive learning theory, Vygotsky, 1978) which itself is said to influence L2 learning (Long, 1996 or Warschauer and Meskill, 2000).

Therefore, the activities undertaken as a result of pedagogical choices as well as the type of actions generated by social connections between distant classes are analysed in each DEP (with a focus on the French side). Then a crossed analysis follows. Our grid refers to situated action (Lave and Wenger, 1991; Bandura, 1997) and situated learning theories (Tardif, 1998). Thus, first, we consider the context in which action and co-action take place to interpret them theoretically on social and psychological grounds. We refer to the actors' representations of the project and of the tools viewed to mediate communication. Then, we analyse the material resources that are used to confront them with the L2 learning process (Bange, 1992; Dausendschön-Gay, 2006), and more particularly we explore the link between participation and appropriation.

5   Findings

Among our findings we notice that even when young learners are beginners in the target language, when involved in distance exchange projects, provided they are guided through active pedagogy (which proves to be inherent to this practice), their roles may be enhanced in the context of a joint action. Each of the four projects is grounded on a socio-constructivist paradigm that refers to a situated perspective (Lave and Wenger, 1991; Tardif, 1998). In other words, our hypothesis is confirmed since their activities are guided by intentions and communicative needs that are created through the dynamics emerging between the two distant groups (see examples of their activities below). Learners take into account what their learning environment is and the nature of the relationships that link the two distant groups (Choffat-Dürr and Macaire, 2012).

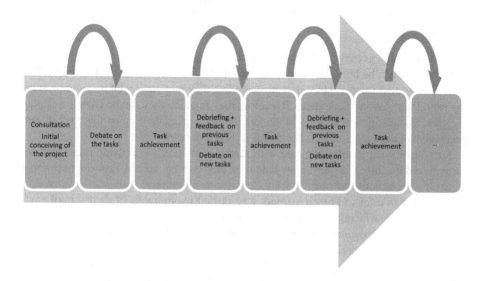

Fig. 1. Cycle based on the teaching method observed in the four partnerships

We observe that in their conceiving of the project, teachers on both sides agree to give an active role to their students. The latter are therefore consulted all along the project. The new pedagogical organisation initiates a new space for learners to engage actively.

The following is an excerpt from an interview with one of the teachers of our cohorts:

> From my point of view, this project wouldn't be successful unless the pupils subscribe to it. It means that at the beginning we should explain what a project is without influencing them, without telling them what they have to do. If they agree with the idea and have ideas to develop they have to have enough space to express their goals, their needs (what they have to learn in the foreign language to be able to achieve the task they focus on), what they feel like doing. Then we can build a program from their ideas.

Consultation appears to be the mode adopted to elaborate the different tasks or activities within each class. As for the teachers, they interact as intermediaries between the two groups. However, each group influences the other (cf. the arrows on figure 1). Data collected through interviews at the beginning of the project with the learners show very positive opinions.

> I would be pleased if they taught me English and I would teach them my French but we could also help them on other things if we can and I think that they have a beautiful country (in French, Lila, class A/F).

The students' initial aims may be grouped under three entries:

- Communicate to discover the others, their environment
- Engage in mutual teaching of the language and culture
- Play together

Their ambition goes further than the teachers'. First, they envisage the link as a social construct that can be built upon social relationships. They appear to identify themselves with their foreign partners since they perceive that they may have a lot in common starting from their age and their status. Therefore they imagine they can be friends and play together. The distinction also lies in the fact that they take into account that their distant peers are language learners too. Their goal is therefore twofold.

First, they want to communicate with their distant peers to provide them with informative data, input in the target language that can be treated (information about their identity, school and outside school environment, cultural facts, etc.). As an illustration we can refer to French learners who posted photographs of their school environment on the eTwinning platform so as to provide their English peers with an oriented topic of conversation for an approaching videoconference. The English learners therefore worked collectively on questions that the pictures raised. Their project being based on a principle of reciprocity, the latter also took pictures of their school to make a book that they submitted for further online exchanges.

Besides, engaged in a crossed relation, learners perceive that they can also contribute to their partners' language learning by engaging themselves in teaching activities. Following the principles of an implicit contract that would be that each group alternatively helps the other in learning its culture and its language, they opt for collective activities, conducted with the whole class or in smaller groups. They provide various items of input in their first language to be treated by their peers. In one DEP, they went as far as conducting lessons reproducing models that their teachers used for their own learning of the language to teach their partners. For example, they created flashcards to teach lexical items during a videoconference, and then intended to check the impact of their teaching during another online meeting, organizing a bingo game.

Thanks to the tools that are available, they prove creative and develop strategies to reach their aims. As an illustration, we can quote the use of voki.com. It is an online application that is used to create avatars that can be given a voice through various means (via phone, microphone, text to speech or by uploading a file). The students had previously used it as a means to provide themselves with a voice recorder. Yet, unexpectedly, while they were faced with the difficulty to decipher orally scripts that they had written, one student found the text-to-speech option and showed it to his classmates. This tool happened to be relevant to improve pronunciation skills so as to feel sufficiently prepared for oral communication with their distant peers. We witnessed many episodes of such collective dynamics emerging and favouring their learning process. In one PED, we observe that within an institutional context, the project focusing on computer-mediated communication generates "focus on form" not mediated by the teachers but by peers. During asynchronous or synchronous exchanges participants are sensitive to errors that punctuate messages. Their self-questioning concerning the norm in both languages make them collectively produce asynchronous corrective feedback.

The use of the tools responds to active and strategic choices in relation to learners' intentions or needs and their environment, either material or social. As another illustration we can refer to their use of traditional paper correspondence that the four partnerships favour at the beginning of their projects. In a letter accompanied with a drawing, they view a more relevant tool for a first "meeting" as each individual could receive a concrete token. A letter has therefore to be viewed as a tangible objet symbolizing the link. Likewise, in the use of digital video recorders, they see a means for self-assessment when preparing themselves for a videoconference, etc. Whatever the tools used, either for synchronous or asynchronous interaction, we observe that learners primarily seek to use them to strengthen the social link between the distant groups in various directions. They use them to improve their skills, to produce items to be shared and to mediate their interaction.

Their posture appears to favour a metacognitive process and a shift in attitudes leading them to perform in a socio-constructivist context. Not only do they speak the language in a pragmatic way but they also speak about the language, and explore the different means to reach their goals (social, material, organisational, learning, etc.).

Pragmatics is at stake in environments which appear to favour their learning, beyond what is usually at stake with early-language learners.

6   Conclusion

Our findings shed some light on the value of PEDs and more particularly their socio-educational benefits. Grounded on active pedagogy, thanks to which early learners have their words (and world) to say, the representation of the language evolves toward a constructive view of it. As Goffin and al. (2009) say "linguistic questions are charged with affect. The picture that one figure out of a language and of the people who speak it has an undoubtable impact on its learning process" (in French). Young learners are able to perceive the benefit they may draw engaging themselves in a collaborative link abroad, the accent being brought on social interaction phenomenon in a new interschool context. Communication is no longer false or artificial (Gaonac'h, 1991). Its social and learning purposes are embedded in the same dynamics. It means that action is perceived through a more holistic perspective that involves each participant of the collective project. The benefit would therefore go beyond the scope of language teaching at school that is therefore questioned.

References

1. Audin, L. (dir.): Enseigner l'anglais de l'école au collège. Comment aborder les principaux obstacles à l'apprentissage. Hatier, Paris (2005)
2. Alziary, H., Freinet, C.: Les correspondances interscolaires. Brochures d'Education Nouvelle Populaire 32 (1947)
3. Bandura, A.: Self-efficacy: The exercise of control. Freeman, New York (1997)
4. Bange, P.: A propos de la communication et de l'apprentissage en L2, notamment dans ses formes institutionnelles. AILE 1, 53–85 (1992)
5. Bourguignon, C.: Apprendre et enseigner les langues dans la perspective actionnelle. Le scénario d'apprentissage-action. APLV (2007),
   http://www.aplv-languesmodernes.org/?article865
6. Choffat-Dürr, A., Macaire, D.: "I'm* two rabbits / J'ai un rouge pullover*. How corrective feedback is handled in collaborative exchange programmes between earl y language learners". Eurocall Review 20(1), 41–44 (2012)
7. Choffat-Dürr, A.: School-to-school correspondence – then and now. Paper Presented at WorldCALL 2013, Glasgow, Scotland (2013)
8. Council of Europe: Common European Framework of Reference for Languages: Learning, Teaching, Assessment. Council of Europe (2001),
   http://www.coe.int/t/dg4/linguistic/Source/Framework_EN.pdf
9. Dausendschön-Gay, U.: Pratiques communicatives et appropriation de langues à l'école primaire. In: Faraco, M. (ed.) La classe de langue. Théories, méthodes et pratiques, pp. 71–91. Aix-en-Provence, PUP (2006)
10. Dillenbourg, P.: Over-scripting CSCL: The risks of blending collaborative learning with instructional design. Three worlds of CSCL. Can we support CSCL, 61–91 (2002)
11. Galisson, R., Puren, C.: La formation en questions. CLE International, Paris (1999)

12. Gaonac'h, D.: Théories d'apprentissage et acquisition d'une langue étrangère. Hatier/Didier, Paris (1991)
13. Goffin, C., Fagnant, A., Blondin, C.: Les langues des voisins: des langues toujours appréciées? Lidil, 40 (2009), http://lidil.revues.org/index2897.html
14. Lave, J., Wenger, E.: Situated learning: Legitimate peripheral participation. Cambridge University Press, Cambridge (1991)
15. Long, M.H.: The role of the linguistic environment in second language acquisition. In: Ritchie, W.C., Bahtia, T.K. (eds.) Handbook of Second Language Acquisition, pp. 413–468. Academic Press, New York (1996)
16. Ollivier, C.: Mettre en œuvre une approche interactionnelle sur le Web 2.0. In: Lirria, P. (ed.) L'approche actionnelle dans l'enseignement des langues, Difusión, Barcelona, pp. 263–285 (2009)
17. Tardif, J.: Intégrer les nouvelles technologies de l'information / Quel cadre pédagogique? Paris. ESF, 54–56 (1998)
18. Vygotsky, L.S.: Mind in society: The development of higher psychological processes. Harvard University Press, Cambridge (1978)
19. Warschauer, M., Meskill, C.: Technology and second language teaching. In: Rosenthal, J. (ed.) Handbook of Undergraduate Second Language Education, pp. 303–318 (2000)

Applying Gianni Rodari Techniques to Develop Creative Educational Environments

Habib M. Fardoun[1], Iyad A. Kateb[1],
Antonio Paules Ciprés[2], and Jaime Ramírez Castillo[3]

[1] Faculty of Computing and Information Technology, King Abdulaziz University (KAU),
Jeddah, Saudi Arabia
{hfardoun,iakatib}@kau.edu.sa
[2] European University of Madrid, Madrid, Spain
apcipres@gmail.com
[3] ITKnowingness, Madrid, Spain
jaime.ram@gmail.com

Abstract. In this article we will conduct a study of the Gianni Rodari School, a technique used in the initial educational levels of pre-schools and primary schools, but in this case for the use in the development of new creative ideas for the college projects, and vocational training subjects. For this we define and justify the essence of creativity as ideas, using a structure that can be stored in the cloud. To validate the system, we present a case study by using abstract concepts of human knowledge in the cloud. The presented work takes into consideration the interaction and collaborative work to promote creativity and the generation of new ideas in a clear and ordered way for the students.

Keywords: Creativity, Teaching Techniques, Cloud Computing, developing ideas, education environments.

1   Introduction

In this article we will conduct a study of the Gianni Rodari School [1], a technique used in the initial educational levels of pre-schools and primary schools, but in this case for the use in the development of new creative ideas for the college projects, and vocational training subjects.

Gianni Rodari is an inventor of children's stories, that aim to develop basic skills and general primary cycles through the children read of those stories. This technique facilitates learning of children by the use of techniques that foster creativity. Our idea is to apply this technique in the vocational training level, in order to encourage creativity and imagination in the course of advanced vocational training projects. The study of this technique by the teachers and the implementation of methods that foster creativity and imagination are important in the industrial products development and innovation of new ideas. Gianni Rodari in his book "Grammar of Fantasy"[1] uses his personal experience of working with children. This book is based on the explanation of many creative techniques that help children, to allow their imagination, to create

P. Zaphiris and A. Ioannou (Eds.): LCT 2014, Part I, LNCS 8523, pp. 388–397, 2014.

fanciful stories in which anything can happen. As he does not limit the children thoughts, he encourage creative thinking which helps them look for different options to solve problems throughout life. The next sentence, captured from Gianni book describes his technique about creativity in childhood education centers:

> *"It is one more propose to put off all those who try to enrich the stimulus of the environment (home or school, whatever) in which the child grows. The mind is only one. His creativity must be cultivated in all directions."*

Our labor as teachers is to be able to help students through techniques that promote creativity, and educate students in the development of new designs, new products and new technologies. For that, During these past courses, we have conducted researches on educational environments in the cloud on the documentation of learning units, from creation to evaluation [4], and on employing methods of interaction in the cloud systems [5] considering the usability in collaborative environments in the cloud [6]. After considering the technical part of the research, we develop the "Montessori Method" as the application of ICT in the classroom [7]. As we appointed, we dispose the technology to develop such methods. So, our goal in this article is to establish a set of guidelines for the development of a technique using Rodari School for project subjects, which our university sets as follows:

> *"... Individual or collective work with well-defined roles, predominantly creative and design side, which will take place in a university department, institution or company, domestic or foreign, or at another university as part of a mobility agreement..."*

2   State of Art

In our quest searching for tools that enable the collaborative work, defined to encourage creativity and document the entire process, we found many of these, based on conceptual design, logical design, and modeling languages, that allow capturing the students' ideas on paper. Thus, the achievement would be getting questions that may not have answers, as any question could be a new idea or a new product.

For example, In software engineering methodology, we can find the client requirements: starting from a discussion of customer requirements, when the analyst develops cases with the need for future implementation, *Rational Requisite Pro* is the used tool [8] which interfaces with *Rational Enterprise Pro* [9], these known engineers software tools allow defining the functional requirements through users interaction in an technology information environment. The rest of the Web 2.0 tools are premises where documents are shared and collaborative online environments are limited to working with similar tools as *Google Docs* [10]. By performing a search in the Web, we can find many Web Sites that use these type of tools and explain it in detail, as we all know, some of these are: Wikis, Blogs, Forums, and Moodle.

3   Resume of the Creativity Technique

Rodari technique is presented throughout its literature [3]. From these texts, the basic premises of the Rodari School extracted are as follow:

- The belief in the transformative power of language.
- Trust in the game as possibility of freedom and the most natural expression of childhood.
- Calls for a happy school, not a boring one.
- Considers magic and knowledge as two interacting components.
- Squeezing the language to sprout new ways of understanding reality.

The techniques developed in the books written by the author are:

- **Fantastic Hypothesis:** What if...? Ask a known situation where a foreign element is introduced. For example, what would happen if an alien landed our school?
- **Tales backwards:** From a well-known story is to imagine what would happen if things happened in that story backwards or if a change in the characteristic element occurs.
- **Creative Analysis:** Many stories have secondary characters we know nothing about them. These characters can be taken as a starting point of a new imaginary story, to try to imagine what are their stories: where he/she comes from? , What was their role in the story, etc.
- **Salad stories:** tales mix, allows other story characters to participate in other stories.
- **Creative Error:** it is about taking note of the mistakes made by people when answering questions, writing, or other school situations, and try to explore its possibilities. For example, if I write the word "ures" (instead of "user") ... what world " ures" could be? What are its characteristics, what would it mean? ...

As we can see, these techniques and their description are designed for schools and exposes a new method:

- Encourage creativity and imagination since childhood.
- It shows the transformative power of language
- It transmits to us the importance of training for the world transformation.

4   Definition

In section 3 we have seen the various techniques developed by Rodari, we can observe that these techniques are of the question-answer type, with a point text, a word game, and interaction of various techniques. In this paper we will transfer these techniques for the identification of projects, so that the creative process is able to focus on the definition of objectives and its idea.

Creativity in our case concerns the creation and definition of milestones project, as it is in these phases where students can make new products, for expanding the objectives. Where the objects in the cloud systems interact with each other, and growth depending on user need. So, the question here can these ideas be represented in the cloud? For that, first we have to identify the meaning of an idea. According to the classic notions as Platon's theory of ideas, taken from his works "The Republic", "Phaedo" and "Phaedrus"[11] is:

> *"The Idea is the object of an intellectual intuition and represents the immutable and eternal essence of reality (that is alien to change, therefore), and having independent existence of sensible reality (i.e., which is subsisting). The Idea is a real object that exists independently of sensible reality and thoughts. In the dual theory of ideas, is the term of the universal definition represent the " essence " of the objects of knowledge, i.e., that which is in the concept, but with the peculiarity that can not be confused with the concept, so the Platonic Ideas are not mental contents, but objects that mental contents designated by the concept relate and express through language. "*

As we can see, the ideas are immutable in time and do not change, while the concept changes, and where the mental contents become the objects that define the ideas. According to Rodari School, ideas come from the techniques that work through contents, so we can use the content to define ideas that results in a product associated with it.

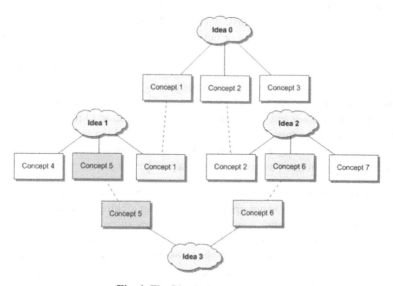

Fig. 1. The Idea and the concepts

As we can see in Figure 1, the ideas consist of concepts that define the idea itself. Furthermore, there are ideas that can arise from different composition concepts of other ideas, graphically and according to the level of the problem we are defining we can see the relationship with the Rodari School. Rodari performs his techniques according to the concepts and that is why these concepts help defining the ideas as their realization and development within the cloud of ideas. Working creative can help developing ideas by defining concepts. The concepts developed by students based on their needs and the content of the materials. And by this Rodari technique streamline the process of creating and defining ideas.

Figure 2. shows how the ideas and creativity in the university environment can be obtained from:

- The content of the subjects taught in the classroom.
- From the path chosen the mistake-test and the questions we have.
- From the current technology and its applications, the fact of considering new uses of technology makes us think about the development of a new technology, a new product.
- The working experience in the field.
- The collaborative work to share ideas.

Rodari adapt techniques to the projects subject, which we are all familiar within the computer terminology:

- **Hypothesis doubt:** we propose the doubt to the student on the technological future and let him consider the off-label use, as a new way to interact with a device, regardless of the labeled technology used.
- **Backwards Engineering:** From selected scientific texts, we try to motivate students to wonder what would have happened if something had changed. Could be realized from made applications or outdated applications that could be changed, or starting from the same prototypes.
- **Creative Analysis:** An analysis of market requirements, the project itself, or searching for projects that are being conducted.
- **Salad of Contents:** using a selected content from the courses, the student may have more motivation and focused thoughts on the creation of products.
- **Error:** Defining the mistakes they have committed and the analysis with the techniques described above, we can reach the solution to the error and encourage the student interrogations as a way to solve to a problem.

As we can observe, we have just made a translation of the method to another education level. In our case, it is not grammar or creating children's stories, we are developing a technique that fosters creativity for students in college and also allow the creation of new products to the industry. Rodari technique is widespread and tested in primary and pre-school lessons; we are only upgrading it for higher educational and to the students cognitive level. Thus, the rapid evolution in the information technology and the emergence for new products in the market requires us to experiment with techniques like this one.

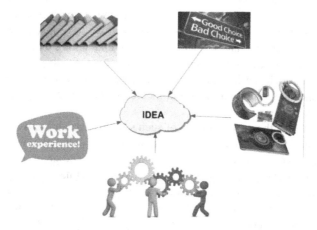

Fig. 2. Development and creation of an idea

5   Architecture

We have developed an architecture that can deploy and develop ideas. In addition, it allows us to have a repository of ideas that permits linking the present ideas with new ideas so that it can emerge. In the previous section, we said that ideas are objects that are made up of concepts, then following this definition, we can say that a cloud where ideas are represented as objects with no relationship between different objects, are defined by a set of concepts where Rodari technique would facilitate the extension of these ideas.

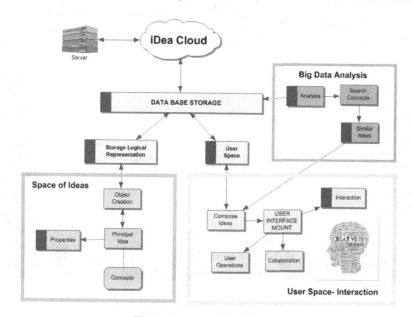

Fig. 3. Conceptual Architecture

As a result, we have the following parts in the logical objects storage where we have a representation of objects and ideas, and then we have a space for the shared work of users where users interact with the system and among them with permission to work in groups. On the other hand, we have a section for the analysis of the network of ideas through the link, also, for associating concepts and ideas in order to modify the existence of proven ideas and its feedback to produce creativity throughout the creative process.

Figure 3. contains the different parts of such system, a database, we choose object-oriented database. In order to reduce the complexity, we only have two objects in the system of ideas and the concepts associated with users. The green area includes reserved space for ideas and concepts. As we see, the ideas have some properties and consist of concepts that define the logical storage. The structure, detailed in the Figure 3, is similar to an indexed list in a file system; these ideas are stored with a unique identifier where the database is associated with users or group of users who are using the system.

In the blue area, we can find the section for the analysis of data in the database. With this, we managed to extract new ideas by associations of ideas through the concepts that define these ideas. By this way, we make the system offers new possibilities created from the analysis of these characteristics. This point is important because the system feeds itself on the new definitions and associations, the authorized users will have the ability to visualize these results and derive these ideas to those responsible for them or for the system, which developed these ideas over time from the definitions of users.

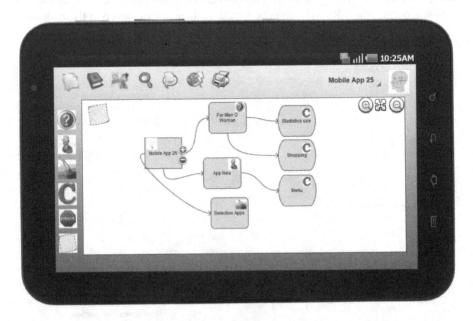

Fig. 4. Desiging creative idea

In yellow we find the logic of interaction. The logic interaction of a system assemble and compose the ideas that the user has made over time to adapt the way the user has determined. This is a personal workspace where Rodari technique is applied; the graphical interface ensures collaboration and interaction from any mobile device, anywhere, because the cloud system is the one that provides the resources by means of a viewer in the user device.

Running a system with these characteristics is easy once the user has started with the creation of ideas in the application, it is stored in the reserved space for it, and so the structure would be saved in the cloud system. The cloud replicates in the database and keep in sync all the information. From the interaction point of view, its not complex for the viewers to access these systems by creating web service, services that transfer information from the client side, cloud system, as parameters or by passing through remote programming methods for sending information. Assigning permissions to the object can perform collaborative work and by this all the users can work in the same session and view the changes. The System growth is guaranteed as the accommodation in cloud systems is dynamic and can increase over time and even in different machines.

6   Study Case

We present the case study of a student who wants to make a mobile application. This interface shows the different parts the student can perform the modeling of the idea, based on the Rodari method, Table 2.

Table 1. Applications options

	With this menu the user creates a new idea that will be stored in the cloud.
	The user can access the resource bank of the school, where he access to both projects for an inquiry as to the works of the subjects listed, in order to be able to get filtered and quality information for the realization of his idea.
	Search users who share his idea with and share the space of thought on that particular idea in order to streamline the process through collaborative work.
	Text search on the entire system returns the items that are in accordance with the entered text in order to expedite the navigation in a specific content.
	Establish communication using text or voice audio with his companion to share experiences.
	Once the idea is set, the user may search for similar trips in the system in order to be able to associate these ideas. In this way the system allows the user to take ideas from other ideas in order to improve them or redesign the existing one.
	Print the diagram; everyone likes to put something on the wall.

Table 2. Menu options using Rodari Terminology

	Hypothesis doubt		Backward Engineering		Error
	Creative Analysis		Content Salad		Tip note to remember

Figure 4., represents an editor where the user develops his ideas graphically. This editor has graphic content to identify the element of the method; it is simple. Further interaction tablet allows the user to work comfortably anywhere in order to enable him ordering his ideas at any time. Table 1. shows the menu options of the application, and Table 2. Show the options of menu options using Rodari terminology.

7   Conclusions

In this paper we have represent an approach for the creation of an application according to *Rodari Technique* for the development of ideas, using our expertise in cloud computing, educational environments and considering what teachers have already apply these techniques in primary schools. We don't find in universities, the use of specific techniques for this issue; we understand the need for these techniques and we consider adapting and applying them for other educational levels, due to its size and use along large time.

Once again, we have used cloud computing during the creation of this application, but in this case it is the definition of the system itself, which determines the architecture design, as we have seen it couldn't be simpler to perform. Usually, cloud systems work in a complex way, with hundreds of thousands of users and data, but in this case the system is simplified by creating a user space each time the user accesses the application. In this way, we cheapen costs and provide a space for independent work.

The application is being created and tested now in several courses in the University of Castilla-La Mancha (Spain).

References

1. Biografía Gianno Rodari,
   http://muse.jhu.edu/login?auth=0&type=summary&url=/
   journals/lion_and_the_unicorn/v026/26.2salvadori.pdf
2. Gramatica De La Fantasia: Introduccion Al Arte De Contar Historias Gianni Rodari, Ed Bronce (2002) ISBN 9788484531647
3. Álvarez, M.: Reseña de" Gramática de la fantasía" de Gianni Rodari. Sapiens. Revista Universitaria de Investigación 7(1), 233–234 (2006)

4. Fardoun, H.M., Cipres, A.P., Mashat, A.S.: Cataloguing Teaching Units: Resources, Evaluation and Collaboration. Knowledge and Information Systems: An International Journal, by Springer. Impact Factor 2.225. ©2012 (2013); Thomson Reuters, 2010 Journal Citation Reports®.
5. Fardoun, H.M., Ciprés, A.P., Alghazzawi, D.M.: CSchool - DUI for Educational System using Clouds. In: Proceedings of the 2nd Workshop on Distributed User Interfaces: Collaboration and Usability, in Conjunction with CHI 2012 Conference, Austin, Texas, USA, May 2012, pp. 35–39. ACM (May 2012) ISBN 84-695-3318-5
6. Fardoun, H.M., Alghazzawi, D.M., Cipres, A.P.: Distributed User Interfaces: Usability and Collaboration. Distributed User Interfaces. In: Human–Computer Interaction Series 2013, pp. 151–163. Springer, London (2013)
7. Fardoun, H.M., AL-Malaise, A., Paules, A.: Creating new Teaching Techniques with ITCs Following the Montessori Method for Uneducable Young Students. In: Proceedings of the 2nd International Workshop on Interaction Design in Educational Environments, IDEE 2013, in Conjunction with ICEIS 2013, SCOPUS (2013)
8. Rational REquisite Pro, link:
   http://www-03.ibm.com/software/products/en/reqpro
9. Rational Rose Enterprise, link:
   http://www-03.ibm.com/software/products/es/enterprise/
10. https://docs.google.com
11. http://www.webdianoia.com/platon/platon_fil.htm

Happy Girls Engaging with Technology: Assessing Emotions and Engagement Related to Programming Activities

Michail N. Giannakos[1,2], Letizia Jaccheri[1], and Ioannis Leftheriotis [1,3]

[1] Department of Computer and Information Science, Norwegian University of Science and Technology, Trondheim, Norway
[2] Department of Computer Science, Old Dominion University, Norfolk, VA, USA
[3] Department of Informatics, Ionian University, Corfu, Greece
mgiannak@cs.odu.edu, letizia@idi.ntnu.no, iolef@acm.org

Abstract. The advent of programming languages for students (i.e., Scratch) combined with accessible programmable hardware platforms (i.e., Arduino) is becoming an emerging practice for computer science education (CSE). Robots and interactive installations are some of the most widespread artifacts for increasing students' adoption in CSE. But what kind of emotions motivate students to participate in such creative development activities? In this paper we present the results of an empirical investigation regarding the key emotions and their impact on a creative learning context. In our empirical evaluation, a group of researchers and artists designed, implemented, and evaluated three workshop programs. The workshops were based on the Reggio Emilia education principles, open source software Scratch and Arduino and were conducted in creative centers. We designed a survey, based on the main Emotional factors identified from the literature as important on the technology context. Responses from 37 twelve-year-old girls were used to examine the effect of Enjoyment, Happiness and Anxiety on students' intention to participate on similar creative development activities. Results confirmed the positive effects of Happiness and the negative effect of Anxiety. Moreover, the results indicated that students' Enjoyment has no relation with students' intention to re-participate in an activity. The overall outcomes are expected to contribute to design practices and promote the acceptance of creative development activities

Keywords: Creativity, Scratch, Programming, Girls in programming, Students' intentions, Emotions, Engagement, Workshop program, Reggio Emilia principles.

1 Introduction

Despite the economic crisis, demand for IT-professionals persists. Currently, several efforts to broaden participation in Computer Science (CS) and introduce computational literacy to young students [6] [22] [33] are in progress. School education plays an important role in raising young students' interest in IT, and particularly in CS subjects. Another notable aspect is the low number of female students in CS subjects.

P. Zaphiris and A. Ioannou (Eds.): LCT 2014, Part I, LNCS 8523, pp. 398–409, 2014.

Women more often than men choose disciplines like linguistics, cultural studies, and arts. In the last decades, attention has been drawn to the imbalance between the males and females in computing; and many initiatives have been taken to that direction [5] [23] [29]. School girls typically show less interest in CS topics; something that later deters them from studying and attaining a CS career [31].

Studies conducted by the (1) Association for Computing Machinery (ACM) and the Computer Science Teachers Association (CSTA) [1], and (2) ACM ITiCSE Working Group Informatics in Secondary Education [17] revealed that CS education faces problems regarding lack of exposure and motives, which are essential for the students. Although students use computers for many tasks both at home and at school, the majority of them never quite understand what computer science is and how it relates to algorithmic thinking and problem solving. Their exposure to computers in school most likely consists of text editors and media presentation tools. Few upper secondary education schools have a mandatory (or even a selective) computer science course and even fewer lower secondary education schools offer a CS course, at a time that is considered crucial for students to think about careers choices and plan future decisions.

The lack of exposure to CS in schools leads to fewer students choosing computer science as a career. To increase the interest, engagement and participation in CS in general, and for females in particular, numerous approaches and projects have been initiated; such as the CS Unplugged [6], Alice [7], Scratch [22] and Greenfoot [16]. Building upon previous research motivating and engaging students with CS in terms of creativity [2] [3], our approach introduces a program which is based on creative activities as a means to facilitate a particular process for teaching youth how to program.

Based on the recent developments of computer science education (CSE) [8] [4], many tools, activities and environments that support CS learning have been developed and were successfully deployed [3] [5] [14]. Although many of these activities are focusing on female students (e.g., female-only events), a possible reason for the lack of success of these intervention strategies is that their evaluation is apparently not usually carried out [9].

Our main research goal is to determine whether female students' (hereinafter students) emotions revealed during the activity can provide a means to increase their intention to adopt a similar activity in the future. Using a quantitative approach, we gained insight on students' emotions towards the activity and then we examined any potential relation of students' emotions and their intention to participate on any similar events in the future. In our line of research, we measure and understand students' emotions regarding creative development activities, in order to be able to:

- Investigate what emotions motivate or distract students to adopt creative programming activities.

The clarification of students' emotions during these activities is expected to contribute to the understanding of their intentions to pursue creative development activities in the future.

2   Related Work

2.1   Creativity in Computer Science Education

In the last decades, various attempts in introducing creativity in CS teaching have been made. One of the earliest is that of Niguidula and van Dam [25]. Perhaps some of the most successful efforts to date are those of using media computation as a context [15] and utilizing Alice to introduce non-majors to computing [7]. These approaches have since been expanded into introductory CS courses (e.g., CS1) with documented success [5]. Other notable efforts in the area include: a course in Introduction to Interactive Multimedia at The College of New Jersey and the Artbotics project which also uses robotics to engage students in creating creative artifacts [34]. On the same direction, the Computational Thinking course at Colby College taught by Bruce Maxwell uses Python and Turtle Graphics for 2D graphics as a medium of creativity, expression, communication and experimentation. Despite its appeal, the concept of generative art and creative computing are relatively underutilized in creating introductory computing curricula.

Numerous projects are focused on creativity and design using computational techniques (e.g., VVVV, PD, Scratch, Processing, Panda3D, Arduino, Wiring). Most of these projects build on the context of robotics, interactive installations and creativity. Their uses in formal computing education are mostly localized to the development groups and their institutions or their immediate communities. However, they represent an exciting direction for bringing computing to a much larger community of students and practitioners.

As we aforementioned, there are many tools to support creativity and idea generation. In our study, we chose to use Scratch (scratch.mit.edu), as the main cornerstone of our study, enabling students to create their own physical characters. Scratch is a media-rich programming language that allows youth to design and share programs in form of stories, movies and games. Students engaging with Scratch use building block command structures; in addition programmable objects can be any imported two-dimensional graphic image, digitally or physically made. This makes it particularly amenable to an array of young creative students who want to build their own software and engage in the participatory culture [19]. With 1.3 million registered members and over 2.8 million projects shared to date, the Scratch website is one of the most vibrant online communities. Scratch can also be used in small group formats (e.g., pair programming).

2.2   Students Emotions

Different emotions arise during the learning procedure and affect students' behavior. As a general categorization, these emotions might either be positive or negative. Previous studies (e.g., [24] [26] [32]) have showed that emotions and feelings in general affect people's intentions and future decisions. Koo and Ju [21] found that pleasure and arousal that derive from atmospherics affect positively computer use. Besides the more generalized positive and negative emotions, it is essential to examine the specific types-categories of emotions and how they affect students while they are learning through different processes.

Students' emotional reactions are very important for the learning process. Hedonic motivations have been found to affect learners' experience and their future decisions and achievements [3] [28]. The different emotions that arise on students during a learning activity can affect students' behavior. However, there is limited research on the different emotional aspects that occur during learning and how these aspects influence the learner. It has been argued that emotions are comprised of different constructs, however, it is generally agreed that in technology education, happiness and anxiety can provide useful insights and are representative of positive and negative emotions [20]. Happiness is defined as to which extend the student feels satisfied, excited and curious, whereas anxiety refers to which extent the student feels anxious, helpless, nervous and insecure; during the learning activity.

Among the various feelings that arise during the learning process, enjoyment is considered of high importance, as it can usually affect students' future behavior and decisions [3] [28]. Enjoyment is generally defined as the degree to which the activity is perceived to be personally enjoyable. The enjoyment that a student feels when studying, sometimes affects positively his attitude towards learning [32].

Previous studies point out the importance of anxiety while using technology [20].Specifically, low levels of anxiety lead to more positive attitudes. Moreover, anxiety has a negative effect on students' intention to use many forms of technology (e.g., mobile applications) [18]. In the context of technology enhanced learning (TEL), previous studies have found that higher levels of happiness and lower levels of anxiety may lead to increased TEL use [20].

Our study is based on prior findings regarding the importance of students' emotions and feelings [3] [27] [28]. In particular, we selected to examine the relation of enjoyment, happiness and anxiety on students' intention to participate on creative development activities. The main reason of this selection was the central role of enjoyment during the creative activity and the representative nature of happiness and anxiety on positive and negative emotions respectively.

2.3   Our Research Hypotheses and Approach

The aim of this study is to assess students' enjoyment, happiness and anxiety during a creative development activity and test the effect of these factors on students' intention to participate in future similar activities.

We formulate the three following research hypotheses:

H1. Students' Enjoyment during the activity is positively related with their intention to participate on future similar activities.

H2. Students' Happiness during the activity is positively related with their intention to participate on future similar activities.

H3. Students' Anxiety during the activity is negatively related with their intention to participate on future similar activities.

In particular, our research is intended to fill the gap on the topic of students' emotions on CSE and in particular on creative development activities. We conducted field studies, collecting empirical data and providing insights that enable scholars and educators to efficiently design and develop programs based on creative and open source activities. Our research follows a three-step process (Figure 1). In the three consecutive steps, we proceed with the sampling, data collection and data analysis. After the workshop and the data collection and analysis, we were able to provide insights regarding the impact of students' emotions on the creative activities adoption from young students. In the following section, the methodology of our research will be presented in more detail.

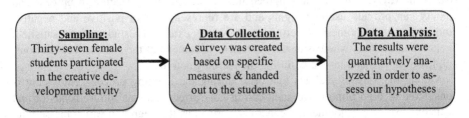

Fig. 1. Overview of the research process

3   Methodology

3.1   Procedures and Participants

In order to introduce students with creativity in CS we organized a series of workshops. The workshops took place at creative centers of University and ReMida centers. ReMIda is a center which collects and offers a variety of materials for use in creative and educational projects. The center is a cooperation between the municipality, the education project Reggio Children, the municipal waste company (recycling) and the local business community. Students' worked according to Reggio Emilia education principles [11]. The main idea is that the initiative for creative actions should spring from the student itself. The centers we used are creative places with a lot of appealing objects where students start to work without being activated by adults. The adults act as assistants.

The creative development program was composed of three workshops. The first and the second workshop lasts two days and the third lasts one day. Each workshop was formed up by 12, 10 and 15 girls respectively, students worked on dyads (with one exception) and each dyad had one computer. In the first and the second workshop 12-year-old girls (last class of primary school) participated, whereas in the third workshop 17- year-old girls participated; however all workshops followed the same schedule.

During the workshop students worked with Scratch for Arduino (S4A); which is a special version that allows the use of actuators (motors and lights) and not only sensors. In particular, the workshop program consisted of four steps:

Creative Session 1: Create physical characters (Figure 2a)

Tutorial: S4A tutorial, learn how to control Arduino, sensors, and motors

Creative Session 2: Make Scratch programs which animate the physical characters with S4A and Arduino boards (Figure 2b, 2c)

Presentation: When students have completed their artworks, they gave them names and presented them to the other teams

At the end of the workshop, a final discussion was held. Students' artworks of the workshop program have been collected and presented in an official exhibition in the university. Figure 2d presents a concrete example of the artworks.

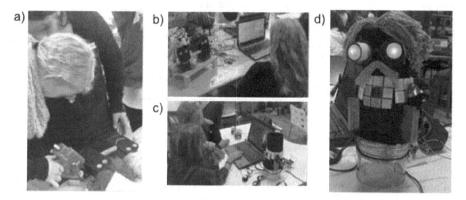

Fig. 1. a) Physical activity; b-c) giving life on the physical characters by programming; c) Example of interactive artworks

3.2   Data Collection

The questionnaire handed out to the students was divided into two parts. The first included questions on the demographics of the sample (age and gender) and the second part included measures of the various factors regarding students' intentions and emotions. Table 1 lists the questionnaire factors with their items, their operational definition, and the source from the literature review. In all cases, 7-point Likert scales were used to measure the variables.

Table 1. The factors used on the survey, their operational definitions, their items and the source

Constructs	Definition	Items (Questions)	Source Adopted
Intention to Participate	The degree of students' intention to participate in a similar activity.	I intend to participate in similar activities in the future (ItP1)	[13]
		My general intention to participate in similar activities in the future is very high (ItP2)	
		I will regularly participate similar activities in the future (ItP3)	
		I will think about participating similar activities (ItP4)	

Table 1. (*continued*)

Enjoyment	The degree to which the activity is perceived to be personally enjoyable.		Attending the activity was enjoyable (ENJ1)	[32]
			Attending the activity was exciting (ENJ2)	
			I was feeling good in the activity (EN3J)	
Happiness	The degree to which a person felt happy during the activity.	In general during the activity I felt:	Satisfied (HAP1)	[19]
			Excited (HAP2)	
			Curious (HAP3)	
Anxiety	The degree to which a person felt anxious during the activity		Insecure (ANX1)	[19]
			Helpless (ANX2)	

4   Data Analysis and Results

Fornell and Larcker [12] proposed three procedures to assess the convergent validity of any measure in a study: a) Composite reliability of each construct, b) Item reliability of the measure and c) The Average Variance Extracted (AVE).

First, we carried out an analysis of composite reliability and dimensionality to check the validity of the scale used in the questionnaire. Regarding the reliability of the scales, Cronbach`s α indicators was applied [12] and inter-item correlations statistics for the items of the variable. As Table 3 demonstrates, the result of the test revealed acceptable indices of internal consistency in all the factors.

In the next stage, we proceeded to evaluating the reliability of the measures. The reliability of an item was assessed by measuring its factor loading onto the underlying construct. Fornell and Larcker [12] recommended a factor loading of 0.5 to be good indicator of validity at the item level. The factor analysis identified four distinct factors (Table 2):

1. Intention to Participate (ItP)
2. Enjoyment (ENJ)
3. Happiness (HAP)
4. Anxious (ANX)

The third step for assessing the convergent validity is the average variance extracted (AVE); AVE measures the overall amount of variance that is attributed to the construct in relation to the amount of variance attributable to measurement error. Convergent validity is found to be adequate when the average variance extracted is equal or exceeds 0.50 [30].

Table 2. Summary of measurement scales

Factors	Item	Mean	S.D	CR	Load	AVE
Intention to Participate (ItP)	ItP1	4.37	1.37	0.849	0.849	0.74
	ItP2	4.43	1.27		0.873	
	ItP3	3.47	1.54		0.898	
	ItP4	4.49	1.48		0.817	
Enjoyment (ENJ)	ENJ1	6.56	0.73	0.867	0.843	0.79
	ENJ2	6.25	1.08		0.910	
	ENJ3	6.06	0.92		0.913	
Happiness (HAP)	HAP1	6.22	0.80	0.717	0.710	0.60
	HAP2	5.31	1.24		0.793	
	HAP3	5.78	1.20		0.813	
Anxious (ANX)	ANX1	2.33	0.93	0.702	0.936	0.59
	ANX2	1.69	0.89		0.555	

SD, Standard Deviation; CR, Cronbach α; AVE, Average Variance Extracted.

Even though these factors arise from an orthogonal rotation and are separable in terms of item loadings, they are correlated (Table 3). Pearson's correlation coefficient between the factors was used, which is about quantifying the strength of the relationship between the variables. Pearson's test suggests all the factors are related relatively strong (Table 3).

Table 3. Pearson's correlation coefficient between factors (n = 86)

Factors	ItP	ENJ	HAP	ANX
ItP	1	0.204	0.511*	-0.467*
ENJ		1	0.519*	-0.500*
HAP			1	-0.501*
ANX				1

* Correlation is significant at the 0.01 level.

To examine the research questions regarding the effect of the Emotion factors on students' ItP we divided ENJ, HAP and ANX on low and high categories using median split approach. And then we used Analysis of Variances (ANOVA) including students' ItP as dependent variables and the three confidence factors (ENJ, HAP, ANX) as independent variable. All statistical analyses reported in this research were conducted in a significance level of 0.05. As we can see from the outcomes in Table 4, 'Enjoyment has indicated insignificant influence and Happiness and Anxiety have indicated significant influence on students' intention to participate on similar activities in the future, as such H1 hypotheses was rejected and H2 and H3 were supported.

Table 4. Hypotheses testing using Analysis of Variances (ANOVA)

Dependent Variable	Mean (S.D.)		F	Results
	Low	High		
Intention to Participate (ItP)	Enjoyment (ENJ)			
	4.02 (1.12)	4.42 (1.29)	0.89	H1 (Rejected)
	Happiness (HAP)			
	3.54 (0.67)	4.93 (1.26)	**16.25***	H2 (Accepted)
	Anxiety (ANX)			
	4.89 (1.39)	3.83 (0.90)	**-7. 05***	H3 (Accepted)

* Correlation is significant at the 0.01 level.

Observing Figure 3, we can easily notice the positive influence of Happiness, the negative influence of Anxiety and the neutrality of Enjoyment.

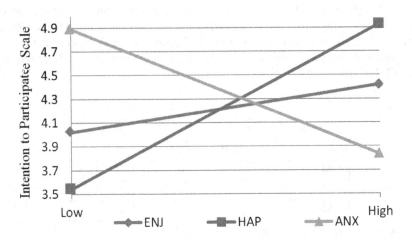

Fig. 2. The effect of enjoyment, happiness and anxiety in students' intention to participate to the programming activity

5   Discussion and Conclusions

In order to attract more students to the CS and IT disciplines, creative development activities have been designed and successfully applied in the last years [2, 5, 8]. In addition, recent studies have reported the crucial role of students' emotions and feelings on their behavior [3, 24]. To this end, a vital issue on that direction is: how emotions can increase students' intention to participate on creative development activities?

In the current paper we attempt to provide insights on the direction of using creative development activities to attract and engage students within the CS. The first step was to design and deploy a series of creative development activities. In particular, students engaged in programming languages (i.e., Scratch) and programmable hardware platforms (i.e. Arduino), which enabled them to engage in the world of creativity with digital enriched artifacts, like robots and interactive installations. In the next step, we used the empirical data obtained from students' experience with the activity in order to evaluate the effect of the key emotions on their intention to adopt on similar future activities.

Specifically in this study, three hypotheses (H1–H3) which help in understanding the role of emotions, and their contribution on creative development activities adoption from students were presented. The findings indicate that happiness has a positive effect, anxious has negative effect and enjoyment has no effect (neutral) on students' intention to participate on similar activities in the future. As such, by increasing students' happiness and decreasing anxiety we will be able to increase participation on creative development activities.

Based on the above findings, practices for increasing happiness (e.g., using humor in instructing, eliminate what students normally do not like, giving them positive feedback) must be performed by activities designers and instructors. Along with increasing students' happiness, practices to decrease their anxiety during the activity are highly recommended. For example, instructors must set attainable goals, praise about students' developing skills and use scenarios for increasing collaboration.

As with any empirical study, there are some limitations. First, in this study the respondents were students, in the frames of Norwegian educational system; this may limit the extent of the generalization of the findings. Secondly, the data are based on self-reported method, other methods such as depth interviews and observations could provide a complimentary picture of the findings through data triangulation. Thirdly, there are numerous emotions (e.g., sadness, anger) affecting students' behavior and intentions, but this study focused on Enjoyment, Happiness and Anxiety, as they are considered the most representative and important from the literature. Last, there is an age difference on the participants of one workshop, this was made because we wanted to see if there is a difference on that group on the under investigation effects. However, the distribution of the responses was the same and there was no moderation effect. Therefore, we decided that there is no reason to distinguish the responses obtained from that group.

In the next step of this ongoing project we will continue our research with qualitative methods, and aim to improve and optimize the workshop experience for our young participants. As such, future studies with larger sample from different classes and educational systems using wide variety of measures (i.e., observations, interviews) would valuably contribute on the understanding and improving the creative development activities and the role of students' emotions.

Acknowledgements. The authors wish to thank the participants of the study and their teachers who kindly spent their time and effort. Our very special thanks go to Pal Bøyesen, Audun Eriksen and Roberta Proto. The project has been recommended by the Data Protection Official for Research, Norwegian Social Science Data Services (NSD).

References

1. ACM and CSTA: Running on empty: The failure to teach k-12 computer science in the digital age, http://www.acm.org/Runningonempty/
2. Adams, J.: Alice, Middle-Schoolers, & The Imaginary Worlds Camps. In: Proceedings of SIGCSE 2007, pp. 307–311. ACM, NY (2007)
3. Apiola, M., et al.: Creativity and intrinsic motivation in computer science education: experimenting with robots. In: Proceedings of ITICSE 2010, pp. 199–203. ACM, NY (2010)
4. Balter, O., Bailey, D.: Enjoying Python, processing, and Java in CS1. ACM Inroads 1(4) (2010)
5. Buechley, L., Eisenberg, M., Catchen, J., Crockett, A.: The LilyPad Arduino: Using Computational Textiles to Investigate Engagement, Aesthetics, and Diversity in Computer Science Education. In: Proceedings of the SIGCHI 2008, pp. 423–432. ACM, NY (2008)
6. Computer Science Unplugged, http://csunplugged.org (retrieved from September 20 (2012)
7. Cooper, S., et al.: Teaching Objects-first in Introductory Computer Science. In: Proceedings of SIGCSE 2003, pp. 191–195. ACM, NY (2003)
8. Cooper, S., Dann, W., Pausch, R.: Alice: a 3-D tool for introductory programming concepts. Journal of Computing Sciences in Colleges 15(5), 107–116 (2000)
9. Craig, A., Fisher, J., Forgasz, H.: Evaluation framework underpinning the digital divas programme. In: Proceedings of ITiCSE 2011, pp. 313–317. ACM, NY (2011)
10. Cronbach, L.J.: Coefficient alpha and the internal structure of tests. Psychometrika 16(3), 297–334 (1951)
11. Edwards, C., Gandini, L., Foreman, G.: The hundred languages of children: the Reggio Emilia approach to early childhood education, 2nd edn. Ablex Publishing (1998)
12. Fornell, C., Larcker, D.F.: Evaluating structural equation models with unobservable variables and measurement error. Journal of Marketing Research 48, 39–50 (1981)
13. Giannakos, M.N., Hubwieser, P., Chrisochoides, N.: How Students Estimate the Effects of ICT and Programming Courses. In: Proceedings of SIGCSE 2013, pp. 717–722. ACM Press (2013)
14. Giannakos, M.N., Jaccheri, L.: What motivates children to become creators of digital enriched artifacts? In: Proceedings C&C 2013, pp. 104–113. ACM, NY (2013)
15. Guzdial, M.: Teaching Computing to Everyone. Communications of the ACM (CACM) 52(5), 31–33 (2009)
16. Henriksen, P., Kölling, M.: Greenfoot: combining object visualisation with interaction. In: Conf. on Object Oriented Prog. Systems Languages and Applications, pp. 73–82 (2004)
17. Hubwieser, P., et al.: Computer science/informatics in secondary education. In: Proc. of the 16th ITiCSE-WGR 2011, pp. 19–38. ACM, NY (2011)
18. Hwang, Y., Kim, D.J.: Customer self-service systems: The effects of perceived Web quality with service contents on enjoyment, anxiety, and e-trust. Decision Support Systems 43, 746–760 (2007)

19. Kafai, J.B., Peppler, K.A.: Youth, technology, and DIY: Developing participatory competencies in creative media production. Review of Research in Educ. 35, 89–119 (2011)
20. Kay, R., Loverock, S.: Assessing emotions related to learning new software: the computer emotion scale. Comput. Hum. Behav. 24, 1605–1623 (2008)
21. Koo, D.M., Ju, S.H.: The interactional effects of atmospherics and perceptual curiosity on emotions and online shopping intention. Comp. in Hum. Beh. 26, 377–388 (2010)
22. Maloney, J., Resnick, M., Rusk, N., Silverman, B., Eastmond, E.: The scratch programming language and environment. Trans. Comput. Educ. 10(16), 1–15 (2010)
23. Margolis, J., Fisher, A.: Unlocking the Clubhouse: Women in Computing. MIT Press, Cambridge (2002)
24. Metcalfe, J., Finn, B.: Evidence that judgments of learning are causally related to study choice. Psychonomic Bulletin & Review 15, 174–179 (2008)
25. Niguidula, D., van Dam, A.: Pascal on the Macintosh: A Graphical Approach. Addison Wesley (1987)
26. Pappas, I.O., Giannakos, M.N., Kourouthanassis, P.E., Chrissikopoulos, V.: Assessing emotions related to privacy and trust in personalized services. In: Douligeris, C., Polemi, N., Karantjias, A., Lamersdorf, W. (eds.) Collaborative, Trusted and Privacy-Aware e/m-Services. IFIP AICT, vol. 399, pp. 38–49. Springer, Heidelberg (2013)
27. Papert, S.: Mindstorms: Children, Computers and Powerful Ideas. Basic Books, Inc., New York (1980)
28. Razon, S., Turner, J., Johnson, T.E., Arsal, G., Tenenbaum, G.: Effects of a collaborative annotation method on students' learning and learning-related motivation and affect. Computers in Human Behavior 28(2), 350–359 (2012)
29. Rich, L., Perry, H., Guzdial, M.: A CS1 course designed to address the interests of women. In: Proceedings of SIGCSE, pp. 190–194 (2004)
30. Segars, A.H.: Assessing the unidimensionality of measurement: A paradigm and illustration within the context of information systems research. Omega International Journal of Management Science 25(1), 107–121 (1997)
31. Tai, R.T., et al.: Planning early for careers in science. Science 312(5777), 1143–1144 (2006)
32. Venkatesh, V., Speier, C., Morris, M.G.: User acceptance enablers in individual decision making about technology: toward an integrated model. Decis. Sciences 33, 297–316 (2002)
33. Webb, D.C., Repenning, A., Koh, K.H.: Toward an emergent theory of broadening participation in computer science education. In: Proceedings of SIGCSE, pp. 173–178. ACM (2012)
34. Yanco, H., et al.: Artbotics: Combining Art and Robotics to Broaden Participation in Computing. In: Workshop on Research in Robots for Education at the Robotics Science and Systems (2007)

Dialogue, Knowledge Work and Tabletops: Lessons from Preservice Teacher Education

Andri Ioannou[1], Maria Zenios[1], and Agni Stylianou[2]

[1] Cyprus University of Technology, Cyprus Interaction Lab,
Department of Multimedia and Graphic Arts, Limassol, Cyprus
[2] University of Nicosia, Nicosia, Cyprus
andri.i.ioannou@cut.ac.cy, mkzenios@gmail.com,
stylianou.a@unic.ac.cy

Abstract. This pilot study is concerned with the exploration of tabletops in preservice teacher education, through the lens of sociocultural theories. An educational tabletop application designed to facilitate dialog and collaborative decision making, so called IdeasMapping, was enacted in the context of proposing a solution plan for a case study classroom problem. Students' responses to a questionnaire showed that they positively endorsed the technology for this type of collaborative activity. Moreover, analysis of video recordings of groups' discussions and interactions showed that the technology enhanced students' communication as they took turns in sharing their ideas, and provided structure and organization of these ideas linked to possible solutions on the problems embedded in the case.

Keywords: collaborative learning, collaborative decision making, surface computing, interactive tables, tabletops, preservice teacher education, case based learning, educational technology, technology integration.

1 Introduction

The emergence of technologies as part of our increasingly networked world has influenced higher education offering new exciting approaches to collaborative activities. Multitouch interactive tables (or tabletops) have been extensively discussed for their potential to support collaboration and learning. As discussed by [15], tabletops afford cooperative gestures which can enhance users' sense of teamwork, while the technology 'invites' interaction and willingness to participate in group work [17]. Despite its promise, integration and appropriate use of this technology in everyday school settings and in higher education classrooms is very limited.

As [14] recently argued there is "a problematic gap between what could be effective technology-enhanced learning (TEL) in theory, and what can be effective TEL in practice." In this pilot study, we view tabletops as a source of innovation in teacher education, that is also possible and practical today, in terms of supporting existing knowledge and practices within a shared physical space that allows the team to remain focused on the task at hand. We present an exploration of the use of tabletops in

P. Zaphiris and A. Ioannou (Eds.): LCT 2014, Part I, LNCS 8523, pp. 410–418, 2014.

preservice teacher education within a classroom environment. The tabletop used in the study is equipped with IdeasMapping, an application that enables participants to develop a taxonomy of their ideas as they brainstorm (see section 1.3). Using the tabletop, groups of students discussed a case study classroom scenario and eventually created a taxonomy of ideas on how the teacher needs to respond to the problems embedded in the case.

2   Theoretical Framing

We explore the use of tabletops in pre-service teacher education through the lens of the Vygotskian sociocultural theory. The sociocultural perspective in education argues that human understanding and meaning is constructed through experiences and as part of a social context. It favors collaboration among peers while learning happens in situ, being located within tools and artifacts that play a pivotal role in the process. From a sociocultural perspective the use of tools plays an important role in extending human abilities and in enhancing thinking processes i.e., as in helping to create a representation of ideas or explicate one's thoughts. In this context, collaborative learning has been considered as key to knowledge creation in problem solving situations as it requires participation in shared activities, negotiation of ideas and decision making. As such, collaborative learning is essentially situated, contextual and discursive [20]. Further, collaborative learning has been claimed as one of the key skills that higher education institutions need to develop as, in today's society, problems which professionals need to tackle are often multi-faceted and need to be explored and targeted by multi-disciplinary groups. Researchers [7] have argued about the need of higher education to induct students into knowledge-building practices across different communities. Such practices often involve dialogical activities organised as part of learning environments potentially supported by technologies.

3   Tabletops in Education

In a recent review, [10] discussed the technological characteristics of interactive tabletops as well as their pedagogical affordances, drawing evidence from the education and computer science literature. Overall, as pointed out by the authors, most of what we know in this area concerns technical issues related to interaction of users with the technology, while we know little about the use and value of multitouch tabletops in formal and informal educational settings. Below we summarize some recent empirical evidence from the education arena.

Multitouch tabletops have been used with special user groups to promote development of social skills. SIDES, for example, is a four-player cooperative computer game designed to support adolescents with Asperger's syndrome practise social skills and effective group work during their group therapy sessions [16]. SIDES provided an engaging experience for this audience who remained engaged in the activity the entire time and learned from the activity (unlike typical behavior of this population). Similarly, StoryTable [5] has been used to facilitate collaboration and social interaction for children with autistic spectrum disorder with positive effects. StoryTable [2] was initially designed to support children's storytelling activity in groups; evaluation of StoryTable showed that it enforced cooperation between children during the storytelling activity, by allowing simultaneous work on different tasks, while encouraging them to perform crucial operations together in order to progress [2].

Furthermore, multitouch tabletops have been studied for their added benefits compared to singletouch tabletops in educational settings. Authors [8] contrasted groups of children in multitouch and singletouch conditions and found that children talked more about the task in the multitouch condition while, in the singletouch condition, they talked more about turn taking. A different study by [12] concerned the impact of particular tabletop interaction techniques on the type of talk during collaborative learning. The researchers found that different interaction techniques (direct touch, pantograph and non-digital table) resulted in different types of communication patterns during collaborative learning.

With regards to using tabletops in formal educational settings, a series of studies was conducted as part of the SynergyNet project [10] going beyond using single tabletops to studying a network of tabletops that can communicate with each other. SynergyNet undertook the development of curricula and tabletop applications for classroom integration focusing on how tabletops can best support collaboration in small groups. One SynergyNet study contrasted groups of children in multitouch and paper-based conditions to examine differences in their collaborative learning strategies [10]. The authors found that student groups in the multitouch condition maintained better joint attention on the task than groups in the paper-based condition. Another recent SynergyNet study examined NumberNet, a tool designed to promote within and between group collaboration in a mathematic classroom using a network of tabletops [9]; pilot results from 32 students showed significant knowledge gains from pre to post testing.

Last but not least, tabletops are considered engaging and fun. Researchers [1] assessed overall (perceived) usefulness and benefit of using tabletops in collaboration contexts with 80 participants. The study showed that groups in the tabletop experimental condition had improved subjective experience and increased motivation to engage in the task.

4   Method

IdeasMapping. This tabletop application is designed to support collaborative decision making by allowing the participants to analyze a problem and brainstorm around possible solutions, while they actively construct a consensus artifact, namely, a taxonomy of their ideas. The detailed functionality of the application, design methodology and user experience evaluation are reported elsewhere [19]. In IdeasMapping, collaboration is enforced in three stages:

Stage 1: With a problem at hand, each collaborator generates new ideas. Ideas are typed into a web application through the use of a mobile device such as a laptop or tablet (brainstorming stage).

Stage 2: The ideas are presented one-by-one, as digital post-it notes on the table-top surface and become subject to discussion amongst the collaborators. For each idea, collaborators make an effort to categorize it in a thematic unit; thematic units can be created by any participant (collaborative decision making stage).

Stage 3: Participants can finalize their taxonomy by editing ideas or generating new ones, deleting ideas or thematic units that are less promising, and relocating ideas into thematic units for a better fit until all collaborators are satisfied (consensus decision making stage).

Fig. 1. Working in IdeasMapping

Participants. The participants were 20 undergraduate students, mainly females (80%) between 20 and 22 years of age, in an Educational Psychology course, taught over 16 weeks at a private University in Cyprus. All of them were preservice teacher education candidates.

Procedures. Students were randomly assigned in five groups of four students each and were tasked to work collaboratively in their groups on a case study classroom scenario. They were to apply concepts learned in the course and argue for plausible solutions to the problem embedded in the case.

To ensure quality, the case scenario was adopted from a book specialized on the case study method by [6]. The scenario presented an ambiguous classroom problem concerning a 'divided' classroom where about 1/3 of the students read below grade level (prefer worksheets), 1/3 read at grade level, and 1/3 read above grade level (prefer reading), leading to emotions of frustration and boredom for many students and making teaching very difficult.

Stage 1 of IdeasMapping (brainstorming stage) was carried out in distance. Students were given a week to read the case, think and record their ideas into the IdeasMapping web application. Then, Stages 2 and 3 involved collocated collaboration around the table. Each group met face-to-face and engaged in dialog and interaction around the table in an effort to categorize their different views and ideas into thematic units (see Fig. 1). Ultimately each group created consensus taxonomy of 4-5 main areas the educator needs work on to create a classroom environment for all students (see Fig. 1).

Data Collection. A questionnaire was administered to all the participants at the completion of the activity. The questionnaire aimed to assess the perceived value of tabletop technology and IdeasMapping specifically for collocated collaboration on case study problems. Moreover, the sessions of all five groups were video recorded for subsequent video analysis.

5   Analysis and Results

Questionnaire Data. The questionnaire included 6 Likert-type items, with a 7-point agreement response scale (from 1: completely disagree to 7: completely agree), measuring the extent to which students thought the technology supported their collaboration. As shown in Table 1, means were well above the midpoint for all items, suggesting that the technology was positively endorsed by the participants.

Table 1. Descriptive statistics (N=20)

Questionnaire Item	Mead (SD)
1. The tabletop met my needs as a collaborator.	6.00 (.89)
2. The tabletop allowed me to work effective in my team.	5.81 (.66)
3. The tabletop reinforced my participation in the activity.	6.40 (.63)
4. The tabletop helped promote collaboration between group members.	6.19 (.54)
5. As an educator, I would use tabletops to support collaborative learning.	6.25 (.93)
6. I would recommend tabletops to an educator aiming to promote collaborative learning.	6.38 (.89)

The questionnaire also included two open-ended questions concerning the pros and cons of using a tabletop for this type of collaborative activity. Using open coding [18] we found a couple of themes (codes) in students' responses, as described below:

The tabletop enabled physical communication, joined attention and awareness. Students pointed out how the physical shared workspace promoted collaboration by enabling physical communication, shared awareness, and shared attention on the group artifact. Some indicative student quotes on this idea include:

Group 1 participant: "Sitting together at one place and discussing and working together on the same artifacts kept our attention focused."

Group 2 participant: "I think the power of this technology is the shared digital display. Everyone can see and interact with artifacts on the tabletop and there is full awareness of everyone's actions."

Group 3 participant: "I felt the tabletop forced collaboration by bringing the teammates first physically closers and subsequently mentally closer. It was not too large like a typical round table, around which people get distracted. It was small enough to get us physically close and large enough to get us working together and thus, mentally close."

Shared power. Students also pointed out how the tabletop allowed 'power' to be shared and distributed over the display, thus enabling participation by all collaborators, for example:

Group 2 participant: "I liked how each of us could delete and add ideas. With the multitouch capability all participated and everyone's voice was heard."

Group 4 participant: "If we were to do this activity around a regular table I can see one student taking the lead and doing all the writing and making the decisions. I can see maybe another one somewhat contributing and the other two students looking outside the window! The tabletop discouraged one member from taking over, but encouraged everyone to contribute instead."

Last but not least, as one would expect with the integration of any new technology in the classroom, a novelty effect was also evident in students' responses. Several students commented how the tabletop was different, original, interesting and enjoyable among others. Of course, we consider this aspect less interesting, as technology should be intergraded to improve the nature of collaboration and learning, not because of its novelty.

Video Data. Analysis of video recordings of groups' discussions and interactions showed that the technology enhanced students' communication as they took turns in sharing their ideas, and provided structure and organization of these ideas linked to possible solutions on the problems embedded in the case. Below, we provide three examples of episodes demonstrating how ideas and thematic units were discussed and evolved as part of the collaboration process.

Group 2 video episode (IdeasMapping Stage 1):
P1: "With this idea I refer to the need for discipline. The teacher continuously threatens the students that there will be a sanction, but this does not occur ever. And the problematic behavior goes on and on. At least 3 students need to be punished based on what I read in the case." (originator of the idea)
P3: "Yes there are 2 boys...they fight during the recesses and continue their fight in the classroom. With sanctions, the rest of the students will also get the message...that the teacher is serious about punishment."
P2: "Should we create a theme named 'controlling behaviors'? Indeed there is a problem with students' behavior. Remember when a poor reader did the reading? Others were laughing at him, and this was very inappropriate."
P3: "Maybe we use a more general description of this theme to include actions towards addressing all these kinds of problematic behaviors?"
P4: "Let's name it 'behavior modification'. The teacher has to work on 'changing' students' behavior for the best."

Group 1 episode (IdeasMapping Stage 1):

P1: "I feel collaboration will be a plus in Karen's lessons. Students have diffident abilities. With mixed-ability groups the strong readers may have a positive influence on the poor readers." (originator of the idea)

P4: "Did you pay attention to the details? …that poor readers (1/3 of the students) enjoy completing worksheets. And another 1/3 are neutral about both reading and worksheets. Indeed, Karen has to somehow mix these abilities. Instead of doing reading vs. worksheets, she should give them a group task of different nature, on which good readers and good worksheet-workers could work together and support each other."

P2: "How should we name this category? It does not fit with our other categories, right? It has to do with a change in the instructional methods and learning environment.

P1: "More specifically it has to do with promoting collaboration or even promoting interaction".

P3/P4 (together): "Let's name it 'promoting interaction'. It is more inclusive and may include other ideas too."

Group 3 video episode (IdeasMapping Stage 1):

P3: "My idea involves promoting collaboration using mixed-ability groups. She could create teams of poor and strong readers and give them tasks that require them to work together." (originator of the idea)

P2: "I have a similar idea coming up [refers to a post-it note not appeared yet]. I suggest that she integrates social tools into her lesson to promote communication across students and make it more interactive and fun."

P4: "Could this be named 'new instructional methods'? Collaboration in terms of peer-feedback would also help, I am thinking. Can we add this thought?"

P1: "I think we can add it later on…in Stage 2 of the app."

P2: "Yes, let's do 'new instructional methods' and we can add more ideas in there as we keep thinking."

6   Discussion and Conclusions

Overall, the results of this pilot study indicate that multitouch interactive tabletops provide a revolutionary approach to collaborative learning in preservice teacher education as they can enable the development of a shared space and physical communication between group members. The tabletop allowed the participants to add and delete ideas, and to take turns on discussing and critiquing thoughts until they agreed on a final taxonomy.

In particular, the results from the questionnaire data analysis showed that users' experience was very positive. Students thought the technology supported their collaboration and there was added value into using a tabletop for this kind of collaborative activity. Consistent with prior work on tabletops, these results provide further evidence of the affordances of tabletop systems to support dialog and collaboration on a group artifact in the context of problem based activities by enabling physical communication, joined attention and awareness (see also [4],[10]) and by distributing 'power' over the display (see also [4], [11], [13]). Further, results from the video analysis demonstrated how the interactive tabletop enabled multiple points of control, in contrast to laptops and computers where team members have to negotiate their participation and often wait for their turn in using the devices (see also [8]). To this extent it can facilitate co-located collaboration and co-ordination as well as sharing of external representations among members that help them explicate their thinking as new developing teachers.

Dimensions of collaborative learning include interactivity, synchronicity and negotiability [3]. Work supported through tabletops enables learners being aware of the interactions among them that seems to influence co-participants' cognitive processes. Also, it shows the effort of an individual to model the knowledge state of a co-participant. Further, it helps participants engage in dialogue and reach consensus. This occurs by enabling participants to create arguments in order to support alternative viewpoints, justify positions, negotiate meaning and attempt to convince each other.

However, it should be noted that at times the process was challenging for the students as they encountered difficulties in engaging in these tasks on their own. The role of the tutor was valuable in stimulating the participants in creating the appropriate linkages between their ideas while they used the multitouch tabletop. Further research needs to identify examples and types of teaching activities that will support student teachers in their use of tabletops. The pedagogic uses of tabletops in classrooms need to show how these activities can be designed, implemented and supported within a classroom.

Acknowledgments. Partially supported by the Cyprus Research Promotion Foundation (DESMI 2009-2010) under the "Bilateral Cooperation" between Slovenia and Cyprus (ΔΙΑΚΡΑΤΙΚΕΣ/ΚΥ-ΣΛΟ/0411).

References

1. Buisine, S., Besacier, G., Aoussat, A., Vernier, F.: How do Interactive Tabletop Systems Influence Collaboration? Computers in Human Behavior 28, 49–59 (2012)
2. Cappelletti, A., Gelmini, G., Pianesi, F., Rossi, F.: Zancanaro.: Enforcing Cooperative Storytelling: First Studies. In: Proceedings of the 4th IEEE Intentional Conference in Advanced Learning Technologies, pp. 281–285 (2004)
3. Dillenbourg, P.: What Do You Mean by 'Collaborative Learning'? In: Dillenbourg, P. (ed.) Collaborative Learning, Cognitive and Computational Approaches, pp. 1–16. Elsevier Science, Amsterdam (1999)
4. Fleck, R., Rogers, Y., Yuill, N., Marshall, P., Carr, A., Rick, J., Bonnet, V.: Actions Speak Loudly with Words: Unpacking Collaboration Around the Table. In: Proceedings of ITS 2009, Banff, Alberta, Canada (2009)
5. Gal, E., Bauminger, N., Goren-Bar, D., Pianesi, F., Stock, O., Zancanaro, M., Weiss, P.: Enhancing Social Communication of Children with High-functioning Autism Through a Co-located Interface. AI & Society 24, 75–84 (2009), doi:10.1007/s00146-009-0199-0
6. Greenwood, G.E., Fillmer, H.T., Parkay, F.W.: Educational Psychology Cases, 2nd edn. Merrill Prentice Hall, Upper Saddle River (2002)

7. Goodyear, P., Zenios, M.: Discussion, Collaborative Knowledge Work and Epistemic Fluency. British Journal of Educational Studies 55(4), 351–368 (2007)
8. Harris, A., Rick, J., Bonnett, V., Yuill, N., Fleck, R., Marshall, P., et al.: Around the Table: Are Multipletouch Surfaces Better than Single-touch for Children's Collaborative Interactions? In: Proceedings of the 9th International Conference on Computer Supported Collaborative Learning, pp. 335–344. ISLS (2009)
9. Hatch, A., Higgins, S., Joyce-Gibbons, A., Mercier, E.: NumberNet: Using Multi-touch Technology to Support Within and Between Group Mathematics Learning. In: Proceedings of the 9th International Conference on Computer Supported Collaborative Learning, pp. 176–183. International Society of the Learning Sciences (2011)
10. Higgins, S.E., Mercier, E.M., Burd, E., Hatch, A.: Multi-touch Tables and the Relationship with Collaborative Classroom Pedagogies: A Synthetic Review. International Journal of Computer-Supported Collaborative Learning 6(4), 515–538 (2011), doi:10.1007/s11412-011-9131-y
11. Ioannou, A., Zaphiris, P., Loizides, F., Vasiliou, C.: Let's talk about Technology for Peace: A Systematic Assessment of Problem-based Group Collaboration Around an Interactive Tabletop. Interacting with Computers (2013)
12. Jamil, I., O'Hara, K., Perry, M., Karnik, A., Subramanian, S.: The Effects of Interaction Techniques on Talk Patterns in Collaborative Peer Learning around Interactive Tables. In: Proc. CHI 2011, pp. 3043–3052. ACM (2011)
13. Marshall, P., Hornecker, E., Morris, R., Sheep Dalton, N., Rogers, Y.: When the fingers do the talking: A study of group participation with varying constraints to a tabletop interface. In: 3rd IEEE International Workshop on Horizontal Interactive Human Computer Systems 2008, pp. 33–40 (2008)
14. McKenney, S.: Designing and Researching Technology-Enhanced Learning for the Zone of Proximal Implementation. Research in Learning Technology 21 (2013), http://www.researchinlearningtechnology.net/index.php/rlt/article/view/17374 (retrieved February 2014)
15. Morris, M.R., Huang, A., Paepcke, A., Winograd, T.: Cooperative gestures: Multi-user Gestural Interactions for Co-located Groupware. In: Proc. CHI, pp. 1201–1210. ACM (2006)
16. Piper, A.M., O'Brien, E., Morris, M.R., Winograd, T.: SIDES: A Cooperative Tabletop Computer Game for Social Skills Development. In: Proceedings of the 6th International Conference on Computer Supported Cooperative Work, Alberta, Canada (2006)
17. Rogers, Y., Lindley, S.: Collaborating around vertical and horizontal displays: Which way is best? Interacting With Computers 16(6), 1133–1152 (2004)
18. Strauss, A., Corbin, J.: Basics of Qualitative Research: Grounded Theory Procedures and Techniques. Sage, London (1990)
19. Zaphiris, P., Ioannou, A., Loizides, F., Vasiliou, C.: User Experience in Using Surface Computing for Collaborative Decision Making. Interactive Technology and Smart Education (2013)
20. Zenios, M.: Epistemic Activities and Collaborative Learning: Towards an Analytical Model for Studying Knowledge Construction in Networked Learning Settings. Journal of Computer-Assisted Learning 27(3), 259–268 (2011)

Simulation Training in Self-Regulated Learning: Investigating the Effects of Dual Feedback on Dynamic Decision-Making Tasks

Jung Hyup Kim

Department of Industrial and Manufacturing Systems Engineering,
University of Missouri, USA
kijung@missouri.edu

Abstract. Self-Regulated Learning (SRL) is a popular concept in the research area of the education. However, most researchers who have studied SRL focus on the theoretical aspects of metacognition or the educational application such as children's learning and academic performance. The purpose of this research is to investigate the SRL effects of dual feedback (retrospective confident judgments and task performances) in a dynamic task environment. A human-in-the-loop simulation experiment was conducted to collect real-time task performance data from participants and compared the self-regulated learning effects between different feedback conditions. We found that an improvement in the accuracy of their performance prediction might promote an increase in their situation awareness on dynamic decision-making tasks. This research will contribute design faster and more effective training algorism to inexperienced operators in the computer simulation training environment.

Keywords: Simulation Training, Self-Regulated Learning, Human-in-the-loop simulation.

1   Introduction

Developing the next generation simulation training methods that account for improving both task performances and situational awareness in dynamic-decision making tasks is an important goal for the computerized training research. To design a more advanced simulation-based training which satisfies this goal, we chose to study the Self-Regulated Learning (SRL) on different feedback conditions. Feedback plays a central role in many learning models and theories (Hawk & Shah, 2008). Especially, most research about feedback in a dynamic environment demonstrates that only appropriate feedback can provide valuable information to operators (Norman, 1990). However, it is hard to understand the various learning patterns caused by different feedback conditions in a dynamic environment. Hence, we initiated an investigation to understand the different learning patterns based on the Self-Regulated Learning in the computer simulation training environment.

P. Zaphiris and A. Ioannou (Eds.): LCT 2014, Part I, LNCS 8523, pp. 419–428, 2014.
© Springer International Publishing Switzerland 2014

In this research, we focused on the SRL effects of dual feedback (retrospective confident judgments and task performances) within the Anti-Air Warfare Coordinator (AAWC) simulation domain. The retrospective confident judgments (RCJ) monitoring feedback informed the score of the participants' confidence level for their responses before knowing whether they were correct or incorrect about the given tasks. The task performances monitoring feedback provided the trainees with information on their decision-making and task strategies. Two different types of task performances were recorded during the experiment. One was called Situation Awareness (SA); another one was called Operator Action Performance (OAP). Our results showed that the experimental groups (1th group: monitoring dual feedback with RCJ and SA, and 2th group: monitoring dual feedback with RCJ and OAP) could predict their situational awareness more accurate than other two control groups (1th group: monitoring dual feedback with SA and OAP, and 2th group: no feedback). In addition, the experimental groups' SA accuracy scores were significantly higher than the control groups. These findings could support that trainee' incremental belief about their decision-making process is important to improve the ability to recognize their situational awareness for the given tasks

2   Background

The theoretical framework for Self-Regulated Learning (SRL) is based on the Dunlosky and Hertzog's memory-training research (Dunlosky & Hertzog, 1998). The key point of SRL is how to direct the students' ability to understand their own learning (Zimmerman & Schunk, 1989). The concept consists of series of self-generated thoughts, feelings, and actions, which are systematically generated by students in order to achieve their goals. One of the strengths to being self-regulated learners is that they are more recognizable for their academic strengths and weaknesses than non-self-regulated learners. Hence, feedback about how well people understand what they learned during the task could be the critical point of the self-regulated learning process. Hacker, Bol, Horgam, and Rakow prove that the poorest performers are the most overconfident (Hacker, Bol, Horgan, & Rakow, 2000). It means that poor performers are not only unskilled but also unaware. In the research area of the education, monitoring retrospective confident judgments feedback from study and test plays an important role to influence in updating the SRL process because the updated data from the feedback can affect not only trainees' decision making process to improve their performance but also the prediction about their self-improvement.

3   Methods

3.1   Dynamic Decision-Making Task

To find the answer to the research question, a human-in-the-loop simulation AAWC simulation test bed was used (Kim, Rothrock, Tharanathan, & Thiruvengada, 2011).

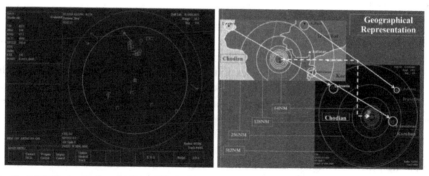

Fig. 1. AAWC simulation (left) and Relationship between geographical map and AAWC interface (right) (Kim et al., 2011)

It is similar to an air traffic controller simulation within the context of military command and control. The AAWC is an interactive simulation in which a controller must defend his/her ship against hostile aircraft. Each aircraft within the simulator presents specific cues that relate to the identity of the aircraft. Participants were required to identify unknown aircraft and take appropriate action on those aircraft based on the Rules of Engagement (RoE). Participants must focus on identifying unknown aircraft correctly in order to defend the ship. Figure 1(left) shows the screen shot of AAWC simulation.

The details of the Rules of Engagement are shown below:

- Identification Rules (Unknown aircraft only)

— Make a primary identification of air contact (i.e., friendly, hostile, assumed hostile/friendly)
— Make an AIR identification of air contact (i.e., Strike, Missile, Helicopter, etc.)

- Warning Rules (Hostile or Assumed hostile only)

— Issue Level 1 Warning at 50NM
— Issue Level 2 Warning at 40NM
— Issue Level 3 Warning at 30NM

- Assign / Illuminate aircraft (at 30NM; Hostile or Assumed hostile only)

The AAWC test bed is used to simulate a complex command-and-control task environment in the laboratory setting to promote decision making under dynamic task conditions. Eight scenarios were developed to conduct the experiment. Realistic geographical representation was used to create authentic experimental scenarios (see Fig 1 right). All events occurred in specific time sequences and were tied to Situation Awareness probes.

3.2   Procedure

A total of 64 students (age 18 or older) participated. Total experimental time for each person took about 4.5 hours. Participants were asked to control resources in order to perform tasks during the simulation. The experiment consisted of two sessions – a training session and an actual trial session. During the training session (Day 1), the participants were trained in task specific skills and were given feedback on their performance. In addition to these, participants also received an instructor's feedback about their tasks during the experiment. The practice scenario took 5 minutes to complete; the total number of unknown aircrafts in practice scenarios was smaller than in experimental scenarios. Based on the result of the pilot test, participants who completed the practice simulation three times were considered ready to engage in actual trials. The participants underwent two experiment sessions (Day 2 and 3). Each person was exposed to 8 test scenarios and required to take the NASA TLX test to measure their task workload. Each experiment session lasted approximately 90 minutes.

During the experiment session, the participants were asked specific situation awareness questions in each test scenario, which was designed to run for 15 minutes. The simulation was frozen automatically at a random time between 10 and 15 minutes after the simulation start time. After this freeze, participants answered situation awareness probe questions. Participants also answered a retrospective confident judgment probe two times (one for Operator Action Performance, called "OAP-RCJ"; another one for Situation Awareness, called "SA-RCJ").

3.3   Experimental Design

In this experiment, we considered a situation in which three factors (**A**: Retrospective Confident Judgment (RCJ), **B**: Situation Awareness (SA), and **C**: Operator Action Performance (OAP)) were of interest. The plus and minus signs for the one-half fractions of the 2^3 design is shown in Table 1 and Figure 2.

In this experiment, there were two experimental groups: RCJ + SA and RCJ + OAP feedback group. Participant who was assigned in the experimental groups monitored both his/her self-evaluation regarding the AAWC performance result and one of their actual task performances (SA or OAP) together. There were also two control groups: SA + OAP and No feedback. Participants in the control groups were monitored for only task performance feedbacks based on SA and OAP or no feedback. Exposure time for the feedback screen for each group was constrained to limit effect of bias due to uneven exposure to the feedback between feedback groups. In this experiment, participants were allowed to view the feedback screen for three minutes.

Table 1. The one-half fractions of the 2^3 design

A	B	C	Treatment Combination	Feedback Group
	−	−	(1)	No feedback
+	+	−	ab	RCJ + SA
+	−	+	ac	RCJ + OAP
	+	+	bc	SA + OAP

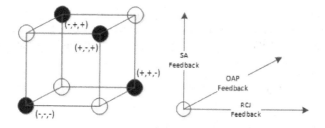

Fig. 2. Projection of the experimental design

4   Performance Metrics

4.1   Retrospective Confidence Judgment (RCJ) Rating

This is the participants' confidence level for their responses before knowing whether they are correct or incorrect.   RCJ rating comes from metacognitive monitoring processes associated more directly with retrieval (Dougherty, Scheck, Nelson, & Narens, 2005). We collected Self-rating scores (scale: 1 to 100) for OAP-RCJ and SA-RCJ during the testing sessions. The following was asked in the probe for OAP-RCJ & SA-RCJ:

- *OAP-RCJ: "How well do you think you are aware of the objects and events in your airspace?"*
- *SA-RCJ: "How well do you think you have performed the Rules of Engagement (RoE) in your airspace?"*

4.2   Situation Awareness (SA) Accuracy

SA accuracy is the most well-known measure of Situation Awareness (Endsley, 1988). It is designed for real time human-in-the-loop simulation such as a radar monitoring or military cockpit. This technique was used in our dynamic system to collect objective data of SA across all operators. In this experiment, SA probes were presented to participants in order to determine their situation awareness after the simulation was stopped at random times, after 10 minutes passed from the beginning of the simulation. Their responses were compared with the correct answers that had been collected in the computer database. The accuracy of operator's situation awareness (SA Accuracy) is calculated by

$$SA\ accuracy = (Number\ of\ correct\ response \times 100) / Total\ number\ of\ SA\ probes \qquad (1)$$

4.3   Operator Action Performance(OAP) Accuracy

This is defined as the degree of on-time correct action of a dynamic control task. In this experiment, we adopted a Time Window (TW) concept to evaluate trainees' task performance. TW is a construct that specifies a functional relationship between a required situation and the time interval that specifies the availability of an action opportunity which leads to the required situation (Rothrock, 2001). By using the concept of a TW, we measured the operator's OAP accuracy in terms of Rules of Engagements (RoE). It is calculated by

$$\text{OAP accuracy} = \text{(Number of correct actions} \times 100) / \text{Total number of TW based on RoE} \qquad (2)$$

4.4 NASA Task Load Index (NASA-TLX)

A multidimensional subjective workload rating technique, NASA TLX is commonly used to measure operators' workload (Hancock, Williams, & Manning, 1995). There are six dimensions for subjective workload: mental demand, physical demand, temporal demand, perceived performance, effort, and frustration level (close to 100 - high workload; close to 0 - low workload). We collected participants' cognitive task workload for each scenario.

4.5 Self-Regulation (SR) Effect

Self-Regulation refers to one's ability to understand and control one's learning environment. Hacker, Bol, Horgam, and Rakow (2000) report that the poorest performers are the most overconfident, and this group has the largest deviation between retrospective confidence judgment score and task performance while the best performers who are self-regulated learners show the smallest deviation between retrospective confidence judgment (RCJ) scores and task performances. We computed the deviation between RCJ scores and task performances. These prediction errors (called SR effect) are calculated by:

$$\text{Self-Regulation (SR)} = |RCJ_i - \text{Performance}_i| \qquad (3)$$

Where $i = 1$ is related to Operator Action Performance; $i = 2$ is related to Situation Awareness.

5   Results

5.1   Descriptive Statics

We compared participants' OAP-RCJ and SA-RCJ rating, SA accuracy, and OAP accuracy, and operator's workload (NASA TLX) between all four groups: No feedback, RCJ + SA, RCJ + OAP, SA + OAP. For OAP-RCJ and SA-RCJ, there were significant differences between groups; OAP-RCJ ($p < 0.01$), SA-RCJ ($p < 0.01$). For SA and OAP accuracy, there were significant difference between groups; SA ($p < 0.01$), OAP ($p < 0.01$). However, NASA-TLX was similar between groups ($p = 0.095$).

Table 2. Performance results

Feedback Group	Metrics	Mean	StDev	Median
RCJ + SA (n = 16)	OAP-RCJ	59.41	20.86	60.00
	SA-RCJ	51.28	20.80	50.00
	SA accuracy	50.69	19.85	55.56
	OAP accuracy	21.65	13.31	21.45
	NASA-TLX	58.29	16.67	57.73
RCJ + OAP (n = 16)	OAP-RCJ	62.42	21.26	70.00
	SA-RCJ	57.25	22.08	60.00
	SA accuracy	54.84	19.01	55.00
	OAP accuracy	30.22	21.51	27.67
	NASA-TLX	54.34	19.57	58.10
SA+OAP (n = 16)	OAP-RCJ	64.84	20.91	70.00
	SA-RCJ	58.06	23.45	60.00
	SA accuracy	46.39	24.27	44.00
	OAP accuracy	30.97	23.43	28.50
	NASA-TLX	58.54	18.85	61.00
No feedback (n = 16)	OAP-RCJ	55.00	28.37	65.00
	SA-RCJ	46.82	28.32	50.00
	SA accuracy	36.36	24.11	33.00
	OAP accuracy	16.56	12.84	15.33
	NASA-TLX	59.72	17.24	59.50

5.2   Main Effects

In this experiment, we used three different feedback factors for our main effect. In terms of the one-way ANOVA result of the learning improvement[1] by testing session (see Table 3), RCJ monitoring feedback significantly affected operators' ability to take on-time correct actions while SA feedback affected operators' understanding level of the given tasks. For OAP feedback, it influenced both SA and OAP accuracy.

Table 3. ANOVA results by learning (*$p<0.05$)

Feedback Condition	OAP-RCJ	SA-RCJ	SA accuracy	OAP accuracy	NASA-TLX
RCJ (A)	0.052	0.26	0.206	**0.019***	0.235
SA (B)	0.796	0.704	**0.012***	0.165	0.897
OAP (C)	0.616	0.897	**0.004***	**0.000***	0.713

5.3   Interaction Effects

We also observed several significant interactions of feedback type. The interaction effect of (A) + (B) feedback showed that means of Day 3 performance (both SA and OAP accuracy) were significantly improved as compared to Day 2 performance. (A) + (C) feedback could significantly influence participants' SA accuracy. On the other hand, (B) + (C) feedback was significantly influence OAP accuracy (see Table 4).

---

[1] Day 3 performance – Day 2 performance.

Table 4. Two-way interaction results (*p<0.05)

Interaction	OAP-RCJ	SA-RCJ	SA accuracy	OAP accuracy	NASA-TLX
(A) + (B)	0.615	0.877	**0.004***	**0.000***	0.714
(A) + (C)	0.795	0.704	**0.012***	0.154	0.897
(B) + (C)	0.052	0.261	0.200	**0.016***	0.236

5.4   Self-Regulation Effect

We found a significant difference between the experimental groups and control groups in terms of the prediction error from SA accuracy. However, there was no significant difference between groups in terms of the prediction error from OAP accuracy. Figure 3 shows that participants who were exposed to the RCJ monitoring feedback could surmise their situation awareness ability more accurately than others.

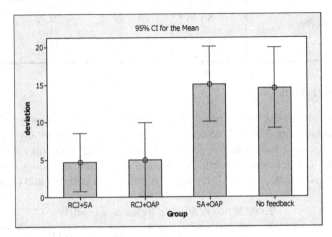

Fig. 3. Prediction Error from SA accuracy

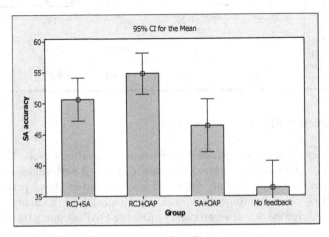

Fig. 4. SA means comparison between groups

Figure 4 shows that the experimental groups' prediction errors from SA accuracy were significantly lower than the control groups. Moreover, both experimental groups' SA means were higher than the control groups (see Figure 5).

6   Discussion

According to the results, we found that different combinations of dual feedback influence task performances differently in a dynamic environment. However, the dual feedback did not influence participants' cognitive workload. By monitoring the RCJ component on the feedback screen, participants' accuracy of judgments regarding a situational awareness was significantly improved. In addition, the RCJ could significantly influence OAP accuracy (see Table 3). This means that participants who were exposed to the concurrent attention to both retrospective confident judgments regarding self-evaluation of the given task and their actual task performances could improve not only their correct decision-making process but also situational awareness in a dynamic environment. Hence, the dual feedback with RCJ and SA or OAP conditions can guide trainees' self-regulated learning behavior more effectively in the computer simulation training environment. This result can be supported by Kuiper and Pesut's research in nursing practice. They found that developing both cognitive and metacognitive skill acquisition methods by using self-regulation learning could significantly influence the reflective clinical reasoning in nursing practice (Kuiper & Pesut, 2004). The present study compared participants' learning performance between different types of dual feedback. We found that an improvement in the accuracy of their performance prediction might promote an increase in their SA performance. It might be interpreted that the feedback of metacognitive monitoring such as retrospective confident judgments rating is an integral part of self-regulated learning processes in the computer-based dynamic decision-making training. The initial findings of our study provide a better understanding of the self-regulated learning process in simulation training within a dynamic environment. The next step of this research will be developing a more advanced feedback training algorithm to more effectively improve operators' learning performance in the computer-based training simulation. One limitation of this study is that the participants performed the AAWC simulation in three days. It will be necessary to consider the long term SRL effects of metacognitive monitoring feedback in dynamic control tasks.

References

1. Dougherty, M.R., Scheck, P., Nelson, T.O., Narens, L.: Using the past to predict the future. Memory & Cognition 33(6), 1096–1115 (2005)
2. Dunlosky, J., Hertzog, C.: Training programs to improve learning in later adulthood: Helping older adults educate themselves (1998)
3. Endsley, M.R.: Situation awareness global assessment technique, SAGAT (1988)
4. Hacker, D.J., Bol, L., Horgan, D.D., Rakow, E.A.: Test prediction and performance in a classroom context. Journal of Educational Psychology 92(1), 160 (2000)

5. Hancock, P., Williams, G., Manning, C.: Influence of task demand characteristics on workload and performance. The International Journal of Aviation Psychology 5(1), 63–86 (1995)
6. Hawk, T.F., Shah, A.J.: A revised feedback model for task and self-regulated learning. The Coastal Business Journal 7(1), 66–81 (2008)
7. Kim, J.H., Rothrock, L., Tharanathan, A., Thiruvengada, H.: Investigating the effects of metacognition in dynamic control tasks. In: Jacko, J.A. (ed.) Human-Computer Interaction, Part I, HCII 2011. LNCS, vol. 6761, pp. 378–387. Springer, Heidelberg (2011)
8. Kuiper, R.A., Pesut, D.J.: Promoting cognitive and metacognitive reflective reasoning skills in nursing practice: self-regulated learning theory. Journal of Advanced Nursing 45(4), 381–391 (2004)
9. Norman, D.A.: The 'problem' with automation: inappropriate feedback and interaction, not 'over-automation'. Philosophical Transactions of the Royal Society of London. Series B, Biological Sciences 327(1241), 585–593 (1990)
10. Rothrock, L.: Using time windows to evaluate operator performance. International Journal of Cognitive Ergonomics 5(1), 1–21 (2001)
11. Zimmerman, B.J., Schunk, D.H.: Self-regulated learning and academic achievement: Theory, research, and practice. Springer-Verlag Publishing (1989)

Development of a Fieldwork Support System for Group Work in Project-Based Learning

Mikihiko Mori[1] and Akihisa Tatsumi[2]

[1] Kyoto University
[2] Kyoto City University of Arts

Abstract. This paper describes the Fieldwork Support System (FSS) for project-based Learning. The FSS is an essential tool for students who are new to fieldwork activities. They need to take notes on events that occur in the field and reflect on what people did and what they talked about in interviews. In addition, students should collaborate to learn using the data they collected. Therefore, we developed the FSS, which was constructed to use a combination of portable terminals during the students' time in the field and a Web-based management application upon their return. We also conducted a practical experiment on PBL in which students explored local communities. The results of a posterior questionnaire showed the students enjoyed being able to view their current locations and the locations of data they had collected on the FSS terminal map. However, they had complaints about the user interface.

1 Introduction

Amid the rapid progress in technology and diversification of individual values, people who offer services or productions should identify individuals' wants and needs. To do this, they should observe the events that occur in their field to determine what the problems are. Therefore, in the work process of value creation, such as designing production or service, designers need to have the skills of finding and solving problems. As an approach to developing these skills, a pedagogical methodology named problem-based learning (PBL)[1] is spreading in the fields of education and business.

Fieldwork has long been carried out in cultural anthropology and sociology[2]. Researchers visit a target site, called "the field," to gather firsthand data on real problems. Similarly, fieldwork is also carried out in the field of design. Fieldworkers in design collect materials about the target site through a preliminary survey before they arrive. Then, during their fieldwork on-site, they observe how people act and behave. In addition, they interview people in the field according to their data and results of observation. After the fieldwork, they organize the data collected from observations and interviews[3,4]. They posit explanations for the behavior of people observed at the field site, form hypotheses, and then return to the field for a more detailed survey.

In this sequence of fieldwork, researchers often record their field notes by hand, using a pen and paper, copy them onto notecards after leaving the field,

P. Zaphiris and A. Ioannou (Eds.): LCT 2014, Part I, LNCS 8523, pp. 429–440, 2014.

and finally, arrange them on a large paper or organize the notecards for the data compilation. Recently, however, portable digital devices have become commonplace. By using such devices, researchers can easily record visual data that is difficult to describe in handwritten notes. They can also carry all the fieldwork equipment they need in a single device.

In this paper, we propose a support system for fieldwork activities in education, mostly intended for use in group work for PBL. We describe a practical experiment in which students used this system to explore local communities in PBL. Finally, we present the results of a posterior questionnaire.

2   Fieldwork Support System

The investigation seeks to answer the following two questions about the use of digital devices for fieldwork activities in the context of group work in PBL.

1. What interface is easiest for students to use? We consider important functions such as collecting field data, collaborating with other students, and organizing information.
2. What information helps teachers understand students' progress? We consider functions such as finding the students' locations and viewing the information students have collected.

Similar studies have previously explored the use of mobile devices in education. Takenaka et al. proposed a Fieldwork Support System with the same name, but different from ours, for elementary school children[5]. Children took pictures using a mobile phone equipped with a camera and emailed the pictures as attachments to the Web server. However, this system cannot follow children's locations, and the task of attaching the pictures in an e-mail requires additional work. Sugimoto et al. proposed a field research system named SketchMap for elementary school children[6]. The children were asked to create a map of the area around their school. They used a tablet PC with modules of a GPS sensor and a camera. A pen-based interaction feature allowed them to add image pictures and draw. They also took pictures for the map using the camera module. However, SketchMap specialized in creating the map. Sumi et al. developed a chatting system named PhotoChat[7] that enables users to draw anyone's pictures or pictures already drawn by people. It was designed to support users' communication through photographic pictures. Yet, although it enables greater communication, PhotoChat is not always sufficient to record and store information on the field.

Furthermore, some recent applications may make it easy to record fieldwork. Evernote[1] is a well-known cloud-based system for PCs and mobile devices. Evernote enables users to record the location of a note when it is taken. Skitch[2] is an application for drawing on pictures, including blank pictures. A Skitch picture is synchronized as an Evernote note.

---

[1] http://evernote.com/
[2] http://evernote.com/skitch/

We conducted a preliminary experiment to test whether the existing systems can adequately support fieldwork. We introduced a combination of Evernote and Skitch. These systems were executed on 4.3-inch smartphones and 10-inch smart tablets. The results are summarized as follows.

Skitch enables users to take pictures, and draw on the pictures to write notes. The drawings are an easy way for students to collect information. Evernote enables collaboration among students; that is, it allows them to share the information they have collected. However, Skitch requested many steps to operate for completing up to synchronization. Thus, we determined that the existing systems were not always fit for fieldwork.

We also found that display-size of the device affected the drawing operation significantly. Although the 4.3-inch smartphone was portable, its small display was less user-friendly than that of the 10-inch tablet. On the other hand, the 10-inch tablet was less portable.

Therefore, we decided to construct an appropriate system for fieldwork activities in group work of PBL. The Fieldwork Support System (FSS) was developed taking into account the above questions and experimental results.

The FSS uses a combination of portable terminals for students' time in the field and a Web-based management application upon the students' return. When students go to the field, they each carry their own FSS terminal, which they use to take pictures (using the camera module) and write notes. Using GPS, the FSS terminal displays a map with the student's current location and the locations for which he/she has taken pictures or notes. We consider the pictures and notes, along with their locations, present location, and past trajectory as the student's activity log. The terminal communicates the activity log to a server computer to store through a third-generation (3G) mobile phone network. When a student accesses the server through the Web by PC, the FSS displays his/her activity log and can also display the activity logs of other members in the same group. Teachers can see all the students' activity logs.

Based on the results of the preliminary experiment, we decided to use a 7-inch tablet, which was considered a good size for in terms of both display and portability. Also for portability in the field, we chose tablet terminals based on Android OS, which is equipped with a camera, GPS sensor, and touch panel.

As shown in Fig. 1, the terminal initially shows the map as the main screen when a student runs the FSS application. The main screen displays buttons for various activities. For example, when the student taps the "Picture" button, the terminal runs the inner camera function to take pictures. When he/she taps the "Notes" button, it runs a canvas screen for note taking. Similarly, when he/she taps the "Notes on picture" button, it also runs a canvas screen, preparing a particular picture that the student has selected beforehand. On the canvas screen, the student is able to directly draw on the screen using a finger or write notes using the touch screen system. These note-taking functions allow the student to choose a color for drawing and to erase only what has been drawn. If he/she has taken notes or pictures, it shows their location on the map on the main screen. The terminal can also show a configuration menu to communicate with the server computer.

Fig. 2 shows the FSS's Web-based service for PCs. After logging in, every student and teacher is shown this screen. They can sort collected information by date or user. In this instance, pictures are sorted by user. A user named "Test1" has taken 7 pictures, 1 note on a picture, and 2 notes, which are sorted by the time they were taken. Each of them is shown on the map as a pin mark. The student's trajectory from 15 minutes before is also shown. When a student marks the checkbox next to a picture, the picture is downloaded into his/her local storage. Teachers, as administrators, have access to the "User Information" page, where they can view a list of all the students and their groups and edit information about them.

3   Practical Experiment

The practical experiment empirically investigated the FSS's usability for students. We used the FSS in a seminar named "The exploration of the fascinating Nishikyo," which was attended by 19 students in a design course of an art university. Nishikyo is a ward of Kyoto city, Japan, and it comprises several communities. The students were divided into three groups, each corresponding to a different local community. The seminar lasted four months. The activities using the FSS took place within the first two months. During this time, the students visited the field many times.

In total, they took 214 pictures, 9 notes, and 4 notes on pictures. For the purpose of evaluating the FSS, we administered a questionnaire after the end of the seminar. The questionnaire asked students how they used the FSS and what they felt about its usability at the time of use. Some questions were in a multiple-choice format that allowed more than one answer to be selected. The others asked for a free response.

All of the 19 students answered the questionnaire. Figs. 3–9 presents the questionnaire results. These figures plot the number of students as the axis of ordinate or abscissa.

As shown in Fig. 3, the students reported how often they took the FSS terminal to the field. No one answered that he/she had brought it more times than he/she had wanted. The answer "others" means that the student did not have a terminal because he/she had broken it early in the seminar and did not yet have a replacement. Hence, the student would be willing to carry a terminal at least that time. All but two of the students who did not carry it at all utilized the FSS.

The second question was about the terminal's usability; the results are shown in Fig. 4. The question was constructed to evaluate each function of the FSS as easy or awkward to use. The camera function and location-showing functions earned relatively good ratings. Meanwhile, the students had little appreciation for the note-taking functions, which half or more of them did not even use. The third question was about the usability of the Web-based service, evaluated

The mark of present location

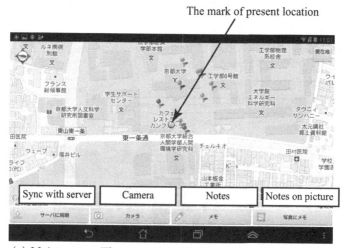

(a) Main screen: The operational buttons and a location map.

(b) Note-taking function screen: It shows the menu when the user taps the three-dot button in the bottom right corner.

Fig. 1. Screenshots of the FSS terminal application.

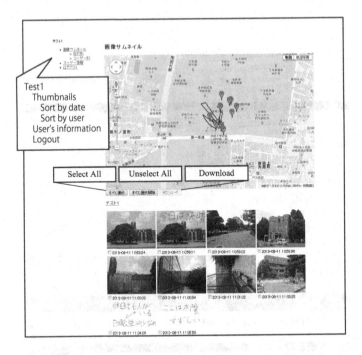

Fig. 2. Screenshot of the FSS Web-based service.

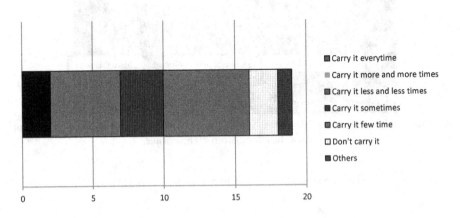

Fig. 3. Question 1: How often did you take the FSS terminal to the field?

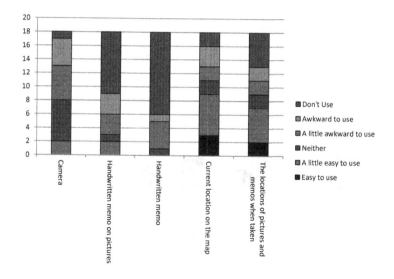

Fig. 4. Question 2: How did you feel about the usability of the FSS terminal?

in the same way as the terminals. As shown in Fig. 5, more than a third of students did not use this service. About half answered that it was awkward or a little awkward. In regard to this service, they also thought about the location functions more positively.

The fourth question asked to answer all items something recording the field when they had gone with them. As shown in Fig. 6, most students still brought notebooks and pens/pencils along. More than half also carried paper maps and their own cameras. Many brought their own smartphones. On the other hand, half of the students decided to utilize the FSS terminal. This result is related to the frequency of use as queried by the first question and is obtained similarly. The histogram in Fig. 7 shows the number of items as the abscissa and the number of students as the ordinate. Most students took more than four items with them.

The fifth question asked about when the students looked at the notes or the pictures they had taken on the PC, as shown in Fig. 8. It was a multiple-choice question. About one half of the students answered that they had looked in their group meeting, and about a quarter of them reported looking the same day they had taken the notes/pictures by the next meeting. The individual data showed that the students who answered they had looked after finishing all the fieldwork also indicated they had not looked before finishing. The students who answered they had not looked at all did not answer any other Question 5 items.

The sixth question asked what the students did with their notes, pictures, and data on their locations and trajectories. As shown in Fig. 9, about a half of them utilized their notes to recall information. In addition, about a half referred to notes written by other group members. About a third of the students returned

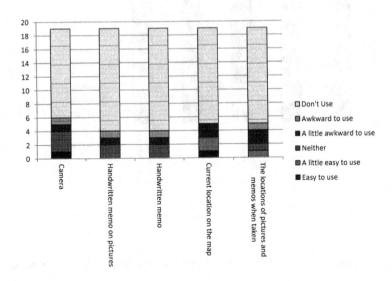

Fig. 5. Question 3: How do you feel about the usability of the PC component?

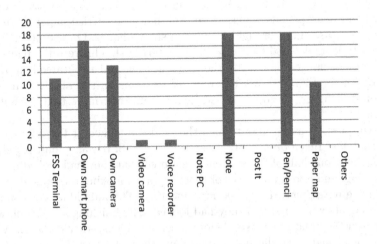

Fig. 6. Question 4: What did you bring to document your observations in the field?

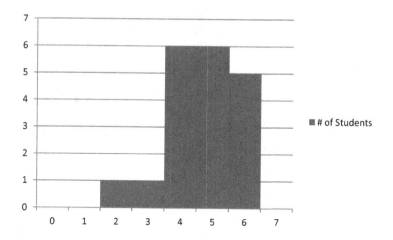

Fig. 7. This histogram shows the number of items as the abscissa and the number of students as the ordinate.

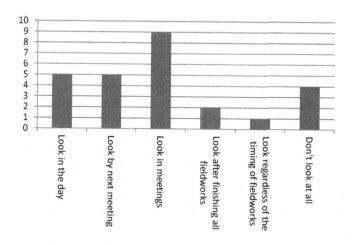

Fig. 8. Question 5: What time did you look at your notes or pictures on the PC?

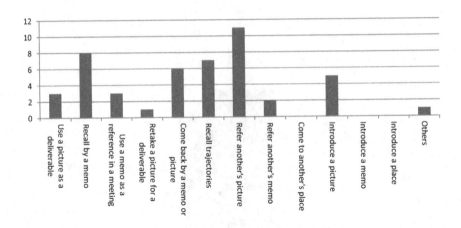

Fig. 9. Question 6: What did you do with your notes and pictures, or their locations?

to where they had taken a note or picture. Also, about a third utilized the data to recall their trajectories. However, none of the students visited a new place or another student's previous location. This result, when considered along with the result of the fifth question, suggests only a few of the students used the Web-based service.

The seventh question, which allowed a free response, was about the difference between the students' experiences using the FSS versus others method of field documentation. They preferred the FSS function for recording locations. Specifically, they described that seeing their current location and trajectories were useful because they did not read paper maps. One student commented that it was easier not having to record locations manually when taking pictures or notes. The students also expressed that the FSS enabled them to share information easily. One student described attempting to record more actively. On the other hand, another student described that operating the terminal was sometimes interfered with making observations of the field.

The eighth question asked the students to suggest ways to improve the FSS. First, one student asked for an additional function would allow users to share pictures and notes while in the field. Second, some students described that the user interfaces was not intuitive and that it required them to go through unnecessary steps. Since the current version of the FSS terminal uses Android's default camera module and photographic library application, which are delegated by the FSS application, one or more steps are required. The students also requested making it easier to switch to the note-taking function from the camera module, or vice versa. Third, although the FSS terminals meet a certain level of accuracy, the GPS sensor was less accurate in the residential areas that the students visited. Therefore, they described that the terminals did not log the correct locations. They also described that the sensor took too long to find the current location when the terminal came back from sleeping mode. Fourth, the students had to carry the terminal in their hands because it was too large to fit in a pocket. As indicated by the responses to the fifth question, the students carried various items in their hands, pockets, or bags, and in addition, they had to take the 7-inch tablet, which could not fit within the palm of their hand. Fifth, the battery ran out quickly. The FSS application in the terminal did not take into account reducing battery drain. Turning on the display led to drain, and then the students could not view the map for as long as they wanted. Sixth, there were the problems of the thermal runaway phenomenon and difficulty looking at the display under direct sunshine. This activity began during mid-summer and late autumn of 2013, when Japan was experiencing exceptionally hot temperatures nationwide. We should reduce the problems of heat and sunlight reflection. Also related to weather, some students asked for water-proof terminals to carry in the rain.

The final question asked the students for any remaining comments. Some suggested making the FSS compatible with their own smartphone (e.g., iPhone). Others requested a carrying case for the terminal to avoid dropping or scratching it.

The results of the questionnaire indicate that the location functions were favorably accepted by the students. The idea of sharing pictures and notes was also welcomed. These functions have not yet been realized as a dedicated system for fieldwork in PBL. However, the students still used their own tools for fieldwork. Although this may be due in part to their anxiety in the unfamiliar field environment, the FSS interface's lack of intuitiveness played a role in their decision to use other tools. Especially, the interface for taking pictures and writing notes needs to be improved.

4   Conclusion

For fieldwork in group work in the context of PBL, we proposed the FSS. The FSS was constructed to use a combination of portable terminals during the students' time in the field and a Web-based management application upon their return. We also described a practical experiment on the use of the FSS in PBL, in which students were asked to explore local communities of Nishikyo ward. The results of a posterior questionnaire showed that the students enjoyed being able to view their current locations and the locations of data they had collected on the FSS terminal map. However, they had complaints about the user interface. In particular, they requested fewer steps to take pictures or notes. They also expressed concerns about the accuracy of the GPS sensor.

In our future work, we will improve the usability and user interface of the FSS. We will develop the camera module and add a function for students to adjust the location value of data on the map. We will also explore the FSS usability for teachers in future investigations.

References

1. Blumenfeld, P.C., Soloway, E., Marx, R.W., Krajcik, J.S., Guzdial, M., Palincsar, A.: Motivating project-based learning: Sustaining the doing, supporting the learning. Educational Psychologist 26, 369–398 (1991)

2. Kuklick, B.H.: Personal equations: Reflections on the history of fieldwork, with special reference to sociocultural anthropology. Isis 102, 1–33 (2011)
3. Kawakita, J.: Hassouhou. Chukou (1967) (in Japanese)
4. McAleese, R.: The knowledge arena as an extension to the concept map: Reflection in action. Interactive Learning Environments 6, 251–272 (1998)
5. Takenaka, M., Ohkubo, M., Inagaki, S., Kuroda, H.: Development and pilot study of a mobile phone-aided mutual monitoring support system, pp. 39–45 (2006)
6. Sugimoto, M., Ravasio, P., Enjoji, H.: Sketchmap: A system for supporting outdoor collaborative learning by enhancing and sharing learners' experiences. In: ICCE Workshop on Design and Experiments of Mobile and Ubiquitous Learning Environments, pp. 1–8 (2006)
7. Sumi, Y., Ito, J., Nishida, T.: Photochat: Communication support system based on sharing photos and notes. In: CHI 2008 Extended Abstracts on Human Factors in Computing Systems, CHI EA 2008, pp. 3237–3242. ACM, New York (2008)

Novel Didactic Proof Assistant for First-Order Logic Natural Deduction

Jorge Pais* and Álvaro Tasistro

Universidad ORT Uruguay

Abstract. We present a proof assistant designed to help learning formal proof, particularly in the system of Natural Deduction for First-Order Logic. The assistant handles formulas and derivations containing meta-variables and allows to maintain a library of instanciable lemmas. It possesses a graphical interface presenting proofs as trees and handles multiple simultaneous derivations that can be dragged and dropped into one another.

1 Introduction

This paper is about technology that helps learning *formal proof*. Proof is the main constituent of the practice of Mathematics, but it is certainly also performed in other disciplines. Particularly, it is, as we argue below, of utmost importance in software construction, despite being therein generally neglected. *Formal* proof, on the other hand, is proof framed within a formal language, or as it is traditionally called, a *formal system* of inference rules. The use of these systems in practice has been awakened, precisely by the needs of the software construction activity of acquiring certainty about the behaviour of computing systems. Out of this situation a field of research within Computing Science has begun to thrive, namely that of the design and development of *proof assistants*.

Learning proof, and especially formal proof, is therefore acquiring increasing importance, especially within the software community. Learning proof, generally, is of course of great interest for students in several disciplines and also, at least in some countries, for those at High School. In this paper we make the claim that certain systems of formal proof, most notably Natural Deduction, are useful also for learning proof in the widest sense, i.e. for developing organized manners of approaching their understanding and construction. Therefore there is some interest too in investigating the technology helping to learn formal proof through practice, i.e. that of the *didactic proof assistants*.

In [1] we presented a novel didactic proof assistant, here to be named Andy 0, for the system of Natural Deduction of Propositional Logic. One of its most interesting features was the handling of a library of *lemmas* that could be reused by instantiating them within other proofs. As pointed out in the paper, the natural continuation of that work was to extend the system to First-Order Logic,

---

* Currently at Northeastern University, Boston.

P. Zaphiris and A. Ioannou (Eds.): LCT 2014, Part I, LNCS 8523, pp. 441–451, 2014.

which is a standard formal language for Mathematics. However, to correspondingly extend the capacity of instantiating lemmas was far from trivial, a fact which is reflected in the absence of such feature in existent proof assistants for the mentioned language.

In this paper we present a solution to this problem, embodied in Andy $1\frac{1}{2}$, the successor to Andy 0. It keeps the general outlook of the latter, being based on a graphical interface that displays formal proofs as trees, allowing for any number of draft proofs that can be dragged and dropped into others, and admitting combined strategies of proof development. Its main advance is the ability to work at the level of *schematic* formulas, i.e. ones that are actual patterns containing meta-variables that stand for arbitrary formulas and terms. It is a fact that the actual practice of First-Order Logic is carried out at this level, as witnessed by any textbook on the matter. It is also this feature that allows to properly handle reusable general lemmas. To our knowledge, Andy $1\frac{1}{2}$ is the first proof assistant to allow for this level of abstraction in the formal language. Its name derives from the fact that it is actually an assistant for (an adaptation of) One-and-a-Halfth Logic, as presented in [2].

The structure of this paper is the following: In section 2 we extend ourselves on the relevance of learning proof and formal proof, which justifies our interest in the related technology. We also try to present the relevant features of First-Order Logic Natural Deduction in a manner accesible to the general reader. In section 3 we describe the features that are in our opinion to be required of a didactic proof assistant. In particular, we try to give a detailed account of the technical problem involved in handling schematic formulas and proofs in the context of First-Order Logic. Having given the preceding motivation, we describe in section 4 the design of Andy $1\frac{1}{2}$, focusing on its most prominent feature as explained above. Finally, the last section comments on the use that we have been able to make of the assistant, as well as on forthcoming work. In comparison to [1], the present paper is more detailed in motivations and of course on the technical aspects concerning the novel extension to schematic First-Order Logic. We enumerate the features common to the predecessor tool Andy 0, giving only summarized descriptions.

2   Learning (Formal) Proof

Proof is the activity of arriving at knowledge deductively, i.e. starting off from self-evident, postulated or simply supposed principles and performing successive inferences, each of which extracts a conclusion out of previously arrived at premises. It constitutes the identifying feature of Mathematics, but is of course also of central importance in other disciplines, like Philosophy and Science generally. Students of all these branches of knowledge surely will benefit from endeavours directed to ease their path towards an increased understanding and mastery of the practice of proof. This should include students not only at college or university level, but also those in high school.

Formal Logic, on the other hand, is the *theory* of the activity of proving. As such it has, since the very beginning, striven to put forward the rules that govern such activity, i.e. the rules of correct reasoning. In its contemporary mathematical variety, it has formulated several artificial languages into which to formulate the (deductive) practice of Mathematics. According to such scientific programme, there should be a language for expressing every conceivable mathematical proposition and also a language (or, as it has been called, proof system) for expressing proofs —of the true propositions.

It was Frege who first formulated such a device, in 1879 [3]. His intent was to complete the work of the foundational movement that had taken over Mathematics since the early XIX century. This movement was firstly directed towards providing a firm basis to the differential and integral calculus. Frege, in turn, intended to reach the most fundamental level by axiomatizing the very concept of proof. It is worthwhile to spend some effort trying to understand the implications of such endeavour, for they are remarkable. Systems of axioms were already a established practice in Mathematics, e.g. in Geometry, and their accomplishment was to make explicit *the starting points* of the deductive activity. But of course each proof had still to be understood, individually. That is to say, the *logic* validating such proof was left implicit, as something that any mathematician (any human being with adequate training) would certainly possess. Now what Frege was pursuing was a manner of making such logic explicit. Hence, and this is the important consequence, *no logic* ought to be necessary to validate a proof as arranged in his system. That is to say, validation or rejection of purported proofs would be immediate by just *reading* them, i.e. what we now call a purely *formal* procedure. Frege could not put it in these terms, but his ideal amounted to providing a language for Mathematics whose correct use could be checked by an automaton. Moreover, such a system ought also to ensure that syntactic validity entailed logical validity, for a correctly written proof should be also logically correct. Hence such a language could be characterized in current computational jargon as one satisfying the lemma *if it compiles, it works*[1].

Formal proof systems are of course of prime importance to logicians, be they of the mathematical or the philosophical extraction. However, these scholars take towards them a stand that is generally external or "from above", i.e. they are mainly interested in the properties of the formal machinery as a whole, not in its actual use. They need only a basic dexterity and certainly not an efficient method for their exploitation. Now, on the other hand, it is a readily perceived fact that the use of formal proof in reasoning about the correctness of computer programs brings about the possibility of having *verifying compilers*, i.e. of programming systems in which syntactic correctness entails functional or behavioural correctness, and that thus realize for software the seemingly utopic motto *if it compiles, it works*. Several such systems have already been developed and constitute a toolkit for practitioners of the branch of Software Engineering called Formal Methods. The approach certainly requires to develop not just executable code, but also *mathematical code*, i.e. formally verifiable evidence of

---

[1] Unfortunately, Frege's system did not satisfy this property, as its logical principles were actually defective. But of course many other sound proof systems have been devised since then.

the correctness of the former. The cost of development is thus increased, but there is still certainly a pay off in many important cases, mainly as the cost of failure approaches infinity.

Thus Computing Science and Software Engineering do already provide an increasingly ample field of demand for adequate systems of formal proof together with appropriate technology for their efficient use. A useful tool for composing formal proofs should of course verify their correctness, but also offer appropriate assistance in their construction. It could be asked whether such assistance could get as far as to just the fully automatic proof of the desired theorems, but this is generally impossible already for the most basic branches of Mathematics that bear some interest. And, moreover, it is arguable not desirable in many cases, for proving is but understanding and therefore essential to the activity of the practitioner, be her a mathematician, a scientist or an engineer. Nevertheless, certainly not all proofs are equally interesting and one would expect effective technology to efficiently take care of the more clerical obligations, among other services. All this has then given rise to the interesting research field of *proof assistants* within Computing Science.

Now, a further interesting side of formal proof systems to which we would like to call attention is their potential to contribute to the understanding and mastery of proof, generally. As said in the beginning this could be of interest to a large audience of students, from high school to college, spanning a diverse range of disciplines. Certainly included among the latter is software construction, since it is a fact that understanding of program code and therefore certainty about its behavior amounts to nothing less than proof. Particularly useful in connection to this educational aspect of formal proof systems is the Calculus of Natural Deduction [4], devised with the aim of closely mimicking common practice in informal, natural proof. We proceed now to give a summary description of its most important features.

First, we shall take First-Order Logic as the formal language for expressing propositions. This is just standard, in the sense that any mathematician, when urged about the ultimate foundations of her activity may, and generally will, safely lean on Set Theory and its formalisation (encoding) in First-Order Logic. It is also quite natural, as its symbolism has permeated normal mathematical practice. For instance, $(\forall x)P(x)$ means "all individuals satisfy the property P" and $\alpha \to \beta$ means "the proposition α entails (implies) the proposition β". It is the fact that $\forall$ can only refer to the universe of individuals, and not to collections of propositions or properties, that is responsible for the "First-Order" part of the name of this language. $\forall$ is the universal *quantifier*, whereas $\to$ is a *connective* (specifically, the implication). Quantifiers and connectives are collectively named the *logical constants*. The letters $P, Q, \ldots$ used to represent properties form a *vocabulary* for a particular application, together with symbols for specific individuals and functions defined over the latter. The expressions representing propositions are the *formulas*, whereas those representing individuals are the *terms* of the language.

Now, as to the language or system of proofs, the system of Natural Deduction presents as characteristic feature the existence of rules that allow the use of temporary additional assumptions. For instance, to prove a formula that states an implication $\alpha \to \beta$ it is possible to use a rule that allows to assume α in order to prove β from it, just as in common practice. Specifically, this rule states that if one possesses a proof of β which depends on the assumption of α, then one can infer that $\alpha \to \beta$, thereby obtaining a proof which does not anymore depend on the aforementioned assumption. This assumption is said to be discharged, i.e. dispensed with in the newly formed proof.

Further, the rules of inference are organized around the logical constants and are of one of two classes in each case, i.e. a rule is either:

- An *introduction* rule stating how a formula having the logical constant in question as principal operator can be derived in a direct, canonical manner, or
- An *elimination* rule, stating how such a formula can be employed to derive further consequences from it.

For example, the rule described just above is the introduction rule for the implication $\to$. The elimination rule for this connective is:

$$\frac{\alpha \to \beta \qquad \alpha}{\beta}$$

which states that from $\alpha \to \beta$ one can infer β provided α is also proven. Another interesting rule is that of introduction of $\forall$: To conclude $(\forall x)\alpha$, where the formula α will in general depend on the variable x, it is enough to prove just α, provided that no assumption used in this latter proof depends on x. The proviso ensures that x represents an indeed *arbitrary* individual, i.e. one about which no particular property has been assumed. The elimination rule for $\forall$ makes use of the (meta-)operation of *substitution*:

$$\forall e \ \frac{\forall x \alpha}{\alpha[x := t]}$$

Here $\forall e$ is just the name of the rule, included for later reference. The conclusion of the rule says that the (universally) quantified variable can be just instantiated at any term (representing some individual). This is of course evidently correct, since we have just proven that the proposition α holds for any such individual. The instantiation is realized by the operation of substitution. The intent here is that this operation is defined outside the proof system and performed "silently". That is to say, it is assumed that the user knows how to perform it (because the explanation is given at some place during the setting up of the language of formulas) and, therefore, she just needs to execute it for applying this inference rule.

Rules have in general several premises and always one conclusion and therefore the formal proofs (technically called *derivations*) are naturally arranged as trees. It is natural to read inference as proceeding from the premises above to the conclusion below, and therefore the trees are written with the root, which is the conclusion of the theorem, at the bottom, and the initial assumptions at the leaves on the top. Generally, the derivations prove judgements of the form $\alpha_1, \ldots, \alpha_n \vdash \alpha$ where the formulas to the left of $\vdash$ are the assumptions (or hypotheses) of the theorem and α its conclusion (thesis). The use of the rules inside a tree follows a quite characteristic pattern: Reading the tree from the top, one first applies elimination rules to obtain information from the given premises in a phase that could be called of *analysis*. At some level during the derivation one starts a *synthesis* forming new conclusions from the data obtained, by employing the introduction rules. The full system is well explained in [5].

So Natural Deduction actually consists in an orderly arrangement of rules of inference, where the organizing concept is the collection of logical constants. Indeed, with basis on the understanding of the meaning of each logical constant one can easily reconstruct the logical system of rules. That is to say that there is really no need of going through a painful recollection of an at first sight long list of inference rules when using the system. It is rather more convenient to *think* about the *meaning* of the formula at hand, and specifically about that of its principal logical constant. Further, the general structure of the proofs as explained earlier reflects the existence of a well founded strategy for selecting introduction or elimination rules at each step: At first, one goes backwards from conclusion to new conclusions-to-be-proven, generally by selecting appropriate introduction rules. This is carried out until no further rules of this kind can be applied or they would lead to conclusions which are not sensible to try. At such point one starts combining the available hypotheses in a forward manner, i.e. going from known premises to further inferred conclusions, trying to obtain the pending results. This is done by applying elimination rules. Hence the tree is generally constructed first from the root and upwards, until some point which roughly corresponds to the completion of the synthetic part of the proof as depicted above in the description of the general strcture of derivations. Then one proceeds from the assumptions and downwards, constructing the analytic part of the proof. Such order of proceeding looks somehow opposite to the one suggested by the analytic-synthetic structure of the proofs that has been mentioned earlier. But then one must keep in mind that the way a proof is presented or read is generally different from the way it is conceived. And also that the strategy just explained is not claimed to be the only one appropriate to employ but just a generally useful one, especially to start finding one's way about carrying out this kind of constructions.

We believe that all these features bear a favourable effect not only as to the mastery of the formal system, but also as to the understanding of mathematical propositions generally, especially as to what concerns the comprehension and development of their proofs.

3   Technology for Learning Formal Proof

What a student should learn about the use of Natural Deduction is not just to be able to come out with syntactically well formed derivations, but also to endow each of the rules with *meaning*, which is to say that they carry out the proofs according to a well determined *intent*. Teaching, i.e. helping to learn, such mastery, conveniently begins with a detailed explanation of the system of rules, since it is important that the student gets to see the entire structure of the system, identifying the organizing principle. But it must quickly follow on promoting extensive practice. Such practice has to be, to the greatest possible extent, autonomous, because the students should not depend on the teacher's judgement for achieving certainty about the correctness of their constructions. Needless to say, this kind of practice is greatly favoured by the use of a computerized tool, which has given rise to the investigation of *didactic* proof assistants.

Clearly, the requirements on didactic proof assistants are different from those on those destined to professional use. Generally, it could be said that a student ought to be plainly in command of the proof process and only get help at those points where it does not stand in the place of understanding. More specifically, a number of tasks that are a nuisance for a professional constitute significant learning items for a student. A didactic assistant should first of all provide motivation. In this respect, a good deal is already achieved by the mere possibility of having the derivations constructed and checked. But there are also a number of other desired features that rapidly turn out to be necessary: The assistant should significantly improve over the paper-and-pencil experience, which means that it should allow:

1. Draft derivations to be initiated, discarded and connected at any moment.
2. Alternating backwards and forward derivation at will.
3. To manipulate the formalism at the right abstraction level.
4. Proof reuse, i.e. storage and instantiation of lemmas.

A detailed explanation of all these points has been given by the authors in [1]. However, the third point needs now some expansion, since the work cited reports on an assistant for the much simpler system of Natural Deduction for Propositional Logic. The point is that the right level of abstraction in using First-Order Logic is that of *schematic* formulas and theorems. The idea can be easily explained by the following claim: The theorems that one proves when teaching and learning First-Order Logic are *not* of the form $\forall x(P(x) \land Q(x)) \vdash \forall x P(x) \land \forall x Q(x)$, but of the form $\forall x(\alpha \land \beta) \vdash \forall x \alpha \land \forall x \beta$, i.e. they are formulated schematically (that is to say, generically) on formulas (and terms). This is due to the simple fact that the interesting results in First-Order Logic are independent of the particular predicate or function symbols employed, i.e. independent of any specific vocabulary. So one is naturally led to reason generically on formulas and terms, i.e. to work at the schematic level. It is important to remark that this *is* the normal practice, as witnessed by direct experience or by the contents of textbooks.

Moreover, we want the schematic theorems to be used directly in inference steps in other proofs. Specifically, each schematic theorem stands for an infinite family of theorems (its instances). We naturally wish to justify any of these by direct appeal to a schematic theorem of which it is an instance. This is equivalent to saying that (schematic) theorems can be used as rules of inference.

These latter considerations bring about a considerable technical problem, whose solution is explained below and turns our tool into a significant innovation in the field of assistants for First-Order Logic. The point is that the logical language is being modified, as can be inferred after consideration of the following examples ($\vee$ is the symbol for disjunction):

$$\forall x(\alpha \vee \beta) \vdash \alpha \vee \forall x\beta \quad (\alpha \text{ not depending on } x)$$

$$\forall x(\alpha \rightarrow \beta), \alpha[x := t] \vdash \beta[x := t].$$

The two preceding judgements are actual theorems that we wish to be able to derive using the assistant. They present:

1. Meta-variables (α and β ranging on formulas, t ranging on terms).
2. Side-conditions (restricting dependence on variables of certain formulas, that generally are or contain meta-variables).
3. Explicit substitution (since meta-variables are symbols standing for yet unknown formulas the substitution can no longer just silently operate on formulas or terms).

Already these observations lead to the necessity of formulating another language and proof system. In addition, a rule of *equality* of formulæ has to be available for explicit use, as in:

$$\forall e \; \frac{\forall x\alpha}{\alpha[x := x]}$$
$$eq \; \frac{}{\alpha.}$$

Notice that one cannot skip the intermediate judgement $\alpha[x := x]$ because the substitution cannot be "silently" performed at the meta-level. Therefore the last step is necessary, in which the rule eq is applied. This allows to infer a formula from another if it can be checked that they are in fact equal modulo a theory that embodies the properties of the substitution together with the interchange of bound names. This rule is mostly left implicit in ordinary practice, i.e. it is used "silently", performing the necessary conversions "on the fly". But to do this correctly requires mastery of the properties of the language, so we think it advantageous that the rule has to emerge explicit in the new formal system.

The problem of formulating this new logic has been solved in [2] where *One-and-a-Halfth Order Logic* is introduced. It is precisely the logic of the schematic theorems of First-Order Logic as described above. One-and-a-Halfth Order Logic is founded in turn upon the syntax of Nominal Terms [6] which is a framework for languages with binding operators (e.g. the logical quantifiers) that incorporates meta-variables with explicit substitutions.

From a strictly technical point of view, the problem of handling schematic theorems could have been solved by stepping up to Second-Order Logic, for then a meta-variable ranging over formulæ can be represented as an object variable ranging over propositional functions. But this approach conducts to modifying the logic itself, i.e. we would be teaching Second-Order instead of First-Order Logic. We would rather stay at First-Order Logic or, as we should say, at the normal practice with First-Order Logic, which is actually the intermediate One-and-a-Halfth level.

4   The Design.

The design of Andy $1\frac{1}{2}$ rests upon the preceding considerations. Most of its features are similar to those of its ancestor Andy 0 and so we just summarize them here, giving also a comment about their presence in other proof assistants. We give some more detail on the new significant feature, which is the ability to deal with schematic First-Order logic.

1. Tree-like display of derivations. This is preferred because it is the notation that corresponds to writing rules of inference in the most natural way, i.e. with the premises on top of a bar which represents the act of inference of the conclusion appearing below. It is rather uncommon in elsewhere available systems.
2. Main proof and draft proofs. There exists a main proof together with draft subsidiary proofs which can be as many as desired. Draft proofs can be adjoined to the main proof by doing just *drag-and-drop*. Not known to be present in other proof assistants.
3. Backwards and forward reasoning. These have already been explained and can be alternated without restriction. They are pretty common in other proof assistants.
4. Library of Lemmas. This has also already been explained. Lemmas are generally schematic theorems and proper instantiation is carried out by the assistant, resting on the algorithms to be described below for the manipulation of the schematic formulas. This feature is rare in other assistants. At most they allow recovering lemmas but instantiation has to be done manually.

As already said, the main contribution of the present work consists in allowing to construct and check *schematic derivations*. For accomplishing this we have based ourselves on the already mentioned One-and-a-Halfth Order Logic. The formal system in [2] is a so-called Sequent Calculus, rather than a Natural Deduction system. We therefore have given it the latter formulation, proving it equivalent to the original one. As a consequence of this result, the logical soundness proven in [2] for the original system is inherited by ours. We also proved two basic properties of our system, which altogether justify the use of lemmas as inference rules. These are a so-called Generalized Cut and an Instantiation result that proves inference closed under substitution of formulas and terms for corresponding meta-variables.

Checking validity of rule application requires to check:

1. Side-conditions concerning the non-dependence of formulas on variables.
2. Equality of formulas, under laws that characterize (explicit) substitution and renaming of bound variables.

These checks are decidable and therefore performed by the assistant. Now, on didactic considerations, we have chosen not to do so silently, i.e. to force the student to explicitly command the assistant to perform the checks. In that way, she is permanently in command of the proof process. The corresponding algorithms pertain to a module dealing with nominal abstract syntax which, as already mentioned, is the framework within which the present language is formulated.

Further, in order to implement the instantiation of lemmas it is necessary to *match* a schematic formula (the one to be proven) against another one (the conclusion of the chosen lemma, officiating as a pattern). Matching requires defining a criterion of identity of formulas, which within this language can be formulated in the following three manners:

1. Up to the laws of explicit substitution and renaming of bound variables.
2. Up to renaming of bound variables only.
3. Just as plain syntactic identity.

Our choice is for the latter, again based on didactic considerations: We want the student to explicitly indicate the need of renaming bound variables or using a susbtitution law. If the matching employed by the assistant were more powerful we would be saving the student from applications of the eq rule, already commented on. This is an example of an arguably clerical task, certainly uninteresting in professional practice, that bears some significance in educational terms. It is also worthwhile to mention that matching algorithms for the most powerful notion of formula equality above (number 1) are yet not known.

5   Conclusions

Andy $1\frac{1}{2}$ is then, to our knowledge, the first proof assistant to allow handling of schematic First-Order Logic, particularly within the calculus of Natural Deduction. It is also quite novel in offering the possibility of developing a library of reusable, instantiable lemmas, and maintains from its predecessor Andy 0, a graphical interface with proofs as trees, and several draft proofs that can be dragged and dropped into one another.

Currently it is being tested in seminars with advanced students. This experience is being used to adjust a number of details concerning especially the graphical interface. The system will be fully operating next semester in the course on Logic pertaining to the Software Engineering programme of our university. This is a standard course comprising Propositional and First-Order Logic. As reported in [1] the experience with Andy 0 is quite satisfactory as can be concluded from several interviews with the students involved. In particular, they were coincident in highlighting the motivating potential of the assistant, as it makes proof development and experimentation much more comfortable. We expect therefore a still better outcome from the experience with Andy $1\frac{1}{2}$, especially since it can be used in both parts of the course. Practice with actual formal proof takes two weeks within the 16 weeks of the entire course, but the students go back to it at the time of preparing the final tests. Our main concern is the permanent risk that the tool becomes the theory, in the sense that they take logical validity to be "Andy" validity. This is another manifestation of the purely formalistic attitude of composing proofs by just fitting trees into one another and missing the sense of the rules. We are also in the search for methodologies for properly assessing the effect of this practice on the general understanding and handling of proofs by the students. Finally, we are currecntly planning to introduce programming practice into the course, posing the students problems of manipulation of formulas and proofs. It will be interesting to study the effect of this activity in their understanding of proof in the widest sense.

References

1. Pais, J., Tasistro, Á.: Proof Assistant Based on Didactic Considerations. Journal of Universal Computer Science 19(11), 1570–1596 (2013)
2. Gabbay, M.J., Mathijssen, A.: One-and-a-Halfth-Order Logic. Journal of Logic and Computation 18, 521–562 (2008)
3. Frege, G.: Beggriffsschrift, eine der aritmetischen nachgebildete Formelsprache des reinen Denkens. Louis Nebert, Halle A.S. (1879); Translated as Bauer-Mengelberg S.: Concept Script: A formal language of pure thought modeled upon that of Arithmetic. In: van Heijenoort, J. (eds.) From Frege to Gödel: A Source Book in Mathematical Logic (1879-1931). Harvard University Press, Cambridge (1967)
4. Gentzen, G.: Untersuchungen über das logische Schliessen. Matematische Zeitsschrift 39 (1935); Translated as Investigations into logical deduction. In: Szabo, M. (ed.) Collected Papers of Gerhard Gentzen. North Holland (1969)
5. van Dalen, D.: Logic and Structure. Springer (2008)
6. Urban, C., Pitts, A.M., Gabbay, M.J.: Nominal Unification. In: Baaz, M., Makowsky, J.A. (eds.) CSL 2003. LNCS, vol. 2803, pp. 513–527. Springer, Heidelberg (2003)

The Evolvement of Constructionism:
An Overview of the Literature

Antigoni Parmaxi and Panayiotis Zaphiris

Cyprus Interaction Lab, Department of Multimedia and Graphic Arts,
Cyprus University of Technology, Cyprus
{antigoni.parmaxi,panayiotis.zaphiris}@cut.ac.cy

Abstract. This paper reviews the theory of constructionism from its evolvement in 1980s towards its more recent implementations. By reviewing recent research conducted under the framework of constructionism, we set off in understanding its key ideas and their evolution over time. At the same time this paper acknowledges obstacles, challenges and critiques towards implementing constructionism in the teaching and learning practice. The paper is organized around three sections: constructionism, distributed constructionism and social constructionism. The findings of this study reveal the dynamic progression of constructionism and its potential to be used as a pervasive theoretical framework for instructional technology in various settings.

Keywords: theory of learning, Papert, Logo, microworlds construction, artifact, object-to-think-with, social technologies.

1   Introduction

Whilst educators, practitioners and researchers express high interest in making available technological tools that enable their students to learn through experimentation rather than lecturing, designing and implementing such tools under the appropriate framework is hardly realized [27]. Resnick [27] provides three threads of thought, which need to be taken into consideration whilst designing such tools: firstly, learners' experiences, needs and expectations; secondly understanding of domain knowledge and finally, understanding of computational ideas and paradigms. On the same line, Ruschoff and Ritter [29] raise the need of "a radical change in our approaches to teaching and learning in order to best prepare future generations for living and working in tomorrow's world". From this perspective, constructionism can offer "the guiding principles for curriculum design, materials development, and classroom practice" [29].

The term constructionism originates from Papert [16-20] and captures the concept of construction of knowledge by engaging in the making of concrete and public artifacts. Papert's theory can be summarized in his vision of a new educational environment in which learners build meaningful knowledge artifacts by taking advantage of the ubiquity of new technologies around them. This study reviews the theoretical

P. Zaphiris and A. Ioannou (Eds.): LCT 2014, Part I, LNCS 8523, pp. 452–461, 2014.

framework of constructionism from its infancy towards its more recent applications and provides support for its privileged status for supporting the use of technological tools in learning.

2   Constructionism

2.1   Constructivism and Constructionism

Constructionism [16-20] builds and expands the Piagetian theory of constructivism [24]. For both constructivism and constructionism, knowledge is built by the learner; instead of being presented and imposed to students by an expert, such as the teacher. As an alternative, they maintain that teachers should enhance students' active learning. Constructionism adds to the constructivist perspective the idea of artifact construction. Where constructivists view the learner as an active builder of knowledge, constructionism places a critical emphasis on having learners engage in artifacts constructions that are external and shared. In contrast to Piaget who focuses on cognitive processes of learning, Papert's constructionism focuses on learning through making and emphasizes on individual learners' interactions with their artifacts that are mostly built through the assistance of digital media and computer based technologies:

> *Constructionism--the N word as opposed to the V word--shares constructivism's connotation of learning as 'building knowledge structures' irrespective of the circumstances of the learning. It then adds the idea that this happens especially felicitously in a context where the learner is consciously engaged in constructing a public entity, whether it's a sand castle on the beach or a theory of the universe* [20].

Constructionists argue that learners' engagement with external artifact construction involves a creative and re-creative activity that represents a developmental cycle. Papert has seen the critical role of the cultural surrounding whilst building internal cognitive structures pointing out that surrounding cultures can inform and facilitate constructive Piagetian learning [16]. Papert views the difficulty in understanding certain concepts in the deficiency of education in materials that would make an idea or concept simple and concrete:

> *All builders need materials to build with. Where I am at variance with Piaget is in the role I attribute to the surrounding cultures as a source of these materials. In some cases the culture supplies them in abundance, thus facilitating constructive Piagetian learning. For example, the fact that so many important things (knives and forks, mothers and fathers, shoes and socks) come in pairs is a "material" for the construction of an intuitive sense of number. But in many cases where Piaget would explain the slower development of a particular concept by its greater complexity or formality, I see the critical factor as the relative poverty of the culture in those materials that would make the concept simple and concrete. In yet other cases the culture may provide materials but block their use* [16].

Wilensky [33] took this point further providing a new perspective into our understanding of concrete elucidating that "concreteness is not a property of an object but rather a *property of a person's relationship to an object*. Concepts that were hopeless-ly abstract at one time can become concrete for us if we get into the "right relationship" with them" [33]. In light of this perspective, any idea, concept or piece of knowledge can become concrete provided that a person develops a set of represen-tations, interactions and connections with the idea, concept or piece of knowledge [33]. The constructionist paradigm offers a fertile ground for promoting concreteness since "when we construct objects in the world, we come into engaged relationship with them and the knowledge needed for their construction. It is especially likely then that we will make this knowledge concrete" [33]. Wilenksy [33] also emphasizes the importance of social relations between people since "it is through people's own idio-syncratically personal ways of connecting to other people that meaningful relation-ships are established" [33].

2.2   Constructionist Concepts

Constructionism is underpinned by three key ideas [12]: appropriation, knowledge construction and learning cultures. Appropriation emphasizes the importance of hav-ing learners seize new knowledge and begin to identify with it [12]. Knowledge con-struction is closely connected to learning through constructing one's own knowledge whilst engaging in creating meaningful artifacts. Finally, constructionism also values the importance of learning culture. A popular example of a learning community is the samba school, an informal social setting in which people come together for something that involves "social cohesion, a sense of belonging to a group, and a sense of com-mon purpose" [16]. In a setting such as a school of samba, constructionists focus on how the social context fortifies the building of connections to what is being learned. Papert [16] has seen the critical role of the cultural surrounding whilst building inter-nal cognitive structures pointing out that surrounding cultures can inform and facili-tate constructive Piagetian learning.

2.3   Potentials and Challenges of Artifact Construction

Digital media and computer based technologies provide a rich teaching instrument, in Papert's words an "object-to-think-with" that can be shared in the world, probed and admired [18]. Constructionism is closely connected with the Logo programming lan-guage which is seen by researchers as "a testing bed for engaging students in prob-lems solving and learning to learn" [12]. Logo is a programming language developed at the Massachusetts Institute of Technology in the late 1960s. Logo is renowned for its turtle graphics which provide an "object-to-think-with" [16]. In its early years, the most popular use of Logo involved a "floor turtle" (robot) and with the burst of per-sonal computers in the late 1970s the Logo turtle shifted to its screen version. Both the floor (robot) and screen turtle were controlled through a computer keyboard. The initial commands that were used with Logo to make the turtle move were: forward, back, left, right, pen up, pen down. These commands made the turtle move and draw whatever the user wanted.

For constructionists Logo provides a vehicle and a language for thinking about thinking, an activity that promotes the development of higher levels of thinking and problem-solving performance [1, 3]. Moreover, learners' engagement with the use of computer "offers children the opportunity to become more like adults, indeed like professionals, in their relationship to their intellectual products and themselves" [16]. Advocates of Logo claim that Logo is a developer of creativity, divergent thinking, metacognitive ability, ability to describe direction well [4, 6-7] and an enhancement of students' mathematical understanding [9, 5]. Moreover, research also indicated that Logo can enhance the development of social and emotional development [10, 13] and promote spontaneous social interaction [11].

On the other hand, Logo has received criticism mainly because what it provokes outstrips its actual performance. A growing body of research at the Education's Centre for Children and Technology (CCT) at the Bank Street College failed to identify Logo effects. Pea [22] conducted a longitudinal pre-post study with children who worked with Logo language over a school year. The results showed no cognitive benefits for the children who worked with Logo language. Moreover, two other quantitative studies conducted at the CCT showed that the knowledge acquired within Logo has limited or no potential in transferring easily to any other kind of learning [14, 23]. As an attempt to elucidate these negative results, CCT researchers explored what happens whilst students explore Logo [15]. The study showed that programming experience (as opposed to expertise) does not transfer to other domains which share analogous formal properties. Finally, advocates against Logo also demonstrate that Logo is a limited instructional tool that inhibits other kinds of thinking [2, 8].

Papert entails this criticism as a "poor way to talk about Logo" [17] grounding his argument on his view of technocentrism from Piaget's use of the word egocentrism:

Egocentrism for Piaget does not, of course, mean "selfishness"--it means that the child has difficulty understanding anything independently of the self. Technocentrism refers to the tendency to give a similar centrality to a technical object-for example computers or Logo [17].

Papert [17] points that this technocentric thinking which emphasizes the centrality of the computer as agent that acts directly on thinking and learning, underestimates other significant elements of the learning practice, people and culture:

Does wood produce good houses? If I built a house out of wood and it fell down, would this show that wood does not produce good houses? Do hammers and saws produce good furniture? These betray themselves as technocentric questions by ignoring people and the elements only people can introduce: skill, design, aesthetics [17].

For Papert this tendency has led to questions like "What is THE effect of THE computer on cognitive development?" which position computer or Logo as the most important component of educational situations whereas people and cultures gain a facilitating role. For Papert, human development is situated within its culture and people:

In the presence of computers, cultures might change and with them people's ways of learning and thinking. But if you want to understand (or influence) the change, you have to center your attention on the culture-- not on the computer [17].

2.4   Other Construction Environments

In the years that followed, several new versions of Logo were developed, amongst which MultiLogo, StarLogo, StarLogo 2.0 and the most common commercial version of Logo called Microworlds Logo developed by Logo Computer Systems Inc. Multi-Logo is a parallel version of Logo, supporting simultaneous creation and execution of multiple processes with a new programming construct: the "agent" [28]. Each agent can control a computational process, thus by using multiple agents the user can control multiple process at the same time. A new version of Logo, called StarLogo, extends the Logo programming language, used by students to model the behavior of decentralized systems [27]. StarLogo extends Logo in three ways: first it has thousands of turtles who can move at the same time, in parallel; secondly, StarLogo turtles expand the senses of the Logo turtle that could only dray geometrical shapes and thirdly, concretize the turtles' world.

Few decades later, Resnick [26] discusses an advanced construction environment developed at the MIT Media Lab known as LEGO/Logo. LEGO/Logo links the LEGO construction kit with the Logo programming language. Whilst using LEGO/Logo children start by making machines out of Lego pieces, with additional pieces such as gears, motors and sensors. Then children can connect their machine on a computer and through a modified version of Logo to control their machine.

Another construction kit developed at the MIT Media Lab is known as Programmable Brick. Programmable Brick is a large LEGO brick, specially designed for interacting with the world. The Brick can control four motors of light at a time and it can receive inputs from eight sensors [26, 30]. To work and play with the Programmable Brick, children need to write programs on their personal computer and then connect the Programmable Brick with their computer through a cable. Then children can disconnect the cable and take the Brick with them, having the program stored in the Brick.

3   Distributed Constructionism

The theoretical underpinning of distributed constructionism was introduced at the MIT Media Laboratory and draws on research on constructionism and distributed cognition [25]. Distributed constructionism focuses on situations in which learning occurs when a person is interacting with its surrounding environment for designing and sharing meaningful artifacts; thus distributed constructionism develops the constructionist theory towards the direction of distributed construction activities. Resnick [25] focuses on three main categories of activities: discussing constructions, sharing constructions, and collaborating on constructions. Table 1 demonstrates how computer networks can be used in order to support the aforementioned distributed construction activities.

Stemming from Resnick's [25] concept of Distributed Constructionism, Zaphiris et al. [34] explored the implementation of Distributed Constructionism through a Participatory Design methodology for an Online Learning Community. Throughout this study, the learners collaborated in developing the content of an online Modern Greek language course, peer review and publish content contributions, and involve in participatory design teams. In this study the Participatory Design was implemented as a four step process, namely: (a) build bridges with the intended users; (b) define user needs and recommendations to the system; (c) develop a prototype and (d) incorporate feedback and carry on the iteration. Additionally, Distributed Constructionism was employed to enhance the learning experience and community development. The findings revealed that Distributed Constructionism enhanced the learning experience of both the passive users and the Participatory Design team, whose contributions included replying to other students' language enquiries, helping out students to cope with technical problems and helping them explore resources to enhance their learning of the Greek language.

Table 1. Distributed construction activities through computer networks [25]

Category of Distributed Construction Activity	Clarification	Examples
Discussing constructions	Students use computer networks for discussing, exchanging ideas for their construction	Discussion through email, newsgroups, bulletin boards
Sharing constructions	Students use computer networks for sharing/distributing constructions (text, images, videos) amongst people in the community and make it part of shared knowledge	Create page on the web that displays artifacts
Collaborating on constructions	Students use computer networks to collaborate with fellow-students in real time for the design and development of their construction	Use of MUDs - text-based virtual worlds where participants can work together

4   Social Constructionism

Shaw [31] first launches the term social constructionism emphasizing the importance of the social setting whilst engaging in constructing external and shared outcomes and artifacts. Shaw [31] views social constructionism as a strong tie between Vygotskian sociocultural theory [32] and constructivist leaning processes informed by Piaget [24], since socially constructive activities may provide developmental activity of the individual for constructing an artifact in a social setting. Shaw [31] in his study reports on MUSIC (Multi-User Sessions In Community), a community computer networking system that was designed for enduring constructionist social environments. MUSIC is a neighborhood based community that facilitates sharing of information and organizing programs run by neighborhood residents. The aim of this system is to encourage members in an urban social setting to invest in their relationships in order to make use of each other's services. MUSIC has been successful in organizing and managing neighborhood programs. In total the network facilitated the organization of eleven projects such as, a group trip to Jamaica, a poetry collection, a summer jobs program for neighborhood teenagers, crime watch information updates etc.

Few decades later, the advent of the social web gave a new perspective to social constructionism as Shaw [31] firstly envisioned it. Parmaxi et al. [21] explored how the construction of an online artifact manifests in practice within social technologies, providing its core dimensions that were sorted out in three high-level categories: exploration of ideas, construction of artifact and evaluation of artifact. In this study, various types of social technologies were used, that is wikis, blogs, Facebook Google documents and Dropbox. Learners used the aforementioned technologies for working together and build artifacts throughout a process that included nine actions: orientation, brainstorming, material exploration, outlining, editing material, revising, peer reviewing, instructor reviewing and presenting/publishing. Overall, this study demonstrated the potential of social technologies to act as social constructionist platforms that can enhance learners' thinking and understanding of abstract ideas by relating them to their shared artifact.

5   Discussion

Figure 1 demonstrates the evolvement of constructionism towards distributed and social constructionism. Digital media offer a rich environment of materials that provide a vehicle for promoting the development of higher levels of thinking, problem solving skills, divergent thinking, metacognitive ability and social interaction.

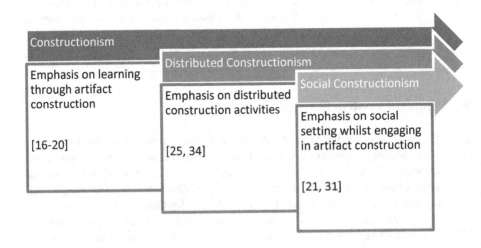

Fig. 1. The evolvement of constructionism

The dynamic progression of constructionism is prevalent not only by its continuous development but also from the various technological tools that evolve as social constructionist tools. A sound mathetic advice in constructionism is *"Look for connections"* which leads to the suggestion of establishing connections between abstract and concrete knowledge by engaging in the making of objects in the world [19]. Through improving the connectivity, we come into engaged relationship both with the artifact and with the knowledge needed for its construction.

6   Conclusion

This study reviewed the theoretical framework of constructionism from its infancy towards its more recent applications. After three decades of theoretical and applied research, constructionism is gaining ground as a comprehensive framework that could ground the use of technology in several settings.

The dynamic progression of constructionism leans towards distributed and social constructionism. This study demonstrated that despite its challenges, constructionism can offer a number of approaches for placing learners as active designers and constructors of knowledge by confronting them with the building of an artifact.

References

1. Battista, M.T., Clements, D.H.: The effects of Logo and CAI problem-solving environments on problem-solving abilities and mathematics achievement. Computers in Human Behavior 2(3), 183–193 (1986)
2. Broughton, J.M.: The surrender of control: Computer literacy as political socialization of the child. In: Sloan, D. (ed.) The Computer in Education: A Critical Perspective, pp. 102–122. Teachers College Press, New York (1985)
3. Clements, D.H.: Effects of Logo and CAI environments on cognition and creativity. Journal of Educational Psychology 78(4), 309 (1986)
4. Clements, D.H.: Longitudinal study of the effects of Logo programming on cognitive abilities and achievement. Journal of Educational Computing Research 3(1), 73–94 (1987)
5. Clements, D.H., Battista, M.T.: The effects of Logo on children's conceptualizations of angle and polygons. Journal for Research in Mathematics Education, 356–371 (1990)
6. Clements, D.: Research on Logo in education: is the turtle slow but steady, or not even in the race? In: Maddux, C.D. (ed.) Computers in the Schools, pp. 55–71. Haworth, New York (1985)
7. Clements, D.H., Gullo, D.F.: Effects of computer programming on young children's cognition. Journal of Educational Psychology 76(6), 1051–1058 (1984)
8. Davy, J.: Mindstorms in the Lamplight. In: Sloan, D. (ed.) The Computer in Education: A Critical Perspective, pp. 11–30. Teachers College, New York (1984)
9. Feurzeig, W.: Algebra slaves and agents in a Logo-based mathematics curriculum. Instructional Science 14(3-4), 229–254 (1986)
10. Fletcher, B.C.: Group and individual learning of junior school children on a microcomputer-based task: social or cognitive facilitation? Educational Review 37(3), 251–261 (1985)
11. Hoyles, C., Sutherland, R.: Logo mathematics in the classroom (revised edition). Routledge, New York (1992)

12. Kafai, Y.B.: Constructionism. In: Sawyer, R.K. (ed.) The Cambridge Handbook of the Learning Sciences, pp. 35–46. Cambridge University Press, New York (2006)

13. Kull, J.A.: Learning and logo. In: Campbell, P., Fein, G. (eds.) Young Children and Microcomputers, pp. 103–130. Prentice Hall, Englewood Cliffs (1986)

14. Kurland, D.M., Pea, R.D.: Children's mental models of recursive LOGO programs. Journal of Educational Computing Research 1(2), 235–243 (1985)

15. Kurland, D.M., Pea, R.D., Clement, C., Mawby, R.: A study of the development of programming ability and thinking skills in high school students. Journal of Educational Computing Research 2(4), 429–458 (1986)

16. Papert, S.: Mindstorms: Children, computers, and powerful ideas. Basic Books, Inc. (1980)

17. Papert, S.: Computer Criticism vs. Technocentric Thinking. Educational Researcher 16(1), 22–30 (1987)

18. Papert, S.: The children's machine: Rethinking school in the age of the computer. Basic Books (1993)

19. Papert, S.: A word for learning. In: Kafai, Y., Resnick, M. (eds.) Constructionism in Practice, pp. 9–24. Lawrence Erlbaum associates Inc., New Jersey (1996)

20. Papert, S., Harel, I.: Situating Constructionism. In: Papert, S., Harel, I. (eds.) Constructionism, pp. 1–11. Ablex Publishing, NJ (1991)

21. Parmaxi, A., Zaphiris, P., Michailidou, E., Papadima-Sophocleous, S., Ioannou, A.: Introducing New Perspectives in the Use of Social Technologies in Learning: Social Constructionism. In: Kotzé, P., Marsden, G., Lindgaard, G., Wesson, J., Winckler, M. (eds.) INTERACT 2013, Part II. LNCS, vol. 8118, pp. 554–570. Springer, Heidelberg (2013)

22. Pea, R.D.: Logo programming and problem solving. In: O'Shea, T., Scanlon, E. (eds.) Technology. Center for Children and Technology, vol. 606(1) (1987), http://eric.ed.gov/ERICWebPortal/recordDetail?accno=ED319371

23. Pea, R.D., Kurland, D.M.: On the cognitive effects of learning computer programming. New Ideas in Psychology 2(2), 137–168 (1984)

24. Piaget, J.: The construction of reality in the child. Ballantine Books, New York (1954)

25. Resnick, M.: Distributed Constructionism. In: Computing, pp. 280–284. International Society of the Learning Sciences (1996)

26. Resnick, M.: Behavior construction kits. Communications of the ACM 36(7), 64–71 (1993)

27. Resnick, M.: New Paradigms for Computing, New Paradigmns for Thinking. In: Kafai, Y., Resnick, M. (eds.) Constructionism in Practice, pp. 255–267. Lawrence Erlbaum Associates Inc., New Jersey (1996)

28. Resnick, M.: MultiLogo: A study of children and concurrent programming. Interactive Learning Environments 1(3), 153–170 (1990)

29. Ruschoff, B., Ritter, M.: Technology-Enhanced Language Learning: Construction of Knowledge and Template-Based Learning in the Foreign Language Classroom. Computer Assisted Language Learning 14(3-4), 219–232 (2001)

30. Sargent, R., Resnick, M., Martin, F., Silverman, B.: Building and learning with programmable bricks. In: Kafai, Y., Resnick, M. (eds.) Constructionism in Practice, pp. 161–173. Lawrence Erlbaum Associates Inc., New Jersey (1996)

31. Shaw, A.: Social constructionism and the inner city: Designing environments for social development and urban renewal. In: Kafai, Y., Resnick, M. (eds.) Constructionism in Practice, pp. 175–206. Lawrence Erlbaum Associates Inc., New Jersey (1996)

32. Vygotsky, L.: Mind in society: The development of higher psychological processes. Harvard University Press, Cambridge (1978)

33. Wilensky, U.: Abstract meditations on the concrete and concrete implications for mathematics education. In: Harel, I., Papert, S. (eds.) Constructionism, pp. 193–203. Ablex Publishing Corporation, Norwood (1991)

34. Zaphiris, P., Zacharia, G., Rajasekaran, M.: Distributed Constructionism through Participatory Design. Group, 164–179 (2003), http://books.google.com/books?hl=en&lr=&id=GaUGjcpjo7AC&oi=fnd&pg=PA164&dq=Distributed+Constructionism+through+Participatory+Design&ots=nr3a7UZes7&sig=Mwum2xiy41oDbi2x4zrRUe-0Z8M (retrieved)

Examining an Online Collaboration Learning Environment with the Dual Eye-Tracking Paradigm: The Case of Virtual Math Teams

Selin Deniz Uzunosmanoğlu[1] and Murat Perit Çakir[2]

[1] Computer Education and Instructional Technology Department, METU, Ankara, Turkey
sdeniz@metu.edu.tr
[2] Cognitive Sciences Department, METU, Ankara, Turkey
perit@metu.edu.tr

Abstract. The aim of this study is to investigate the computer supported collaborative problem solving processes using the dual eye-tracking method. 18 university students participated in this study, and 9 pairs tried to solve 10 geometry problems using Virtual Math Team (VMT) online environment. Which situations the participants' eye movements, and eye gazes overlap, and how usability of VMT environment affect the problem solving processes are tried to identify. After experiments with two eye-trackers, a questionnaire including System Usability Scale and open-ended questions was filled by participants. Eye-tracker data were analyzed both quantitatively using cross-recurrence analysis, and qualitatively using interaction analysis. Analysis of eye-tracker data and open-ended questions are consistent, and support to each other. Results show that pairs collaborating with higher level have more gazes overlapping, more shared understanding, and anticipatory gazes than pairs having with low level. Also, usability of the system and awareness tools affect the collaboration processes.

Keywords: computer supported collaborative learning, collaborative problem solving, joint attention, gaze overlap, dual eye tracking.

1 Introduction

People around the world can communicate with each other with the developments of Information and Communication Technology (ICT). Particularly young people have shown great interest to ICT based communication tools like instant messaging, chat and social networking sites (Lenhart et al., 2007). This allows various peer groups to build knowledge together and further their understanding by engaging in collective discussions online. As a research paradigm that has attracted increasing interest within Instructional Technology, Computer-Supported Collaborative Learning (CSCL) specifically focuses on how ICT technologies can be designed and used to better support collective meaning-making practices of learners (Stahl, Koschmann & Suthers, 2006).

P. Zaphiris and A. Ioannou (Eds.): LCT 2014, Part I, LNCS 8523, pp. 462–472, 2014.

The design of effective awareness mechanisms is a fundamental usability concern in CSCL research since such features enable learners to monitor and coordinate each other's' actions as they gradually achieve a sense of joint attention, which is considered as a prerequisite for productive collaboration (Barron, 2003). Achievement of joint attention is particularly challenging when learners are engaged with multiple interaction spaces where they can exchange not only text messages but also shared drawings (Cakir, Zemel & Stahl, 2009). Most CSCL systems aim to help users monitor each other's actions by providing annotation features, color-coded text, referencing tools; system generated messages that display who is currently typing/drawing or present in the environment as well as visualizations that mirror the state of ongoing collaboration (Soller et al., 2003).

The influence of such features on collaboration is often assessed via outcome measures or discourse analysis of interaction logs. Outcome measures are important for making an overall assessment of the effectiveness of collaboration, but they provide an indirect assessment of the influence of designed interactive features on the collaboration process (Dillenbourg et al., 1995). Discourse analysis of logs partly addresses this issue by focusing on the sequential organization of exchanged messages/drawings, but it requires analysts to make inferences regarding how the message production process might have been influenced by interface features based on what is said or done. In particular, when there is no explicit response or uptake, it is ambiguous whether a message or a drawing action had actually succeeded in eliciting the attention of other members. Analysis of such cases are important as they may point to serious usability issues, and this kind of analysis requires further information regarding where participants allocate their attention while they produce their own messages and monitor those of others.

The aim of this study is to investigate joint eye gaze features for assessing the collaboration processes and evaluating Virtual Math Team (VMT), (Stahl, 2009; Stahl, Mantoan & Weimar, 2013), which is a CSCL environment designed to support collaborative math problem-solving activities online by providing a text-based chat tool together with a shared drawing area with GeoGebra based dynamic geometry features, using dual eye-tracking paradigm. Dual eye-tracking is a promising technique to investigate the collaboration and interaction processes among two people. There are two eye-trackers recording the eye movements of two people working together.

In this study, some important uses of dual eye-tracking method are presented such as the collaboration level between pairs, and difficulties that pairs face during collaborative problem solving processes. This kind of methods provides researchers with not only assessment of collaborative problem solving processes, but also guidance for usability studies to improve CSCL environments in terms of ease of use. Designing automated support for the assessment of collaborative learning is becoming an important need given the recent interest towards collaborative learning pedagogy and systems that support such activities. PISA exam will, also, include questions evaluating collaboration skills (OECD, 2013). So there is an important need for designing useful and effective collaborative environments, and assessing them in order to support the collaborative learning pedagogy and systems. Some of the measures searched in this study can be improved to meet the need for large scale applications, evaluate them, and developing advanced awareness features to help learners to develop coordination skills necessary to work together as a team.

Research questions are presented below;

1. To what extent VMT's features facilitate joint attention? When and where gaze overlaps occur?
2. Is there a relationship between the amount of gaze overlap and success in joint problem solving and collaboration?
3. How does the usability of VMT environment affect collaborative problem solving processes?

The aim of this study is to identify in which situations participants' gaze patterns overlap, and how the percentage of this overlap correlate with the degree of attention paid to awareness features and with the overall success of the collaborative problem solving process.

2 Method

18 students (9 pairs) from the Middle East Technical University (METU) were recruited for this study. While forming the pairs, some criteria were considered such as they know each other, and both of them are from the same department, and same educational level. The reason why these criteria were used is that, the more partners know their level of knowledge, the more interaction between pair increases, because this awareness provides partners with better understanding among them (Nüssli, 2011). In addition to this, according to Sangin (2009), since partners have awareness about their knowledge, they have better estimation about their actions. Because this study focuses on technological factors on joint work, these kinds of pairs are more appropriate to control the social factors. Each pair attempted 10 geometry problems on VMT environment. During the experiments, the eye movements of the participants were recorded with two Tobii eye-trackers. In VMT environment, there are chat rooms which provide participants with communication via chat section. For this study, chat rooms were created for each pair. In these chat rooms, there are 3 tabs: Questions, GeoGebra, and Results. Question tab includes 10 questions. GeoGebra tab consists of algebra view providing participants with monitoring the coordinates of drawings, and construction area providing participants with drawing construction. In GeoGebra tab, only one participant can take control, and draw the construction. In result tab, participants were asked to write their results on whiteboard and proof after they solve the problems. Before the solving questions part, there were a training part lasting approximately 10 minutes which explains the VMT environment, GeoGebra tools used frequently while solving geometry problems, and gives an example.

After the experiments, a questionnaire with System Usability Scale (SUS) (Brooke, 1986) open-ended questions was filled to obtain participants' comments about the collaboration process and the online environment features, so mixed method research design is used for this study.

2.1   Data Analysis

Eye-tracker data were analyzed both quantitatively and qualitatively. The cross-recurrence analysis method (Richardson & Dale, 2005; Richardson et al., 2007) was used for the quantitative analysis of eye gaze data. Interaction analysis method was used to qualitatively examine the synchronized video recordings of sessions to explore interactional and design factors that facilitate joint attention.

For the qualitative analysis eye-tracker data were used in order to measure the degree of gaze overlap among collaborating pairs. Recording time stamps, local time stamps, coordination of gaze points and area of interests (AOI) of the eye movements were considered, and exported from Tobii Studio Software. This method is called cross-recurrence analysis, and was used in the studies of Richardson and Dale (2005) and Richardson et. al. (2007). A customize program written in Java was used for performing this analysis. The screen was divided into AOI in Tobii Software Studio. Then Java program gets the raw data extracted from Tobii Studio, and gives a scarf plot which presents the information about which AOI partners' look, when their eye gazes overlapped. After generating scarf plots for each pair, Java program produces gaze overlap distribution plot for each question of both partners with the time lag between -4000 and 4000 msec. It is formed using the total gaze overlap duration among the participants, when one participant's gaze sequence is shifted x msec where x ranges between -4000 and 4000 msec, and is incremented in 100 msec. Then, these values are converted into percentage values in accordance with the segment's length. The recurrence plot also represents the recurrence percentage distribution when the gaze sequences are randomly shuffled in order to provide a baseline for comparing against the random recurrence.

Finally, a separate and single recurrence graphs are produced for each pair containing whole session shown in recurrence analysis results part. Point 0 indicates the recurrence percentage of the pairs for exactly synchronous gaze, -200 indicates the recurrence percentage in which second participant gazes with a 200 msec delay with respect to first participant, and vice versa. The blue part represents the same info with a shuffled gaze data used as a baseline. The vertical lines are the standard error bars indicating the amount of deviation in the data for the corresponding time.

3   Results

3.1   Recurrence Analysis Results

The recurrence graphs for Pair-8 which has the best quality collaboration and for Pair-4 which has the lowest level of collaboration are presented. Each data point represents the overlap in specified time lag value while calculating the recurrence percentage. For example; there is no lag in 0 point, so both participants look at the same AOI. Then one participant's gaze data is shifted 100 msec, and gaze overlap is calculated again in order to identify the overlapping of one participant's gaze at the same area as the other participant with a 100 msec delay. Then duration is divided by segment length, and recorded -100 msec data point. Finally, for each pair, overall curve calculated using mean values of each question for 80 data points between -4000 msec and

+4000 msec. The reason why time lag value is stated between -4 and +4 seconds is that listeners' tend to look at the same location where speakers looked at a delay of 2 seconds (Richardson & Dale, 2005). In this study, communication was performed via a chat tool, so we extend the time interval to +4 and -4 seconds in order to explore gaze overlapping for the chat case. Graphs shown below are formed.

The graphs can be interpreted as:

- If the red circle line (percentage of recurrence) is far from, and has higher percentage than the blue triangle line (random baseline), it means that this pair performs high level of gaze coordination.
- If there is symmetry around the 0 point, partners follow each other's actions equivalently.
- If there is a skew on the right side of the 0 point, the participant whose eye-movement data are chosen firstly follows the second participant more. If there is a skew on the left side of the 0 point, the participant whose eye-movement data are chosen firstly is followed by the second participant more.

Fig.1 represents the recurrence percentage graph of Pair-4 which has the lowest recurrence percentage in this study. Two lines are very close to each other, intersect at some points, and recurrence percentage level is very low.

Fig. 2 shows the recurrence percentage of Pair-8 which has the highest recurrence percentage level in this study. There is symmetry around the 0 point, so we can say that both participants follow other's action at similar level. Furthermore, the distance between recurrence percentage line and random baseline increases between -2400 msec and +2800 msec, so we can say that these participants follow each other with the approximately 2 seconds time lag.

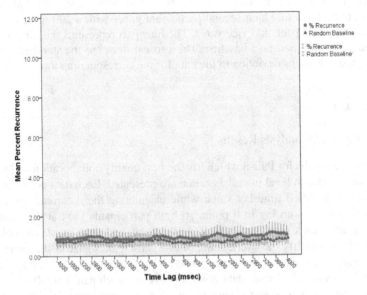

Fig. 1. Recurrence percentage graph of Pair-4

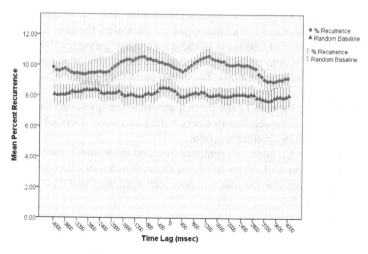

Fig. 2. Recurrence percentage of Pair-8

3.2   Interaction Analysis Results

In this part, some excerpts are presented to show the collaboration process with antic-ipatory gazes, where gaze overlaid video recording indicate that some participants estimate the location of next possible action of the team member before s/he per-forms. Suchexamples can be considered as a strong evidence for the achievement of common ground and mutual understanding. Furthermore, gaze overlap, and uses of awareness tools are the evidence of good quality collaboration.

Considering the recurrence analysis, pair-8 has the highest gaze overlap, because before starting solving the problem, they reasoned together communicating via chat element. The second highest collaboration level belongs to Pair-5. While solving the

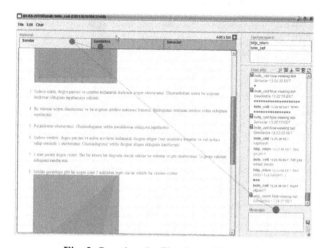

Fig. 3. Question-6 – Fixations of bote_ceit

problems, they used awareness messages such as following "... is typing" messages, and "Now viewing tab GeoGebra" messages which shows the one participant's tab changes on chat element. In addition to these awareness messages, VMT has awareness elements at the bottom of the screen; one represents the last usage tool, and the other one represents who has control. These two pairs used these awareness elements and messages to follow partner's actions.

In question-6 (Pair-8), both of the participants read the question. Then bilgi_islem viewed GeGebra tab, bote_ceit saw this action, and he viewed GeoGebra tab, too (see Fig. 3), so he followed his partner's action.

In question-4 (Pair-8), bote_ceit took control, and drew an equilateral triangle using equilateral polygon tool. Then he stated the midpoints of all edges (see Fig. 4). Meanwhile, bilgi_islem saw the tool that bote_ceit used, and looked at the midpoints' of the edges (see Fig. 5).

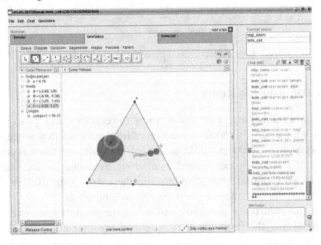

Fig. 4. Question-4 – Fixations of bote_ceit

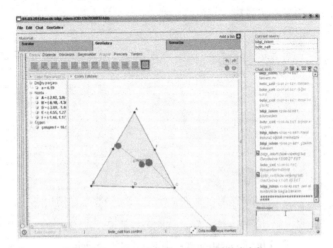

Fig. 5. Question-4 – Fixations of bilgi_islem

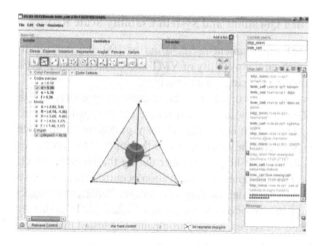

Fig. 6. Question-4 – Fixations of bote_ceit

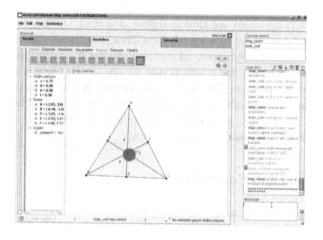

Fig. 7. Question-4 – Fixations of bilgi_islem

In question-4 (Pair-8), before bote_ceit stated the center point (G) (see Fig. 6), bilgi_islem anticipated this action, and looked at this location (see Fig. 7).

There are, also, some cases where there was no gaze coordination. Pair-4 has the lowest gaze occurrence. The main reason is that while one partner was writing the answers on the Results tab, the other worked on the next question, so partners could not follow their actions because they were working different tabs. The other reason is that while bilgi_islem was solving the problem, she did not look at the chat section, and could not see what her partner wrote. So gaze overlapping either did not occur in those cases or occurred by chance.

To sum up, our aim is to support the results of cross recurrence analysis by closely analyzing gaze patterns of pairs.

3.3   Open-Ended Questions and System Usability Scale Results

SUS score of VMT environment is 52,30 out of 100, but this result does not give detail information about the usability of VMT and collaboration process, because it is designed for evaluating the single user interface.

Answers of open-ended questions were examined to understand the participants' experiences, difficulties they faced, their ideas, and suggestions about VMT. Participants stated that chat section is the main element of collaboration process. If someone fails to solve the problem, the other one takes the control, and continues to solve problem. They, also, direct, and help each other during the process, but chat element has some difficulties. For example; communication occurred text-based, so it causes time loss, and sometimes misunderstanding may occur. Participants suggested that communication should be provided via video-based channel. In addition to these, pairs missed the partner's messages. Some participants suggested that when a chat message is sent, it should be a notification voice, so the messages attract attention of other participant.

The colors of the text messages are different for each person, but because the colors are similar, text messages are hard to follow, and read. On the other hand, some participants stated that "Now viewing tab GeoGebra" awareness message is useful to follow their partners. Furthermore, take control button is useful, because just one person constructs drawings, and confliction is prevented. This button is, also, useful for awareness among partners. The other main problem is that participants had difficulties about usage of GeoGebra tools. Participants stated that GeoGebra tools should be more easy to use. Finally, some of the participants stated that the construction area was slide, and the partner's actions were not seen.

4   Discussion and Conclusion

In this part, results are discussed according to research questions. For the first research question, it is observed that some VMT features provide coordination of joint attention to the users. Chat tool is one of these tools, participants used it for communication, and they directed each other while solving the problems. For example, "... is typing" awareness feature help participants with facilitating joint attention, because when one was constructing the solution, the other wrote messages, and suggest solution, or asked something. In addition to this, when a participant changes the tab, "... view ... tab" awareness message is seen. It, also, provides users with joint attention, because when one sees this tab changes, s/he changes tab, too, and follows his/her partner. Furthermore, construction area on GeoGebra tab makes the on-going construction visible to all users. Eye-tracking videos show us these gazes and joint attention. Thus, gaze overlapping especially occur on construction area, and chat tool by using awareness messages.

For the second research question, results of the recurrence analysis and interaction analysis show that there is relationship between the amount of gaze overlap and success in joint problem solving and collaboration. This finding is consistent with the literature, and reported by some other studies that high-quality collaboration is related with high level gaze recurrence (Jermann, Nüssli, Mullins & Dillenbourg, 2011; Richardson & Dale, 2005; Jermann & Nüssli, 2012). Pairs having high quality of collaboration show more gaze overlap than the pair having low quality of collaboration, because good pairs usually followed partner's action, reasoned together, suggested solutions to each other. But pairs with low quality of collaboration just divided the work as constructing solution and writing solution, and did their sub-work, so they work cooperatively, not collaboratively. As Dillenbourg (1999a) stated that they worked cooperatively, because they divided the whole work into sub-work, work individually and finally united the final work.

For the third research question, open-ended question results are used. Participants stated that they faced with some difficulties, because of the some VMT features. Some participants said that it was difficult to follow construction area and chat area simultaneously. There are some reasons of this difficulty. For example, colors of each user's messages are different, but very similar, so participants faced difficulty in identifying which messages belongs to whom, and they had to read last few messages. This difficulty slows down the communication process. Because color selection is an important factor affecting users' perception, interface should be designed according to design principles. The other reason about difficulty is about awareness messages about changing tab action and their crowded view. Although this awareness messages support collaboration, and following the partner's action, the design of them is not suitable, because color tone is similar to participants' message, and people see their own changing tab action. It is not necessary. Another reason of difficulty is about the construction area. When a user zooms in, zooms out or moves the construction area, other user cannot see these actions, so "what you see is what I see" design principle for collaborative systems fails. This usability problem affects the collaboration process.

Because there is a big problem about understanding users' motivation regarding to using collaborative environment (Holtzblatt, Damianos & Weiss, 2010; Matthews, Whittaker, Moran, Yuen & Judge, 2011), users' experiences and their feedback about the environment should be considered well, and reflected to the design of user interface. Because SUS is designed for single user interface usability evaluation, it is inadequate to assess the usability of collaborative environment. Although there are some rating schemes for assessing the quality of collaborative environment such as developed by Meier, Spada and Rummel (2007), there is a big need to develop scale for evaluating usability of collaborative environment.

References

1. Barron, B.: When smart groups fail. The Journal of the Learning Sciences 12(3), 307–359 (2003)
2. Brooke, J.: System Usability Scale (SUS): A Quick-and-Dirty Method of System Evaluation User Information. Digital Equipment Co. Ltd., Reading (1986)
3. Çakir, M.P., Zemel, A., Stahl, G.: Interaction analysis of dual-interaction CSCL environments. Paper presented at the International Conference on Computer Support for Collaborative Learning (CSCL), Rhodes, Greece (2009), http://GerryStahl.net/pub/cscl2009cakir.pdf

4. Dillenbourg, P.: What do you mean by "collaborative learning"? In: Dillenbourg, P. (ed.) Collaborative Learning: Cognitive and Computational Approaches, pp. 1–16. Pergamon, Elsevier Science, Amsterdam, NL (1999a)
5. Dillenbourg, P., Baker, M., Blaye, A., O'Malley, C.: The evolution of research in collaborative learning. In: Reiman, P., Spada, H. (eds.) Learning in Humans and Machines: Towards and Interdiciplinary Learning Science, pp. 189–211. Elsevier, Oxford (1995)
6. Holtzblatt, L., Damianos, L., Weiss, D.: Factors impeding wiki use in the enterprise: A case study. In: Collective Intelligence Workshop at CSCW (2010)
7. Jermann, P., Nüssli, M.A.: Effects of sharing text selections on gaze recurrence and interaction quality in a pair programming task. In: Computer Supported Cooperative Work, Seattle (2012)
8. Jermann, P., Nüssli, M.A., Mullins, D., Dillenbourg, P.: Collaborative gaze footprints: correlates of interaction quality. In: Proceedings of CSCL 2011, Hong Kong (2011)
9. Lenhart, A., Madden, M., Macgill, A.R., Smith, A.: Teens and social media (2007), http://www.pewinternet.org/~/media/Files/Reports/2007/PIP_Teens_Social_Media_Final.pdf.pdf (retrieved)
10. Matthews, T., Whittaker, S., Moran, T., Yuen, S., Judge, T.: Productive interrelationships between collaborative groups ease the challenges of dynamic and multi-teaming. CSCW Journal (2011), doi:10.1007/s10606-011-9154-y
11. Meier, A., Spada, H., Rummel, N.: A rating scheme for assessing the quality of computer-supported collaboration processes. International Journal of Computer-Supported Collaborative Learning 2(1), 63–86 (2007), doi:10.1007/s11412-006-9005-x
12. Nüssli, M.A.: Dual eye-tracking methods for the study of remote collaborative problem-solving. PhD thesis, École Polytechnique Fédérale de Lausanne (2011)
13. OECD (2013), http://www.oecd.org/pisa/pisaproducts/Draft%20PISA%202015%20Collaborative%20Problem%20Solving%20Framework%20.pdf (retrieved)
14. Richardson, D.C., Dale, R.: Looking to understand: the coupling between speakers' and listeners' eye movements and its relationship to discourse comprehension. Cognitive Science 29, 1045–1060 (2005)
15. Richardson, D.C., Dale, R., Spivey, M.J.: Eye movements in language and cognition: A brief introduction. In: Gonzalez- Marquez, M., Coulson, S., Mittelberg, I., Spivey, M.J. (eds.) Methods in Cognitive Linguistics. John Benjamins, Amsterdam (2007)
16. Sangin, M.: Peer Knowledge Modeling in Computer Supported Collaborative Learning. PhD thesis, École Polytechnique Fédérale de Lausanne (2009)
17. Soller, A., Martínez, A., Jermann, P., Muehlenbrock, M.: From mirroring to guiding: A review of state of the art technology for supporting collaborative learning. International Journal of Artificial Intelligence in Education 15(4), 261–290 (2005)
18. Stahl, G.: Studying virtual math teams. Springer, New York (2009)
19. Stahl, G., Koschmann, T., Suthers, D.: Computer-supported collaborative learning: An historical perspective. In: Sawyer, R.K. (ed.) Cambridge Handbook of the Learning Sciences, pp. 409–426. Cambridge University Press, Cambridge (2006), http://GerryStahl.net/cscl/CSCL_English.pdf
20. Stahl, G., Mantoan, A., Weimar, S.: Demo: Collaborative dynamic mathematics in virtual math teams. Presented at the International Conference of Computer-Supported Collaborative Learning (CSCL, Madison, WI (2013), http://GerryStahl.net/pub/cscl2013demo.pdf

Author Index